*Myth and the
American Experience*

Myth and the American Experience

Volume Two

THIRD EDITION

Edited and with an Introduction by
Nicholas Cords and Patrick Gerster

Lakewood Community College

HarperCollins*Publishers*

Sponsoring Editor: Lauren Silverman/Bruce Borland
Project Editor: Susan Goldfarb
Art Direction: Lucy Krikorian
Text Design Adaptation and Cover Design: Graphnick
Cover Coordinator: Lucy Krikorian
Photo Research: Mira Schachne/Liza Caldwell
Production: Willie Lane/Sunaina Sehwani
Compositor: David Seham Associates
Printer and Binder: R. R. Donnelley & Sons Company
Cover Printer: Lynn Art Offset Corporation

Myth and the American Experience (Volume Two), Third Edition

Library of Congress Cataloging-in Publication Data

Myth and the American experience / edited and with an introduction by
 Nicholas Cords and Patrick Gerster.—3rd ed.
     p.   cm.
   ISBN 0-06-041379-4 (v. 1). —ISBN 0-06-041380-8 (v. 2)
   1. United States—History.   2. United States—Historiography.
 I. Cords, Nicholas.   II. Gerster, Patrick.
 E178.6.M94   1991   90-5004
 973—dc20   CIP

90   91   92   93   9 8 7 6 5 4 3 2 1

To
Maggie and Carole

Mundus vult decipi
[The world wants to be deceived.]

All America lies at the end of the wilderness road, and our past is not a dead past, but still lives in us. Our forefathers had civilization inside them, the wild outside. We live in the civilization they created, but within us the wilderness still lingers. What they dreamed, we live, and what they lived, we dream.

T. K. Whipple, *Study Out the Land*

Contents

Preface

The enthusiastic response to previous editions of *Myth and the American Experience* has made this new edition possible. In receiving both words of praise and suggestions for improvement from users of earlier editions, our conviction about the viability of a mythic perspective on American history has, if anything, become more firm. The mythological approach to American history continues to be both relevant and exciting. It most assuredly has come of age, or at least it has assumed its proper place alongside more traditional contemporary perspectives on the American past.

Since the publication of the first edition of *Myth and the American Experience,* we have had occasion to comment further—in classroom lectures, during the presentation of professional papers, and with the publication of articles, books, and reviews—on the elusive relationship between myth and American history. Those experiences have led us to an even deeper awareness of myth's reality. We continue to see myth and reality as complementary elements of the historical record.

The selected historical myths discussed and analyzed in this work can best be understood as a series of *false beliefs* about America's past. They are false beliefs, however, which have been accepted as true and acted upon as real. Thus, one comes to see that myths remain both true and false simultaneously. They are false in the sense that they often enjoy only a remote relationship to what most informed historians consider to have actually happened; they are true in the sense that people believe them and that they form bases for action. It is well to remember that there is a point at which myth and reality intersect; at that given point, they become one and the same. A myth becomes reality precisely when people base their beliefs upon it and act as if the myth were true. In fact, the making of myths is a twofold process by which a culture structures its world and by which it perpetuates its grandest dreams.

The idea for *Myth and the American Experience* grew out of our own teaching experiences. In continually dealing with students who for the most part were beginning their collegiate study of American history, we found that a thematic approach to the nation's past was useful, even stimulating, for those intent on understanding the past of which they were a continuing part. More specifically, the theme of "myth"—a thread by which to trace the diverse tapestry of our cultural experience—proved to be especially engaging.

In creating a third edition of *Myth and the American Experience*, we are necessarily reminded of the history of the book itself—for without its own successful history, this new edition would never have come to pass. We have sought to retain the vitality and integrity of earlier editions, while remaining sensitive to recent scholarly trends. More specifically, while offering an especially strong foundation of "classic" historical writing and interpretation, we have sought to better reflect those habitually underrepresented, both in American society and in history texts. Thus, we have included several new selections on Indians and women; new material on the Great Awakening, the Chicano experience, and the social realities of the Jacksonian era; new studies of Andrew Jackson, Abraham Lincoln, Reconstruction, and the two Roosevelts; and fresh perspectives on such topics as workers, Victorian sexuality, the melting pot, Japanese Americans, John F. Kennedy, and the very nature of myth itself. We have found good reason to retain the basic organization of the previous edition and have been guided in our final selections by a desire to offer articles that voice our mythic theme in a scholarly way: articles that offer students readability and current interest without sacrificing the demands of thorough historical scholarship. Our emphasis on historiography remains, for historians continue to maintain their seemingly contradictory roles as mythmakers and, at the same time, myth-debunkers.

NICHOLAS CORDS
PATRICK GERSTER

Acknowledgments

As the historical past itself is a collaborative enterprise, so too is this book. While we claim the mythic theme applied across the entire landscape of American history to be uniquely ours, we gratefully acknowledge those whose efforts came in various ways to be reflected in the final product. Our greatest thanks must be extended to our professional colleagues; the results of their many years of scholarly effort comprise the very heart of this work. Without their intellectual skills and narrative talents, this book would not have been possible. Students have helped us both to hone our ideas and to gauge better the critical reception of individual selections. Our families have granted us both support and a sounding board for the joys and problems that cumulatively accrue to such a project. The reviewers of this edition—Carol Jensen, University of Wisconsin at La Crosse; Charles Wilson, University of Mississippi; Tom Jones, Metropolitan State University; Bruce Dierenfield, Canisius College; and Marlette Rebhorn, Austin Community College—by their constructive criticism, also have made this a better project. The publishing support system of HarperCollins was most helpful in bringing our ideas from mind to printed page. Lauren Silverman, our original sponsoring editor, in particular showed early enthusiasm and added consistent strategic support to our efforts. Bruce Borland, sponsoring editor, and Susan Goldfarb, project editor, guided the work through its editorial journey. To all of these we offer thanks.

NICHOLAS CORDS
PATRICK GERSTER

*Myth and the
American Experience*

Introduction: Myth and History

"Human Being is a featherless, storytelling animal. . . ." We tell stories—myths— about who we are, where we come from, where we are going and how we should live. And the myths we tell become who we are and what we believe—as individuals, families, whole cultures.[1]

The appearance of this third edition of *Myth and the American Experience* strongly suggests that many readers of our earlier editions have found myth an especially useful perspective from which to view the nation's past. In the interest of making this mythic perspective more explicit, we address these questions: What is myth? What is myth's relationship to history? Why study American history in terms of myth? And how does this third edition aid in answering these questions?

Myth and history always have enjoyed a close relationship. In preliterate societies, a sense of origins and traditions was preserved in cultural memory through stories told by elders whose task it was to be custodians of the past and the past's interpreters to the present. In ancient societies, myths were thus the "storied" explanations in both oral and, later, written form of the past order of things and how the culture had come through time to its current circumstance. While not always—or even often—completely "true" renditions of the culture's past, myths' power lay more with their capacity to provide a sense of cultural continuity. In brief, myths always have been the traditional stories a culture tells itself about itself.

Today the fashion regarding myth is to associate it with the ancient world—as Greek myths, for example, told fantastic tales of gods and heroes and collective cultural accomplishments. Also dating to classical times is the common historic usage of *myth* as a pejorative term, a synonym for "lie," "fabrication," or "false belief." Plato often emphasized this highly negative view towards myths, declaring them to be little more than silly beliefs on false parade. Aristotle, on the other hand, thought of myths as more serious—even useful—as a treasury of cultural stories about the past that provide meaning for the present. Myths function, he concluded, as a kind of cultural glue that holds a people together—however great their diversity. Aristotle's view was that a mythic tale may well be factually suspect even as it conveys the under-

1

lying realities of the culture. A myth could then be factually false and psychologically true simultaneously. Those who associate myth with falsehood wish to invalidate it historically; but as Aristotle and others began to recognize, such attacks are powerless against myth's psychological potency within the context of the culture that chooses to believe it. Since Greek times, then, the understanding and use of myth have been ambivalent—implying both falsehood and truth. To the degree that a uniform opinion had formed in the Greek world regarding myth, it was simply that myth was a traditional story—perhaps false, perhaps true.

Throughout subsequent history, the view continued to be voiced that myth was a mutation of historical fact, and thus more false than true. Just as creditable over time, however, has been the view that myth is allegorical, discussing cultural values under other images containing a special brand of truth. Thus, as with so many other features of Western culture, the shaping of opinion and attitude about myths bears a distinct Hellenic imprint. Armed with these countervailing approaches to myth begun by the Greeks, the West has since sat Janus-faced, viewing myth as both negative and positive, as both profane and sacred.

So it has been, too, that a dialectical use of the term *myth* in American historical studies mirrors this ambivalence with which Western culture has long contended. Reflecting this tradition, the term *myth*, as presented in this set of readings, is utilized in two ways. In many instances the material, at least implicitly, reflects what one might call a Platonic tradition. This tradition has been rearticulated by the American historian Thomas A. Bailey, who over two decades ago wrote, "A historical myth is . . . an account or belief which is demonstrably untrue in whole or substantial part."[2] Historians reflecting this definition choose to emphasize the negative aspects of myth, to isolate and debunk what they regard as erroneous belief and misguided scholarship. The goal of historical study, as those of the Plato/Bailey tradition would have it, lies especially with recording history "as it actually happened." The historian, they insist, must stand as a transparent witness to the occurrences of the past. The truth, if diligently sought and recorded, will out.

Other American historians, however, deal with myth in a way fundamentally sympathetic to Aristotelian thinking, as did Henry Nash Smith in his famous study *Virgin Land: The American West as Symbol and Myth.* For Smith, a cultural or social myth, even while often factually false, needs to be sympathetically reckoned with, in that it contains an internal treasure—a culture's ideological foundations. Thus are myths useful fictions for a culture. When sensitively deconstructed, they can be shown to embody American culture's basic beliefs and highest aspirations—honesty, unpretentiousness, optimism, tolerance, hard work, sympathy for the underdog, dedication to God and country, an abiding concern for all, and a special esteem for freedom. Myths are especially powerful, rich, and revealing for students and scholars to study because they are inspiring tales ripe with culturally received wisdom. Myth, says Smith, is culturally significant in that it is "an intellectual construction that fuses concept and emotion into an image."[3] Myth is, so to speak, a mental movie, with accompanying script, which Americans carry around in their heads regarding their heritage and sense of special destiny. The American past is therefore scarcely a dead past; the past effects a presiding influence over the present. It continues to live within us. Myth lays claim to preserving, repeating, and defending the treasury of wisdom our forebears entrusted to us.

In summary, then, one school of thought on American historical myth seeks to emphasize historical inaccuracies, while the other approaches myth from the vantage point of social psychology. One sees myth as the by-product of historical scholarship (or lack of it), while the other demonstrates a marked concern for the ways in which myth serves the decidedly positive function of unifying cultural experience, providing, in the words of the literary scholar Mark Schorer, "a large controlling image that gives philosophical meaning to the facts of ordinary life. . . ."[4] Certainly at times both senses of myth are present; on occasion they tend to blend to the point of becoming nearly indistinguishable. Both notions of myth are germane to the study of American history.

University of Chicago historian William H. McNeill further observes that "myth and history are close kin inasmuch as both explain how things got to be the way they are by telling some sort of story."[5] In this way, history is "mythic" in Aristotle's and Henry Nash Smith's sense of the word, for history offers by its very nature a narrative reconstruction, a *story* of the past. This clear linkage of *story* and *history* is rather clearly recognized in some cultures. In the Italian and Spanish languages, for example, the words *history* and *story* are interchangeable. Historians are essentially the storytellers of the "tribe," functioning as purveyors of cultural stories. In this sense, surely, historians are mythmakers.

Historians also function as mythmakers in that, being human, they reflect their personal backgrounds, their times, their methodologies, their current interests—including biases and prejudices, and sometimes even their whims. All historical interpretation, in other words, is both personally contemporary and ideological—such is the nature of what has been called "the politics of interpretation." Moreover, historians constantly revise each other's work and sometimes even their own. This process of mythmaking by professional historians—myths as a critical by-product of what historians do—is given major emphasis in this work.

In addition to formal, academic study of American history, a sense of the past is frequently derived from a vast array of informational sources constantly assaulting the average citizen with a barrage of historical "facts" with implicit interpretations. These, too, structure and sustain the illusions and traditional stories—the myths—about America's past. Television and film especially, two of American culture's favorite recreations, transmit images and "re-creations" of the past in appealing sight and sound to eager audiences, most often with an eye to drama rather than solid research and scholarly validity. Similarly, "historical" novels, poetry, political rhetoric, children's literature, paintings, ballads, oral traditions, folklore, political cartoons, tourist shrines, and culturally induced sexist and racist stereotypes contribute in their own ways to our collective impression of the past. In the aggregate, they probably represent as consistent and enduring a fund of "historical" information as what we learn in more formalized educational settings. As Americans "make up their mind" about their cultural traditions, they fashion a colorful mental mosaic of their history. Song, story, nostalgia, and the ever-present media reinforce the picture. Such "mythic" history works its way to a level of operational reality when people act as if the myths are true. Policies—even laws—are based on them. In this way, the making of myths is a process by which a culture perpetuates its grandest illusions as it gives substance, order, and stability to its world.

Taking all of the above considerations into account, this new edition of *Myth and the American Experience* views myth on two levels—as a matter of correcting what is false or at least highly suspect about one's sense of the past, even while realizing myth to be highly emblematic of the nation's desires, dreams, and values. As the mathematician-turned-philosopher Alfred North Whitehead succinctly put the matter to a Virginia audience over half a century ago:

> The art of a free society consists first in the maintenance of the symbolic code; and secondly in a fearlessness of revision, to secure that the code serves those purposes which satisfy an enlightened reason. Those societies which cannot combine reverence to their symbols with freedom of revision, must ultimately decay either from anarchy, or from the slow atrophy of a life stifled by useless shadows.[6]

Seeking to offer cautionary comment as to American culture's many "useless shadows" while still cultivating a decent respect for "the symbolic code," this new edition offers much fresh material: on American Indians, the Great Awakening, colonial women, the American Revolution, Andrew Jackson, the Chicano experience, southern women, slavery, Abraham Lincoln, Reconstruction, the Gilded Age, Victorian sexuality, the American working class, the two Roosevelts, women's suffrage and feminism, immigration and minorities, the Great Depression, Pearl Harbor and Japanese Americans, the Eisenhower presidency, and the contemporary American scene—among other topics. Together with the many classic essays from earlier editions of this work, these new readings ought to contribute to a clearer yet critical vision of the nation's past. It is hoped that this selective study of myth and the American experience will launch the reader on an especially rewarding journey through America's storied mythic past.

Notes

1. Sam Keen, "Personal Myths Guide Daily Life: The Stories We Live By," *Psychology Today* (December 1989), p. 44.
2. Thomas A. Bailey, "The Mythmakers of American History," *The Journal of American History*, 55 (June 1968), p. 5.
3. Henry Nash Smith, *Virgin Land: The American West as Symbol and Myth* (New York, 1950), p. v.
4 Mark Schorer, "The Necessity of Myth," in Henry A. Murray (ed.), *Myth and Mythmaking* (New York, 1960), p. 355.
5. William H. McNeill, "Mythistory, or Truth, Myth, History, and Historians," *The American Historical Review*, 91 (February 1986), p. 1.
6. Alfred North Whitehead, *Symbolism: Its Meaning and Effect* (New York, 1959), p. 88.

Myths of the Civil War and Reconstruction

A great literature will yet arise out of the era of those four [Civil War] years, those scenes—era compressing centuries of native passion, first-class pictures, tempests of life and death—an inexhaustible mine for the histories, drama, romance, and even philosophy, of peoples to come—indeed the verteber of poetry and art (of personal character too) for all future America—far more grand, in my opinion, to the hands capable of it, than Homer's siege of Troy, or the French wars to Shakespeare.
Walt Whitman   *(1879)*

There they are, cutting each other's throats, because one half of them prefer hiring their servants for life, and the other by the hour.
Thomas Carlyle

The Glorious: John A. Logan in action. [Virginia State Library and Archives.]

The Terrible: Union dead after Gettysburg. [Reproduced from the collections of the Library of Congress.]

*T*oday the Civil War remains central to America's historical experience. For many Americans, the War Between the States represents the greatest single event in their history. From the epic struggle emerges a gallery of heroic figures and memorable episodes—Lincoln and Lee, Shiloh and Gettysburg. "The War" enjoys the status of an American *Iliad*. As novelist and poet Robert Penn Warren suggests, the Civil War marked America's "Homeric Age." To Warren, the War Between the States quickly became the great synthesis of the American experience and the inexhaustible reservoir of American symbol and myth:

> From the first, Americans had a strong tendency to think of their land as the Galahad among nations, and the Civil War, with its happy marriage of victory and virtue, has converted this tendency into an article of faith nearly as sacrosanct as the Declaration of Independence.

As Warren implies, ideas concerning the past often combine with emotion. Because of this, time,, which is supposed to bring detachment and objectivity to one's historical understanding, very often has the opposite effect. The American Civil War proves an interesting case in point. Images of either the heroic (the war itself) or the tragic (the period of Reconstruction that followed) have supplanted a proportioned view. Civil War and Reconstruction history has been an exceptionally fertile breeding ground for distortion and myth.

Recognizing what people think happened as against what actually happened—the discrepancy between history as perceived and history as actuality—is particularly significant, then, in our historical judgments concerning the war and its aftermath. A proper view of our "Homeric Age" requires that the American penchant for overemphasizing both the heroic and the tragic elements of history be challenged. A proper understanding of the era of the Civil War must yield much more than the pageantry and legend of the martyred and the Christ-like Lee. It must supply more than the tragic legend of the war's aftermath. One can begin to appreciate the entire era in its proper historical perspective only by noting the war's multiple causes, the complexity of Lincoln both as politician and as cultural hero, the conflict in both its glorious and its terrible aspects, Reconstruction's importance to the course of American race relations, the war's importance to American industrial development, and the encounter between the Plains Indians and white America. In the end, the Civil War and its heritage can indeed remain central to our national historical experience, but for reasons other than those we might previously have imagined.

Abraham Lincoln: The Man Behind the Myths

Stephen B. Oates

As the Richard Hofstadter selection earlier noted, important elements of the "Lincoln myth" are attributable to and were rather consciously sustained by Abraham Lincoln himself. Beyond this, however, it is necessary to take account as well of associated myths—and mythmakers—after Lincoln. For ever since his tragic assassination, both his accomplishments and his memory have strongly affected the emotional and political life of the nation. The Lincoln who *was* largely remains the Lincoln who *is,* so strongly has his mythic reputation persisted—for poets (Walt Whitman), for sculptors (Gutzon Borglum, who fashioned Mount. Rushmore), for foreign novelists (Leo Tolstoy), and for the American people at large. Finding the myths of Lincoln essentially benign—if taken as myths, not history—Professor Stephen B. Oates of the University of Massachusetts at Amherst tries to sustain a careful distinction between the two as he notes how "democracy's mythic hero" came to succeeding generations of Americans as the Man of the People, the Great Commoner, and Father Abraham. The poet Carl Sandburg, especially, had the greatest hand in crafting these images, emotionally shaping the contours of Lincoln's memory for a nation eager to reconstruct itself and carry on the traditions of democracy.

In 1858, against a backdrop of heightening sectional tensions over slavery, Abraham Lincoln stood in the Great Hall of the Illinois House of Representatives, warning his countrymen that a house divided against itself could not stand. Across Illinois that year, in a series of forensic duels with Stephen A. Douglas, this tall and melancholy man addressed himself boldly to the difficult problems of his day: to the haunting moral contradiction of slavery in a nation based on the Declaration of Independence . . . to the combustible issue of Negro social and political rights . . . to the meaning and historic mission of America's experiment in popular government. This same man went on to the presidency, charged with the awesome task of saving the Union—and its experiment in popular government—in the holocaust of civil war. In the end, after enduring four unendurable years, he himself became a casualty of that conflict, gunned down by John Wilkes Booth just when the war was won and popular government preserved for humankind the world over.

The man who died that dark and dismal day had flaws as well as

---

strengths, made mistakes and suffered reversals just as surely as he enjoyed his remarkable achievements. But in the days that followed his assassination, the man became obscured in an outpouring of flowery orations and tear-filled eulogies. As the seasons passed, Lincoln went on to legend and martyrdom, inflated by the myth makers into a godly Emancipator who personified America's ideal Everyman.

Before proceeding, I had best try to define myth as I am using it here. Above all, I do not mean some preposterous story. Nor do I mean a story that is uncontaminated by life. Myth, as I am using the term, is a grandiose projection of a people's experience. As X. J. Kennedy has put it, "Myths tell us of the exploits of the gods—their battles, the ways in which they live, love, and perhaps suffer—all on a scale of magnificence larger than our life. We envy their freedom and power; they enact our wishes and dreams." In other words, the grandiose dimensions and symbol-building power of the myths we create reveal our deepest longings as a people. And this is especially true of the myths we Americans have fashioned about the powerful figure who presided over the Civil War, our greatest trial as a nation. Our extravagant projections of Lincoln in myth suggest a great deal about the spiritual and psychological needs of our culture ever since.

As historian David Donald has noted, two traditions of Lincoln mythology developed after the war. The first began on "Black Easter," April 16, 1865, when ministers across the North portrayed the slain President as an American Christ who died to expiate the sins of his guilty land. For them, it was no coincidence that he had fallen on Good Friday. Did not the times of his shooting and death—just after ten in the evening and just after seven-twenty the next morning—make on the clock an outline of the crucifix? "Oh, friends," cried the Reverend C. B. Crane from the pulpit of Broadway Tabernacle, "it was meet that the martyrdom should occur on Good Friday. It is no blasphemy against the Son of God and the Saviour of men that we declare the fitness of the slaying of the second Father of our Republic on the anniversary of the day on which He was slain. Jesus Christ died for the world, Abraham Lincoln died for his country."

Blacks, too, viewed Lincoln with uninhibited reverence. "We mourn for the loss of our great and good President," a Negro soldier wrote his fiancée. "Humanity has lost a firm advocate, our race its Patron Saint, and the good of all the world a fitting object to emulate. . . . The name Abraham Lincoln will ever be cherished in our hearts, and none will more delight to lisp his name in reverence than the future generations of our people." In truth, black Americans came to regard Lincoln as a perfect, personal emancipator and kept pictures of him pasted on the walls above their mantelpieces. "To the deeply emotional and religious slave," as one man explained, "Lincoln was an earthly incarnation of the Saviour of mankind."

And so one body of writings depicted him in the ensuing decades. Typical of this school was Josiah Gilbert Holland's *The Life of Abraham Lincoln*, which appeared in 1866 and sold more than 100,000 copies. Holland's Lincoln is a model youth and an impeccable Christian gentleman. When war clouds gather in 1860, he supposedly tells an Illinois associate: "I know there is a God and that he hates injustice and slavery. I see the storm coming, and I know that His hand is in it. If he has a place for and work for me—and I think he has—I believe I am ready. I am nothing, but truth is everything. I know I am right, because I know that liberty is right, for Christ teaches it and Christ is God." For Holland and other writers, ministers, and orators of this tradition, Lincoln was a martyr-saint, as pure and perfect a spirit as the Almighty ever created. He was "savior of the republic, emancipator of a race, true Christian, true man."

Sheer nonsense! thundered William H. Herndon, Lincoln's nervous, besotted law partner, when he read Holland's book. This prettified character was not the Lincoln he had known in Illinois. That Lincoln had never belonged to a church. He was *"an infidel,"* a prairie lawyer who told stories that made the pious wince. Determined to correct Holland's portrait, Herndon set out "to write the life of Lincoln as I saw him—honestly—truthfully—co[u]rageously— fearlessly cut whom it may." He jotted down his own impressions and interviewed old settlers in Indiana and Illinois who remembered Lincoln. They spun yarns about "Old Abe" that made Herndon's eyes hang out on his shirt front. Their Lincoln was an Illinois Paul Bunyan who could hoist a whiskey barrel overhead, a prairie Davy Crockett who roared that he was "the big buck of the lick." No historian, Herndon embraced such tales as zealously as he did actual fact. As a consequence, *Herndon's Lincoln: The True Story of a Great Life,* which came out in 1889, brimmed with gossip, hearsay, and legend, all mixed in with Herndon's own authentic observations of Lincoln in their law office, in Springfield's muddy streets, in courthouses and on the platform.

In sharp contrast to Holland's Christian gentleman, Herndon's Lincoln is a Western folk hero, funny, ambitious, irreverent, and sorrowful by turns. He is born in a "stagnant, putrid pool," the son of a shiftless poor white and "the illegitimate daughter" of a prominent Virginia planter. Though he rises above his impoverished origins, Herndon's Lincoln still has the stamp of the frontier on him: he plays practical jokes and performs legendary feats of strength. Still, he fears that he is illegitimate, too, and that and other woes often make him depressed. In New Salem, Herndon's Lincoln has the only love affair of his life. This is the Ann Rutledge story, a chimerical story which Herndon popularized and which subsequent biographies shamelessly repeated. In Herndon's telling, Lincoln falls deeply in love with Ann and almost goes mad when she dies. As she lies in her grave, he moans miserably, "My heart is buried there." If his heart is buried there, then he cannot possibly love Mary Todd. Herndon certainly bears her no love; in fact, he detests the woman; she is *"the female wildcat of the age."* What follows about Lincoln and Mary is mostly malicious gossip. In Springfield, Herndon's Lincoln does promise to wed Mary, only to plummet into despair. How can he marry this nasty little woman? Still, his sense of honor torments him. He has given his word. Sacrificing domestic happiness, Herndon's Lincoln goes ahead with the marriage, and Mary, a "tigress," "soured," "insolent," "haughty," and "gross," devotes herself to making Lincoln miserable. For him, life with Mary is "worse punishment . . . than burning by the stake." He finds escape in law and politics, and through adversity rises to "the topmost rung of the ladder." No haloed saint, Herndon's Lincoln in sum is a product of the great Western prairies, a religious skeptic, open, candid, energetic, trusting, and brave.

Herndon had promised that his *Lincoln* would "cause a squirm," and he was right. From across American Christendom came a fierce and unrelenting cry, "Atheist! Atheist! Herndon's an atheist!" With that, Herndon's partisans took on those of the Holland school in what David Donald has termed "a religious war." And so the two mythical conceptions—one portraying Lincoln as a frontier hero, the other as a martyr-saint—battled one another into the twentieth century.

By 1909, the centennial year of Lincoln's birth, the two traditions had begun to blend into "a composite American ideal," as Donald has said. But it remained for Carl Sandburg, in his epochal *Abraham Lincoln*, to combine the saint and folklore Lincoln and capture the mythic figure more vividly and consistently than any other folk biographer. In truth, Sandburg's became the most popular Lincoln work ever written, as a procession of plays, motion pictures, novels, children's books, school texts, and television shows purveyed Sandburg's Lincoln to a vast American public, until that Lincoln became for most Americans the real historical figure.

Yet, ironically enough, Sandburg did not set out to write an enduring epic. When he began his project in 1923, he intended only to do a Lincoln book for teenagers. He had collected Lincoln materials since his days at Lombard College in Galesburg, Illinois. Now he read voraciously in the sources, particularly in *Herndon's Lincoln*. And he retraced Lincoln's path across Illinois, chatting with plain folk as Herndon had done, looking for the Lincoln who lived in their imaginations and memories. As he worked, Sandburg strongly identified with "Abe" and even dressed, acted, and physically resembled the figure taking shape in his mind. "Like him," Sandburg said, "I am a son of the prairie, a poor boy who wandered over the land to find himself and his mission in life." Both were commoners from Illinois, both champions of the underdog, both great storytellers, and "both poets withal," as Stuart Sherman said.

As it happened, another poet had the most influence on Sandburg as a Lincoln biographer. This was Walt Whitman, who before the Civil War had actually anticipated the kind of mythic Lincoln who subsequently emerged. In the rollicking preface to *Leaves of Grass*, first published in 1855, Whitman's Poet Hero was "the equable man," simple, generous, and large, who spoke for the common people and for national union. In 1856, with uncanny foresight, Whitman asserted that "I would be much pleased to see some heroic, shrewd, fully-informed, healthy bodied, middle-aged, beard-faced American blacksmith come down from the West across the Alleghanies, and walk into the Presidency, dressed in a clean suit of working attire, and with the tan all over his face, breast, and arms." Four years later, Republican campaign propaganda depicted the rail-splitter candidate as almost exactly such a man.

In February, 1861, Whitman saw the President-elect as he passed through New York City on his way to Washington. Lincoln's "look and gait" captivated Whitman—"his dark-brown complexion, seam'd and wrinkled yet can-ny-looking face, his black, bushy head of hair, disproportionately long neck, and his hands held behind him as he stood observing the people." Here was a hero fit for the author of *Leaves of Grass.* From that moment on, Whitman idolized Lincoln and insisted that only the combined genius of Plutarch, Aes-chylus, and Michelangelo—"assisted by Rabelais"—could have captured Lin-coln's likeness. A true portrait, in other words, must have the dimensions and powerful symbols of myth.

"He has a face like a hoosier Michel Angelo," Whitman wrote three years later, "so awful ugly it becomes beautiful, with its strange mouth, its deep cut, criss-cross lines, and its doughnut complexion." Then he wrote something that was to affect Carl Sandburg enormously: "My notion is, too, that under-neath his outside smutched mannerism, and stories from third-class country bar-rooms (it is his humor,) Mr. Lincoln keeps a fountain of first-class practical telling wisdom. I do not dwell on the supposed failures of his government; he has shown, I sometimes think, an almost supernatural tact in keeping the ship afloat at all, with head steady, not only not going down, and now certain not to, but with proud and resolute spirit, and flag flying in sight of the world, menacing and high as ever." Here was the mythic "equalizer of his age and land" who inhabited Whitman's *Leaves of Grass,* a poet leader who in peace "speaks in the spirit of peace," but in war "is the most deadly force of the war."

In Lincoln, Whitman saw the archetypical Captain who was destined to lie "fallen cold and dead." And after Lincoln did fall, the poet poured out his grief in "When Lilacs Last in the Dooryard Bloom'd," a melodic farewell to the leader he loved, "O powerful western fallen star!" "the sweetest, wisest soul of all my days and lands." In 1886, broken down from a stroke, this "tender mother-man" with whiskered face and luminous blue-gray eyes, smelling of soap and cologne, wearing his gray felt hat tilted straight back, gave a memorial lecture about Lincoln which he repeated almost every year until his death in 1892. It was a ritual reenactment of Lincoln's assassination, a poet's celebration of a "sane and sacred death" that filtered "into the nation and race" and gave "a cement to the whole People, subtler, more underlying, than anything in written Constitution, or courts or armies."

In Whitman's writings, Sandburg found the central themes of the life he wanted to tell. He was already publishing verse that reflected Whitman's influ-ence and would soon be known as his heir, describing him as "the only distin-guished epic poet in America." But it was Whitman's mythic vision of Lincoln that most captured Sandburg's imagination, setting many of the expectations in treatment, mood, and archetype, as Justin Kaplan has pointed out, which Sandburg would try to satisfy in his biography. "In Lincoln," Sandburg himself wrote, "the people of the United States could finally see themselves, each for himself and all together." And he intended, Sandburg said, "to take Lincoln away from the religious bigots and the professional politicians and restore him to the common people."

Sandburg became completely absorbed in his Lincoln enterprise, so much so that at times he "felt as if in a trance, saw automobiles as horses and wagons, and saw cities of brick and stone dissolve into lumber cottages and shanties." What began as a teenagers' book swelled into a massive "life and times" that took fifteen years to complete and ran to 3,765 pages in six published volumes: the two-volume *Prairie Years*, which appeared in 1928, and the four-volume *War Years*, which followed in 1939. Sandburg's was a sprawling panorama, the literary equivalent of a Cecil B. DeMille motion-picture spectacular, with Lincoln himself alternately disappearing and reappearing in a rush of crowded scenes and events. And the Lincoln that emerges is not only a composite of the patron saint and Western hero; he is democracy's mythic hero, a great commoner who rises to the White House from utter obscurity, an "All-American" President who personifies the American ideal that "a democracy can choose a man," as Sandburg writes, "set him up with power and honor, and the very act does something to the man himself, raises up new gifts, modulations, controls, outlooks, wisdoms, inside the man, so that he is something else again than he was before they sifted him out and anointed him . . . Head of the Nation."

Sandburg's *Lincoln* captured the hearts of an entire generation of Americans, a generation that came of age in the cynical twenties, with its gang wars and brassy speakeasies, unbridled speculation and declining moral values, and that struggled through the Great Depression of the thirties, the worst crisis of American democracy since the Civil War. Small wonder that Sandburg won near universal acclaim. For poet Stephen Vincent Benét, Sandburg's "mountain range of biography" was "a good purge for our own troubled time and for its wild-eyed fears. For here we see the thing working, clumsily, erratically, often unfairly, attacked and reviled by extremists of left and right, yet working and surviving nevertheless." For Henry Bertram Hill of the Kansas City *Star*, Sandburg's Lincoln was "an apotheosis of the American people as well as of Lincoln as the greatest exemplar of their essential worth and goodness." For historian Henry Steele Commager, poets had always understood Lincoln best, and so it was "fitting that from the pen of a poet should come the greatest of all Lincoln biographies." For playwright Robert E. Sherwood, it was "a monument that would live forever."

Yet, as some critics pointed out, Sandburg's Lincoln could not be regarded as authentic biography, as an approximation of the real-life Lincoln based on accurate detail. No, Sandburg was not after that Lincoln. He was after the mythic figure—the Man of the People who had always fascinated him the most. And proven fact and sound documentation did not impede the poet in his search. "He suggests," as one critic said, "a bard sitting before a rude fireplace, chanting his hero tale with a poet's repetitions and refrains."

As *The Prairie Years* opens, we find the future Head of the Nation born of ordinary pioneer stock on the cutting edge of the Kentucky frontier. What follows is a gripping story, a poetic story, and it abounds in fictional scenes and lyrical apocrypha. As a boy, Sandburg's Lincoln shucks corn from early dawn till sundown and then reads books all night by the flickering fire. He kisses Green Taylor's girl. He once fights William Grigsby and cries out (as did Herndon's Lincoln), "I'm the big buck of this lick." He lifts barefoot boys so they can leave muddy footprints on the ceiling of the Lincoln cabin. Later, as a New Salem clerk, he walks six miles to return a few cents a customer has overpaid on her bill. And of course, he loves Ann Rutledge with an aching heart. "After the first evening in which Lincoln had sat next to her and found that bashful words tumbling from his tongue's end really spelled themselves out into sensible talk, her face, as he went away, kept coming back. So often all else would fade out of his mind and there would be only this riddle of a pink-fair face, a mouth and eyes in a frame of light corn-silk hair. He could ask himself what it meant and search his heart for an answer and no answer would come. A trembling took his body and dark waves ran through him sometimes when she spoke so simple a thing as, 'The corn is getting high, isn't it?' " Which prompted Edmund Wilson to remark, "The corn is getting high indeed!"

When Ann dies, Sandburg's Lincoln, like Herndon's, is stricken with a lover's grief: he wanders absently in the forest; he makes his way to the burying ground outside New Salem and lies with an arm across Ann's grave. "In the evenings it was useless to try to talk with him," Sandburg writes. "He sat by the fire one night as the flames licked up the cordwood and swept up the chimney to pass out into a driving storm-wind. The blowing weather woke some sort of lights in him and he went to the door and looked out into a night of fierce stumbling wind and black horizons. And he came back saying, 'I can't bear to think of her out there alone.' And he clenched his hands, mumbling, 'The rain and the storm shan't beat on her grave.' "

Though he eventually recovers from Ann's death, Sandburg's Lincoln never forgets the love he felt for her.*

As he grows to maturity, Sandburg's Lincoln is indigenously American, utterly shaped by the sprawling, unruly, pungent democracy of his day. He is simple, honest and ambitious, practical and wise. Professionally he is a homespun village lawyer and politician, always dressed in a rumpled suit and an old stovepipe hat. It is noticed among men that he has "two shifting moods," one when he lapses into "a gravity beyond any bystander to penetrate," the other when he recounts a "rollicking, droll story," usually to illustrate some point about people or politics. In the company of his male friends, he can tell offcolor jokes, too, and indulge in an expletive like "son-of-a-bitch." He is a colorful and yet mystic man, a kind of prairie Socrates brimming with wilderness wit and prairie sagacity. Above all, his heart beats with the pulse of rural, working-class America, and he loves the common folk and revels in daily contact with them.

But behind his bucolic plainness is a profound and mystical spirit awaiting its call to greatness. And that call comes in the grim and terrible years that

---

*There is not a scintilla of evidence for Sandburg's scenes about Lincoln and Ann. In fairness, though, Sandburg did delete a lot of this material in a one-volume condensation of the *Prairie* and *War Years.* But even there he persists in suggesting a romance between Lincoln and Ann and even quotes Edgar Lee Masters's ridiculous poem about how Ann Rutledge, "beloved in life of Abraham Lincoln," was wedded to him in her grave. Later Sandburg was sorry that he had fallen for the legend. He should have known it was out of character for Lincoln, he said.

follow the Kansas-Nebraska Act of 1854. Now Sandburg's Lincoln is a ghost on the platform, explaining to the people that the Revolution and freedom really mean something and reminding them of forgotten oaths and wasted sacrifices. In his great debates with Stephen A. Douglas, Sandburg's Lincoln is always one with the people, thrilling them with his "stubby, homely words." For the folk masses, he is both "the Strange Friend and Friendly Stranger." He is "something out of a picture book for children"—tall, bony, comical, haunted-looking, and sad. Already stories about him are spreading among the plain folk, and many sit brooding and talking about this "fabulous human figure of their own time." By 1861, history has called him to his tragic destiny: his is "a mind, a spirit, a tongue, and a voice" for an American democracy caught in its greatest trial. As he leaves Illinois for Washington, the presidency, and the war years, voices cry out on the wind, "Good-bye, Abe."

When he wrote *The War Years*, Sandburg abandoned poetical imaginings and produced a kind of symphonic documentary of the war and the man at its center. Though marred by a plethora of unauthenticated scenes and stories, the four volumes are full of the blood and stench—the sound and fury—of Civil War. And they capture all the immense tumult and confusion through which Lincoln day by day had to make his way. When we see the President, in between extensive passages on military and political developments in North and South alike, he is entirely an external Lincoln, an observed hero filtered to us through the vision and sensibilities of hundreds of witnesses who called at his White House office, from generals and politicians and office seekers to the infirm, the destitute, and the ordinary. By revealing Lincoln through the observations of others and relating him to almost everything that happened in his shell-torn land, Sandburg is trying to demonstrate that "the hopes and apprehensions of millions, their loves and hates, their exultation and despair, were reflected truthfully in the deep waters of Lincoln's being," as Robert Sherwood said.

In the "tornado years" of civil war, Sandburg's Lincoln is both the hero and the instrument of the people. He is the umpire of an embattled Union, patiently sticking to the cherished middle way. When it comes to emancipation, he always follows the pulse of the people: with a genius for timing, he issues his proclamation only when that is what they want. Now "a piece of historic drama" has been played, and across the world, among the masses of people who create folk gods out of slender fact, there runs the story of "the Strong Man who arose in his might and delivered an edict, spoke a few words fitly chosen, and thereupon the shackles and chains fell from the arms and ankles of men, women, and children born to be chattels for toil and bondage."

As the war rages on, Lincoln's "skilled referee hand" guides the ship of state through cross winds of passion and cross plays of hate. Throughout he has the folk masses behind him. He is still their Friendly Stranger in a storm of death and destruction. Even during his lowest ebb in 1864, he remains the people's President: he retains their love and loyalty even as Republican leaders raise a howl against his renomination and reelection. And he wins in 1864 because the wisdom of the people prevails.

Moreover, in the last long year of the war, Sandburg's Lincoln does battle with the so-called radicals of the party—vindictive cynics like Charles Sumner and old Thad Stevens, who in Sandburg's view want to exterminate the South's ruling class and convert Dixie into "a vast graveyard of slaughtered whites, with Negro State governments established and upheld by Northern white bayonets." But a mild and moderate Lincoln refuses to go along with them. He is now in his grandest hour, this Lincoln of *The War Years*, as he plans to reconstruct the South with tender magnanimity. He is the only man in the entire country who can peaceably reunite the sections. But, as in a Greek tragedy, Lincoln is murdered before he can bind up the nation's wounds and heal the antagonisms of his divided countrymen. In North and South, common people weep aloud, realizing the painful truth of the old folk adage that a tree is measured best when it is down.

"To a deep river," writes Sandburg, "to a far country, to a by-and-by whence no man returns, had gone the child of Nancy Hanks and Tom Lincoln, the wilderness boy who found far lights and tall rainbows to live by, whose name even before he died had become a legend inwoven with men's struggle for freedom the world over." There was the story of how Count Leo Tolstoy, traveling into the Caucasus of czarist Russia, encountered tribesmen demanding to know about Lincoln, the "greatest general and greatest ruler of the world." Says Sandburg: "To Tolstoy the incident proved that in far places over the earth the name of Lincoln was worshipped and the personality of Lincoln had become a world folk legend."

Sandburg ended his narrative with Lincoln's funeral in Springfield. But others have added an epilogue implied by Sandburg's story. Without Father Abraham, the epilogue goes, the nation foundered in the harsh years of reconstruction, as an all-too-mortal President succumbed to "vengeful radicals" on Capitol Hill. Alas, how much better reconstruction would have been had Father Abraham only lived. How much more easily a divided nation would have set aside the war years and come together again in a spirit of mutual respect and harmony. There would never have been an impeachment trial, never a radical reconstruction, never an army of occupation, never a Ku Klux Klan, never all those racial troubles to haunt later generations, if only Father Abraham had not died that terrible day in 1865.

And so Lincoln comes to us in the mists of mythology. Still, I have no quarrel with this Lincoln, so long as we make a careful distinction between myth and history. Myth, after all, is not an untrue story to be avoided like some dread disease. On the contrary, myth carries a special truth of its own— a truth, however, that is different from historical truth, from what actually happened. In the case of Lincoln, the myth is what Americans wish the man had been, not necessarily the way he was in real life. That is why Sandburg's Lincoln has such irresistible appeal to us. He is a "baffling and completely inexplicable" hero who embodies the mystical genius of our nation. He possesses what Americans have always considered their most noble traits—honesty, unpretentiousness, tolerance, hard work, a capacity to forgive, a compassion for the underdog, a clear-sighted vision of right and wrong, a dedication to God and country, and an abiding concern for all. As I have said elsewhere, no real-life person has ever risen to such mythic proportions, to epitomize all that we have longed to be since 1776. No real-life person can ever rise to such proportions. So we have invented a Lincoln who fulfills our deepest needs as a people—a Father Abraham who in the stormy present still provides an example and shows us the way. The Lincoln of mythology carries the torch of the American dream, a dream of noble idealism, of self-sacrifice and common humanity, of liberty and equality for all.

Our folly as a nation, though, is that we too often confuse myth with history, mistake our mythologized heroes for their real-life counterparts, regard the deified frontiersman as the actual frontiersman. As a consequence, we too often try to emulate our mythical forebears, to be as glorious, as powerful, as incapable of error, as incessantly right, as we have made them. As journalist Ronnie Dugger has reminded us, those who live by the lessons of mythology rather than the lessons of history—as Lyndon Johnson did in the Vietnam era—are apt to trap themselves in catastrophe.

This is not to say that myths have no function in our cultural life. On the contrary, if we Americans can accept our myths as inspiring tales rather than as authentic history, then surely myths can serve us as they have traditional myth-bound societies. Like fiction and poetry, they can give us insight into ourselves, help us understand the spiritual needs of our country, as we cope with the complex realities of our own time. In that event, the Lincoln of mythology—the Plain and Humble Man of the People who emerged from the toiling millions to guide us through our greatest national ordeal—can have profound spiritual meaning for us.

The New View of Reconstruction

Eric Foner

Generations of American college students, at least those schooled prior to the 1960s, were rather comfortably conveyed the impression that Reconstruction—the era after the Civil War involved with "binding up the nation's wounds" opened by civil conflict—was an era of America's past simply portrayed in shades of black and white. It was said to offer a tale of black rule (the "Africanization" of southern politics), resultant corruption, political subordination of southern whites, military despotism, and radical congressional control of Reconstruction policy. Offering a summary of new research findings, Columbia University professor Eric Foner demonstrates how almost every previous assumption regarding Reconstruction has been overturned. Black supremacy was a myth, the era was far more conservative than radical, southern whites were not categorically disenfranchised, and military despotism was hardly the rule. Moreover, recent scholarship has formulated a new agenda for Reconstruction study, emphasizing social rather than political issues, noting the continuing relevance of Reconstruction issues to American society, and, most important, conceding the role of blacks as active agents in the profound changes of the time.

In the past twenty years, no period of American history has been the subject of a more thoroughgoing reevaluation than Reconstruction—the violent, dramatic, and still controversial era following the Civil War. Race relations, politics, social life, and economic change during Reconstruction have all been reinterpreted in the light of changed attitudes toward the place of blacks within American society. If historians have not yet forged a fully satisfying portrait of Reconstruction as a whole, the traditional interpretation that dominated historical writing for much of this century has irrevocably been laid to rest.

Anyone who attended high school before 1960 learned that Reconstruction was an era of unrelieved sordidness in American political and social life. The martyred Lincoln, according to this view, had planned a quick and painless readmission of the Southern states as equal members of the national family. President Andrew Johnson, his successor, attempted to carry out Lincoln's policies but was foiled by the Radical Republicans (also known as Vindictives or Jacobins). Motivated by an irrational hatred of Rebels or by ties with North-

From "The New View of Reconstruction" by Eric Foner. Reprinted with permission from *American Heritage*, Volume 34, No. 6. Copyright 1983 by American Heritage Publishing Co. Inc.

ern capitalists out to plunder the South, the Radicals swept aside Johnson's lenient program and fastened black supremacy upon the defeated Confederacy. An orgy of corruption followed, presided over by unscrupulous carpetbaggers (Northerners who ventured south to reap the spoils of office), traitorous scalawags (Southern whites who cooperated with the new governments for personal gain), and the ignorant and childlike freedmen, who were incapable of properly exercising the political power that had been thrust upon them. After much needless suffering, the white community of the South banded together to overthrow these "black" governments and restore home rule (their euphemism for white supremacy). All told, Reconstruction was just about the darkest page in the American saga.

Originating in anti-Reconstruction propaganda of Southern Democrats during the 1870s, this traditional interpretation achieved scholarly legitimacy around the turn of the century through the work of William Dunning and his students at Columbia University. It reached the larger public through films like *Birth of a Nation* and *Gone With the Wind* and that best-selling work of myth-making masquerading as history, *The Tragic Era* by Claude G. Bowers. In language as exaggerated as it was colorful, Bowers told how Andrew Johnson "fought the bravest battle for constitutional liberty and for the preservation of our institutions ever waged by an Executive" but was overwhelmed by the "poisonous propaganda" of the Radicals. Southern whites, as a result, "literally were put to the torture" by "emissaries of hate" who manipulated the "simple-minded" freedmen, "inflaming the negroes' egotism" and even inspiring "lustful assaults" by blacks upon white womanhood.

In a discipline that sometimes seems to pride itself on the rapid rise and fall of historical interpretations, this traditional portrait of Reconstruction enjoyed remarkable staying power. The long reign of the old interpretation is not difficult to explain. It presented a set of easily identifiable heroes and villains. It enjoyed the imprimatur of the nation's leading scholars. And it accorded with the political and social realities of the first half of this century. This image of Reconstruction helped freeze the mind of the white South in unalterable opposition to any movement for breaching the ascendancy of the Democratic party, eliminating segregation, or readmitting disfranchised blacks to the vote.

Nevertheless, the demise of the traditional interpretation was inevitable, for it ignored the testimony of the central participant in the drama of Reconstruction—the black freedman. Furthermore, it was grounded in the conviction that blacks were unfit to share in political power. As Dunning's Columbia colleague John W. Burgess put it, "A black skin means membership in a race of men which has never of itself succeeded in subjecting passion to reason, has never, therefore, created any civilization of any kind." Once objective scholarship and modern experience rendered that assumption untenable, the entire edifice was bound to fall.

The work of "revising" the history of Reconstruction began with the writings of a handful of survivors of the era, such as John R. Lynch, who had served as a black congressman from Mississippi after the Civil War. In the

1930s white scholars like Francis Simkins and Robert Woody carried the task forward. Then, in 1935, the black historian and activist W. E. B. Du Bois produced *Black Reconstruction in America,* a monumental reevaluation that closed with an irrefutable indictment of a historical profession that had sacrificed scholarly objectivity on the altar of racial bias. "One fact and one alone," he wrote, "explains the attitude of most recent writers toward Reconstruction; they cannot conceive of Negroes as men." Du Bois's work, however, was ignored by most historians.

It was not until the 1960s that the full force of the revisionist wave broke over the field. Then, in rapid succession, virtually every assumption of the traditional viewpoint was systematically dismantled. A drastically different portrait emerged to take its place. President Lincoln did not have a coherent "plan" for Reconstruction, but at the time of his assassination he had been cautiously contemplating black suffrage. Andrew Johnson was a stubborn, racist politician who lacked the ability to compromise. By isolating himself from the broad currents of public opinion that had nourished Lincoln's career, Johnson created an impasse with Congress that Lincoln would certainly have avoided, thus throwing away his political power and destroying his own plans for reconstructing the South.

The Radicals in Congress were acquitted of both vindictive motives and the charge of serving as the stalking-horses of Northern capitalism. They emerged instead as idealists in the best nineteenth-century reform tradition. Radical leaders like Charles Sumner and Thaddeus Stevens had worked for the rights of blacks long before any conceivable political advantage flowed from such a commitment. Stevens refused to sign the Pennsylvania Constitution of 1838 because it disfranchised the state's black citizens; Sumner led a fight in the 1850s to integrate Boston's public schools. Their Reconstruction policies were based on principle, not petty political advantage, for the central issue dividing Johnson and these Radical Republicans was the civil rights of freedmen. Studies of congressional policy-making, such as Eric L. McKitrick's *Andrew Johnson and Reconstruction,* also revealed that Reconstruction legislation, ranging from the Civil Rights Act of 1866 to the Fourteenth and Fifteenth Amendments, enjoyed broad support from moderate and conservative Republicans. It was not simply the work of a narrow Radical faction.

Even more startling was the revised portrait of Reconstruction in the South itself. Imbued with the spirit of the civil rights movement and rejecting entirely the racial assumptions that had underpinned the traditional interpretation, these historians evaluated Reconstruction from the black point of view. Works like Joel Williamson's *After Slavery* portrayed the period as a time of extraordinary political, social, and economic progress for blacks. The establishment of public school systems, the granting of equal citizenship to blacks, the effort to restore the devastated Southern economy, the attempt to construct an interracial political democracy from the ashes of slavery, all these were commendable achievements, not the elements of Bowers's "tragic era."

Unlike earlier writers, the revisionists stressed the active role of the freedmen in shaping Reconstruction. Black initiative established as many schools as did Northern religious societies and the Freedmen's Bureau. The right to vote was not simply thrust upon them by meddling outsiders, since blacks began agitating for the suffrage as soon as they were freed. In 1865 black conventions throughout the South issued eloquent, though unheeded, appeals for equal civil and political rights.

With the advent of Radical Reconstruction in 1867, the freedmen did enjoy a real measure of political power. But black supremacy never existed. In most states blacks held only a small fraction of political offices, and even in South Carolina, where they comprised a majority of the state legislature's lower house, effective power remained in white hands. As for corruption, moral standards in both government and private enterprise were at low ebb throughout the nation in the postwar years—the era of Boss Tweed, the Credit Mobilier scandal, and the Whiskey Ring. Southern corruption could hardly be blamed on former slaves.

Other actors in the Reconstruction drama also came in for reevaluation. Most carpetbaggers were former Union soldiers seeking economic opportunity in the postwar South, not unscrupulous adventurers. Their motives, a typically American amalgam of humanitarianism and the pursuit of profit, were no more insidious than those of Western pioneers. Scalawags, previously seen as traitors to the white race, now emerged as "Old Line" Whig Unionists who had opposed secession in the first place or as poor whites who had long resented planters' domination of Southern life and who saw in Reconstruction a chance to recast Southern society along more democratic lines. Strongholds of Southern white Republicanism like east Tennessee and western North Carolina had been the scene of resistance to Confederate rule throughout the Civil War; now, as one scalawag newspaper put it, the choice was "between salvation at the hand of the Negro or destruction at the hand of the rebels."

At the same time, the Ku Klux Klan and kindred groups, whose campaign of violence against black and white Republicans had been minimized or excused in older writings, were portrayed as they really were. Earlier scholars had conveyed the impression that the Klan intimidated blacks mainly by dressing as ghosts and playing on the freedmen's superstitions. In fact, black fears were all too real: the Klan was a terrorist organization that beat and killed its political opponents to deprive blacks of their newly won rights. The complicity of the Democratic party and the silence of prominent whites in the face of such outrages stood as an indictment of the moral code the South had inherited from the days of slavery.

By the end of the 1960s, then, the old interpretation had been completely reversed. Southern freedmen were the heroes, the "Redeemers" who overthrew Reconstruction were the villains, and if the era was "tragic," it was because change did not go far enough. Reconstruction had been a time of real progress and its failure a lost opportunity for the South and the nation. But the legacy of Reconstruction—the Fourteenth and Fifteenth Amendments—endured to inspire future efforts for civil rights. As Kenneth Stampp wrote in *The Era of Reconstruction*, a superb summary of revisionist findings published in 1965, "if it was worth four years of civil war to save the Union, it was worth a few years of radical reconstruction to give the American Negro the ultimate promise of equal civil and political rights."

As Stampp's statement suggests, the reevaluation of the first Reconstruction was inspired in large measure by the impact of the second—the modern civil rights movement. And with the waning of that movement in recent years, writing on Reconstruction has undergone still another transformation. Instead of seeing the Civil War and its aftermath as a second American Revolution (as Charles Beard had), a regression into barbarism (as Bowers argued), or a golden opportunity squandered (as the revisionists saw it), recent writers argue that Radical Reconstruction was not really very radical. Since land was not distributed to the former slaves, they remained economically dependent upon their former owners. The planter class survived both the war and Reconstruction with its property (apart from slaves) and prestige more or less intact.

Not only changing times but also the changing concerns of historians have contributed to this latest reassessment of Reconstruction. The hallmark of the past decade's historical writing has been an emphasis upon "social history"—the evocation of the past lives of ordinary Americans—and the downplaying of strictly political events. When applied to Reconstruction, this concern with the "social" suggested that black suffrage and officeholding, once seen as the most radical departures of the Reconstruction era, were relatively insignificant.

Recent historians have focused their investigations not upon the politics of Reconstruction but upon the social and economic aspects of the transition from slavery to freedom. Herbert Gutman's influential study of the black family during and after slavery found little change in family structure or relations between men and women resulting from emancipation. Under slavery most blacks had lived in nuclear family units, although they faced the constant threat of separation from loved ones by sale. Reconstruction provided the opportunity for blacks to solidify their preexisting family ties. Conflicts over whether black women should work in the cotton fields (planters said yes, many black families said no) and over white attempts to "apprentice" black children revealed that the autonomy of family life was a major preoccupation of the freedmen. Indeed, whether manifested in their withdrawal from churches controlled by whites, in the blossoming of black fraternal, benevolent, and self-improvement organizations, or in the demise of the slave quarters and their replacement by small tenant farms occupied by individual families, the quest for independence from white authority and control over their own day-to-day lives shaped the black response to emancipation.

In the post–Civil War South the surest guarantee of economic autonomy, blacks believed, was land. To the freedmen the justice of a claim to land based on their years of unrequited labor appeared self-evident. As an Alabama black convention put it, "The property which they [the planters] hold was nearly all earned by the sweat of *our* brows." As Leon Litwack showed in *Been in the*

Storm So Long, a Pulitzer Prize–winning account of the black response to emancipation, many freedmen in 1865 and 1866 refused to sign labor contracts, expecting the federal government to give them land. In some localities, as one Alabama overseer reported, they "set up claims to the plantation and all on it."

In the end, of course, the vast majority of Southern blacks remained propertyless and poor. But exactly why the South, and especially its black population, suffered from dire poverty and economic retardation in the decades following the Civil War is a matter of much dispute. In *One Kind of Freedom,* economists Roger Ransom and Richard Sutch indicted country merchants for monopolizing credit and charging usurious interest rates, forcing black tenants into debt and locking the South into a dependence on cotton production that impoverished the entire region. But Jonathan Wiener, in his study of postwar Alabama, argued that planters used their political power to compel blacks to remain on the plantations. Planters succeeded in stabilizing the plantation system, but only by blocking the growth of alternative enterprises, like factories, that might draw off black laborers, thus locking the region into a pattern of economic backwardness.

If the thrust of recent writing has emphasized the social and economic aspects of Reconstruction, politics has not been entirely neglected. But political studies have also reflected the postrevisionist mood summarized by C. Vann Woodward when he observed "how essentially nonrevolutionary and conservative Reconstruction really was." Recent writers, unlike their revisionist predecessors, have found little to praise in federal policy toward the emancipated blacks.

A new sensitivity to the strength of prejudice and laissez-faire ideas in the nineteenth-century North has led many historians to doubt whether the Republican party ever made a genuine commitment to racial justice in the South. The granting of black suffrage was an alternative to a long-term federal responsibility for protecting the rights of the former slaves. Once enfranchised, blacks could be left to fend for themselves. With the exception of a few Radicals like Thaddeus Stevens, nearly all Northern policy-makers and educators are criticized today for assuming that, so long as the unfettered operations of the marketplace afforded blacks the opportunity to advance through diligent labor, federal efforts to assist them in acquiring land were unnecessary.

Probably the most innovative recent writing on Reconstruction politics has centered on a broad reassessment of black Republicanism, largely undertaken by a new generation of black historians. Scholars like Thomas Holt and Nell Painter insist that Reconstruction was not simply a matter of black and white. Conflicts within the black community, no less than divisions among whites, shaped Reconstruction politics. Where revisionist scholars, both black and white, had celebrated the accomplishments of black political leaders, Holt, Painter, and others charge that they failed to address the economic plight of the black masses. Painter criticized "representative colored men," as national black leaders were called, for failing to provide ordinary freedmen with effective political leadership. Holt found that black officeholders in South Carolina mostly emerged from the old free mulatto class of Charleston, which shared many assumptions with prominent whites. "Basically bourgeois in their origins and orientation," he wrote, they "failed to act in the interest of black peasants."

In emphasizing the persistence from slavery of divisions between free blacks and slaves, these writers reflect the increasing concern with continuity and conservatism in Reconstruction. Their work reflects a startling extension of revisionist premises. If, as has been argued for the past twenty years, blacks were active agents rather than mere victims of manipulation, then they could not be absolved of blame for the ultimate failure of Reconstruction.

Despite the excellence of recent writing and the continual expansion of our knowledge of the period, historians of Reconstruction today face a unique dilemma. An old interpretation has been overthrown, but a coherent new synthesis has yet to take its place. The revisionists of the 1960s effectively established a series of negative points: the Reconstruction governments were not as bad as had been portrayed, black supremacy was a myth, the Radicals were not cynical manipulators of the freedmen. Yet no convincing overall portrait of the quality of political and social life emerged from their writings. More recent historians have rightly pointed to elements of continuity that spanned the nineteenth-century Southern experience, especially the survival, in modified form, of the plantation system. Nevertheless, by denying the real changes that did occur, they have failed to provide a convincing portrait of an era characterized above all by drama, turmoil, and social change.

Building upon the findings of the past twenty years of scholarship, a new portrait of Reconstruction ought to begin by viewing it not as a specific time period, bounded by the years 1865 and 1877, but as an episode in a prolonged historical process—American society's adjustment to the consequences of the Civil War and emancipation. The Civil War, of course, raised the decisive questions of America's national existence: the relations between local and national authority, the definition of citizenship, the balance between force and consent in generating obedience to authority. The war and Reconstruction, as Allan Nevins observed over fifty years ago, marked the "emergence of modern America." This was the era of the completion of the national railroad network, the creation of the modern steel industry, the conquest of the West and final subduing of the Indians, and the expansion of the mining frontier. Lincoln's America—the world of the small farm and artisan shop—gave way to a rapidly industrializing economy. The issues that galvanized postwar Northern politics—from the question of the greenback currency to the mode of paying holders of the national debt—arose from the economic changes unleashed by the Civil War.

Above all, the war irrevocably abolished slavery. Since 1619, when "twenty negars" disembarked from a Dutch ship in Virginia, racial injustice had haunted American life, mocking its professed ideals even as tobacco and cotton, the products of slave labor, helped finance the nation's economic development. Now the implications of the black presence could no longer be ignored. The Civil War resolved the problem of slavery but, as the Philadelphia diarist Sydney George Fisher observed in June 1865, it opened an even more intractable problem: "What shall we do with the Negro?" Indeed, he went on, this was a problem *incapable* of any solution that will satisfy both North and South."

As Fisher realized, the focal point of Reconstruction was the social revolution known as emancipation. Plantation slavery was simultaneously a system of labor, a form of racial domination, and the foundation upon which arose a distinctive ruling class within the South. Its demise threw open the most fundamental questions of economy, society, and politics. A new system of labor, social, racial, and political relations had to be created to replace slavery.

The United States was not the only nation to experience emancipation in the nineteenth century. Neither plantation slavery nor abolition were unique to the United States. But Reconstruction was. In a comparative perspective Radical Reconstruction stands as a remarkable experiment, the only effort of a society experiencing abolition to bring the former slaves within the umbrella of equal citizenship. Because the Radicals did not achieve everything they wanted, historians have lately tended to play down the stunning departure represented by black suffrage and officeholding. Former slaves, most fewer than two years removed from bondage, debated the fundamental questions of the polity: What is a republican form of government? Should the state provide equal education for all? How could political equality be reconciled with a society in which property was so unequally distributed? There was something inspiring in the way such men met the challenge of Reconstruction. "I knew nothing more than to obey my master," James K. Greene, an Alabama black politician later recalled. "But the tocsin of freedom sounded and knocked at the door and we walked out like free men and we met the exigencies as they grew up, and shouldered responsibilities."

"You never saw a people more excited on the subject of politics than are the negroes of the south," one planter observed in 1867. And there were more than a few Southern whites as well who in these years shook off the prejudices of the past to embrace the vision of a new South dedicated to the principles of equal citizenship and social justice. One ordinary South Carolinian expressed the new sense of possibility in 1868 to the Republican governor of the state: "I am sorry that I cannot write an elegant stiled letter to your excellency. But I rejoice to think that God almighty has given to the poor of S. C. a Gov. to hear to feel to protect the humble poor without distinction to race or color. . . . I am a native borned S. C. a poor man never owned a Negro in my life nor my father before me. . . . Remember the true and loyal are the poor of the whites and blacks, outside of these you can find none loyal."

Few modern scholars believe the Reconstruction governments established in the South in 1867 and 1868 fulfilled the aspirations of their humble constituents. While their achievements in such realms as education, civil rights, and the economic rebuilding of the South are now widely appreciated, historians today believe they failed to affect either the economic plight of the

emancipated slave or the ongoing transformation of independent white farmers into cotton tenants. Yet their opponents did perceive the Reconstruction
governments in precisely this way—as representatives of a revolution that had
put the bottom rail, both racial and economic, on top. This perception helps
explain the ferocity of the attacks leveled against them and the pervasiveness
of violence in the postemancipation South.

   The spectacle of black men voting and holding office was anathema to
large numbers of Southern whites. Even more disturbing, at least in the view
of those who still controlled the plantation regions of the South, was the emergence of local officials, black and white, who sympathized with the plight of
the black laborer. Alabama's vagrancy law was a "dead letter" in 1870, "because those who are charged with its enforcement are indebted to the vagrant
vote for their offices and emoluments." Political debates over the level and
incidence of taxation, the control of crops, and the resolution of contract disputes revealed that a primary issue of Reconstruction was the role of government in a plantation society. During presidential Reconstruction, and after
"Redemption," with planters and their allies in control of politics, the law
emerged as a means of stabilizing and promoting the plantation system. If Radical Reconstruction failed to redistribute the land of the South, the ouster of
the planter class from control of politics at least ensured that the sanctions of
the criminal law would not be employed to discipline the black labor force.

An understanding of this fundamental conflict over the relation between government and society helps explain the pervasive complaints concerning corruption and "extravagance" during Radical Reconstruction. Corruption there
was aplenty; tax rates did rise sharply. More significant than the rate of taxation, however, was the change in its incidence. For the first time, planters and
white farmers had to pay a significant portion of their income to the government, while propertyless blacks often escaped scot-free. Several states, moreover, enacted heavy taxes on uncultivated land to discourage land speculation
and force land onto the market, benefiting, it was hoped, the freedmen.

   As time passed, complaints about the "extravagance" and corruption of
Southern governments found a sympathetic audience among influential
Northerners. The Democratic charge that universal suffrage in the South was
responsible for high taxes and governmental extravagance coincided with a
rising conviction among the urban middle classes of the North that city government had to be taken out of the hands of the immigrant poor and returned
to the "best men"—the educated, professional, financially independent citizens unable to exert much political influence at a time of mass parties and
machine politics. Increasingly the "respectable" middle classes began to retreat from the very notion of universal suffrage. The poor were no longer perceived as honest producers, the backbone of the social order; now they became
the "dangerous classes," the "mob." As the historian Francis Parkman put it,
too much power rested with "masses of imported ignorance and hereditary
ineptitude." To Parkman the Irish of the Northern cities and the blacks of the

South were equally incapable of utilizing the ballot: "Witness the municipal corruptions of New York, and the monstrosities of negro rule in South Carolina." Such attitudes helped to justify Northern inaction as, one by one, the Reconstruction regimes of the South were overthrown by political violence.

In the end, then, neither the abolition of slavery nor Reconstruction succeeded in resolving the debate over the meaning of freedom in American life. Twenty years before the American Civil War, writing about the prospect of abolition in France's colonies, Alexis de Tocqueville had written, "If the Negroes have the right to become free, the [planters] have the incontestable right not to be ruined by the Negroes' freedom." And in the United States, as in nearly every plantation society that experienced the end of slavery, a rigid social and political dichotomy between former master and former slave, an ideology of racism, and a dependent labor force with limited economic opportunities all survived abolition. Unless one means by freedom the simple fact of not being a slave, emancipation thrust blacks into a kind of no-man's land, a partial freedom that made a mockery of the American ideal of equal citizenship.

Yet by the same token the ultimate outcome underscores the uniqueness of Reconstruction itself. Alone among the societies that abolished slavery in the nineteenth century, the United States, for a moment, offered the freedmen a measure of political control over their own destinies. However brief its sway, Reconstruction allowed scope for a remarkable political and social mobilization of the black community. It opened doors of opportunity that could never be completely closed. Reconstruction transformed the lives of Southern blacks in ways unmeasurable by statistics and unreachable by law. It raised their expectations and aspirations, redefined their status in relation to the larger society, and allowed space for the creation of institutions that enabled them to survive the repression that followed. And it established constitutional principles of civil and political equality that, while flagrantly violated after Redemption, planted the seeds of future struggle.

Certainly, in terms of the sense of possibility with which it opened, Reconstruction failed. But as Du Bois observed, it was a "splendid failure." For its animating vision—a society in which social advancement would be open to all on the basis of individual merit, not inherited caste distinctions—is as old as America itself and remains relevant to a nation still grappling with the unresolved legacy of emancipation.

Did the Civil War Retard Industrialization?

Thomas C. Cochran

Nations in the twentieth century tend to define their existence largely in economic terms. We as Americans see our economic strength and fate invariably linked to "capitalism" as both an economic and a political way of life. Thus it is not surprising that, historically speaking, the nation has come to attach considerable importance to the development of the American economy. In the traditional view, the Civil War was always considered basic to American economic development. It served as the convenient dividing line between limited economic growth and massive industrial expansion. In the selection here reprinted, however, Thomas C. Cochran, Professor of Economic History at the University of Pennsylvania, posits that the Civil War, rather than generating economic growth, actually retarded its development.

In most textbooks and interpretative histories of the United States the Civil War has been assigned a major role in bringing about the American Industrial Revolution. Colorful business developments in the North—adoption of new machines, the quick spread of war contracting, the boost given to profits by inflation, and the creation of a group of war millionaires—make the war years seem not only a period of rapid economic change but also one that created important forces for future growth. The superficial qualitative evidence is so persuasive that apparently few writers have examined the available long-run statistical series before adding their endorsement to the conventional interpretation. The following quotations taken from the books of two generations of leading scholars illustrate the popular view.

"The so-called Civil War," wrote Charles A. and Mary R. Beard in 1927, ". . . was a social war . . . making *vast changes* in the arrangement of classes, in the accumulation and distribution of wealth, *in the course of industrial development.*" Midway between 1927 and the present, Arthur M. Schlesinger, Sr., wrote: "On these tender industrial growths the Civil War *had the effect of a hothouse.* For reasons already clear . . . nearly every branch of industry grew lustily." Harold U. Faulkner, whose textbook sales have ranked near or at the top, said in 1954: "In the economic history of the United States the Civil War was extremely important. . . . In the North *it speeded the Industrial*

From "Did the Civil War Retard Industrialization?" by Thomas C. Cochran, in *Mississippi Valley Historical Review*, September 1961. Reprinted by permission of the *Journal of American History.*

Revolution and the development of capitalism by the prosperity which it brought to industry." The leading new text of 1957, by Richard Hofstadter, William Miller, and Daniel Aaron, showed no weakening of this interpretation: "The growing demand for farm machinery as well as for the 'sinews of war' led to American industrial expansion. . . . Of necessity, *iron, coal, and copper* production boomed during the war years." A sophisticated but still essentially misleading view is presented by Gilbert C. Fite and Jim E. Reese in a text of 1959: "The Civil War proved to be a boon to Northern economic development. . . . Industry, for example, was not created by the war, but wartime demands *greatly stimulated and encouraged industrial development* which already had a good start." In a reappraisal of the Civil War, in *Harper's Magazine* for April, 1960, Denis W. Brogan, a specialist in American institutions, wrote: "It may have been only a catalyst but the War *precipitated the entry* of the United States *into the modern industrial world*, made 'the take-off' (to use Professor W. W. Rostow's brilliant metaphor) come sooner."

In all of these reiterations of the effect of the Civil War on industrialism, statistical series seem to have been largely neglected. None of the authors cited reinforce their interpretations by setting the war period in the context of important long-run indexes of industrial growth. Since 1949, series of the period 1840 to 1890 that would cast doubt on the conventional generalizations have been available in *Historical Statistics of the United States, 1789–1945.* In 1960 a new edition of *Historical Statistics* and the report of the Conference on Research in Income and Wealth in *Trends in the American Economy in the Nineteenth Century* have provided additional material to support the argument that the Civil War retarded American industrial development. These volumes give data for many growth curves for the two decades before and after the war decade—in other words, the long-run trends before and after the event in question. The pattern of these trends is a mixed one which shows no uniform type of change during the Civil War decade, but on balance for the more important series the trend is toward retardation in *rates* of growth rather than toward acceleration. The fact is evident in many series which economists would regard as basic to economic growth, but in order to keep the discussion within reasonable limits only a few can be considered here.

Robert E. Gallman has compiled new and more accurate series for both "total commodity output," including agriculture, and "value added by manufacture," the two most general measures of economic growth available for this period. He writes: "Between 1839 and 1899 total commodity output increased elevenfold, or at an average decade rate of slightly less than 50 percent. . . . Actual rates varied fairly widely, high rates appearing during the decades ending with 1854 and 1884, and a very low rate during the decade ending with 1869." From the overall standpoint this statement indicates the immediately retarding effect of the Civil War on American economic growth, but since most of the misleading statements are made in regard to industrial growth, or particular elements in industrial growth, it is necessary to look in more detail at "value added by manufacture" and some special series. Gallman's series for value added in constant dollars of the purchasing power of 1879 shows a rise of 157 percent from 1839 to 1849; 76 percent from 1849 to 1859; and only 25 percent from 1859 to 1869. By the 1870's the more favorable prewar rates were resumed, with an increase of 82 percent for 1869–1879, and 112 percent for 1879–1889. Thus two decades of very rapid advance, the 1840's and the 1880's, are separated by thirty years of slower growth which falls to the lowest level in the decade that embraces the Civil War.

Pig-iron production in tons, perhaps the most significant commodity index of nineteenth-century American industrial growth, is available year-by-year from 1854 on. Taking total production for five-year periods, output increased 9 percent between the block of years from 1856 to 1860 and the block from 1861 to 1865. That even this slight increase might not have been registered except for the fact that 1857 to 1860 were years of intermittent depression is indicated by an 81 percent increase over the war years in the block of years from 1866 to 1870. If annual production is taken at five-year intervals, starting in 1850, the increase is 24 percent from 1850 to 1855; 17 percent from 1855 to 1860; 1 percent from 1860 to 1865; and 100 percent from 1865 to 1870. While there is no figure available for 1845, the period from 1840 to 1850 shows 97 percent increase in shipments, while for the period 1870 to 1880 the increase was 130 percent. To sum up, depression and war appear to have retarded a curve of production that was tending to rise at a high rate.

Bituminous coal production may be regarded as the next most essential commodity series. After a gain of 199 percent from 1840 to 1850 this series shows a rather steady pattern of increase at rates varying from 119 to 148 percent each decade from 1850 to 1890. The war does not appear to have markedly affected the rate of growth.

In the mid-nineteenth century copper production was not a basic series for recording American growth, but since three distinguished authors have singled it out as one of the indexes of the effect of the war on industry it is best to cite the statistics. Before 1845 production of domestic copper was negligible. By 1850 the "annual recoverable content" of copper from United States mines was 728 tons, by 1860 it was 8,064 tons, by 1865 it was 9,520 tons, and by 1870 it was 14,112 tons. In this series of very small quantities, therefore, the increase from 1850 to 1860 was just over 1,000 percent, from 1860 to 1865 it was 18 percent, and from 1865 to 1870 it was 48 percent.

Railroad track, particularly in the United States, was an essential for industrialization. Here both the depression and the war retarded the rate of growth. From 1851 through 1855 a total of 11,627 miles of new track was laid, from 1856 through 1860, only 8,721 miles, and from 1861 through 1865, only 4,076 miles. After the war the rate of growth of the early 1850's was resumed, with 16,174 miles constructed from 1866 through 1870. Looked at by decades, a rate of over 200 percent increase per decade in the twenty years before the war was slowed to 70 percent for the period from 1860 to 1870, with only a 15 percent increase during the war years. In the next two decades the rate averaged about 75 percent.

Next to food, cotton textiles may be taken as the most representative consumer-goods industry in the nineteenth century. Interference with the flow of southern cotton had a depressing effect. The number of bales of cotton consumed in United States manufacturing rose 143 percent from 1840 to 1850 and 47 percent from 1850 to 1860, but *fell* by 6 percent from 1860 to 1870. From then on consumption increased at a little higher rate than in the 1850's.

While woolen textile production is not an important series in the overall picture of industrial growth, it should be noted that, helped by protection and military needs, consumption of wool for manufacturing more than doubled during the war, and then *fell* somewhat from 1865 to 1870. But Arthur H. Cole, the historian of the woolen industry, characterizes the years from 1830 to 1870 as a period of growth "not so striking as in the decades before or afterwards."

Immigration to a nation essentially short of labor was unquestionably a stimulant to economic growth. Another country had paid for the immigrant's unproductive youthful years, and he came to the United States ready to contribute his labor at a low cost. The pattern of the curve for annual immigration shows the retarding effect of both depression and war. In the first five years of the 1850's an average of 349,685 immigrants a year came to the United States. From 1856 through 1860 the annual average fell to 169,958, and for the war years of 1861 to 1865 it fell further to 160,345. In the first five postwar years the average rose to 302,620, but not until the first half of the 1870's did the rate equal that of the early 1850's. Had there been a return to prosperity instead of war in 1861, it seems reasonable to suppose that several hundred thousand additional immigrants would have arrived before 1865.

In the case of farm mechanization the same type of error occurs as in the annual series on copper production. "Random" statistics such as the manufacture of 90,000 reapers in 1864 are frequently cited without putting them in the proper perspective of the total number in use and the continuing trends. Reaper and mower sales started upward in the early 1850's and were large from 1856 on, in spite of the depression. William T. Hutchinson estimates that most of the 125,000 reapers and mowers in use in 1861 had been sold during the previous five years. While the business, without regard to the accidental coming of the war, was obviously in a stage of very rapid growth, the war years presented many difficulties and may actually have retarded the rate of increase. Total sales of reapers for the period 1861–1865 are estimated at 250,000—a quite ordinary increase for a young industry—but the 90,000 figure for 1864, if it is correct, reinforces the evidence from the McCormick correspondence that this was the one particularly good year of the period. During these years William S. McCormick was often of the opinion that the "uncertainties of the times" made advisable a suspension of manufacturing until the close of the war.

For a broader view of agricultural mechanization the series "value of farm implements and machinery" has special interest. Here the census gives a picture which, if correct, is explicable only on the basis of wartime destruction. Based on constant dollars the dollar value of all loans was more than 15 percent lower than just before the war. If instead of examining loans one looks at total assets of all banks the decline in constant dollars from 1860 to 1870 is reduced to 10 percent, the difference arising from a larger cash position and more investment in government bonds.

Net capital formation would be a more proper index of economic growth than bank loans or assets. Unfortunately, neither the teams of the National Bureau of Economic Research nor those of the Census Bureau have been able to carry any reliable series back of 1868. From colonial times to 1960, however, the chief single form of American capital formation has undoubtedly been building construction. Farm houses, city homes, public buildings, stores, warehouses, and factories have year-by-year constituted, in monetary value, the leading type of capital growth. Gallman has drawn up series for such construction based on estimating the flow of construction materials and adding what appear to be appropriate markups. Admittedly the process is inexact, but because of the importance of construction in reflecting general trends in capital formation it is interesting to see the results. The rate of change for the ten-year period ending in 1854 is about 140 percent; for the one ending in 1859 it is 90 percent; for 1869 it is 40 percent; and for 1879 it is 46 percent. Taking a long view, from 1839 to 1859 the average decennial rate of increase was about 70 percent, and from 1869 to 1899 it was about 40 percent. The *rate* of advance in construction was declining and the war decade added a further dip to the decline.

Since the decline in rate is for the decade, the exact effect of the war years can only be estimated, but the logic of the situation, reinforced by the record of sharp cut-backs in railroad building, seems inescapable: the Civil War, like all modern wars, checked civilian construction. The first year of war was a period of depression and tight credit in the Middle West, which checked residential and farm construction in the area that grew most rapidly before and after the war. In both the East and the West the last two years of the war were a period of rapid inflation which was regarded by businessmen as a temporary wartime phenomenon. The logical result would be to postpone construction for long-term use until after the anticipated deflation. The decline in private railroad construction to a small fraction of the normal rate exemplifies the situation.

Lavish expenditure and speculation by a small group of war contractors and market operators gambling on the inflation seem to have created a legend of high prosperity during the war years. But the general series on fluctuations in the volume of business do not bear this out. Leonard P. Ayres's estimates of business activity place the average for 1861 through 1865 below normal, and Norman J. Silberling's business index is below its normal line for all years of the war. Silberling also has an intermediate trend line for business, which smooths out annual fluctuations. This line falls steadily from 1860 to 1869. Much of Silberling's discussion in his chapter "Business Activity, Prices, and Wars" is in answer to his question: "Why does it seem to be true that despite a temporary stimulating effect of war upon some industries, wars are generally associated with a long-term retarding of business growth . . .?" He puts the Civil War in this general category.

Collectively these statistical estimates support a conclusion that the Civil War retarded American industrial growth. Presentation of this view has been the chief purpose of this article. To try to judge the non-measurable or indirect effects of the war is extremely difficult. But since further discussion of the conventional qualitative factors may help to explain the prevailing evaluation in American texts, it seems appropriate to add some conjectural obiter dicta.

Experience with the apparently stimulating effects of twentieth-century wars on production makes the conclusion that victorious war may retard the growth of an industrial state seem paradoxical, and no doubt accounts in part for the use of detached bits of quantitative data to emphasize the Civil War's industrial importance. The resolution of the paradox may be found in contemporary conditions in the United States and in the nature of the wartime demand. The essential wastefulness of war from the standpoint of economic growth was obscured by the accident that both of the great European wars of the twentieth century began when the United States had a high level of unemployment. The immediate effect of each, therefore, was to put men to work, to increase the national product, and to create an aura of prosperity. Presumably, the United States of the mid-nineteenth century tended to operate close enough to full employment in average years that any wasteful labor-consuming activities were a burden rather than a stimulant.

By modern standards the Civil War was still unmechanized. It was fought with rifles, bayonets, and sabers by men on foot or horseback. Artillery was more used than in previous wars, but was still a relatively minor consumer of iron and steel. The railroad was also brought into use, but the building of military lines offset only a small percentage of the overall drop from the prewar level of civilian railroad construction. Had all of these things not been true, the Confederacy with its small industrial development could never have fought through four years of increasingly effective blockade.

In spite of the failure of direct quantitative evidence to show accelerating effects of the war on rates of economic growth, there could be long-run effects of a qualitative type that would gradually foster a more rapid rate of economic growth. The most obvious place to look for such indirect effects would be in the results of freeing the slaves. Marxists contended that elimination of slavery was a necessary precursor of the bourgeois industrialism which would lead to the socialist revolution. The creation of a free Negro labor force was, of course, of great long-run importance. In the twentieth century it has led to readjustment of Negro population between the deep South and the northern industrial areas, and to changes in the use of southern land.

But economically the effects of war and emancipation over the period 1840 to 1880 were negative. Richard A. Easterlin writes: "In every southern state, the 1880 level of per capita income originating in commodity production and distribution was below, or at best only slightly above that of 1840. . . . [This] attests strikingly to the impact of that war and the subsequent disruption on the southern economy." In general the Negroes became sharecroppers or wage laborers, often cultivating the same land and the same crops as before the war. In qualification of the argument that free Negro labor led to more rapid industrialization it should be noted that the South did not keep up with the national pace in the growth of non-agricultural wealth until after 1900.

Two indirect effects of the war aided industrial growth to degrees that cannot accurately be measured. These were, first, a more satisfactory money market, and, secondly, more security for entrepreneurial activity than in the prewar period. The sharp wartime inflation had the usual effect of transferring income from wage, salary, and interest receivers to those making profits. This meant concentration of savings in the hands of entrepreneurs who would invest in new activities; and this no doubt helps to explain the speculative booms of the last half of the 1860's and first two years of the 1870's which have been treated as the prosperity resulting from the war. Inflation also eased the burdens of those railroads which had excessive mortgage debts. But a great deal of new research would be needed to establish causal connections between the inflationary reallocation of wealth, 1863 to 1865, and the high rate of industrial progress in the late 1870's and the 1880's.

The National Banking Act, providing a more reliable currency for interstate operations, has been hailed as a great aid to business expansion although it would be hard to demonstrate, aside from a few weeks during panics, that plentiful but occasionally unsound currency had seriously interfered with earlier industrial growth. The existence of two and a half billion dollars in federal bonds also provided a basis for credit that was larger than before the war. This led to broader and more active security markets as well as to easier personal borrowing. But two qualifications must be kept in mind. First, local bank lending to favored borrowers had probably tended to be too liberal before the war and was now put on a somewhat firmer basis. In other words, since 1800 a multiplication of banks had made credit relatively easy to obtain in the United States, and in the North this continued to be the situation. Second, the southern banking system was largely destroyed by the war and had to be rebuilt in the subsequent decades. It should also be remembered that by 1875 some 40 percent of the banks were outside the national banking system.

Because of a few colorful speculators like Jay Gould, Daniel Drew, and Jim Fisk, and the immortality conferred on them, initially by the literary ability of the Adams brothers, the New York stock exchange in the postwar decade appears to have mirrored a new era of predatory wealth. But one has only to study the scandals of the London and New York stock exchanges in 1854 to see that there was little growth in the sophistication or boldness of stock operators during these fifteen years. In any case, the exploits of market operators were seldom related in a positive way to economic growth. Even a record of new issues of securities, which is lacking for this period, would chiefly reflect the flow of capital into railroads, banks, and public utilities rather than into manufacturing. Very few "industrial" shares were publicly marketed before the decade of the 1880's; such enterprises grew chiefly from the reinvestment of earnings.

There was strong government encouragement to entrepreneurial activity during the Civil War, but to ascribe to it unusual importance for economic growth requires both analysis of the results and comparison with other periods. Government in the United States has almost always encouraged entrepreneurs. The federal and state administrations preceding the Civil War could certainly be regarded as friendly to business. They subsidized railroads by land grants, subscribed to corporate bond issues, and remitted taxes on new enterprise. Tariffs were low, but railroad men and many bankers were happy with the situation. Whether or not American industrialism was significantly accelerated by the high protection that commenced with the war is a question that economists will probably never settle.

The building of a subsidized transcontinental railroad, held back by sectional controversies in the 1850's, was authorized along a northern route with the help of federal loans and land grants when the southerners excluded themselves from Congress. Putting more than a hundred million dollars into this project in the latter half of the 1860's, however, may have had an adverse effect on industrial growth. In general, the far western roads were built for speculative and strategic purposes uneconomically ahead of demand. They may for a decade, or even two, have consumed more capital than their transportation services were then worth to the economy.

To sum up this part of the obiter dictum, those who write of the war creating a national market tied together by railroads underestimate both the achievements of the two decades before the war and the ongoing trends of the economy. The nation's business in 1855 was nearly as intersectional as in 1870. Regional animosities did not interfere with trade, nor did these feelings diminish after the war. By the late 1850's the United States was a rapidly maturing industrial state with its major cities connected by rail, its major industries selling in a national market, and blessed or cursed with financiers, security flotations, stock markets, and all the other appurtenances of industrial capitalism.

But when all specific factors of change attributable to the war have been deflated, there is still the possibility that northern victory had enhanced the capitalist spirit, that as a consequence the atmosphere of government in Washington among members of both parties was more friendly to industrial enterprise and to northern-based national business operations than had formerly been the rule. It can be argued that in spite of Greenbackers and discontented farmers legislation presumably favorable to industry could be more readily enacted. The Fourteenth Amendment, for example, had as a by-product greater security for interstate business against state regulation, although it was to be almost two decades before the Supreme Court would give force to this protection. By 1876, a year of deep depression, the two major parties were trying to outdo each other in promises of stimulating economic growth. This highly generalized type of argument is difficult to evaluate, but in qualification of any theory of a sharp change in attitude we should remember that industrialism was growing rapidly from general causes and that by the 1870's it was to be expected that major-party politics would be conforming to this change in American life.

Massive changes in physical environment such as those accompanying the rise of trade at the close of the Middle Ages or the gradual growth of industrialism from the seventeenth century on do not lend themselves readily to exact or brief periodization. If factory industry and mechanized transportation be taken as the chief indexes of early industrialism, its spread in the United

States was continuous and rapid during the entire nineteenth century, but in general, advance was greater during periods of prosperity than in depression. The first long period without a major depression, after railroads, canals, and steamboats had opened a national market, was from 1834 to 1857. Many economic historians interested in quantitative calculations would regard these years as marking the appearance of an integrated industrial society. Walter W. Rostow, incidentally, starts his "take-off" period in the 1840's and calls it completed by 1860. Others might prefer to avoid any narrow span of years. Few, however, would see a major stimulation to economic growth in the events of the Civil War.

Finally, one may speculate as to why this exaggerated conception of the role of the Civil War in industrialization gained so firm a place in American historiography. The idea fits, of course, into the Marxian frame of revolutionary changes, but it seems initially to have gained acceptance quite independently of Marxian influences. More concentrated study of the war years than of any other four-year span in the nineteenth century called attention to technological and business events usually overlooked. Isolated facts were seized upon without comparing them with similar data for other decades. The desire of teachers for neat periodization was probably a strong factor in quickly placing the interpretation in textbooks; thus, up to 1860 the nation was agricultural, after 1865 it was industrial. Recent study of American cultural themes suggests still another reason. From most standpoints the Civil War was a national disaster, but Americans like to see their history in terms of optimism and progress. Perhaps the war was put in a perspective suited to the culture by seeing it as good because in addition to achieving freedom for the Negro it brought about industrial progress.

The Winning of the West: The Expansion of the Western Sioux

Richard White

The image of the fierce mounted warrior astride his fleet pony—silhouetted against an austere western landscape, surveying the inexorable advance of white civilization's "manifest destiny"—is surely the most enduring stereotype of the American Indian, thanks especially to nineteenth-century pulp fiction and the twentieth-century media. The "winning of the West," however, involves a set of historical complexities that fit the strictures of the stereotype scarcely at all. The process whereby the Plains Indians came to be dispossessed of their lands and cultures during and by virtue of the Plains Wars, argues Professor Richard White of the University of Utah, needs to be more methodically scrutinized and reassessed. Violent episodes between Indians and whites—often bred by cultural misunderstandings—were both a symptom and a foreshadowing of the false beliefs that continued to haunt white-Indian relations. Most needed as a historical corrective, White concludes, is a proper understanding of intertribal relations, especially the rise of the western Sioux to imperial supremacy. Although we have been inclined to view Indian resistance to the whites' "winning of the West" as a short story with a simple plot—the Indian stoically suffering tragic retreat, the inevitable consequence of white territorial ambition—the true story is rather more complex. Close scrutiny of the historical facts yields a different picture, for the western Sioux had already "won the West" by intertribal warfare before the period of white advancement. In fact, traders, and then settlers, *followed* the Sioux, who had largely subdued other Indian tribes militarily prior to the whites' arrival. The "winning of the West" was in great measure, then, a conflict between the two remaining major expanding powers in the area—the Sioux and the white Americans.

The mounted warrior of the Great Plains has proved to be the most enduring stereotype of the American Indian, but like most stereotypes this one conceals more than it reveals. Both popularizers and scholars have been fascinated with the individual warrior to the neglect of plains warfare itself. Harry Turney-

From "The Winning of the West: The Expansion of the Western Sioux in the Eighteenth and Nineteenth Centuries," by Richard White, in *Journal of American History*, 65 (September 1978), pp. 319–343. Copyright © 1985 Organization of American Historians. Reprinted by permission. The author wishes to acknowledge the financial assistance of the Center for the History of the American Indian, Newberry Library.

High, in his classic *Primitive Warfare*, provided the most cogent justification of this neglect. The plains tribes, he contended, were so loosely organized that they remained below the "military horizon"; there really was no warfare on the plains, only battles that were little more than "a mildly dangerous game" fought for largely individual reasons. In much of the literature, intertribal warfare has remained just this: an individual enterprise fought for individualistic reasons—glory, revenge, prestige, and booty. Robert Lowie's statement on warfare, in what is still the standard work on the Plains Indians, can be taken as typical of much anthropological thought: "The objective was never to acquire new lands. Revenge, horse lifting, and lust for glory were the chief motives. . . ."

There is, however, a second group of anthropologists, W. W. Newcomb, Oscar Lewis, Frank Secoy, and more recently Symmes Oliver, who have found this explanation of intertribal warfare unconvincing. These scholars, making much more thorough use of historical sources than is common among anthropologists, have examined warfare in light of economic and technological change. They have presented intertribal warfare as dynamic, changing over time; wars were not interminable contests with traditional enemies, but real struggles in which defeat was often catastrophic. Tribes fought largely for the potential economic and social benefits to be derived from furs, slaves, better hunting grounds, and horses. According to these scholars, plains tribes went to war because their survival as a people depended on securing and defending essential resources.

Historians have by and large neglected this social and economic interpretation of plains warfare and have been content to borrow uncritically from the individualistic school. Western historians usually present intertribal warfare as a chaotic series of raids and counter-raids; an almost irrelevant prelude to the real story: Indian resistance to white invasion. The exaggerated focus on the heroic resistance of certain plains tribes to white incursions has recently prompted John Ewers, an ethnologist, to stress that Indians on the plains had fought each other long before whites came and that intertribal warfare remained very significant into the late nineteenth century.

The neglect by historians of intertribal warfare and the reasons behind it has fundamentally distorted the historical position of the Plains Indians. As Ewers has noted, the heroic resistance approach to plains history reduces these tribes who did not offer organized armed resistance to the white American invaders, and who indeed often aided them against other tribes, to the position of either foolish dupes of the whites or of traitors to their race. Why tribes such as the Pawnee, Mandan, Hidatsa, Oto, Missouri, Crow, and Omaha never took up arms against white Americans has never been subject to much historical scrutiny. The failure of Indians to unite has been much easier to deplore than to examine.

The history of the northern and central American Great Plains in the eighteenth and nineteenth centuries is far more complicated than the tragic retreat of the Indians in the face of an inexorable white advance. From the perspective of most northern and central plains tribes the crucial invasion of the plains during this period was not necessarily that of the whites at all. These tribes had few illusions about American whites and the danger they presented, but the Sioux remained their most feared enemy.

The Teton and Yanktonai Sioux appeared on the edges of the Great Plains early in the eighteenth century. Although unmounted, they were already culturally differentiated from their woodland brothers, the Santee Sioux. The western Sioux were never united under any central government and never developed any concerted policy of conquest. By the mid-nineteenth century the Plains Sioux comprised three broad divisions, the Tetons, Yanktons, and Yanktonais, with the Tetons subdivided into seven component tribes—the Oglala, Brulé, Hunkpapa, Miniconjou, Sans Arc, Two Kettles, and Sihaspas, the last five tribes having evolved from an earlier Sioux group—the Saones. Although linked by common language, culture, interest, and intermarriage, these tribes operated independently. At no time did all the western Sioux tribes unite against any enemy, but alliances of several tribes against a common foe were not unusual. Only rarely did any Teton tribe join an alien tribe in an attack on another group of Sioux.

Between approximately 1685 and 1876 the western Sioux conquered and controlled an area from the Minnesota River in Minnesota, west to the head of the Yellowstone, and south from the Yellowstone to the drainage of the upper Republican River. This advance westward took place in three identifiable stages: initially a movement during the late seventeenth and early eighteenth centuries onto the prairies east of the Missouri, then a conquest of the middle Missouri River region during the late eighteenth and nineteenth centuries, and, finally, a sweep west and south from the Missouri during the early and mid-nineteenth century. Each of these stages possessed its own impetus and rationale. Taken together they comprised a sustained movement by the Sioux that resulted in the dispossession or subjugation of numerous tribes and made the Sioux a major Indian power on the Great Plains during the nineteenth century. . . .

The conquests of the western Sioux during the nineteenth century were politically united in only the loosest sense. The various Sioux tribes expanded for similar demographic, economic, and social reasons, however, and these underlying causes give a unity to the various wars of the Sioux.

Unlike every other tribe on the Great Plains during the nineteenth century, the Sioux appear to have increased in numbers. They were not immune to the epidemics that decimated the other tribes, but most of the Tetons and Yanktonais successfully avoided the disastrous results of the great epidemics, especially the epidemic of 1837 that probably halved the Indian population of the plains. Through historical accident the very conquests of the Sioux protected them from disease. This occurred in two opposite ways. The advance of Oglalas and Brulés to the southwest simply put them out of reach of the main epidemic corridor along the Missouri. Furthermore, Pilcher, the Indian agent on the Missouri, succeeded in giving them advance warning of the danger in 1837, and, unlike the Blackfeet and other nomadic tribes that suffered heavily from the epidemic, they did not come in to trade. The Tetons were infected, and individual tribes lost heavily, but the losses of the Sioux as a whole were comparatively slight. The Yanktons, Yanktonais, and portions of the Saone Tetons, however, dominated the Missouri trade route, but paradoxically this probably helped to save them. In 1832 the Office of Indian Affairs sent doctors up the river to vaccinate the Indians. Many of the Sioux refused to cooperate, but well over a thousand people, mostly Yanktonais, received vaccinations. Only enough money was appropriated to send the doctors as far upriver as the Sioux; so the Mandans and Hidatsas further upriver remained unvaccinated. As a result, when smallpox came, the Yanktonais were partially protected while their enemies in the villages once again died miserably in great numbers. The renewed American efforts at mass vaccination that followed the epidemic came too late for the Mandans, but in the 1840s thousands more Sioux were given immunity from smallpox.

The combination of freedom from disease, a high birth rate (in 1875 estimated as capable of doubling the population every twenty years), and continued migration from the Sioux tribes further east produced a steadily growing population for the western Sioux. Although the various censuses taken by the whites were often little more than rough estimates, the western Sioux appear to have increased from a very low estimate of 5,000 people in 1804 to approximately 25,000 in the 1850s. This population increase, itself partly a result of the new abundance the Sioux derived from the buffalo herds, in turn fueled an increased need for buffalo. The Sioux used the animals not only to feed their expanding population, but also to trade for necessary European goods. Since pemmican, buffalo robes, hides, and tongues had replaced beaver pelts as the main Indian trade item on the Missouri, the Sioux needed secure and profitable hunting grounds during a period when the buffalo were steadily moving west and north in response to hunting pressure on the Missouri.

Increased Indian hunting for trade contributed to the pressure on the buffalo herds, but the great bulk of the destruction was the direct work of white hunters and traders. The number of buffalo robes annually shipped down the Missouri increased from an average of 2,600 between 1815 and 1830 to 40,000 to 50,000 in 1833, a figure that did not include the numbers slaughtered by whites for pleasure. In 1848 Father Pierre-Jean De Smet reported the annual figure shipped downriver to St. Louis to be 25,000 tongues and 110,000 robes.

Despite what the most thorough student of the subject has seen as the Indians' own prudent use of the buffalo, the various tribes competed for an increasingly scarce resource. By the late 1820s the buffalo had disappeared from the Missouri below the Omaha villages, and the border tribes were already in desperate condition from lack of game. The Indians quickly realized the danger further up the Missouri, and upper Missouri tribes voiced complaints about white hunters as early as 1833. By the 1840s observations on the diminishing number of buffalo and increased Indian competition had become commonplace. Between 1833 and 1844 buffalo could be found in large numbers on the headwaters of the Little Cheyenne, but by the mid-1840s they were receding rapidly toward the mountains. The Sioux to a great extent simply had to follow, or move north and south, to find new hunting grounds. Their survival and prosperity depended on their success.

But buffalo hunting demanded more than territory; it also required horses, and in the 1820s, the Sioux were hardly noted for either the abundance or the quality of their herds. Raids and harsh winters on the plains frequently depleted Sioux horse herds, and the Sioux had to replenish them by raiding or trading farther to the south. In this sense the economy of the Sioux depended on warfare to secure the horses needed for the hunt. As Oscar Lewis has pointed out in connection with the Blackfeet, war and horse raiding became important economic activities for the Plains Indians.

The Yanktonais, Yanktons, and Saone Tetons had a third incentive for expansion. Power over the sedentary villagers secured them what Tabeau had called their serfs. Under Sioux domination these villages could be raided or traded with as the occasion demanded, their corn and beans serving as sources of supplementary food supplies when the buffalo failed. A favorite tactic of the Sioux was to restrict, as far as possible, the access of these tribes to both European goods and the hunting grounds, thus forcing the village peoples to rely on the Sioux for trade goods, meat, and robes. To escape this exploitation, the villagers, in alliance with the nomadic tribes who traded with them, waged a nearly constant, if often desultory, war.

It is in this context of increasing population, increasing demand for buffalos and horses, the declining and retreating bison populations, and attempted domination of the sedentary villagers that the final phase of Sioux expansion during the nineteenth century took place. And, as the Omahas had found out, the loose structural organization of the western Sioux worked to make the impetus of their advance even more irresistible. Accommodation with one band or tribe often only served to increase inroads from others. There was no way for a tribe to deal with the whole Sioux nation.

On the Missouri the Sioux had long feared the logical alliance of all the village tribes against them, and they worked actively to prevent it. After 1810, the Arikaras sporadically attempted to break away from Sioux domination by allying themselves with the Mandans and Hidatsas. In response, the Sioux blockaded the villages, cutting them off from the buffalo and stopping the white traders who came up the Missouri from supplying them. The Mandan-Arikara alliance, in turn, sent out war parties to keep the river open. But these alliances inevitably fell apart from internal strains, and the old pattern of oscillating periods of trade and warfare was renewed.

But if the Sioux feared an alliance of the sedentary village tribes, these tribes had an even greater fear of a Sioux-American partnership on the Missouri. The Arikaras, by attacking and defeating an American fur trading party under William Ashley in 1823, precipitated exactly the combination from which they had most to fear. When 1,500 Sioux warriors appeared before their village that year, they were accompanied by United States troops under Colonel Henry Leavenworth. This joint expedition took the Arikara village and sacked it, but the Sioux were disgusted with the performance of their American auxiliaries. They blamed American cautiousness for allowing the Arikaras to escape further upstream. Although they remained friendly to the United States, the whole affair gave them a low estimation of the ability of white soldiers that would last for years. They finished the removal of the Arikaras themselves, forcing them by 1832 to abandon both their sedentary villages and the Missouri River and to move south to live first with, and then just above, the Skidi Pawnees. The Yanktonais, 450 lodges strong, moved in from the Minnesota River to take over the old Arikara territory.

With the departure of the Arikaras, the Mandans and Hidatsas alone remained to contest Sioux domination of the Missouri. In 1836 the Yanktonais, nearly starving after a season of poor hunts, began petty raids on the Mandans and Hidatsas. In retaliation, a Mandan-Hidatsa war party destroyed a Yanktonai village of forty-five lodges, killing more than 150 people and taking fifty prisoners. The Sioux counterattacks cost the Mandans dearly. During the next year they lost over sixty warriors, but what was worse, when the smallpox hit in 1837, the villagers could not disperse for fear of the hostile Yanktonais who still occupied the plains around the villages. The Mandans were very nearly destroyed; the Hidatsas, who attempted a quarantine, lost over half their people, and even the luckless Arikaras returned in time to be ravaged by the epidemic. The villages that survived continued to suffer from Yanktonai attacks and could use the plains hunting grounds only on sufferance of the Sioux.

The Oglala-Brulé advance onto the buffalo plains southwest of the Missouri was contemporaneous with the push up the Missouri and much more significant. Here horse raids and occasional hunts by the Sioux gave way to a concerted attempt to wrest the plains between the Black Hills and the Missouri from the Arapahos, Crows, Kiowas, and Cheyennes. By 1825, the Oglalas, advancing up the drainage of the Teton River, and the Brulés, moving up the drainage of the White River, had dispossessed the Kiowas and driven them south, pushed the Crows west to Powder River, and formed with the Cheyennes and Arapahos an alliance which would dominate the north and central plains for the next half century.

Historians have attributed the movement of the Sioux beyond the Black Hills into the Platte drainage to manipulations of the Rocky Mountain Fur Company, which sought to capture the Sioux trade from the American Fur Company. But, in fact, traders followed the Sioux; the Sioux did not follow the traders. William Sublette of the Rocky Mountain Fur Company did not lure the Sioux to the Platte. He merely took advantage of their obvious advance toward it. He was the first to realize that by the 1830s Brulé and Oglala hunting grounds lay closer to the Platte than to the Missouri, and he took advantage of the situation to get their trade. The arrival of the Sioux on the Platte was not sudden; it had been preceded by the usual period of horse raids. Nor did it break some long accepted balance of power. Their push beyond the Black Hills was merely another phase in the long Sioux advance from the edge of the Great Plains.

What probably lured the Sioux toward the Platte was an ecological phenomenon that did not require the total depletion of game in the area they already held and that was not peculiar to the plains. Borders dividing contending tribes were never firm; between the established hunting territory of each people lay an indeterminate zone, variously described as war grounds or neutral grounds. In this area only war parties dared to venture; it was too dangerous for any band to travel into these regions to hunt. Because little pressure was put on the animal populations of these contested areas by hunters, they provided a refuge for the hard-pressed herds of adjacent tribal hunting grounds. Since buffalo migrations were unpredictable, a sudden loss of game in a large part of one's tribe's territory could prompt an invasion of these neutral grounds. Thus, throughout the nineteenth century, there usually lay at the edges of the Sioux-controlled lands a lucrative area that held an understandable attraction for them. In the contest for these rich disputed areas lay the key not only to many of the Sioux wars, but also to many other aboriginal wars on the continent.

These areas were, of course, never static. They shifted as tribes were able to wrest total control of them from other contending peoples, and so often created, in turn, a new disputed area beyond. Between 1830 and 1860, travelers on the plains described various neutral or war grounds ranging from the Sand Hills north of the Loup River in Nebraska down to the Pawnee Fork of the Arkansas. But for the Sioux four areas stand out: the region below Fort Laramie between the forks of the Platte in dispute during the 1830s; the Medicine Bow–Laramie plains country above Fort Laramie, fought over in the 1840s; the Yellowstone drainage of the Powder, Rosebud, and Big Horn rivers initially held by the Crows but reduced to a neutral ground in the 1840s and 1850s; and portions of the Republican River country contested from the 1840s to the 1870s. Two things stand out in travelers' accounts of these areas: they were disputed by two or more tribes and they were rich in game.

Francis Parkman vividly described and completely misinterpreted an episode of the Sioux conquest of one of these areas, the Medicine Bow Valley, in 1846. He attributed the mustering of the large expedition that went, according to his account, against the Shoshones, and according to others against the Crows, to a desire for revenge for the loss of a son of Whirlwind, an important Sioux chief, during a horse raid on the Shoshones. But in Parkman's account, Whirlwind, who supposedly organized the expedition, decided not to accompany it, and the Oglalas and Saones who went ended up fighting neither the Crows nor the Shoshones. What they did, however, is significant. They moved into disputed Medicine Bow country west of Fort Laramie, land which all of these tribes contested.

The Sioux entered the area warily, took great precautions to avoid, not seek out, Crow and Shoshone war parties, and were much relieved to escape unscathed after a successful hunt. Parkman was disgusted, but the Sioux were immensely pleased with the whole affair. They had achieved the main goal of their warfare, the invasion and safe hunting of disputed buffalo grounds without any cost to themselves. White Shield, the slain man's brother, made another, apparently token, attempt to organize a war party to avenge his loss, but he never departed. The whole episode—from the whites' confusion over what tribe was the target of the expedition, to their misinterpretation of Indian motives, to Parkman's failure to see why the eventual outcome pleased the Sioux—reveals why, in so many accounts, the logic of Indian warfare is lost and wars are reduced to outbursts of random bloodletting. For the Sioux, the disputed area and its buffalo, more that the Shoshones or Crows, were the targets of the expedition; revenge was subordinate to the hunt. Their ability to hunt in safety, without striking a blow, comprised a strategic victory that more than satisfied them. To Parkman, intent on observing savage warriors lusting for blood revenge, all this was unfathomable.

Not all expeditions ended so peacefully, however. Bloodier probes preceded the summer expedition of 1846, and others followed it. When the Sioux arrived in strength on the Platte in the mid-1830s, their raiding parties were already familiar to peoples from the Pawnee south to the Arkansas and the Santa Fe Trail. As early as the 1820s, their allies, the Cheyennes and Arapahos, had unsuccessfully contested hunting grounds with the Skidi Pawnees. But by 1835, these tribes had agreed to make peace.

The arrival of the Oglalas and Brulés at the Laramie River presented both the Pawnees and the Crows with more powerful rivals. The Crows were by now old enemies of the Tetons. Initially as allies of the Mandans and Hidatsas, and later as contestants for the hunting grounds of the plains, they had fought the Sioux for at least fifty years. By the 1840s, however, the once formidable Crows were a much weakened people. As late as the 1830s they had possessed more horses than any other tribe on the upper Missouri and estimates of their armed strength had ranged from 1,000 to 2,500 mounted men, but the years that followed brought them little but disaster. Smallpox and cholera reduced their numbers from 800 to 460 lodges, and rival groups pressed into their remaining hunting grounds. The Blackfeet attacked them from the north while the Saones, Oglalas, and Brulés closed in on the east and south. Threatened and desperate, the Crows sought aid west of the Rockies and increasingly allied themselves with the Shoshones and Flatheads.

The Pawnees, the last powerful horticultural tribe left on the plains, did not have a long tradition of warfare with the Sioux. The four Pawnee tribes—the Republicans, Skidis, Tapages, and Grands—lived in permanent earth-lodge villages on the Platte and Loup rivers, but twice a year they went on extended hunts in an area that stretched from between the forks of the Platte in the north to the Republican, Kansas, and Arkansas rivers in the south. Sioux horse raids had originally worried them very little, but, after the wars with Arapahos and Cheyennes, the growing proximity of the Sioux and their advantage in firearms had begun to concern the Pawnees enough to ask Americans to act as intermediaries in establishing peace. In the 1830s they remained, in the words of their white agent, along with the Sioux, one of the "two master tribes in the Upper Indian Country . . . who govern nearly all the smaller ones."

Under BullBear the Oglalas spearheaded the conquest of the Platte River hunting grounds of the Skidi Pawnees. By 1838, the Pawnee agent reported that the Skidis, fearing the Sioux would soon dominate the entire buffalo country, were contesting "every inch of ground," and, he added, "they are right for the day is not far off when the Sioux will possess the whole buffalo region, unless they are checked." In 1838, smallpox struck both the Oglalas and the Pawnees, but, as happened further north, the populous horticultural villages of the Pawnees suffered far more than the nomadic Sioux bands. The next year the intertribal struggle culminated in a pitched battle that cost the Pawnees between eighty and one-hundred warriors and led to the *de facto* surrender of the Platte hunting grounds by the Skidis.

The murder of BullBear in 1841 during a factional quarrel prompted a split in the Oglalas. One band, the Kiyuskas, BullBear's old supporters, continued to push into the Pawnee lands along the Platte and Smoky Hill rivers, while the other faction, the Bad Faces, moved west and north often joining with the Saone bands who were pushing out from the Missouri in attacks on the Crows. During these advances the Utes and Shoshones would be added to the ranks of Teton enemies, and further north the Yanktonais and Hunkpapas pushed into Canada, fighting the Metis, Plains Crees, and Assiniboines.

The Oregon, California, and Utah migrations of the 1840s made the Platte River Valley an American road across the plains. Like the traders on the Missouri before them, these migrants drove away game and created a new avenue for epidemic diseases, culminating in the cholera epidemic of 1849–1850. For the first time, the whites presented a significant threat to Sioux interests, and this conflict bore as fruit the first signs of overt Teton hostility since Chouteau's and Pryor's expeditions. But on the whole whites suffered little from the initial Teton reaction to the Oregon trail. The Crows and Pawnees bore the consequences of the decline of the Platte hunting grounds.

The Brulé and Kiyuska Oglalas attacked the Pawnee on the South Platte and the Republican. The Tetons did not restrict their attacks to the buffalo grounds; along with the Yanktons and Yanktonais from the Missouri, they attacked the Pawnees in their villages and disrupted the whole Pawnee economy. While small war parties stole horses and killed women working in the fields, large expeditions with as many as 700 men attacked the villages themselves. This dual assault threatened to reduce the Pawnees to starvation, greatly weakening their ability to resist.

The Sioux struck one of their most devastating blows in 1843, destroying a new village the Pawnees had built on the Loup at the urging of the whites. They killed sixty-seven people and forced the Pawnees back to the Platte, where they were threatened with retribution by whites for their failure to remove as agreed. The Pawnees vainly cited American obligations under the treaty of 1833 to help defend them from attacks by other tribes; and they also repeatedly sought peace. Neither availed. Unlike the Otos, Omahas, and Poncas, who eventually gave up all attempts to hunt on the western plains, the Pawnees persisted in their semiannual expeditions. The tribal census taken in 1859 reveals the price the Pawnees paid. When Zebulon Pike had visited the Pawnees in 1806 he found a roughly equivalent number of men and women in each village. In his partial census, he gave a population of 1,973 men and 2,170 women, exclusive of children. In 1859, agent William Dennison listed 820 men and 1,505 women; largely because of war, women now outnumbered men by nearly two to one.

The final blow came in 1873, three years before the Battle of the Little Bighorn, when the Sioux surprised a Pawnee hunting party on the Republican River, killing about 100 people. The Pawnees, now virtually prisoners in their reservation villages, gave in. They abandoned their Nebraska homeland and, over the protests of their agents, moved to Indian Territory. White settlers may have rejoiced at their removal, but it was the Sioux who had driven the Pawnees from Nebraska.

The experience of the Crows was much the same. Attacked along a front that ran from the Yellowstone to the Laramie Plains, they were never routed, but their power declined steadily. The Sioux drove them from the Laramie Plains and then during the 1850s and 1860s pushed them farther and farther up the Yellowstone. In the mid-1850s, Edwin Denig, a trapper familiar with the plains, predicted their total destruction, and by 1862 they had apparently been driven from the plains and into the mountains. They, too, would join the Americans against the Sioux.

In a very real sense the Americans, because of their destruction of game along the Missouri and Platte, had stimulated this warfare for years, but their first significant intervention in intertribal politics since the Leavenworth expedition came with the celebrated Laramie Peace Conference of 1851. Although scholars have recognized the importance of both intertribal warfare and the decline of the buffalo in prompting this conference, they have, probably because they accepted without question the individualistic interpretation of Indian wars, neglected the Indian political situation at the time of the treaty. They have failed to appreciate the predominance of the Sioux-Cheyenne-Arapaho alliance on the northern and central plains.

By 1851, American Indian officials has recognized that white travel and trade on the Great Plains had reduced the number of buffalo and helped precipitate intertribal wars. They proposed to restore peace by compensating the Indians for the loss of game. Their motives for this were hardly selfless, since intertribal wars endangered American travelers and commerce. Once they had established peace and drawn firm boundaries between the tribes, they could hold a tribe responsible for any depredations committed within its allotted area. Furthermore, by granting compensation for the destruction of game, the government gave itself an entrée into tribal politics: by allowing or withholding payments, they could directly influence the conduct of the Indians.

Although American negotiators certainly did not seek tribal unity in 1851, it is ethnocentric history to contend that the Fort Laramie Treaty allowed the Americans to "divide and conquer." Fundamentally divided at the time of the treaty, the plains tribes continued so afterward. The treaty itself was irrelevant; both the boundaries it created and its prohibition of intertribal warfare were ignored from the beginning by the only tribal participants who finally mattered, the Sioux.

Indeed the whole conference can be interpreted as a major triumph for the Tetons. In a sense, the Fort Laramie Treaty marked the height of Sioux political power. Of the 10,000 Indians who attended the conference, the great majority of them were Sioux, Cheyennes, and Arapahos. Sioux threats kept the Pawnees and all but small groups of Crows, Arikaras, Hidatsas, and Assiniboines from coming to Fort Laramie. The Shoshones came, but the Cheyennes attacked their party and part turned back. With the Sioux and their allies so thoroughly dominating the conference, the treaty itself amounted to both a recognition of Sioux power and an attempt to curb it. But when American negotiators tried to restrict the Sioux to an area north of the Platte, Black Hawk, an Oglala, protested that they held the lands to the south by the same right the Americans held their lands, the right of conquest: "These lands once belonged to the Kiowas and the Crows, but we whipped those nations out of them, and in this we did what the white men do when they want the lands of the Indians." The Americans conceded, granting the Sioux hunting rights, which, in Indian eyes, confirmed title. The Sioux gladly accepted American presents and their tacit recognition of Sioux conquests, but, as their actions proved, they never saw the treaty as a prohibition of future gains. After an American war with the Sioux and another attempt to stop intertribal warfare in 1855, Bear's Rib, a Hunkpapa chief, explained to Lieutenant G. K. Warren that the Tetons found it difficult to take the American prohibition of warfare seriously when the Americans themselves left these conferences only to engage in wars with other Indians or with the Mormons.

After the treaty, the lines of conflict on the plains were clearly drawn. The two major powers in the area, the Sioux and the Americans, had both advanced steadily and with relatively little mutual conflict. Following the treaty they became avowed and recognized rivals. Within four years of the treaty, the first American war with the Tetons would break out; and by the mid-1850s, American officers frankly saw further war as inevitable. The Sioux, in turn, recognized the American threat to their interests, and the tribes, in a rare display of concerted action, agreed as a matter of policy to prohibit all land cessions and to close their remaining productive hunting grounds to American intrusions. These attempts consistently led to war with the Americans. After a century of conquest the Sioux had very definite conceptions of the boundaries of their tribal territory. Recent historians and some earlier anthropologists contended that Indians never fought for territory, but if this is so, it is hard to explain the documented outrage of the Saones, Oglalas, and Brulés at the cession of land along the Missouri by the Yanktons in 1858. The Tetons had moved from this land decades before and had been replaced by the Yanktons, but from the Teton point of view the whole western Sioux nation still held title to the territory and the Yanktons had no authority to sell it. Fearing that acceptance of annuities would connote recognition of the sale, the Saone tribes refused them, and the cession provoked a crisis on the western plains and hardened Teton ranks against the Americans.

The warfare between the northern plains tribes and the United States that followed the Fort Laramie Treaty of 1851 was not the armed resistance of a people driven to the wall by American expansion. In reality these wars arose from the clash of two expanding powers—the United States, and the Sioux and their allies. If, from a distance, it appears that the vast preponderance of strength rested with the whites, it should be remembered that the ability of the United States to bring this power to bear was limited. The series of defeats the Sioux inflicted on American troops during these years reveals how real the power of the Tetons was.

Even as they fought the Americans, the Sioux continued to expand their domination of plains hunting grounds, as they had to in order to survive. Logically enough, the tribes the Sioux threatened—the Crows, Pawnees, and Arikaras especially—sided with the Americans, providing them with soldiers and scouts. For white historians to cast these people as mere dupes or traitors is too simplistic. They fought for their tribal interests and loyalties as did the Sioux.

It is ironic that historians, far more than anthropologists, have been guilty of viewing intertribal history as essentially ahistoric and static, of refusing to examine critically the conditions that prompted Indian actions. In too much Indian history, tribes fight only "ancient" enemies, as if each group were doled out an allotted number of adversaries at creation with whom they battled mindlessly through eternity. Historians have been too easily mystified by intertribal warfare, too willing to see it as the result of some ingrained cultural pugnacity. This is not to argue that the plains tribes did not offer individual warriors incentives of wealth and prestige that encouraged warfare, but, as Newcomb pointed out, the real question is why the tribe placed such a premium on encouraging warriors. This is essentially a historical question. Without an understanding of tribal and intertribal histories, and an appreciation that, like all history, they are dynamic, not static, the actions of Indians when they come into conflict with whites can be easily and fatally distorted.

American Myths at Century's End

An honest politician is one who when he is bought will stay bought.
Simon Cameron

The United States is the only country since the Middle Ages that has created a legend to set beside the story of Achilles, Robin Hood, Roland and Arthur.
Denis Brogan

It is a glorious history our God has bestowed upon His chosen people; a history whose keynote was struck by Liberty Bell; a history heroic with faith in our mission and our future; a history of statesmen, who flung the boundaries of the Republic out into unexplored lands and savage wildernesses; a history of soldiers, who carried the flag across blazing deserts and through the ranks of hostile mountains, even to the gates of sunset; a history of multiplying people, who overran a continent in half a century; a history divinely logical, in the process of whose tremendous reasoning we find ourselves today. . . . [I]t is ours to execute the purpose of a fate that has driven us to be greater than our small intentions.
Senator Albert Beveridge, "The March of the Flag" (1898)

THE PLEASURES OF THE COUNTRY.
SWEET HOME

"The Pleasures of the Country": Home Sweet Home. [Currier & Ives lithograph, 1869. Reproduced from the collections of the Library of Congress.]

Preparing for the American Dream: prayer time at the nursery of the Five Points Industrial School. [Photo by Jacob A. Riis, c. 1889. Jacob A. Riis Collection, Museum of the City of New York.]

The pleasures of the country: Home Sweet Home. [Nebraska, c. 1889. Solomon D. Butcher Collection, Nebraska State Historical Society.]

"Tipple boy," West Virginia coal mine. The bitter cry of the children: an American reality. [Photo by Lewis Hine, 1908. The Bettmann Archive.]

53

*A*ccording to Henry Steele Commager's seminal book *The American Mind*, the 1890s were especially significant to the development of American institutions and traditions. The span of the nineties, Commager contends, marked the transition from the "old" to the "new" America. It was at this "watershed" in American historical consciousness that the two faces of America stood exposed:

> On the one side . . . lies an America predominantly agricultural; concerned with domestic problems . . . an America still in the making, physically and socially; an America on the whole self-confident, self-contained, self-reliant, and conscious of its unique character and of a unique destiny. On the other side lies the modern America, predominantly urban and industrial; inextricably involved in world economy and politics . . . experiencing profound changes in population, social institutions, economy, and technology; and trying to accommodate its traditions and institutions and habits of thought to conditions new and in part alien.

Thus, as America reached the conclusion of one century and the beginning of another, new forces were astir in all areas of American life—forces that were to produce a period of trauma and urgent readjustment for the American mind.

At century's end, America's self-image was being strongly conditioned by a curious mixture of anticipation and nostalgia. It was at once an age of confidence and an age of doubt. Such conditions served to create an environment conducive to the myth building of both contemporaries and future historians. Thus, the cluster of myths that appears in the late nineteenth century speaks clearly not only to America's confrontation with the new but also, perhaps as importantly, to the nation's desire to secure something that seemed about to be lost. It was as the frontier was ending, for example, that Americans began to picture it as something it had rarely been, and its people became obvious candidates for national hero worship. The cowboy in particular symbolized the golden past and a preindustrial age, and the West now came to rival the South as a major source of American symbol and myth. It was of little concern that this inflated image did not conform to reality. Similarly, it was as America's agricultural past was being challenged and the rural life was becoming increasingly subject to business practices and mechanization that it too became an inexhaustible resource for the American romantic imagination. The American novelist Hamlin Garland reflected this state of mind in recalling an element of his own rural experience:

> It all lies in the unchanging realm of the past—this land of my childhood. Its charm, its strange domination cannot return save in the poet's reminiscent dream. No money, no railway train can take us back to it. It did not in truth exist—it was a magical world, born to the vibrant union of youth and firelight, of music and the voice of moaning winds.

In such fashion did America repress the tragic and cruel elements of her rural-agricultural heritage in favor of an idealized Jeffersonian version of the yeoman farmer. So also did the country create a flurry of myths concerning the self-made man, workers, the Gilded Age, American Indians, the alleged gaiety of the decade of the 1890s, and revisions regarding Victorian sexuality.

Ten-Gallon Hero

David Brion Davis

The cowboy as folk hero, the product of commercial convention and psychological need, has enjoyed sustained vitality in American mythology since the end of the nineteenth century. Indeed, ever since the solidification of the myth of the "ten-gallon hero," America has responded to it with a poignant impulse. To David Brion Davis of Yale University, the haunting nostalgia the cowboy elicits is a synthesis of two American traditions—the myths of the Western scout and the antebellum South. Though the portrait of the cowboy-hero has been incompletely drawn, and although he therefore represents in many ways an essentially false tradition, when compared with other folk heroes the cowboy is perhaps among the least obnoxious of the lot.

In 1900 it seemed that the significance of the cowboy era would decline along with other brief but romantic episodes in American history. The Long Drive lingered only in the memories and imaginations of old cowhands. The "hoe-men" occupied former range land while Mennonites and professional dry farmers had sown their Turkey Red winter wheat on the Kansas prairies. To be sure, a cattle industry still flourished, but the cowboy was more like an employee of a corporation than the free-lance cowboy of old.[1] The myth of the cowboy lived on in the Beadle and Adams paperback novels, with the followers of Ned Buntline and the prolific Colonel Prentiss Ingraham. But this seemed merely a substitution of the more up-to-date cowboy in a tradition which began with Leatherstocking and Daniel Boone.[2] If the mountain man had replaced Boone and the forest scouts, if the cowboy had succeeded the mountain man, and if the legends of Mike Fink and Crockett were slipping into the past, it would seem probable that the cowboy would follow, to become a quaint character of antiquity, overshadowed by newer heroes.

Yet more than a half-century after the passing of the actual wild and woolly cowboy, we find a unique phenomenon in American mythology. Gaudy-covered Western or cowboy magazines decorate stands, windows, and shelves in "drug" stores, bookstores, grocery stores and supermarkets from Miami to Seattle. Hundreds of cowboy movies and television shows are watched and lived through by millions of Americans. Nearly every little boy demands a cowboy suit and a Western six-shooter cap pistol. Cowboys gaze out at you with steely eye and cocked revolver from cereal packages and television screens. Jukeboxes in Bennington, Vermont, as well as Globe, Arizona, moan and warble the latest cowboy songs. Middle-age folk who had once thought of William S. Hart, Harry Carey, and Tom Mix as a passing phase, have lived to see several Hopalong Cassidy revivals, the Lone Ranger, Tim McCoy, Gene Autry, and Roy Rogers. Adolescents and even grown men in Maine and Florida can be seen affecting cowboy, or at least modified cowboy garb, while in the new airplane plants in Kansas, workers don their cowboy boots and wide-brimmed hats, go to work whistling a cowboy song, and are defiantly proud that they live in the land of lassos and six-guns.

When recognized at all, this remarkable cowboy complex is usually defined as the distortion of once-colorful legends by a commercial society.[3] The obvious divergence between the real West and the idealized version, the standardization of plot and characters, and the ridiculous incongruities of cowboys with automobiles and airplanes, all go to substantiate this conclusion.

However, there is more than the cowboy costume and stage setting in even the wildest of these adventures. Despite the incongruities, the cowboy myth exists in fact, and as such is probably a more influential social force than the actual cowboy ever was. It provides the framework for an expression of common ideals of morality and behavior. And while a commercial success, the hero cowboy must satisfy some basic want in American culture, or there could never be such a tremendous market. It is true that the market has been exploited by magazine, song, and scenario writers, but it is important to ask why similar myths have not been equally profitable, such as the lumbermen of the early northwest, the whale fishermen of New Bedford, the early railroad builders, or the fur traders. There have been romances written and movies produced idealizing these phases of American history, but little boys do not dress up like Paul Bunyan and you do not see harpooners on cereal packages. Yet America has had many episodes fully as colorful and of longer duration than the actual cowboy era.

The cowboy hero and his setting are a unique synthesis of two American traditions, and echoes of this past can be discerned in even the wildest of the modern horse operas. On the one hand, the line of descent is a direct evolution from the Western scout of Cooper and the Dime Novel; on the other, there has been a recasting of the golden myth of the antebellum South.[4] The two were fused sometime in the 1880's. Perhaps there was actually some basis for such a union. While the West was economically tied to the North as soon as the early canals and railroads broke the river-centered traffic, social ties endured longer. Many Southerners emigrated West and went into the cattle business, and of course, the Long Drive originated in Texas.[5] The literary synthesis of two traditions only followed the two social movements. It was on the Great Plains that the descendants of Daniel Boone met the drawling Texas cowboy.

Henry Nash Smith has described two paradoxical aspects of the legendary Western scout, typified in Boone himself.[6] This woodsman, this buckskin-clad wilderness hunter is a pioneer, breaking trails for his countrymen to follow, reducing the savage wilderness for civilization. Nevertheless, he is also represented as escaping civilization, turning his back on the petty materialism of the world, on the hypocritical and self-conscious manners of community life, and seeking the unsullied, true values of nature.

These seemingly conflicting points of view have counterparts in the woodsman's descendant, the cowboy. The ideal cowboy fights for justice, risks his life to make the dismal little cowtown safe for law-abiding, respectable citizens, but in so doing he destroys the very environment which made him a heroic figure. This paradox is common with all ideals, and the cowboy legend is certainly the embodiment of a social ideal. Thus the minister or social reformer who rises to heroism in his fight against a sin-infested community would logically become a mere figurehead once the community is reformed. There can be no true ideal or hero in a utopia. And the civilization for which the cowboy or trailblazer struggles is utopian in character.

But there is a further consideration in the case of the cowboy. In our mythology, the cowboy era is timeless. The ranch may own a modern station wagon, but the distinguishing attributes of cowboy and environment remain. There is, it is true, a nostalgic sense that this is the last great drama, a sad knowledge that the cowboy is passing and that civilization is approaching. But it never comes. This strange, wistful sense of the coming end of an epoch is not something outside our experience. It is a faithful reflection of the sense of approaching adulthood. The appeal of the cowboy, in this sense, is similar to the appeal of Boone, Leatherstocking, and the later Mountain Man. We know that adulthood, civilization, is inevitable, but we are living toward the end of childhood, and at that point "childness" seems eternal; it is a whole lifetime. But suddenly we find it is not eternal, the forests disappear, the mountains are settled, and we have new responsibilities. When we shut our eyes and try to remember, the last image of a carefree life appears. For the nation, this last image is the cowboy.

The reborn myth of the antebellum South also involves nostalgia; not so much nostalgia for something that actually existed as for dreams and ideals. When the Southern myth reappeared on the rolling prairies, it was purified and regenerated by the casting off of apologies for slavery. It could focus all energies on its former rôle of opposing the peculiar social and economic philosophy of the Northeast. This took the form of something more fundamental than mere agrarianism or primitivism. Asserting the importance of values beyond the utilitarian and material, this transplanted Southern philosophy challenged the doctrine of enlightened self-interest and the belief that leisure time is sin.

Like the barons and knights of Southern feudalism, the large ranch owners and itinerant cowboys knew how to have a good time. If there was a time for work, there was a time for play, and the early rodeos, horse races, and wild nights at a cowtown were not occasions for reserve. In this respect, the cowboy West was more in the tradition of fun-loving New Orleans than of the Northeast. Furthermore, the ranch was a remarkable duplication of the plantation, minus slaves. It was a hospitable social unit, where travelers were welcome even when the owner was absent. As opposed to the hard-working, thrifty, and sober ideal of the East, the actual cowboy was overly cheerful at times, generous to the point of waste, and inclined to value friendly comradeship above prestige.[7]

The mythical New England Yankee developed a code of action which always triumphed over the more sophisticated city slicker, because the Yankee's down-to-earth shrewdness, common sense, and reserved humor embodied values which Americans considered as pragmatically effective. The ideal cowboy also had a code of action, but it involved neither material nor social success. The cowboy avoided actions which "just weren't done" because he placed a value on doing things "right," on managing difficult problems and situations with ease, skill, and modesty. The cowboy's code was a Western and democratic version of the Southern gentleman's "honor."

In the early years of the twentieth century, a Philadelphia lawyer, who affected a careless, loose-tied bow instead of the traditional black ribbon and who liked to appear in his shirt-sleeves, wrote: "The nomadic bachelor west is over, the housed, married west is established."[8] In a book published in 1902 he had, more than any other man, established an idealized version of the former, unifying the Southern and Western hero myths in a formula which was not to be forgotten. Owen Wister had, in fact, liberated the cowboy hero from the Dime Novels and provided a synthetic tradition suitable for a new century. *The Virginian* became a key document in popular American culture, a romance which defined the cowboy character and thus the ideal American character in terms of courage, sex, religion, and humor. The novel served as a model for hundreds of Western books and movies for half a century. In the recent popular movie "High Noon" a Hollywood star, who won his fame dramatizing Wister's novel, reenacted the same basic plot of hero rejecting heroine's pleas and threats, to uphold his honor against the villain Trampas. While this theme is probably at least a thousand years old, it was Owen Wister who gave it a specifically American content and thus explicated and popularized the modern cowboy ideal, with its traditions, informality, and all-important code.

Of course, Wister's West is not the realistic, boisterous, sometimes monotonous West of Charlie Siringo and Andy Adams. The cowboy, after all, drove cattle. He worked. There was much loneliness and monotony on the range, which has faded like mist under a desert sun in the reminiscences of old cowhands and the fiction of idealizers. The Virginian runs some errands now and then, but there are no cattle-driving scenes, no monotony, no hard work. Fictional cowboys are never bored. Real cowboys were often so bored that they memorized the labels on tin cans and then played games to see how well they could recite them.[9] The cowboys in books and movies are far too busy making love and chasing bandits to work at such a dreary task as driving cattle. But then the Southern plantation owner did no work. The befringed hero of the forests did not work. And if any ideal is to be accepted by adolescent America, monotonous work must be subordinated to more exciting pastimes. The fact that the cowboy hero has more important things to do is only in keeping with his tradition and audience. He is only a natural reaction against a civilization which demands increasingly monotonous work, against the approaching adulthood when playtime ends.

And if the cowboy romance banishes work and monotony, their very opposite are found in the immensity of the Western environment. To be sure, the deserts and prairies can be bleak, but they are never dull when used as setting for the cowboy myth. There is always an element of the unexpected, of surprise, of variety. The tremendous distances either seclude or elevate the particular and significant. There are mirages, hidden springs, dust storms, hidden identities, and secret ranches. In one of his early Western novels William MacLeod Raine used both devices of a secret ranch and hidden identity, while Hoffman Birney combined a hidden ranch, a secret trail, and two hidden identities.[10] In such an environment of uncertainty and change men of true genius stand out from the rest. The evil or good in an individual is quickly revealed in cowboy land. A man familiar with the actual cowboy wrote that "brains, moral and physical courage, strength of character, native gentlemanliness, proficiency in riding or shooting—every quality of leadership tended to raise its owner from the common level.[11]

The hazing which cowboys gave the tenderfoot was only preliminary. It was a symbol of the true test which anyone must undergo in the West. After the final winnowing of men, there emerge the heroes, the villains, and the clowns. The latter live in a purgatory and usually attach themselves to the hero group. Often, after stress of an extreme emergency, they burst out of their caste and are accepted in the élite.

While the Western environment, according to the myth, sorts men into their true places, it does not determine men. It brings out the best in heroes and the worst in villains, but it does not add qualities to the man who has none. The cowboy is a superman and is adorable for his own sake. It is here that he is the descendant of supernatural folk heroes. Harry Hawkeye, the creator of an early cowboy hero, Calvin Yancey, described him as:

> . . . straight as an arrow, fair and ruddy as a Viking, with long, flowing golden hair, which rippled over his massive shoulders, falling nearly at his waist; a high, broad forehead beneath which sparkled a pair of violet blue eyes, tender and soulful in repose, but firm and determined under excitement. His entire face was a study for a sculptor with its delicate aquiline nose, straight in outline as though chiselled from Parian marble, and its generous manly mouth, with full crimson and arched lips, surmounted by a long, silken blonde mustache, through which a beautiful set of even white teeth gleamed like rows of lustrous pearls.[12]

While the Virginian is not quite the blond, Nordic hero, he is just as beautiful to behold. His black, curly locks, his lean, athletic figure, his quiet, unassuming manner, all go to make the most physically attractive man Owen Wister could describe. Later cowboy heroes have shaved their mustaches, but the great majority have beautiful curly hair, usually blond or red, square jaws, cleft chins, broad shoulders, deep chests, and wasp-like waists. Like the Virginian, they are perfect men, absolutely incapable of doing the wrong thing unless deceived.[13]

Many writers familiar with the real cowboy have criticized Wister for his concentration on the Virginian's love interest and, of course, they deplore the present degeneration of the cowboy plot, where love is supreme. There were few women in the West in the Chisholm Trail days and those few in Dodge City, Abilene, and Wichita were of dubious morality. The cowboy's sex life was intermittent, to say the least. He had to carry his thirst long distances, like a camel, and in the oases the orgies were hardly on a spiritual plane.[14] Since earlier heroes, like the woodsman, led celibate lives, it is important to ask why the cowboy depends on love interest.

At first glance, there would seem to be an inconsistency here. The cowboy is happiest with a group of buddies, playing poker, chasing horse thieves, riding in masculine company. He is contemptuous of farmers, has no interest in children, and considers men who have lived among women as effete. Usually he left his own family at a tender age and rebelled against the restrictions of mothers and older sisters. Neither the Virginian nor the actual cowboys were family men, nor did they have much interest in the homes they left behind. Thus it would seem that courting a young schoolteacher from Vermont would be self-destruction. At no place is the idealized cowboy further from reality than in his love for the tender woman from the East. Like the law and order he fights for, she will destroy his way of life.

But this paradox is solved when one considers the hero cowboy, not the plot, as the center of all attention. Molly Wood in *The Virginian,* like all her successors, is a literary device, a *dea ex machina* with a special purpose. Along with the Western environment, she serves to throw a stronger light on the hero, to make him stand out in relief, to complete the picture of an ideal. In the first place, she brings out qualities in him which we could not see otherwise. Without her, he would be too much the brute for a real folk hero, at least in a modern age. If Molly Wood were not in *The Virginian,* the hero might seem too raucous, too wild. Of course, his affair with a blonde in town is handled genteelly; his boyish pranks such as mixing up the babies at the party are treated as good, clean fun. But still, there is nothing to bring out his qualities of masculine tenderness, there is nothing to show his conscience until Molly Wood arrives. A cowboy's tenderness is usually revealed through his kindness to horses, and in this sense, the Eastern belle's rôle is that of a glorified horse. A woman in the Western drama is somebody to rescue, somebody to protect. In her presence, the cowboy shows that, in his own way, he is a cultural ideal. The nomadic, bachelor cowboys described by Andy Adams and Charles Siringo are a little too masculine, a little too isolated from civilization to become the ideal for a settled community.

While the Western heroine brings out a new aspect of the cowboy's character, she also serves the external purpose of registering our attitudes toward him. The cowboy is an adorable figure and the heroine is the vehicle of adoration. Female characters enable the author to make observations about cowboys which would be impossible with an all-male cast.[15] This rôle would lose its value if the heroine surrendered to the cowboy immediately. So the more she struggles with herself, the more she conquers her Eastern reservations and surmounts difficulties before capitulating, the more it enhances the hero.

Again, *The Virginian* is the perfect example. We do not meet Molly Wood in the first part of the book. Instead, the author, the I, who is an Easterner, goes to Wyoming and meets the Virginian. It is love at first sight, not in the sexual sense, of course (this was 1902), but there is no mistaking it for anything other than love. This young man's love for the Virginian is not important in itself; it heightens our worship of the hero. The sex of the worshiper is irrelevant. At first the young man is disconsolate, because he cannot win the Virginian's friendship. He must go through the ordeal of not knowing the Virginian's opinion of him. But as he learns the ways of the West, the Virginian's sublime goodness is unveiled. Though increasing knowledge of the hero's character only serves to widen the impossible gulf between the finite Easterner and the infinite, pure virtue of the cowboy, the latter, out of his own free grace and goodness recognizes the lowly visitor, who adores him all the more for it. But this little episode is only a preface, a symbol of the drama to come. As soon as the Virginian bestows his grace on the male adorer, Molly Wood arrives. The same passion is reenacted, though on a much larger frame. In this rôle, the sex of Molly *is* important, and the traditional romance plot is only superficial form. Molly's coyness, her reserve, her involved heritage of Vermont tradition, all go to build an insurmountable barrier. Yet she loves the Virginian. And Owen Wister and his audience love the Virginian through Molly Wood's love. With the male adorer, they had gone about as far as they could go. But Molly offers a new height from which to love the Virginian. There are many exciting possibilities. Molly can save his life and nurse him back to health. She can threaten to break off their wedding if he goes out to fight his rival, and then forgive him when he disobeys her plea. The Virginian marries Molly in the end and most of his descendants either marry or are about to marry their lovely ladies. But this does not mean a physical marriage, children, and a home. That would be building up a hero only to destroy him. The love climax at the end of the cowboy drama raises the hero to a supreme height, the audience achieves an emotional union with its ideal. In the next book or movie the cowboy will be the carefree bachelor again.

The classic hero, Hopalong Cassidy, has saved hundreds of heroines, protected them, and has been adored by them. But in 1910 Hopalong, "remembering a former experience of his own, smiled in knowing cynicism when told that he again would fall under the feminine spell."[16] In 1950 he expressed the same resistance to actual marriage:

> "But you can't always move on, Hoppy!" Lenny protested. "Someday you must settle down! Don't you ever think of marriage?" "Uh-huh, and whenever I think of it I saddle Topper and ride. I'm not a marrying man, Lenny. Sometimes I get to thinkin' about that poem a feller wrote, about how a woman is only a woman but—" "The open road is my Fate!" she finished. "That's it. But can you imagine any woman raised outside a tepee livin' in the same house with a restless man?"[17]

The cowboy hero is the hero of the pre-adolescent, either chronologically or mentally. It is the stage of revolt against femininity and feminine standards. It is also the age of hero worship. If the cowboy romance were sexual, if it implied settling down with a real *girl*, there would be little interest. One recent cowboy hero summarized this attitude in terms which should appeal strongly to any ten-year-old: "I'd as soon fight a she-lion barehanded as have any truck with a gal."[18] The usual cowboy movie idol has about as much social presence in front of the leading lady as a very bashful boy. He is most certainly not the lover-type. That makes him lovable to both male and female Americans. There can be no doubt that Owen Wister identified himself, not with the Virginian, but with Molly Wood.

While some glorifiers of the actual cowboy have maintained that his closeness to nature made him a deeply religious being, thus echoing the devoutness of the earlier woodsman hero who found God in nature, this tradition has never carried over to the heroic cowboy. Undoubtedly some of the real cowboys were religious, though the consensus of most of the writers on the subject seems to indicate that indifference was more common.[19] Intellectualized religion obviously had no appeal and though the cowboy was often deeply sentimental, he did not seem prone to the emotional and frenzied religion of backwoods farmers and squatters. Perhaps his freedom from family conflicts, from smoldering hatreds and entangled jealousies and loves, had something to do with this. Despite the hard work, the violent physical conflicts, and the occasional debaucheries, the cowboy's life must have had a certain innocent, Homeric quality. Even when witnessing a lynching or murder, the cowboy must have felt further removed from total depravity or original sin than the farmer in a squalid frontier town, with his nagging wife and thirteen children.

At any rate, the cowboy hero of our mythology is too much of a god himself to feel humility. His very creation is a denial of any kind of sin. The cowboy is an enunciation of the goodness of man and the glory which he can achieve by himself. The Western environment strips off the artifice, the social veneer, and instead of a cringing sinner, we behold a dazzling superman. He is a figure of friendly justice, full of self-reliance, a very tower of strength. What need has he of a god?

Of course, the cowboy is not positively anti-religious. He is a respecter of traditions as long as they do not threaten his freedom. The Virginian is polite enough to the orthodox minister who visits his employer's ranch. He listens respectfully to the long sermon, but the ranting and raving about his evil nature are more than he can stand. He knows that his cowboy friends are good men. He loves the beauty of the natural world and feels that the Creator of such a world must be a good and just God. Beyond that, the most ignorant cowboy knows as much as this sinister-voiced preacher. So like a young Greek god leaving Mount Olympus for a practical joke in the interest of justice, the Virginian leaves his rôle of calm and straightforward dignity, and engages in some humorous guile and deceit. The minister is sleeping in the next room and the Virginian calls him and complains that the devil is clutching him. After numerous sessions of wrestling with his conscience, the sleepy minister acting as referee, morning comes before the divine finds he has been tricked. He leaves the ranch in a rage, much to the delight of all the cowboys. The moral, observes Wister, is that men who are obsessed with evil and morbid ideas of human nature, had better stay away from the cowboy West. As Alfred Henry Lewis put it, describing a Western town the year *The Virginian* was published, "Wolfville's a hard practical outfit, what you might call a heap obdurate, an' it's goin' to take more than them fitful an' o'casional sermons I aloodes to,—to reach the roots of its soul."[20] The cowboy is too good and has too much horse sense to be deluded by such brooding theology. Tex Burns could have been describing the Virginian when he wrote that his characters "had the cow hand's rough sense of humor and a zest for practical jokes no cow hand ever outgrows."[21]

Coming as it did at the end of the nineteenth century, the cowboy ideal registered both a protest against orthodox creeds and a faith that man needs no formal religion, once he finds a pure and natural environment. It is the extreme end of a long evolution of individualism. Even the individualistic forest scout was dependent on his surroundings, and he exhibited a sort of pantheistic piety when he beheld the wilderness. The mighty captain of industry, while not accountable to anyone in this world, gave lip-service to the generous God who had made him a steward of wealth. But the cowboy hero stood out on the lonely prairie, dependent on neither man nor God. He was willing to take whatever risks lay along his road and would gladly make fun of any man who took life too seriously. Speaking of his mother's death, a real cowboy is supposed to have said:

> With almost her last breath, she begged me to make my peace with God, while the making was good. I have been too busy to heed her last advice. Being a just God, I feel that He will overlook my neglect. If not, I will have to take my medicine, with Satan holding the spoon.[22]

While the cowboy hero has a respect for property, he does not seek personal wealth and is generous to the point of carelessness. He gives money to his friends, to people in distress, and blows the rest when he hits town on Saturday night. He owns no land and, in fact, has only contempt for farmers, with their ploughed fields and weather-beaten buildings. He hates the slick professional gambler, the grasping Eastern speculator, and the railroad man. How are these traits to be reconciled with his regard for property rights? The answer lies in a single possession—his horse. The cowboy's horse is what separates him from vagabondage and migratory labor. It is his link with the cavalier and plumed knight. More and more, in our increasingly property-conscious society, the cowboy's horse has gained in importance. A horse thief becomes a symbol of concentrated evil, a projection of all crime against property and, concomitantly, against social status. Zane Grey was adhering to this tradition when he wrote, "In those days, a horse meant all the world to a man. A lucky strike of grassy upland and good water . . . made him rich in all that he cared to own." On the other hand, "a horse thief was meaner than a poisoned coyote."[23]

When a cowboy is willing to sell his horse, as one actually does in *The Virginian*, he has sold his dignity and self-identity. It is the tragic mistake which will inevitably bring its nemesis. His love for and close relationship with his horse not only make a cowboy seem more human, they also show his respect for propriety and order. He may drift from ranch to ranch, but his horse ties him down to respectability. Yet the cowboy hero is not an ambitious man. He lacks the concern for hard work and practical results which typifies the

Horatio Alger ideal. Despite his fine horse and expensive saddle and boots, he values his code of honor and his friends more than possessions. Because the cowboy era is timeless, the hero has little drive or push toward a new and better life. He fights for law and order and this implies civilization, but the cowboy has no visions of empires, industrial or agrarian.

One of the American traits which foreign visitors most frequently described was the inability to have a good time. Americans constantly appear in European journals as ill-at-ease socially, as feeling they must work every spare moment. Certainly it was part of the American Protestant capitalistic ethic, the Poor Richard, Horatio Alger ideal, that spare time, frivolous play, and relaxation were sins which would bring only poverty, disease, and other misfortunes. If a youth would study the wise sayings of great men, if he worked hard and made valuable friends but no really confidential ones, if he never let his hair down or became too intimate with any person, wife included, if he stolidly kept his emotions to himself and watched for his chance in the world, then he would be sure to succeed. But the cowboy hero is mainly concerned with doing things skillfully and conforming to his moral code for its own sake. When he plays poker, treats the town to a drink, or raises a thousand dollars to buy off the evil mortgage, he is not aiming at personal success. Most cowboy heroes have at least one friend who knows them intimately, and they are seldom reserved, except in the presence of a villain or nosey stranger.

Both the hero and real cowboy appear to be easy-going and informal. In dress, speech, and social manner, the cowboy sets a new ideal. Every cowboy knows how to relax. If the villains are sometimes tense and nervous, the hero sits placidly at a card game, never ruffled, never disturbed, even when his archrival is behind him at the bar, hot with rage and whisky. The ideal cowboy is the kind of man who turns around slowly when a pistol goes off and drawls, "Ah'd put thet up, if Ah were yew." William MacLeod Raine's Sheriff Collins chats humorously with some train robbers and maintains a calm, unconcerned air which amuses the passengers, though he is actually pumping the bandits for useful information.[24] Previously, he had displayed typical cowboy individualism by flagging the train down and climbing aboard, despite the protests of the conductor. Instead of the eager, aspiring youth, the cowboy hero is like a young tomcat, calm and relaxed, but always ready to spring into action. An early description of one of the most persistent of the cowboy heroes summarizes the ideal characteristics which appeal to a wide audience:

> Hopalong Cassidy had the most striking personality of all the men in his outfit; humorous, courageous to the point of foolishness, eager for fight or frolic, nonchalant when one would expect him to be quite otherwise, curious, loyal to a fault, and the best man with a Colt in the Southwest, he was a paradox, and a puzzle even to his most intimate friends. With him life was a humorous recurrence of sensations, a huge pleasant joke instinctively tolerated, but not worth the price cowards pay to keep it. He had come onto the range when a boy and since that time he had laughingly carried his life in his open hand, and . . . still carried it there, and just as recklessly.[25]

Of course, most cowboy books and movies bristle with violence. Wild fist fights, brawls with chairs and bottles, gun play and mass battles with crashing windows, fires, and the final racing skirmish on horseback, are all as much a part of the cowboy drama as the boots and spurs. These bloody escapades are necessary and are simply explained. They provide the stage for the hero to show his heroism, and since the cowboy is the hero to the pre-adolescent, he must prove himself by their standards. Physical prowess is the most important thing for the ten- or twelve-year-old mind. They are constantly plagued by fear, doubt, and insecurity, in short, by evil, and they lack the power to crush it. The cowboy provides the instrument for their aggressive impulses, while the villain symbolizes all evil. The ethics of the cowboy band are the ethics of the boy's gang, where each member has a rôle determined by his physical skills and his past performance. As with any group of boys, an individual cowboy who had been "taken down a peg" was forever ridiculed and teased about his loss in status.[26]

The volume of cowboy magazines, radio programs and motion pictures would indicate a national hero for at least a certain age group, a national hero who could hardly help but reflect specific attitudes. The cowboy myth has been chosen by this audience because it combines a complex of traits, a way of life, which they consider the proper ideal for America. The actual drama and setting are subordinate to the grand figure of the cowboy hero, and the love affairs, the exciting plots, and the climactic physical struggles present opportunities for the definition of the cowboy code and character. Through the superficial action, the heroism of the cowboy is revealed, and each repetition of the drama, like the repetition of a sacrament, reaffirms the cowboy public's faith in their ideal.

Perhaps the outstanding cowboy trait, above even honor, courage, and generosity, is the relaxed, calm attitude toward life. Though he lives intensely, he has a calm self-assurance, a knowledge that he can handle anything. He is good-humored and jovial.[27] He never takes women too seriously. He can take a joke or laugh at himself. Yet the cowboy is usually anti-intellectual and anti-school, another attitude which appeals to a younger audience.[28]

Above all, the cowboy is a "good joe." He personifies a code of personal dignity, personal liberty, and personal honesty. Most writers on the actual cowboy represented him as having these traits.[29] While many of these men obviously glorify him as much as any fiction writers, there must have been some basis for their judgment. As far as his light-hearted, calm attitude is concerned, it is amazing how similar cowboys appear, both in romances and non-fiction.[30] Millions of American youth subscribed to the new ideal and yearned for the clear, Western atmosphere of "unswerving loyalty, the true, deep affection, and good-natured banter that left no sting."[31] For a few thrilling hours they could roughly toss conventions aside and share the fellowship of ranch life and adore the kind of hero who was never bored and never afraid.

Whether these traits of self-confidence, a relaxed attitude toward life and good humor, have actually increased in the United States during the past fifty years is like asking whether men love their wives more now than in 1900.

Certainly the effective influence of the cowboy myth can never be determined. It is significant, however, that the cowboy ideal has emerged above all others. And while the standardization of plot and character seems to follow other commercial conventions, the very popularity of this standard cowboy is important and is an overlooked aspect of the American character. It is true that this hero is infantile, that he is silly, overdone, and unreal. But when we think of many past ideals and heroes, myths and ethics; when we compare our placid cowboy with, say, the eager, cold, serious hero of Nazi Germany (the high-cheekboned, blond lad who appeared on the Reichsmarks); or if we compare the cowboy with the gangster heroes of the thirties, or with the serious, self-righteous and brutal series of Supermen, Batmen, and Human Torches; when, in an age of violence and questioned public and private morality, we think of the many possible heroes we might have had—then we can be thankful for our silly cowboy. We could have chosen worse.

Notes

1. Edward Douglas Branch, *The Cowboy and His Interpreters* (New York: D. Appleton & Company, 1926), p. 69.
2. Henry Nash Smith, *Virgin Land* (Cambridge: Harvard University Press, 1950), pp. v, vi.
3. Smith, *Virgin Land*, p. 111.
4. Emerson Hough, *The Story of the Cowboy* (New York: D. Appleton & Company, 1901), p. 200.
5. Edward E. Dale, *Cow Country* (Norman, Okla.: University of Oklahoma Press, 1942), p. 15.
6. Smith, *Virgin Land*, p. v.
7. Alfred Henry Lewis, *Wolfville Days* (New York: Stokes, 1902), p. 24.
8. Branch, *The Cowboy and His Interpreters*, pp. 190 ff.
9. Philip Ashton Rollins, *The Cowboy* (New York: Charles Scribner's Sons, 1922), p. 185.
10. William MacLeod Raine, *Bucky O'Connor* (New York: Grosset & Dunlap, 1907); Hoffman Birney, *The Masked Rider* (New York: Penn, 1928).
11. Rollins, *The Cowboy*, p. 352.
12. Branch, *The Cowboy and His Interpreters*, p. 191.
13. A Zane Grey hero is typical and is also seen through the eyes of a woman: "She saw a bronzed, strong-jawed, eagle-eyed man, stalwart, superb of height." Zane Grey, *The Light of Western Stars* (New York: Harper & Brothers, 1914), pp. 29–30.
14. Charles A. Siringo, *A Lone Star Cowboy* (Santa Fe: C. A. Siringo, 1919), p. 64.
15. No male character could observe that " 'cowboys play like they work or fight,' she added. 'They give their whole souls to it. They are great big simple boys.' " Grey, *The Light of Western Stars*, p. 187.
16. Clarence E. Mulford, *Hopalong Cassidy* (Chicago: A. C. McClurg & Company, 1910), p. 11.
17. Tex Burns, pseud. (Louis L'Amour), *Hopalong Cassidy and the Trail to Seven Pines* (New York: Doubleday, 1951), p. 187.
18. Davis Dresser, *The Hangmen of Sleepy Valley* (New York: Jefferson House, 1950), p. 77.

19. Hough, *The Story of the Cowboy*, p. 199; Branch, *The Cowboy and His Interpreters*, p. 160; Rollins, *The Cowboy*, p. 84; Lewis, *Wolfville Days*, p. 216.

20. Lewis, *Wolfville Days*, p. 216.

21. Burns, *Hopalong Cassidy*, p. 130.

22. Siringo, *A Lone Star Cowboy*, p. 37.

23. Zane Grey, *Wildfire* (New York: Harper & Brothers, 1917), pp. 10, 7.

24. Raine, *Bucky O'Connor*, p. 22.

25. Mulford, *Hopalong Cassidy*, p. 65.

26. Sam P. Ridings, *The Chisholm Trail* (Medford, Okla.: S. P. Ridings, 1936), p. 297.

27. The cowboy hero was judged to be "out of sorts when he could not vent his peculiar humor on somebody or something." Grey, *The Light of Western Stars*, pp. 118–19.

28. This anti-intellectualism in the Western myth is at least as old as Cooper's parody of the scientist, Obed Bat, in *The Prairie*. More recently, Will James took pride in his son's poor attitude and performance in school. Will James, *The American Cowboy* (New York: Charles Scribner's Sons, 1942), p. 107.

29. Ridings, *The Chisholm Trail*, pp. 278–94; Rollins, *The Cowboy*, p. 67; Dale, *Cow Country*, pp. 122, 153.

30. According to Alfred Henry Lewis, surly and contentious people were just as unpopular in Wolfville as they appear to be in fiction. Lewis, *Wolfville Days*, p. 217.

31. Mulford, *Hopalong Cassidy*, p. 155.

The Myth of the Happy Yeoman

Richard Hofstadter

For centuries humankind has cherished the notion that agriculture is the most basic of industries and the yeoman farmer the most virtuous of individuals. Though certainly not alone in viewing the farmer as a folk hero, Americans have perhaps been the most persistent in articulating their support for this romantic vision. A commitment to the yeoman farmer as ideal type and ideal citizen can be found in the views of such diverse Americans as Benjamin Franklin, Thomas Jefferson, Alexander Hamilton, and Calvin Coolidge. Richard Hofstadter, late Dewitt Clinton Professor of American History at Columbia University, here comments on the yeoman myth as it evolved from a literary to a popular ideal.

The United States was born in the country and has moved to the city. From the beginning its political values as well as ideas were of necessity shaped by country life. The early American politician, the country editor, who wished to address himself to the common man, had to draw upon a rhetoric that would touch the tillers of the soil; and even the spokesman of city people knew that his audience had been in very large part reared upon the farm.

But what the articulate people who talked and wrote about farmers and farming—the preachers, poets, philosophers, writers, and statesmen—liked about American farming was not, in every respect, what the typical working farmer liked. For the articulate people were drawn irresistibly to the noncommercial, nonpecuniary, self-sufficient aspect of American farm life. To them it was an ideal.

Writers like Thomas Jefferson and Hector St. John de Crèvecoeur admired the yeoman farmer not for his capacity to exploit opportunities and make money but for his honest industry, his independence, his frank spirit of equality, his ability to produce and enjoy a simple abundance. The farmer himself, in most cases, was in fact inspired to make money, and such self-sufficiency as he actually had was usually forced upon him by a lack of transportation or markets, or by the necessity to save cash to expand his operations.

For while early American society was an agrarian society, it was fast becoming more commercial, and commercial goals made their way among its agricultural classes almost as rapidly as elsewhere. The more commercial this society became, however, the more reason it found to cling in imagination to the noncommercial agrarian values. The more farming as a self-sufficient way of life was abandoned for farming as a business, the more merit men found in what was being left behind. And the more rapidly the farmers' sons moved into the towns, the more nostalgic the whole culture became about its rural past. Throughout the nineteenth and even in the twentieth century, the American was taught that rural life and farming as a vocation were something sacred.

This sentimental attachment to the rural way of life is a kind of homage that Americans have paid to the fancied innocence of their origins. To call it a "myth" is not to imply that the idea is simply false. Rather the "myth" so effectively embodies men's values that it profoundly influences their way of perceiving reality and hence their behavior.

Like any complex of ideas, the agrarian myth cannot be defined in a phrase, but its component themes form a clear pattern. Its hero was the yeoman farmer, its central conception the notion that he is the ideal man and the ideal citizen. Unstinted praise of the special virtues of the farmer and the special values of rural life was coupled with the assertion that agriculture, as a calling uniquely productive and uniquely important to society, had a special right to the concern and protection of government. The yeoman, who owned a small farm and worked it with the aid of his family, was the incarnation of the simple, honest, independent, healthy, happy human being. Because he lived in close communion with beneficent nature, his life was believed to have a wholesomeness and integrity impossible for the depraved populations of cities.

His well-being was not merely physical, it was moral; it was not merely personal, it was the central source of civic virtue; it was not merely secular but religious, for God had made the land and called man to cultivate it. Since the yeoman was believed to be both happy and honest, and since he had a secure propertied stake in society in the form of his own land, he was held to be the best and most reliable sort of citizen. To this conviction Jefferson appealed when he wrote: "The small land holders are the most precious part of a state."

In origin the agrarian myth was not a popular but a literary idea, a preoccupation of the upper classes, of those who enjoyed a classical education, read pastoral poetry, experimented with breeding stock, and owned plantations or country estates. It was clearly formulated and almost universally accepted in America during the last half of the eighteenth century. As it took shape both in Europe and America, its promulgators drew heavily upon the authority and the rhetoric of classical writers—Hesiod, Xenophon, Cato, Cicero, Virgil, Horace, and others—whose works were the staples of a good education. A learned agricultural gentry, coming into conflict with the industrial classes, welcomed the moral strength that a rich classical ancestry brought to the praise of husbandry.

Chiefly through English experience, and from English and classical writers, the agrarian myth came to America, where, like so many other cultural importations, it eventually took on altogether new dimensions in its new setting. So appealing were the symbols of the myth that even an arch-opponent of the agrarian interest like Alexander Hamilton found it politic to concede in his *Report on Manufactures* that "the cultivation of the earth, as the primary and most certain source of national supply . . . has intrinsically a strong claim to pre-eminence over every other kind of industry." And Benjamin Franklin, urban cosmopolite though he was, once said that agriculture was "the only *honest way*" for a nation to acquire wealth, "wherein man receives a real increase of the seed thrown into the ground, a kind of continuous miracle, wrought by the hand of God in his favour, as a reward for his innocent life and virtuous industry."

Among the intellectual classes in the eighteenth century the agrarian myth had virtually universal appeal. Some writers used it to give simple, direct, and emotional expression to their feelings about life and nature; others linked agrarianism with a formal philosophy of natural rights. The application of the natural rights philosophy to land tenure became especially popular in America. Since the time of Locke it had been a standard argument that the land is the common stock of society to which every man has a right—what Jefferson called "the fundamental right to labour the earth"; that since the occupancy and use of land are the true criteria of valid ownership, labor expended in cultivating the earth confers title to it; that since government was created to protect property, the property of working land-holders has a special claim to be fostered and protected by the state.

At first the agrarian myth was a notion of the educated classes, but by the early nineteenth century it had become a mass creed, a part of the country's political folklore and its nationalist ideology. The roots of this change may be found as far back as the American Revolution, which, appearing to many Americans as the victory of a band of embattled farmers over an empire, seemed to confirm the moral and civic superiority of the yeoman, made the farmer a symbol of the new nation, and wove the agrarian myth into his patriotic sentiments and idealism.

Still more important, the myth played a role in the first party battles under the Constitution. The Jeffersonians appealed again and again to the moral primacy of the yeoman farmer in their attacks on the Federalists. The family farm and American democracy became indissolubly connected in Jeffersonian thought, and by 1840 even the more conservative party, the Whigs, took over the rhetorical appeal to the common man, and elected a President in good part on the strength of the fiction that he lived in a log cabin.

The Jeffersonians, moreover, made the agrarian myth the basis of a strategy of continental development. Many of them expected that the great empty inland regions would guarantee the preponderance of the yeoman—and therefore the dominance of Jeffersonianism and the health of the state—for an unlimited future. The opening of the trans-Allegheny region, its protection from slavery, and the purchase of the Louisiana Territory were the first great steps in a continental strategy designed to establish an internal empire of small farms. Much later the Homestead Act was meant to carry to its completion the process of continental settlement by small homeowners. The failure of the Homestead Act "to enact by statute the fee-simple empire" was one of the original sources of Populist grievances, and one of the central points at which the agrarian myth was overrun by the commercial realities.

Above all, however, the myth was powerful because the United States in the first half of the nineteenth century consisted predominantly of literate and politically enfranchised farmers. Offering what seemed harmless flattery to this numerically dominant class, the myth suggested a standard vocabulary to rural editors and politicians. Although farmers may not have been much impressed by what was said about the merits of a noncommercial way of life, they could only enjoy learning about their special virtues and their unique services to the nation. Moreover, the editors and politicians who so flattered them need not in most cases have been insincere. More often than not they too were likely to have begun life in little villages or on farms, and what they had to say stirred in their own breasts, as it did in the breasts of a great many townspeople, nostalgia for their early years and perhaps relieved some residual feelings of guilt at having deserted parental homes and childhood attachments. They also had the satisfaction in the early days of knowing that in so far as it was based upon the life of the largely self-sufficient yeoman the agrarian myth was a depiction of reality as well as the assertion of an ideal.

Oddly enough, the agrarian myth came to be believed more widely and tenaciously as it became more fictional. At first it was propagated with a kind of genial candor, and only later did it acquire overtones of insincerity. There survives from the Jackson era a painting that shows Governor Joseph Ritner of Pennsylvania standing by a primitive plow at the end of a furrow. There is no pretense that the Governor has actually been plowing—he wears broad-cloth pants and a silk vest, and his tall black beaver hat has been carefully laid in the grass beside him—but the picture is meant as a reminder of both his rustic origin and his present high station in life. By contrast, Calvin Coolidge posed almost a century later for a series of photographs that represented him as haying in Vermont. In one of them the President sits on the edge of a hay rig in a white shirt, collar detached, wearing highly polished black shoes and a fresh pair of overalls; in the background stands his Pierce Arrow, a secret service man on the running board, plainly waiting to hurry the President away from his bogus rural labors. That the second picture is so much more preten-tious and disingenuous than the first is a measure of the increasing hollowness of the myth as it became more and more remote from the realities of agricul-ture.

Throughout the nineteenth century hundreds upon hundreds of thou-sands of farm-born youths sought their careers in the towns and cities. Particu-larly after 1840, which marked the beginning of a long cycle of heavy country-to-city migration, farm children repudiated their parents' way of life and took off for the cities where, in agrarian theory if not in fact, they were sure to succumb to vice and poverty.

When a correspondent of the *Prairie Farmer* in 1849 made the mistake of praising the luxuries, the "polished society," and the economic opportunities of the city, he was rebuked for overlooking the fact that city life *"crushes, enslaves,* and *ruins so many thousands of our young men* who are insensibly made the victims of *dissipation,* of *reckless speculation,* and of *ultimate crime."* Such warnings, of course, were futile. "Thousands of young men," wrote the New York agriculturist Jesse Buel, "who annually forsake the plough, and the honest profession of their fathers, if not to win the fair, at least from an opinion, too often confirmed by mistaken parents, that agriculture is not the road to wealth, to honor, nor to happiness. And such will continue to be the case, until our agriculturists become qualified to assume that rank in society to which the importance of their calling, and their numbers, entitle them, and which intelligence and self-respect can alone give them."

Rank in society! That was close to the heart of the matter, for the farmer was beginning to realize acutely not merely that the best of the world's goods were to be had in the cities and that the urban middle and upper classes had much more of them than he did but also that he was losing in status and respect as compared with them. He became aware that the official respect paid to the farmer masked a certain disdain felt by many city people. "There has . . . a certain class of individuals grown up in our land," complained a farm writer in 1835, "who treat the cultivators of the soil as an inferior caste . . . whose utmost abilities are confined to the merit of being able to discuss a boiled potato and a rasher of bacon." The city was symbolized as the home of loan sharks, dandies, fops, and aristocrats with European ideas who despised farmers as hayseeds.

The growth of the urban market intensified this antagonism. In areas like colonial New England, where an intimate connection had existed between the small town and the adjacent countryside, where a community of interests and even of occupations cut across the town line, the rural-urban hostility had not developed so sharply as in the newer areas where the township plan was never instituted and where isolated farmsteads were more common. As settlement moved west, as urban markets grew, as self-sufficient farmers became rarer, as farmers pushed into commercial production for the cities they feared and distrusted, they quite correctly thought of themselves as a vocational and economic group rather than as members of a neighborhood. In the Populist era the city was totally alien territory to many farmers, and the primacy of agriculture as a source of wealth was reasserted with much bitterness. "The great cities rest upon our broad and fertile prairies," declared Bryan in his "Cross of Gold" speech. "Burn down your cities and leave our farms, and your cities will spring up again as if by magic; but destroy our farms, and the grass will grow in the streets of every city in the country." Out of the beliefs nourished by the agrarian myth there had arisen the notion that the city was a parasitical growth on the country. Bryan spoke for a people raised for generations on the idea that the farmer was a very special creature, blessed by God, and that in a country consisting largely of farmers the voice of the farmer was the voice of democracy and of virtue itself.

The agrarian myth encouraged farmers to believe that they were not themselves an organic part of the whole order of business enterprise and specu-lation that flourished in the city, partaking of its character and sharing in its risks, but rather the innocent pastoral victims of a conspiracy hatched in the distance. The notion of an innocent and victimized populace colors the whole history of agrarian controversy.

For the farmer it was bewildering, and irritating too, to think of the great contrast between the verbal deference paid him by almost everyone and the real economic position in which he found himself. Improving his economic position was always possible, though this was often done too little and too late; but it was not within anyone's power to stem the decline in the rural values and pieties, the gradual rejection of the moral commitments that had been expressed in the early exaltations of agrarianism.

It was the fate of the farmer himself to contribute to this decline. Like almost all good Americans he had innocently sought progress from the very beginning, and thus hastened the decline of many of his own values. Elsewhere the rural classes had usually looked to the past, had been bearers of tradition and upholders of stability. The American farmer looked to the future alone, and the story of the American land became a study in futures.

In the very hours of its birth as a nation Crèvecoeur had congratulated America for having, in effect, no feudal past and no industrial present, for hav-ing no royal, aristocratic, ecclesiastical, or monarchical power, and no manu-facturing class, and had rapturously concluded: "We are the most perfect soci-ety now existing in the world." Here was the irony from which the farmer suffered above all others: the United States was the only country in the world that began with perfection and aspired to progress.

To what extent was the agrarian myth actually false? During the colonial period, and even well down into the nineteenth century, there were in fact large numbers of farmers who were very much like the yeomen idealized in the myth. They were independent and self-sufficient, and they bequeathed to their children a strong love of craftsmanlike improvisation and a firm tradition of household industry. These yeomen were all too often yeomen by force of circumstance. They could not become commercial farmers because they were too far from the rivers or the towns, because the roads were too poor for bulky traffic, because the domestic market for agricultural produce was too small and the overseas markets were out of reach. At the beginning of the nineteenth century, when the American population was still living largely in the forests and most of it was east of the Appalachians, the yeoman farmer did exist in large numbers, living much as the theorists of the agrarian myth portrayed him.

But when the yeoman practiced the self-sufficient economy that was ex-pected of him, he usually did so not because he wanted to stay out of the market but because he wanted to get into it. "My farm," said a farmer of Jeffer-son's time, "gave me and my family a good living on the produce of it; and left me, one year with another, one hundred and fifty dollars, for I have never spent more than ten dollars a year, which was for salt, nails, and the like. Nothing to wear, eat, or drink was purchased, as my farm provided all. With this saving, I put money to interest, bought cattle, fatted and sold them, and made great profit." Great profit! Here was the significance of self-sufficiency for the characteristic family farmer. Commercialism had already begun to enter the American Arcadia.

For, whatever the spokesman of the agrarian myth might have told him, the farmer almost anywhere in early America knew that all around him there were examples of commercial success in agriculture—the tobacco, rice, and indigo, and later the cotton planters of the South, the grain, meat, and cattle exporters of the middle states.

The farmer knew that without cash he could never rise above the hardships and squalor of pioneering and log-cabin life. So the savings from his self-sufficiency went into improvements—into the purchase of more land, of herds and flocks, of better tools; they went into the building of barns and silos and better dwellings. Self-sufficiency, in short, was adopted for a time in order that it would eventually be unnecessary.

Between 1815 and 1860 the character of American agriculture was transformed. The rise of native industry created a home market for agriculture, while demands arose abroad for American cotton and foodstuffs, and a great network of turnpikes, canals, and railroads helped link the planter and the advancing western farmer to the new markets. As the farmer moved out of the forests onto the flat, rich prairies, he found possibilities for machinery that did not exist in the forest. Before long he was cultivating the prairies with horse-drawn mechanical reapers, steel plows, wheat and corn drills, and threshers.

The farmer was still a hardworking man, and he still owned his own land in the old tradition. But no longer did he grow or manufacture almost everything he needed. He concentrated on the cash crop, bought more and more of his supplies from the country store. To take full advantage of the possibilities of mechanization, he engrossed as much land as he could and borrowed money for his land and machinery. The shift from self-sufficient to commercial farming varied in time throughout the West and cannot be dated with precision, but it was complete in Ohio by about 1830 and twenty years later in Indiana, Illinois, and Michigan. All through the great Northwest, farmers whose fathers might have lived in isolation and self-sufficiency were surrounded by jobbers, banks, stores, middlemen, horses, and machinery.

This transformation affected not only what the farmer did but how he felt. The ideals of the agrarian myth were competing in his breast, and gradually losing ground, to another, even stronger ideal, the notion of opportunity, of career, of the self-made man. Agrarian sentiment sanctified labor in the soil and the simple life; but the prevailing Calvinist atmosphere of rural life implied that virtue was rewarded with success and material goods. Even farm boys were taught to strive for achievement in one form or another, and when this did not take them away from the farms altogether, it impelled them to follow farming not as a way of life but as a *career*—that is, as a way of achieving substantial success.

The sheer abundance of the land—that very internal empire that had been expected to insure the predominance of the yeoman in American life for centuries—gave the *coup de grâce* to the yeomanlike way of life. For it made of the farmer a speculator. Cheap land invited extensive and careless cultivation. Rising land values in areas of new settlement tempted early liquidation and frequent moves. Frequent and sensational rises in land values bred a boom psychology in the American farmer and caused him to rely for his margin of profit more on the appreciation in the value of his land than on the sale of crops. It took a strong man to resist the temptation to ride skyward on lands that might easily triple or quadruple their value in one decade and then double in the next.

What developed in America, then, was an agricultural society whose real attachment was not, like the yeoman's, to the land but to land values. The characteristic product of American rural society, as it developed on the prairies and the plains, was not a yeoman or a villager, but a harassed little country businessman who worked very hard, moved all too often, gambled with his land, and made his way alone.

While the farmer had long since ceased to act like a yeoman, he was somewhat slower in ceasing to think like one. He became a businessman in fact long before he began to regard himself in this light. As the nineteenth century drew to a close, however, various things were changing him. He was becoming increasingly an employer of labor, and though he still worked with his hands, he began to look with suspicion upon the working classes of the cities, especially those organized in trade unions, as he had once done upon the urban fops and aristocrats. Moreover, when good times returned after the Populist revolt of the 1890's, businessmen and bankers and the agricultural colleges began to woo the farmer, to make efforts to persuade him to take the businesslike view of himself that was warranted by the nature of his farm operations. "The object of farming," declared a writer in the *Cornell Countryman* in 1904, "is not primarily to make a living, but it is to make money. To this end it is to be conducted on the same business basis as any other producing industry."

The final change, which came only with a succession of changes in the twentieth century, wiped out the last traces of the yeoman of old, as the coming first of good roads and rural free delivery, and mail order catalogues, then the telephone, the automobile, and the tractor, and at length radio, movies, and television largely eliminated the difference between urban and rural experience in so many important areas of life. The city luxuries, once so derided by farmers, are now what they aspire to give to their wives and daughters.

In 1860 a farm journal satirized the imagined refinements and affectations of a city girl in the following picture:

> Slowly she rises from her couch. . . . Languidly she gains her feet, and oh! what vision of human perfection appears before us: Skinny, bony, sickly, hipless, thighless, formless, hairless, teethless. What a radiant belle! . . . The ceremony of enrobing commences. In goes the dentist's naturalization efforts; next the witching curls are fashioned to her "classically molded head." Then the womanly proportions are properly adjusted; hoops, bustles, and so forth, follow in succession, then a profuse quantity of whitewash, together with a "permanent rose tint" is

applied to a sallow complexion; and lastly the "killing" wrapper is arranged on her systematical and matchless form.

But compare this with these beauty hints for farmers' wives from the *Idaho Farmer*, April, 1935:

> Hands should be soft enough to flatter the most delicate of the new fabrics. They must be carefully manicured, with none of the hot, brilliant shades of nail polish. The lighter and more delicate tones are in keeping with the spirit of freshness. Keep the tint of your fingertips friendly to the red of your lips, and check both your powder and your rouge to see that they best suit the tone of your skin in the bold light of summer.

Nothing can tell us with greater finality of the passing of the yeoman ideal than these light and delicate tones of nail polish.

From Rags to Respectability: Horatio Alger

John G. Cawelti

The notion that through hard work, luck, and moral rectitude one can become president of United States remains one of the sacred dogmas of the American creed. To think that the idea of the "self-made man" was born in America is, itself, a myth; yet the concept has enjoyed surprising durability within American social and political folklore. The myth of rags to riches is of course a reflection of truth. Upward mobility—the rise of men and women to higher social and economic stations—has occurred and continues to occur in America, but perhaps not with the frequency or in the manner generally presumed. John G. Cawelti, Professor of English and Humanities at the University of Chicago, here explains how the myth of "rags to respectability" is related to the myths surrounding Horatio Alger's writings—a myth upon a myth, if you will.

Luke Walton is not puffed up by his unexpected and remarkable success. He never fails to recognize kindly, and help, if there is need, the old associates of his humbler days, and never tries to conceal the fact that he was once a Chicago Newsboy.

Horatio Alger, *Luke Walton*

Today his books are read more often by cultural historians than by children, and such erstwhile classics as *Struggling Upward* and *Mark, the Match Boy* are no longer on the shelves of libraries, but the name of Horatio Alger has become synonymous with the self-made man. American businessmen who commission brief biographies often are described in the following manner:

> The Horatio Alger quality of William J. Stebler's rise to the presidency of General American Transportation Corporation makes one almost pause for breath.

There is even a Horatio Alger award presented annually by the American Schools and Colleges Association to eight Americans who have reached positions of prominence from humble beginnings. In recent years, this award, a bronze desk plaque, has been presented to such leading industrialists and financiers as Benjamin F. Fairless, retired chairman of the United States Steel Corporation; James H. Carmichael, chairman of Capital Airlines; and Milton G. Hulme, president and chairman of a large investment banking firm in Pittsburgh. The creator of *Ragged Dick* has become a familiar idol to Americans concerned about the decline of what they refer to as "individualistic free enterprise." *Advertising Age* in December, 1947, tired of "government interference" in business, begged for a new Horatio Alger to inspire American youth with the independence and enterprise of their fathers.

Many of those who parade under Alger's mantle know little about their hero beyond the fact that he wrote books about success. They would probably be startled if they read one, for Alger was not a partisan of "rugged individualism," and only within limits an admirer of pecuniary success. For a patron saint of success, his life was rather obscure. Born in 1832 in Revere, Massachusetts, he was trained for the ministry at the insistence of his domineering father. He soon gave this up when he found he could support himself by writing children's books. He published a collection of sentimental tales in 1856, and his first widely popular juvenile, *Ragged Dick*, was published serially in Oliver Optic's (William T. Adams) *Student and Schoolmate* magazine, and as a book, in 1867. Alger moved to New York about 1866 and, aside from an occasional trip West and to Europe, spent most of his life in and around the Newsboys' Lodging House, an institution which figures in many of his stories. Its superintendent, Charles O'Connor, was one of his few close friends. Alger, whose books made fortunes for several publishers, died a relatively poor man. He sold most of his books outright for small sums, and spent what money he received in acts of spontaneous and unflagging charity to help almost anyone who applied to him. His amazingly rapid composition of books like *Grit, the Young Boatman of Pine Point* and *Jed, the Poorhouse Boy* was interspersed with occasional efforts at a serious novel, desultory participation in various reform movements—New York Mayor A. Oakey Hall, member of the Tweed ring, once named him chairman of an anti-vice commission—and brief forays into education (he sometimes tutored boys in Greek and Latin to supplement the income from his books).

Alger's death in 1899 did not put an end to the publication of Alger books. Publishers hired ghosts like Edward Stratemeyer, later the author of the Rover Boys series, to capitalize on Alger's popularity. Inevitably, there were signs of a reaction. Parents began to protest against what they considered the false values and unreality of the Alger stories, and a number of libraries removed his books from the shelves. They were republished less often in the second decade of the twentieth century, and, after World War I, sales declined rapidly. At the centennial of Alger's birth, in 1932, a survey of New York working children showed that less than 20 percent of the "juvenile proletariat" had ever heard of Alger; only 14 percent had read an Alger book; and, even more threatening, a "large number" dismissed the theory of "work and win" as "a lot of bunk." A similar survey taken in the forties revealed that only 1 percent of 20,000 children had read an Alger book.

Alger and His Predecessors

There was a marked difference between Alger's work and that of his most important predecessor in the field of juvenile fiction. Jacob Abbott, author of the "Rollo" and "Caleb" books, began his extremely successful career as a writer of children's books in the early 1830's with a long, rather heavily theological, tome discussing the Christian duties of young boys and girls. A strong emphasis on evangelical Protestantism remained the central element in his work. Alger, on the other hand, was not so concerned with the role of religion in the lives of his young heroes. There were other important differences between the Abbott boy and the Alger boy. A firm believer in the ethic of industry, frugality, integrity, and piety, Abbott rarely made ambition itself a significant element in his stories. Rollo and Caleb were not poor boys but the scions of well-to-do middle-class families. The typical Abbott book concerns everyday events from which Rollo or Caleb learns an important moral lesson. In *Rollo at Work*, for example, the hero learns how to work through a Lockean course of instruction which instills in him a progressively greater capacity for sustained effort.

Unlike Alger, Abbott chose to write about younger boys from well-established families for whom social mobility was not a significant problem, and his stories reflect the more conservative social views of the upper middle-class audience for which he wrote. As he presents American life, there are rightful and fundamental class distinctions, each class has its particular role, and there is relatively little movement between classes. At the same time, there is no conception of a leisure class in the Abbott books, and, in terms of worldly luxuries, the gulf between the higher and lower ranks is not great. According to Abbott, since every rank has its proper work, there should be no idlers.

In Alger's stories, on the other hand, rising and falling in society are characteristic phenomena. This is not the first appearance in American children's literature of the idea of mobility. Even in the period of Abbott's dominance, some juvenile authors began to write tales anticipating those of Alger. An interesting halfway house can be seen in the works of Mrs. Louisa M. Tuthill in the period 1830–50. Like Abbott, Mrs. Tuthill generally wrote about boys from well-established families, not the street boys who were Alger's favorite subjects. As an adherent of the Jeffersonian ideal of natural aristocracy, Mrs. Tuthill believed that American institutions properly encouraged the rise of talented and virtuous young men to whatever positions of eminence their merits entitled them. In her *I Will Be a Gentleman*, for example, she attacks the idea of hereditary distinction:

> Having no hereditary titles in the United States, there can be no higher distinction than that which belongs to moral worth, intellectual superiority, and refined politeness. A republican gentleman, therefore need acknowledge no superior; he is a companion for nobles and kings, or, what is better, for the polite, the talented, the good. Since such are an American's only claims to distinction, it becomes the more important for him to cultivate all those graces which elevate and dignify humanity. No high ancestral claims can he urge for his position in society.

Wealth he may possess, and there are those who will acknowledge that claim; but if the possessor have not intelligence and taste to teach him how to use his wealth, it will only make him a more conspicuous mark for ridicule. Those glorious institutions of New England, common schools, afford to every boy the opportunity to acquire that intelligence and taste, and his associates there are from every class of society. There is no unsurmountable obstacle in any boy's way; his position in society must depend mainly upon himself.

Mrs. Tuthill puts the same limits on rising in society as the didactic novelists of the same period. The candidate for distinction must be talented, virtuous, and refined, although he need not spring from an aristocratic family tradition. This emphasis on gentility and refinement, however acquired, also has an important role in the Alger books. Alger constantly emphasizes neatness, good manners, and the proper clothes, and yet his conception of gentility is far less elevated than Mrs Tuthill's. In spite of her frequent protestations that the way was open to all, Mrs. Tuthill's heroes spring from respectable families who have the means to educate their children.

Most of the children's literature of the pre–Civil War period deals with the offspring of secure, middle-class families, but the orphaned boy of the city streets is not without his bards. As early as 1834, a putative autobiography of a bootblack who rose from poverty to be a member of Congress was published with the delightful title *A Spur to Youth; or, Davy Crockett Beaten.* In the following year, Charles F. Barnard published *The Life of Collin Reynolds, the Orphan Boy and Young Merchant.* In this tearful tale, dedicated to the pupils of the Hollis Street Sunday School in Boston, the hero is orphaned when his mother dies and his father goes to sea. Undaunted, he determines to support himself by peddling candy, peanuts, and sundries on the New York ferries. In good Alger fashion, he soon meets the wealthy Mr. J., who is impressed by the boy's history, his industry, and his enterprise and adopts him. Entering Mr. J.'s store, Collin is doing well when the opportunity to sigh forth a highly sentimental deathbed scene proves more attractive to his creator than the fulfilment of material promise. Poor Collin is disposed of in a fall from a horse.

Even closer to the Alger formula is J. H. Ingraham's *Jemmy Daily: or, The Little News Vender,* published in 1843. Ingraham, a hack writer of astonishing fertility, made sentimental romance out of almost any subject. Ingraham's treatment of the newsboy foreshadowed both Alger's characteristic material and his method of treating it. Jemmy Daily and his noble mother, reduced to starvation by a drunken father, are saved when, in a chance encounter, the lovely daughter of a wealthy merchant gives Jemmy food and a sixpence. As a newsboy, Jemmy manages to support his mother. When father becomes intolerable, Jemmy and his mother leave him, a shock which happily reforms the drunkard. The rest of the story concerns Jemmy's fight with a bully and his foiling of the quack Dr. Wellington Smoot's lascivious designs on his mother. Once reformed, the father is granted a convenient death, and Jemmy takes over the family, becoming a clerk under the benevolent tutelage of Mr. Weldon. Jemmy's reward is the promise of a junior partnership and the hand of Mr. Weldon's daughter, the girl who had originally befriended him.

The difference between Ingraham's tale and the typical Alger story is largely a matter of emphasis. The plot and characters are essentially the same, but Ingraham stresses religious conversion and "the great moral temperance reform, which is without question one of the agents of God in ameliorating the condition of fallen man." Jemmy Daily's rise in society and his gradual acquisition of respectability are not as important to him as they were to Alger.

In the 1850's, as urban phenomena became of increasing interest and concern, newsboys and bootblacks were common figures in popular fiction. A. L. Stimson's *Easy Nat* includes an Alger-like street boy adopted by a benevolent farmer, and Seba Smith's wife, a sentimental novelist of considerable popularity, published a long novel, *The Newsboy*, in 1854. This is a typical romantic adventure, containing as one of its many plots the narrative of a poor newsboy's rise to some prominence, through, as usual, the patronage of a benevolent merchant. One writer in the 1850's went so far as to proclaim the newsboy the symbol of a new age:

> Our clarion now, more potent than the Fontabrian horn, is the shrill voice of the news-boy, that modern Minerva, who leaped full blown from the o'erfraught head of journalism; and, as the news-boy is in some respects the type of the time—an incarnation of the spirit of the day,—a few words devoted to his consideration may not be deemed amiss. [Joseph C. Neal, *Peter Ploddy*]

Alger had considerable precedent for his dramatization of the street boy's rise to social respectability. Nor was he the only writer of his time to employ this subject. In fact, Alger neither created the Alger hero nor was he his only exponent. A flood of children's books by such authors as Oliver Optic, Mrs. Sarah Stuart Robbins, Mrs. Madeline Leslie, and the Rev. Elijah Kellog dealt with the rise to moderate security of a poor boy. Alger, however, outsold them all. Somehow he was able to seize upon just those combinations of characters and plot situations that most engrossed adolescent American boys of the nineteenth century.

Alger's Message

Alger's contemporary position as a symbol of individualistic free enterprise has obscured the actual characteristics of his stories. A number of misconceptions must be cleared away before we can get to the heart of the Alger version of what constitutes success. Here, for example, is a typical interpretation of the Alger hero in a recent book:

> Alone, unaided, the ragged boy is plunged into the maelstrom of city life, but by his own pluck and luck he capitalizes on one of the myriad opportunities available to him and rises to the top of the economic heap. Here, in a nutshell, is the plot of every novel Alger ever wrote; here, too, is the quintessence of the myth. Like many simple formulations which nevertheless convey a heavy intellectual and emotional charge to vast numbers of people, the Alger hero represents a triumphant combination—and reduction to the lowest common denominator—of

the most widely accepted concepts in nineteenth-century American society. The belief in the potential greatness of the common man, the glorification of individual effort and accomplishment, the equation of the pursuit of money with the pursuit of happiness and of business success with spiritual grace: simply to mention these concepts is to comprehend the brilliance of Alger's synthesis.

This passage illustrates several important misconceptions concerning Alger's books. In the first place, Alger's heroes are rarely "alone and unaided," and do not win their success entirely through individual effort and accomplishment. From the very beginning of his career, the Alger boy demonstrates an astounding propensity for chance encounters with benevolent and useful friends, and his success is largely due to their patronage and assistance. In the course of his duties Fred Fenton, the hero of *The Erie Train Boy,* meets a wealthy young girl named Isabel Archer—presumably named in homage to Alger's literary idol, Henry James—who gives him money to pay his mother's rent. In addition, he encounters an eccentric miner, who later helps him sell some land belonging to his late father, and the uncle of a wealthy broker, who gives young Fred his chance in business. Alger's heroes are well aware of their indebtedness to these patrons, and modestly make no pretense of success through their own efforts, although Alger assures his readers that they deserve their advancement. Ragged Dick, congratulated on his achievement by one of the innumerable wealthy men who befriended him, replies: " 'I was lucky,' said Dick, modestly, 'I found some good friends who helped me along.' " [*Mark, the Match Boy*]

Nor did the Alger hero rise "to the top of the economic heap." Some years ago a writer for *Time,* in a mathematical mood, calculated that the average Alger hero's fortune is only $10,000. Usually the hero is established in a secure white-collar position, either as a clerk with the promise of a junior partnership or as a junior member of a successful mercantile establishment. None achieve anything resembling economic or political prominence. Moderate economic security would best summarize the pecuniary achievements of the typical Alger hero, in spite of such tantalizing titles as *Fame and Fortune, Striving for Fortune,* and *From Farm to Fortune.* For example, at the end of *Fame and Fortune,* the hero is in possession of a magnificent income of $1,400 a year, plus the interest on about $2,000 in savings. In Alger's mind, this was "fame and fortune."

We may admit that Alger's representation of economic reality was highly sentimentalized, but it is unfair to call him an uninhibited adulator of wealth who equated spiritual grace with business success. The true aim of the Alger hero is respectability, a happy state only partially defined by economic repute. Nor was Alger unaware that many men were successful as the result of questionable practices. He may have lacked knowledge of these practices, but Alger frequently reminded his readers that many wealthy and successful men were undeserving of their fortunes. One of the favorite villains is the wealthy, unscrupulous banker who accumulates wealth by cheating widows and orphans. On the whole, Alger's formula is more accurately stated as middle-class respectability equals spiritual grace.

Alger was no more an unrestrained advocate of the "potential greatness" of the common man than he was of the uninhibited pursuit of financial success. His heroes are ordinary boys only in the sense of their lowly origin. In ability and personal character they are far above average. Many boys in the Alger books are unable, in spite of their earnest efforts, to rise above a lowly position. Micky McGuire, a young slum boy who is a secondary character in the *Ragged Dick* series, is reformed at last through the efforts of Dick and his patron Mr. Rockwell. But the old maxim "No Irish Need Apply" still held for Alger.

> Micky has already turned out much better than was expected, but he is hardly likely to rise much higher than the subordinate position he now occupies. In capacity and education he is far inferior to his old associate, Richard Hunter, who is destined to rise much higher than at present. [*Mark, the Match Boy*]

Who, then, is the Alger hero, and what is the nature of the adventures in which he is involved? Alger has two types of heroes. The first, and probably the more popular, is the poor, uneducated street boy—sometimes an orphan, more frequently the son of a widowed mother—who rises to moderate affluence. The second is a well-born and well-educated middle-class youth whose father dies, leaving the son to fend for himself. In some cases a villainous squire or distant relative attempts to cheat the hero out of his rightful legacy, but, in the end, the hero is restored to his inheritance or succeeds in rising to his proper place.

Alger made desultory attempts to vary the character of his hero in each story, but such an achievement was beyond his skill, and the reader could be certain that, whatever the situation, and whether the hero smokes or uses slangy language, the same solid core of virtue is present. Alger's heroes, who range in age from around twelve to eighteen, are in the tradition of the didactic novels of self-improvement. One must give Alger some credit for making his young paragons a little less earnest and more likely than the placid prigs of T. S. Arthur. The Alger hero might begin as an intemperate spendthrift like Ragged Dick, but soon he becomes a master of the traditional virtues of industry, economy, integrity, and piety. He is manly and self-reliant—two of Alger's favorite words—and, in addition, kind and generous. Never a genius, he is usually a boy of above-average intelligence, particularly in the area of mathematics, and is also a strenuous devotee of self-culture. The Alger hero is never snobbish or condescending; indeed, he is the veritable apothcosis of modesty. Thoroughly democratic in his tastes, he befriends other poor boys and is uniformly courteous to people of all classes. The Alger hero demonstrates to a high degree those traits that might be called the employee virtues: fidelity, punctuality, and courteous deference. It is upon these latter traits that Alger places the greatest stress.

Against his hero, Alger sets three types of boys who serve as foils to the hero's sterling qualities. One of these may be called the lesser hero. He is usually a slightly younger and less vigorous edition of the major figure. The lesser hero often has greater advantages than his friend, but he lacks the enterprise, the courage, and the self-reliance of the hero, and frequently depends on him for protection against the harsh urban world, enabling the hero to demonstrate his courage and generosity. Another boy who appears in almost all the Alger books is the snob. Insisting that he is a gentleman's son, the snob looks down his nose at the hero's willingness to work at such lowly trades as that of bootblack or newsboy. Sometimes the snob is the son of a rich but grasping relative of the hero's, envious of his greater capabilities and endeavoring to get him into trouble. The young snob shows the obverse of all the hero's virtues: he is lazy, ignorant, arrogant, and unwilling to work because he considers it beneath his station. He is overtly contemptuous and secretly envious of the hero's successes. Alger delights in foiling this little monster, usually by arranging for his father to fail in business, thereby forcing the snob to go to work at a salary lower than the hero's.

Another type appearing somewhat less frequently in the Alger books is the poor boy who lacks the intelligence and ability of the hero and is more susceptible to the corruption of his environment. Often he becomes involved in plots against the hero, but is usually won over when he recognizes his true manliness and forgiving character. Although sometimes reformed through the hero's efforts, the Micky McGuire type is doomed to remain in a subordinate but respectable position by his lack of intelligence and enterprise. Curiously enough, these dim-minded characters are Alger's most interesting and vivid creations, and foreshadow the "bad boy" heroes of later juvenile books. In addition, they frequently represent immigrant groups—Irish, Italians, Germans— who, not all bad, play a distinctly inferior role in Alger's version of America.

The adult characters vary no more than the boys in the typical Alger book. The central adult figure is the benevolent businessman whose chance encounter with the hero gives him his big opportunity. Like all adults in Alger, this figure is thinly characterized, his major traits being the ability to recognize and reward the hero's potentialities. He is called upon to deliver long homilies on the virtues requisite to success. Generally, he is a merchant or a highly reputable stockbroker. In his business dealings he is honest and upright, scorning all but the most elevated commercial practices. In effect his role is to serve as an ideal adoptive father for the hero.

The second most important male adult in the Alger books is the villain, who usually has some important hold over the hero. Sometimes he is a mean stepfather, more often a grasping uncle or cousin who becomes the hero's guardian, and frequently a cruel, miserly squire who holds a mortgage on the family property. Whatever his mask, he invariably attempts to assert his tyrannical authority over the hero, and fails. One is tempted to describe him in Freudian terms as the overbearing father-figure whose authority the adolescent hero rejects and overthrows.

Few of the Alger heroes are orphans; the majority have a widowed mother dependent upon them for support. Here Alger differs appreciably from his predecessors. The Alger mother stands in a very different relationship to her doughty young offspring than do the mothers in the novels of T. S. Arthur. The "Arthurian" mother is pre-eminently a source of moral authority, an instructor and preceptor, whose gentle commands the young hero is expected to obey. In Alger, the mother rarely commands or instructs; although she presumably has some hand in her son's development, her authoritative function is mentioned only rarely. On the contrary, she is both a dependent and an admiring onlooker. Always gentle and supremely confident in her son's ability, she never criticizes or disciplines. Indeed, occasionally she is weak and indecisive, qualities which might lead the family into difficulty were it not for the manly self-reliance of her son. Characteristic of the Alger version of maternity is this interchange between Paul the peddler and his mother:

> "You see, mother, Phil would be sure of a beating if he went home without his fiddle. Now he doesn't like to be beaten, and the padrone gives harder beatings than you do, mother."
> "I presume so," said Mrs. Hoffman, smiling. "I do not think I am very severe."
> "No, you spoil the rod and spare the child."
>
> *[Phil, the Fiddler]*

The benevolent merchant, the villainous father-figure, and the gentle and appreciative mother are at the center of most Alger books. They are joined by a variety of minor figures, all of whom can be traced to the traditional stereotypes of the sentimental novel: the warm-hearted Irish woman, poor and crude, kind and generous, who helps the hero escape from the villain; the snobbish female with aristocratic pretensions; the "stage Yankee" who appears in an occasional novel as a friend of the hero; and a variety of minor villains, such as the miserly moneylender, the petty swindler, and, in the Western stories, the stagecoach robber.

From such material, together with carefully accumulated local color—the books are filled with detailed descriptions of New York City—Alger constructed his tales. Almost invariably, they follow the same formula: by an amazing series of coincidences, and a few acts of personal heroism and generosity, the hero escapes from the plots laid by his enemies—usually an unholy alliance between the snobbish boy and the villainous father-figure—and attains the patronage of the benevolent merchant. In generating the action, chance and luck play a dominant role. Alger was apparently aware that the unbelievable tissue of coincidences which ran through his stories put some strain on the tolerance of his youthful readers. In *Struggling Upward,* for example, Linton Tomkins, the lesser hero, chances upon practically every other character in the book in the course of a twenty-minute promenade. Somewhat amazed at this feat, Alger can only remark that "Linton was destined to meet plenty of acquaintances." At the book's conclusion he confesses:

> So closes an eventful passage in the life of Luke Larkin. He has struggled upward from a boyhood of privation and self-denial into a youth and manhood of prosperity and honor. There has been some luck about it, I admit, but after all he is indebted for most of his good fortune to his own good qualities.

However much the hero's good qualities may have been involved, and they often seem incidental, Alger is obsessed with luck. The chapter which contains the crucial turning point of the book is invariably entitled ——'s *Luck,* and every accession to the hero's fortunes stems from a coincidence: the land thought to be worthless suddenly becomes valuable because a town has been built around it; the strongbox which the hero saves from thieves turns out to belong to an eccentric and wealthy old man who rewards the hero; the dead father's seemingly worthless speculation in mining stock is in fact a bonanza.

Alger's emphasis on luck resembles that found in the stories of T. S. Arthur and other apostles of the self-made man in the pre–Civil War era. Like them, he represents American society as an environment in which sudden and unaccountable prosperity frequently comes to the deserving like manna from heaven. To some extent, this reliance on luck or Providence is a literary shortcoming. Both Alger and Arthur turned out books at a tremendous rate; sloppiness and inadequacies in plotting and motivation could be concealed in part by defending coincidence. Furthermore, accident, luck, and chance have always played a large role in folk and popular literature, for they allow for exciting plot manipulation and the maintenance of suspense. It is equally true that the form which the accidental takes in a given work is some indication of the beliefs of an author and his intended audience.

In the case of Arthur and his contemporaries, the accidental assumes the form of the more or less direct intervention of Divine Providence. God acts to reward the deserving, punish the evil, and convert the doubting to a faith in his powers. Alger ignores the religious implications of the accidental. In his stories, luck is seemingly independent of the divine, inhering in the particular social environment of America, with its absence of hereditary class distinctions and the freedom it allows. Because most of the great merchants had been poor boys themselves, they were always on the lookout for deserving young men to assist. If the hero has the daring and self-assurance to seize one of his many opportunities to come to the attention of a benevolent patron, and is also blessed with the virtues of industry, fidelity, and good manners, he is certain to get ahead.

Religion itself does not play a major role in the life of the Alger hero. His heroes pray and go to Sunday School willingly enough, but Alger places greater stress on their obligations to others—loyalty to family and employer, and personal assistance to the less fortunate. His books encourage humanitarianism in their emphasis on practical good works and frequent insistence that Americans extend opportunities for worldly success to the juvenile proletariat of the cities. Although, like most writers in the tradition of self-improvement, Alger attributes success and failure to qualities within the individual, he occasionally points out to his young readers that a stifling and corrupting environment can be a major cause of vice and failure. An important factor in the rise of his street-boy heroes is their removal from the streets, where, if they remain, moral decay and poverty are certain. Alger can hardly be granted a profound understanding of the contemporary scene, but sympathy for the underprivileged is strong in his books. Judging from the prominence of his themes, there is as much evidence that Alger was an important influence on future reformers as a popular model for incipient robber barons.

Luck is not the only element in the success of the Alger hero. He has to deserve his luck by manifesting certain important traits which show him to be a fit candidate for a higher place in society. He carries the full complement of middle-class virtues, but these are not solely industry, frugality, and piety. Far more important are those qualities of character and intellect which make the hero a good employee and a reputable member of middle-class society. To his hero's cultivation of these qualities Alger devotes much of his attention. The hero has to learn how to dress neatly and modestly, to eliminate slang and colloquialisms from his speech, and to develop a facility with the stilted and pretentious language that Alger took to be the proper medium of verbal intercourse among respectable Americans. In addition, he has to educate himself. Alger's conception of the liberally educated man is also closely tied to social respectability. It is particularly desirable for the hero to have a neat hand and mathematical ability, but it is also important that he show a smattering of traditional culture. A foreign language is usually the prescribed curriculum. Ragged Dick studies French, for example. Since a foreign language plays no part in the hero's economic life, it is apparently intended by Alger as a certificate of a certain kind of respectability. The ability to learn French or Latin, although he might never have an opportunity to use such a skill, shows that the hero has a respect for learning as an end in itself and is no mere materialist. Thus, the Alger hero is a pale reflection of the ideal of self-culture as well as a devotee of rising in society.

Inner attainments are marked by characteristic external signs. The most crucial event in the hero's life is his acquisition of a good suit. The good suit, which is usually presented to the hero by his patron, marks the initial step in his advancement, his escape from the dirty and ragged classes and his entry upon respectability. It immediately differentiates the hero from the other bootblacks, and often leads to a quarrel with such dedicated proletarians as Micky McGuire. A second important event follows on the first: he is given a watch. The new watch marks the hero's attainment of a more elevated position, and is a symbol of punctuality and his respect for time as well as a sign of the attainment of young manhood. Alger makes much of the scene in which his hero receives from his patron a pocket watch suitably engraved.

Perhaps the most important group of qualities which operate in the hero's favor are those which make him the ideal employee: fidelity, dependability, and a burning desire to make himself useful. In a common Algerine situation, the hero, entrusted with some of his employer's money, is confronted by a villainous robber. At great risk to his own life, he defends his employer's property, preferring to lose his own money, or even his life, rather than betray his patron's trust. Under lesser stress, the hero demonstrates his superiority over the snobs by showing his willingness to perform any duties useful to his employer, and by going out of his way to give cheerful and uncomplaining service without haggling over wages. In *Fame and Fortune*, Roswell Crawford, a snob, is fired from his position as errand boy in a dry goods store when he not only complains of being required to carry packages—work too low for a "gentleman's son"—but has the additional temerity to ask for a raise. Ragged Dick, on the other hand, generously offers to carry Roswell's packages for him. Needless to say, Dick receives a raise without asking for it, because his patron recognizes his fidelity and insists on a suitable reward.

Emphasis on fidelity to the employer's interests is perhaps the worst advice Alger could have given his young readers if financial success was of major interest to them. Contrast the Alger hero's relations with his employers and Benjamin Franklin's as described in the *Memoirs*. Franklin keeps his eyes on his own interests when he works for his brother, and for the Philadelphia printers, Bradford and Keimer; indeed, he shows considerable satisfaction at his ability to turn Keimer's faults to his own benefit. By studying the inadequacies of his former employer he is able to make his own business a success. The Alger hero would never resort to such a self-serving device.

Placed against Emerson and his philosophy of self-reliance, Alger is simply another exponent of the idealized version of the self-made man found in the novels of T. S. Arthur, Sylvester Judd, and other sentimentalists of the 1840's and 1850's. His understanding of social mobility is on the same level of abstraction and idealization. Emerson, in comparison, has a much more profound understanding of the implications of social mobility and the actual characteristics likely to lead to economic and social advancement, as well as a broader ideal of self-culture. It is as true of Alger as of Arthur that he presents the mobile society through the rose-colored glasses of the middle-class ethical tradition of industry, frugality, and integrity, and the sentimental Christian version of a benevolent Providence.

The great attainment of Alger's hero is to leave the ranks of the "working class" and become an owner or partner in a business of his own. Yet few of Alger's heroes have any connection with such enterprises as mining, manufacturing, or construction, the industries in which most of the large fortunes of the late nineteenth century were made. Alger's favorite reward is a junior partnership in a respectable mercantile house. This emphasis is a throwback to the economic life of an earlier period, when American business was still dominated by merchants whose economic behavior in retrospect seemed refined and benevolent in comparison to the devastating strategies of transcontinental railroad builders, iron and steel manufacturers, and other corporate giants. Alger's version of success is, in effect, a reassertion of the values of a bygone era in an age of dramatic change and expansion.

Alger's Popularity

Today one would hardly expect adolescent boys to respond to Alger's vision of a dying past. His popularity with many older Americans—a phenomenon that continues into the present time—is certainly nostalgic. Alger is a teacher of traditional manners and morals rather than an exponent of free enterprise. His fictions embody the values that middle-class Americans have been taught to revere: honesty, hard work, familial loyalty; good manners, cleanliness, and neatness of appearance; kindness and generosity to the less fortunate; loyalty and deference on the part of employees, and consideration and personal interest on the part of employers. These "bourgeois virtues" are strenuously displayed by the Alger hero and his benevolent patron, along with that strong respect for education and self-culture which is a considerable part of the middle-class heritage. On the other hand, the Alger villains represent those vices particularly reprehensible to many nineteenth-century Americans: they have aristocratic pretensions and try to adopt the airs of the leisure-class; they frequent theaters and gaming houses and are intemperate; they are disloyal to their families and often try to cheat their relatives; they are avaricious, miserly, and usurious; and they lack integrity and are unscrupulous in business affairs. The conflict between middle-class virtues and vices is played out against a background of unlimited opportunities in which the virtues ultimately show themselves to be indispensable and the vices trip up their possessors.

At the time when Alger wrote, traditional commercial practices and ethics had been undermined by economic expansion. A lifetime of hard work often left a man worse off than when he began. The growing gulf between millionaire and employee and the increasing development of complex economic hierarchies were so circumscribing individual ownership and control that a clerk was better off working for others than attempting to found and operate his own business. Alger reasserts an older economic model, one that had begun to be out of date as early as 1830, but which still lingered in the minds of Americans as the ideal form of economic organization: a multiplicity of small individual businesses or partnerships. He certainly had little idea of the actuality of business enterprise in his day—nowhere in his novels do industrial corporations or the character types they produce appear—but he does have enough personal knowledge of New York City to give a certain plausibility and contemporaneity to his representation of American life. He is able to present the traditional pattern of middle-class economic ideals in late nineteenth-century dress and fill the bustling streets and thoroughfares of a nineteenth-century industrial metropolis with a nostalgic reincarnation of the ideal *eighteenth-century* merchant and his noble young apprentice. This moral and economic anachronism is an important source of Alger's popularity with adults. When, a generation or so later, the accumulation of social and economic change made it no longer tenable, even in fantasy, the books began to come down from the library shelves, classed as unrealistic and misleading, perhaps even dangerous, fairy tales.

Although parents encouraged their children to read Alger because he seemed to reassert the validity of hard work, economy, integrity, and family loyalty, this is probably not the source of his popularity with young boys. There were a great many reasons why children liked Alger. He writes of places that they were interested in. In these locales he places a set of characters whose activities have enough of the fantastic and unusual to be exciting, yet always retain enough connection with the ordinary activities of American boys to encourage an emotionally satisfying empathy. Alger's glorification of financial success has been overemphasized by commentators, but many of his young readers enjoyed dreaming of the day when they would be rich enough to buy gold watches, good clothes, and have others dependent on their beneficences. Furthermore, Alger has a simple and unsophisticated sense of justice, which punishes the enemies of boyhood. The snobs, the bullies, the uncles and spinster aunts who do not like boys get their comeuppances in ways that must have appealed to a juvenile audience. Alger is hardly a master stylist, but his narrative and dialogue are simple, clear, and relatively fast-moving; and his diction, if formal and stilted, is not arcane or difficult.

These elements were undoubtedly important factors in Alger's popularity with his juvenile audience; and there was a further dimension to the Alger formula. Legion are the dangers of Freudian interpretation of literary works, but Alger cries out for this kind of treatment. Consider the following brief summary, which can apply with variations to almost any of the Alger books: an adolescent boy, the support of a gentle, loving, and admiring mother, is threatened by a male figure of authority and discipline. Through personal heroism he succeeds in subverting the authority of this figure and in finding a new male supporter who makes no threats to his relationship with the mother and does not seek to circumscribe his independence. The pattern is too obvious to require extended comment. When we recall that the late nineteenth century was an era of relatively strict paternal discipline and control, it does not seem farfetched to suggest that the Alger books may have been appreciated as phantasies of father-elimination. The rapid decline in the popularity of Alger books after World War I probably resulted in part from the changing character of familial relationships in the twenties and thirties. When new ideals of parent-child relationship became generally accepted, the Alger hero's victory over the villainous father-figure must have lost much of its bite.

The Workers' Search for Power

Herbert G. Gutman

Somewhat paradoxically, the study of the American worker has largely been the study of elites. Much attention has been drawn to the holders of power and their antilabor tactics—the Fisks, Goulds, Vanderbilts, Carnegies, and Rockefellers. Attention also has been directed toward sensational conflicts between labor and capital—the Haymarket Riot, the exploits of the "Molly Maguires," the Homestead steel and Pullman strikes—freighted with brutality and destruction. Following trails blazed by the likes of John R. Commons, the study of organized labor has mostly involved craft unionism, almost exclusively in the form of the American Federation of Labor and its founder-leader, Samuel Gompers. Ironically, craft workers, because of the demand for their skills and the paucity of their numbers, needed unions far less than semiskilled and unskilled workers. The irony compounds when one carefully examines the structure, goals, and operations of the AFL, and finds them not unlike those of big business itself and extremely exclusionary toward nonmember laborers. Thanks to the "New Left" historians and the "new social history," interest has increased in the semiskilled and unskilled workers of the post–Civil War period, for the most part unorganized yet needing the benefits of unionism certainly more than the craft workers. In this article, the late Herbert Gutman of City College, City University of New York, and a pioneer in both labor history and "new social history" analyzes the industrial workers against the above-outlined mythology and finds its many strictures to be much less hardened than previously believed. It was an age of new and complex developments, unsettling to employer as well as employee—a state of ferment. He does find strong antilabor animosities coming into existence and solidifying early in large cities such as New York, Boston, and Chicago. In the smaller industrial towns, however, he finds an entirely different picture—more mutual concern and respect between employer and employee, a neutral and occasionally even prolabor press, and far fewer obstacles to unionism. Gutman goes on to issue a call to reexamine stereotypes and clichés regarding labor in the Gilded Age, for example its supposed "impotence and division before the iron hand of oppressive capitalism." Also, reflecting the spirit of the "new social history," Professor Gutman underscores the need to study the worker *per se*, not just the power brokers, be they employers or union leaders. Following this advice will yield a much richer social history of American workers and their search for power.

Until very recent times, the worker never seemed as glamorous or important as the entrepreneur. This is especially true of the Gilded Age, where attention focuses more readily upon Jim Fisk, Commodore Vanderbilt, or John D. Rocke-

From "Industrial Workers Struggle for Power" (orig. chap. 3, "The Workers' Search for Power") by Herbert G. Gutman. From *The Gilded Age,* revised and enlarged edition, edited by H. Wayne Morgan (Syracuse, N.Y.: Syracuse University Press, 1970), pp. 31–53. Copyright © 1970 by Syracuse University Press. Reprinted by permission of the publisher.

feller than on the men whose labor built their fortunes. Most studies have devoted too much attention to too little. Excessive interest in the Haymarket riot, the "Molly Maguires," the great strikes of 1877, the Homestead lockout, and the Pullman strike has obscured the more important currents of which these things were only symptoms. Close attention has also focused on the small craft unions, the Knights of Labor, and the early socialists, excluding the great mass of workers who belonged to none of these groups and creating an uneven picture of labor in the Gilded Age.

Labor history had little to do with those matters scholars traditionally and excessively emphasize. Too few workers belonged to trade unions to make the unions important. There was a fundamental distinction between wage earners as a social class and the small minority of the working population that belonged to labor organizations. The full story of the wage earner is much more than the tale of struggling craft unions and the exhortations of committed trade unionists and assorted reformers and radicals. A national perspective often misrepresented those issues important to large segments of the post-bellum working population and to other economic and social groups who had contact with the wage earners. Most of the available literature about labor in the Gilded Age is thin, and there are huge gaps in our knowledge of the entire period. Little was written about the workers themselves, their communities, and the day-to-day occurrences that shaped their outlook. Excessive concern with craft workers has meant the serious neglect of the impact of industrial capitalism—a new way of life—upon large segments of the population.

A rather stereotyped conception of labor and of industrial relations in the Gilded Age has gained widespread credence, and final and conclusive generalizations about labor abound: "During the depression from 1873 to 1879, employers sought to eliminate trade unions by a *systematic* policy of lock-outs, blacklists, labor espionage, and legal prosecution. The *widespread* use of blacklists and Pinkerton labor spies caused labor to organize *more or less* secretly and *undoubtedly* helped bring on the violence that *characterized* labor strife during this period." One historian asserts: "Employers *everywhere* seemed determined to rid themselves of 'restrictions upon free enterprise' by smashing unions." The "*typical* [labor] organization during the seventies," writes another scholar, "was secret for protection against intrusion by outsiders." Such seemingly final judgments are questionable: How *systematic* were lockouts, blacklists, and legal prosecutions? How *widespread* was the use of labor spies and private detectives? Was the secret union the *typical* form of labor organization? Did violence *characterize* industrial relations?

It is widely believed that the industrialist exercised a great deal of power and had almost unlimited freedom of choice when dealing with his workers after the Civil War. Part of this belief reflects the weakness or absence of trade unions. Another justification for this interpretation, however, is more shaky—the assumption that industrialism generated new kinds of economic power which immediately affected the social structure and ideology. The supposition that "interests" rapidly reshaped "ideas" is misleading. "The social pyramid," Joseph Schumpeter pointed out, "is never made of a single substance, is never seamless." The economic interpretation of history "would at once become untenable and unrealistic . . . if its formulation failed to consider that the manner in which production shapes social life is essentially influenced by the fact that human protagonists have always been shaped by past situations."

In postbellum America, the relationship between "interest" and "ideology" was very complex and subtle. Industrial capitalism was a new way of life and was not fully institutionalized. Much of the history of industrialism is the story of the painful process by which an old way of life was discarded for a new one so that a central issue was the rejection or modification of a set of "rules" and "commands" that no longer fitted the new industrial context. Since so much was new, traditional stereotypes about the popular sanctioning of the rules and values of industrial society either demand severe qualification or entirely fall by the wayside. Among questionable commonly held generalizations are those that insist that the worker was isolated from the rest of society; that the employer had an easy time and a relatively free hand in imposing the new disciplines; that the spirit of the times, the ethic of the Gilded Age, worked to the advantage of the owner of industrial property; that workers found little if any sympathy from nonworkers; that the quest for wealth obliterated nonpecuniary values; and that industrialists swept aside countless obstacles with great ease.

The new way of life was more popular and more quickly sanctioned in large cities than in small one- or two-industry towns. Put another way, the social environment in the large American city after the Civil War was more often hostile toward workers than that in smaller industrial towns. Employers in large cities had more freedom of choice than counterparts in small towns, where local conditions often hampered the employer's decision-making power. The ideology of many nonworkers in these small towns was not entirely hospitable toward industrial, as opposed to traditional, business enterprise. Strikes and lockouts in large cities seldom lasted as long as similar disputes outside of urban centers. In the large city, there was almost no sympathy for the city worker among the middle and upper classes. A good deal of pro-labor and anti-industrial sentiment flowed from similar occupational groups in the small towns. Small-town employers of factory labor often reached out of the local environment for aid in solving industrial disputes, but diverse elements in the social structure and ideology shaped such decisions.

The direct economic relationships in large cities and in small towns and outlying industrial regions were similar, but the social structures differed profoundly. Private enterprise was central to the economy of both the small industrial town and the large metropolitan city, but functioned in a different social environment. The social structure and ideology of a given time are not derived only from economic institutions. In a time of rapid economic and social transformation, when industrial capitalism was relatively new, parts of an ideology alien to industrialism retained a powerful hold on many who lived outside large cities.

Men and their thoughts were different in the large cities. "The modern town," John Hobson wrote of the large nineteenth-century cities, "is a result of the desire to produce and distribute most economically the largest aggregate of material goods: economy of work, not convenience of life, is the object." In such an environment, "anti-social feelings" were exhibited "at every point by the competition of workers with one another, the antagonism between employer and employed, between sellers and buyers, factory and factory, shop and shop." Persons dealt with each other less as human beings and more as objects. The *Chicago Times*, for example, argued that "political economy" was "in reality the autocrat of the age" and occupied "the position once held by the Caesars and the Popes." According to the *New York Times*, the "antagonistic . . . position between employers and the employed on the subject of work and wages" was "unavoidable. . . . The object of trade is to get as much as you may and give as little as you can." The *Chicago Tribune* celebrated the coming of the centennial in 1876: "Suddenly acquired wealth, decked in all the colors of the rainbow, flaunts its robe before the eyes of Labor, and laughs with contempt at honest poverty." The country, "great in all the material powers of a vast empire," was entering "upon the second century weak and poor in social morality as compared with one hundred years ago."

Much more than economic considerations shaped the status of the urban working population, for the social structure in large cities unavoidably widened the distance between social and economic classes. Home and job often were far apart. A man's fellow workers were not necessarily his friends and neighbors. Face-to-face relationships became less meaningful as the city grew larger and production became more diverse and specialized. "It has always been difficult for well-to-do people of the upper and middle classes," wrote Samuel Lane Loomis, a Protestant minister, in the 1880s, "to sympathize with and to understand the needs of their poorer neighbors." The large city, both impersonal and confining, made it even harder. Loomis was convinced that "a great and growing gulf" lay "between the working-class and those above them." A Massachusetts clergyman saw a similar void between the social classes and complained: "I once knew a wealthy manufacturer who personally visited and looked after the comforts of his invalid operatives. I know of no such case now." The fabric of human relationships was cloaked in a kind of shadowed anonymity that became more and more characteristic of urban life.

Social contact was more direct in the smaller post–Civil War industrial towns and regions. *Cooper's New Monthly*, a reform trade union journal, insisted that while "money" was the "sole measure of gentility and respectability" in large cities, "a more democratic feeling" prevailed in small towns. "The most happy and contented workingmen in the country," wrote the *Iron Molder's Journal*, "are those residing in small towns and villages. . . . We want more towns and villages and less cities." Except for certain parts of New England and the mid-Atlantic states, the post–Civil War industrial towns and regions were relatively new to that kind of enterprise. Men and women who lived and worked in these areas usually had known another way of life, and they contrasted the present with the past.

The nineteenth-century notion of enterprise came quickly to these regions after the Civil War, but the social distance between the various economic classes that characterized the large city came much more slowly and hardly paralleled industrial developments. In the midst of the new industrial enterprise with its new set of commands, men often clung to older "agrarian" attitudes, and they judged the economic and social behavior of local industrialists by these values.

The social structure of the large city differed from that of the small industrial town because of the more direct human relationships among the residents of the smaller towns. Although many persons were not personally involved in the industrial process, they felt its presence. Life was more difficult and less cosmopolitan in small towns, but it was also less complicated. This life was not romantic, since it frequently meant company-owned houses and stores and conflicts between workers and employers over rights taken for granted in agricultural communities and large cities. Yet the nonurban industrial environment had in it a kind of compelling simplicity. There the inhabitants lived and worked together, and a certain sense of community threaded their everyday lives.

The first year of the 1873 depression sharply suggested the differences between the large urban center and the small industrial town. There was no question about the severity of the economic crisis. Its consequences were felt throughout the entire industrial sector, and production, employment, and income fell sharply everywhere. The dollar value of business failures in 1873 was greater than in any other single year between 1857 and 1893. Deflation in the iron and steel industry was especially severe: 266 of the nations's 666 iron furnaces were out of blast by January 1, 1874, and more than 50 percent of the rail mills were silent. A New York philanthropic organization figured that 25 percent of the city's workers—nearly 100,000 persons—were unemployed in the winter months of 1873–74.

"The simple fact is that a great many laboring men are out of work," wrote the *New York Graphic*. "It is not the fault of merchants and manufacturers that they refuse to employ four men when they can pay but one, and decline to pay four dollars for work which they can buy for two and a half." Gloom and pessimism settled over the entire country, and the most optimistic predicted only that the panic would end in the late spring months of 1873. James Swank, the secretary of the American Iron and Steel Association, found the country suffering "from a calamity which may be likened to a famine or a flood."

A number of serious labor difficulties occurred in small industrial towns and outlying industrial regions during the first year of the depression, revealing much about the social structure of these areas. Although each had its own unique character, a common set of problems shaped them all. Demand fell away and industrialists cut production and costs to sell off accumulated inventory and retain shrinking markets. This general contraction caused harsh industrial conflict in many parts of the country. "No sooner does a depression in trade set in," observed David A. Harris, the conservative head of the Sons of Vulcan, a national craft union for puddlers and boilermen, "than all expressions of friendship to the toiler are forgotten."

The *New York Times* insisted that the depression would "bring wages down for all time," and advised employers to dismiss workers who struck against wage reductions. This was not the time for the "insane imitations of the miserable class warfare and jealousy of Europe." The *Chicago Times* stated that strikers were "idiots" and "criminals." Its sister newspaper, the *Chicago Evening Journal*, said the crisis was not "an unmixed evil," since labor would finally learn "the folly and danger of trade organizations, strikes, and combinations . . . against capital." *Iron Age* was similarly sanguine. "We are sorry for those who suffer," it explained, "but if the power of the trade unions for mischief is weakened . . . the country will have gained far more than it loses from the partial depression of industry." Perhaps "simple workingmen" would learn they were misled by "demagogues and unprincipled agitators." Trade unions "crippled that productive power of capital" and retarded the operation of "beneficent natural laws of progress and development." James Swank was somewhat more generous. Prices had fallen, and it was "neither right nor practicable for all the loss to be borne by the employers." "Some of it," he explained, "must be shared by the workingmen. . . . We must hereafter be contented with lower wages for our labor and be more thankful for the opportunity to labor at all."

In cutting costs in 1873 and 1874, many employers found that certain aspects of the social structure and ideology in small industrial towns hindered their freedom of action. It was easy to announce a wage cut or refuse to negotiate with a local trade union, but it was difficult to enforce such decisions. In instance after instance, and for reasons that varied from region to region, employers reached outside of their environment to help assert their authority.

Industrialists used various methods to strengthen their local positions with workers. The state militia brought order to a town or region swept by industrial conflict. Troops were used in railroad strikes in Indiana, Ohio, and Pennsylvania; in a dispute involving iron heaters and rollers in Newport, Kentucky; in a strike of Colorado ore diggers; in two strikes of Illinois coal miners; and in a strike of Michigan ore workers.

Other employers aggravated racial and nationality problems among workers by introducing new ethnic groups to end strikes, forcing men to work under new contracts, and destroying local trade unions. Negroes were used in coal disputes. Danish, Norwegian, and Swedish immigrants went into mines in Illinois, and into the Shenango Valley and the northern anthracite region of Pennsylvania. Germans went to coal mines in northern Ohio along with Italian workers. Some Italians also were used in western Pennsylvania as coal miners, and in western and northern New York as railroad workers. A number of employers imposed their authority in other ways. Regional, not local, blacklists were tried in the Illinois coal fields, on certain railroads, in the Ohio Valley iron towns, and in the iron mills of eastern Pennsylvania. Mine operators in Pennsylvania's Shenango Valley and Tioga coal region used state laws to evict discontented workers from company-owned houses in midwinter.

The social structure in these small towns and the ideology of many of their residents, who were neither workers nor employers, shaped the behavior of those employers who reached outside local environments to win industrial disputes. The story was different for every town, but had certain similarities. The strikes and lockouts had little meaning in and of themselves, but the incidents shed light on the distribution of power in these towns, on important social and economic relationships which shaped the attitudes and actions of workers and employers.

One neglected aspect of the small industrial town after the Civil War is its political structure. Because workers made up a large proportion of the electorate and often participated actively in local politics, they influenced local and regional affairs more than wage earners in the larger cities. In 1874, few workers held elected or appointed offices in large cities. In that year, however, the postmaster of Whistler, Alabama, was a member of the Iron Molder's International Union. George Kinghorn, a leading trade unionist in the southern Illinois coal fields, was postmaster of West Belleville, Illinois. A local labor party swept an election in Evansville, Indiana. Joliet, Illinois, had three workers on its city council. A prominent official of the local union of iron heaters and rollers sat on the city council in Newport, Kentucky. Coal and ore miners ran for the state legislature in Carthage, Missouri, in Clay County, Indiana, and in Belleville, Illinois. The residents of Virginia City, a town famous in western mythology, sent the president of the local miners' union to Congress. In other instances, town officials and other officeholders who were not wage earners sympathized with the problems and difficulties of local workers or displayed an unusual degree of objectivity during local industrial disputes.

Many local newspapers criticized the industrial entrepreneur, and editorials defended *local* workers and demanded redress for their grievances. Certain of these newspapers were entirely independent; others warmly endorsed local trade union activities.

The small businessmen and shopkeepers, lawyers and professional people, and other nonindustrial members of the middle class were a small but vital element in these industrial towns. Unlike the urban middle class they had direct and everyday contact with the new industrialism and with the problems and outlook of workers and employers. Many had risen from a lower station in life and knew the meaning of hardship and toil, and could judge the troubles of both workers and employers by personal experience. While they invariably accepted the concepts of private property and free entrepreneurship, their judgments about the *social* behavior of industrialists often drew upon noneconomic considerations and values. Some saw no necessary contradiction between private enterprise and gain and decent, humane social relations between workers and employers.

In a number of industrial conflicts, segments of the local middle class sided with workers. A Maryland weekly newspaper complained in 1876: "In the changes of the last thirty years not the least unfortunate is the separation of personal relations between employers and employees." While most metropolitan newspapers sang paeans of joy for the industrial entrepreneur and the new way of life, the *Youngstown Miner and Manufacturer* thought it completely wrong that the "Vanderbilts, Stewarts, and Astors bear, in proportion to their resources, infinitely less of the burden incident to society than the poorest worker." The *Ironton Register* defended dismissed iron strikers as "upright and esteemed . . . citizens" who had been sacrificed "to the cold demands on business." The *Portsmouth Times* boasted: "We have very little of the codfish aristocracy, and industrious laborers are looked upon here with as much respect as any class of people. . . ."

Nothing better illustrated the differences between the small town and large city than attitudes toward public works for the unemployed. Urban newspapers frowned upon the idea, and relief and welfare agents often felt that the unemployed were "looking for a handout." The jobless, one official insisted, belonged to "the degraded class . . . who have the vague idea that 'the world owes them a living.' " Unemployed workers were lazy, many said, and trifling.

Native-born radicals and reformers, a few welfare officers, ambitious politicians, responsible theorists, socialists, and "relics" from the pre–Civil War era all agitated for public works during the great economic crisis of 1873–74. The earliest advocates urged construction of city streets, parks and playgrounds, rapid transit systems, and other projects to relieve unemployment. These schemes usually depended on borrowed money or fiat currency, or issuance of low-interest-rate bonds on both local and national levels. The government had aided wealthy classes in the past; it was time to "legislate for the good of all not the few." Street demonstrations and meetings by the unemployed occurred in November and December of 1873 in Boston, Cincinnati, Chicago, Detroit, Indianapolis, Louisville, Newark, New York, Paterson, Pittsburgh, and Philadelphia. The dominant theme at all these gatherings was the same: unemployment was widespread, countless persons were without means, charity and philanthropy were poor substitutes for work, and public aid and employment were necessary and just.

The reaction to the demand for public works contained elements of surprise, ridicule, contempt, and genuine fear. The Board of Aldermen refused to meet with committees of jobless Philadelphia workers. Irate Paterson taxpayers put an end to a limited program of street repairs the city government had started. Chicago public officials and charity leaders told the unemployed to join them "in God's work" and rescue "the poor and suffering" through philanthropy, not public employment.

The urban press rejected the plea for public works and responsibility for the unemployed. Men demanding such aid were "disgusting," "crazy," "loudmouthed gasometers," "impudent vagabonds," and even "ineffable asses." They were ready "to chop off the heads of every man addicted to clean linen." They wanted to make "Government an institution to pillage the individual for the benefit of the mass." Hopefully, "yellow fever, cholera, or any other blessing" would sweep these persons from the earth. Depressions, after all, were normal and necessary adjustments, and workers should only "quietly bide their time till the natural laws of trade" brought renewed prosperity. Private charity and alms, as well as "free land," were adequate answers to unemployment. "The United States," said the *New York Times*, "is the only 'socialistic,' or more correctly 'agrarian,' government in the world in that it offers good land at nominal prices to every settler" and thereby takes "the sting from Communism." If the unemployed "prefer to cling to the great cities to oversupply labor," added the *Chicago Times*, "the fault is theirs."

None of the proposals of the jobless workers met with favor, but the demand by New York workers that personal wealth be limited to $100,000 was criticized most severely. To restrict the "ambition of building up colossal fortunes" meant an end to all "progress," wrote the *Chicago Times*. The *New York Tribune* insisted that any limitation on personal wealth was really an effort "to have employment without employers," and that was "almost as impossible . . . as to get into the world without ancestors."

Another argument against public responsibility for the unemployed identified this notion with immigrants, socialists, and "alien" doctrine. The agitation by the socialists compounded the anxieties of the more comfortable classes. Remembering that force had put down the Paris Communards, the *Chicago Times* asked: "Are we to be required to face a like alternative?" New York's police superintendent urged his men to spy on labor meetings and warned that German and French revolutionaries were "doing their utmost to inflame the workingman's mind." The *Chicago Tribune* menacingly concluded, "The coalition of foreign nationalities must be for a foreign, non-American object. The principles of these men are wild and subversive of society itself."

Hemmed in by such ideological blinders, devoted to "natural laws" of economics, and committed to a conspiracy theory of social change so often attributed only to the lower classes, the literate nonindustrial residents of large cities could not identify with the urban poor and the unemployed. Most well-to-do metropolitan residents in 1873 and 1874 believed that whether men rose or fell depended on individual effort. They viewed the worker as little more than a factor of production. They were sufficiently alienated from the urban poor to join the *New York Graphic* in jubilantly celebrating a country in which republican equality, free public schools, and cheap western lands allowed "intelligent working people" to "have anything they all want."

The attitude displayed toward the unemployed reflected a broader and more encompassing view of labor. Unlike similar groups in small towns, the urban middle- and upper-income groups generally frowned upon labor disputes and automatically sided with employers. Contact between these persons and the worker was casual and indirect. Labor unions violated certain immutable "natural and moral laws" and deterred economic development and capital accumulation. The *Chicago Times* put it another way in its discussion of workers who challenged the status quo: "The man who lays up not for the morrow, perishes on the morrow. It is the inexorable law of God, which neither legislatures nor communistic blatherskites can repeal. The fittest alone survive, and those are the fittest, as the result always proves, who provide for their own survival."

Unions and all forms of labor protest, particularly strikes, were condemned. The *New York Times* described the strike as "a combination against long-established laws," especially "the law of supply and demand." The *New York Tribune* wrote of "the general viciousness of the trades-union system," and the *Cleveland Leader* called "the labor union kings . . . the most absolute tyrants of our day." Strikes, insisted the *Chicago Tribune*, "implant in many men habits of indolence that are fatal to their efficiency thereafter." Cleveland sailors who protested conditions on the Great Lakes ships were "a motley throng and a wicked one," and when Cuban cigar makers struck in New York, the *New York Herald* insisted that "madness rules the hour."

City officials joined in attacking and weakening trade unions. The mayor forbade the leader of striking Philadelphia weavers from speaking in the streets. New York police barred striking German cigar workers from gathering in front of a factory whose owners had discharged six trade unionists, including four women. Plain-clothes detectives trailed striking Brooklyn plasterers. When Peter Smith, a nonunion barrel maker, shot and wounded four union men—killing one of them—during a bitter lockout, a New York judge freed him on $1,000 bail supplied by his employers and said his employers did "perfectly right in giving Smith a revolver to defend himself from strikers."

Brief review of three important labor crises in Pittsburgh, Cleveland, and New York points out different aspects of the underlying attitude toward labor in the large cities. The owners of Pittsburgh's five daily newspapers cut printers' wages in November, 1873, and formed an association to break the printers' union. After the printers rejected the wage cut and agreed to strike if nonunion men were taken on, two newspapers fired the union printers. The others quit in protest. The *Pittsburgh Dispatch* said the strikers "owe no allegiance to society," and the other publishers condemned the union as an "unreasoning tyranny." Three publishers started a court suit against more than seventy union members charging them with "conspiracy." The printers were held in $700 bail, and the strike was lost. Pittsburgh was soon "swarming with 'rats' from all parts of the country," and the union went under. Though the cases were not pressed after the union collapsed, the indictments were not dropped. In 1876, the *Pittsburgh National Labor Tribune* charged, "All of these men are kept under bail *to this day* to intimidate them from forming a Union, or asking for just wages." A weekly organ of the anthracite miners' union attacked the indictment and complained that it reiterated "the prejudice against workingmen's unions that seems to exist universally among officeholders."

In May, 1874, Cleveland coal dealers cut the wages of their coal heavers more than 25 percent, and between four- and five-hundred men struck. Some new hands were hired. A foreman drew a pistol on the strikers and was beaten.

He and several strikers were arrested, and the coal docks remained quiet as the strikers, who had started a union, paraded up and down and neither spoke nor gestured to the new men. Police guarded the area, and a light artillery battery of the Ohio National Guard was mobilized. Lumber heavers joined the striking workers, and the two groups paraded quietly on May 8. Although the strikers were orderly, the police jailed several leaders. The strikers did not resist and dispersed when so ordered by the law. In their complaint to the public, they captured the flavor of urban-industrial conflict:

> The whole thing is a calumny, based upon the assumption that if a man be poor he must necessarily be a blackguard. Honest poverty can have no merit here, as the rich, together with all their other monopolies, must also monopolize all the virtues. We say now . . . we entertain a much more devout respect and reverence for our public law than the men who are thus seeking to degrade it into a tool of grinding oppression. We ask from the generosity of our fellow citizens . . . to dispute [sic] a commission of honest men to come and examine our claims. . . . We feel confident they will be convinced that the authorities of Cleveland, its police force, and particularly the formidable artillery are all made partisans to a very dirty and mean transaction.

The impartial inquiry proved unnecessary; a few days later several firms rescinded the wage cut, and the strikers thanked these employers.

Italian laborers were used on a large scale in the New York building trades for the first time in the spring of 1874. They lived "piled together like sardines in a box" and worked mainly as ragpickers and street cleaners. They were men of "passionate dispositions" and, "as a rule, filthy beyond the power of one to imagine." Irish street laborers and unskilled workers were especially hard on Italians, and numerous scuffles between the two groups occurred in the spring of 1874. In spite of the revulsion toward the Italians as a people, the *New York Tribune* advised employers that their "mode of life" allowed them to work for low wages.

Two non-Italians, civil engineers and contractors, founded the New York Italian Labor Company in April, 1874. It claimed 2,700 members, and its superintendent, an Italian named Frederick Guscetti, announced: "As peaceable and industrious men, we claim the right to put such price upon our labor as may seem to us best." The firm held power of attorney over members, contracted particular jobs, provided transportation, supplied work gangs with "simple food," and retained a commission of a day's wages from each monthly paycheck. The company was started to protect the Italians from Irish "adversaries," and Guscetti said the men were willing to work "at panic prices." The non-Italian managers announced the men would work for 20 percent less in the building trades. Employers were urged to hire them "and do away with strikes."

Protected by the city police and encouraged by the most powerful newspapers, the New York Italian Labor Company first attracted attention when it broke a strike of union hod carriers. Irish workers hooted and stoned the Italians, but the police provided them with ample protection. *Cooper's New*

Monthly complained that "poor strangers, unacquainted with the laws and customs and language of the country," had been made "the dupes of unprincipled money sharks" and were being "used as tools to victimize and oppress other workingmen." This was just the start. The firm advertised its services in *Iron Age.* By the end of July, 1874, it had branched out with work gangs in New York, Massachusetts, and Pennsylvania.

There is much yet to learn about the attitude toward labor that existed in large cities, but over all opinion lay a popular belief that "laws" governed the economy and life itself. He who tampered with them through social experiments or reforms imperiled the whole structure. The *Chicago Times* was honest, if callous, in saying: "Whatever cheapens production, whatever will lessen the cost of growing wheat, digging gold, washing dishes, building steam engines, is of value. . . . The age is not one which enquires when looking at a piece of lace whether the woman who wove it is a saint or a courtesan." It came at last almost to a kind of inhumanity, as one manufacturer who used dogs and men in his operation discovered. The employer liked the dogs. "They never go on strike for higher wages, have no labor unions, never get intoxicated and disorderly, never absent themselves from work without good cause, obey orders without growling, and are very reliable."

The contrast between urban and rural views of labor and its fullest role in society and life is clear. In recent years, many have stressed "entrepreneurship" in nineteenth-century America without distinguishing between entrepreneurs in commerce and trade and those in industrial manufacturing. Reflecting the stresses and strains in the thought and social attitudes of a generation passing from the old pre-industrial way of life to the new industrial America, many men could justify the business ethic in its own sphere without sustaining it in operation in society at large or in human relationships. It was one thing to apply brute force in the marketplace, and quite another to talk blithely of "iron laws" when men's lives and well-being were at stake.

Not all men had such second thoughts about the social fabric which industrial capitalism was weaving, but in the older areas of the country the spirits of free enterprise and free action were neither dead nor mutually exclusive. Many labor elements kept their freedom of action and bargaining even during strikes. And the worker was shrewd in appealing to public opinion. There is a certain irony in realizing that small-town America, supposedly alien and antagonistic toward city ways, remained a stronghold of freedom for the worker seeking economic and social rights.

But perhaps this is not so strange after all, for pre-industrial America, whatever its narrowness and faults, had always preached personal freedom. The city, whose very impersonality would make it a kind of frontier of anonymity, often practiced personal restriction and the law of the economic and social jungle. As industrialism triumphed, the businessman's powers increased, yet he was often hindered—and always suspect—in vast areas of the nation which cheered his efforts toward wealth even while condemning his methods.

Facile generalizations are easy to make and not always sound, but surely the evidence warrants a new view of labor in the Gilded Age. The standard stereotypes and textbook clichés about its impotence and division before the iron hand of oppressive capitalism do not quite fit the facts. Its story is far different when surveyed in depth, carrying in it overtones of great complexity. And even in an age often marked by lust for power, men did not abandon old and honored concepts of human dignity and worth.

The Myth of the Gild

H. Wayne Morgan

The period from 1868 to the turn of the century, christe...
contemporary writer Mark Twain, long suffered from a glittering yet unsavory
reputation. It was, said those in the Twain tradition, an era of conspicuous
consumption, one typified by mindless entrepreneurial greed and corruption and by
lush yet crass extravagance. The commercial spirit and ethic prevailed at the expense
of the masses, whose lives were filled with discrimination, low wages, and the very
worst features of an emerging urban and industrial America. A notable revision of
this view, however, is offered here by H. Wayne Morgan, George Lynn Cross
Research Professor of History at the University of Oklahoma. Reflecting much new
work in quantitative and social history as well as new study centering on architecture,
art, and literature, Morgan etches a more positive portrait of the Gilded Age focused
on small business and labor. Moreover, he notes the high relevance of studying the
age, since it displayed a set of social concerns and questions similar to our own—
the position of minorities in American life, the rights of women, and the role of
government in social development, as well as issues in monetary and tariff policy.
Through a closer study of the Gilded Age, we stand to learn how American society
sought to adjust to accelerating social change.

Anyone who recalls the Gilded Age from an American history course taken
twenty or more years ago would be surprised at how the treatment of that era
has changed. Most historians used to hold a rather low opinion of the period.
Remember Grover Cleveland's illegitimate child, who figured in the campaign
of 1884? And how business appeared dominant in every sphere of life? How
Andrew Carnegie and John D. Rockefeller amassed huge fortunes with monopolistic "trusts"? And how, toward the era's end, when lightning seemed to
strike everywhere at once, farmers staged a revolt that frightened almost everyone else half to death?

The facts about the Gilded Age have not changed, but historians' views
have. The first scholarly interpretations of any period have a lasting impact,
and every generation tends to be critical of its immediate predecessor. In this
case, the determining views first came from some famous contemporaries.
Mark Twain gave the period (which lasted roughly from 1868 to 1900) its textbook name in *The Gilded Age* (1873), the novel he wrote with Charles Dudley
Warner. As literature it was a weak performance, but it produced some durable

From "The Gilded Age" by H. Wayne Morgan. Reprinted with permission from *American Heritage Magazine*, Volume 35, No. 5. Copyright 1984 by American Heritage Publishing Co. Inc.

images of social climbing and shady political dealings. The book also encapsulated the country's traditional boomer spirit based on mindless expansion, which the period seemed to typify. The English diplomat James Bryce added the weight of analytical thought to that stereotype with *The American Commonwealth* (1888). Bryce admired the nation's economic dynamism and social flexibility but feared that democracy too often bred mediocrity and wondered if a civilization that so emphasized material gain could produce any true culture. Above all American tolerance of weak and shabby behavior in public life disturbed him.

The first historians of the Gilded Age built upon these contemporary views. Early textbooks couched the period in terms of wars between labor and capital, of settled Americans rising against immigrants, of outmoded ideas facing new social problems. They described politics as corrupt, and government, especially the federal government, as weak and unconcerned with human problems. The nation's blacks had been trapped in segregation and poverty, and the surviving Indians had been isolated on reservations. Perhaps most disturbing to early historians, the period had begun with a society on a scale that people could comprehend, yet it ended with an economic system based on corporations, chaotic cities, and feeble government at all levels. The historian Charles Beard maintained much of the stereotype in *The Rise of American Civilization* (1927) and *America in Midpassage* (1939), which influenced generations of college students. The radical writer Matthew Josephson excoriated the period in two widely read books, *The Robber Barons* (1934), whose thesis was its title, and *The Politicos* (1938), which depicted Gilded Age politicians as the flunkies of the corporations.

There was an alternative viewpoint, a thoughtful approach, which Allan Nevins, more than any other student of the period, fostered. Influential both as a biographer and as a professor of history at Columbia University, Nevins edited a major group of books about the era's leading figures. His own Pulitzer Prize–winning biography, *Grover Cleveland: A Study in Courage* (1932), was the most famous of these, and many others remain the standard biographies of their subjects. Nonetheless, the pace of development in Gilded Age studies was slow, partly because historians emphasized other periods and problems.

By the late 1950s, a new generation of scholars started to rethink the issues of the Gilded Age. Their first focus was on politics. No era had debated partisan questions more fervently. The issues had seemed remote and unimportant to scholars later, but they had fascinated and moved voters at the time.

On such issues as the levying of tariffs on foreign imports, which the early historians portrayed as simply a tool for helping big business, the new writers pointed out that this protection had *not* especially benefited the railroads or the oil industry, two of the supposed villains of the age. Supporters of high tariffs, who included workers in many industries, had defended them as a means of safeguarding American jobs, of helping producers of certain raw materials, and of shielding small business from foreign competition. Politically, the policy had been central to the Republican coalition, since it promised to promote economic growth among various likely GOP voters.

The political debate over the currency—tight money versus easy money—had equally bewildered early historians. Many Gilded Age farmers favored inflation to counteract the growing value of their debts after wheat and cotton prices nose-dived; some businessmen also liked easy money because low interest rates enabled them to expand operations. This issue tended to pit Westerners and Southerners, who needed cash for economic development, against the East, but it also had a powerful moral component. Those who favored a currency based on some intrinsic value such as gold stood divided from those who saw money as a flexible device for regulating the nation's economic health. In the broadest sense, the currency debate highlighted the complexity of the national economy and the growing difference of opinion over the role of government in it. In 1964 Irwin Unger elucidated the subject in a Pulitzer Prize–winning analysis, *The Greenback Era.*

By the 1960s some historians had begun to argue that scholars in the 1930s, who revered a powerful Executive and an interventionist federal government, had read their biases into the study of the Gilded Age. Congress had remained more powerful than the Presidency during the period, and as often as not, one or both houses had not been of the President's party; this explained the partisan deadlocks and compromises of the time. The national political scene had been one long struggle to build a new majority, a battle the Republicans finally won in 1894 and 1896. The highest rate of voter participation in American history occurred in the 1880s and 1890s, and the closeness of most elections and the sense of a major struggle for power reflected people's intense interest in politics. If voting, public dicussion of issues, and legislative enactments constitute democracy, the Gilded Age was one of the most democratic periods in American history.

In 1963 I published a symposium, *The Gilded Age: A Reappraisal,* in which leading young scholars presented new views of the era's major public issues. (A second edition appeared in 1970.) Then in 1969 I brought out a narrative account of Gilded Age politics, *From Hayes to McKinley.* I liked the Republicans better than the Democrats because of their record against slavery and because they had attempted to build a truly national economy during the late nineteenth century. The Democrats seemed to me to have been a loose coalition of local and often conflicting interests. The party had feared and opposed federal authority because it threatened Democratic urban machines in the North and white rule in the South.

The traditional historian's criticism of the lack of federal action in solving social problems during this period was ahistorical. Neither the consensus nor the machinery for such activity was available. Most Gilded Age Americans were content to leave such matters as public health, housing, and welfare to local government and private philanthropy. The typical citizen thought of the federal government only when picking up the mail, paying a modest excise tax on whiskey or tobacco, or seeing a serviceman in uniform. Nonetheless, the government did slowly get more involved in social problems, with much debate, as Ari Hoogenboom noted when delineating the struggle over civil service reform in *Outlawing the Spoils* (1961), and as Morton Keller recounted in

Affairs of State (1979). Congress laid substantial groundwork for expanded action with the Sherman Anti-Trust Act, the Interstate Commerce Commission, and civil service reform.

In the 1960s and 1970s the computer allowed historians to ask and answer many new questions about Gilded Age politics. Using methods of quantification borrowed from other social sciences, some scholars turned from studying party battles to analyzing the composition of the electorate, and from the national to the local scene. They concluded that political preferences had often been rooted less in economic positions than in ethnic and religious tensions. Tariff and currency questions had not been as important to voters as the compulsory teaching of English in public schools or the drive for Prohibition, which touched deeply held beliefs. (Catholics, for instance, had tended to oppose Prohibition, which they saw as an attempt to make them conform to a standard of personal conduct that Protestants upheld, and since Prohibitionists were often Republicans, Catholics usually voted Democratic.) The most influential scholar promoting this new theory has been Samuel P. Hays, author of *American Political History as Social Analysis* (1980).

By the 1980s this approach was widely accepted but had its critics. It was based mostly on studies of Midwestern states such as Ohio, Indiana, and Illinois. Would it appear equally valid elsewhere? The quantifiers had produced a sharper picture of who voted but not necessarily of why they voted as they did. And did it really follow that national politics was secondary to local affairs? Perhaps the two were merely different. The quantifiers' books were filled with statistics and complicated jargon and focused on groups and trends rather than on individuals. Surely something was missing. Their tone was that of the metronome, but Gilded Age politics had marched to the sound of the calliope and brass band.

Any new synthesis of Gilded Age politics will be convincing only if it recognizes voting behavior as both culturally determined and a product of the complex national political system. It is important to remember, for instance, that politicians of the Gilded Age set the agenda. And people responded strongly to personalities, just as they do today. Furthermore, people's hopes and fears about their own jobs were important. Local contests and presidential elections had different dynamics, and voters, as always, had multiple personalities. The best syntheses of the various new approaches are found in Richard J. Jensen's *The Winning of the Midwest* (1971) and R. Hal Williams's *Years of Decision* (1978).

Historians' treatments of business and economic development during the Gilded Age have changed as much as their ideas about politics. Most scholars remain suspicious of large corporations and continue to disapprove of the great wealth that a few industrialists acquired during the period. Standard accounts usually have contained descriptions of lavish mansions where the feckless rich disported themselves, oblivious of the working classes. But such types no more reflect the typical entrepreneur of the time than flashy jet setters reflect most businessmen of today. The typical Gilded Age businessman ran a small company, and many of the antisocial actions of businessmen large and small resulted less from greed or malice than from a desperate need to "meet the competition."

Josephson's *The Robber Barons*, a best seller in the 1930s, soundly established the antibusiness view. Once again Nevins provided a corrective, with his monumental biography of the era's most famous entrepreneur, *John D. Rockefeller* (1940). Nevins did not whitewash Rockefeller or the practices of the Standard Oil Company, but he pointed out that Rockefeller and his partners faced ruthless competition and an uncertain economy and worked in a milieu that emphasized struggle, not regulation. Nevins portrayed the corporation as a complex institution. Not all big businesses were entirely honest, in his view, but the scope and complexity of the Gilded Age economy had made their evolution inevitable.

Nevins's book on Rockefeller sparked considerable controversy, and many historians did not approve of it. But like it or not, the book forced them to reconsider their moralistic ideas about business history. The most impressive economic revisionist of Nevins's generation was probably Edward C. Kirkland. In *Dream and Thought in the Business Community, 1860–1900* (1956), he showed how bewildered businessmen had had to adapt their inherited attitudes and ideals, rooted in a world of farms and small towns, to modern industrial society. His magisterial work *Industry Comes of Age* (1961) is basic to understanding the era.

Kirkland excelled at dealing with important subjects that earlier scholars had slighted. He showed how the inventions of Alexander Graham Bell, George Westinghouse, and Thomas A. Edison created entire industries, and how improvements in education helped prepare a generation of workers for the kinds of jobs the new economy required. He pointed out that while the country was wealthier than ever in the Gilded Age, it went through cycles of boom and bust that made planning difficult and the future uncertain. Productivity increased, but too often profits declined. Businessmen were not the lords of creation that Josephson had described but fallible human beings at the mercy of inscrutable market forces.

Kirkland also shifted the focus in economic studies, making the total economy the star of the show. He noted that the new industrial order was much too large and complex for any one set of people to understand or control. He showed the cumulative nature of much economic development—Edison's work on electricity, for instance, produced not only a successful electric light bulb, with all its ramifications in human affairs, but also a whole range of new industries that relied on electrical power. Time and again Kirkland demonstrated how economic processes had changed society at large, and he revealed the difficulties inherent in trying to predict or manage these changes. He was especially careful to remind readers that less noticed developments, such as expanded educational facilities, had often aided growth and diversification as much as had widely touted and debated public policies.

As time passed and the literature on economic development grew in volume and sophistication, historians turned from tycoons and corporations to the anonymous people who had made the economy work. Alfred D. Chandler, in *The Visible Hand: The Managerial Revolution in American Business* (1977), described the activities and ideas of corporate managers who had often been below-decks engineers rather than captains, yet had made the ships go. Chandler's approach made business history more human and portrayed both the individual business and the total economic system as much more complex and tenuous than had earlier studies.

Parallel tendencies animate modern labor history. Strikes and union organization marked the Gilded Age, but nowadays historians look beyond these events to the social composition of the labor force, the nature of the workplace, and economic mobility. They have shown how workers influenced economic development, how accommodation often modified the antagonism between capital and labor. Trade unionism did improve the workers' lot, but fraternal and community organizations also helped them cope with social and economic change. And most workers believed that they, or at least their children, could move up the ladder, not necessarily to be a boss, but at least to be a foreman. Historians' emphasis on how workers lived has made the labor movement more real, more personal, and more logical in its relationship to later labor matters.

Gilded Age revisionism extends to literature and art. Here progress has been slow because of the unfortunate division between historians of culture and historians of public affairs. This breach must close before a unified view of the period can emerge. Late-nineteenth-century fiction, for instance, has much to offer the historian seeking to understand the period's intangible moods, fears, and aspirations. William Dean Howells's prodigious output constitutes a magnificent survey of relationships among various classes. There are few better ways to understand the struggle between capital and labor than through Howells's novel *A Hazard of New Fortunes* (1890). This great story pivots on a violent streetcar workers' strike in New York City and depicts the reactions of the new urban middle class to supposedly radical immigrants. Most of Howells's works reflect the social, economic, and geographic interdependence and human strains that industrialization created.

Painting is an equally valuable source for historians. The canvases of the Gilded Age richly illustrate the period's appearance, customs, and activities. Genre studies, portraits, and landscapes say much about how people saw themselves. Beginning in the late 1870s, an increasing number of young people, many of them women, chose art as an alternative to business or a professional career. Study in Paris, London, or Munich offered them an artistic tradition as well as technical training.

New York became the nation's cultural capital during the era, but the arts flourished in most large cities. Gradually a clientele of middle-class buyers emerged, along with professional critics who described and analyzed artistic developments in the popular press and magazines. The art world was the scene of debates as fierce as those that raged in politics and economics, and the succession of styles—realism, impressionism, abstractionism—reflected social as well as aesthetic changes. Viewed in its full context, the art world of the Gilded Age poses fascinating questions for the student of American society.

Buildings have faced a harsher test, being more durable and visible, and until recently historians were unkind to much of the era's architecture. The period's transitional nature showed in its buildings. The new industrial order based on machine goods and congested cities called for new kinds of factories and commercial edifices, but people were more traditional when it came to designing homes or public structures. A need for reassurance and familiarity made historical associations popular in architecture. The society's fluidity and individualism also enhanced the appeals of eclecticism, so that Grecian, Gothic, and other historical styles each had a day, sometimes all at once. Meanwhile, both patrons and architects sought a form of expression that would be appropriate to American ideals and practices and would express modern energy yet would not leave the mainstream of Western history and culture.

The result was often a jumble. Many houses and skyscrapers boasted the latest mechanical contrivances on the inside—central heating, electric lighting, and a planned flow pattern—while juggling a variety of tastes and associations with the past on the outside. They were not organic, according to many contemporary critics and later historians, and therefore were not genuine or suited to modern times. As one Gilded Age observer said of the so-called Queen Anne style, which incorporated many echoes of the past, it was Queen Anne in front and Mary Anne behind. Much urban housing, built hastily and without planning, took on a sameness in the brownstone front. Yet these buildings seem both suitable and charming today. At its best, well-made middle-class housing allowed for color, variety, and even whimsy, traits lacking in the styles that followed, when standardization triumphed.

In public building, the period produced several important architects. Henry Hobson Richardson's use of rough stone and his emphasis on mass reflected a national respect for power and scope and thus more than echoed the Romanesque style that inspired him. McKim, Mead and White's urbane variations on Italian Renaissance Classicism reflected an attachment to grand ideals in a time of rapid change. Many architects hoped to soften the commercial spirit with historical associations in architecture. They also wanted buildings to function in an emotional as well as technical sense. A university, for instance, should reflect inherited ideals about learning. Government buildings should express traditional ideas of legitimacy and power. At the same time, many architects were trying to adapt to the new demand for tall buildings in confined spaces, designing structures that use familiar ornament and proportion to reassure both the passerby outside and the worker inside.

Historians have criticized this conflict of styles and purposes, but the triumph of the later International style, making almost every city in the country look somewhat alike, has finally provoked a reexamination of Gilded Age building. A strong public preservation movement has arisen to save and use many of the artifacts in question, and the best Gilded Age architecture has become both more understandable and more attractive.

Despite all the interesting work that has been done on the Gilded Age in recent years, a sense of uncertainty dominates the field. No fresh synthesis of information and ideas has appeared. The historians have shaken old generalizations but have produced no totally convincing new ones and have too often made the period seem bland or abstract.

Transition is a catchword for describing confusing epochs, but it fits this one perfectly. In one generation a nation of farms, workshops, and small towns became a society of cities, factories, and complex social and economic organizations, whose operations challenged inherited ideals. The people of the Gilded Age displayed great energy and were certain of themselves in some spheres while very uncertain in others. They produced and acted upon familiar compromises and struggled to balance individualism with the ever-growing tendency toward mass in an industrial society.

In politics, parochial interests confronted the need for national policies, and contesting groups often prevented planned responses to crises. But the political system remained flexible; no group was permanently alienated, and that was no mean achievement. In the economic sphere people hoped to retain the advantages of competition while enjoying the benefits of large-scale production. The system produced about as much regulation as the general public wanted and allowed the rise of the world's most productive economy. In cultural affairs, the generation could boast many distinctive figures, a broad range of activity in the literary and plastic arts, and a steadily growing level of public appreciation.

Studying this fascinating era reminds us of how slowly people adapt to change. It is a great mistake to suppose that the Gilded Age could somehow have prevented the problems that confront us today, but it merits close attention because in many ways it resembles our own generation. We, too, are moving rapidly into a new economy, with all the consequent human and societal upheavals. Many of the public questions we grapple with today resemble those of the Gilded Age—the place of minorities in society; the problems of a wave of foreign immigration; women's rights; government's role in shaping social development. Questions of monetary policy and tariff protection are also very much alive. Like our predecessors in the Gilded Age, we face a changing social and economic order whose future seems glamorous and filled with potential for good but is also tinged with danger and uncertainty.

The Ghost Dance and the Battle of Wounded Knee

Dee Alexander Brown

The anthropologist Oliver La Farge has argued that upon first encounter white Europeans created myths concerning the American Indians. These myths usually fell into two contradictory categories—noble and ignoble. On the one hand, Indians were seen as children of God and nature, innocents in a "garden" environment; on the other hand, they were viewed as bloodthirsty savages, children of the devil and the netherworld. These two images have persisted throughout American history, although certainly the ignoble image has dominated, with tragic consequences for Indians. By seeing the Indians as basically either noble or ignoble, whites developed a universal, simplistic, mythic view of these peoples that tended to rob them of their human identity and thus at the same time of their history. A classic case in point involves the Battle of Wounded Knee, fought on the Pine Ridge Sioux Reservation in South Dakota in December 1890. Wounded Knee is also considered to be the last "battle" in the long series of Plains wars, a topic itself laden with myth and involving what appeared to be a concerted effort on the part of the United States War Department to transform the "vanishing American" image into a reality. Here, Dee Alexander Brown of the University of Illinois argues that this incident—which resulted in the deaths of 146 Indian men, women, and children (their bodies thrown into a common grave) and 25 soldiers—need not have happened. The Ghost Dance religion of the Paiute chief Tavibo and his son Wovoka was essentially therapeutic, offering relief to depressed Plains Indians in the final throes of defeat. The religion was "opposed to all forms of violence, self-mutilation, theft, and falsehood." Yet failing to see this reality, the War Department viewed it as threatening and moved to stamp it out, thus injecting the element of violence. It was perhaps grimly fitting that the "battle," which was triggered by the death of Sitting Bull (a recent convert) at the hands of reservation Indian police, took place among Sioux followers of the great Sioux chief at Pine Ridge. To continue the grim coincidence, the "effectives" on the American side were members of the U.S. Seventh Cavalry, Custer's old outfit. The spark was provided as troopers attempted to disarm the Sioux, and thinking themselves protected from bullets because of the ghost shirts they wore, the Indians opened fire—the "battle" was drawn. There were those at the time and since who, adhering to the noble image, viewed the clash at Wounded Knee Creek as a massacre; and those adhering to the ignoble image who viewed it as a triumph of brave soldiers over treacherous Indian savages. The reality is that it was another confrontation of misunderstood mythologies, particularly on the part of the Americans; in this case the side with the Hotchkiss guns prevailed—by now an all too traditional way of resolving issues such as these.

During the decade following Custer's defeat on the Little Big Horn, the warring tribes of Indians in the American West were gradually shorn of their power and locked within reservations. Many of the great chiefs and mighty warriors were dead. The buffalo and antelope had almost vanished; the old ceremonies of the tribes were becoming rituals without meaning.

For the survivors it was a time without spirit, a time of despair. One might swap a few skins for the trader's crazy-water and dream of the old days, the days of the splendid hunts and fighting. One might make big talk for a little while but that was all.

In such times, defeated peoples search for redeemers, and soon on many reservations there were dreamers and swooning men to tell of approaching redemption. Most of them were great fakers, but some were sincere in their vagaries and their visions.

As early as 1870 the defeated Paiutes of Nevada had found a redeemer in Tavibo, a petty chief, who claimed to have talked with divine spirits in the mountains. All the people of the earth were to be swallowed up, the spirits told him, but at the end of three days the Indians would be resurrected in the flesh to live forever. They would enjoy the earth which was rightfully theirs. Once again there would be plenty of game, fish, and piñon nuts. Best of all, the white invaders would be destroyed forever.

When Tavibo first told his vision to the Paiutes, he attracted very few believers. But gradually he added other features to his story, and he went up into the mountains again for further revelations. It was necessary for the Indians to dance, everywhere; to keep on dancing. This would please the Great Spirit, who would come and destroy the white men and bring back the buffalo.

Tavibo died shortly after he told of these things, but his son, Wovoka, was considered the natural inheritor of his powers by those Paiutes who believed in the new religion of the dance. Wovoka, who was only 14 when his father died, was taken into the family of a white farmer, David Wilson, and was given the name of Jack Wilson. In his new home the boy's imagination was fired by Bible stories told to him; he was fascinated by the white man's God.

On New Year's Day of 1889, a vision came to Jack Wilson (Wovoka) while he lay ill with fever; he dreamed that he died and went to heaven. God spoke to him, commanding him to take a message back to earth. Wovoka was to tell the Indians that if they would follow God's commandment and perform a "ghost dance" at regular intervals their old days of happiness and prosperity would be returned to them.

In January 1889 on the Walker Lake Reservation, the first Ghost Dance was performed on a dancing ground selected by Wovoka. The ceremony was simple, the Paiutes forming into a large circle, dancing and chanting as they constricted the circle, the circle widening and constricting again and again. The

From "The Ghost Dance and the Battle of Wounded Knee," by Dee Alexander Brown, in *American History Illustrated* (December 1966). Reprinted through the courtesy of Cowles Magazines, Inc., publishers of *American History Illustrated*.

dancing continued for a day and a night, Wovoka sitting in the middle of the circle before a large fire with his head bowed. He wore a white striped coat, a pair of trousers, and moccasins. On the second day he stopped the dancing and described the visions that God had sent to him. Then the dancing commenced again and lasted for three more days.

When a second dance was held soon afterward, several Utes visited the ceremony out of curiosity. Returning to their reservation, the Utes told the neighboring Bannocks about what they had seen. The Bannocks sent emissaries to the next dance, and within a few weeks the Shoshones at Fort Hall Reservation saw a ritual staged by the Bannocks. They were so impressed they sent a delegation to Nevada to learn the new religion from Wovoka himself.

Perhaps more than any other of the tribes, the Cheyenne and Sioux felt the need for a messiah who could lead them back to their days of glory. After the story of Wovoka was carried swiftly to their reservations, several medicine men decided to make pilgrimages. It was a mark of prestige for them to travel by railroad, and as soon as they could raise enough money, they purchased tickets to Nevada. In the autumn of 1889, a Cheyenne named Porcupine made the journey, and a short time later Short Bull, Kicking Bear, and other Sioux leaders traveled all the way from Dakota.

The Sioux accepted the Ghost Dance religion with more fervor than any of the other tribes. On their return to the Dakota reservations, each delegate tried to outdo the others in describing the wonders of the messiah. Wovoka came down from heaven in a cloud, they said. He showed them a vision of all the nations of Indians coming home. The earth would be covered with dust and then a new earth would come upon the old. They must use the sacred red and white paint and the sacred grass to make the vanished buffalo return in great herds.

In the spring of 1890 the Sioux began dancing the Ghost Dance at Pine Ridge Reservation, adding new symbols to Wovoka's original ceremony. By June they were wearing ghost-shirts made of cotton cloth painted blue around the necks, with bright-colored thunderbirds, bows and arrows, suns, moons, and stars emblazoned upon them.

To accompany the dancing they made ghost songs:

> The whole world is coming,
> A nation is coming, a nation is coming.
> The Eagle has brought the message to the tribe.
> The father says so, the father says so.
> Over the whole earth they are coming,
> The buffalo are coming, the buffalo are coming.

Mainly because they misunderstood the meaning of the Ghost Dance religion, the Government's policy makers who ran the reservations from Washington decided to stamp it out. If they had taken the trouble to examine its basic tenets, they would have found that in its original form the religion was opposed to all forms of violence, self-mutilation, theft, and falsehood. As one

Army officer observed: "Wovoka has given these people a better religion than they ever had before."

The Ghost Dance might have died away under official pressure had not the greatest maker of medicine among the Sioux, Sitting Bull, chosen to come forth from his "retirement" near Standing Rock agency and join the new religion of the dance. Sitting Bull was the last of the great unreconciled chiefs. Since his return from Canada, where he had gone after the Custer battle, he had been carrying on a feud with the military as well as with civilian reservation agents.

When Kicking Bear, one of the early emissaries to Wovoka, visited Sitting Bull in late 1890 to teach him the Ghost Dance, Agent James McLaughlin ordered Kicking Bear escorted off the reservation. Sitting Bull may or may not have believed in the messiah, but he was always searching for opportunities to bedevil the authorities. Kicking Bear was hardly off the reservation before Sitting Bull set up a dance camp and started instructing his followers in the new religion. In a short time the peaceful ghost songs became warlike chants.

Efforts of authorities to put a stop to ghost dancing now led to resentment and increased belligerency from the Indians. Inevitably the Army was drawn into the controversy, and in the late autumn of 1890 General Nelson Miles ordered more troops into the plains area.

Suspecting that Sitting Bull was the leading trouble-maker, Miles arranged informally with Buffalo Bill Cody to act as intermediary. Cody had scouted with Miles in former years and had also employed Sitting Bull as a feature attraction with his Wild West show. "Sitting Bull might listen to you," Miles told Cody, "when under the same conditions he'd take a shot at one of my soldiers."

Buffalo Bill went at once to Fort Yates on the Standing Rock Reservation, but authorities there were dismayed when they read Miles's written instructions to Cody: "Secure the person of Sitting Bull and deliver him to the nearest commanding officer of U.S. troops." James McLaughlin, the reservation agent, and Lieutenant Colonel William Drum, the military commander, both feared that Cody's actions might precipitate a general outbreak throughout the area. The military authorities immediately took it upon themselves to get Buffalo Bill drunk, send a wire to Washington, and have his orders rescinded.

"All the officers were requested to assist in drinking Buffalo Bill under the table," Captain A. R. Chaplin later recorded. "But his capacity was such that it took practically all of us in details of two or three at a time to keep him interested and busy throughout the day." Although the rugged Cody managed to keep a clear head through all this maneuvering, he had scarcely started out to Sitting Bull's encampment before a telegram came from Washington canceling his orders.

Meanwhile Agent McLaughlin had decided to take Sitting Bull into custody himself, hoping to prevent a dangerous disturbance which he felt would result if the military authorities forced the issue and tried to make an arrest.

McLaughlin gave the necessary orders to his Indian police, instructing them not to permit the chief to escape under any circumstances.

Just before daybreak on December 15, 1890, forty-three Indian police surrounded Sitting Bull's log cabin. Lieutenant Bull Head, the Indian policeman in charge of the party, found Sitting Bull asleep on the floor. When he was awakened, the old war leader stared incredulously at Bull Head. "What do you want here?" he asked.

"You are my prisoner," said Bull Head calmly. "You must go to the agency."

Sitting Bull yawned and sat up. "All right," he said, "let me put on my clothes and I'll go with you." He called one of his wives and sent her to an adjoining cabin for his best clothing, and then asked the policeman to saddle his horse for him.

While these things were being done, his ardent followers, who had been dancing the Ghost Dance every night for weeks, were gathering around the cabin. They outnumbered the police four to one, and soon had them pressed against the walls. As soon as Lieutenant Bull Head emerged with Sitting Bull, he must have sensed the explosive nature of the situation.

While they waited for Sitting Bull's horse, a fanatical ghost dancer named Catch-the-Bear appeared out of the mob. "You think you are going to take him," Catch-the-Bear shouted at the policemen. "You shall not do it!"

"Come now," Bull Head said quietly to his prisoner, "do not listen to anyone." But Sitting Bull held back, forcing Bull Head and Sergeant Red Tomahawk to pull him toward his horse.

Without warning, Catch-the-Bear suddenly threw off his blanket and brought up a rifle, firing point-blank at Bull Head, wounding him in the side. As Bull Head fell, he tried to shoot his assailant, but the bullet struck Sitting Bull instead. Almost simultaneously Red Tomahawk shot Sitting Bull through the head. A wild fight developed immediately, and only the timely arrival of a calvary detachment saved the police from extinction.

News of Sitting Bull's death swept across the reservations, startling the Indians and the watchful military forces in the Dakotas. Most of the frightened followers of the great chief immediately came into Standing Rock agency and surrendered. Others fled toward the southwest.

Those who were fleeing knew exactly where they were going. They were seeking to join forces with a Ghost Dance believer, an aging chief named Big Foot. For some time, Big Foot had been gathering followers at a small village near the mouth of Deep Creek on Cheyenne River. As the Ghost Dance craze had increased, so had Big Foot's forces, and even before the fatal shooting of Sitting Bull, a small party of cavalrymen under Lieutenant Colonel Edwin V. Sumner, Jr. had been assigned to watch his movements.

As soon as news of Sitting Bull's death reached Big Foot, he began preparations to break camp. Lieutenant Colonel Sumner accepted the chief's explanation that the Indians were preparing to proceed eastward to the Cheyenne River agency where they would spend the winter. Big Foot was unusually friendly, and declared that the only reason he had permitted the fugitives from Sitting Bull's camp to join his people was that he felt sorry for them and wanted them to return to the reservation with him. Sumner was so convinced of Big Foot's sincerity that he permitted the band to keep their arms—a decision that was to precipitate the tragedy of Wounded Knee.

Before dawn the next day, December 23, Big Foot and his ever-increasing band were in rapid flight, moving in the opposite direction from the Cheyenne River agency. The question has never been settled as to whether they were heading for the Pine Ridge agency, as Big Foot's followers later claimed, or for the Sioux recalcitrants' stronghold in the Badlands. Perhaps Big Foot did not know that Kicking Bear and Short Bull had withdrawn to the stronghold in the Badlands. But it is a fact that a few days earlier those two leaders, who had once visited the messiah in Nevada, were in the Badlands. And they had with them several hundred fanatical followers, keyed up to a high frenzy as a result of their continual dancing and chanting.

Learning of Big Foot's escape from Sumner's cavalry, General Miles ordered Major Samuel M. Whitside of the 7th Cavalry to intercept the Indians, disarm them, and return them to a reservation. On December 28, Whitside's scouts found the fugitives on Porcupine Creek and when the major sighted a white flag fluttering from a wagon, he rode out to meet it. He was surprised to find Big Foot lying in the bed of the wagon, swathed in blankets, suffering severely from pneumonia.

Whitside shook hands with the ailing chief, and told him that he must bring his people to the cavalry camp on Wounded Knee Creek. In a hoarse voice that was almost a whisper, Big Foot agreed to the order. Whitside, on the advice of one of his scouts, decided to wait until the band was assembled beside the cavalry camp before disarming them.

During the ensuing march, none of the cavalrymen suspected that anything was amiss. The Indians seemed to be in good humor; they talked and laughed with the soldiers, and smoked their cigarettes. Not one of the cavalrymen seemed to have been aware that almost all of these Indians were wearing sacred ghost shirts which they believed would protect them from the soldiers' weapons. And the soldiers seemed to be completely ignorant of the fact that their prisoners were obsessed with the belief that the day of the Indians' return to power was close at hand. One of the most fanatical members of the band was a medicine man, Yellow Bird, who all during the march was moving stealthily up and down the line, occasionally blowing on an eagle-bone whistle and muttering Ghost Dance chants.

When the column reached Wounded Knee, the Indians were assigned an area near the cavalry camp. They were carefully counted; 120 men and 230 women and children were present. Rations were issued, and they set up their shelters for the night. For additional cover, Major Whitside gave them several army tents. The troop surgeon, John van R. Hoff, went to attend the ailing Big Foot, and a stove was set up in the chief's tent. Whitside, however, did not entirely trust Big Foot's band. He posted a battery of four Hotchkiss guns, training them directly on the Indians' camp.

It was a cold night. Ice was already an inch thick on the tree-bordered creek, and there was a hint of snow in the air. During the night, Colonel James W. Forsyth of the 7th Cavalry rode in and took command. Significantly there were now at Wounded Knee five troop commanders—Moylan, Varnum, Wallace, Godfrey, and Edgerly—who had been with Reno and Custer at the Little Big Horn. With Big Foot were warriors who had fought in the same battle. Much would be made of that in days to come.

In Forsyth's command was a young lieutenant, James D. Mann, who was to witness the opening shots of the approaching fight. "The next morning," Mann said afterwards, "we started to disarm them, the bucks being formed in a semi-circle in front of the tents. We went through the tents looking for arms, and while this was going on, everyone seemed to be good-natured, and we had no thought of trouble. The squaws were sitting on bundles concealing guns and other arms. We lifted them as tenderly and treated them as nicely as possible.

"While this was going on, the medicine man [Yellow Bird] who was in the center of the semi-circle of bucks, had been going through the Ghost Dance, and making a speech, the substance of which was, as told me by an interpreter afterwards, 'I have made medicine of the white man's ammunition. It is good medicine, and his bullets cannot harm you, as they will not go through your ghost shirts, while your bullets will kill.'

"It was then that I had a peculiar feeling come over me which I can not describe—some presentiment of trouble—and I told the men to 'be ready: there is going to be trouble.' We were only six or eight feet from the Indians and I ordered my men to fall back.

"In front of me were four bucks—three armed with rifles and one with bow and arrows. I drew my revolver and stepped through the line to my place with my detachment. The Indians raised their weapons over their heads to heaven as if in votive offering, then brought them down to bear on us, the one with the bow and arrow aiming directly at me. Then they seemed to wait an instant.

"The medicine man threw a handful of dust in the air, put on his war bonnet, and an instant later a gun was fired. This seemed to be the signal they had been waiting for, and the firing immediately began. I ordered my men to fire, and the reports were almost simultaneous."

Things happened fast after that first volley. The Hotchkiss guns opened fire and began pouring shells into the Indians at the rate of nearly fifty per minute. What survivors there were began a fierce hand-to-hand struggle, using revolvers, knives, and war clubs. The lack of rifles among the Indians made the fight more bloody because it brought the combatants to closer quarters. In a few minutes, 200 Indian men, women and children and sixty soldiers were lying dead and wounded on the ground, the ripped tents blazing and smoking around them. Some of the surviving Indians fled to a nearby ravine, hiding among the rocks and scrub cedars. Others continued their flight up the slopes to the south.

Yellow Bird, the medicine man, concealed himself in a tent, and through a slit in the canvas began shooting at the soldiers. When one of the 7th Cavalry troopers ran forward to slash open the tent, Yellow Bird killed him by pumping bullets into his stomach. Angry cavalrymen responded with heavy fire, then piled hay around the tent and set it to blazing.

Big Foot died early in the fighting from a bullet through his head. Captain Edward Godfrey, who had survived the Little Bighorn (he was with Benteen), was shocked when he discovered he had ordered his men to fire on women and children hidden in a brush thicket. Captain George Wallace, who also had survived the Custer fight (with Reno's battalion), was shouting his first order to fire when a bullet carried away the top of his head.

On the bloody campground, Surgeon Hoff did what he could for the wounded. He disarmed a wounded Indian who was still trying to fire his rifle. The warrior staggered to his feet and looked down fixedly at the burned body of Yellow Bird. "If I could be taken to you," the wounded Indian muttered to the dead medicine man, "I would kill you again."

Disillusionment over the failure of the ghost shirts had already affected most of the other survivors. With blood flowing from her wounds, one of the squaws tore off her brilliantly colored shirt and stamped upon it.

As it was apparent by the end of the day that a blizzard was approaching, the medical staff hastily gathered the wounded together to carry them to a field hospital at Pine Ridge. In the affair 146 Indians and 25 soldiers had been killed, but the full totals would not be known until several days afterward because of the snowstorm that blanketed the battlefield.

After the blizzard, when a burial party went out to Wounded Knee, they found many of the bodies frozen grotesquely where they had fallen. They buried all the Indians together in a large pit. A few days later, relatives of the slain came and put up a wire fence around the mass grave; then they smeared the posts with sacred red medicine paint.

By this time the nation's press was having a field day with the new "Indian war." Some journalists pictured the Wounded Knee tragedy as a triumph of brave soldiers over treacherous Indians; others declared it was a slaughter of helpless Indians by a regiment searching for revenge since the Little Big Horn. The truth undoubtedly lay somewhere between these opposite points of view. Certainly it was a tragic accident of war.

At Wounded Knee, the vision of the peaceful Paiute dreamer, Wovoka, had come to an end. And so had all the long and bitter years of Indian resistance on the western plains.

The Gay Nineties—Reconsidered

Reynold M. Wik

Nostalgia has often distorted the view that Americans hold of their historical past. Few stereotyped views, however, are more out of line with fact than that labeled the Gay Nineties. The very mention of the phrase conjures up a series of mythical images: the corner ice cream parlor, the penny arcade, Victorian brownstone houses, the bicycle built for two, Gibson Girls, and the colorful sights and sounds of vaudeville and Tin Pan Alley—the "good old days." Indeed the decade of the 1890s is thought to have been a fun-loving and charming era from America's golden past. However, as discussed by Reynold M. Wik, Morrison Professor of American History Emeritus at Mills College, the enthusiastic razzmatazz of the era was for the great mass of Americans simply a brittle veneer that hid many sober realities of American life. The mythical notion that the Nineties bubbled with gusto and excitement completely omits the frustration and despair evident in rural America, the grim conditions in the nation's cities, and the depressed social and economic position of the country's minorities. Viewed more closely, the latter years of what Mark Twain critically labeled the Gilded Age were considerably less buoyant and "gay" than they have since appeared. On closer analysis, the period loses much of its golden luster and reveals instead a large amount of self-deception and make-believe on the part of both those who lived at the time and those who later came to remember it fondly after the trauma of World War I.

Of all the labels pinned on past decades none became more indelibly stereotyped than the "Gay Nineties." The expression embedded itself in the American mind, it captured a people's faith. Today it conjures up all the nostalgia of the so-called good old days, the confident years, the golden age.

Needless to say, this image grew out of varied circumstances. A dynamic technology created the bicycle built for two, the phonograph, the kinescope in the penny arcade, the sputtering "Red Devils" constructed by Duryea, Haynes, Winton, and Ford and the electric dynamo which Henry Adams regarded "the most expressive among a thousand symbols of ultimate energy." Meanwhile, a rabid nationalism enveloped a public fanned by such spectaculars as the Chicago World's Fair, the Spanish American War, Roosevelt's charge up San Juan Hill, the scramble for an overseas empire, and the dash of 6,000 miners to the Klondike.

From "The Gay Nineties—Reconsidered," by Reynold M. Wik, in *Mid-America*, Vol. 44, No. 2 (April 1962), pp. 67–79. Reprinted by permission.

But the notion that the 90's reeked with levity springs largely from the entertainment of the time. Vaudeville reigned with its loquacious master of ceremonies, the burnt cork darky musicales, the strumming banjo, ragtime, the can-can chorus, melodramas, and perhaps the rendition of "Casey at the Bat." Popular songs flourished. Sigmund Spaeth insists more songs were written in the 1890's than in any previous decade. These ranged from "The Bowery" and "Daisey Bell" to "They'll Be a Hot Time in the Old Town Tonight," "Ta ra ra Boom De Aye," and the barbershop quartet favorite, "Only a Bird in a Gilded Cage."

Yet, the musical gaiety of the era may not have reflected the mood of the average American. Perhaps "After the Ball," or Gussie L. Davis's "In the Baggage Coach Ahead," more accurately depicted the times. Mr. Dooley, decrying hasty observations, commented, "I know history isn't true, Hennessey, because it ain't like what I see every day on Halsted Street." How did America look to those on city streets? Did the common man laugh himself to sleep every night? Were the 90's good? Good for whom?

Ample evidence suggests that the 90's were not particularly gay for large segments of the population. On the contrary, millions experienced frustration and despair. For these any suggestion to the effect that the nation wallowed in mirth would have been deemed pure nonsense.

In 1900, the sixty percent of the population living on farms had faced one of the worst economic decades in agriculture. In the Northeast crops were abandoned because of cheaper land in the West. Southern planters struggled against almost universal poverty. In the West, those who had taken Greeley's advice, met recurring drouths, low prices, and mounting indebtedness. Farmers complained of 14-cent corn, 5-cent cotton, and 12 percent interest. From 1889 to 1893, 11,000 Kansas farmers were foreclosed, and by the end of the decade the loan companies owned 90 percent of the land in the state. Tom Watson of the Southern Alliance observed that people who once had plenty now lost their homes. "You took down the family pictures from the walls," he lamented. "You picked some favorite flowers and took your weary march into the strange cold world. You walked the roads looking for work. I have done it too."

William Allen White writing for the *Emporia Gazette* in 1896 noted thousands were leaving the state. "Kansas isn't in the civilized world," he fumed. "She has taken the place of Arkansas and Timbucktoo." Hamlin Garland, after bitter experience in Dakota, insisted he was tired of high-sounding cliches about the virtues of the American farmer. Writers and orators were blind to the fact that agrarian folk were the hardest working and poorest paid people in America. They lived in hovels, their wives filled insane asylums, they were dreary peasants with a well-nigh hopeless future. When Mary Lease urged the raising of less corn and more hell, farmers responded by singing:

> My country 'tis of thee
> Once land of liberty
> Of thee I sing
> Land of the millionaire
> Farmers with pockets bare
> Caused by the cursed snare
> The Money Ring.

Meanwhile, those working for wages suffered a similar fate. According to the United States Bureau of the Census, the average annual wage of all workers in the nation in 1890 was $438.00. Ten years later the figure stood at $428.00, actually a loss in wage income during the decade. Hired hands on farms and factory workers in the South received less than $250.00 a year. Negroes got fifty cents a day. Half the women in industry received less than five dollars a week. A Columbia University professor in 1924 described the 1890's as a time when 32 percent of all wage earners were underfed, 57 percent ill-clothed and 52 percent ill-housed.

Moreover, working conditions remained intolerable with factory employees forced to work a 60-hour week under hazardous conditions. Since only half the states had safety inspection laws in 1900, industrial accidents claimed 20,000 lives annually. During the 90's, approximately 7,500 railroad workers were killed each year. In the mines 45 men lost their lives for each 10,000 employed, a death rate three times greater than in Europe. All this in a land where people bragged about the democratic tradition emphasizing the value of the individual. One cynic remarked that in America everything was cheap, especially human life.

When labor attempted to organize to improve working conditions, to escape the incubus of the company town and to share in the wealth they had helped create, management offered stiff resistance. The Homestead strike erupted in the Carnegie steel mills in 1892 when the company cut wages and refused to recognize the union. Two years later the Pullman strike broke out in Chicago when wages were cut one-third in spite of a four-million-dollar surplus in the company treasury. Injunctions were issued, Debs went to prison, federal troops broke the strike and the public excoriated Governor Altgeld and Clarence Darrow. In the 1890's there were 14,191 strikes involving four million workers, making the decade one of the most violent in labor-management relations.

Nor did white collar workers find Utopia in the gay 90's. Even though apartments rented for $8.00 a month and suits sold for $10.00, the salaries paid were, in purchasing power, less than half of what they are today. Besides, office rules were often dictatorial. One firm warned that a person's integrity would be questioned if he smoked cigars, used liquor in any form, got shaved in a barber shop, or frequented pool halls. Young men would get one evening off a week for courting purposes; however, leisure time should be spent in reading good books and contemplating the glories of the Kingdom of God.

In addition, the panic of 1893, the most serious depression of the century, added to the collective misery. With over two million unemployed in 1894, soup kitchens were set up in New York, wood-chopping projects in Denver, and street-sweeping jobs in San Francisco. Hoping to get Congress to enact a national public works program, Jacob Coxey led his motley army of unemployed on the long hike from Massillon, Ohio, to Washington, D.C. Delegates from Los Angeles and Oakland, including Jack London, joined the demonstration. After reaching the capitol, the leaders were arrested for, as the legal jargon put it, "stepping on certain plants, shrubs, and turf."

Frequently the pleas of working people were met with arrogance. One entrepreneur claimed the masses did not suffer because they could not even speak English. Another suggested that strikers be fed bullets. A Chicago newspaper hinted that the unemployment problem be solved by giving handouts in which there had been placed a little strychnine.

Although the 90's were difficult for farmers, factory workers, and office employees, the notion persisted that the decade was good for the businessman. Free enterprise prevailed, governmental restrictions were limited and the graduated income tax nonexistent. In the language of the Chamber of Commerce, these were the grand days of laissez-faire capitalism which had made America great.

Still, even here generalizations must be viewed with caution because he who generalizes, generally lies. A distinction must be made between small and big business. Whereas giant corporations usually made good profits, the small partnerships and individually owned companies suffered the same financial stringencies felt by those in other occupations. Small business firms lacked capital. The treasurer of the Huber Manufacturing Company of Marion, Ohio, writing to the board of directors in 1896, explained, "We are practically at the end of our string. I have done everything in my power to meet the payroll, but now I must recommend that the plant be closed down. This is not a question of sympathy for workers but of life and death for the company. . . ." During the 1890's, 160,320 companies failed. This is the highest figure for any decade in the nineteenth century. In fact the ratio of business failures to the total number of firms existing in the 90's was higher than in the 1930's following the crash of 1929. In this sense, the gay 90's were not good for the small business man. Those talking so glibly about the halcyon days when businessmen had freedom apparently never think about the freedom to go bankrupt.

However, big business through consolidation, by freezing out competition, and by exploiting the vast resources of the country piled up fantastic profits. James Bryce thought it paradoxical that the most individualistic peoples should excel in the art of combination. Conspicuous consumption graced the social life of the Four Hundred, and manifested itself in Gould's $500,000 yacht, Morgan's $100,000 private car, Vanderbilt's two-million-dollar home with its $50,000 paintings and $20,000 bronze doors. The *Methodist Quarterly Review* estimated that if the original Adam had saved $500 every day since his introduction to Eve 6,000 years ago, he would still be $200,000 behind John D. Rockefeller.

While industrial tycoons produced miracles, they caused anxiety by seizing political power and creating an inequitable distribution of wealth. Twenty-two millionaires sat in the Senate in 1900 and men of wealth dominated many state legislatures. Theodore Roosevelt thought amalgamated wealth threatened to make government itself captive. "It matters not one iota which political party is in power," boasted one plutocrat. "We are rich. We own America." "Gas" Adricks claimed the senatorship in Delaware saying, "I've bought it. I paid for it. I'm going to have it." The *Arena* in 1901 claimed one-half of the people owned practically nothing because one percent of the population owned 54 percent of the nation's wealth. The *Fortnightly Review* said America had been overrun by robber barons. Henry D. Lloyd in his *Wealth Against Commonwealth* saw civilization being destroyed by the great moneymakers at the top, not by the barbarians from below. John M. Harlan of the Supreme Court in 1911 said those recalling the 1890's would remember the unrest which prevailed by the aggregation of capital in the hands of a few. Vernon Parrington in retrospect termed the spectacle the great barbecue. These days were wonderful except that they almost ruined the country. Ralph Gorman, a journalist writing in 1957, held that "nobody would want to go back to 1900, not even the smooth orators before managerial groups."

In spite of the revisionist school of business historians such as Edward Kirkland, Allan Nevins, Henrietta Larson, Richard Overton, Ralph Hidy, and Harold Williamson, the fact remains that after all that is favorable has been said to justify the actions of the industrial magnates of this era, the new looks are never completely convincing. None of these experts believe the distribution of wealth in the 90's was beneficial to society. None insist the nation return to laissez-faire capitalism with an absence of governmental controls. Nor do the revisionists think the muckrakers' efforts were detrimental to the general welfare. The consensus remains that this was a dangerous epoch in the nation's life which should never be repeated. Even Allan Nevins, a most prolific historian, writing for *Life* in January, 1950, confessed that "It was not a just or good society and there are statistics and men to prove it was not."

Similarly, much remained deplorable in cultural matters. Senator Henry W. Blair of New Hampshire filled large sections of the *Congressional Record* in 1890 with his concern for education. He cited census returns proving one-third of the children in the United States were growing up without schooling. In 1890, six million Huckleberry Finns were not enrolled in school, in 1900 the figure reached nine million. In Oakland, 26 percent of the children were out of school, in San Francisco, 29 percent; Jacksonville, 42 percent; Chicago, 43 percent; and Milwaukee 55 percent. Among adults, six million could neither read nor write. In fact, the colonists in 1776 were twice as literate as the population in 1890. Blair urged the appropriation of ten million dollars of federal funds to help build 120,000 rural schools costing $300 each. Since teachers' salaries were a national disgrace, he called for governmental aid for this purpose. All proposals died because most Congressmen believed such assistance would kill initiative and destroy character.

Medical standards likewise needed improvement. At the turn of the century the life expectancy was only 48 years. Quack medicine flourished with Sears, Roebuck selling the following nostrums: Dr. Rowland's lung restorer, Dr. Betz's worm syrup, Dr. Rose's Arsenic Complex Wafers for radiant complexions, and Dr. Pasteur's "Death to Microbes," guaranteed to cure tuberculosis, rheumatism, shingles, hives, malaria, blood poisoning, catarrh, and opium addiction.

Many suffered ill health because of dietary problems resulting from urbanization. Farmers usually ate a heavy diet rich in bacon, molasses, fried potatoes, pork, and pancakes. In moving to town, folks took their eating habits with them. The greasy food without rigorous exercise led to indigestion, dyspepsia, and various kinds of stomach trouble. Many plagued by this gastro-nomical difficulty went to consult the Mayo brothers at Rochester, Minnesota, who had gained fame as daring surgeons with a particular skill in performing abdominal operations. They did 54 of these in 1885, 612 in 1900, and 2,157 in 1905. Their reputation merited the compliment, "Dr. Will is a wonderful surgeon; Dr. Charles is a surgical wonder."

Another solution to the "national bellyache" called for a visit to the health sanatoriums at Battle Creek, Michigan. Following the Civil War, the Adventists led a crusade to end piggery by encouraging vegetarianism. Sanatoriums were built in Battle Creek specializing in baths, massages, and health diets. Dr. John Harvey Kellogg, while working in one of these sanatoriums, produced the first pre-cooked flaked cereal health food in 1894. In the same year, C. W. Post concocted a cereal coffee called Postum designed to produce red blood. By accident both men discovered they could sell their health foods to the general public, thus opening the way for a breakfast food business which was to reach 400 million in 1956—a revolution in the eating habits of the American people.

In some respects the 1890's became the most vicious in our history. In 1892, 231 people were lynched. During the decade, 1,540 victims met the same fate, the highest totals for any decade during the last century. Frenzied mobs participated in these nauseating crimes where the scaffold, the noose, and the burning pyre silenced the shrieks of the condemned. At times the charges were as minor as slander, wife beating, swindling, fraud, refusing to give evidence, or writing insulting letters. Lynch leaders prided themselves on their work, often posing for pictures at the scene of death. While Americans mouthed religion, these miscarriages of justice continued with disgusting regularity. To those trapped in the extralegal proceedings, the 90's were not very gay.

Furthermore, social conditions gave little cause for ecstasy. Booker T. Washington in 1900 stated that not more than one Negro in twenty owned the land he cultivated. Jacob Riis, investigating conditions in lower New York City, mordantly announced, "The slum is the measure of civilization." Robert Hunter, the sociologist, in 1904 reported ten million of the nation's 83 million people living in poverty. Joseph Kirkland, looking at Chicago in 1892 said, "It is hard to imagine just how filthy, how squalid, how noisome, how abhorrent it all is." Jane Addams counted 55 saloons in her ward in the same city, one for every 28 voters. Rudyard Kipling after viewing the Windy City in 1899 called the place a splendid chaos. He explained, "Having seen it, I urgently desire never to see it again."

Over all hung a cloud of jingoistic chauvinism fed by men like Senator Albert J. Beveridge, who claimed God had marked the Americans as a chosen people—a master race to lead in the regeneration of the world. Cabot Lodge urged the annexation of Canada because it was the tendency to consolidate and small nations were a thing of the past. One imperialist suggested that statesmanship was the art of seeing where God was going and then getting things out of His way.

Then too, intolerance, bigotry, anti-intellectualism, and reactionary thought abounded. Peter Viereck described the 90's as seething in xenophobia, Jew baiting, intellectual baiting, thought control, lynch spirit, negrophobia, and anti-Catholicism. Reformers succumbed to militant reactionaries who dominated the social and economic welfare of millions. Senator Joseph H. Choate called the income tax the beginnings of socialism, communism, and the destruction of the Constitution itself. Apparently the Supreme Court concurred, for it declared such a law unconstitutional in 1894. In the *Plessy v. Ferguson* case in 1896, the Court enunciated the "separate but equal" decision to sanctify segregation in the Southern states. Theodore Roosevelt, as Police Commissioner of New York, called the Populists subversives and recommended their top twelve leaders be "shot dead against a wall." Senator George F. Hoar lectured the members of the American Historical Association in 1895 asking them to refrain from criticizing public officials. Since all politicians were honest and upright, historians should spend their time defending the heroes of representative government. When women demanded the vote to help eliminate the graft in politics, critics hollered socialism. A minister sourly intoned that since all women looked alike, universal suffrage would lead to multiple voting. Ex-president Grover Cleveland insisted that sensible women did not want to vote and Father Vaughan of Boston thought those who did were "jackasses."

If the 1890's were less gay than commonly believed, there may also be less validity in the long-accepted belief that all Americans at the end of the nineteenth century were imbued with glowing optimism and a confirmed faith in progress. Obviously there is evidence to support the inevitable progress theme. Darwinian principles were applied to the social order by Herbert Spencer and reaffirmed by William Sumner, Andrew Carnegie, John Fiske, and others. Reverend Newell D. Hollis in 1900 preached that laws were more just, rulers more humane, music sweeter, and books wiser. He asserted, "Art, industry, invention, literature, learning and government all are marching in Christ's triumphal procession up the hill of fame." H. G. Wells in 1906 said our national temper reflected a sort of optimistic fatalism.

However, some Americans doubted the faith in progress thesis. Frederick Jackson Turner reading his paper, "The Significance of the Frontier in American History," at the meeting of the American Historical Association in Chicago in 1893, suggested the end of free land had closed the frontier, thus terminating a 400-year span of unlimited opportunity. All this implied a less hopeful future.

In like vein, H. D. Sedgwick, writing for *The Atlantic Monthly* in 1902, protested the superficiality, the conformity, the vulgar tastes, and the low standards of morality in American life. An industrialized society squeezed everyone into the same mold. Since materialism denoted the chief duty of man, dogmas grew, developed, and petrified. Men of great vigor appeared but good manners and gracious behavior declined. The United States had retrogressed.

Look at our religion, read our poetry, witness our national joy in papier mâché arches and Dewey celebrations. Our morals are cribbed and confined . . . our poets express trepidity and lassitude. Look at our Christianity. We honor riches, oppress our neighbors and keep a pecuniary account with righteousness.

The editor, Albert Bushnell Hart, in 1898 thought Americans were ignorant of their own past while Brooks Adams believed the whole world was rotting. Henry Adams beheld a doleful society, not much hurt, but like a cow before a railroad locomotive, somewhat discouraged. He concluded in 1895 that politics, religion, and statistics had led to nothing. Congressmen were disorganized, stupid, and childlike. In Cuba we were beaten and hopeless. Education had proved futile and one had just as well try to educate a gravel pit. Above all nothing could be more tiresome than a superannuated pedagogue. Indeed, our so-called civilization was likely to disintegrate. E. L. Godkin said he came to America with high ideals but they were all shattered, forcing him to look elsewhere for even moderate hopes about keeping the human race alive. Thorstein Veblen in *Theory of the Leisure Class*, published in 1899, claimed the capitalistic system retarded progress because the wealthy resisted change while the poor worked so hard to make a living that they had no energy left to strive for progress. The middle class remained too small to initiate progressive policies. Veblen, in criticizing the vulgarity of the 90's, insisted that the backs of buildings were more attractive than the fronts. He joined Greenough and Sullivan in the hope that form would follow function. Henry George's *Progress and Poverty* pictured capitalism widening the gap between the rich and poor. Although tax revision might prove beneficial, the author rejected the Spencer-Sumner formula of automatic, evolutionary progress. In *Looking Backward,* Edward Bellamy envisioned Utopia, but prophesied its arrival by way of improved technology and the government ownership of the means of production. In fact, Bellamy, writing for the *North American Review* in 1890, quoted the French economist Emil de Loveley as saying Bellamy had proved that the optimism of the old-fashioned economists had lost its authority. People no longer believed in the laissez-faire principle in which everything would arrange itself for the best in the best of all possible worlds. The good things were not divided according to the laws of justice and discontent grew more profound.

In addition, those who accepted orthodox religious views were skeptical about society being on an escalator in an ever-improving universe. Leather-lunged evangelical preachers stressed the sinful nature of men who had been conceived in iniquity and born in sin. All like sheep had gone astray and would continue to do so. Dwight L. Moody, Gypsy Smith, and Sam Jones traversed the land propounding the old-time religion and exhorting the repentant to hit the sawdust trail. Hope resided in salvation and good works, but straight was the way and narrow the gate leading to glory and broad the way leading to destruction. Thus only a remnant would be saved, leaving the majority floundering down the slippery road to perdition. Then too, *Revelation* as a prophetic book depicted a future afflicted with wars and rumors of war, earthquakes, pestilence, and the nefarious antics of the Anti-Christ. Evil would multiply until the universe plunged into the fiery battle of Armageddon—a view diametrically opposed to the faith in progress theory. The conservative religionists in the rural regions and small towns tended to reject evolution either because they had never heard of Darwin or else because they could not accept the notion that man emerged from lower forms of life. Numerically, this bloc remained strong, forming the backbone of the Fundamentalist movement in the 1920's.

Likewise, opposition to progress characterized the thinking of most agrarians who believed the migration of rural youth to the wicked city led to moral degradation. Farm journals begged young people to stay on the old homestead. *The Nebraska Farmer* in 1900 warned that city slickers loafing on city streets would lure country boys into saloons and gambling dens where they would hurtle down the slippery road of ruin as fast as the wheels of destruction could carry them. Even James Bryce, speaking at the University of California in Berkeley where he received the third honorary degree granted by the university, spoke of the ideal rural life where there was plenty of fresh air and healthy exercise. Farmers gave stability to political life because they were less excitable than city people cooped up on the crowded streets. He repeated the tired cliche, "God made the country and man made the town." Since the rise of the city seemed inevitable, progress in terms of morality seemed to be on the skids.

In retrospect, the 1890s were years of rapid change brought on by accelerated industrialization, urbanization, and technological innovation. How could the ethics of an individualistic, agrarian America be applied to an increasingly highly integrated social order? Could new techniques in social engineering cope with the rise of cities? Could wealth be distributed more equitably? How could dirty politics be reformed? From this maelstrom many were flexible enough to land on their feet; others became confused, discouraged, and filled with pessimism. Mark Twain had plenty of evidence to reinforce his growing qualms about society in his later years.

Perhaps it is impossible to prove that the 90's were less gay than other decades in our history because national sentiment is virtually impossible to measure accurately. Scholars lack the techniques with which to make quantitative judgments about the thoughts of millions of people living . . . years ago. Too often the views of a few are taken as representative of all society. Nor need the voices of the erudite reflect the ideas of the multitudes. The tendency to oversimplify the past becomes a formidable temptation. It can be argued that the most significant contribution that experts can make over the long pull is to demonstrate that the patterns of human behavior fluctuate less violently than commonly supposed. We may ultimately reach the position of the famous Arnold Toynbee, who, after a lifetime of study of the world's civilizations, concluded that "history proves that life is just one damn thing after another."

Victorian Sexuality: Can Historians Do It Better?

Carol Z. Stearns and Peter N. Stearns

A major emphasis of recent historical studies has been what has come to be called the "new social history." Its principal task has been to uncover and illuminate largely ignored aspects of the nation's social life—especially those formerly sequestered regions often referred to as the "underside" or "private side" of American history. Representative of this attempt to stand conventional history on its head, to view history from the bottom up, is the renewed interest in the history of women, minorities, the poor, the habitually disempowered and disadvantaged, and formerly taboo topics such as insanity and human sexuality. Regarding the last of these, Carol Z. Stearns of the Western Psychiatric Institute and Peter N. Stearns of Carnegie-Mellon University offer a reevaluation of Victorian sexuality—especially as revealed in the now-famous Stanford University Mosher survey. Antedating the more famous Kinsey Report and the era of Masters and Johnson, the Mosher study—conducted from 1892 to 1920 but not widely published until 1980—as initially interpreted by historians in both the United States and Europe (primarily Carl Degler and Peter Gay) strongly suggested a need to dismiss the myth that "Victorianism" is properly synonymous with moral severity, middle-class stuffiness, and pompous conservatism in sexual matters. Allegedly, "God's frozen people"—Victorians both here and abroad—were far more sexually liberated and progressive than formerly supposed. They courted sexual experience and found intercourse and orgasm not disgusting but rather normal in the course of human events. Stearns and Stearns, however, beg to differ, shifting the emphasis on this issue back in the direction of the conventional, allegedly "mythical" view of Victorianism. Claiming the Mosher survey was not truly representative, and granting the power of the then conventional wisdom conveyed in prescriptive literature that female sexuality was "abnormal," they conclude that the Victorian reputation for repression and prudery and the Victorian legacy of circumspect sexual behavior are, after all, rather well deserved.

Starting with Carl Degler's path-breaking article in the *American Historical Review* in 1974, and following with the publication of the now widely cited Mosher report, in 1980, we have been told that Victorian women, far from being revolted or frightened by sex, took it as a normal and pleasurable part of married life and were often orgasmic. Most recently the sexual revisionists have been joined by Peter Gay, who in his *The Bourgeois Experience, Victoria to Freud, Education of the Senses,* uses the material from the Mosher report and adds compelling corroboration from the diary of Mabel Loomis Todd. This lady, who recorded her sexual encounters with a shorthand that includes notation for orgasms, enjoyed a heady and successful relationship for many years with her husband, and then went on to employ the same sexual athleticism in a long-lasting affair with Austin Dickinson, Emily's brother.

The Mosher report, unpublished in Mosher's own time, was the result of a survey by a female physician on the sexuality of her compeers. Based on questionnaires answered by 45 women, 70% born before 1870, the forms were completed between 1892 and 1920. Most of those who answered were upper middle class college graduates, and as such not necessarily typical of Victorian females. The fact that they replied to the survey at all also suggests that they may not have been typical. Still, neither Degler nor Gay is naive, and they are far from making the claim that all Victorian women had a great time in bed. Nonetheless, they are both asking us, on the basis of just the type of evidence we have cited, to revise our views of Victorian female sexuality. Thus, Degler:

> A frank and sometimes enthusiastic acceptance of sexual relations was the response from most of the women . . . [intercourse was seen as part] of healthy living and frequently a joy . . . the great majority of them . . . experienced orgasm as well as sexual desire.

And thus again, Gay:

> The answers Dr. Mosher elicited carry conviction and have a meaning beyond the group of forty-five . . . they have the authenticity of awkwardness. Their artless and earnest candor is a clue to desires and fulfillments of which they were only partially aware . . . it is congruent with other, more informal testimony . . . Mabel Todd, in short, spoke for a substantial population of married middle-class women.

Degler read Mosher to say that 35% of the respondents usually or always had orgasms in intercourse, and another 40% sometimes did. Gay reads this to mean that a third almost always did and another 40% were only marginally less satisfied.

Neither Gay nor Degler dismisses all traces of a distinctive Victorianism. Degler notes, from Mosher, the women who had to abstain from sex during periods when conception could not be risked. Gay rather approvingly discusses the hypocrisy of Victorian culture, which said one thing about sex while doing another. But both interpretations present actual sexual behavior and values in a strikingly modern guise. It would be easy, reading them, to assume that Victorianism barely existed, describing nineteenth-century sexuality no more than, say, papal pronouncements describe the birth control attitudes and practices of contemporary American Catholics.

For the most part, the response of the historical community to this revisionist view has been favorable. To be sure, the new interpretation is still ignored by those who enjoy using Victorianism as a foil for a critique of modern males and modern medicine. But few critics have actually attacked the central findings about middle-class sexual behavior. There are several reasons for this. Historians learned some time ago that Victorianism was not as pervasive as once believed. It never described mainstream working-class sexuality during most of the nineteenth century, and indeed was partly directed at some fairly accurate perceptions of working-class indulgence in premarital sex and rising rates (to 1870) of illegitimacy. It does not come as a total surprise, then, to find the Victorian code even less descriptive than this first modification allowed.

And historians do like revisions. We may have grown bored with the stereotype of uptight Victorians and open to a newer and hence more interesting stereotype. Some implicit dismay about contemporary sexuality, which derives part of its justification from ringing attacks on Victorian prudery (see Gay Talese for a recent example), may also fuel the revision. A statement that Victorians were, in the main, sexually healthy might restrain contemporary penchants for sexual experimentation. Certainly it is a useful corrective for some exaggerations to know that Victorianism was partly invented in order to make twentieth-century sexual achievements look good. Scholars like Carl Degler, sympathetic to feminism, may have been uncomfortable with the notion that female sexuality could have been so totally annihilated by a repressive culture as historians like Cominos had claimed. Or a Freudian true believer like Gay can enjoy the idea that biology or anatomy, even female biology/anatomy, must override culture; certainly a large portion of Gay's particular interpretation rests on assumptions of psychological constants such that history, rather than seriously testing a particular theory, must simply confirm it.

But, however attractive, revisionism often goes too far. In this case, we believe that significant interpretive problems remain which have not yet been addressed with any seriousness. It is amusing to reverse images, and we would certainly agree that some modification of the older conventions is now essential. But several problems remain, before we abandon Victorianism as an ill-tempered artifact.

Three avenues of inquiry tend to shed some doubt on the idea of the sexy middle-class Victorian. One, most obvious, is the evidence that Gay has chosen to ignore, and Degler to minimize, about Victorian preachments. Two, which follows in part, is what we know or suspect about the way children's sexuality is socially influenced. Three is the accumulated wisdom we have about rates of sexual dissatisfaction among contemporary women, which raises vital questions about the relationship between nineteenth-century sexuality and more recent trends. Let us examine each of these areas.

First we have the problem of the massive literature the Victorians published on the lack of female sexuality. These views were not buried in academic treatises or even medical journals; they entered into popular manuals, magazines and fiction. Female sexuality was seen by many Victorian physicians, clergymen and novelists as abnormal. To be sure, Acton himself, the most noted proponent of the asexual view of women, has been overquoted. Degler and Gay discuss authors such as Dr. George H. Napheys and Dr. Elizabeth Blackwell who believed quite differently, arguing that female sexuality was normal and expected. A large middle ground embraced authorities who admitted the possibility of female sexual pleasure but found the female sex drive, nevertheless, much less vigorous than the male, and usefully so in keeping sexuality within proper bounds. In sum, the Actonites themselves were hardly silent, and their views were echoed in part by a still larger group. Without pretending to know exactly which school of thought was most popular, it is fair to note that the few who really undertook a more radical view of female sexuality knew full well that they were bucking the mainstream. So if we are going to revise our views of Victorian female sexuality, we need to explain how it was that a substantial literature existed which denied that the sexuality existed, supplemented by other works which were only slightly less extreme in judging women's sexual needs. What was the function of this literature in its culture? . . .

Victorian views on sexuality—if not always rigorously Actonite—certainly went beyond intellectual discourse alone. They affected, indeed largely determined, longstanding legislation on censorship and the publicity of birth control, both of which could influence actual sexual behavior. And a similar Victorianism pervaded middle-class childrearing, such that well into the twentieth century school authorities, listing problems with female charges, attended to sexual issues above all. During the Victorian period itself, we still have every reason to believe that girls were taught about the horrors of masturbation, frightened about bodily functions such as menstruation, and denied frank discussions about female anatomy and the prerequisites of sexual satisfaction. And we have every reason to believe that this childrearing style is a good way to inhibit the enjoyment of adult sexuality. Degler and Gay give us no indication that they challenge the historical wisdom in this area, which is that Victorian girls would have been forcibly corrected if caught fondling themselves; that they would not have been encouraged to examined their own bodies or to discuss the sexual functions of their own bodies; that nobody would have taught them about the pleasures or necessity of foreplay. In helping women who are sexually dysfunctional today, Masters and Johnson and others have stressed the importance of undoing just these Victorian deficiencies. Self-examination of the female organs, then masturbation and learning to reach orgasm are now seen as important way stations toward orgasmic satisfaction with a partner. How did Victorian women manage to function so well when they were forbidden from childhood to do exactly what we think women need to do in order to function well today? If Degler and Gay know, they certainly do not explain.

Finally, there is the issue of the ongoing problem of female sexuality even in our own more open society—an issue easy enough to understand if we assume a genuine Victorian legacy in childrearing, but far harder if we are to believe in widespread female satisfaction a century ago. Shere Hite gained national attention in 1976 by claiming that more than two thirds of married women never achieve orgasm with sexual intercourse alone, and by recounting the great difficulty with which many others managed to achieve that potential for pleasure. Hite was widely criticized for taking a sample of women who had a complaint to typify all women, and in fact her problem was not unlike that of Dr. Mosher years earlier: how do we know if the women who answer a survey are typical of women in general? But in the contemporary case, more scientifically organized inquiries into the question of female orgasmic dysfunction have produced startling results not dissimilar to those of Hite. Three University of Pittsburgh researchers inquired about sexual function from 100 predominantly white, well-educated couples defining themselves as happily married. The questions relating to sexual adjustment were a small part of a large questionnaire covering many aspects of marriage. The project was specifically designed so as to avoid selecting for those who had a particular sexual axe to grind, as Hite's respondents may have had. This study, published in the *New England Journal of Medicine* in 1978, revealed that 46% of the women had difficulty, and an additional 15% reported a complete inability to have an orgasm—in total 63% reporting some difficulty with orgasm. Since these researchers did not discuss the method used to reach orgasm, it is possible that those who easily attained orgasm with intercourse alone may have been even fewer than the remaining 37%. In short, although disagreeing on the importance of sexual difficulties in marriage, this scientific study was in substantial accord with Hite's findings on the specific subject of the statistics of orgasmic achievement.

Obviously, this accord, juxtaposed with the new reading of the Victorian experience, raises fascinating interpretive problems. For women, at least, the twentieth century becomes not even a tentative step forward, but a massive regression in terms of sexual pleasure and orgasmic ability. Here is a reversal, not only of standard teachings about Victorianism, but of successive twentieth-century proclamations of sexual revolution or at least increasing sexual freedom, stretching from the Bloomer girls of the late nineteenth century to the flappers to the premarital adepts among middle-class girls of the 1960s. Could it really be true that for all our hype about the sexual revolution, and the undeniable improvements in middle-class birth control knowledge and technology, the female majority, at least, is less orgasmic than their Victorian great-grandmothers? The prospect is worth considering, if only because of excessive brainwashing about our sexual prowess today. It can feed some recent feminist complaints that the current sexual revolution is actually male-dominated, for all the public concern about greater equality of pleasure. And the possibility of a sexual reversal, as against our ingrained expectations of progress in this area at least, is genuine; it cannot be dismissed out of hand. But possibility does not make certainty; the problem must be discussed, particularly in light of the undeniably different sexual culture and probably somewhat different socialization of the Victorian period. It is odd and unsatisfactory that the historians who have rediscovered Victorian sexuality not only have not offered a plausible interpretation of the Victorian-contemporary relationship, but do not seem to have noticed what a strange problem they have created for our understanding of ourselves. . . .

Without pretending to have all the answers to the new questions raised about Victorian sexuality, we do confess some hesitation in totally reversing the commonplace assumptions about the contemporary relationship to past sexuality. And there are two other, possibly related ways to deal with the Victorian evidence.

One approach to the newly discussed sources, particularly the Mosher report, is to question that these women meant the same thing we do when they talked about orgasm. In our reading of Mosher, of those who say they "always" had an orgasm, we find more than half (10/18) difficult to take at face value. We doubt that these women mean the same thing modern women mean by orgasm when we find that they consistently wish for a lower frequency of sex, are skeptical that pleasure is an important part of the sexual relationship, and are either silent or strikingly unenthusiastic in describing how orgasm makes them feel. We know that many of Hite's women report being uncertain as to what an orgasm is and are often confused as to whether they have had one or not. Seymour Fisher also attested to the great variety of experience which is actually encompassed when women use the word orgasm. It is clear that Mosher's respondents were trained to think of sex as part of a total marital experience, and that it was very important to them to view that marital experience as satisfactory. We wonder, then, if they did not overestimate rather than underestimate in their claims to orgasm. Their precision may also have been hampered by embarrassment at dealing with sexuality at all openly, even though their survey participation was voluntary.

What we can surmise about Victorian sexual practices is certainly in accord with our doubts. Marriage manuals and childhood training would certainly have prepared neither husband nor wife to think in terms of lengthy foreplay and clitoral stimulation, especially during the act of coitus. (Interestingly, even doctors daringly interested in female orgasm seemed confused about the functioning of the clitoris.) How can it be that Hite's subjects so often have needed clitoral stimulation during coitus, while Mosher's, reporting no concomitant clitoral stimulation, had less difficulty? Interestingly enough, those few of Mosher's subjects who do discuss the need for foreplay or difficulties of timing, also seem more frank in answering that they don't "always" but do "sometimes" reach orgasm. They also seem to have more to say about what an orgasm does for them than those who claim "perfect" satisfaction.

It is unpleasant to assume the role of sexual interrogator to the Mosher women, but one cannot help wondering if there was not a self-deluding quality in some of their responses. There is always reason for skepticism about what people say about themselves on surveys, and Degler and Gay have been surprisingly naive in their reading of this one, admittedly fascinating, Victorian approximation of survey data. . . .

A note of caution must assuredly be introduced into the "new" interpretation of Victorian sexuality, and more complicated questions explored than have been undertaken to date. Victorian culture cannot be dismissed too lightly. It had purpose, not only as a lament against modernity (which it was for some advocates), but also an encouragement to birth control and a protest against lower-class behavior patterns. The impact of prescriptive literature—

repressive in the Victorian period, permissive and sometimes even erotic during the past three decades—poses a difficult interpretive problem, but one that must be faced. If it is true that early histories of Victorianism simplified the prescriptive literature and took it too much at face value, scholars like Gay and Degler have gone too far in the other direction. In fact, we know that prescriptions had real impact on some individuals, like the Frenchwoman described by Theodore Zeldin who tried to divorce her husband for seemingly modest sexual advances, or the many parents who punished masturbation. The Mosher report certainly suggests that the number of middle-class women who took Victorianism literally may have been limited. But we argue that it also suggests that, compared to contemporary expectations of orgasm, the attitudes of most such women also incorporated a large slice of modified Victorianism, which made them look at their sexual experience in distinctive ways. To be sure, another minority undoubtedly defied Victorianism altogether, and wrote diaries to prove it. But the most interesting group, the complex majority, must be sought with subtlety, through evidence that includes prescriptive advice and socialization, evaluative language as well as apparently measurable experience.

Myths of Progressivism and the 1920s

America is everywhere. For an isolationist nation it is remarkable how she gets about.
Edward Crankshaw, *Russia and the Russians*

France was a land, England was a people, but America, having about it still the quality of the idea, was harder to utter. . . . It was a willingness of the heart. . . .
F. Scott Fitzgerald

Our country—this great republic—means nothing unless it means the triumph of a real democracy, the triumph of popular government, and, in the long run, of an economic system under which each man shall be guaranteed the opportunity to show the best that there is in him. That is why the history of America is now the central feature of the history of the world; for the world has set its face hopefully toward our democracy; and, O my fellow citizens, each one of you carries on your shoulders not only the burden of doing well for the sake of your own country, but the burden of doing well and of seeing that this nation does well for the sake of mankind.
Theodore Roosevelt, *Speech at Osawatomie, Kansas (August 31, 1910)*

Teddy Roosevelt: the progressive pioneer. [The Bettmann Archive.]

FROM THE DEPTHS

"From the Depths": the progressive paradox. [William Balfour-Ker, *From the Depths* (1906). Reproduced from the collections of the Library of Congress.]

*T*he study of United States history is in a constant state of revision. Those ubiquitous revisionists among American historians have been particularly active since the end of World War II. Almost every historical personage, event, topic, or chronological period has come in for some sort of reinterpretation; many revisionists have lived to be revised—even by themselves.

One of the major twentieth-century revisions deals with the subject of progressivism. Once considered rather easily definable, "progressives" were simply all those who, philosophically or actively, sought reform during the early part of the twentieth century. Within the last twenty-five years, however, historians have seen the necessity of reworking this definition. Perhaps the earlier definition was too simplistic, too all-inclusive; perhaps not all progressives supported every reform. Thus a southern progressive might not get exercised over civil rights reform; a midwestern rural progressive might lack a burning impulse to get involved in ghetto reform on New York's Lower East Side. Perhaps the historian should approach the subject with a little more caution, recognize the diversity and complexity of progressivism, delineate and analyze the various progressive groups, and still be prepared for much irony and paradox.

Largely as a result of its complexity, irony, and paradox, the progressive period is richly laden with myth. One of the chief reasons is that during the progressive era, more than in any previous period in American history, the development of myth was aided and abetted by professional historians themselves. At times, one might argue, they acted as the movement's high priests—at intervals announcing total victory for their ideology. Indeed at one point, many historians heralded the arrival of a "New Republic" by their contributions to a nascent magazine of that name.

The study of the progressive period necessarily becomes involved in myth as one attempts to find out who the progressives really were and to focus on their central areas of action. And one must attempt to understand and demythologize the two major brands of progressivism—the New Nationalism and the New Freedom—along with their chief proponents, Theodore Roosevelt and Woodrow Wilson. One must come to grips with the issue of progressivism as a movement reformist or conservative in nature. A body of myths has also grown up concerning the progressives and their relation to imperialism, and certainly around Woodrow Wilson, the president who is thought to have arrived at a synthesis of the New Nationalism and the New Freedom. Issues surrounding the United States' entry into World War I and Wilson's role in it have also provided fertile ground for distortion and myth. In addition, feminism and the life span of progressivism have been popular subjects for mythmakers. Did progressivism die with the close of the Great War, or did it live on into the 1920s and even beyond, albeit in a somewhat altered form? Further, how were the myths of the decade reflected in the concept of the melting pot and in its heroes, and how complete was the nation's isolation in the 1920s? Is it possible to see the decade as one of more, rather than less, involvement in foreign affairs?

Answers to these questions, which take into account the body of myths surrounding them, will lead to a clearer understanding of progressivism and the 1920s.

The Progressive Profile

George E. Mowry

A writer of history is always tempted to make his rendition a story of elites in which only the most visible, the most articulate, or the most powerful are given adequate representation. Of course, such a tendency provides a climate ripe for the development of myth and a one-dimensional view of the past in which simplicity supplants complexity. It remains the province of the historian, then, to counter myth and to draw a fair representational view of the past. Such an unbiased cross-sectional treatment is afforded by George E. Mowry's progressive profile. The late Professor Mowry of the University of North Carolina, Greensboro, is perhaps the best-known historian of progressivism. Here, he isolates the essential ideas and assumptions of progressivism yet demonstrates its ambivalence and paradox. Progressivism was not an exercise in conformity. Its essence was its great complexity.

As a group, the reform mayors and governors, their prominent supporters, and the muckrakers were an interesting lot. Considering the positions they held, they were very young. Joseph W. Folk was only thirty-five when elected governor, Theodore Roosevelt forty, Charles Evans Hughes and Hiram Johnson forty-four, and Robert La Follette forty-five. The average age of the important progressive leaders who upset the Southern Pacific Railroad machine in California was a little over thirty-eight. The tale of a rather typical young reformer was that of Joseph Medill Patterson of the Chicago *Tribune* family. Patterson's grandfather founded the *Tribune*, his father was general manager of the paper, and his cousin was Robert McCormick, who controlled the paper for over thirty years. Patterson sharply reacted against the reigning conservatism by winning a seat in the Illinois legislature at the age of twenty-four on a platform advocating the municipal ownership of all city utilities in the state. Two years later he resigned from the Chicago Commission of Public Works to become a Socialist because, he announced, it was impossible to reform the city and the country under capitalism. In 1906 he published a diatribe against wealth in the *Independent* entitled "The Confessions of a Drone," and followed it two years later with a book of similar tone. Obviously, this was a period, like the ones after the War of 1812 and in the 1850's, when energetic and incautious youth took command. And in each instance the departure of the elder statesmen portended great changes.

Some of these reformers, like Golden Rule Jones, Charles Evans Hughes, and Tom Johnson, were self-made men, although Hughes's father was a minister, and Johnson's, a Confederate colonel, had come from the upper stratum of Kentucky society. A surprising number of them came from very wealthy families, with names like du Pont, Crane, Spreckels, Dodge, Morgenthau, Pinchot, Perkins, McCormick, and Patterson. The quip was made that this was a "millionaire's reform movement." But the great majority of the reformers came from the "solid middle class," as it then was called with some pride. That their families had been of the economically secure is indicated by the fact that most of them had had a college education in a day when a degree stamped a person as coming from a special economic group. It is interesting to note that most of the women reformers and social workers had gone to college. Occupationally also the reformers came from a very narrow base in society. Of a sample of over four hundred a majority were lawyers, as might be expected of politicians, and nearly 20 percent of them newspaper editors or publishers. The next largest group was from the independent manufacturers or merchants, with the rest scattered among varied occupations, including medicine, banking, and real estate. A statistical study of sixty of the wealthier reformers reveals that the largest single group of twenty-one were manufacturers or merchants, ten lawyers, six newspaper publishers, while nineteen more had inherited their wealth. Quite a few among the latter group had no definite occupation save that of preserving their family fortune and indulging in reform. Of the sixty only about half attended college, a figure much lower than that for the entire group of reformers. Of this number just 50 percent came from three institutions, Harvard, Princeton, and Yale.

If names mean anything, an overwhelming proportion of this reform group came from old American stock with British origins consistently indicated. Except for the women, who were predominantly Midwestern, the reformers' places of origin were scattered over the country roughly in proportion to population densities. Practically all of them by 1900, however, lived in northern cities, most of the Southerners having left their section during early manhood. Religious affiliations were surprisingly difficult to get, and no really trustworthy national sample was obtained. The figures collected were not all consonant with national church membership statistics. Representatives of the Quaker faith bulked large among the women reformers, as did members of the Jewish religion among the very wealthy. But for the group as a whole the religious descendants of Calvin and Knox predominated, with the Congregationalists, Unitarians, and Presbyterians in the vast majority. Thus it seems likely that the intellectual and religious influence of New England was again dominating the land.

Whether Democrats or Republicans, the overwhelming number of this group of twentieth-century reformers had been conservatives in the nineties. If Republican, they had almost to a man followed the way of Theodore Roosevelt, Robert La Follette, Lincoln Steffens, and William Allen White to support William McKinley. Most of the progressive Democrats had been supporters of Bryan, but, like Woodrow Wilson, Tom Johnson, and Hoke Smith of Georgia, had either followed the Gold Democratic ticket or had remained silent during the election of 1896. Yet from four to six years later most of these men were ardent advocates of municipal gas and water socialism, and were opposed to their regular party machines to the extent of leading either nonpartisan movements in the municipalities or rebellious splinter groups in the states. Moreover, the new century found most of them, except on the currency issue, supporting many of the 1896 Populist and Bryanite demands. Before the Progressive years were finished they and their kind had not only secured the inception of a host of the Populists' reforms, but had contributed a few of their own.

Obviously, a good many questions arise about the motivation of this economically secure, well-educated, middle-class group. On the surface it looked as if the progressive movement was simply a continuation, under different leadership, of the Populist cause. According to William Allen White, Populism had "shaved its whiskers, washed its shirt, put on a derby, and moved up into the middle class. . . ." But White's remark scarcely probed beneath the surface. Populism arose from farmer distress in a period of acute depression. Its reforms were belly reforms. The movement was led by angry men and women not too far removed from the Grange hall. Except for the western silver men, they were incensed at the mounting figures of farm foreclosures and a withering countryside. To the contrary, progressivism arose in a period of relative prosperity. Its reforms were more the results of the heart and the head than of the stomach. Its leaders were largely recruited from the professional and business classes of the city. A good many were wealthy men; more were college graduates. As a group they were indignant at times, but scarcely ever angry. What caused them to act in the peculiar way they did? A part of the answer lies in the peculiar economic and social position in which this middle-class group found itself at about the turn of the century, a part in the intellectual and ethical climate of the age, a part in the significant cluster of prejudices and biases that marked the progressive mind.

"The world wants men, great, strong, harsh, brutal men—men with purpose who let nothing, nothing, nothing stand in their way," Frank Norris wrote in one of his novels. This worship of the strong man, so characteristic of the age, produced a cult of political leadership with ominous overtones for later years. Tempered at this time with the ethics of the social gospel, the cult produced an image far less frightening: an image of men dedicated to the social good, an image approximating the hope of Plato for his guardians. These strong good men, "the changemakers," Harold Frederic wrote, were the protectors of morality, the originators of progress. They were ambitious men and ruthless, but only ruthless in their zeal for human advancement. They were supremely alone, the causative individuals. Far from being disturbed when isolated, David Graham Phillips's hero Scarborough was only concerned when he was "propped up" by something other than his own will and intelligence. "I propose," he commented, "never to 'belong' to anything or anybody."

In 1872 a future progressive, Henry Demarest Lloyd, confessed that he wanted power above all things, but "power unpoisoned by the presence of obligation." That worship of the unfettered individual, the strong pride of self, the strain of ambition, and the almost compulsive desire for power ran through progressive rhetoric like a theme in a symphony. From Frank Norris's strong-minded heroes to Richard Harding Davis's men of almost pure muscle these feelings were a badge of a restless, sensitive, and troubled class. They were never far below the surface in the character of Theodore Roosevelt. Robert La Follette knew them, and Woodrow Wilson had more than his share of them. While still a scholar and teacher, Wilson poured out his frustration with the contemplative life: "I have no patience with the tedious world of what is known as 'research,' " he wrote to a friend. "I should be complete if I could inspire a great movement of opinion. . . ."

A few progressive leaders like William Jennings Bryan and Golden Rule Jones really thought of themselves as servants of the people, and almost completely identified themselves with their constituents. But most progressives set themselves apart from the crowd. Mankind was basically good and capable of progress, but benign change scarcely issued from the masses. Rather it was only accomplished through the instrumentality of a few great and good men. Woodrow Wilson believed that efficient government could come only from "an educated elite," William Kent thought that progress never came from the bottom, and Roosevelt often spoke of government as the process of "giving justice from above." Occasionally, when the electorate disagreed with them, the progressives contented themselves with the thought that truth "was always in the minority" and a possession alone of the "few who see." In 1912 Walter Lippmann wrote that since men could do anything but govern themselves, they were constantly looking for some "benevolent guardian." To the progressive politician that guardian, of course, was patterned after his image of himself.

"I am so sick of fraud and filth and lies," David Graham Phillips plaintively wrote to Senator Beveridge in 1902, "so tired of stern realities. I grasp at myths like a child." The myths Phillips reached for were the supposed realities of an older day, a day when the individual presumably had been able to make his way to the top by the strength of his abilities, and yet a day when there was enough opportunity left at the bottom so that mass poverty, slums, and crime were never evident enough to assault either the eye or the conscience of the successful. Things were different now even in the Valley of Democracy.

The Indiana town where Booth Tarkington's Magnificent Ambersons had benevolently ruled from their big house on Amberson Boulevard had now become a city. In the process of growth spanning the lives of just one generation, the fortunes of the Ambersons had declined until the grandson George was working as a clerk in a factory. As all the young George Ambersons set about to reassert their rightful power and prestige, they were confronted both by enormous and monopolizing wealth and by the rising labor unions. The United States, it seemed, had become almost what Bellamy's historian in *Equality* called it, a world of organized degraded serfs run by a plundering and tightly knit plutocracy. The continual clash between the serfs and the plutocrats engulfed almost everyone. It was enough to disenchant the bystander whose loyalties were neither to the plunderers nor the plundered, but rather to an older America where such social extremes, it was felt, had not existed. Morosely, Professor Barrett Wendell observed that America had sold her democratic, equalitarian birthright and was becoming "just another part of the world." Europe no longer learned at America's feet, Walter Weyl, the economist and publicist, wrote with an air of nostalgia, but rather in some respects had become "our teacher." Obviously something needed to be done. Should it be the "return or reversion . . . to certain elementary doctrines of common sense" and the simple rural institutions of the past, as some progressives hoped, or a going forward to something approaching Howells's utopia, which combined the new urban industrialism and a concern for human values in a new type of ethical socialism?

A small reform-minded minority in 1900 was outspoken in defense of the large industrial and commercial city as the creator of the good life. Some of them saw the city as a place of refuge from an ugly countryside and from a hostile natural environment. Remembering his own bleak and lonely boyhood on an upstate New York farm, the novelist Harold Frederic condemned a daily communion with nature that starved the mind and dwarfed the soul. Theodore Dreiser bluntly described the natural processes as inimical to man as a species. Others felt the fascination of the city, a place of excitement and of opportunity. Lincoln Steffens recalled that he felt about the concrete canyons of New York as other youths felt about the wild West. For people like Jane Addams, Jacob Riis, and Hutchins Hapgood the city offered a place to work and an avenue to opportunity.

For the great majority of the new century's reformers, however, the city contained almost the sum of their dislikes. It was a "devilsburg of crime" sucking into its corrupt vortex the "young, genuine, strong and simple men from the farm." There, if successful, they became "financial wreckers" who made their money strangling legitimate enterprises and other human beings. If they were failures—that is, if they remained factory workers—they gradually became like the machine they tended, "huge, hard, brutal, strung with a crude blind strength, stupid, unreasoning." At the worst such unfortunates became the flotsam of the slums, making the saloon their church and the dive their home. The native American lost not only his morals in the city but also his talent for creative work and his sense of beauty. "Sometimes, I think, they'se poison in th' life in a big city," Mr. Dooley remarked, "the flowers won't grow there. . . ." If a man stayed in the city long enough, one of David Graham Phillips's characters remarked, he would almost inevitably lose those qualities that made him an American: one had to go West to see a "real American, a man or a woman who looks as if he or she would do something honest or valuable. . . ."

With such intense anti-urban feeling, it is small wonder that the United States began to romanticize its pioneer past and its agrarian background. Following the Spanish War historical novels fairly poured from the publishers. The public appetite for western stories had one of its periodic increases, and the virtues of the countryside were extolled in even the best literature. In one of Ellen Glasgow's first novels the country, "with its ecstatic insight into the sacred plan of things," is contrasted with the city's "tainted atmosphere." Almost repeating William Jennings Bryan in 1896, Miss Glasgow wrote that the country was the world as God had planned it, the city as man had made it. The cult of the frontier, first introduced into historical scholarship by Frederick Jackson Turner in 1890, and the new emphasis upon agrarian virtues were zealously reflected by the more sensitive politicians. William Jennings Bryan, Theodore Roosevelt, Robert La Follette, and Woodrow Wilson all showed to varying degrees this national nostalgia, this reactionary impulse. Roosevelt in particular saw the great city as the creator of national weakness and possible disintegration, and the countryside as the nation's savior. It was the man on the farm, he wrote, who had consistently done the nation the "best service in governing himself in time of peace and also in fighting in time of war." Dangerous elements to the commonwealth lurked in every large city, but among the western farmers of the West "there was not room for an anarchist or a communist in the whole lot." What Professor Richard Hofstadter has called the agrarian myth, but which might better be called the agrarian bias, was one of the more important elements that went into the making of the progressive mind.

A part of the progressive's romantic attraction to the countryside at this particular time can be explained by the alien character of the urban population. In 1903 the Commissioner of Immigration reported that the past year had witnessed the greatest influx of immigrants in the nation's history. But far from being pleased, the Commissioner was plainly worried. An increasing percentage of these newcomers, he pointed out, belonged to an "undesirable foreign element," the "indigestible" aliens from south Europe. The public was neither surprised at the figures of the report nor shocked by its adjectives. It had been made increasingly sensitive to the changing patterns of immigration by numerous periodical articles and newspaper items calling attention to the alien nature of the eastern seaboard cities. As the immigrant tide welled stronger each year, the nativist spirit that had been so obviously a part of the mental complex leading to the Spanish War increased in intensity. Throughout the decade editors, novelists, and politicians competed with each other in singing the praises of the "big-boned, blond, long-haired" Anglo-Saxon with the blood of the berserkers in his veins, and in denigrating Jack London's "dark pigmented things, the half castes, the mongrel bloods, and the dregs of long conquered races. . . ." In Frank Norris's novels the really despicable characters run all to a type. Braun, the diamond expert in *Vandover*; Zerkow, the junk dealer in *McTeague*; the flannel-shirted Grossman in *The Pit*; and Behrman in *The Octopus* were all of the same religion and approximately from the same regions in Europe. One of the themes in Homer Lea's *The Vermillion Pencil* was the extranational loyalty of the Catholic bishop who intrigued endlessly for the Church and against the State. Although Chester Rowell frankly admitted that California needed "a class of servile labor," he was adamantly opposed to the admission of Orientals, who were dangerous to the state and to "the blood of the next generation."

The progressives, of course, had no monopoly of this racism. Such conservatives as Elihu Root, Henry Cabot Lodge, and Chauncey Depew, and even radicals like Debs, shared their views to a degree. But for one reason or another neither conservative nor radical was as vocal or as specific in his racism as was the reformer. No more eloquent testimony to the power of racism over the progressive mind is evident than in the writings of the kindly, tolerant Middle Westerner William Allen White. In a book published in 1910 White explained nearly all of America's past greatness, including its will to reform, in terms of the nation's "race life" and its racial institutions, "the home and the folk moot." Nor would this genius, this "clean Aryan blood," White promised, be subjected to a debilitating admixture in the future despite the incoming hordes. "We are separated by two oceans from the inferior races and by an instinctive race revulsion to cross breeding that marks the American wherever he is found." Such diverse reformers as Theodore Roosevelt, Albert J. Beveridge, Chester Rowell, Frank Parsons, Hoke Smith, Richard W. Gilder, and Ray Stannard Baker, with more or less emphasis, echoed White's sentiments.

The attitude of the progressive toward race, religion, and color, and his attending views of the great city, was to have profound effects on both internal and external policy. Its consequences were already obvious by 1905 in the South; it was to provoke an international storm in California, and it was to keep alive and possibly nourish a strain of bigotry that was to bear bitter fruit for the United States after the First World War and for the entire world in post-depression Germany. But this is far from saying that the progressive was a spiritual father of either the Ku Klux Klan of the twenties or the Nazi of the thirties. He might well have been anti-immigrant, anti-Catholic, and anti-Jewish, and he might have thought of himself as one of the racial lords of creation, but he was also extremely responsive to the Christian ethic and to the democratic tradition. It was just not in his character to be ruthless toward a helpless minority, especially when the minority was one of his own. The progressive's response to the big-city slum was the settlement-house movement and housing, fire, and sanitary regulations, not the concentration camp. It was probably not entirely politics that prompted Theodore Roosevelt to invite the first Negro to lunch in the White House or to appoint people of Jewish or of Catholic faith to the Cabinet. Roosevelt thoroughly sympathized with California's Oriental problem. But he insisted that the state live up to the nation's international agreements and to the Constitution in its treatment of American Orientals. True, he was worried about Japan's reaction, but elsewhere in international politics he was not so careful of the sensibilities of other nations.

The progressive had reasons beyond racial ones for disliking the big city. For him the metropolis was the home of great wealth, and excessive wealth was as much an enemy to civilization as excessive poverty. A surprising number of very wealthy men supported the progressive cause, and their feelings toward their wealth produced a most interesting psychic state. Taken together, their statements sounded something like those in a confessional session of an early Puritan congregation. Explaining that he had acquired his wealth by "special privilege," Joseph Fels sought expiation by proposing "to spend the damnable money to wipe out the system by which I made it." Medill Patterson and William Kent produced similar variations on the same theme, and Tom Johnson repeatedly used coups from his own career of money-making to illustrate the social viciousness of the system he was contending against in Cleveland. Professor Hofstadter has ascribed this sense of guilt to the Protestant mind as it made the transit from rural and village life to the urban world where great extremes of economic circumstance were the common condition. It is also probable that as the Protestant upper middle class lost its mystical religion, it compensated by more fiercely adhering to the Protestant ethic. It may be of note that the very wealthy who maintained their belief in a mystical religion were never as earnest in social well-doing as their erring brothers. If no one is as zealous as a convert, then perhaps no one conserves what is left of his ideological inheritance more than the man who has lost part of it.

The less well-circumstanced progressive was just as critical of great wealth as his more fortunate colleague. Theodore Roosevelt, who had been left a comfortable but not a great fortune, disliked the American multimillionaire and felt that a society that created an ideal of him was in a very "rotten condition." Bryan once declared that great wealth and personal goodness was something of a paradox. And a reforming journalist from the midlands raised the question whether a man could honestly earn more than a few million dollars in one lifetime. By 1913 Walter Lippmann noted that great wealth, along with "the economic man of the theorists," was in public disrepute.

The reasons for this antimaterialistic crusade of the progressive are an interesting study in complex human motivation. Some of the sentiment undoubtedly came from personal frustration and personal envy. Perhaps to the point is Lincoln Steffens's experience with the stock market. In 1900 he wrote his father that the boom in stocks had made him considerable profits and that he was joining the Republican organization in his district. A year later, after some reverses, he insisted that character was the important desideratum for a young man and not wealth, which often meant the loss of character. The rising intensity of competition for the small merchants and industrialists also played a part in the attack on great wealth. Occasionally one found a reformer who had lost his business. But more often than not in the new century such men were moderately prosperous. Their resentment, if it arose from economic causes, came not from despair but from other feelings, from their sense of lessened power, perhaps, from their regard for their good name, from their sensitivity to the opinion of their fellows. Their relative status and power in society had been going down consistently since the rise of the economic moguls following the Civil War. The gap between them and the Morgans and the Rockefellers had been steadily increasing, and their hopes for attaining the top of the economic heap were progressively dimming. As one commentator noted, the ambitious middle classes in society had "suffered a reduction less in income than in outlook."

This reduction in outlook that Walter Weyl perceived was even more acute for another class, the old American elite whose wealth, family, name, and social power had been secure long before the rise of the relatively new multimillionaires. The Adamses, the Lodges, the Roosevelts, the Bonapartes, and their local counterparts in the hinterlands were a self-consciously proud group. Although Theodore Roosevelt was well down academically in his 1880 Harvard class, he observed that "only one gentleman stands ahead of me." The turbulent and revolutionary waves of the new industrialism and finance had washed up on such polished shores some exceedingly rough gravel. The Rockefellers, the Hannas, and the Harrimans, to say nothing of the Jay Goulds, had not importuned for power in either industry or politics; they had seized it. As their names dominated the newspaper headlines and their ladies laid violent siege to formal society, old families and old ways seemed to have been forgotten. To the recent plutocrats, Henry Cabot Lodge acidly observed from the historic shores of Nahant, "the old American family" and society's long-tested "laws and customs" meant nothing. And far to the west in Cincinnati, it was reported, a social war had broken out between "the stick-ems" and "the stuckems." The first group was a "barbarous new class" of millionaires, just risen from the packing industry, who had assaulted an older class of "thousandaires," who had inherited their wealth made two generations before in the same industry.

In the nineties New England's Brooks Adams had written a book about the fall of Rome. The volume contributed little to historical scholarship, but it revealed with remarkable clarity one facet of the American patrician mind at the end of the century. Fundamental to the work was a hypothesis that human history moved in a two-staged evolutionary scheme. The first stage was one reminiscent of the early days of the Republic, of an expanding progressive society dominated by a military, religious, and artistic mind with an emphasis upon loyalty to the state and containing a superstitious strain, which led the adventurous spirit to the creative act. A second stage of decay, clearly identified with Adams's own day, was characterized by an acquisitive, greedy, and feminine personality which resulted in a static and defensive upper class and a sullen, idle mass below, whose loyalty to the state was as uncertain as its livelihood.

In 1905 a young hunchbacked Californian, Homer Lea, decided that a local Los Angeles reform movement was too tame for his impetuous, adventurous spirit. Lea dropped politics to sail to the Orient, where he eventually became a general in the Chinese revolutionary armies and military adviser to Sun Yat-sen. During his short, incredible career Lea wrote two books, the first of which indicted commercialism as "the natural enemy" of national militancy. Pure industrialism Lea approved of as "incidental to national progress." But industrialism as a vehicle of "individual avarice" was a national cancer because it tended to destroy "the aspirations and world-wide career open to the nation." Herbert Croly, sometimes described as the theorist of the progressive movement, echoed Lea's sentiments a few years later. Modern democracy, unlike economic individualism, he argued, impelled men to forget their self-interest and to transfer their devotion away from acquisitiveness toward "a special object," the nation-state and its "historic mission." This distrust of materialism and emphasis upon romantic nationalism were reflected in a good many progressives, especially those with more collectivist inclinations. It was almost completely absent in the thinking of such Midwesterners as Robert La Follette and George W. Norris. But something of the same spirit had sent Theodore Roosevelt to the Cuban shores in 1898 and something akin to it perhaps was to lead Woodrow Wilson into his great crusade for international idealism in 1917.

The idea that value was created only by the production of things or in rendering service, and that there was something dishonest in making money on other men's products, was an old American one. In part it stemmed from religious origins, in part from an unsophisticated system of agrarian economics. It was implicit in the thought of Henry George; it was basic to the progressive attitude toward great wealth. In apologizing to his constituents for his wealth, the progressive Congressman William Kent admitted that he was not entitled to the money he had out of speculation. Andrew Carnegie, who late in life became something of a progressive, agreed with the attitude. It was time, he felt, that the honest businessman, who made money "legitimately," should refuse to recognize those of his fellows who made money and rendered no value for it. Speculators, to the progressive, were immoralists, men with fat hands sitting in mahogany offices who had acquired the dishonest art of taking money away from the earth's real producers. They believed, said the hero of one of Winston Churchill's novels, that "the acquisition of wealth was exempt from the practice of morality."

In reviewing Professor [E.R.A.] Seligman's *The Economic Interpretation of History*, the editors of *The Outlook* vehemently denied that progress primarily depended upon materialist forces. The history of society, they argued, was like the history of individuals, composed of a struggle between the moral and the material forces, and "only through the subordination of material ends to moral ends has humanity advanced." There was something corrosive about great wealth, the progressive believed, and in acquiring it a man usually had to sacrifice moral values to overriding material ambitions. In the world of progressive fiction this sloughing off of morality usually produced the hero's economic collapse and his return to morality. But in the less well-ordered practical world the progressive was sure that the multimillionaire remained unredeemed, trapped by the very ethics he had used to acquire his fortune. The world of the great rich was usually an idle one, a sensuous one, and often a vicious one. The lives of its people, Theodore Roosevelt observed, often "vary from rotten frivolity to rotten vice." The way to rescue them from their state of moral degradation, a Midwest editor wrote, was "to put them to work."

Since the progressive usually came from a comfortable part of society and a general attack upon property was usually furthest from his mind, this assault upon great wealth put him in a rather ambiguous position. The one way out of the paradox was to draw a line between good and bad wealth. For some the limit of private fortunes was the total that man could "justly acquire." For others the measurement was made in terms of service to society. Tom Johnson, for example, believed that the law could be so drawn that men would be able "to get" only the amount "they earned." Still others argued that there must be a point where additional money ceased to be salubrious for a man's character and became instead a positive evil force. Wayne MacVeagh, Garfield's Attorney General, suggested that all people could be divided into three classes: those who had more money than was good for them, those who had just enough, and those who had much less than was morally desirable. Just where the exact lines should be drawn, most progressives would not say. But the imputation that the state ought to redivide wealth on a morally desirable basis found a receptive audience. To George F. Baer's claim that coal prices should be the sum of "all the traffic will bear," the editors of *The Outlook* replied that property was private not by any natural right but by an "artificial arrangement made by the community." "If under those artificial arrangements," the editorial continued, "the community is made to suffer, the same power that made them will find a way to unmake them." Thus in the progressive mind the classical economic laws repeatedly described in the past as natural had become artificial arrangements to be rearranged at any time the community found it morally or socially desirable. Admittedly the formulations of new ethical standards for a division of national wealth were to be extremely difficult. But once the progressive had destroyed the popular sanction behind the "laws" of rent, prices, and wages, there was to be no complete turning back. A revolution in human thought had occurred. Man, it was hoped, would now become the master and not the creature of his economy. And the phrases punctuating the next fifty years of history—the "square deal," the New Deal, the Fair Deal, the just wage, the fair price—attested to his efforts to make the reality square with his ambitions.

After revisiting the United States in 1905, James Bryce, the one-time ambassador from Great Britain, noted that of all the questions before the public the ones bearing on capital and labor were the most insistent and the most discussed. Certainly for many a progressive the rise of the labor union was as frightening as the rise of trusts. True, he talked about them less because nationally they were obviously not as powerful as were the combines of capital. But emotionally he was, if anything, more opposed to this collectivism from below than he was to the collectivism above him in the economic ladder.

"There is nothing ethical about the labor movement. It is coercion from start to finish. In every aspect it is a driver and not a leader. It is simply a war movement, and must be judged by the analogues of belligerence and not by industrial principles." This statement by a Democratic progressive illustrates the ire of the small and uncertain employer who was being challenged daily by a power he often could not match. In their lawlessness and in their violence, remarked another, unions were "a menace not only to the employer but to the entire community." To the small employer and to many middle-class professionals unions were just another kind of monopoly created for the same reasons and having the same results as industrial monopoly. Unions, they charged, restricted production, narrowed the available labor market, and raised wages artificially in the same manner that trusts were restricting production, narrowing competition, and raising their own profits. "Every step in trade unionism has followed the steps that organized capital has laid down before it," Clarence Darrow observed in a speech before the Chicago Henry George

Association. The ultimate direction of the two monopolies was as clear to the individual entrepreneur as it was to Darrow. Either trade unionism would break down, a Midwestern editor argued, or it would culminate in "a dangerously oppressive partnership" with the stronger industrial trusts. The end result was equally obvious to such men: a steady decrease in opportunity for the individual operating as an individual, an economy of statics, an end to the open society. The burden of the industrial revolution, Darrow said in concluding his speech, "falls upon the middle class." And Howells's traveler from Altruria put the case even more graphically: "the struggle for life has changed from a free fight to an encounter of disciplined forces, and the free fighters that are left get ground to pieces between organized labor and organized capital."

On the whole, the average progressive preferred to talk in moral rather than in economic terms. Orally, at least, he reacted more quickly to appeals based upon abstractions than the usual ones connected with day-to-day livelihood. Characteristically, he denounced more vehemently the philosophic overtones of unionism than its pragmatic economic gains. He was almost obsessed with the class consciousness implicit in unionism and flaunted by the more radical parties of the left. Almost to a man the progressive fervently agreed with one of Harold Frederic's heroes that "the abominable word 'class' could be wiped out of the English language as it is spoken in America." Sociologists, economists, preachers, politicians, and publishers all joined the chorus. Economic classes, according to the sociologist Cooley, were characterized by a "complacent ignorance." Other progressives regarded them as "greedy," "arrogant," "insolent," "ruthless," "unsocial," and "tyrannical." Morality did not know them, declared one editor, because morality could only come from the individual who had not succumbed to "the economic temptation" manifested by the class. But the ultimate in the way of devastating criticism of the class spirit came from Ray Stannard Baker. Although sympathetic with the economic plight of the garment workers, Baker observed that in devotion to their class they were "almost more unionists than Americans."

" 'I am for labor,' or 'I am for capital,' substitutes something else for the immutable laws of righteousness," Theodore Roosevelt was quoted as saying in 1904. "The one and the other would let the class man in, and letting him in is the one thing that will most quickly eat out the heart of the Republic." Roosevelt, of course, was referring to class parties in politics. Most progressives agreed with Herbert Croly that a "profound antagonism" existed between the political system and a government controlled by a labor party. In San Francisco in 1901, in Chicago in 1905, and in Los Angeles in 1911, when labor used or threatened direct political action, the progressive reacted as if touched by fire. Chicago was a "class-ridden" city, remarked one progressive journal, which would not redeem itself until the evil pretensions of both organized capital and labor had been suppressed. In Los Angeles, where a Socialist labor group came within a hair's breadth of controlling the city, the progressives combined with their old enemies, the corporation-dominated machine, to fight off the challenge, and as a result never again exerted the power they once had in the city. Apropos of that struggle punctuated by a near general strike, dynamite, and death, the leading California progressive theorist, Chester Rowell, expostulated that no class as a class was fit to rule a democracy; that progress came only from activities of good citizens acting as individuals. Class prejudice and class pride excused bribery, mass selfishness, lawlessness, and disorder. This class spirit emanating from both business and labor was "destroying American liberty." When it became predominant, Rowell concluded, "American institutions would be dead, for peaceful reform would no longer be possible, and "nothing but revolution" would remain.

At various times and places the progressive politician invited the support of organized labor, but such co-operation was almost invariably a one-way street. Somewhat reminiscent of the early relations between the British Liberal and Labor parties, it worked only if the progressive rather than the labor politician was in the driver's seat. In Maine, for example, when labor attempted to lead a campaign for the initiative and referendum, it was defeated in part by progressives, who two years later led a successful campaign on the same issues. In the progressive literature the terms "captain of industry" and "labor boss" were standard, while "labor statesman" was practically unknown. Roosevelt's inclination to try labor lawbreakers in a criminal court is well known; his administration's failure to indict criminally one corporation executive is eloquent of the limits of his prejudice. Progressive literature contained many proposals for permitting corporations to develop until they had achieved quasi-monopoly status, at which time federal regulation would be imposed. No such development was forecast for labor. Unions were grudgingly recognized as a necessary evil, but the monopolistic closed shop was an abomination not to be tolerated with or without government regulation. In the Chicago teamsters' strike of 1905 Mayor Dunne ordered the city police to be "absolutely impartial" toward both capital and labor. But he also insisted that the strikers not be allowed to block the teams of nonunion men or the delivery of nonunion-marked goods.

A few progressives, of course, hailed the rise of labor unions as an advance in democracy. But the majority, while sincerely desirous of improving the plight of the individual workingman, were perhaps basically more hostile to the union than to corporate monopoly. If the progressive attention was mostly centered on the corporation during the decade, it was largely because the sheer social power of the corporation vastly overshadowed that of the rising but still relatively weak unions. When confronted with a bleak either-or situation, progressive loyalties significantly shifted up and not down the economic ladder.

Emotionally attached to the individual as a causative force and to an older America where he saw his group supreme, assaulted economically and socially from above and below, and yet eager for the wealth and the power that flowed from the new collectivism, the progressive was at once nostalgic, envious, fearful, and yet confident about the future. Fear and confidence together for a time inspired this middle-class group of supremely independent individuals with a class consciousness that perhaps exceeded that of any other group in the nation. This synthesis had been a long time developing. Back in the early 1890's Henry George had remarked that the two dangerous classes to the state were "the very rich" and "the very poor." Some years afterward a Populist paper referred to the "upper and lower scum" of society. At about the same time the acknowledged dean of American letters had inquired just where the great inventions, the good books, the beautiful pictures, and the just laws had come from in American society. Not from the "uppermost" or "lowermost" classes, Howells replied. They had come mostly from the middle-class man. In the first decade of the twentieth century the progressive never questioned where ability and righteousness resided. Nor was he uncertain of the sources of the nation's evils. "From above," one wrote, "come the problems of predatory wealth. . . . From below come the problems of poverty and pig-headed and brutish criminality."

As the progressive looked at the sharply differentiated America of 1900, he saw "pyramids of money in a desert of want." For William Allen White the world was full of "big crooks" and the "underprivileged." The polar conditions of society assaulted the progressive conscience and threatened progressive security. Supremely individualistic, the progressive could not impute class consciousness, or, as he would have phrased it, class selfishness, to himself. His talk was therefore full of moral self-judgments, or phrases like "the good men," "the better element," "the moral crowd." From the Old Source, he paraphrased, "Thou shalt not respect the person of the poor, nor honor the person of the great; in righteousness shalt thou judge they neighbor." His self-image was that of a "kind-hearted man" dealing in justice. William Kent publicly stated that he could not believe in the class struggle because every great reform of the past had been wrought by men who were not "selfishly interested." "I believe," he concluded, "altruism is a bigger force in the world than selfishness."

Since the progressive was not organized economically as was the capitalist and the laborer, he chose to fight his battles where he had the most power—in the political arena. And in large terms his political program was first that of the most basic urge of all nature, to preserve himself, and secondly to refashion the world after his own image. What the nation needed most, wrote a Midwestern clergyman, was an increase in the number of "large-hearted men" to counteract the class organization of both capital and labor. "Solidarity," Herbert Croly stated, "must be restored." The point of reconcentration around which the hoped-for solidarity was to take place, of course, was the middle class. It was to "absorb" all other classes, thought Henry Demarest Lloyd. It was to be both the sum and substance of the classless state of the future.

The progressive mentality was a compound of many curious elements. It contained a reactionary as well as a reform impulse. It was imbued with a burning ethical strain which at times approached a missionary desire to create a heaven on earth. It had in it intense feelings of moral superiority over both elements of society above and below it economically. It emphasized individual dynamism and leadership. One part of it looked backward to an intensely democratic small America; another looked forward to a highly centralized nationalistic state. And both elements contained a rather ugly strain of racism.

The progressive mentality was generated in part from both a fear of the loss of group status and a confidence in man's ability to order the future. Had progressive militancy come in a more despondent intellectual and ethical climate and in a bleaker economic day, group fear might have won over group hope. Its more benign social ends might then have been transmuted into something more malignant. But in the warm and sunny atmosphere of 1900 the optimistic mood prevailed. For the year marking the beginning of the new century was a year of progressive success in the cities and the states. And within another year, by the ugly agent of an assassin's gun. Theodore Roosevelt had become President. With the shot in Buffalo, progressivism achieved a spokesman in the White House.

Theodore Roosevelt and the Mythos of the Presidency

Morton Keller

Theodore Roosevelt was many things to many people—ornithologist, historian, cowboy, pugilist, language expert, legislator, police commissioner, naval expert, Rough Rider, governor, vice-president, president, and general all-around character. A cartoonist's delight, he was also a tempting target for mythmakers. His malleable talents and interests formed a combustible compound, especially when combined with the times in which he lived. For like the progressive era itself, Theodore Roosevelt embodied many contradictions—an aristocrat turned cowboy aficionado, one "born to the manor" and a believer in the necessity of elite leadership who fashioned government policy to function as watchdog for the middle and lower classes. He assumed a conservative and pro-business stance yet was a progressive Republican who busted trusts. Necessarily, the matter of sifting through the conflicting evidence on Roosevelt and distinguishing legend from fact has been a most difficult enterprise. Morton Keller, Spector Professor of History at Brandeis University, here attempts a balanced interpretation of Theodore Roosevelt and the times he affected. Most notably, concludes Keller, Roosevelt proves the adage that presidents are both leaders and symbols. Given Roosevelt's vivid tenure in public life, the "mythos of the office"—the idea that the person who occupies the White House must shoulder the mythic burden of being "the embodiment of the people"— carries special weight.

We cling to the memory of our Presidents for two reasons. One has to do with the idea that the chief executive is the sum of the national character, is in some way the embodiment of his people and his time. Then, too, there is the aura of power that surrounds the office. The man who is President of the United States has a unique and awesome access to the instruments of national sovereignty, of political power, of public opinion. A President who responds to these potentialities, or at least appears to do so, cannot help but pique the imagination.

Presidents, in short, are both symbols and leaders. Theodore Roosevelt was the first chief executive after Lincoln to lay claim to attention as a major figure in the mythos of the office and as an important shaper of national policy. . . . [T]hese [are the] central themes of Roosevelt and his Presidency.

I

A certain degree of personal drama and historical significance accrues to every President; it is inherent in the office. But Theodore Roosevelt's impact as an evocative figure in American life had little to do with his title. He made the American Presidency into something new and arresting, not the reverse. Presidents since Andrew Jackson's time had come of humble or middling origins; not since John Quincy Adams could they lay claim to distinguished birth or high culture. Roosevelt broke the established pattern. He was as much the aristocrat and intellectual as American society would permit one of its leaders to be. To old-family New York and Harvard he added the unique ingredients of gentlemanly adventuring in the West and in the Spanish-American War. He united a passion for blood sports with respectable attainments as a historian and naturalist. His flamboyant personality was worlds away from those of his comfortable, phlegmatic predecessors.

Even more dramatic was the abrupt transition of generations that occurred when Roosevelt entered the Presidency on William McKinley's death in 1901. The average age of incoming Presidents to this time was about sixty; T.R., the youngest chief executive in our history, was not yet forty-three when he took office. (Some idea of what this age difference meant in experience— and could mean in outlook—comes when we recall that McKinley had been a major and a hero in the Civil War; T.R. as a boy of seven had watched Abraham Lincoln's New York City funeral procession in 1865.)

The style of Roosevelt's Presidency reinforced this sense of sharp and sudden change. He behaved in a manner quite unlike anything Americans had come to expect of their chief executives. Not since Jefferson, and not again until Kennedy, was the White House so open to men of diverse accomplishments. T.R., most of all, infused a vitality, almost an electric intensity, in everything he did—politics, science, scholarship, sports. Henry Adams, who did not like Roosevelt, summed him up in a classic observation: "[He] showed the singular primitive quality that belongs to ultimate matter—the quality that medieval theology assigned to God—he was pure act."

Roosevelt's hypertension was real enough. He died worn out at sixty, a victim of "malignant endocarditis, and an embolism in the coronary arteries." But his instinctive flair for the full, dramatic life was made to serve the hard, grubby purposes of politics and policy. What might otherwise have been a colorful but frivolous personality became, in the office of the Presidency, a subject of profound concern for contemporaries and later commentators. It was for this reason that the critical Stuart Sherman found Roosevelt to be "the most interesting man of our times."

That unabashed admirer William Allen White saw a single theme in Roosevelt's personal style and Presidential role: the uplifting of American life. Others, less kind, have decided that T.R.'s baroque public performance served as a façade for essentially empty or regressive policies. But all observers of Roosevelt have been struck by a peculiar, pervasive paradox. The man who had one of the most remarkable careers in American history had also, it would seem, an extraordinary ability to represent, to address himself to the American average: to be, in Richard Hofstadter's words, "the master therapist of the middle classes." White looked on Roosevelt not only as a revered leader but as a kindred spirit; as a man who was at one with the disturbed petite bourgeoisie. H. L. Mencken found T.R., for all the fact that he was a consummate showman, to be "a perfectly typical politician." Dixon Wecter, treating Roosevelt as one of America's mythic heroes, nevertheless was struck by his essential ordinariness. John Dewey noted at the time of Roosevelt's death that as the Man of Action he was the "typical representative," indeed the "living embodiment" of the generation that came to its maturity around 1900.

For all the color and sophistication of his life, Roosevelt remains best remembered for an underlying, an almost eccentric simplicity. The Rough Rider, the tamer of the Dakota badlands and the Dakota badmen, Hemingway's great American boy-child romping in the White House: this is the Roosevelt that has persisted in the memory of Americans.

And yet, as John M. Blum and Howard K. Beale among others have noted, there are sufficient grounds for arguing that Roosevelt went about his policy-making with considerable subtlety of style and purpose. The interesting question, of course, is why Roosevelt for so long, and on so many different levels of apprehension, has been regarded as a classic American innocent. The answer lies in the nature and function of his Presidential performance.

II

For all the fascination of Roosevelt's personality, it is his career as a politician and a shaper of public policy that is the primary measure of his historical significance. And again we find an elusive relationship between form and substance—between promise and performance—commanding the attention of commentators.

For contemporary—and later—idolators he is the great figure of the Progressive movement of reform that swept over American life in the early twentieth century. White, for one, has no doubts as to the significance and substance of Roosevelt's Presidential achievement. He sees T.R. as the wise and effective overseer of the transition—"critical, dangerous, and but for him terrible"—from rural individuality to the highly industrialized, urbanized social order of the twentieth century. But even for White there are difficulties when one examines this performance in detail. "For some strange reason," he muses, "the labor movement never followed in his train." Nor did the administration that succeeded T.R.'s triumphal election in 1904 seem, in retrospect, to hold very much of substance, and White is forced to resort to rhetoric: "The actual list of achievements of Roosevelt in his second term, viewed as a legislative or administrative program, is not imposing; viewed as a crusade for justice it is a revolution." Another admirer, the literary critic Harry Thurston Peck, said much the same thing of T.R. in October, 1908: "He will be remembered as the

President who stirred the conscience of the people to a righteous indignation. He has accomplished little except this; and yet there was nothing else so absolutely needed at the time."

Others have found it far more difficult to see him as a significant figure in the tradition of American political reform. The First World War, and Roosevelt's important public role in it as a spokesman of preparedness, intervention, and militant Americanism, colored many early evaluations of his career. Because of Roosevelt's role in the conflict, Stuart Sherman declared, "he can never again greatly inspire the popular liberal movement in America." Indeed, in retrospect T.R.'s major political contribution was the regressive one of transforming "the unimaginative plutocratic psychology . . . into the psychology of efficient, militant, imperialistic nationalism."

Mencken took T.R. less seriously. He concerned himself with Roosevelt's style as a political demagogue rather than with his substance as a national leader—which, of course, was in itself a comment on that leadership. "He didn't believe in democracy; he believed simply in government," declared the great iconoclast. T.R.'s policies existed only to serve his demagoguery: "The issues that won him most votes were issues that, at bottom, he didn't believe in."

Consideration of Roosevelt flagged during the 1920's. He had, it seemed, equally little to offer those who followed George W. Norris and Robert La Follette and those who followed Harding and Coolidge. He was remembered chiefly as the exemplification of sterling American virtues—Hermann Hagedorn and the Roosevelt Memorial Association fostered the cult of the Rough Rider—or as a figure of fun. Henry F. Pringle's often caustic Pulitzer Prize biography in 1931 portrayed an amusing but hardly a major figure in American history.

The Great Depression of the 1930's and the appearance of the New Deal stimulated a renewed interest in F.D.R.'s cousin and the Progressive movement of which he was so prominent a part. But he remained an unattractive figure to angry critics of American life. John Chamberlain, comparing Roosevelt and La Follette in a Marxist interpretation of Progressivism, found T.R. distinctly less significant than the Wisconsin Senator. Roosevelt's conception of himself as the spokesman of a core middle class preyed upon by capital and labor had little viability, said Chamberlain. The true American reality, rather, was that of oppressed labor confronting avaricious corporations; and to this Roosevelt did not address himself. The radical Chamberlain of the early 1930's found T.R.'s romanticism not exhilarating but unscientific and hence destructive: Roosevelt, he complained, "never understood the spirit of the laboratory—which was the one hope of the Progressive, or Liberal, movement." Matthew Josephson, in *The President Makers*, was more inclusive and concrete in rejecting Roosevelt as a reformer. He drew a picture of T.R. as the close associate—and in many respects the spokesman—of the great finance capitalists and corporation lawyers of the time.

Louis Filler, too, in 1939 had little patience with Roosevelt's evident insufficiency in the face of the problems of an industrial society. "Each year," he observed, "Roosevelt becomes less impressive in retrospect, and it is unlikely that he will ever resume the stature he enjoyed in his days of triumph." The coming of F.D.R. and the New Deal gave T.R. legitimacy as a reformer, but little more: "Roosevelt was a promise rather than a fulfillment. The excitement that attended him was mainly the excitement of anticipation." Richard Hofstadter, writing in the wake of World War II, added to the well-established theme of Roosevelt's inadequacy as a shaper of public policy in an industrial age the element that had concerned Stuart Sherman and H. L. Mencken in 1919: T.R.'s authoritarianism and militarism.

In recent years interpretations of Theodore Roosevelt have taken an interesting turn. The Second World War, and the mix of welfare and warfare that has characterized American government since then, gives new significance to the Roosevelt policies. American society—in which social order, administrative efficiency, and an intermixed devotion to international *Realpolitik* and domestic reform are highly prized—inevitably finds in Roosevelt's career something more than therapy and entertainment.

One can see the change at work in Hamilton Basso's World War II assessment of T.R. The ironic amusement of Pringle and the angry disapproval of Chamberlain are gone. In their place is a respectful consideration of Roosevelt as the first American President to propose using the state to discipline and democratize the economy and to bring order into international power politics.

John M. Blum develops the ramifications of this new appreciation of Roosevelt. Nelson Aldrich's estimate of T.R. as "the greatest politician of his time" was a gauge of derision in the 1920's and contempt in the 1930's; by the 1950's it had become a measure of his significance. The political art took on increasing importance as an instrument of social betterment—and of social control. Blum's Roosevelt emerges as the archetypal enlightened conservative: "an institutionalist, a gradualist, a moralist" whose prime achievement lay in the fact that he created a viable governmental response to the tremendous economic, intellectual, and demographic forces that were transforming American life. Roosevelt's goals—and now they have come to seem important and desirable ones—were consolidation, conservation, stability: "He broadened power precisely for the purpose of establishing order." His great lack, says Blum, was an equivalent commitment to the pursuit of happiness: to a dynamic rather than a static vision of the Good Society. Carleton Putnam, Roosevelt's most recent biographer, echoes Blum's conclusions: "three traits . . . were the pillars of Roosevelt's personality—a belief in the leadership principle, a stern respect for duly constituted authority and a devotion to the ideal of freedom and self-dependence for the individual."

Another recent appraisal of Roosevelt as a sophisticated conservative dwells on these traits with less satisfaction than those of Blum and Putnam. Gabriel Kolko, elaborating upon the earlier insights of Matthew Josephson and John Chamberlain, sees Roosevelt as the spokesman of a large-scale financial and industrial capitalism seeking a more rationalized and controllable economic order. In his view, Roosevelt's relationships to men such as George W. Perkins of J. P. Morgan and Company, and his readiness to support forms of government regulation that major corporate interests—railroad, insurance, banking, and the like—themselves wanted constitute the central theme of his Presidency.

Closely analogous in spirit is Howard K. Beale's examination of T.R.'s foreign policy. Here, too, *Machtpolitik* and *Realpolitik* coincide. Beale concedes that Roosevelt's conduct of American international relations was restrained by a strong sense of social responsibility and by an underlying commitment to persuasion and the democratic process. But he is disturbed by Roosevelt's desire "for sufficient power to be able to do as he pleases without restraint."

III

What can be said in sum of a man who for half a century has been the subject of such diverse opinion? Surely—especially since the publication of the magnificent edition of *The Letters of Theodore Roosevelt* in the 1950's—the important facts about T.R. the man and the President are available to us. And presumably we are sufficiently removed from his generation to evaluate his place in history without the strong sense of personal involvement that he engendered in so many of his contemporaries.

What first commands recognition is the extraordinary vividness of Roosevelt's life. Poseur or genius, T.R. remains one of the commanding personalities in American history. Judgments may vary as to the nature and worth of the use to which he put his great personal talents. But there can be no question of his impact as a dramatic human being upon his contemporaries. For the first time since Lincoln, the Presidency became a meaningful institution for Americans who were accustomed to regard national politics as bencath—or above—their concern. Men of education and social conscience generally found T.R. a sympathetic figure. Those who had cause to account themselves among the dispossessed of American life could not help but respond to a President who lunched with Booker T. Washington, appointed a Jew to his cabinet, and publicly sided with a labor union during a strike. As the first chief executive explicitly to recognize the fact that the United States was becoming a nation of cities, of workers, of great ethnic diversity, Roosevelt's place in American history is secure.

The precise weight and direction of his policy-making is more difficult to determine. Certainly no legislation of great significance to twentieth-century American life came about under his aegis. The proposals for business regulation and conservation that were such important parts of his Presidency hardly compare with the institutional changes of the New Deal and after. Nor do his adventures in thc field of foreign policy, for all the clamor that attended them, rank in significance with the activities of Woodrow Wilson or of Franklin D. Roosevelt and his successors. T.R. cannot even be accounted, for all his incontestable political skill, a seminal figure in the history of party politics. His effort to bring the Republican party to a sophisticated apprehension of the realities of twentieth-century American life hardly achieved success. Finally, for all the token recognition that he accorded Negroes, Jews, Catholics, organized labor—and reformers—the fact remains that he presided over an America where racist assumptions (among them his own) remained strong, where unions remained weak, where the conditions of life of the industrial and agrarian poor improved little.

The quality that makes Roosevelt a significant President despite this litany of insufficiencies is precisely the one that has been the subject of fiercest criticism: his ideological and political fluidity. He seems to lend himself with equal facility to each of a bewildering lot of interpretations: as the representative of a middle class that is fearful of change—or is demanding it; as the front man of sophisticated finance capitalism; as the first spokesman of the new America or the last great defender of the old.

If in his career Roosevelt seemed to speak with so many voices, to represent so many divergent yet contemporaneous interests, this may be a measure not of his duplicity but of his skill. Perhaps this is what sets him apart from other great figures of his time, who represented narrower, more parochial points of view: La Follette, Debs, Bryan. But he belongs in their company insofar as the central theme of his political career was to respond to the conditions imposed on American life by massive industrialization, urbanization, and immigration.

Ultimately he was no better able than these others, or his successor Woodrow Wilson, to ride out the political storms of early twentieth-century American life. After his last great effort of 1912 ended in defeat he became a frivolous, restless, and unsettled figure, vainly trying to reassert his place in the political order. The hysterical, chauvinistic Roosevelt of the wartime years has much in common with the shrilly fundamentalist Bryan of the 1920's, or the shattered, vindictive Wilson after Versailles.

Even before he was borne under, Roosevelt's response to the social changes of his time was less concrete and specific, less materially creative, than those of his distinguished contemporaries. In consequence his role in that story of political adaptation to the conditions of modern America is especially difficult to fix, to categorize. It is obscured, too, by the highly-colored huckster's manner with which he went about the business of national leadership. But it is well to bear in mind how overwhelming was the need to adapt old and deeply entrenched social values to spectacularly new social conditions, and how great was the potential for social chaos. In this context Roosevelt's flamboyance and adaptability become not impediments but instruments: the instruments of the great political teacher-broker of the Progressive era.

Woodrow Wilson: A Profile
Arthur S. Link

Woodrow Wilson, like other great American presidents, has attracted many biographers, some of whom have contributed myths in reconstructing his "life and times." The Wilson mystique, however, seems to have drawn a wider spectrum of biographers—thus resulting, if not in more myths, at least in an increased variety. For example, Wilson has been analyzed by none other than the great Sigmund Freud himself. Arthur S. Link, Professor of History at Princeton University and America's premier Wilson scholar, critically examines several of the myth builders, including Ray Stannard Baker, Robert Lansing, and Colonel E. M. House; he even fires a salvo at the Bullitt-Freud study. Link argues that it is possible to know the real Wilson, perhaps even better than he knew himself, if one cultivates detachment and makes use of the large and growing amount of information available on the subject.

It is by no means impossible for a diligent researcher to discover the public facts about most important individuals, but it is always extraordinarily difficult to get behind the facade and to study, describe, and re-create verbally the personality of a subject. It requires several years of intense analysis for a psychiatrist to probe into the psyche of a live subject. How much more difficult it is for the scholar who has to rely only upon the written word!

Ordinary difficulties aside, it is little wonder that the personality of Woodrow Wilson has so long remained a mystery or been only imperfectly understood. Ray Stannard Baker, Wilson's authorized biographer, was originally partially responsible for the mystification. Baker had exclusive possession of what were thought to be the entire body of the Wilson Papers until he completed his biography in the late 1930's. His eight-volume *Woodrow Wilson: Life and Letters* (1927–1939) was for many years the only full-scale biography available. Indispensable though it was, Baker's work embodied a portrait of the Wilsonian personality that was something of a caricature.

Baker labored under some obvious handicaps. First, his long acquaintance with and intense admiration of Wilson not only influenced him in obvious ways but also profoundly affected his reading of the documentary evidence. Second, Baker *was* writing the authorized biography, and writing it under Mrs. Wilson's watchful eye. Third, Baker, because of his own limitations, was never fully sensitive to the subtleties and changes in Wilson's religious thought and their manifestations in Wilson's personal and public conduct. Finally, as Robert Bannister's acute study *Ray Stannard Baker: The Mind and Thought of a Progressive* has recently shown, Baker to a large degree imposed his own personality profile upon Wilson.

Whatever the cause, the result was a portrait that was scarcely credible to critical readers. The Wilson of the Baker biography is too good to be true—or human. By robbing Wilson of his humanity, Baker unconsciously created a less interesting as well as a less credible character. For example, Baker was so intent upon protecting Wilson's reputation against contemporary slanderers that he ended by portraying his subject as being mainly feminine in personality, if not virtually a sexual neuter. Perhaps this statement is too strong. In any event, Baker refused either to come to grips with or to describe the strong masculine drive that was one of the great sources of Wilson's life power.

It was very difficult for biographers to get a clear view of the Wilsonian personality for years after the completion of Baker's biography simply because the essential biographical materials were either missing or unavailable. Such absolutely indispensable collections as the letters between Wilson and his first and second wives, Ellen Axson Wilson and Edith Bolling Wilson, and Wilson's letters to his friend and intimate correspondent, Mary Allen Hulbert, were closed to all scholars until the 1960's. Even worse, the great body of the Wilson Papers for the first forty years of Wilson's life were hidden in trunks in the Wilson house on S Street in Washington. Only after the discovery of this collection was it possible, for example, to understand the relationship between Wilson and his father, the Reverend Dr. Joseph Ruggles Wilson. Enough was known for all biographers to affirm that this relationship was indubitably the most important force during the formative years of Woodrow Wilson's life. And yet all biographers, Baker included, had never seen the relationship with anything but very imperfect and distorted vision.

Biographers and historians in pursuit of truth necessarily have to use whatever evidence is at hand. In Wilson's case, the unavailability of the most elementary personal documents forced historians and biographers to rely heavily upon the letters, diaries, etc., of his contemporaries. These sources are of course indispensable: without them, we could never see many facets of Wilson's personality. However, the light from these sources is distorted by the prisms of the contemporary's own prejudices, varying ability to understand personality, and above all his purpose in writing a letter, memorandum, or diary entry. There is distortion both ways, to be sure. Contemporaries who ardently admired Wilson tended to leave documentary evidence just as distorted as that left by individuals who had strong feelings against Wilson.

There are numerous examples of the dangers of relying too much on the testimony left by Wilson's close associates. One such example among the serious works is a psychological study of Wilson by Alexander L. and Juliette L. George, *Woodrow Wilson and Colonel House*, published in 1956. This study, like many others of the Wilson era, is based heavily on the diary of Colonel Edward M. House, Wilson's intimate adviser. This massive diary is one of the

most important sources of Wilsonian biography. Yet we are only now beginning to see the degree to which Colonel House wrote for the specific purpose
of creating his own version of the historical record. Portions of the House diary
are simply unreliable, and the truth about any particular episode can be determined only when one is able to compare House's account with accounts left
by other participants. It is more important to say that House's numerous comments on Wilson's actions and personality have to be read in light of House's
unrelenting effort to defend, through his diary, the superiority of his own
mind, intellect, and policies against Wilson's.

One has to be equally careful in using the various memoranda left by
Wilson's Secretary of State from 1915 to 1920, Robert Lansing—the papers
usually referred to as the Lansing diary. I quoted one of these memoranda—a
personality profile—at length in my *Wilson: The New Freedom* (1956). Were
I rewriting that book, I would probably use the extract again. But I would be
careful to point out that it was the testimony of a bitter man, and that the
bitterness that Lansing felt was not by any means justified by Wilson's treatment of his Secretary of State.

Is it possible really to know Woodrow Wilson? And is it possible to construct a full and accurate profile of his personality?

One has to begin the answer to the first question by saying that many of
the major contours of Wilson's personality have been long known and written
about. Virtually all contemporaries and historical writers, friendly and hostile,
have agreed that Wilson was different from the run of ordinary men. His personality was, in short, strong, aggressive, dominant, and, to many persons,
compelling. He had the power to command loyalty, to charm, and also to repel.
The testimony of his contemporaries, from his student days to the end of his
life, is so unanimous on this point as to be conclusive.

In addition, all observers, contemporary and historical, agree that Wilson
was an extraordinarily intense person. He was not merely a well-disciplined
and hard worker, but a person who was always driving, never satisfied with
momentary achievements and triumphs. Psychologists have attributed this inner drive to Wilson's highly developed superego, derived particularly from the
demands and expectations of his father.

The great majority of Wilson's contemporaries also agree that he had a
first-class mind, though one more adept at synthesizing ideas than originating
them. He was, as Gamaliel Bradford, Jr., put it, a "creature of brains." But, as
Bradford and other writers have made clear, Wilson was interested in ideas for
the practical use to which they might be put, and hardly at all in abstract
speculation.

All observers strongly affirm that Wilson was an idealist, and all his close
friends agree that he had a strong conscience, a highly developed ethical system, and deep Christian faith. However, very few of Wilson's contemporaries
understood the nature of Wilson's idealism, and some secondary writers have
followed them in incorrectly interpreting it as being largely moralism and slav-
ish obedience to an ethical system. Recent research has put this whole matter

in a new perspective. Wilson, at least in his mature years, was not, technically, an idealist, even though he continued to use the language of idealism. On the contrary, he had little use for ethical abstractions or ideals as these terms have been defined by philosophers. Having discovered the meaning of justification by faith in about 1905 and 1906, Wilson became increasingly afterward a Christian realist whose ethics were very much affected by the context and circumstances of any particular situation demanding a moral decision.

Most contemporaries and biographers also agree that Wilson was by nature headstrong, opinionated, and combative. Some critics have asserted that he had no capacity for self-criticism or understanding, would brook no opposition, and cut off friends who disagreed with him.

Finally, views of Wilson the man in day-to-day relationships have varied according to the subjective reactions of contemporaries and biographers. To persons who did not like him, Wilson seemed cold, even capable of some personal cruelty. To members of his family and to his friends, on the other hand, Wilson was outgoing, warmhearted, and generously capable of friendship.

The foregoing generalizations summarize a fairly extensive and intimate understanding of Wilson's personality—a much better understanding, indeed, than we possess about most historic personages. Is it possible to know Wilson even better? Is it possible to define sharply what is now described imprecisely in talking about various aspects of his personality? Can we probe behind the facade of behavior to the wellsprings of motivation? Or is what Wilson once said about Lincoln also true of himself? "That brooding spirit had no real familiars. I get the impression that it never spoke out in complete self-revelation, and that it could not reveal itself completely to anyone."

Wilson was not describing himself. We are now in a position to know him better than probably any other important individual in history. We are in a position to know him better than any of his contemporaries did, even members of his family. We can now probably know him better than he knew himself.

From his student days onward, Wilson wrote constantly—in letters, lectures, articles, editorials, essays, and diaries. He never held anything back because he was incapable of successful dissimulation. He poured out his thoughts in torrents of words. The form did not particularly matter. To be sure, he expressed himself more fully and frankly in diaries and in letters to members of his family and to intimate friends. As he once put it in a letter, "I am apt to let my thoughts and feelings slip more readily from the end of my pen than from the end of my tongue." He revealed himself differently but perhaps just as importantly in essays in literary criticism, lectures on the Reformation, diplomatic notes, sermons, and political speeches.

Wilson rarely threw anything away. He saved not only letters and the things that one usually finds in personal papers, but also thousands of envelopes, loose pages, scraps of paper, etc., as well as his books. On many of these he jotted down thoughts as they came from his mind. Even though he did not usually keep copies of his personal letters, many of his correspondents did save them, and it has been possible to reconstruct virtually a complete Wilsonian archive.

The present writer and his colleagues at Princeton University are now deep into this vast collection, and the early fruits of their work, the first three volumes of *The Papers of Woodrow Wilson*, are in print. In addition, four other volumes in various stages of production cover Wilson's life to 1893.

It would require a fairly sizable volume adequately to relate what the documents in these first volumes of *The Papers* tell us about the formation and maturing of Wilson's personality. One can say in summary that it is evident that:

1. The relationship between Wilson and his father was very determinative. The letters show plainly enough why Wilson later called his father "the best instructor, the most inspiring companion . . . that a youngster ever had." The relationship during its early stages was of course that of father and son, master and pupil. Dr. Wilson had exacting standards and gave the most extraordinary attention to his son's intellectual and literary development. However the extant letters indicate very strongly that Dr. Wilson was more intent upon drawing out his son's own talent than upon imposing ideas and techniques upon him, and that he evoked these talents with measured encouragement and love. This relationship was, actually, liberating and creative for both partners. It had become a relationship between equals by the time of Woodrow Wilson's maturity, and from this time forward the father increasingly drew strength and ideas from his son.

2. Wilson's mother, Janet Woodrow Wilson, was in her own quiet way a much greater influence upon her son than we had ever known. Indeed, it is clear that Wilson derived his ideal of womanhood in large measure from the example set by his mother.

3. Dr. and Mrs. Wilson were proud, sensitive, and quick to resent alleged slights. Midwesterners who had moved to the South before the Civil War, they had warmly embraced the Southern cause. Even so, they were obviously never fully accepted by the extremists called "Southrons" and "unreconstructed rebels," and this antagonism, if not hostility, accentuated the Wilsons' sensitivity and caused them to find self-protection in family clannishness and pride. Woodrow Wilson came by his own pride and sensitivity quite naturally.

4. Wilson was a precocious child. Family tradition had it that he was a slow starter—this tradition says, for example, that he did not learn to read until he was nine. This may or may not be correct. But Wilson learned rapidly enough once he began, and by his eighteenth year he had acquired the fundamental habits of hard work and incredible self-discipline that were to characterize everything that he did from his undergraduate days at Princeton onward.

5. Wilson's education in ancient history and ancient and modern languages, modern history, political science, economics, legal studies, and literature was much more extensive and profound than we had ever imagined. To be sure, much of his undergraduate education was self-motivated and self-acquired, and this fact is another early evidence of his iron self-discipline. But

at The Johns Hopkins University he acquired what was probably as good an education in the social sciences as it was possible to acquire at the time, the 1880's.

6. During the formative years of his life, Wilson had a keen capacity for self-criticism and seems to have suffered from insecurity on account of his inability to achieve as rapidly as he thought he should. However, he seems to have come to full self-realization—and to terms with himself, at least temporarily—by 1890. Wilson's self-realization, incidentally, did not do full justice to his intellectual powers.

7. Normal insecurity during his early years drove Wilson to depend upon the love of his family and friends, but he also clearly developed a high capacity for wholehearted friendship. His own numerous comments about his inability to give himself in friendship are to be taken with some large grains of salt.

8. Wilson was from his youth onward, as I have said, extraordinarily intense; that is to say, he worked with unrelenting efforts to achieve his self-appointed goals. His superego undoubtedly set these goals, but power came from his own life force, and one can only conclude that the genes combined with family influences and environment to make him what he was.

9. The incidence and intensity of Wilson's psychosomatic illnesses during these formative years have been much exaggerated by Baker, and particularly by Sigmund Freud and William C. Bullitt in their *Thomas Woodrow Wilson, A Psychological Study* (1967). Ironically, insufficient attention has been paid to the exact nature and effects of Wilson's strokes in 1906 and 1919. Edwin A. Weinstein, M.D., of the Washington School of Psychiatry, has begun what promises to be a thorough investigation. His tentative conclusions to date are that Wilson suffered a severe stroke with accompanying brain damage in 1906, that he achieved substantial and almost miraculous recovery through sheer determination, and that he suffered a massive stroke with considerable damage to the brain in 1919. We know that subtle but very important changes occurred in Wilson's personality in 1906; that, for example, he became less tractable than he had been before and more intense than ever in pursuing goals. It seems likely that Wilson's almost self-destructive behavior during the controversies at Princeton from 1907 to 1910 and over ratification of the Treaty of Versailles from 1919 to 1920 was profoundly if not decisively influenced by certain brain damage. But we will not be able to speak authoritatively on this matter until Dr. Weinstein and other medical experts have completed their work.

10. His personal advantages and precocity aside, Wilson seems to have been a remarkably normal person during the first forty years of his life. His childhood was serene in spite of growing up in the South during the Civil War and Reconstruction. He may or may not have been robust as a boy—we simply have no good evidence on this point—but he knew most of the pleasures of boyhood. He played baseball, and football to a lesser degree, and maintained an avid interest in sports. He dreamed of building great warships and of commanding large armies in the field. Like most boys from the same kind of families in the Victorian era, he was something of a prig, at least by our own stan-

dards. He fell deeply in love and knew all the joys of romance and courtship. He had numerous male friends.

Students of personality, and particularly of Wilson's personality, will be able to make their own analyses and form their own conclusions as the evidence becomes available in *The Papers of Woodrow Wilson*. Indeed, we will soon have the evidence in print for a detailed study of Wilson's mature personality. . . .

American Intervention: 1917

Ernest R. May

This article, which deals with the United States' entry into World War I, is historiographical in nature. Ernest R. May, a distinguished diplomatic historian from Harvard University, considers the great debate between proadministration authors such as Walter H. Page and Colonel House and isolationists such as Walter Millis and Charles C. Tansill. This confrontation resulted in considerable myth building on both sides. May himself represents a more "realistic" school of historians, which seeks to avoid the probably insoluble question of whether intervention was good or bad and simply attempts to "set forth the tragic dilemmas in which the men of 1917 found themselves." He amply demonstrates how one's perspective can easily taint one's view of historical reality.

For Marxists, only socialist states can be "peace-loving." "Aggressive capitalist-imperialist" countries cannot. On the historical record, however, America deserves such a label at least as much as any other nation. Having led most modern peace movements, including those for arbitration and disarmament, and having insisted until very recently that their government pursue isolationist foreign policies and maintain only minimal military forces, Americans could be said not only to love peace but to have been infatuated with it.

Not least among evidences of this romance is their remorse over departures from peaceful ways. Bitter self-recrimination followed the Mexican War, the Civil War, the Spanish American War, and especially the two world wars.

In historical writing, it is true, the reaction usually developed slowly. After World War I, according to most observers, disillusionment qu i kly settled over the public. Books dealing with the war continued nevertheless to express pride and satisfaction in American intervention. The most widely read were two semiautobiographies: *The Life and Letters of Walter H. Page* (3 volumes; Garden City, New York: Doubleday, Page & Company, 1922–26), edited by Burton J. Hendrick, and *The Intimate Papers of Colonel House* (4 volumes: Boston, Massachusetts: Houghton Mifflin, 1926–28), edited by Charles Seymour. According to the extracts from diaries and letters published in these volumes, Page, who had been American ambassador in London, and House,

Reprinted by permission of the American Historical Association, from Ernest R. May, *American Intervention: 1917 and 1941*, Washington, D.C. 1969, pp. 1–13 and 25–26.

who had been President Wilson's confidant and unofficial ambassador at large, both had advocated intervention and rejoiced that it had taken place. Though the collections consisted more of raw materials for history than of narrative and analysis, they set forth one interpretation of Wilson's diplomacy.

Both works divided the years 1914–1917 into two periods, broken by the *Lusitania* crisis of May–June 1915. In the first period, according to both Page and House, the United States did not yet face a moral imperative to intervene. The issue was simply whether or not to obstruct the Allies. Wilson and his official aids, Secretary of State William Jennings Bryan and State Department Counselor Robert Lansing, inclined to be overly legalistic. They pressed, in particular, for acceptance by the belligerents of the unratified Declaration of London of 1909, a code of rules for naval warfare, which, by protecting American trade with continental Europe, would seriously limit the Allies' ability to cut off food and supplies for Germany. Page fought such a policy with all his resources. On one occasion he visited the Foreign Secretary, Sir Edward Grey, read him a formal note from the State Department, and then said, "I have now read the dispatch, but I do not agree with it; let us consider how it should be answered!" House, meanwhile, carried on the same battle in Washington, quietly advising Wilson and going behind the back of the State Department to work out a compromise with the British ambassador. The United States eventually ceased to press for acceptance of the Declaration of London and declared that it would simply stand by the traditional rule of international law. This gave Britain greater freedom to block German imports, and both Page and House celebrate this victory as the first among many that kept the United States from obstructing the Allies.

In the second phase, after the sinking of the *Lusitania*, according to both works, benevolent neutrality ceased to be enough. Page actually had become convinced earlier that German militarism represented a threat to American democracy; House on occasion had the same conviction. After the spring of 1915, Page rarely doubted that it was his country's duty to get into the war as soon as possible. House urged breaking relations with Germany. When Wilson allowed the issue of the *Lusitania* to cool, House advised that the next submarine incident, the sinking of the *Arabic* in August 1915, be made the occasion for the break. He made the same plea after an attack on the Channel steamer *Sussex* in the spring of 1916. At moments of crisis, House and Page stood together in urging that opportunity be seized for a rupture in relations or a declaration of war.

House meanwhile recommended that Wilson plan for possible intervention. In the winter of 1915–1916 he induced the President to send him to Europe on an extraordinary mission. He sought an agreement with the Allies under which Wilson would make a public appeal for peace negotiations. If the Germans either refused or declined to meet conditions satisfactory to the Allies, the United States would then intervene. Though actually initialed by House and Grey in February 1916 and endorsed conditionally by Wilson, this agreement never went into effect. When Wilson made a public appeal for peace in December 1916, he regarded the agreement out of date. To House, this appeal seemed a mistake; it fortunately came to nought. And in 1917 the President finally yielded, broke diplomatic relations, and asked Congress to declare war on Germany.

Through both the Page and House accounts ran a contention that American intervention had been the right course, at least after the sinking of the *Lusitania.* This contention rested in part on an assumption that the Allies had morality on their side and that Germany, absolutist and aggressively militarist, represented principles antithetic to those of the United States and the Western Allies. Page and House judged that the war had tested which code, which set of political abstractions, would prevail, and the United States had to join in preventing a German victory in order to defend representative government and individual freedom. Indeed, defeat of Imperial Germany, a malignant survival of feudalism, had been necessary if the world were to be made safe for democracy.

But the Page and House view drew on another line of reasoning, occasionally in evidence at the time, but best articulated later by Walter Lippmann in *U.S. Foreign Policy: Shield of the Republic* (Boston, Massachusetts: Little, Brown, 1943). In this argument the security of the United States depended on there being no dominant power in Europe. Wilhelmine Germany, like Napoleonic France, threatened to master all the Continent's immense war potential. If that occurred, the United States would confront an enemy stronger than itself, not only capable of challenging its hemispheric supremacy but of jeopardizing its very existence. As Page and House hinted and Lippmann, among others, said explicitly, the United States had a vital security interest in helping the Allies to prevent German triumph.

Only toward the end of the 1920's did another version of American intervention begin to gain currency. It grew out of the revisionism of Americans, Englishmen, and Germans who re-examined the wartime assumption that Germany had been responsible for starting the war. Drawing on the forty volumes of *Diplomatischen Akten des Auswätigen Amtes, 1871–1914,* better known as *Die Grosse Politik,* these writers portrayed Imperial Germany as no worse than its opponents. Bickering among erstwhile allies, coupled with the consolidation of Soviet power and the rise of Fascism in Italy, meanwhile, made it seem doubtful if the war had in fact made democracy more secure in the world. As Warren I. Cohen shows in *The American Revisionists* (Chicago, Illinois: University of Chicago Press, 1967), these new perceptions led to the questioning of moral premises so confidently accepted by Page and House.

In the late 'twenties C. Hartley Grattan published a detailed indictment of Wilson's diplomacy entitled *Why We Fought* (New York: Vanguard Press, 1929). Contending that neither the United States nor the world had gained anything from the war, he asked how and why America had given up its policy of neutrality. He found Wilson's abandonment of the Declaration of London and retreat from an initial ban on private loans to belligerent governments explicable only as reflecting, first, the sentimental Anglophilism of Page, House, and Wilson and, second, the influence of capitalists, financiers, and munitions makers who profited from supplying the Allies. Wilson had taken a stand against German submarine warfare more because it menaced trade than because it threatened neutral rights, Grattan argued, and had pressed his case to the point of war in order to protect America's investment in the Allied cause. Citing a senile congressman's tendentious testimony that Wilson had called a "sunrise conference" early in 1916 to tell congressional leaders that he wanted war, Grattan charged the President with having planned this step long in advance. The final prod to action he found in a telegram of 1917 from Page warning that Britain faced economic collapse if America did not enter the war. And the public followed, Grattan reasoned, because it had been subjected to a barrage of English propaganda and frightened by tales contrived by the administration of German espionage and sabotage. Though this crude summary does not do justice to Grattan's skillfully argued indictment, it suffices to indicate his themes—that the administration worked in the interest of munitions makers and bankers and that the people had been tricked into an irrational and almost hysterical frame of mind.

Such views won wide credence during the Great Depression. In 1936 and 1937 Ray Stannard Baker, who had worked with Wilson at Versailles and later, reached the years of neutrality in Volumes V and VI of his eight-volume authorized biography. Despite his continuing reverence for Wilson, Baker assailed the follies of Page and House, deplored the abandonment of the Declaration of London, ridiculed the House-Grey understanding, and lamented the final decision to intervene. Walter Millis of the New York *Herald Tribune* meanwhile devoted his lively pen and studious mind to a one-volume account of the background of intervention, *Road to War, 1914–1917* (Boston, Massachusetts: Houghton Mifflin, 1935). A popular bestseller, Millis' book also ridiculed the illusions of the interventionists and suggested that American intervention had been due to a combination of folly, sentimentalism, and greed. In 1936 the United States Senate set up a special committee under the chairmanship of Senator Gerald P. Nye of North Dakota to investigate the influence of munitions makers on foreign policy. The committee interrogated representatives of such firms as J. P. Morgan and Company and the National City Bank of New York and ransacked the files of the State and Treasury Departments. International lawyers, such as Edwin M. Borchard of Yale University and the elderly John Bassett Moore, meanwhile assailed the legal theories upon which Wilson had acted. Borchard and William P. Lage published *Neutrality for the United States* (New Haven, Connecticut: Yale University Press, 1937), denouncing any and all efforts to safeguard "freedom of the seas." In the midst of this climate of opinion, Congress passed Neutrality Acts, designed, as someone said, to prevent any future President from getting the United States into the war of 1914–1918.

Scholars also joined in the clamor. Joseph V. Fuller, a historian for the Department of State and the author of a monograph on Bismarckian diplomacy, published an article asking why the Germans had not abandoned submarine warfare and thus deprived Wilson of his excuse for intervention ("The Genesis of the Munitions Traffic," *Journal of Modern History,* VI [1934]). He answered that Germany had to stop munitions from reaching the Allies and that the provocation was therefore Wilson's refusal to heed pleas for an embargo on arms. In the late 'thirties H. C. Peterson of the University of Oklahoma wrote *Propaganda for War* (Norman: University of Oklahoma Press, 1939), a lengthy monograph on how Sir Gilbert Parker and agencies in Wellington House entrapped the American public. Among other such articles and monographs, Charles Callan Tansill's *America Goes to War* (Boston, Massachusetts: Little, Brown, 1938) was foremost. Eventually a professor at Fordham University and then at Georgetown University, Tansill previously had published monographs on American relations with Santo Domingo and on the acquisition of the Virgin Islands. Though not allowed to use the Wilson manuscripts, which Baker still hoarded, he had seen parts of the unpublished House diaries and had been given free access to the information gathered by the Nye Committee. Correspondence from an obliging officer in the Berlin *Marine-Archiv* enabled him to sketch the German side. His bibliography, though including some items not actually used, was full and impressive.

Tansill's volume stressed the enormous growth of American trade in munitions and other war supplies and the extent of American private loans to the Allies. Portraying House, Page, and even Lansing as influenced by these interests and moved by blind hatred for Germany, he showed how they frustrated true neutrality, as he conceived it, persuading the President to abandon the Declaration of London, give up his early opposition to loans, resist pressure for an embargo on arms, and take an unjustifiable stand against German submarine warfare. Some of the chapter titles indicate the thread of his argument: "War Profits Beckon to 'Big Business,' " "England Looks upon the Declaration of London as a 'Mere Scrap of Paper,' " "Mr. Lansing Leads the President Along the Road to War," "Colonel House Blocks a Path to Peace," "The Kaiser Chooses Peace with America Rather Than Victory at Verdun." Though reviewers in scholarly journals did not call his book dispassionate, most found it solid and convincing.

The interpretation popularized by Grattan and Millis and footnoted by Tansill had, of course, its own foundation in faith. It rested on the premise that the United States had no reason, moral or material, for opposing Germany or helping the Allies. Some members of this school assumed that if the United States had remained neutral a negotiated peace would have resulted, with happier results than those of the Versailles *Diktat*. Even if Germany had been absolutist, militaristic, and imperialistic, which these writers doubted, and even if it had been on the edge of triumph, still they felt that the outcome of the war should have remained a matter of indifference to Americans. As many writers asserted, among them Charles A. Beard in his eloquent *Open Door at Home* (New York: Macmillan, 1934), the United States was strong precisely because it did not involve itself in European diplomatic chicanery and waste its substance in preparations for war. From this premise it followed that the intervention of 1917 had been at least a blunder and probably a crime.

Though most writing on 1914–1917 in the twenty years after Versailles resembled either that in Page's *Letters* and the House *Papers* or Grattan and Tansill, a third approach already had been discovered. In 1923 Malbone W. Graham published a University of Texas Ph.D. dissertation entitled *The Con-*

troversy between the United States and Allied Governments Respecting Neutral Rights and Commerce During the Period of American Neutrality, 1914– 1917 (Austin: University of Texas Press, 1923). It neither glorified American policy nor recriminated against its architects. Graham found that with slight departures in one direction or another the United States had tried to follow the applicable rules of international law. Another scholar, Richard Van Alstyne, writing in the *Journal of Modern History* (VII [November 1935], 434–47), reached much the same conclusion about the abandonment of the Declaration of London. But, curiously enough, it was Seymour, the editor of the House *Papers*, who published the first book-length study dealing with intervention as a historical episode rather than a question of moral doctrine.

In *American Diplomacy During the World War* (Baltimore, Maryland: Johns Hopkins University Press, 1934), the Albert Shaw Lectures for 1933, and in supplementary essays published as *American Neutrality, 1914–1917* (New Haven, Connecticut: Yale University Press, 1935), Seymour analyzed Wilson's policies toward the Allies, his efforts to mediate, and his opposition to submarine warfare. He reported that the President and his advisers, while influenced by belief in the moral superiority of the English and French, had adhered to international law as they understood it and, indeed, had taken risks to prevent inroads upon it. In the interval between the *Sussex* pledge and the coming of war, when German submarines were under control, Seymour pointed out, American relations with Britain had become so troubled that Wilson talked vexedly of employing economic sanctions against the Allies.

The submarine issue alone, Seymour contended, brought intervention. Wilson saw German undersea warfare as a challenge that could not be ignored. If a belligerent could extend its operations anywhere, interfere with the trade of neutral states, and imperil the lives of neutral citizens, then neither neutrality nor international law had meaning. The President felt compelled in conscience to oppose the Germans on this issue and, paradoxically, to risk neutrality for the sake of neutrality. He was not entirely altruistic, for American lives and property were at stake. Though the German government respected Wilson's wishes for a time, it eventually ceased to do so. At Spa on January 7, 1917, the Kaiser and his advisers decided to launch a campaign of unrestricted submarine warfare in defiance of the United States and in conscious certainty that war would result. The decisive roles were played by these German leaders, not by Page, House, Lansing, or even Wilson.

Much the same view of intervention appeared in a bulkier study, Harley F. Notter's *The Origins of the Foreign Policy of Woodrow Wilson* (Baltimore, Maryland: Johns Hopkins University Press, 1937). Setting Wilson's diplomacy in the context of his earlier life and thought, Notter's volume tended to highlight Wilson's preoccupation with moral issues. But Notter's work was more diffuse, less studied, and less incisive than Seymour's volumes.

When World War II called attention to more immediate problems of neutrality, debate tended to diminish. After Pearl Harbor the parallels of 1919 seemed more relevant than those of 1917, and scholarly work centered on the armistice, the Peace Conference, and the fight over the League of Nations.

After World War II a generation with different attitudes and preoccupations began to restudy problems of World War I. Lippmann already had provided one new point of departure by suggesting that intervention had been necessary for the rescue of the balance of power and the protection of American security. In various popular and scholarly periodicals and in a book, *In Defense of the National Interest* (New York: Alfred A. Knopf, 1951), a University of Chicago political scientist, Hans J. Morgenthau, attacked the Wilson administration for having failed to concentrate on realistic goals. In lectures printed as *American Diplomacy, 1900–1950* (Chicago, Illinois: University of Chicago Press, 1950), the erudite and sophisticated career diplomat George Frost Kennan put the same charge into captivating phrases. He accused Wilson and other American leaders of excessive moralism and legalism. Taking a position halfway between the major prewar schools, he argued that while intervention might have been justified by the national interest, the overlay of other excuses had ruined its purpose. As a result, the United States became

> uncomfortably similar to one of those prehistoric monsters with a body as long as this room and a brain the size of a pin; he lies there in his comfortable primeval mud and pays little attention to his environment; he is slow to wrath—in fact, you practically have to whack his tail off to make him aware that his interests are being disturbed; but, once he grasps this, he lays about him with such blind determination that he not only destroys his adversary but largely wrecks his native habitat.

While prewar writers had argued over whether intervention had been right or wrong, Morgenthau and Kennan suggested instead that it had been right, but for the wrong reasons.

This hypothesis intrigued a number of young scholars. Robert E. Osgood, a political scientist in Morgenthau's Chicago Center for the Study of American Foreign Policy, investigated it in *Ideals and Self-Interest in America's Foreign Relations* (Chicago, Illinois: University of Chicago Press, 1953). In several chapters devoted to World War I, he amplified the theses that Morgenthau and Kennan had sketched. Another political scientist, Edward H. Buehrig of the University of Indiana, in *Woodrow Wilson and the Balance of Power* (Bloomington: Indiana University Press, 1955), assessed these criticisms as not altogether fair. The submarine issue symbolized a clash of national interests, he said, and while American leaders, did concern themselves with legal and moral issues, Wilson, House, and especially Lansing showed acute awareness of the balance of power. Daniel M. Smith, in *Robert Lansing and American Neutrality, 1914–1917* (Berkeley and Los Angeles: University of California Press, 1958), detailed the evidence regarding Lansing, stressing that Lansing's opinions derived from a mixture of political, economic, and moral considerations. In a subsequent article, "National Interest and American Intervention, 1917: An Historiographical Appraisal" (*Journal of American History*, LIX [June 1965]), Smith carefully weighed the support for the balance of power thesis to be found in known evidence; he concluded that it neglected much and therefore belonged among the "more simplistic" interpretations.

Like the tortoise competing with the hare, the separate line of scholarship started by Graham, Van Alstyne, and Seymour meanwhile kept up its plodding pace. Arthur S. Link, professor of history at Princeton University, Northwestern University, and then Princeton again, launched a magisterial biography of Wilson. In a shorter work, *Woodrow Wilson and the Progressive Era* (New York: Harper, 1954), and in *Wilson, the Diplomatist* (Baltimore, Maryland: Johns Hopkins University Press, 1957), the Albert Shaw Lectures for 1956, Link sketched his tentative findings about the period 1914–1917. By 1965 he had finally completed the fifth volume of *Wilson* (Princeton, N.J.: Princeton University Press, 1947–) carrying the narrative to the declaration of war. By that time, my own *The World War and American Isolation* (Cambridge, Massachusetts: Harvard University Press, 1959) had appeared. In that book, I argued that in nearly every case requiring a decision by the President, considerations of law, morality, power, national prestige, and domestic politics all had to be taken into account. Neither Wilson nor his advisers could ever see clearly the probable results of their decisions. In each instance, the weight of argument seemed to commend the course finally adopted. Each time, however, the decision tended to close out one or more alternatives until in 1917 there seemed no real option except war. The Germans, whom I tried to study in some detail, found themselves similarly driven into a corner from which they too could see no exit. Karl E. Birnbaum, a Swedish scholar, in *Peace Moves and U-Boat Warfare, 1916–1917* (Stockholm: Almquist & Wiksell, 1958), more fully described German diplomatic maneuvers in the crucial final stage, suggesting that there might have been moments when better communications between Berlin and Washington could have altered the outcome. But the necessary understanding of the other side simply did not exist within the Kaiser's councils or, equally importantly, among leaders in the *Reichstag.* The German decision to force a crisis, compelling Wilson either to make war or to concede that he had bluffed, therefore had a quality of tragic inevitablility.

The central themes of Link's vast and nearly definite biographical volumes proved not to differ markedly from those foreshadowed in his shorter works and set forth in my own book. By meticulous analysis of data, some of which was uniquely available to him (notably French diplomatic archives that remain officially closed), he set the record straight on a number of points where others, including myself, had been in doubt or in error. Thus, for example, he proved that the House-Grey agreement merited less attention than it received. Playing a devious game, House misled Wilson as to what he was seeking, misrepresented the President's views when speaking to the Allies, and then misrepresented their views to Washington. In accepting the document, Wilson had no sense of committing himself to intervention. Link also showed that a public letter sent to Senator William J. Stone by Wilson in 1916, seemingly stating a dogmatic moral position with regard to submarine warfare, was actually a hastily drafted document tailored to fit a particular challenge to presidential leadership of the legislative branch. It neither expressed Wilson's private thoughts nor mirrored the policy he was pursuing. Link showed what a flexible and conciliatory course Wilson actually followed, backing away between 1915 and 1917 from the perilous ground taken in the *Lusitania* correspondence and standing instead on the proposition that submarine operations would become cause for war only in the event of willful attacks on American citizens or ships. Link described better than anyone else the domestic problems that Wilson faced, the difficulties made for him by, on the one hand, near-pacifist Democrats, German-Americans, and Irish-Americans who opposed any resolute defense of American interests or rights against Germany, and, on the other hand, by Roosevelt Republicans, Anglophiles, Francophiles, and chauvinists who clamored against any compromises whatever. The Wilson one sees in Link's biography is many-sided, moved by conscience and by deeply felt religious ideas, by a sense of responsibility for the economic welfare of his country and for its international standing, credit, and influence, and by an additional sense of responsibility as leader of a party and sponsor of domestic reforms, the success of which seemed to depend on his party's continuance in power. The range of alternatives open to him in regard to the European war appears narrower than either the Page and House, the isolationist, or the Morgenthau and Kennan school would concede; Wilson's choices seem the best that, in the circumstances, any prudent man could have made.

It is perhaps significant that most who continue to debate whether intervention in World War I was right or wrong describe themselves as political scientists. Historians by and large now deal with that war much as with the Punic or Napoleonic Wars, seeking rather to achieve some kind of empathy than to assign praise or blame. The chief exceptions, as yet few in number, have some association with what is called the New Left.

Because the New Left accords much attention to businessmen and bankers, it is sometimes confused with an older school of economic interpretation. It is, in fact, quite different. The older group took the view that businessmen constituted a special class. Through force, corruption, and chicanery, this class used government to serve its special interests at the expense of the interests of other classes. Thus, bankers and munitions makers brought about American intervention in order to protect their investment and profits. Although the thought of the New Left owes much to Marxist class struggle analysis, from which most economic interpretation derived, it is also indebted to Louis Hartz, John Higham, and others who challenged traditional assumptions by marshaling evidence that American history had been characterized less by conflict among interest groups or ideologies than by broad consensus. The New Left argues that, from the late nineteenth century onward, America has had a single dominant system of values in which the protection of private property, opportunity for individual enrichment, increase in production, and expansion of markets have been goals above all others. The New Left regards this capitalist system of values as wrong and productive of evil. It leads inevitably, they contend, to varieties of imperialism designed to ensure access to markets and, as a corollary, to conflict with revolutionary movements that espouse other than free market forms of economic and political organization. But the New Left does not, like the "Old Left," charge these outcomes to conspiracies. Its members blame instead the whole society's failure to think objectively and critically about fundamental assumptions. Those who have touched on American intervention in World War I, notably William Appleman Williams in *The Tragedy of American Diplomacy* (revised and enlarged edition; New York: Dell, 1962) and N. Gordon Levin, Jr., in *Woodrow Wilson and World Politics* (New York: Oxford University Press, 1968), concede that each move by the American government was, in the circumstances, logical and understandable. Indeed, they agree that Wilson's actions had a quality of inevitability, given the values accepted by him and by the largest part of the American public. They raise the philosophical question—one that might be raised with regard to Republican Rome or Napoleonic France—whether the results might not have been otherwise if these values had been radically different. . . .

That some new debate will develop seems a safe prediction. Historians still dispute, after all, about the Persian and Peloponnesian Wars. Like little Billie Potts in Robert Penn Warren's poem, all men try to remember when they lost whatever it was they lost and try to retrace their steps from that point. The date 1917 . . . will long remain [a point] at which Americans pause in such a search, and historians will keep going back to [it], seeking at least to understand what was, and sometimes speculating about what might have been.

Separatism as Strategy: Female Institution Building and American Feminism

Estelle Freedman

The sexual division of labor in American society has always been built on and sustained by an ideological foundation of gender mythology proclaiming women to be physically weaker, less mentally gifted, less emotionally stable, less socially adept, and far more politically naive than men. Women, the story traditionally went, were creatures of physical delicacy, procreative potential, spiritual sensibility, and moral force who had special "natural" domestic and nurturing capacities. No need, the story continued, for "true women" to be vocationally creative, politically active, or economically ambitious on their own account. The tyranny, alienation, and slavery of women's culturally defined separate sphere demanded special efforts toward the destruction of a persistent and pernicious social mythology operating in the public sphere. Indeed, the battle still rages. The origins of American feminism, especially during the suffrage movement, argues Estelle Freedman of Stanford University, were strongly tied to organizational necessities, particularly the need for female institution building through the social networking and activism of women's clubs, the Women's Christian Temperance Union, women's colleges, the Women's Trade Union League, and the settlement house movement. What was surely and fundamentally at issue was the cultural definition of what constituted "womanhood"—less in terms of piety, purity, virtue, and domesticity and more in terms of legal rights, equality, full citizenship, and social reform. Yet somewhat ironically, Professor Freedman finds the very success of these women's institutions and reforms was in no small measure due to their purposeful attempts to extend the values of women's private sphere to the ever-broadening public arena. "True womanhood" served to inspire the move to "new womanhood" as suffragists, for example, argued that women needed the vote in order better to perform their traditional tasks. The old mythology regarding women helped energize the rise of a new social order seeking to define a new, more truly democratic social mythology.

In nineteenth-century America, commercial and industrial growth intensified the sexual division of labor, encouraging the separation of men's and women's spheres. While white males entered the public world of wage labor, business, the

From Estelle Freedman, "Separatism as Strategy: Female Institution Building and American Feminism, 1870–1930," in *Feminist Studies*, V (1979), pp. 512–529, by permission of the publisher, Feminist Studies, c/o Women's Studies Program, University of Maryland, College Park, Maryland 20742.

professions and politics, most white middle-class women remained at home where they provided the domestic, maternal, and spiritual care for their families and the nation. These women underwent intensive socialization into their roles as "true women." Combined with the restrictions on women which denied them access to the public sphere, this training gave American women an identity quite separate from men's. Women shared unique life experiences as daughters, wives, childbearers, childrearers, and moral guardians. They passed on their values and traditions to their female kin. They created what Smith-Rosenberg has called "The Female World of Love and Ritual," a world of homosocial networks that helped these women transcend the alienation of domestic life.

The ideology of "true womanhood" was so deeply ingrained and so useful for preserving social stability in a time of flux that those few women who explicitly rejected its inequalities could find little support for their views. The feminists of the early women's rights movement were certainly justified in their grievances and demands for equal opportunity with men. The Seneca Falls Declaration of Sentiments of 1848, which called for access to education, property ownership, and political rights, has inspired many feminists since then, while the ridicule and denial of these demands have inspired our rage. But the equal rights arguments of the 1850s were apparently too radical for their own times. Men would not accept women's entry into the public sphere, but more importantly, most women were not interested in rejecting their deeply rooted female identities. Both men and women feared the demise of the female sphere and the valuable functions it performed. The feminists, however, still hoped to reduce the limitations on women within their own sphere, as well as to gain the right of choice—of autonomy—for those women who opted for public rather than private roles.

Radical feminists such as Elizabeth Cady Stanton and Susan B. Anthony recognized the importance of maintaining the virtues of the female world while eliminating discrimination against women in public. As their political analysis developed at mid-century, they drew upon the concepts of female moral superiority and sisterhood, and they affirmed the separate nature of woman. At the same time, their disillusionment with even the more enlightened men of the times reinforced the belief that women had to create their own movement to achieve independence. The bitterness that resulted when most male abolitionists refused to support women's rights in the 1860s, and when they failed to include Woman Suffrage in the Fifteenth Amendment (as well as the inclusion of the term "male citizen" in the Fourteenth Amendment) alienated many women reformers. When Frederick Douglass proclaimed in defense that "This is the Negro's Hour," the more radical women's rights advocates followed Stanton and Anthony in withdrawing from the reform coalition and creating a separatist organization. Their National Woman Suffrage Association had women members and officers; supported a broad range of reforms, including changes in marriage and divorce laws; and published the short-lived journal, *The Revolution*. The radical path proved difficult, however, and the National Woman Suffrage Association merged in 1890 with the more moderate American Woman Suffrage Association. Looking back on their disappointment after the Civil War, Stanton and Anthony wrote prophetically in 1881:

> Our liberal men counselled us to silence during the war, and we were silent on our own wrongs; they counselled us to silence in Kansas and New York (in the suffrage referenda), lest we should defeat "Negro Suffrage," and threatened if we were not, we might fight the battle alone. We chose the latter, and were defeated. But standing alone we learned our power: we repudiated man's counsels forevermore; and solemnly vowed that there should never be another season of silence until woman had the same rights everywhere on this green earth, as man. . . .
>
> We would warn the young women of the coming generation against man's advice as to their best interests. . . . Woman must lead the way to her own enfranchisement. . . . She must not put her trust in man in this transition period, since while regarded as his subject, his inferior, his slave, their interests must be antagonistic.

The "transition period" that Stanton and Anthony invoked lasted from the 1870s to the 1920s. It was an era of separate female organization and institution building, the result, on the one hand, of the negative push of discrimination in the public, male sphere, and on the other hand, of the positive attraction of the female world of close, personal relationships and domestic institutional structures. These dual origins characterized, for instance, one of the largest manifestations of "social feminism" in the late nineteenth century—the women's club movement.

The club movement illustrated the politicization of women's institutions as well as the limitations of their politics. The exclusion of women reporters from the New York Press Club in 1868 inspired the founding of the first women's club, Sorosis. The movement then blossomed in dozens and later hundreds of localities, until a General Federation of Women's Clubs formed in 1890. By 1910, it claimed over one million members. Although club social and literary activities at first appealed to traditional women who simply wanted to gather with friends and neighbors, by the turn of the century women's clubs had launched civic reform programs. Their activities served to politicize traditional women by forcing them to define themselves as citizens, not simply as wives and mothers. The clubs reflected the societal racism of the time, however, and the black women who founded the National Association of Colored Women in 1896 turned their attention to the social and legal problems that confronted both black women and men.

The Women's Christian Temperance Union had roots in the social feminist tradition of separate institution building. As Ellen DuBois has argued, the WCTU appealed to late nineteenth-century women because it was grounded in the private sphere—the home—and attempted to correct the private abuses against women, namely, intemperance and the sexual double standard. Significantly, though, the WCTU, under Frances Willard's leadership, became a strong prosuffrage organization, committed to righting all wrongs against women, through any means, including the vote.

The women's colleges that opened in these same decades further attest to the importance of separate female institutions during this "transition period." Originally conceived as training grounds of piety, purity, and domesticity, the antebellum women's seminaries, such as Mary Lyon's Mt. Holyoke and Emma Willard's Troy Female Academy, laid the groundwork for the new collegiate institutions of the postwar era. When elite male institutions refused to educate women, the sister colleges of the East, like their counterparts elsewhere, took on the task themselves. In the process they encouraged intimate friendships and professional networks among educated women. At the same time, liberal arts and science training provided tools for women's further development, and by their examples, female teachers inspired students to use their skills creatively. As Barbara Welter noted when she first described the "Cult of True Womanhood," submissiveness was always its weakest link. Like other women's institutions, the colleges could help subvert that element of the Cult by encouraging independence in their students.

The most famous example of the impact of women's colleges may be Jane Addams's description of her experience at Rockford Seminary when she and other students were imbued with the mission of bringing their female values to bear on the entire society. While Addams later questioned the usefulness of her intellectual training in meeting the challenges of the real world, other women did build upon academic foundations when increasingly, as reformers, teachers, doctors, social workers, and in other capacities they left the home to enter public or quasi-public work. Between 1890 and 1920, the number of professional degrees granted to women increased 226 percent, at three times the rate of increase for men. Some of these professionals had attended separate female institutions such as the women's medical colleges in Philadelphia, New York, and Boston. The new female professionals often served women and children clients, in part because of the discrimination against their encroachment on men's domains but also because they sincerely wanted to work with the traditional objects of their concern. As their skills and roles expanded, these women would demand the right to choose for themselves where and with whom they could work. This first generation of educated professional women became supporters of the suffrage movement in the early twentieth century, calling for the citizenship for women.

The process of redefining womanhood by the extension, rather than by the rejection, of the female sphere may be best illustrated by the settlement house movement. Although both men and women resided in and supported these quasi-public institutions, the high proportion of female participants and leaders (approximately three-fifths of the total), as well as the domestic structure and emphasis on service to women and children, qualify the settlements as female institutions. Mary P. Ryan has captured the link which these ventures provided between "true womanhood" and "new womanhood" in a particularly fitting metaphor: "Within the settlement houses maternal sentiments were further sifted and leavened until they became an entirely new variety of social reform." Thus did Jane Addams learn the techniques of the political world through her efforts to keep the neighborhood clean. So too did Florence Kelley of Hull House welcome appointment as chief factory inspector of Illinois, to protect women and children workers, and Julia Lathrop, another Hull House resident, entered the public sphere as director of the United States Children's Bureau; while one-time settlement resident Katherine Bement Davis moved from the superintendency of the Bedford Hills reformatory for women to become in 1914 the first female commissioner of corrections in New York City. Each of these women, and other settlement workers who moved on to professional and public office, eventually joined and often led branches of the National American Woman Suffrage Association. They drew upon the networks of personal friends and professional allies that grew within separate female institutions when they waged their campaigns for social reform and for suffrage.

Separate female organizations were not limited to middle-class women. Recent histories have shown that groups hoping to bridge class lines between women existed within working-class or radical movements. In both the Women's Trade Union League and the National Consumers League, middle-class reformers strived for cooperation, rather than condescension, in their relationships with working women. Although in neither organization were they entirely successful, the Women's Trade Union League did provide valuable services in organizing women workers, many of whom were significant in its leadership. The efforts of the Consumers League, led by Florence Kelley, to improve working conditions through the use of middle-class women's buying power was probably less effective, but efforts to enact protective legislation for women workers did succeed. Members of both organizations turned to suffrage as one solution to the problems workers faced. Meanwhile, both in leftist organizations and in unions, women formed separate female organizations. Feminists within the Socialist Party met in women's groups in the early twentieth century, while within the clothing trades, women workers formed separate local unions which survived until the mid-1920s.

As a final example of female institution building, I want to compare two actual buildings—the Women's Pavilion at the 1876 Centennial Exposition in Philadelphia, analyzed recently by Judith Paine, and the Woman's Building at the 1893 World's Columbian Exposition in Chicago. I think that the origins and functions of each illustrate some of the changes that occurred in the women's movement in the time interval between those two celebrations.

Originally, the managers of the 1876 Centennial had promised "a sphere for woman's action and space for her work" within the main display areas. In return women raised over $100,000 for the fair, at which point the management informed the Women's Centennial Executive Committee that there would not be any space for them in the main building. The women's response surprised the men: they raised money for a separate building, and although they hoped to find a woman architect to design it, there was no such professional at the time. From May through October, 1876, the Women's Pavilion displayed achievements in journalism, medicine, science, art, literature, invention, teaching, business, and social work. It included a library of books by women; an office that published a newspaper for women; and an innovative kindergarten annex, the first such day school in the country. Some radical feminists, however, boycotted the building. Elizabeth Cady Stanton claimed that the pavilion "was no true exhibit of woman's art" because it did not represent the product of industrial labor or protest the inequalities of "political slavery."

By 1893, there was less hesitation about the need for a women's building and somewhat less conflict about its functions. Congress authorized the creation of a Board of Lady Managers for the Columbian Commission, and the women quickly decided on a separate Women's Building, to be designed by a woman architect chosen by nationwide competition. Contests were also held to locate the best women sculptors, painters, and other artists to complete the designs of the building. The Lady Managers also planned and provided a Children's Building that offered nursery care for over ten thousand young visitors to the fair. At this exposition, not only were women's artistic and professional achievements heralded, but industrial organizations were "especially invited to make themselves known," and women's industrial work, as well as the conditions and wages for which they worked, were displayed. Feminists found this exhibit more agreeable; Antoinette Brown Blackwell, Julia Ward Howe, and Susan B. Anthony all attended, and Anthony read a paper written by Elizabeth Cady Stanton at one of the women's symposia. The Board of Lady Managers fought long and hard to combine their separate enterprise with participation in the rest of the fair. They demanded equal representation of women judges for the exhibitions and equal consideration of women's enterprises in all contests. While they had to compromise on some goals, their efforts are noteworthy as an indication of a dual commitment of separate female institutions, but only if they had equal status within the society at large.

The separate institution building of the late nineteenth century rested on a belief in women's unique identity which had roots in the private female sphere of the early nineteenth century. Increasingly, however, as its participants entered a public female world, they adopted the more radical stance of feminists such as Stanton and Anthony who had long called for an end to political discrimination against women.

The generation that achieved suffrage, then, stood on the border of two worlds, each of which contributed to its ideology and politics. Suffragists argued that women needed the vote to perform their traditional tasks—to protect themselves as mothers and to exert their moral force on society. Yet they also argued for full citizenship and waged a successful, female-controlled political campaign to achieve it.

The suffrage movement succeeded by appealing to a broad constituency—mothers, workers, professionals, reformers—with the vision of the common concerns of womanhood. The movement failed, however, by not extending fully the political strengths of woman bonding. For one thing, the leadership allowed some members to exploit popular racist and nativist sentiments in their prosuffrage arguments, thus excluding most black and immigrant women from a potential feminist coalition. They also failed to recognize that the bonds that held the constituency together were not "natural," but social and political. The belief that women would automatically use the vote to the advantage of their sex overlooked both the class and racial lines that separated women. It underestimated the need for continued political organization so that their interests might be united and realized. . . .

What Happened to the Progressive Movement in the 1920s?

Arthur S. Link

The conventional view of the decade of the 1920s holds that the period witnessed the death of idealism, a termination of the progressive spirit, and the triumph of crass materialism and special privilege. Such a rendering of progressivism tends to neglect the fact that the movement never existed at any time as a recognizable entity with common goals. The popular view also ignores the continued importance of progressive sentiment, evidenced by the congressional farm bloc, support for public ownership of electric power, and other progressive achievements such as immigration restriction and Prohibition. In this spirit, Princeton historian Arthur S. Link attempts to counter the governing hypotheses about the period, which, to his mind, have been offered "without fear or much research."

If the day has not yet arrived when we can make a definite synthesis of political developments between the Armistice and the Great Depression, it is surely high time for historians to begin to clear away the accumulated heap of mistaken and half-mistaken hypotheses about this important transitional period. Writing often without fear or much research (to paraphrase Carl Becker's remark), we recent American historians have gone on indefatigably to perpetuate hypotheses that either reflected the disillusionment and despair of contemporaries, or once served their purpose in exposing the alleged hiatus in the great continuum of twentieth-century reform.

Stated briefly, the following are what might be called the governing hypotheses of the period under discussion: The 1920's were a period made almost unique by an extraordinary reaction against idealism and reform. They were a time when the political representatives of big business and Wall Street executed a relentless and successful campaign in state and nation to subvert the regulatory structure that had been built at the cost of so much toil and sweat since the 1870's, and to restore a Hanna-like reign of special privilege to benefit business, industry, and finance. The surging tides of nationalism and mass hatreds generated by World War I continued to engulf the land and were manifested, among other things, in fear of communism, suppression of civil liberties, revival of nativism and anti-Semitism most crudely exemplified by the Ku Klux Klan, and in the triumph of racism and prejudice in immigration legislation. The 1920's were an era when great traditions and ideals were repudiated or forgotten, when the American people, propelled by a crass materialism in their scramble for wealth, uttered a curse on twenty-five years of reform endeavor. As a result, progressives were stunned and everywhere in retreat along the entire political front, their forces disorganized and leaderless, their movement shattered, their dreams of a new America turned into agonizing nightmares.

To be sure, the total picture that emerges from these generalizations is overdrawn. Yet it seems fair to say that leading historians have advanced each of these generalizations, that the total picture is the one that most of us younger historians saw during the years of our training, and that these hypotheses to a greater or lesser degree still control the way in which we write and teach about the 1920's, as a reading of textbooks and general works will quickly show.

This paper has not been written, however, to quarrel with anyone or to make an indictment. Its purposes are, first, to attempt to determine the degree to which the governing hypotheses, as stated, are adequate or inadequate to explain the political phenomena of the period, and, second, to discover whether any new and sounder hypotheses might be suggested. Such an effort, of course, must be tentative and above all imperfect in view of the absence of sufficient foundations for a synthesis.

Happily, however, we do not have to proceed entirely in the dark. Historians young and old, but mostly young, have already discovered that the period of the 1920's is the exciting new frontier of American historical research and that its opportunities are almost limitless in view of the mass of manuscript materials that are becoming available. Thus we have (the following examples are mentioned only at random) excellent recent studies of agrarian discontent and farm movements by Theodore Saloutos, John D. Hicks, Gilbert C. Fite, Robert L. Morlan, and James H. Shideler; of nativism and problems of immigration and assimilation by John Higham, Oscar Handlin, Robert A. Devine, and Edmund D. Cronon; of intellectual currents, the social gospel, and religious controversies by Henry F. May, Paul A. Carter, Robert M. Miller, and Norman F. Furniss; of left-wing politics and labor developments by Theodore Draper, David A. Shannon, Daniel Bell, Paul M. Angle, and Matthew Josephson; of the campaign of 1928 by Edmund A. Moore; and of political and judicial leaders by Alpheus T. Mason, Frank Freidel, Arthur M. Schlesinger, Jr., Merlo J. Pusey, and Joel F. Paschal. Moreover, we can look forward to the early publication of studies that will be equally illuminating for the period, like the biographies of George W. Norris, Thomas J. Walsh, and Albert B. Fall now being prepared by Richard Lowitt, Leonard Bates, and David Stratton, respectively, and the recently completed study of the campaign and election of 1920 by Wesley M. Bagby.

Obviously, we are not only at a point in the progress of our research into the political history of the 1920's when we can begin to generalize, but we have reached the time when we should attempt to find some consensus, however tentative it must now be, concerning the larger political dimensions and meanings of the period.

In answering the question of what happened to the progressive movement in the 1920's, we should begin looking briefly at some fundamental facts about the movement before 1918, facts that in large measure predetermined its fate in the 1920's, given the political climate and circumstances that prevailed.

The first of these was the elementary fact that the progressive movement never really existed as a recognizable organization with common goals and a political machinery geared to achieve them. Generally speaking (and for the purposes of this paper), progressivism might be defined as the popular effort, which began convulsively in the 1890's and waxed and waned afterward to our own time, to insure the survival of democracy in the United States by the enlargement of governmental power to control and offset the power of private economic groups over the nation's institutions and life. Actually, of course, from the 1890's on there were many "progressive" movements on many levels seeking sometimes contradictory objectives. Not all, but most of these campaigns were the work of special interest groups or classes seeking greater political status and economic security. This was true from the beginning of the progressive movement in the 1890's; by 1913 it was that movement's most important characteristic.

The second fundamental fact—that the progressive movements were often largely middle class in constituency and orientation—is of course well known, but an important corollary has often been ignored. It was that several of the most important reform movements were inspired, staffed, and led by businessmen with very specific or special-interest objectives in view. Because they hated waste, mismanagement, and high taxes, they, together with their friends in the legal profession, often furnished the leadership of good government campaigns. Because they feared industrial monopoly, abuse of power by railroads, and the growth of financial oligarchy, they were the backbone of the movements that culminated in the adoption of the Hepburn and later acts for railroad regulation, the Federal Reserve Act, and the Federal Trade Commission Act. Among the many consequences of their participation in the progressive movement, two should be mentioned because of their significance for developments in the 1920's. First, the strong identification of businessmen with good government and economic reforms for which the general public also had a lively concern helped preserve the good reputation of the middle-class business community (as opposed to its alleged natural enemies, monopolists, malefactors of great wealth, and railroad barons) and helped to direct the energies of the progressive movement toward the strengthening instead of the shackling of the business community. Second, their activities and influence served to intensify the tensions within the broad reform movement, because they often opposed the demands of farm groups, labor unions, and advocates of social justice.

The third remark to be made about the progressive movement before

1918 is that despite its actual diversity and inner tensions it did seem to have unity; that is, it seemed to share common ideals and objectives. This was true in part because much of the motivation even of the special-interest groups was altruistic (at least they succeeded in convincing themselves that they sought the welfare of society rather than their own interests primarily); in part because political leadership generally succeeded in subordinating inner tensions. It was true, above all, because there were in fact important idealistic elements in the progressive ranks—social gospel leaders, social justice elements, and intellectuals and philosophers—who worked hard at the task of defining and elevating common principles and goals.

Fourth and finally, the substantial progressive achievements before 1918 had been gained, at least on the federal level, only because of the temporary dislocations of the national political structure caused by successive popular uprisings, not because progressives had found or created a viable organization for perpetuating their control. Or, to put the matter another way, before 1918 the various progressive elements had failed to destroy the existing party structure by organizing a national party of their own that could survive. They, or at least many of them, tried in 1912; and it seemed for a time in 1916 that Woodrow Wilson had succeeded in drawing the important progressive groups permanently into the Democratic party. But Wilson's accomplishment did not survive even to the end of the war, and by 1920 traditional partisan loyalties were reasserting themselves with extraordinary vigor.

With this introduction, we can now ask what happened to the progressive movement or movements in the 1920's. Surely no one would contend that after 1916 the political scene did not change significantly, both on the state and national levels. There was the seemingly obvious fact that the Wilsonian coalition had been wrecked by the election of 1920, and that the progressive elements were divided and afterward unable to agree upon a program or to control the national government. There was the even more "obvious" fact that conservative Republican presidents and their cabinets controlled the executive branch throughout the period. There was Congress, as Eric F. Goldman had said, allegedly whooping through procorporation legislation, and the Supreme Court interpreting the New Freedom laws in a way that harassed unions and encouraged trusts. There were, to outraged idealists and intellectuals, the more disgusting spectacles of Red hunts, mass arrests and deportations, the survival deep into the 1920's of arrogant nationalism, crusades against the teaching of evolution, the attempted suppression of the right to drink, and myriad other manifestations of what would now be called a repressive reaction.

Like the hypotheses suggested at the beginning, this picture is overdrawn in some particulars. But it is accurate in part, for progressivism was certainly on the downgrade if not in decay after 1918. This is an obvious fact that needs explanation and understanding rather than eleborate proof. We can go a long way toward answering our question if we can explain, at least partially, the extraordinary complex developments that converge to produce the "obvious" result.

For this explanation we must begin by looking at the several progressive elements and their relation to each other and to the two major parties after 1916. Since national progressivism was never an organized or independent movement (except imperfectly and then only temporarily in 1912), it could succeed only when its constituent elements formed a coalition strong enough to control one of the major parties. This had happened in 1916, when southern and western farmers, organized labor, the social justice elements, and a large part of the independent radicals who had heretofore voted the Socialist ticket coalesced to continue the control of Wilson and the Democratic party.

The important fact about the progressive coalition of 1916, however, was not its strength but its weakness. It was not a new party but a temporary alliance, welded in the heat of the most extraordinary domestic and external events. To be sure, it functioned for the most part successfully during the war, in providing the necessary support for a program of heavy taxation, relatively stringent controls over business and industry, and extensive new benefits to labor. Surviving in a crippled way even in the months following the Armistice, it put across a program that constituted a sizable triumph for the progressive movement—continued heavy taxation, the Transportation Act of 1920, the culmination of the long fight for railroad regulation, a new child labor act, amendments for prohibition and woman suffrage, immigration restriction, and water power and conservation legislation.

Even so, the progressive coalition of 1916 was inherently unstable. Indeed, it was so wracked by inner tensions that it could not survive, and destruction came inexorably, it seemed systematically, from 1917 to 1920. Why was this true?

First, the independent radicals and antiwar agrarians were alienated by the war declaration and the government's suppression of dissent and civil liberties during the war and the Red scare. Organized labor was disaffected by the administration's coercion of the coal miners in 1919, its lukewarm if not hostile attitude during the great strikes of 1919 and 1920, and its failure to support the Plumb Plan for nationalization of the railroads. Isolationists and idealists were outraged by what they thought was the President's betrayal of American traditions or the liberal peace program at Paris. These tensions were strong enough to disrupt the coalition, but a final one would have been fatal even if the others had never existed. This was the alienation of farmers in the Plains and western states produced by the administration's refusal to impose price controls on cotton while it maintained ceilings on the prices of other agricultural commodities, and especially by the administration's failure to do anything decisive to stem the downward plunge of farm prices that began in the summer of 1920. Under the impact of all these stresses, the Wilsonian coalition gradually disintegrated from 1917 to 1920 and disappeared entirely during the campaign of 1920.

The progressive coalition was thus destroyed, but the components of a potential movement remained. As we will see, these elements were neither inactive nor entirely unsuccessful in the 1920's. But they obviously failed to find common principles and a program, much less to unite effectively for political action on a national scale. I suggest that this was true, in part at least, for the following reasons:

First, the progressive elements could never create or gain control of a political organization capable of carrying them into national office. The Republican party was patently an impossible instrument because control of the GOP was too much in the hands of the eastern and midwestern industrial, oil, and financial interests, as it had been since about 1910. There was always the hope of a third party. Several progressive groups—insurgent midwestern Republicans, the railroad brotherhoods, a segment of the AF of L, and the moderate Socialists under Robert M. La Follette—tried to realize this goal in 1924, only to discover that third party movements in the United States are doomed to failure except in periods of enormous national turmoil, and that the 1920's were not such a time. Thus the Democratic party remained the only vehicle that conceivably could have been used by a new progressive coalition. But that party was simply not capable of such service in the 1920's. It was so torn by conflicts between its eastern, big city wing and its southern and western rural majority that it literally ceased to be a national party. It remained strong in its sectional and metropolitan components, but it was so divided that it barely succeeded in nominating a presidential candidate at all in 1924 and nominated one in 1928 only at the cost of temporary disruption.

Progressivism declined in the 1920's, in the second place, because, as has been suggested, the tensions that had wrecked the coalition of 1916 not only persisted but actually grew in number and intensity. The two most numerous progressive elements, the southern and western farmers, strongly supported the Eighteenth Amendment, were heavily tinged with nativism and therefore supported immigration restriction, were either members of, friendly to, or politically afraid of the Ku Klux Klan, and demanded as the principal plank in their platform legislation to guarantee them a larger share of the national income. On all these points and issues the lower and lower middle classes in the large cities stood in direct and often violent opposition to their potential allies in the rural areas. Moreover, the liaison between the farm groups and organized labor, which had been productive of much significant legislation during the Wilson period, virtually ceased to exist in the 1920's. There were many reasons for this development, and I mention only one—the fact that the preeminent spokesmen of farmers in the 1920's, the new Farm Bureau Federation, represented the larger commercial farmers who (in contrast to the members of the leading farm organization in Wilson's day, the National Farmers' Union) were often employers themselves and felt no identification with the rank and file of labor.

It was little wonder, therefore (and this is a third reason for the weakness of progressivism in the 1920's), that the tension-ridden progressive groups were never able to agree upon a program that, like the Democratic platform of 1916, could provide the basis for a revived coalition. So long as progressive groups fought one another more fiercely than they fought their natural opponents, such agreement was impossible; and so long as common goals were impossible to achieve, a national progressive movement could not take effective form. Nothing illustrates this better than the failure of the Democratic conventions of 1924 and 1928 to adopt platforms that could rally and unite the discontented elements. One result, among others, was that southern farmers voted as Democrats and western farmers as Republicans. And, as Professor Frank Freidel once commented to the author, much of the failure of progressivism in the 1920's can be explained by this elementary fact.

A deeper reason for the failure of progressives to unite ideologically in the 1920's was what might be called a substantial paralysis of the progressive mind. This was partly the result of the repudiation of progressive ideals by many intellectuals and the defection from the progressive movement of the urban middle classes and professional groups, as will be demonstrated. It was the result, even more importantly, of the fact that progressivism as an organized body of political thought found itself at a crossroads in the 1920's, like progressivism today, and did not know which way to turn. The major objectives of the progressive movement of the prewar years had in fact been largely achieved by 1920. In what direction should progressivism now move? Should it remain in the channels already deeply cut by its own traditions, and, while giving sincere allegiance to the ideal of democratic capitalism, work for more comprehensive programs of business regulation and assistance to disadvantaged classes like farmers and submerged industrial workers? Should it abandon these traditions and, like most similar European movements, take the road toward a moderate socialism with a predominantly labor orientation? Should it attempt merely to revive the goals of more democracy through changes in the political machinery? Or should it become mainly an agrarian movement with purely agrarian goals?

These were real dilemmas, not academic ones, and one can see numerous examples of how they confused and almost paralyzed progressives in the 1920's. The platform of La Follette's Progressive party of 1924 offers one revealing illustration. It embodied much that was old and meaningless by this time (the direct election of the President and a national referendum before the adoption of a war resolution, for example) and little that had any real significance for the future. And yet it was the best that a vigorous and idealistic movement could offer. A second example was the plight of the agrarians and insurgents in Congress who fought so hard all through the 1920's against Andrew Mellon's proposals to abolish the inheritance tax and to make drastic reductions in the taxes on large incomes. In view of the rapid reduction of the federal debt, the progressives were hard pressed to justify the continuation of nearly confiscatory tax levels, simply because few of them realized the wide social and economic uses to which the income tax could be put. Lacking any programs for the redistribution of the national income (except to farmers), they were plagued and overwhelmed by the surpluses in the federal Treasury until, for want of any good arguments, they finally gave Secretary Andrew Mellon the legislation he had been demanding. A third and final example of this virtual paralysis of the progressive mind was perhaps the most revealing of all. It was the attempt that Woodrow Wilson, Louis D. Brandeis, and other Democratic leaders made from 1921 to 1924 to draft a new charter for progressivism.

Except for its inevitable proposals for an idealistic world leadership, the document that emerged from this interchange included little or nothing that would have sounded new to a western progressive in 1912.

A fourth reason for the disintergration and decline of the progressive movement in the 1920's was the lack of any effective leadership. Given the political temper and circumstances of the 1920's, it is possible that such leadership could not have operated successfully in any event. Perhaps the various progressive elements were so mutually hostile and so self-centered in interests and objectives that even a Theodore Roosevelt or a Woodrow Wilson, had they been at the zenith of their powers in the 1920's, could not have drawn them together in a common front. We will never know what a strong national leader might have done because by a trick of fate no such leader emerged before Franklin D. Roosevelt.

Four factors, then, contributed to the failure of the progressive components to unite successfully after 1918 and, as things turned out, before 1932: the lack of a suitable political vehicle, the severity of the tensions that kept progressives apart, the failure of progressives to agree upon a common program, and the absence of a national leadership, without which a united movement could never be created and sustained. These were all weaknesses that stemmed to a large degree from the instability and failures of the progressive movement itself.

There were, besides, a number of what might be called external causes for the movement's decline. In considering them one must begin with what was seemingly the most important—the alleged fact that the 1920's were a very unpropitious time for any new progressive revolt because of the ever-increasing level of economic prosperity, the materialism, and the general contentment of the decade 1919 to 1929. Part of this generalization is valid when applied to specific elements in the population. For example, the rapid rise in the real wages of industrial workers, coupled with generally full employment and the spread of so-called welfare practices among management, certainly did much to weaken and avert the further spread of organized labor, and thus to debilitate one of the important progressive components. But to say that it was prosperity *per se* that created a climate unfriendly to progressive ideals would be inaccurate. There was little prosperity and much depression during the 1920's for the single largest economic group, the farmers, as well as for numerous other groups. Progressivism, moreover, can flourish as much during periods of prosperity as during periods of discontent, as the history of the development of the progressive movement from 1901 to 1917 and of its triumph from 1945 to 1956 prove.

Vastly more important among the external factors in the decline of progressivism was the widespread, almost wholesale, defection from its ranks of the middle classes—the middling businessmen, bankers, and manufacturers, and the professional people closely associated with them in ideals and habits—in American cities large and small. For an understanding of this phenomenon no simple explanations like "prosperity" or the "temper of the times" will suffice, although they give some insight. The important fact was that these groups found a new economic and social status as a consequence of the flowering of American enterprise under the impact of the technological, financial, and other revolutions of the 1920's. If, as Professor Richard Hofstadter had claimed, the urban middle classes were progressive (that is, they demanded governmental relief from various anxieties) in the early 1900's because they resented their loss of social prestige to the *nouveaux riches* and feared being ground under by monopolists in industry, banking, and labor—if this is true, then the urban middle classes were progressive in the 1920's for inverse reasons. Their temper was dynamic, expansive, and supremely confident. They knew that they were building a new America, a business civilization based not upon monopoly and restriction but upon a whole new set of business values—mass production and consumption, short hours and high wages, full employment, welfare capitalism. And what was more important, virtually the entire country (at least the journalists, writers in popular magazines, and many preachers and professors) acknowledged that the nation's destiny was in good hands. It was little wonder, therefore, that the whole complex of groups constituting the urban middle classes, whether in New York, Zenith, or Middletown, had little interest in rebellion or even in mild reform proposals that seemed to imperil their leadership and control.

Other important factors, of course, contributed to the contentment of the urban middle classes. The professionalization of business and the full-blown emergence of a large managerial class had a profound impact upon social and political ideals. The acceleration of mass advertising played its role, as did also the beginning disintegration of the great cities with the spread of middle- and upper-class suburbs, a factor that diffused the remaining reform energies among the urban leaders.

A second external factor in the decline of the progressive movement after 1918 was the desertion from its ranks of a good part of the intellectual leadership of the country. Indeed, more than simple desertion was involved here; it was often a matter of a cynical repudiation of the ideals from which progressivism derived its strength. I do not mean to imply too much by this generalization. I know that what has been called intellectual progressivism not only survived in the 1920's but actually flourished in many fields. I know that the intellectual foundations of our present quasi-welfare state were either being laid or reinforced during the decade. Even so, one cannot evade the conclusion that the intellectual-political climate of the 1920's was vastly different from the one that had prevailed in the preceding two decades.

During the years of the great progressive revolt, intellectuals—novelists, journalists, political thinkers, social scientists, historians, and the like—had made a deeply personal commitment to the cause of democracy, first in domestic and then in foreign affairs. Their leadership in and impact on many phases of the progressive movement had been profound. By contrast, in the 1920's a large body of this intellectual phalanx turned against the very ideals they had once deified. One could cite, for example, the reaction of the idealists against the Versailles settlement; the disenchantment of the intellectuals with the extension of government authority when it could be used to justify the

Eighteenth Amendment or the suppression of free speech; or the inevitable loss of faith in the "people" when en masse they hounded so-called radicals, joined Bryan's crusade against evolution, or regaled themselves as Knights of the Ku Klux Klan. Whatever the cause, many alienated intellectuals simply withdrew or repudiated any identification with the groups they had once helped to lead. The result was not fatal to progressivism, but it was serious. The spark plugs had been removed from the engine of reform.

The progressive movement, then, unquestionably declined, but was it defunct in the 1920's? Much, of course, depends upon the definition of terms. If we accept the usual definition for "defunct" as "dead" or "ceasing to have any life or strength," we must recognize that the progressive movement was certainly not defunct in the 1920's; that on the contrary at least important parts of it were very much alive; and that it is just as important to know how and why progressivism survived as it is to know how and why it declined.

To state the matter briefly, progressivism survived in the 1920's because several important elements of the movement remained either in full vigor or in only slightly diminished strength. These were the farmers, after 1918 better organized and more powerful than during the high tide of the progressive revolt; the politically conscious elements among organized labor, particularly the railroad brotherhoods, who wielded a power all out of proportion to their numbers; the Democratic organizations in the large cities, usually vitally concerned with the welfare of the so-called lower classes; a remnant of independent radicals, social workers, and social gospel writers and preachers; and finally, an emerging new vocal element, the champions of public power and regional developments.

Although they never united effectively enough to capture a major party and the national government before 1932, these progressive elements controlled Congress from 1921 to about 1927 and continued to exercise a near control during the period of their greatest weakness in the legislative branch, from 1927 to about 1930.

Indeed, the single most powerful and consistently successful group in Congress during the entire decade from 1919 to 1929 were the spokesmen of the farmers. Spurred by an unrest in the country areas more intense than at any time since the 1890's, in 1920 and 1921 southern Democrats and midwestern and western insurgents, nominally Republican, joined forces in an alliance called the Farm Bloc. By maintaining a common front from 1921 to 1924 they succeeded in enacting the most advanced agricultural legislation to that date, legislation that completed the program begun under Wilsonian auspices. It included measures for high tariffs on agricultural products, thoroughgoing federal regulation of stockyards, packing houses, and grain exchanges, the exemption of agricultural cooperatives from the application of the antitrust laws, stimulation of the export of agricultural commodities, and the establishment of an entirely new federal system of intermediate rural credit.

When prosperity failed to return to the countryside, rural leaders in Congress espoused a new and bolder plan for relief—the proposal made by George N. Peck and Hugh S. Johnson in 1922 to use the federal power to obtain "fair exchange" or "parity" prices for farm products. Embodied in the McNary-Haugen bill in 1924, this measure was approved by Congress in 1927 and 1928, only to encounter vetoes by President Calvin Coolidge.

In spite of its momentary failure, the McNary-Haugen bill had a momentous significance for the American progressive movement. Its wholesale espousal by the great mass of farm leaders and spokesmen meant that the politically most powerful class in the country had come full scale to the conviction that the taxing power should be used directly and specifically for the purpose of underwriting (some persons called it subsidizing) agriculture. It was a milestone in the development of a comprehensive political doctrine that it was government's duty to protect the economic security of all classes and particularly depressed ones. McNary-Haugenism can be seen in its proper perspective if it is remembered that it would have been considered almost absurd in the Wilson period, that it was regarded as radical by nonfarm elements in the 1920's, and that it, or at any rate its fundamental objective, was incorporated almost as a matter of course into basic federal policy in the 1930's.

A second significant manifestation of the survival of progressivism in the 1920's came during the long controversy over public ownership or regulation of the burgeoning electric power industry. In this, as in most of the conflicts that eventually culminated on Capitol Hill, the agrarian element constituted the core of progressive strength. At the same time a sizable and well-organized independent movement developed that emanated from urban centers and was vigorous on the municipal and state levels. Throughout the decade this relatively new progressive group fought with mounting success to expose the propaganda of the private utilities, to strengthen state and federal regulatory agencies, and to win municipal ownership for distributive facilities. Like the advocates of railroad regulation in an earlier period, these proponents of regulation or ownership of a great new natural monopoly failed almost as much as they had succeeded in the 1920's. But their activities and exposures (the Federal Trade Commission's devastating investigation of the electric power industry in the late 1920's and early 1930's was the prime example) laid secure foundations for movements that in the 1930's would reach various culminations.

Even more significant for the future of American progressivism was the emergence in the 1920's of a new objective, that of committing the federal government to plans for large hydroelectric projects in the Tennessee Valley, the Columbia River watershed, the Southwest, and the St. Lawrence Valley for the purpose, some progressives said, of establishing "yardsticks" for rates, or for the further purpose, as other progressives declared, of beginning a movement for the eventual nationalization of the entire electric power industry. The development of this movement in its emerging stages affords a good case study in the natural history of American progressivism. It began when the Harding and Coolidge administrations attempted to dispose of the government's hydroelectric and nitrate facilities at Muscle Shoals, Alabama, to private interests. In the first stage of the controversy, the progressive objective was merely federal operation of these facilities for the production of cheap fertilizer—a reflection of its exclusive special-interest orientation. Then, as

new groups joined the fight to save Muscle Shoals, the objective of public production of cheap electric power came to the fore. Finally, by the end of the
1920's, the objective of a multipurpose regional development in the Tennessee
Valley and in other areas as well had taken firm shape.

In addition, by 1928 the agrarians in Congress, led by Senator George W.
Norris, had found enough allies in the two houses and enough support in the
country at large to adopt a bill for limited federal development of the Tennessee Valley. Thwarted by President Coolidge's pocket veto, the progressives
tried again in 1931, only to meet a second rebuff at the hands of President
Herbert Hoover.

All this might be regarded as another milestone in the maturing of American progressivism. It signified a deviation from the older traditions of mere
regulation, as President Hoover had said in his veto of the second Muscle
Shoals bill, and the triumph of new concepts of direct federal leadership in
large-scale development of resources. If progressives had not won their goal by
the end of the 1920's, they had at least succeeded in writing what would become perhaps the most important plank in their program for the future.

The maturing of an advanced farm program and the formulation of plans
for public power and regional developments may be termed the two most significant progressive achievements on the national level in the 1920's. Others
merit only brief consideration. One was the final winning of the old progressive goal of immigration restriction through limited and selective admission.
The fact that this movement was motivated in part by racism, nativism, and
anti-Semitism (with which, incidentally, a great many if not a majority of progressives were imbued in the 1920's) should not blind us to the fact that it was
also progressive. It sought to substitute a so-called scientific and a planned
policy for a policy of *laissez-faire.* Its purpose was admittedly to disturb the
free operation of the international labor market. Organized labor and social
workers had long supported it against the opposition of large employers. And
there was prohibition, the most ambitious and revealing progressive experiment of the twentieth century. Even the contemned antievolution crusade of
Bryan and the fundamentalists and the surging drives for conformity of
thought and action in other fields should be mentioned. All these movements
stemmed from the conviction that organized public power could and should
be used purposefully to achieve fundamental social and so-called moral
change. The fact that they were potentially or actively repressive does not
mean that they were not progressive. On the contrary, they superbly illustrated the repressive tendencies that inhered in progressivism precisely because it was grounded so much upon majoritarian principles.

Three other developments on the national level that have often been
cited as evidences of the failure of progressivism in the 1920's appear in a
somewhat different light at second glance. The first was the reversal of the
tariff-for-revenue-only tendencies of the Underwood Act with the enactment
of the Emergency Tariff Act of 1921 and the Fordney-McCumber Act of 1922.
Actually, the adoption of these measures signified, on the whole, not a repudiation but a revival of progressive principles in the realm of federal fiscal policy.

A revenue tariff had never been an authentic progressive objective. Indeed, at least by 1913, many progressives, except for some southern agrarians, had concluded that it was retrogressive and had agreed that the tariff laws should be used deliberately to achieve certain national objectives—for example, the crippling of noncompetitive big business by the free admission of articles manufactured by so-called trusts, or benefits to farmers by the free entry of farm implements. Wilson himself had been at least partially converted to these principles by 1916, as his insistence upon the creation of the Federal Tariff Commission and his promise of protection to the domestic chemical industry revealed. As for the tariff legislation of the early 1920's, its only important changes were increased protection for aluminum, chemical products, and agricultural commodities. It left the Underwood rates on the great mass of raw materials and manufactured goods largely undisturbed. It may have been economically shortsighted and a bad example for the rest of the world, but for the most part it was progressive in principle and was the handiwork of the progressive coalition in Congress.

Another development that has often been misunderstood in its relation to the progressive movement was the policies of consistent support that the Harding and Coolidge administrations adopted for business enterprise, particularly the policy of the Federal Trade Commission in encouraging the formation of trade associations and the diminution of certain traditional competitive practices. The significance of all this can easily be overrated. Such policies as these two administrations executed had substantial justification in progressive theory and in precedents clearly established by the Wilson administration.

A third challenge to usual interpretations concerns implications to be drawn from the election of Harding and Coolidge in 1920 and 1924. These elections seem to indicate the triumph of reaction among the mass of American voters. Yet one could argue that both Harding and Coolidge were political accidents, the beneficiaries of grave defects in the American political and constitutional systems. The rank and file of Republican voters demonstrated during the preconvention campaign that they wanted vigorous leadership and a moderately progressive candidate in 1920. They got Harding instead, not because they wanted him, but because unusual circumstances permitted a small clique to thwart the will of the majority. They took Coolidge as their candidate in 1924 simply because Harding died in the middle of his term and there seemed to be no alternative to nominating the man who had succeeded him in the White House. Further, an analysis of the election returns in 1920 and 1924 will show that the really decisive factor in the victories of Harding and Coolidge was the fragmentation of the progressive movement and the fact that an opposition strong enough to rally and unite the progressive majority simply did not exist.

There remains, finally, a vast area of progressive activity about which we yet know very little. One could mention the continuation of old reform movements and the development of new ones in the cities and states during the years following the Armistice: For example, the steady spread of the city manager form of government, the beginning of zoning and planning movements, and the efforts of the great cities to keep abreast of the transportation revolution then in full swing. Throughout the country the educational and welfare activities of the cities and states steadily increased. Factory legislation matured, while social insurance had its experimental beginnings. Whether such reform impulses were generally weak or strong, one cannot say; but what we do know about developments in cities like Cincinnati and states like New York, Wisconsin, and Louisiana justifies a challenge to the assumption that municipal and state reform energies were dead after 1918 and, incidentally, a plea to young scholars to plow this unworked field of recent American history.

Let us, then, suggest a tentative synthesis as an explanation of what happened to the progressive movement after 1918:

First, the national progressive movement, which had found its most effective embodiment in the coalition of forces that reelected Woodrow Wilson in 1916, was shattered by certain policies that the administration pursued from 1917 to 1920, and by some developments over which the administration had no or only slight control. The collapse that occurred in 1920 was not inevitable and cannot be explained by merely saying that "the war killed the progressive movement."

Second, large and aggressive components of a potential new progressive coalition remained after 1920. These elements never succeeded in uniting effectively before the end of the decade, not because they did not exist, but because they were divided by conflicts among themselves. National leadership, which in any event did not emerge in the 1920's, perhaps could not have succeeded in subduing these tensions and in creating a new common front.

Third, as a result of the foregoing, progressivism as an organized national force suffered a serious decline in the 1920's. This decline was heightened by the defection of large elements among the urban middle classes and the intellectuals, a desertion induced by technological, economic, and demographic changes, and by the outcropping of certain repressive tendencies in progressivism after 1917.

Fourth, in spite of reversals and failures, important components of the national progressive movement survived in considerable vigor and succeeded to a varying degree, not merely in keeping the movement alive, but even in broadening its horizons. This was true particularly of the farm groups and of the coalition concerned with public regulation or ownership of electric power resources. These two groups laid the groundwork in the 1920's for significant new programs in the 1930's and beyond.

Fifth, various progressive coalitions controlled Congress for the greater part of the 1920's and were always a serious threat to the conservative administrations that controlled the executive branch. Because this was true, most of the legislation adopted by Congress during this period, including many measures that historians have inaccurately called reactionary, was progressive in character.

Sixth, the progressive movement in the cities and states was far from dead in the 1920's, although we do not have sufficient evidence to justify any generalizations about the degree of its vigor.

If this tentative and imperfect synthesis has any value, perhaps it is high time that we discard the sweeping generalizations, false hypotheses, and clichés that we have so often used in explaining and characterizing political developments from 1918 to 1929. Perhaps we should try to see these developments for what they were—the normal and ordinary political behavior of groups and classes caught up in a swirl of social and economic change. When we do this we will no longer ask whether the progressive movement was defunct in the 1920's. We will ask only what happened to it and why.

The Failure of the Melting Pot

Stanley Coben

Among the most persistent of historical myths is that associated with the idea of modern America as a "melting pot." The phrase has a ring to it, and it was brought to focus by the Israel Zangwill play *The Melting Pot* in 1908. Never really all-inclusive, the myth has been exposed, even debunked, many times, perhaps most notably by Milton Gordon. The reality is better reflected by phrases such as *cultural pluralism* or by the image of America as a mosaic rather than a melting pot. Stanley Coben of the University of California at Los Angeles examines the myth of the melting pot mainly from the perspective of the "new social history" and by focusing on the decade of the 1920s. Fueled and emboldened by post–World War I "Red scare" hysteria, existing "elites" made a concerted effort to melt down America and, failing that, to relegate recalcitrant "unmeltables" to the slag heap (to continue the metaphor). Among the targets were blacks, Orientals (particularly those of Japanese descent), Mexican Americans, and until 1924 what continued to be evident of the "new immigration." These groups many times were associated with other phobias, among them urbanism, Communism, Catholicism, Judaism, and immorality—that of the un-American variety, of course. Throughout Professor Coben's treatment he not only highlights these groups' persisting identities but also demonstrates that in many cases they fought back against the mythology in various ways and with varying degrees of success. Victories resulting from these counterattacks proved to be mainly temporary, however, as by the depressed 1930s most were forced to adopt a more traditional life-style. Yet the stage had been set for future and in many cases more successful and permanent forays to establish cultural identity within the melting pot. Finally, Professor Coben's focus on the seemingly myriad social (and antisocial) activities of the 1920s corrects another grand twentieth-century mythology—that of the decade as a roaring, carefree, fun-loving "Jazz Age."

During the late nineteenth and early twentieth centuries Americans and Western Europeans carried out an insidious type of conquest throughout the world, tearing apart established religious, economic, and political relationships, attempting to replace them with Western cultural forms. Minority ethnic groups in the United States were subject to similar cultural assaults, usually more

"The Failure of the Melting Pot," by Stanley Coben. From *The Great Fear: Race in the Mind of America*, edited by Gary B. Nash and Richard Weiss. Copyright © 1970 by Gary B. Nash and Richard Weiss. Reprinted by permission of Holt, Rinehart and Winston, Inc.

subtle, but in many respects more effective than attacks on cultures in foreign lands. Only the United States, among the Western powers, contained among its population large elements of many races generally believed in the West to be inferior. Nowhere else were nativist organizations and official policies directed against internal minorities which together formed such a substantial portion of the population. Only the United States, therefore, suffered massive counterattacks analogous to the revolts of colonial races elsewhere. There was an element of reality, then, in the terror experienced by millions of Americans when revolution swept eastern and central Europe during 1919 to 1920, and propagandists among hitherto subservient races threatened similar rebellion in the United States.

I

A series of short-term, postwar dislocations further disturbed the psychological equilibrium of large numbers of Americans. Some of these events—runaway prices, a brief economic depression, and a stock market crash—could be connected to racial minorities only by the most prejudiced. But thousands of returning soldiers were disgruntled when they found their old jobs occupied by Negroes and recent immigrants. And other disturbances—race riots, labor strikes, formation of Communist parties, widespread bomb explosions and bombing attempts, and an outpouring of arch-radical propaganda—were easily linked in the public mind with alien races and peoples. The formation of the Comintern in Moscow in 1919 and the revolutions then raging in eastern Europe seemed to give credence to the fear that a new revolutionary force was loose in the world that threatened to overwhelm American institutions. The result was an intensification of nativist patterns of thought. These found expression in a quasi-religious nativist movement aimed at unifying an apparently disintegrating culture against an onslaught by darker, inferior races. Americans who took part in this crusade for "100 percent Americanism," as it was popularly called, hoped to eliminate the intrusive influences felt to be the chief cause of contemporary anxieties, if they could not eliminate the intruders themselves.[1]

A similar movement, less frenzied, perhaps, but with the same objectives, probably would have taken place even without the stimulation provided by postwar disturbances. The real foundation of the movement for 100 percent Americanism was a long-term crisis for the nation's dominant cultural groups: the urbanization of America and the peopling of its great cities by black migrants from the southern states, and by other dark immigrants from Italy, eastern Europe, Mexico, and the Caribbean. These were regarded by white native-born Americans as dangerous, immoral people, easily associated with the immorality they read about and believed they saw all around them in the nation's urban centers.

The dimensions of the problem facing native-born white Americans can be indicated by a few demographic statistics. Of a total population of 106 million in 1920, 54 million lived in urban areas, the first time in the nation's history that the urban exceeded the rural populace. In 1860, only 20 percent of all Americans had lived in towns and cities. Of 106 million Americans in 1920, 23 million were immigrants or the children of immigrants, and over 10 million of these had migrated in the fifteen years before World War I, the height of the exodus from Italy and eastern Europe. In the year before the war, immigrants from southern and eastern Europe outnumbered those from north-western Europe by six to one. The majority of these "new" immigrants settled in the metropolitan centers.[2]

Even more alarming to white Americans was the concurrent movement of southern Negroes to the cities, especially the large northern cities. There they congregated, or were forced to concentrate, in huge ghettos. Of 11 million Negroes in the United States, 2 million lived in the North by 1920, and, like the influx of Europeans, the migration showed signs of continuing if not in-creasing its pace. Tired of low pay, mistreatment, and a losing battle against the boll weevil, at least 600,000 Negroes moved north during the 1920s, and tens of thousands more came from the Caribbean Islands, especially Jamaica, after World War I. The 1930 census revealed that 273,000 Negroes lived in New York City alone, only 9000 of whom had been born in any of the North Atlantic states. Most had come from Virginia and the Carolinas. Harlem, a white, middle-class area in 1910, was inhabited almost entirely by 106,000 blacks in 1930. By that year, also, 232,000 Negroes were settled in Chicago, most of them from states of the Deep South. Another 118,000 Negroes lived in Detroit by 1930. The same kind of movement away from the tenant farms and rural villages took place within the South. According to the 1930 census, 96,000 Negroes lived in Memphis, 35,000 of whom had come from Mississippi alone; 99,000 Negroes lived in Birmingham; 90,000 in Atlanta; 63,000 in Houston, and 38,000 in Los Angeles, only 6700 of whom had been born any-where in California.[3]

White leaders attempted to check the shift in Negro population both at its source and its destination. Mississippi employers, facing a labor shortage, formed an association and hired agents to woo blacks back to the pleasant land they had left. Advertisements promising jobs and transportation were placed in northern newspapers, agents made personal pleas, and even intimidation was tried. Some tactics closely resembled kidnapping. But nothing worked. Those Negroes who did return to the South often acted as labor agents for northern employers, and soon returned to northern cities accompanied by friends and relatives. The most common attitude was that periodic unemploy-ment and freezing weather in the North was preferable to certain peonage and possible lynching in the South. A contemporary folk tale, frequently repeated in northern ghettos, describes an unemployed Negro migrant, cold, wet, and hungry, appealing to God for advice. "Go back to Mississippi," the Lord told him. "You don't mean it, Lord," the poor man replied, "You're jesting." The Lord repeated, "Go back to Mississippi!" Finally, the man relented: "Very well, Lord, if you insist, I'll go. But will you go with me?" The Lord answered: "As far as Cincinnati."

Most of the Negro migrants were young, and, at first, predominantly sin-gle men. The Department of Labor's Division of Negro Economics, established primarily to find the causes and probable duration of the black exodus, gave as a typical example of the process at work, this account by a rural Negro preacher:

> My father [said he] was born and brought up as a slave. He never knew anything else until after I was born. He was taught his place and was content to keep it. But when he brought me up he let some of the old customs slip by. But I know that there are certain things that I must do, and I do them, and it doesn't worry me. Yet in bringing up my own son, I let some more of the old customs slip by. He has been through the eighth grade; he reads easily. For a year I have been keeping him from going to Chicago; but he tells me that this is his last crop; that in the fall he's going. He says, "When a young white man talks rough to me, I can't talk rough to him. You can stand that; I can't. I have some education, and inside I has the feelins of a white man. I'm goin'."[4]

Most northerners were not pleased by their new black neighbors, and thousands organized either to keep Negroes out of their residential areas, or to ensure that the newcomers acted as Negroes were supposed to act—subserviently. A letter sent to a Lenox Avenue, New York City, realty company warned, "We have been informed of your intention to rent your house . . . to Negro tenants. This is wholly un-American, and is totally against our principles. We ask you in a gentlemanly way to rescind your order, or unpleasant things may happen." The note was signed: Ku Klux Klan, Realm 7, Chapter 3. In Chicago, twenty-four bombs were thrown at the houses of Negroes who moved into previously all-white neighborhoods, or at the offices of the real estate agents who sold or rented them the houses. No arrests were made as a result of these bombings.[5]

The extent of residential and school segregation varied widely from city to city. A study published in 1930 found the least segregation in Minneapolis, Buffalo, and New York City, where over 100,000 Negroes lived outside Harlem. In Chicago, the city administration held office by grace of Negro votes, so official racist policies were opposed at the highest level. Nevertheless Chicago's citizens proved adequate to the task of confining Negroes to certain slum areas, and keeping the better schools limited to white children. In Philadelphia, twelve schools had 100 percent Negro student bodies. Other schools in the city contained separate entrances for Negroes. Chester, Pennsylvania, operated parallel school systems for Negroes and whites through junior high school. Segregationists also enjoyed wide success in such midwestern cities as Gary, Dayton, and Indianapolis.[6]

Nevertheless, schools in all the northern cities were far superior to those operated for Negroes in the South. This was an important reason why the harassment mentioned above, and even the race riots described below, tended to stimulate withdrawal into the Negro ghettos and into black nationalist organizations, rather than a mass return to the South.

The hostility these demographic shifts provoked among thousands of whites can be seen most vividly in the pattern of violent racial disturbances which shook a dozen northern urban centers following the end of World War I. Chicago was typical. A teen-aged Negro boy, Eugene Williams, swimming

off a Lake Michigan beach on a hot Sunday afternoon, July 27, 1919, acciden-
tally wandered over the traditional line separating white and black swimming
areas. Whites on the shore began throwing rocks at him. Some apparently
found their target for the boy sank and drowned. Blacks insisted that a policeman at the scene arrest one of the white rock-throwers, but the officer refused
and tried to arrest a Negro instead. Groups of blacks then attacked the policeman; whites came to his rescue, and a wild battle began on the beach. Accounts of the fighting on the Lake Michigan shore quickly spread through the
sweltering south side of Chicago.

That night, white teen-aged gangs captured Negroes who worked in
white areas of the city, and beat, stabbed, or shot them. Two died and over
fifty reported their injuries to hospitals or the police. For the next twelve days,
law and order almost disappeared from Chicago as armed white gangs in automobiles invaded black districts, shooting from their cars into Negro homes
and setting some of them on fire. Snipers fired from rooftops on these cars and
on others driven by whites. Negroes working in white areas continued to be
attacked on the streets and in buses and streetcars. Black gangs retaliated
against whites who made the mistake of venturing into the Negro ghetto
(where hundreds of them worked) on foot. Eventually the state militia restored
relative peace; but by then 23 Negroes and 15 whites were known to have died
in the fighting, at least 520 were seriously injured, and over 1000 were left
homeless by fires set in the Negro district.

Perhaps the most significant statistics from the Chicago race riot were
the number of whites killed and injured. These indicated that from the Lake
Michigan beach to the south side ghetto Negroes were fighting back. In all, six
major race riots and about twenty other racial conflicts erupted in American
cities during the summer and fall of 1919. Some, like the battles in Washington, D.C., and Knoxville, Tennesee, were only slightly less violent than the
conflict in Chicago. A race war in and around Elaine, Arkansas, was the bloodi-
est of all. In every case, whites were the aggressors in the large-scale fighting;
but blacks fought back, which helps account for the ferocity of the riots. Negroes shed most of the blood everywhere, and black spokesmen termed the
months of race riots the "Red Summer" of 1919.[7]

II

Although the major riots took place in the eastern and central sections of the
nation, Americans in the Southwest also were gripped with severe racial fears,
though they could hardly have been alarmed by the comparatively small number of Negroes and "inferior breeds" of European immigrants in their section.
The role that these groups played in the East and Midwest was filled instead
by Orientals and Mexicans. With their yellow and brown skin color, their tendency to speak languages other than English, and their willingness to work
hard for low wages, these peoples clearly established their cultures as inferior
in the view of the white majority.

Chinese immigration to the United States was negligible after passage of
the Exclusion Act of 1882; but Japanese entrants increased sharply at the turn

of the century, setting off demands for further exclusion legislation aimed at this new source of Oriental immigration. "The Japanese are starting the same tide of immigration which we thought we had checked twenty years ago," complained San Francisco's Mayor James Duval Phelan in 1900. "They are not the stuff of which American citizens can be made. . . . Let them keep at a respectful distance." Phelan would continue to inveigh against the presence of Japanese in America for the next thirty years, including a period when he served as United States senator.[8]

Japanese armed forces annihilated the Russian fleet and mangled the Russian army in 1905. Californians, alarmed by this powerful "yellow peril" in the Pacific, joined labor representatives fearful of economic competition and nativists from all classes terrified of "racial mongrelization," to form the influential Asiatic Exclusion League. Under pressure from the league, the San Francisco Board of Education barred Japanese-American children from all but special "Oriental" schools in 1906, creating a major diplomatic issue. To avoid further strife, President Theodore Roosevelt and Secretary of State Elihu Root negotiated the Gentlemen's Agreement with the Japanese government, ending the migration of Japanese laborers to America.

Nonlaborers, especially wives of Japanese men already resident in the United States, continued to enter the country, however. As Japanese families bought land, mostly in the fertile California valleys, demands for anti-Japanese legislation spread from San Francisco throughout the state. An Alien Land Law, passed in 1913, limited Japanese ownership of farms; but in most cases it was evaded easily.

In conformity with the national pattern, the most virulent phase of the agitation against Japanese began in 1919. In September of that year leading California politicians of both parties responded to public clamor for action by meeting "to consider the Japanese question." After the conference, the politicians issued a report stating: "All agreed that their [Japanese-American] loyalty was first to Japan and second, if at all, to America; that they were here in large part in pursuance of a plan to populate the Pacific Slope of America and that they were a peril, economically, politically, and socially."[9]

The California American Legion fought the "peril" by producing a movie, *Shadows of the West*, circulated in 1920. Japanese-American characters in the film were revealed as spies and sex fiends. At the tale's climax, two innocent white girls were rescued from the Oriental fiends by brave Legionnaires—just in time.

The political highlight of this California campaign was an initiative measure placed on the state ballot in 1920, forbidding further purchase of California land by Japanese or their agents. The measure passed by a vote of 668,483 to 222,086. National endorsement of the California position came with the passage of the Immigration Act of 1924, which excluded all Japanese immigration to the United States. California nativists, working for a Constitutional amendment which would deprive American-born Orientals of their citizenship, continued to warn about the menace posed by the "little brown men." But until World War II they were unable to convince even southern congressmen that such drastic action was necessary.

The great fear in the Southwest after the mid-1920s was occasioned by the movement of more than a million Mexicans into that area—at least one-tenth of Mexico's total population. The basis for this migration was the feder-ally financed irrigation of vast stretches of desert land in the area from Califor-nia to Texas. A series of laws, beginning with the Reclamation Act of 1902, made possible this government action. Then, during the 1920s, Americans drastically shifted their eating habits, consuming a much greater quantity of fruits and vegetables. New canning methods and refrigeration cars made it pos-sible to carry perishable crops long distances and to store them for lengthy periods. The irrigated southwestern lands were ideally suited for production of fruits and vegetables; but these required enormous numbers of laborers with special characteristics to prepare the land and harvest the crops.

Growth and harvest of an acre of wheat during the 1920s required 13 man hours; an acre of lettuce, however, took 125 man hours; and an acre of strawberries took 500 man hours. Very cheap labor, therefore, was a necessity in the Southwest. Furthermore, these low-paid workers would have to farm a reclaimed desert, where temperatures frequently rose above 100 degrees, clear-ing and planting a terrain that few white Americans understood.

By 1925, the southwestern states produced 40 percent of the nation's fruits, vegetables, and truck crops, almost all on farms developed during the twentieth century. Only an enormous influx of Mexican labor made this pro-duction possible. The Mexicans, who could withstand the heat, who knew how to clear the many varieties of desert brush, and who would work for infin-itesimal wages at a time when American farm help was scarce, provided about 75 percent of the labor that cultivated the new southwestern crops. They also contributed most of the labor that created cotton fields on irrigated land in Arizona, Texas, and California; as well as 60 percent of the mine workers and approximately 80 percent of the railroad laborers employed in the western states between 1910 and 1930.[10]

Immigration from Mexico, and other Western Hemisphere countries, was not limited by the 1921 and 1924 Immigration Acts, which set quotas for other nations. In 1923 and 1924, Mexican entrants comprised over 12 percent of total immigration to the United States, and in 1927 and 1928 about 20 percent. Almost half a million Mexicans entered the country during the ten-year period from 1920 to 1929, according to official records. However, Labor Department officials estimated illegal entries from Mexico at two to five times the number who passed through immigration stations. Most of these immigrants crossed the border into Texas and the majority remained there; but at least 200,000 moved to California during the 1920s alone.[11]

Until the late 1920s, the Mexicans were almost universally welcome. They seemed content to live in their own communities, and to exist in squa-lor, while earning the contempt of native Americans by working at the most menial labor for wages which seldom rose above an average of $100 a month for an entire family.[12] But the passivity of the Mexican laborers was coming to an end.

A suggestion of what was to come occurred in Arizona during 1920 when 4000 cotton field workers—all migrants from Mexico—struck for higher wages. Scores of workers were arrested, the leaders deported, and the strike broken. Mexican-American farm laborers in Texas and California began organizing on a large scale in 1927. To some observers it seemed that they were protesting against social subordination and humiliation as much as they were attempting to improve their economic condition. The *Confederación de Uniones Obreras Mexicanas,* established in southern California in 1927, was able to call out on strike as many as 5000 Mexican-American field workers in the Imperial Valley. Mexicans also comprised three-quarters of the farm workers' union in the lower San Joaquin Valley.

From Texas to California, the pattern was the same. Strikes were broken with large-scale violence, including the use of tear gas, clubs, and guns. Strikers were arrested by legal authorities or kidnapped and beaten by growers' private armies. The leaders were deported. Starting in 1931, California officials resorted to mass deportations. During 1932, over 11,000 Mexicans were "repatriated" from Los Angeles alone.[13]

This series of events, beginning in the 1920s, changed for decades to come the dominant attitude of western Americans toward the Mexicans who had built the foundations of their agricultural economy. Creation of labor organizations and consequent strikes ended the myth of the docile Mexican laborer. Machinery invented late in the 1920s began to replace human labor in fruit and vegetable harvesting. Then the depression halted the steady rise in demand for those crops.

In response to the unrest among agricultural laborers, the governor of California appointed a "Mexican Fact-Finding Committee" which reported in October 1930. The committee employed as investigators social scientists sympathetic with the Mexicans. Nevertheless, as often happens, the group's final report reflected the prejudices of the government officials named to head the project. Its conclusions provided a rationale for the treatment accorded Mexican-Americans during the following decades. The committee estimated that whites comprised less than 10 percent of Mexico's population. It quoted George P. Clements, Director of the Agricultural Department of the Los Angeles Chamber of Commerce, who stated that 13 of the 15 million inhabitants of Mexico were Indians, "as primitive as our own Indians were when the first colonists arrived in America." These barely civilized Indians, the committee concluded, now were inundating California. Forty percent of all alien immigrants entering the state came from Mexico; and the proportion of Mexican migrants who gave California as their eventual destination when they crossed the border increased annually. The committee reported also that Los Angeles police department records "indicate an increasing proportion of arrests of Mexicans in the city." About 40 percent of the Mexican-Americans in California already lived in Los Angeles.[14]

As in the case of Oriental-Americans, California's treatment of Mexican immigrants and their descendents is among the more dismal chapters in the national history. Mobilized by newspapers, politicians, and official publications like the Mexican Fact-Finding Committee report, Californians resorted to violent means of ridding their state of racial minorities. Almost immediately after Japanese-Americans had been dispatched to "relocation" camps in March 1942, police, servicemen, and other citizens in southern California started a campaign of terror against Americans of Mexican origin, especially Mexican-American youths. Beginning in August 1942, police dragnets in Mexican sections of Los Angeles periodically stopped all cars entering or leaving the districts. As many as 600 persons were arrested in one night for possession of dangerous weapons that included jackknives and equipment for changing automobile tires.

In June 1943, young Mexican-Americans and some Negroes were the victims of what California newspapers and police called "zoot-suit riots." Less prejudiced observers termed these events mob violence, and even mass lynching. For almost a week, mobs of hundreds and even one of several thousand roamed those areas of Los Angeles and nearby cities that were inhabited or frequented by Mexicans, savagely beating and stabbing Mexican-Americans and Negroes. Los Angeles police sometimes followed the mobs, arresting the bleeding or unconscious victims on charges ranging from assault to inciting a riot. In no reported cases did the police intervene, except to help beat Mexicans.[15]

The anxiety generated in native Americans by migrant Negroes, Orientals, and Mexicans closely resembled the panic created at the same time by the vast flow of Italian and Slavic immigrants. Some of the country's politicians, editors, and polemicists made the association explicit. Speaking in favor of immigration restriction legislation, Oscar W. Underwood of Alabama, the most influential Democrat in the House of Representatives, contrasted the pure white blood of those who had made America great with the mixture of African and Asian blood that fixed the character of southern European immigrants. In the Senate, while debating the same issue, Fernifold M. Simmons of North Carolina warned that Anglo-Saxon civilization in America was in danger of destruction from immigrants who "are nothing more than the degenerate progeny of the Asiatic hordes which, long centuries ago, overran the shores of the Mediterranean . . . [and] the spawn of the Phoenician curse." Thomas Abercrombie of Alabama also pointed to *prima facie* evidence of the new immigrants' inferiority: "The color of thousands of them differs materially from that of the Anglo-Saxon."[16]

A torrent of literature expressing this sense of white racial superiority flowed from the presses in the 1920s. The most popular polemic on the subject was Theodore Lothrop Stoddard's *The Rising Tide of Color Against White World Supremacy*, which appeared in 1920. In this and a score of other books, Stoddard parroted the theme developed in prewar racist literature, that progress and civilization were products of "Nordic" blood. This magnificent breed had "clean, virile, genius-bearing blood, streaming down the ages through the unerring action of heredity, which, in anything like a favorable environment, will multiply itself, solve our problems, and sweep us on to higher and nobler destinies." Stoddard warned of the danger to Nordic supremacy from less civilized eastern and southern European, as well as Oriental and other "colored," peoples. Another popular author on the same topic, Henry Pratt Fairchild, a former president of the American Sociological Society, wrote in 1926 that "if America is to remain a stable nation it must continue a white man's country for an indefinite period to come." Fairchild's statement was part of a plea, not for Jim Crow laws in the South, but for immigration restriction directed largely against "inferior" European races.[17]

The alleged relationship between darker peoples and urban problems was made to seem even more menacing during 1919–1920 by those who attempted to associate these groups with the specter of international communism. By mid-1919 almost every nation in eastern and central Europe had undergone a communist revolution, several of them successful, although only the Bolshevik government in Russia retained power. Russian and Baltic language organizations in the United States moved—or were moved by their leaders—into the new American Communist parties, partly out of pride in the Bolshevik achievements. Probably 90 percent of the parties' members in 1919 were eastern European immigrants. Several men who became Bolshevik leaders in Russia during the Revolution, including Leon Trotsky, sat out most of World War I in New York City. Therefore, there was some slight basis in fact for Attorney-General A. Mitchell Palmer's assertion in 1920 that the Bolshevik triumph was led by "a small clique of outcasts from the East Side of New York.... Because a disreputable alien—Leon Bronstein, the man who now calls himself Trotsky—can inaugurate a reign of terror from his throne room in the Kremlin; because this lowest of all types known to New York can sleep in the Czar's bed ... should America be swayed by such doctrines?"[18]

Palmer's alert antiradical division, directed by J. Edgar Hoover, discovered that American Negroes were deeply involved in the Communist conspiracy. Hoover, an avid reader of dissident books, journals, and newspapers, hardly missed an expression of seditious propaganda. Although there is no evidence that Negroes took part in founding the Communist parties in September 1919, or that any joined soon afterward, dozens of black propagandists sounded enough like revolutionists to convince the Justice Department experts that they constituted an authentic menace. The antiradical division's collection of this inflammatory literature was published in the fall of 1919 in a pamphlet entitled "Radicalism and Sedition among the Negroes as Reflected in Their Publications." Among the black radicals cited were A. Philip Randolph, a moderate socialist best known as president of the Pullman Car Porters; and Marcus Garvey, one of the country's more enthusiastic champions of capitalism. Both men had written powerful diatribes against contemporary American white culture, especially its racist aspects, which sounded to Hoover like calls to revolution.[19]

Theodore Lothrop Stoddard also warned his fellow countrymen that the world-wide movement to undermine the Nordic's natural superiority was being encouraged if not directed from Moscow: "In every quarter of the globe ... the Bolshevik agitators whisper in the ears of discontented colored men their gospel of hatred and revenge. Every nationalist aspiration, every political grievance, every social discrimination, is fuel for Bolshevism's hellish incitement to racial as well as to class war."[20]

Almost all the racial fears felt by white Americans after World War I were distilled and promulgated by one organization: the Ku Klux Klan. The Klan gave voice also to the traditional culture—such as the dangers carried by new ideas and moral standards. The KKK of that period was started by a small group in Atlanta during 1915. The time and place were chosen to coincide with excitement generated by the showing of the motion picture "The Birth of a Nation." In that tremendously popular epic, white-hooded Klansmen of the post–Civil War era were depicted redeeming the South and its most cherished values from the clutches of black Reconstruction.

Until the cultural crisis of 1919–1920, however, the twentieth-century Klan remained a small, southern organization. When it expanded, the professional publicists who managed the membership drive discovered that the largest potential source of Klan dues lay not in Georgia or South Carolina, nor even in Alabama and Mississippi, those traditional strongholds of vigilante justice for Negroes. The greatest response to the Klan's brand of racism appeared in growing cities of the Southwest and Midwest: Shreveport, Dallas, Youngstown, Indianapolis, Dayton, and Detroit; and in smaller cities like Joliet, Illinois; Hammond, Indiana; Oklahoma City; San Antonio; Babylon, New York; Camden, New Jersey; and Anaheim, California.

In areas where Klan organizers—or Kleagles, as the invisible empire called them—were most successful in recruiting, they entered towns instructed to discover the prejudices of prospective members, then to exploit these people's complaints. At first it was assumed that the Klan once again would be chiefly a device for keeping southern Negroes and their white friends in place. When he called together the first small group of Klansmen in 1915, William J. Simmons explained that Negroes were getting "uppity." Klan recruiting efforts played cleverly on the Reconstruction Klan's reputation for punishing ambitious Negroes and for protecting white women against threats to their purity. A Klan recruiting lecturer promised: "The Negro, in whose blood flows the mad desire for race amalgamation, is more dangerous than a maddened wild beast and he must and will be controlled."[21]

However, when questions and applications from all over the country poured into Atlanta headquarters during 1920, Imperial Wizard Simmons readily conceded that Negroes were not the only enemies of 100 percent Americans. Furthermore, he announced: "Any real man, any native-born white American citizen who is not affiliated with any foreign institution (that is, not a Catholic) and who loves his country and his flag may become a member of the Ku Klux Klan, whether he lives north, south, east, or west."[22] The only other requirement for membership was a man's willingness to part with a $10 initiation fee, of which $4 went to the Kleagle, $2 to Simmons, $2.50 to the publicists in Atlanta, and the rest to the local Grand Goblin. Further payments were exacted later for membership dues and for uniforms (sheets), which were supplied from Atlanta.

Throughout the nation, Kleagles discovered a fear of Catholics, Jews, and recent immigrants, as well as Negroes. They also found native Americans worried about the erosion of moral standards, and angry about widespread lawlessness. Frequently this laxity was associated with foreign or colored races. Violation of Prohibition statutes especially was blamed on urban minorities. Established governmental institutions seemed incapable of handling these elements—incapable of protecting white, Anglo-Saxon Victorian civilization. So Kleagles received a warm welcome when they came to town and gave native Americans an opportunity to fight back. One of the most effective pieces of Klan recruiting literature read:

> Every criminal, every gambler, every thug, every libertine, every girl ruiner, every home wrecker, every wife beater, every dope peddler, every moonshiner, every crooked politician, every pagan Papist priest, every shyster lawyer, every K. of C., every white slaver, every Rome-controlled newspaper, every black spider—is fighting the Klan. Think it over, which side are you on?[23]

Local chapters took action against what they considered indecent motion pictures and books. They destroyed stills, and attacked prostitutes and gamblers. Groups of hooded men even invaded lovers' lanes and beat up the occupants of cars, in one case beating a young couple to death. This work was considered no less important than political efforts to destroy parochial schools, to enforce Bible reading in classrooms, and to defeat Catholic and Jewish candidates for public office.

Although membership figures remain largely shrouded in secrecy, available records indicate that the hooded empire probably enrolled over 5 million members during the 1920s, with a peak membership of about 2 million in 1924. Because members were concentrated so heavily in certain northern and western areas, the Klan won considerable political power in at least six states, and in large sections of about ten others.

In the great cities, however, and eventually in the country as a whole, the Klan discovered that the time had passed when an organization devoted to the supremacy of white Anglo-Saxon Protestants could operate both violently and safely. In some respects the whole movement for 100 percent Americanism was an anachronism in the post–World War I era; but the Klan especially depended upon a widespread delusion that this was still the world of Wade Hampton and the young Rudyard Kipling.

The Klan's fate in New York City was pathetic—and illustrative. In the world's wealthiest city, the nation's largest by far, with a million native-born white Protestants among its inhabitants, the KKK was treated like a band of shabby criminals. The great majority of New York's population of 6 million were Catholics and Jews; and the Irish Catholics who dominated the city's politics and police force were especially offended when the Klan dared organize in New York. The city seethed with bigotry against Negroes, Catholics, and Jews, including considerable distaste within these groups directed at members of the others. But even among white Protestant New Yorkers eligible for Klan membership, few were so foolhardy during the 1920s as to identify themselves publicly with an organization so clearly marked for disaster. It was not an absence of racial prejudice that doomed the Klan in New York, but rather the fact that in most respects the city already was controlled by the "minority" groups which the Klan aimed to suppress.

A year after Kleagles entered the city, two grand juries commenced investigations of the secret order. Special legislation, directed at the KKK, forced all unincorporated associations to file annual membership lists. New York Mayor John F. Hylan denounced Klan members as "anarchists," and the city police force was ordered to "ferret out these despicable disloyal persons who are attempting to organize a society, the aims and purposes of which are of such a character that were they to prevail, the foundations of our country would be destroyed."[24]

In most of New York City, the customary march of hooded Klansmen, carrying banners with messages that were so popular in Kokomo and Anaheim, would have been a feat of amazing courage. In certain sections—the lower east side and Harlem, for example—such a march would have been the most foolhardy event since General Custer's seventh cavalry left a day early for the Little Bighorn. New York's borough of Queens, however, remained predominantly suburban and Protestant in the 1920s. Although subject to hostile laws and unsympathetic policies there as in the rest of New York City, a Klan chapter continued to operate in Queens. In 1927, it received permission to take part in the Queens County Memorial Day Parade to the local Soldier's Monument.

Both the Boy Scouts and the Knights of Columbus withdrew from the patriotic celebration rather than march in the same line as the KKK. The New York police did their best to stop or divert the Klan members, but something less than their best to hold back angry crowds determined to halt the hooded patriots. After 1500 Klansmen and Klanswomen—including a 100-man paramilitary unit—broke through several police barricades, the police simply left the KKK to the parade audience. According to the *New York Times:* "Women fought women and spectators fought the policemen and the Klansmen, as their desire dictated. Combatants were knocked down. Klan banners were shredded. . . ." Five Klansmen were arrested during the melée. Finally the police ceased holding back traffic as the remnant of the Klan cavalcade passed, and motorists tried to run the white-robed marchers down. The Klan parade disintegrated, although three Klansmen in an automobile managed to reach the war memorial monument and placed a wreath with the KKK signature upon it. The wreath promptly was stolen.[25]

Throughout the Northeast, the Klan found only mild support, and even that sometimes aroused the kind of mob violence for which the Klan itself was so well known in the South. In Boston, Mayor James Michael Curley incited crowds by speaking before flaming crosses—the Klan's favorite symbol—and pointing to the cross while he shouted to his predominantly Irish Catholic audiences: "There it burns, the cross of hatred upon which Our Lord, Jesus Christ, was crucified—the cross of human avarice, and not the cross of love and charity. . . ." Curley declared Klan meetings illegal even in private homes, and in Boston he obtained support in his crusade not only from the City Council, but also from the city's Catholic and Jewish leaders. It was just as well for the Klan that they did not meet in Boston; houses of people only suspected of being Klan members were attacked with bricks and stones.[26]

In Pittsburgh, another center of Catholic population, Kleagles enjoyed great success in recruiting members. Ten thousand Klansmen from the area, led by the national Imperial Wizard, Hiram Wesley Evans, gathered outside the nearby town of Carnegie for an initiation rally in August 1923. When they marched into town, however, they were met not with cheers, but with angry shouts and a hail of rocks and bottles. The Klansmen continued until a citizen started shooting and a Klan member fell dead. There were no further Klan parades in the Pittsburgh area. The Klan chapter in Perth Amboy, New Jersey, obtained substantial police protection for its meetings; but guards availed little in that heavily Catholic and Jewish industrial and resort area. The entire city police and fire departments, protecting a meeting of 500 Knights of the Secret Order, were overwhelmed by a mob of 6000 on the evening of August 30, 1923, and the Ku Kluxers were beaten, kicked, and stoned as they fled.

When the Klan reached its peak strength in 1924, less than 4 percent of its members lived in the Northeast—the entire area from Portland, Maine, through Baltimore, Maryland—despite strenuous organizational efforts. The Klan itself claimed that over 40 percent of its membership lived in the three midwestern states of Indiana, Illinois, and Ohio. Even in that hospitable area, however, the Klan's brand of racism was not welcome everywhere.

For a while it appeared that white Protestants in Chicago, disturbed by a rapid influx of Negroes and immigrants, and by the city's infamous lawlessness during the 1920s, might make it the hub of the Klan empire. By 1922, Chicago had more Klan members than any other city, and initiation fees continued to flow from the midwestern metropolis into Atlanta. When Imperial Kleagle Edward Young Clarke visited the city in June 1922, he announced that 30,000 Chicagoans already belonged to the Klan, and implied that the branch soon would be large enough to help enforce the law in Chicago, thus reducing the city's alarming crime rate. In smaller communities, where violators of Klan mores were easier to intimidate, bootleggers were forced to obey Prohibition laws, and gamblers and other sinners were punished by the secret order. When a major civic association started investigating crime in Chicago, however, the group's leader—a prominent clergyman—was found shot to death in Cicero, Illinois, then the center of Al Capone's operations. After Clarke returned to Atlanta, the Chicago Klan wisely continued to leave the war against crime to the police, the FBI, and the Treasury Department, even though these organizations were overwhelmed by the task.

As soon as the Klan's strength in Chicago became known, powerful enemies sprang up to protect the threatened minority groups. Mayor "Big Bill" Thompson, elected with crucial aid from Negro votes, denounced the Klan. The City Council opened an investigation of the society, and made its findings available to other state and local political bodies. One consequence was a bill prohibiting the wearing of masks in public, that passed the Illinois House of Representatives by a vote of 100 to 2, and the State Senate by 26 to 1. The City Council itself resolved by a vote of 56 to 2 to rid the city's payroll of Kluxers. Within a week, two firemen were suspended and the Klan's attorney had to be rushed from Atlanta to take legal steps halting the purge. Meanwhile the American Unity League, dominated by Catholics, started publishing the

names of Klan members, concentrating on those in business and the professions. Salesmen, milkmen, and even a bank president were forced out of their
jobs when their customers refused to deal with Klan members. The disheart-
ened bank president, complying with his board of directors' request that he
resign, explained, "I signed a petition for membership in the Klan several
months ago, but did not know it was anything else than an ordinary fraternal
order."[27] He may not have realized either how many Jewish, Irish, and Negro
depositors had placed their money in his bank.

A counterattack was also launched in the press. In a front-page editorial
headlined "To Hell with the Ku Klux Klan!" the Chicago *Defender*, the nation's leading Negro newspaper, advised readers to get ready to fight against
"those who now try to win by signs and robes what their fathers lost by fire
and sword." A prominent rabbi warned that "Protestantism is on trial. Protestantism must destroy Ku Kluxism or Ku Kluxism will destroy Protestantism."[28]

Political candidates backed publicly by the Klan fared badly in Chicago.
Enough excitement was generated during the city election of 1924 to bring
forth a series of threatening letters from the Klan. Some of these went to Chicago's largest Negro church, which was completely destroyed one night by
fire. On the other hand, bombs demolished a shop just vacated by the Klan
journal, *Dawn*, and other bombs were exploded against offices of Klan members and of advertisers in Klan periodicals.

The accumulation of outside pressures on the Klan in Chicago—political,
economic, and physical—served to increase internal dissension in the order.
Although the Klan enrolled well over 50,000 members in Chicago by 1924, at
the end of that year the organization was practically dormant in the city. For
similar reasons it already was on the way to destruction as a major political
and social force throughout the United States. The failure of the KKK, after
temporary success in the immediate postwar years, should not be interpreted
as a sign that racism was waning. The Klan simply had tried to take on too
many enemies. The "minorities" which the Klan was organized to suppress
possessed far more members, votes, wealth, and almost every other kind of
power than the Klan itself. The order's fate should have served as a warning
to the American people of the changes taking place in a world in which white
Protestants were far outnumbered; but it did not.

III

Another ominous development for the future of "Nordic" supremacy in
America was the creation after World War I of an impressive movement for
black nationalism and black power. Although dozens of organizations devoted
to those ends were formed during the postwar period, by far the largest was
the Universal Negro Improvement Association, sometimes called the Garvey
movement after its founder Marcus Garvey. The history of the UNIA, and of
black as well as white reaction to it, illuminates many qualities of the ferment
that arose forty years later when Negro protest again tended to move in the
direction of black separatism.

The societal dislocations which gave rise to the movement for 100 percent Americanism affected Negro Americans also. The shift from the rural South to densely populated northern cities, despite the obvious compensations, left even the most adaptable migrants somewhat disoriented. Not only were familiar and loved friends and relatives left behind, but so were southern customs, games, climate, landmarks, and to some extent even language. For those who made the move directly from the farm, all these difficulties were magnified. Certain aspects of the white nativist response—the great increase in lynchings and Klan membership beginning in 1919, the ferocious race riots, the organized hostility of white property owners—also helped make black Americans susceptible to a movement similar, in some respects, to that of the Klansmen. They differed drastically, however, in one crucially important respect: Garvey's movement attempted to uplift a long-exploited people; whereas the Klan intended to continue suppression of racial minorities.

Marcus Garvey repeatedly stated: "I believe in a pure black race, just as all self-respecting whites believe in a pure white race."[29] He scorned attempts at integration and ridiculed Negro leaders who worked in any way toward that objective. Whites respected nothing but power, he insisted, and Negro equality could come only from black unity in America combined with a strong black nation in Africa.

Garvey, a stocky, intense, black-skinned man, born on the West Indian island of Jamaica, was a dynamic orator with all the charismatic qualities of the successful visionary, including an inability to handle administrative details. His speeches, and to a lesser degree his essays in his newspaper, *Negro World*, awakened a pride in their race and color among millions of Negroes throughout the world. Garvey delighted in telling his audiences: "I am the equal of any white man." A black skin, he declared repeatedly, far from being a badge of shame, was a glorious symbol of racial greatness, even superiority; a reminder of the African past when, he claimed, black civilizations were the most advanced in the world. These could be thrilling words to Negroes born and raised in the North as well as the South, who had been trained never to think such thoughts, much less express them publicly.

The 1920 UNIA convention, held in New York, was a memorable event for American Negroes, and a disturbing experience for whites accustomed to Negro subservience. Black delegates attended from almost every nation in the Western Hemisphere, as well as from several African states. The convention opened with a silent march by thousands of delegates through the streets of Harlem. The parade, and all subsequent activities connected with the convention, were pervaded by a fervent spirit of black nationalism.

At the convention's climax, Garvey addressed an overcapacity crowd of 25,000 jammed into Madison Square Garden: "We are the descendants of a suffering people. We are the descendants of a people determined to suffer no longer." In another speech during the convention he warned that Negroes never again would fight in the service of whites, as they had during World War I: "The first dying that is to be done by the black man in the future will be done to make himself free."[30]

Black Americans were far from unanimous in accepting Garvey's leadership. Among New York's Negro intellectuals—vitally involved in creating their own image of the "new Negro"—hostility to Garvey's style, if not the content of his message, was common. Garvey's disdain for the intellectuals, and for all light-skinned Negroes, his enthusiasm for capitalism, and his emphasis on action in Africa rather than in the United States, displeased the men who led the Harlem literary and artistic renaissance of the 1920s. Established Negro politicians in major cities also criticized Garvey and his program, although some important Negro dissident political organizations in Chicago and New York were more sympathetic. This criticism became more intense when Garvey's plans for a steamship line, and then for an industrial corporation, failed.

As Garvey and his lieutenants spoke increasingly of violence, they further antagonized the Negro intellectuals and worried the politicians. The UNIA leader even appeared willing to reach some agreement with the Ku Klux Klan, defending this attempt by explaining: "I regard the Klan, the Anglo-Saxon Clubs and White American Societies as better friends of the race than all other groups of hypocritical whites put together." Garvey's ambassador to the League of Nations, William Sherrill, unsettled some Americans by stating in 1922: "Black folk as well as white who tamper with the Universal Negro Improvement Association are going to die."[31] Not long afterward, one of Garvey's most vociferous critics, James W. H. Eason, was shot and murdered in New Orleans where he had gone to address an anti-Garvey rally. Two of Garvey's henchmen had arrived in New Orleans about the same time as Eason; however, the men were acquitted of complicity in the crime. Nevertheless, the murder, and the growing paramilitary element in Garvey's organization, turned Negro intellectuals increasingly toward open opposition.

A week after Eason's murder, eight of the most highly respected Negro leaders in the country protested to the Justice Department that Garvey's trial for mail fraud already had been postponed for a year and a half. They asked why this "unscrupulous demagogue" was being treated differently than ordinary citizens. Garvey responded by charging that the "Committee of Eight" were almost all octoroons or quadroons, or married to quadroons, and were enemies of the black race. Nevertheless, Garvey soon was tried, convicted, sentenced to prison, and a few years later deported to the West Indies.

Garvey's organization disintegrated after his removal from the scene. By the mid-1920s, however, Garvey's was not the only movement unable to sustain the high promise of 1919–1920. Dozens of smaller black nationalist groups also were fading, including W. E. B. Du Bois's Pan African movement. The African Blood Brotherhood, a propagandistic society whose members included some of the most intelligent and able black leaders in the country, merged and practically disappeared into the Communist Party during this period. A meeting in 1924 of representatives from sixty-four Negro organizations—ranging in the political spectrum from the NAACP to the Blood Brotherhood—seemed to foreshadow unified action on some issues, at least; but the movement toward unity soon faltered.[32]

At about the same time, membership in the Ku Klux Klan began falling rapidly, despite a temporary recovery during the crusade against Al Smith's presidential candidacy in 1928. The massive "Americanization" campaign directed at recent immigrants lost its urgency after passage of immigration restriction legislation in 1924. A marked decline in the publication of pseudo-scientific racist literature was noted about 1925. Even efforts to enforce Prohibition, and to spread and protect the doctrines of fundamentalist religion, were reduced in fervor after the mid-1920s.

It would be an exaggeration to state that "normalcy" had returned; that the movement for 100 percent Americanism was successful enough to obviate the need for organizations like the Klan; that dissident groups like Garvey's and the Communists were doomed by that success. Too many other factors were involved; such simple statements provide only partial explanations. However, they *are* partial explanations. The movement to protect the established culture, which included the maintenance of attitudes and institutions based on the concept of white racial superiority, did accomplish many of its objectives. Nevertheless, it left the major problems facing modern American society basically unsolved, especially those involving racial and cultural differences within the society. The holding action conducted by 100 percent Americans from 1915 to 1930 handed these problems to future generations, who would have to deal with them in even more acute forms, at a time when temporary expedients would not suffice.

Notes

1. These events are described and an attempt made to link them theoretically with similar movements at other times and places, in Stanley Coben, "A Study in Nativism: The American Red Scare of 1919–1920," *Political Science Quarterly*, 79 (March 1964), pp. 52–75.
2. U.S. Bureau of the Census, *Historical Statistics of the United States, Colonial Times to 1957* (Washington, D.C., 1960), chapter C.
3. U.S. Department of Labor, Division of Negro Economics, *Negro Migration in 1916–17* (Washington, D.C., 1919); Louis V. Kennedy, *The Negro Peasant Turns Cityward* (New York, 1930); Bureau of the Census, *Historical Statistics of the United States*, chapter C.
4. Department of Labor, *Negro Migration in 1916–17*, p. 33.
5. Clyde Vernon Kiser, *Sea Island to City* (New York, 1932), p. 22. Chicago Commission on Race Relations, *The Negro in Chicago* (Chicago, 1922; reprinted, New York, 1968), p. 3
6. Kennedy, *The Negro Peasant Turns Cityward*, pp. 193–200.
7. The best account of the Chicago riot can be found in Chicago Commission on Race Relations, *The Negro in Chicago*. The other riots of the period are described in Arthur I. Waskow, *From Race Riot to Sit-In* (Garden City, N.Y., 1966), chapters 1–9. As indicated in earlier chapters, race riots were not a new phenomenon in United States history. But never had riots been even remotely as widespread or as violent on *both* sides as in 1919.
8. In Roger Daniels, *The Politics of Prejudice*, University of California Publications in History, Volume 71 (Berkeley and Los Angeles, 1962), p. 21.

9. In Daniels, *The Politics of Prejudice*, p. 84.

10. Carey McWilliams, *North from Mexico* (New York, 1948, 1968), chapter 9.

11. Bureau of the Census, *Historical Statistics of the United States*, chapter C.

12. McWilliams estimated the average wage at $600 annually per family; but outside of the beet sugar industry the majority of Mexican-American families seem to have earned slightly over $1000 a year. In any case, the average was well below that set by the Bureau of Labor Statistics as the minimum for subsistence. For incomes of large samples of Mexicans in a variety of California agricultural and nonagricultural industries, see *Mexicans in California, Report of Governor C. C. Young's Mexican Fact-Finding Committee* (San Francisco, 1930), chapters 4–5.

13. The report compiled for the Mexican Fact-Finding Committee on the formation of the chief California unions and their treatment by growers and local officials was both detailed and fair. When the committee's chief investigator showed a copy of his account of the cantaloupe pickers' strike to the district attorney of Imperial County, the official complained that "while the report was on the whole correct and accurate as to details, it gave the erroneous impression that the district attorney's office was unreasonable in its conduct during the labor troubles." Actually the report indicated that the county sheriff, not the district attorney, was arresting strikers indiscriminately. *Mexicans in California*, chapters 6, 7; also McWilliams, *North from Mexico*, chapter 10.

14. *Mexicans in California*, pp. 20, 25, 43, 49, 59.

15. McWilliams, *North from Mexico*, chapters 12, 13. McWilliams led efforts first to prevent, then to end, these events.

16. John Higham, *Strangers in the Land: Patterns of American Nativism 1860–1925* (New Brunswick, N.J., 1955), pp. 164–65, 168.

17. Theodore Lothrop Stoddard, *The Rising Tide of Color Against White World Supremacy* (New York, 1920), p. 89; Thomas F. Gossett, *Race: The History of an Idea in America* (Dallas, 1963), pp. 387, 395–96. A recent survey of anti-Negro literature in the United States concluded that "by 1925 a marked change was occurring in the attitude of scientific circles toward the subject of race . . . By 1930 the amount of scientific literature purporting to prove the Negro's alleged inferiority had precipitously declined." A conspicuous reduction in the amount of popular anti-Negro writing followed immediately afterward. I. A. Newby, *Jim Crow's Defense: Anti-Negro Thought in America 1900–1930* (Baton Rouge, La., 1965), pp. 50–51.

18. Palmer is quoted more fully on this subject in Stanley Coben, *A. Mitchell Palmer: Politician* (New York, 1963), p. 198, and chapters 11 and 12, *passim*.

19. A. Mitchell Palmer, "Radicalism and Sedition among the Negroes as Reflected in Their Publications," Exhibit 10, *Investigation Activities of the Department of Justice*, Volume XII, Senate Document 153, 66 Cong. 1 Sess. (Washington, D.C., 1919), pp. 161–87. By far the best account of Negroes' role in the American Communist movement after World War I can be found in Theodore Draper, *American Communism and Soviet Russia* (New York, 1960), chapter 15.

20. Stoddard, *The Rising Tide of Color Against White World Supremacy*, p. 220.

21. In Kenneth T. Jackson, *The Ku Klux Klan in the City, 1915–1930* (New York, 1967), p. 22.

22. In Charles C. Alexander, *The Ku Klux Klan in the Southwest* (Lexington, Ky., 1966), p. 9. The prejudice of Klan leaders against women, who were segregated in separate organizations, deserves more exploration by historians than it has received.

23. Jackson, *The Ku Klux Klan in the City*, p. 19.

24. Jackson, *The Ku Klux Klan in the City*, p. 177.

25. *New York Times*, May 31, 1927, pp. 1, 7.
26. Jackson, *The Ku Klux Klan in the City*, p. 182. The Klan's activities in northern cities like Boston, Pittsburgh, and Chicago are described in Jackson's volume.
27. Jackson, *The Ku Klux Klan in the City*, p. 104.
28. Jackson, *The Ku Klux Klan in the City*, p. 102.
29. Amy Jacques Garvey, ed., *Philosophy and Opinions of Marcus Garvey* (New York, 1923), p. 37.
30. In Edmund David Cronon, *Black Moses, the Story of Marcus Garvey and the Universal Negro Improvement Association* (Madison, Wis., 1955), p. 65.
31. In Cronon, *Black Moses*, pp. 109, 190.
32. Alain Locke, "The Negro Speaks for Himself," *The Survey* (April 15, 1924) pp. 71–72; Draper, *American Communism and Soviet Russia*, chapter 15.

The Meaning of Lindbergh's Flight

John William Ward

Historians have increasingly come to see that the meaning of America often has been reflected in the individuals the nation selects as its heroes. This insight seems to be particularly true regarding the 1920s. By then, for example, Thomas A. Edison's inventive genius had led many to view him as a classic example of the Horatio Alger dream come true. And Henry Ford, seemingly a twentieth-century edition of Benjamin Franklin, captured much the same spirit. However, in the informed opinion of the late John William Ward, former president of Amherst College and professor of history at Princeton, it was Charles A. Lindbergh, Jr.—the Lone Eagle—who most fully symbolized the spirit of his age. As the first aviator to fly solo across the Atlantic Ocean in his famous flight from Roosevelt Field, New York, to Le Bourget airport near Paris in 1927, Lindbergh became an instant legend and his feat triggered "magic on a vast scale" in the American mind. By some he was viewed as but the latest representative of the American pioneer tradition, the trailblazer of a new frontier who had found inspiration for his deeds among the legendary frontiersmen of old. For others, however, he emerged as the new hero of the machine age; his exploits represented a triumph of technology over nature. At one and the same time, then, Lindbergh symbolized the tensions between nostalgia and progress. He symbolized America's continuing love affair with its mythic past and its utopian visions of the future.

On Friday, May 20, 1927, at 7:52 a.m., Charles A. Lindbergh took off in a silver-winged monoplane and flew from the United States to France. With this flight Lindbergh became the first man to fly alone across the Atlantic Ocean. The log of flight 33 of "The Spirit of St. Louis" reads: "Roosevelt Field, Long Island, New York, to Le Bourget Aerodrome, Paris, France. 33 hrs. 30 min." Thus was the fact of Lindbergh's achievement easily put down. But the meaning of Lindbergh's flight lay hidden in the next sentence of the log: "(Fuselage fabric badly torn by souvenir hunters.)"

When Lindbergh landed at Le Bourget he is supposed to have said, "Well, we've done it." A contemporary writer asked "Did what?" Lindbergh "had no idea of what he had done. He thought he had simply flown from New York to Paris. What he had really done was something far greater. He had fired the

From "The Meaning of Lindbergh's Flight," by John William Ward, in *American Quarterly*, Vol. 10 (Spring 1958), pp. 2–16. Copyright 1958.

imagination of mankind." From the moment of Lindbergh's flight people recognized that something more was involved than the mere fact of the physical leap from New York to Paris. "Lindbergh," wrote John Erskine, "served as a metaphor." But what the metaphor stood for was not easy to say. The *New York Times* remarked then that "there has been no complete and satisfactory explanation of the enthusiasm and acclaim for Captain Lindbergh." Looking back on the celebration of Lindbergh, one can see now that the American people were trying to understand Lindbergh's flight, to grasp its meaning, and through it, perhaps, to grasp the meaning of their own experience. Was the flight the achievement of a heroic, solitary, unaided individual? Or did the flight represent the triumph of the machine, the success of an industrially organized society? These questions were central to the meaning of Lindbergh's flight. They were also central to the lives of the people who made Lindbergh their hero.

The flight demanded attention in its own right, of course, quite apart from whatever significance it might have. Lindbergh's story had all the makings of great drama. Since 1919 there had been a standing prize of $25,000 to be awarded to the first aviator who could cross the Atlantic in either direction between the United States and France in a heavier-than-air craft. In the spring of 1927 there promised to be what the *New York Times* called "the most spectacular race ever held—3,600 miles over the open sea to Paris." The scene was dominated by veteran pilots. On the European side were the French aces, Nungesser and Coli; on the American side, Commander Richard E. Byrd, in a big tri-motored Fokker monoplane, led a group of contestants. Besides Byrd, who had already flown over the North Pole, there were Commander Davis, flying a ship named in honor of the American Legion which had put up $100,000 to finance his attempt, Clarence Chamberlin, who had already set a world's endurance record of more than fifty-one hours in the air in a Bellanca tri-motored plane, and Captain René Fonck, the French war ace, who had come to America to fly a Sikorsky aircraft. The hero was unheard of and unknown. He was on the West Coast supervising the construction of a single-engined plane to cost only ten thousand dollars.

Then fate played its part. It seemed impossible that Lindbergh could get his plane built and east to New York in time to challenge his better equipped and more famous rivals. But in quick succession a series of disasters cleared his path. On April 16, Commander Byrd's "America" crashed on its test flight, crushing the leg of Floyd Bennett who was one of the crew and injuring Byrd's hand and wrist. On April 24, Clarence Chamberlin cracked up in his Bellanca, not seriously, but enough to delay his plans. Then on April 26, Commander Davis and his co-pilot lost their lives as the "American Legion" crashed on its final test flight. In ten days, accidents had stopped all of Lindbergh's American rivals. Nungesser and Coli, however, took off in their romantically named ship, "The White Bird," from Le Bourget on May 8. The world waited and Lindbergh, still on the West Coast, decided to try to fly the Pacific. But Nungesser and Coli were never seen again. As rumors filled the newspapers, as reports came in that the "White Bird" was seen over Newfoundland, over

Boston, over the Atlantic, it soon became apparent that Nungesser and Coli had failed, dropping to their death in some unknown grave. Disaster had touched every ship entered in the trans-Atlantic race.

Now, with the stage cleared, Lindbergh entered. He swooped across the continent in two great strides, landing only at St. Louis. The first leg of his flight established a new distance record but all eyes were on the Atlantic and the feat received little notice. Curiously, the first time Lindbergh appeared in the headlines of the New York papers was Friday, the thirteenth. By this time Byrd and Chamberlin were ready once again but the weather had closed in and kept all planes on the ground. Then, after a week of fretful waiting, on the night of May 19, on the way into New York to see "Rio Rita," Lindbergh received a report that the weather was breaking over the ocean. He hurried back to Roosevelt Field to haul his plane out onto a wet, dripping runway. After mechanics painfully loaded the plane's gas by hand, the wind shifted, as fate played its last trick. A muddy runway and an adverse wind. Whatever the elements, whatever the fates, the decisive act is the hero's, and Lindbergh made his choice. Providing chorus to the action, the *Herald Tribune* reported that Lindbergh lifted the overloaded plane into the sky "by his indomitable will alone."

The parabola of the action was as clean as the arc of Lindbergh's flight. The drama should have ended with the landing of "The Spirit of St. Louis" at Le Bourget. That is where Lindbergh wanted it to end. In *"WE,"* written immediately after the flight, and in *The Spirit of St. Louis*, written twenty-six years later, Lindbergh chose to end his accounts there. But the flight turned out to be only the first act in the part Lindbergh was to play.

Lindbergh was so innocent of his future that on his flight he carried letters of introduction. The hysterical response, first of the French and then of his own countrymen, had been no part of his careful plans. In *"WE,"* after Lindbergh's narrative of the flight, the publisher wrote: "When Lindbergh came to tell the story of his welcome at Paris, London, Brussels, Washington, New York, and St. Louis he found himself up against a tougher problem than flying the Atlantic." So another writer completed the account in the third person. He suggested that "the reason Lindbergh's story is different is that when his plane came to a halt on Le Bourget field that black night in Paris, Lindbergh the man kept on going. The phenomenon of Lindbergh took its start with his flight across the ocean; but in its entirety it was almost as distinct from that flight as though he had never flown at all."

Lindbergh's private life ended with his flight to Paris. The drama was no longer his, it was the public's. "The outburst of unanimous acclaim was at once personal and symbolic," said the *American Review of Reviews*. From the moment of success there were two Lindberghs, the private Lindbergh and the public Lindbergh. The latter was the construction of the imagination of Lindbergh's time, fastened on to an unwilling person. The tragedy of Lindbergh's career is that he could never accept the role assigned him. He always believed he might keep his two lives separate. But from the moment he landed at Le Bourget, Lindbergh became, as the *New Republic* noted, "ours. . . . He is no longer permitted to be himself. He is US personified. He is the United States." Ambassador Herrick introduced Lindbergh to the French, saying, "This young man from out of the West brings you better than anything else the spirit of America," and wired to President Coolidge, "Had we searched all America we could not have found a better type than young Lindbergh to represent the spirit and high purpose of our people." This was Lindbergh's fate, to be a type. A writer in the *North American Review* felt that Lindbergh represented "the dominant American character," he "images the best" about the United States. And an ecstatic female in the *American Magazine,* who began by saying that Lindbergh "is a sort of symbol. . . . He is the dream that is in our hearts," concluded that the American public responded so wildly to Lindbergh because of "the thrill of possessing, in him, our dream of what *we* really and truly want to be." The act of possession was so complete that articles since have attempted to discover the "real" Lindbergh, that enigmatic and taciturn figure behind the public mask. But it is no less difficult to discern the features of the public Lindbergh, that symbolic figure who presented to the imagination of his time all the yearnings and buried desires of its dream for itself.

Lindbergh's flight came at the end of a decade marked by social and political corruption and by a sense of moral loss. The heady idealism of the First World War had been succeeded by a deep cynicism as to the war's real purpose. The naïve belief that virtue could be legislated was violated by the vast discrepancy between the law and the social habits of prohibition. A philosophy of relativism had become the uneasy rationale of a nation which had formerly believed in moral absolutes. The newspapers agreed that Lindbergh's chief worth was his spiritual and moral value. His story was held to be "in striking contrast with the sordid unhallowed themes that have for months steeped the imaginations and thinking of the people." Or, as another had it, "there is good reason why people should hail Lindbergh and give him honor. He stands out in a grubby world as an inspiration."

Lindbergh gave the American people a glimpse of what they liked to think themselves to be at a time when they feared they had deserted their own vision of themselves. The grubbiness of the twenties had a good deal to do with the shining quality of Lindbergh's success, especially when one remembers that Lindbergh's flight was not as unexampled as our national memory would have it. The Atlantic was not unconquered when Lindbergh flew. A British dirigible had twice crossed the Atlantic before 1919 and on May 8 of that year three naval seaplanes left Rockaway, New York, and one, the NC-4 manned by a crew of five, got through to Plymouth, England. A month later, Captain John Alcock, an Englishman, with Arthur W. Browne, an American, flew the first heavier-than-air land plane across the Atlantic nonstop, from Newfoundland to Ireland, to win twice the money Lindbergh did, a prize of $50,000 offered by the London *Daily Mail.* Alcock's and Browne's misfortune was to land in a soft and somnolent Irish peat bog instead of before the cheering thousands of London or Paris. Or perhaps they should have flown in 1927.

The wild medley of public acclaim and the homeric strivings of editors make one realize that the response to Lindbergh involved a mass ritual in which America celebrated itself more than it celebrated Lindbergh. Lindbergh's flight was the occasion of a public act of regeneration in which the nation momentarily rededicated itself to something, the loss of which was keenly felt. It was said again and again that "Lindy" taught America "to lift its eyes up to Heaven." Heywood Broun, in his column in the *New York World,* wrote that this "tall young man raised up and let us see the potentialities of the human spirit." Broun felt that the flight proved that, though "we are small and fragile," it "isn't true that there is no health in us." Lindbergh's flight provided the moment, but the meaning of the flight is to be found in the deep and pervasive need for renewal which the flight brought to the surface of public feeling. When Lindbergh appeared at the nation's capital, the *Washington Post* observed, "He was given that frenzied acclaim which comes from the depths of the people." In New York, where 4,000,000 people saw him, a reporter wrote that the dense and vociferous crowds were swept, as Lindbergh passed, "with an emotion tense and inflammable." The *Literary Digest* suggested that the answer to the hero-worship of Lindbergh would "throw an interesting light on the psychology of our times and of the American people."

The *Nation* noted about Lindbergh that "there was something lyric as well as heroic about the apparition of this young Lochinvar who suddenly came out of the West and who flew all unarmed and all alone. It is the kind of stuff which the ancient Greeks would have worked into a myth and the medieval Scots into a border ballad. . . . But what we have in the case of Lindbergh is an actual, an heroic and an exhaustively exposed experience which exists by suggestion in the form of poetry." The *Nation* quickly qualified its statement by observing that reporters were as far as possible from being poets and concluded that the discrepancy between the fact and the celebration of it was not poetry, perhaps, but "magic on a vast scale." Yet the *Nation* might have clung to its insight that the public meaning of Lindbergh's flight was somehow poetic. The vast publicity about Lindbergh corresponds in one vital particular with the poetic vision. Poetry, said William Butler Yeats, contains opposites; so did Lindbergh. Lindbergh did not mean one thing; he meant many things. The image of itself which America contemplated in the public person of Lindbergh was full of conflict; it was, in a word, dramatic.

To heighten the drama, Lindbergh did it alone. He was the "lone eagle" and a full exploration of that fact takes one deep into the emotional meaning of his success. Not only the *Nation* found Sir Walter Scott's lines on Lochinvar appropriate: "he rode all unarmed and he rode all alone." Newspapers and magazines were deluged with amateur poems that vindicated one rhymester's wry comment, "Go conquer the perils / That lurk in the skies—/ And you'll get bum poems / Right up to your eyes." The *New York Times,* that alone received more than two hundred poems, observed in trying to summarize the poetic deluge that "the fact that he flew alone made the strongest impression." Another favorite tribute was Kipling's "The Winners," with its refain, "He travels the fastest who travels alone." The others who had conquered the Atlantic and those like Byrd and Chamberlin who were trying at the same time were not traveling alone and they hardly rode unarmed. Other than Lindbergh, all the contestants in the trans-Atlantic race had unlimited backing, access to the best planes, and all were working in teams, carrying at least one co-pilot to share the long burden of flying the plane. So a writer in the New York *Sun*, in a poem called "The Flying Fool," a nickname that Lindbergh despised, celebrated Lindbergh's flight: ". . . no kingly plane for him; / No endless data, comrades, moneyed chums; / No boards, no councils, no directors grim—/ He plans ALONE . . . and takes luck as it comes."

Upon second thought, it must seem strange that the long distance flight of an airplane, the achievement of a highly advanced and organized technology, should be the occasion for hymns of praise to the solitary unaided man. Yet the National Geographic Society, when it presented a medal to Lindbergh, wrote on the presentation scroll, "Courage, when it goes alone, has ever caught men's imaginations," and compared Lindbergh to Robinson Crusoe and the trailmakers in our own West. But Lindbergh and Robinson Crusoe, the one in his helmet and fur-lined flying coat and the other in his wild goatskins, do not easily co-exist. Even if Robinson Crusoe did have a tidy capital investment in the form of a well-stocked shipwreck, he still did not have a ten thousand dollar machine under him.

Lindbergh, in nearly every remark about his flight and in his own writings about it, resisted the tendency to exploit the flight as the achievement of an individual. He never said "I," he always said "We." The plane was not to go unrecognized. Nevertheless, there persisted a tendency to seize upon the flight as a way of celebrating the self-sufficient individual, so that among many others an Ohio newspaper could describe Lindbergh as this "self-contained, self-reliant, courageous young man [who] ranks among the great pioneers of history." The strategy here was a common one, to make Lindbergh a "pioneer" and thus to link him with a long and vital tradition of individualism in the American experience. Colonel Theodore Roosevelt, himself the son of a famous exponent of self-reliance, said to reporters at his home in Oyster Bay that "Captain Lindbergh personifies the daring of youth. Daniel Boone, David Crocket [*sic*], and men of that type played a lone hand and made America. Lindbergh is their lineal descendant." In *Outlook* magazine, immediately below an enthusiastic endorsement of Lindbergh's own remarks on the importance of his machine and his scientific instruments, there was the statement, "Charles Lindbergh is the heir of all that we like to think is best in America. He is of the stuff out of which have been made the pioneers that opened up the wilderness, first on the Atlantic coast, and then in our great West. His are the qualities which we, as a people, must nourish." It is in this mood that one suspects it was important that Lindbergh came out of the West and rode all alone.

Another common metaphor in the attempt to place Lindbergh's exploit was to say that he had opened a new "frontier." To speak of the air as a "frontier" was to invoke an interpretation of the meaning of American history which had sources deep in American experience, but the frontier of the airplane is hardly the frontier of the trailmakers of the old West. Rather than an escape into the self-sufficient simplicity of the American past, the machine which made Lindbergh's flight possible represented an advance into a complex industrial present. The difficulty lay in using an instance of modern life to celebrate the virtues of the past, to use an extreme development of an urban industrial society to insist upon the significance of the frontier in American life.

A little more than a month after Lindbergh's flight, Joseph K. Hart in *Survey* magazine reached back to Walt Whitman's poem for the title of an article on Lindbergh: "O Pioneer." A school had made Lindbergh an honarary alumnus but Hart protested there was little available evidence "that he was educated in *schools.*" "We must look elsewhere for our explanation," Hart wrote and he looked to the experience of Lindbergh's youth when "everything that he ever did . . . he did by himself. He lived more to himself than most boys." And, of course, Lindbergh lived to himself in the only place conceivably possible, in the world of nature, on a Minnesota farm. "There he developed in the companionship of woods and fields, animals and machines, his audaciously natural and simple personality." The word, "machines," jars as it intrudes into Hart's idyllic pastoral landscape and betrays Hart's difficulty in relating the setting of nature upon which he wishes to insist with the fact that its product spent his whole life tinkering with machines, from motorcycles to airplanes. But except for that one word, Hart proceeds in uncritical nostalgia to show that "a lone trip across the Atlantic was not impossible for a boy who had grown up in the solitude of the woods and waters." If Lindbergh was "clear-headed, naif, untrained in the ways of cities," it was because he had "that 'natural simplicity' which Fenimore Cooper used to attribute to the pioneer hero of his Leatherstocking Tales." Hart rejected the notion that any student "bent to all the conformities" of formal training could have done what Lindbergh did. "Must we not admit," he asked, "that this pioneering urge remained to this audacious youth because he had never submitted completely to the repressions of the world and its jealous institutions?"

Only those who insist on reason will find it strange that Hart should use the industrial achievement of the airplane to reject the urban, institutionalized world of industrialism. Hart was dealing with something other than reason; he was dealing with the emotion evoked by Lindbergh's solitude. He recognized that people wished to call Lindbergh a "genius" because that "would release him from the ordinary rules of existence." That way, "we could rejoice with him in his triumph and then go back to the contracted routines of our institutional ways [because] ninety-nine percent of us must be content to be shaped and moulded by the routine ways and forms of the world to the routine tasks of life." It is in the word "must" that the pathos of this interpretation of the phenomenon of Lindbergh lies. The world had changed from the open society of the pioneer to the close-knit, interdependent world of a modern machine-oriented civilization. The institutions of a highly corporate industrial society existed as a constant reproach to a people who liked to believe that the meaning of its experience was embodied in the formless, independent life of the frontier. Like Thomas Jefferson who identified American virtue with nature and saw the city as a "great sore" on the public body, Hart concluded that "certainly, in the response that the world—especially the world of great cities—has made to the performance of this midwestern boy, we can read of the homesickness of the human soul, immured in city canyons and routine tasks, for the freer world of youth, for the open spaces of the pioneer, for the joy of battling with nature and clean storms once more on the frontiers of the earth."

The social actuality which made the adulation of Lindbergh possible had its own irony for the notion that America's strength lay in its simple uncomplicated beginnings. For the public response to Lindbergh to have reached the proportions it did, the world had by necessity to be the intricately developed world of modern mass communications. But more than irony was involved. Ultimately, the emotion attached to Lindbergh's flight involved no less than a whole theory about American history. By singling out the fact that Lindbergh rode alone, and by naming him a pioneer of the frontier, the public projected its sense that the source of America's strength lay somewhere in the past and that Lindbergh somehow meant that America must look backward in time to rediscover some lost virtue. The mood was nostalgic and American history was read as a decline, a decline measured in terms of America's advance into an urban, institutionalized way of life which made solitary achievement increasingly beyond the reach of ninety-nine per cent of the people. Because Lindbergh's ancestors were Norse, it was easy to call him a "Viking" and extend the emotion far into the past when all frontiers were open. He became the "Columbus" of another new world to conquer as well as the "Lochinvar" who rode all alone. But there was always the brute, irreducible fact that Lindbergh's exploit was a victory of the machine over the barriers of nature. If the only response to Lindbergh had been a retreat to the past, we would be involved with a mass cultural neurosis, the inability of America to accept reality, the reality of the world in which it lived. But there was another aspect, one in which the public celebrated the machine and the highly organized society of which it was a product. The response to Lindbergh reveals that the American people were deeply torn between conflicting interpretations of their own experience. By calling Lindbergh a pioneer, the people could read into American history the necessity of turning back to the frontier past. Yet the people could also read American history in terms of progress into the industrial future. They could do this by emphasizing the machine which was involved in Lindbergh's flight.

Lindbergh came back from Europe in an American man-of-war, the cruiser *Memphis*. It seems he had contemplated flying on, around the whole world perhaps, but less adventurous heads prevailed and dictated a surer mode of travel for so valuable a piece of public property. The *New Republic* protested against bringing America's hero of romance home in a warship. If he had returned on a great liner, that would have been one thing. "One's first trip on an oceanliner is a great adventure—the novelty of it, the many people of all kinds and conditions, floating for a week in a tiny compact world of their own." But to return on the *Memphis*, "to be put on a gray battleship with a collection of people all of the same stripe, in a kind of ship that has as much relation to the life of the sea as a Ford factory has! We might as well have put him in a pneumatic tube and shot him across the Atlantic." The interesting thing about the *New Republic's* protest against the unromantic, regimented life of a battleship is that the image it found appropriate was the Ford assembly line. It was this reaction against the discipline of a mechanized society that probably led to the nostalgic image of Lindbergh as a remnant of a past when romance was possible for the individual, when life held novelty and society was variegated rather than uniform. But what the Ford Assembly Line represents, a society committed to the path of full mechanization, was what lay behind Lindbergh's romantic success. A long piece in the Sunday *New York Times,* "Lindbergh Symbolizes the Genius of America," reminded its readers of the too obvious fact that "without an airplane he could not have flown at all." Lindbergh "is, indeed, the Icarus of the twentieth century; not himself an inventor of his own wings, but a son of that omnipotent Daedalus whose ingenuity has created the modern world." The point was that modern America was the creation of modern industry. Lindbergh "reveres his 'ship' as a noble expression of mechanical wisdom. . . . Yet in this reverence . . . Lindbergh is not an exception. What he means by the Spirit of St. Louis is really the spirit of America. The mechanical genius, which is discerned in Henry Ford as well as in Charles A. Lindbergh, is in the very atmosphere of [the] country." In contrast to a sentiment that feared the enforced discipline of the machine there existed an attitude of reverence for its power.

Lindbergh led the way in the celebration of the machine, not only implicitly by including his plane when he said "we," but by direct statement. In Paris he told newspapermen, "You fellows have not said enough about that wonderful motor." Rarely have two more taciturn figures confronted one another than when Lindbergh returned to Washington and Calvin Coolidge pinned the Distinguished Flying Cross on him, but in his brief remarks Coolidge found room to express his particular delight that Lindbergh should have given equal credit to the airplane. "For we are proud," said the President, "that in every particular this silent partner represented American genius and industry. I am told that more than 100 separate companies furnished materials, parts or service in its construction."

The flight was not the heroic lone success of a single daring individual, but the climax of the co-operative effort of an elaborately interlocked technology. The day after Coolidge's speech, Lindbergh said at another ceremony in Washington that the honor should "not go to the pilot alone but to American science and genius which had given years of study to the advancement of aeronautics." "Some things," he said, "should be taken into due consideration in connection with our flight that have not heretofore been given due weight. That is just what made this flight possible. It was not the act of a single pilot. It was the culmination of twenty years of aeronautical research and the assembling together of all that was practical and best in American aviation." The flight, concluded Lindbergh, "represented American industry."

The worship of the machine which was embodied in the public's response to Lindbergh exalted those very aspects which were denigrated in the celebration of the flight as the work of a heroic individual. Organization and careful method were what lay behind the flight, not individual self-sufficiency and daring romance. One magazine hailed the flight as a "triumph of mechanical engineering." "It is not to be forgotten that this era is the work not so much of brave aviators as of engineers, who have through patient and protracted effort been steadily improving the construction of airplanes." The lesson to be learned from Lindbergh's flight, thought a writer in the *Independent*, "is that the splendid human and material aspects of America need to be organized for the ordinary, matter of fact service of society." The machine meant organization, the careful rationalization of activity of a Ford assembly line, it meant planning, and, if it meant the loss of spontaneous individual action, it meant the material betterment of society. Lindbergh meant not a retreat to the free life of the frontier past but an emergence into the time when "the machine began to take first place in the public mind—the machine and the organization that made its operation possible on a large scale." A poet on this side of the matter wrote, "All day I felt the pull / Of the steel miracle." The machine was not a devilish engine which would enthrall mankind, it was the instrument which would lead to a new paradise. But the direction of history implicit in the machine was toward the future, not the past; the meaning of history was progress, not decline, and America should not lose faith in the future betterment of society. An address by a Harvard professor, picked up by the *Magazine of Business*, made all this explicit. "We commonly take Social Progress for granted," said Edwin F. Gay, "but the doctrine of Social Progress is one of the great revolutionary ideas which have powerfully affected our modern world." There was a danger, however, that the idea "may be in danger of becoming a commonplace or a butt of criticism." The speaker recognized why this might be. America was "worn and disillusioned after the Great War." Logically, contentment should have gone with so optimistic a creed, yet the American people were losing faith. So Lindbergh filled an emotional need even where a need should have been lacking. "He has come like a shining vision to revive the hope of mankind." The high ideals of faith in progress "had almost come to seem like hollow words to us—but now here he is, emblematic of heroes yet to inhabit this world. Our belief in Social Progress is justified symbolically in him."

It is a long flight from New York to Paris; it is a still longer flight from the fact of Lindbergh's achievement to the burden imposed upon it by the imagination of his time. But it is in that further flight that lies the full meaning of Lindbergh. His role was finally a double one. His flight provided an opportunity for the people to project their own emotions into his act and their emotions involved finally two attitudes toward the meaning of their own experience. One view had it that America represented a brief escape from the course of history, an emergence into a new and open world with the self-sufficient individual at its center. The other said that America represented a stage in historical evolution and that its fulfillment lay in the development of society. For one, the meaning of America lay in the past; for the other in the future. For one, the American ideal was an escape from institutions, from the forms of society, and from limitations put upon the free individual; for the other, the American ideal was the elaboration of the complex institutions which made modern society possible, an acceptance of the discipline of the machine, and the achievement of the individual within a context of which he was only a part. The two views were contradictory but both were possible and both were present in the public's reaction to Lindbergh's flight.

The Sunday newspapers announced that Lindbergh had reached Paris and in the very issue whose front pages were covered with Lindbergh's story the magazine section of the *New York Times* featured an article by the British philosopher, Bertrand Russell. The magazine had, of course, been made up too far in advance to take advantage of the news about Lindbergh. Yet, in a prophetic way, Russell's article was about Lindbergh. Russell hailed the rise to power of the United States because he felt that in the "new life that is America's" in the twentieth century "the new outlook appropriate to machinery [would] become more completely dominant than in the old world." Russell sensed that some might be unwilling to accept the machine, but "whether we like this new outlook or not," he wrote, "is of little importance." Why one might not was obvious. A society built on the machine, said Russell, meant "the diminution in the value and independence of the individual. Great enterprises tend more and more to be collective, and in an industrialized world the interference of the community with the individual must be more intense." Russell realized that while the co-operative effort involved in machine technology makes man collectively more lordly, it makes the individual more submissive. "I do not see how it is to be avoided," he concluded.

People are not philosophers. They did not see how the conflict between a machine society and the free individual was to be avoided either. But neither were they ready to accept the philosopher's statement of the prolem. In Lindbergh, the people celebrated both the self-sufficient individual and the machine. Americans still celebrate both. We cherish the individualism of the American creed at the same time that we worship the machine which increasingly enforces collectivized behavior. Whether we can have both, the freedom of the individual and the power of an organized society, is a question that still haunts our minds. To resolve the conflict that is present in America's celebration of Lindbergh in 1927 is still the task of America.

The Legend of Isolationism in the 1920s

William Appleman Williams

The myth of the 1920s as the Jazz Age, a decade of "booze, bobbed hair and the blues," had its origins when the era was indeed "only yesterday." That this view is mostly myth, at least to the extent that it described only certain domestic aspects of the age, has been emphasized so much that we may be coming to believe it. One of the aspects of the Jazz Age myth that has maintained its tenacity is that which characterizes U.S. foreign policy of the period as isolationist. In this article, William Appleman Williams, late professor of history at the University of Oregon and one of the early "New Leftists," attacks this stance as completely mythological—a reflection of "the folklore of American foreign relations." He sees America's approach to foreign affairs during the 1920s as related to other so called isolationist periods in American history when the country, led by the business community and supported by the government and the people, was in fact very much expansionist.

The widely accepted assumption that the United States was isolationist from 1920 through 1932 is no more than a legend. Sir Francis Bacon might have classed this myth of isolation as one of his Idols of the Market-Place. An "ill and unfit choice of words," he cautioned, "leads men aways into innumerable and inane controversies and fancies." And certainly the application of the terms *isolation* and *isolationism* to a period and a policy that were characterized by vigorous involvement in the affairs of the world with consciousness of purpose qualifies as an "ill and unfit choice of words." Thus the purpose of this essay: on the basis of an investigation of the record to suggest that, far from isolation, the foreign relations of the United States from 1920 through 1932 were marked by express and extended involvement with—and intervention in the affairs of—other nations of the world.

It is both more accurate and more helpful to consider the twenties as contiguous with the present instead of viewing those years as a quixotic interlude of low-down jazz and lower-grade gin, fluttering flappers and Faulkner's fiction, and bootlegging millionaires and millionaire bootleggers. For in foreign policy there is far less of a sharp break between 1923 and 1953 than generally is acknowledged. A closer examination of the so-called isolationists of the twenties reveals that many of them were in fact busily engaged in extending American power. Those individuals and groups have not dramatically changed their outlook on foreign affairs. Their policies and objectives may differ with those of others (including professors), but they have never sought to isolate the United States.

This interpretation runs counter to the folklore of American foreign relations. Harvard places isolationism "in the saddle." Columbia sees "Americans retiring within their own shell." Yale judges that policy "degenerated" into isolation—among other things. Others, less picturesque but equally positive, refer to a "marked increase of isolationist sentiment" and to "those years of isolationism." Another group diagnoses the populace as having "ingrained isolationism," analyzes it as "sullen and selfish" in consequence, and characterizes it as doing "its best to forget international subjects." Related verdicts describe the Republican Party as "predominantly isolationist" and as an organization that "fostered a policy of deliberate islation."

Most pointed of these specifications is a terse two-word summary of the diplomacy of the period: "Isolation Perfected." Popularizers have transcribed this theme into a burlesque. Their articles and books convey the impression that the Secretaries of State were in semi-retirement and that the citizenry wished to do away with the Department itself. Columnists and commentators have made the concept an eerie example of George Orwell's double-think. They label as isolationists the most vigorous interventionists.

The case would seem to be closed and judgment given if it were not for the ambivalence of some observers and the brief dissents filed by a few others. The scholar who used the phrase "those years of isolationism," for example, remarks elsewhere in the same book that "expansionism . . . really was long a major expression of isolationism." Another writes of the "return to an earlier policy of isolation," and on the next page notes a "shift in policy during the twenties amounting almost to a 'diplomatic revolution'." A recent biographer states that Henry Cabot Lodge "did not propose . . . an isolationist attitude," but then proceeds to characterize the Monroe Doctrine—upon which Lodge stood in his fight against the League of Nations treaty—as a philosophy of "isolation." And in the last volume of his trilogy, the late Professor Frederick L. Paxton summed up a long review of the many diplomatic activities of the years 1919–1923 with the remark that this was a foreign policy of "avoidance rather than of action."

But a few scholars, toying with the Idol of the Market-Place, have made bold to rock the image. Yet Professor Richard Van Alstyne was doing more than playing the iconoclast when he observed that the "militant manifest destiny men were the isolationists of the nineteenth century." For with this insight we can translate those who maintain that Lodge "led the movement to perpetuate the traditional policy of isolation." Perhaps William G. Carleton was even more forthright. In 1946 he pointed out that the fight over the League treaty was not between isolationists and internationalists, and added that many of the mislabeled isolationists were actually "nationalists and imperialists." Equally discerning was Charles Beard's comment in 1933 that the twenties were marked by a "return to the more aggressive ways . . . [used] to protect and advance the claims of American business enterprise." All these interpretations were based on facts that prompted another scholar to change his earlier conclusion and declare in 1953 that "the thought was all of keeping American freedom of action."

These are perceptive comments. Additional help has recently been supplied by two other students of the period. One of these is Robert E. Osgood, who approached the problem in terms of *Ideals and Self-Interest in American Foreign Relations.* Though primarily concerned with the argument that Americans should cease being naïve, Osgood suggests that certain stereotypes are misleading. One might differ with his analysis of the struggle over the Treaty of Versailles, but not with his insistence that there were fundamental differences between Senators Lodge and William E. Borah—as well as between those two and President Woodrow Wilson. Osgood likewise raises questions about the reputed withdrawal of the American public. Over a thousand organizations for the study of international relations existed in 1926, to say nothing of the groups that sought constantly to make or modify foreign policy.

Osgood gives little attention to this latter aspect of foreign relations, a surprising omission on the part of a realist. But the underlying assumption of his inquiry cannot be challenged. The foreign policy issue of the twenties was never isolationism. The controversy and competition were waged between those who entertained different concepts of the national interest and disagreed over the means to be employed to secure that objective. Secretary of State Charles Evans Hughes was merely more eloquent, not less explicit. "Foreign policies," he explained in 1923, "are not built upon abstractions. They are the result of practical conceptions of national interest arising from some immediate exigency or standing out vividly in historical perspective."

Historian George L. Grassmuck used this old-fashioned premise of the politician as a tool with which to probe the *Sectional Biases in Congress on Foreign Policy.* Disciplining himself more rigorously in the search for primary facts than did Osgood, Grassmuck's findings prompted him to conclude that "the 'sheep and goats' technique" of historical research is eminently unproductive. From 1921 to 1933, for example, the Republicans in both houses of Congress were "more favorable to both Army and Navy measures than . . . Democrats." Eighty-five percent of the same Republicans supported international economic measures and agreements. As for the Middle West, that much condemned section did not reveal any "extraordinary indication of a . . . tendency to withdraw." Nor was there "an intense 'isolationism' on the part of [its] legislators with regard to membership in a world organization." And what opposition there was seems to have been as much the consequence of dust bowls and depression as the product of disillusioned scholars in ivory towers.

These investigations and correlations have two implications. First, the United States was neither isolated nor did it pursue a policy of isolationism from 1920 to 1933. Second, if the policy of that era, so generally accepted as the product of traditional isolationist sentiment, proves non-isolationist, then the validity and usefulness of the concept when applied to earlier or later periods may seriously be challenged.

Indeed, it would seem more probable that the central theme of American foreign relations has been the expansion of the United States. Alexander Hamilton made astute use of the phrase "no entangling alliances" during the negotiation of Jay's Treaty in 1794, but his object was a *de facto* affiliation with the British Fleet—not isolation. Nor was Thomas Jefferson seeking to withdraw when he made of Monticello a counselling center for those seeking to emulate the success of the American Revolution. A century later Senator Lodge sought to revise the Treaty of Versailles and the Covenant of the League of Nations with reservations that seemed no more than a restatement of Hamilton's remarks. Yet the maneuvers of Lodge were no more isolationist in character and purpose than Hamilton's earlier action. And while surely no latter-day Jefferson, Senator Borah was anything but an isolationist in his concept of the power of economics and ideas. Borah not only favored the recognition of the Soviet Union in order to influence the development of the Bolshevik Revolution and as a check against Japanese expansion in Asia, but also argued that American economic policies were intimately connected with foreign political crises. All those men were concerned with the extension of one or more aspects of American influence, power, and authority.

Approached in this manner, the record of American foreign policy in the twenties verifies the judgments of two remarkably dissimilar students: historian Richard W. Leopold and Senator Lodge. The professor warns that the era was "more complex than most glib generalizations . . . would suggest"; and the scholastic politician concludes that, excepting wars, there "never [was] a period when the United States [was] more active and its influence more felt internationally than between 1921 and 1924." The admonition about perplexity was offered as helpful advice, not as an invitation to anti-intellectualism. For, as the remarks of the Senator implied, recognition that a problem is involved does not mean that it cannot be resolved.

Paradox and complexity can often be clarified by rearranging the data around a new focal point that is common to all aspects of the apparent contradiction. The confusion of certainty and ambiguity that characterizes most accounts of American foreign policy in the twenties stems from the fact that they are centered on the issue of membership in the League of Nations. Those Americans who wanted to join are called internationalists. Opponents of that move became isolationists. But the subsequent action of most of those who fought participation in the League belies this simple classification. And the later policies of many who favored adherence to the League cast serious doubts upon the assumption that they were willing to negotiate or arbitrate questions that they defined as involving the national interest. More pertinent is an examination of why certain groups and individuals favored or disapproved of the League, coupled with a review of the programs they supported after that question was decided.

Yet such a re-study of the League fight is in itself insuffient. Equally important is a close analysis of the American reaction to the Bolshevik Revolution. Both the League Covenant and the Treaty of Versailles were written on a table shaken by that upheaval. The argument over the ratification of the combined documents was waged in a context determined as much by Nikolai Lenin's *Appeal to the Toiling, Oppressed, and Exhausted Peoples of Europe* and the Soviet *Declaration to the Chinese People* as by George Washington's Farewell Address.

Considered within the setting of the Bolshevik Revolution, the basic question was far greater than whether or not to enter the League. At issue was what response was to be made to the domestic and international division of labor that had accompanied the Industrial Revolution. Challenges from organized urban labor, dissatisfied farmers, frightened men of property, searching intellectual critics, and colonial peoples rudely interrupted almost every meeting of the Big Four in Paris and were echoed in many Senate debates over the treaty. And those who determined American policy through the decade of the twenties were consciously concerned with the same problem.

An inquiry into this controversy over the broad question of how to end the war reveals certain divisions within American society. These groupings were composed of individuals and organizations whose position on the League of Nations was coincident with and part of their response to the Bolsheviks; or, in a wider sense, with their answer to that general unrest, described by Woodrow Wilson as a "feeling of revolt against the large vested interests which influenced the world both in the economic and the political sphere." Once this breakdown has been made it is then possible to follow the ideas and actions of these various associations of influence and power through the years 1920 to 1933.

At the core of the American reaction to the League and the Bolshevik Revolution was the quandary between fidelity to ideals and the urge to power. Jefferson faced a less acute version of the same predicament in terms of whether to force citizenship on settlers west of the Mississippi who were reluctant to be absorbed in the Louisiana Purchase. A century later the anti-imperialists posed the same issue in the more sharply defined circumstances of the Spanish-American War. The League and the Bolsheviks raised the question in its most dramatic context and in unavoidable terms.

There were four broad responses to this reopening of the age-old dilemma. At one pole stood the pure idealists and pacifists, led by William Jennings Bryan. A tiny minority in themselves, they were joined, in terms of general consequences if not in action, by those Americans who were preoccupied with their own solutions to the problems. Many American business men, for example, were concerned primarily with the expansion of trade and were apathetic toward or impatient with the hullabaloo over the League. Diametrically opposed to the idealists were the vigorous expansionists. All these exponents of the main chance did not insist upon an overt crusade to run the world, but they were united on Senator Lodge's proposition that the United States should dominate world politics. Association with other nations they accepted, but not equality of membership or mutuality of decision.

Caught in the middle were those Americans who declined to support either extreme. A large number of these people clustered around Woodrow Wilson, and can be called the Wilsonites. Though aware of the dangers and temptations involved, Wilson declared his intention to extend American power for the purpose of strengthening the ideals. However noble that effort, it failed for two reasons. Wilson delegated power and initiative to men and organizations that did not share his objectives, and on his own part the President ultimately "cast in his lot" with the defenders of the *status quo.*

Led by the Sons of the Wild Jackass, the remaining group usually followed Senator Borah in foreign relations. These men had few illusions about the importance of power in human affairs or concerning the authority of the United States in international politics. Prior to the world war they supported—either positively or passively—such vigorous expansionists as Theodore Roosevelt, who led their Progressive Party. But the war and the Bolshevik Revolution jarred some of these Progressives into a closer examination of their assumptions. These reflections and new conclusions widened the breach with those of their old comrades who had moved toward a conservative position on domestic issues. Some of those earlier allies, like Senator Albert J. Beveridge, continued to agitate for an American century. Others, such as Bainbridge Colby, sided with Wilson in 1916 and went along with the President on foreign policy.

But a handful had become firm anti-expansionists by 1919. No attempt was made by these men to deny the power of the United States. Nor did they think that the nation could become self-sufficient and impregnable in its strength. Borah, for example, insisted that America must stand with Russia if Japan and Germany were to be checked. And Johnson constantly pointed out that the question was not whether to withdraw, but at what time and under what circumstances to use the country's influence. What these men did maintain was that any effort to run the world by establishing an American system comparable to the British Empire was both futile and un-American.

In this they agreed with Henry Adams, who debated the same issue with his brother Brooks Adams, Theodore Roosevelt, and Henry Cabot Lodge in the years after 1898. "I incline now to anti-imperialism, and very strongly to anti-militarism," Henry warned. "If we try to rule politically, we take the chances against us." By the end of the first world war another generation of expansionists tended to agree with Henry Adams about ruling politically, but planned to build and maintain a similar pattern of control through the use of America's economic might. Replying to these later expansionists, Borah and other anti-expansionists of the nineteen-twenties argued that if Washington's influence was to be effective it would have to be used to support the movements of reform and colonial nationalism rather than deployed in an effort to dam up and dominate those forces.

For these reasons they opposed Wilson's reorganization of the international banking consortium, fearing that the financiers would either influence strongly or veto—as they did—American foreign policies. With Senator Albert B. Cummins of Iowa they voted against the Wilson-approved Webb-Pomerene Act, which repealed the anti-trust laws for export associations. In the same vein they tried to prevent passage of the Edge Act, an amendment to the Federal Reserve Act that authorized foreign banking corporations. Led by Borah, they bitterly attacked the Versailles Treaty because, in their view, it committed the United States to oppose colonial movements for self-government and to support an unjust and indefensible *status quo.* From the same perspective they criticized and fought to end intervention in Russia and the suppression of civil liberties at home.

Contrary to the standard criticism of their actions, however, these anti-expansionists were not just negative die-hards. Senator Cummins maintained from the first that American loans to the allies should be considered gifts. Borah spoke out on the same issue, hammered away against armed intervention in Latin America, played a key role in securing the appointment of Dwight Morrow as Ambassador to Mexico, and sought to align the United States with, instead of against, the Chinese Revolution. On these and other issues the anti-expansionists were not always of one mind, but as in the case of the Washington Conference Treaties the majority of them were far more positive in their actions than has been acknowledged.

Within this framework the key to the defeat of the League treaty was the defection from the Wilsonites of a group who declined to accept the restrictions that Article X of the League Covenant threatened to impose upon the United States. A morally binding guarantee of the "territorial integrity and existing political integrity of all members of the League" was too much for these men. First they tried to modify that limitation. Failing there, they followed Elihu Root and William Howard Taft, both old time expansionists, to a new position behind Senator Lodge. Among those who abandoned Wilson on this issue were Herbert Hoover, Calvin Coolidge, Charles Evans Hughes, and Henry L. Stimson.

Not all these men were at ease with the vigorous expansionists. Stimson, for one, thought the Lodge reservations "harsh and unpleasant," and later adjusted other of his views. Hoover and Hughes tried to revive their version of the League after the Republicans returned to power in 1920. But at the time all of them were more uneasy about what one writer has termed Wilson's "moral imperialism." They were not eager to identify themselves with the memories of that blatant imperialism of the years 1895 to 1905, but neither did they like Article X. That proviso caught them from both sides, it illegalized changes initiated by the United States, and obligated America to restore a *status quo* to some aspects of which they were either indifferent or antagonistic. But least of all were they anxious to run the risk that the Wilsonian rhetoric of freedom and liberty might be taken seriously in an age of revolution. Either by choice or default they supported the idea of a community of interest among the industrialized powers of the world led by an American-British *entente* as against the colonial areas and the Soviet Union.

This postwar concept of the community of interest was the first generation intellectual offspring of Herbert Croly's *Promise of American Life* and Herbert Hoover's *American Individualism.* Croly's opportunistic nationalism provided direction for Hoover's "greater mutuality of interest." The latter was to be expressed in an alliance between the government and the "great trade associations and the powerful corporations." Pushed by the Croly-Hoover wing of the old Progressive Party, the idea enjoyed great prestige during the twenties. Among its most ardent exponents were Samuel Gompers and Matthew Woll of the labor movement, Owen D. Young of management, and Bernard Baruch of finance.

What emerged was an American corporatism. The avowed goals were order, stability, and social peace. The means to those objectives were labor-management co-operation, arbitration, and the elimination of waste and inefficiency by closing out unrestrained competition. State intervention was to be firm, but moderated through the cultivation and legalization of trade associations which would, in turn, advise the national government and supply leaders for the federal bureaucracy. The ideal was union in place of diversity and conflict.

Other than Hoover, the chief spokesmen of this new community of interest as applied to foreign affairs were Secretaries of State Hughes and Stimson. In the late months of 1931 Stimson was to shift his ground, but until that time he supported the principle. All three men agreed that American economic power should be used to build, strengthen, and maintain the co-operation they sought. As a condition for his entry into the [Harding] cabinet, Hoover demanded—and received—a major voice in "all important economic policies of the administration." With the energetic assistance of Julius Klein, lauded by the National Foreign Trade Council as the "international business go-getter of Uncle Sam," Hoover changed the Department of Commerce from an agency primarily concerned with interstate commerce to one that concentrated on foreign markets and loans, and control of import sources. Hughes and Stimson handled the political aspects of establishing a "community of ideals, interests and purposes."

These men were not imperialists in the traditional sense of that much abused term. All agreed with Klein that the object was to eliminate "the old imperialistic trappings of politico-economic exploitation." They sought instead the "internationalization of business." Through the use of economic power they wanted to establish a common bond, forged of similar assumptions and purposes, with both the industrialized nations and the native business community in the colonial areas of the world. Their deployment of America's material strength is unquestioned. President Calvin Coolidge reviewed their success, and indicated the political implications thereof, on Memorial Day, 1928. "Our investments and trade relations are such," he summarized, "that it is almost impossible to conceive of any conflict anywhere on earth which would not affect us injuriously."

Internationalization through the avoidance of conflict was the key objective. This did not mean a negative foreign policy. Positive action was the basic theme. The transposition of corporatist principles to the area of foreign relations produced a parallel policy. American leadership and intervention would build a world community regulated by agreement among the industrialized nations. The prevention of revolution and the preservation of the sanctity of private property were vital objectives. Hughes was very clear when he formulated the idea for Latin America. "We are seeking to establish a *Pax Americana* maintained not by arms but by mutual respect and good will and the tranquillizing processes of reason." There would be, he admitted, "interpositions of a temporary character"—the Secretary did not like the connotations of the word intervention—but only to facilitate the establishment of the United States as the "exemplar of justice."

Extension to the world of this pattern developed in Latin America was more involved. There were five main difficulties, four in the realm of foreign relations and one in domestic affairs. The internal problem was to establish and integrate a concert of decision between the government and private economic groups. Abroad the objectives were more sharply defined: circumscribe the impact of the Soviet Union, forestall and control potential resistance of colonial areas, pamper and cajole Germany and Japan into acceptance of the basic proposition, and secure from Great Britain practical recognition of the fact that Washington had become the center of Anglo-Saxon collaboration. Several examples will serve to illustrate the general outline of this diplomacy, and to indicate the friction between the office holders and the office dwellers.

Wilson's Administration left the incoming Republicans a plurality of tools designed for the purpose of extending American power. The Webb-Pomerene Law, the Edge Act, and the banking consortium were but three of the more obvious and important of these. Certain polishing and sharpening remained to be done, as exemplified by Hoover's generous interpretation of the Webb-Pomerene legislation, but this was a minor problem. Hoover and Hughes added to these implements with such laws as the one designed to give American customs officials diplomatic immunity so that they could do cost accounting surveys of foreign firms. This procedure was part of the plan to provide equal opportunity abroad, under which circumstances Secretary Hughes was confident that "American business men would take care of themselves."

It was harder to deal with the British, who persisted in annoying indications that they considered themselves equal partners in the enterprise. Bainbridge Colby, Wilson's last Secretary of State, ran into the same trouble. Unless England came "to our way of thinking," Colby feared that "agreement [would] be impossible." A bit later Hughes told the British Ambassador that the time had come for London's expressions of cordial sentiment to be "translated into something definite." After many harangues about oil, access to mandated areas, and trade with Russia, it was with great relief that Stimson spoke of the United States and Great Britain "working together like two old shoes."

Deep concern over revolutionary ferment produced great anxiety. Hughes quite agreed with Colby that the problem was to prevent revolutions without making martyrs of the leaders of colonial or other dissident movements. The dispatches of the period are filled with such expressions as "very grave concern," "further depressed," and "deeply regret," in connection with revolutionary activity in China, Latin America, and Europe. American foreign service personnel abroad were constantly reminded to report all indications of such unrest. This sensitivity reached a high point when one representative telegraphed as "an example of the failure to assure public safety . . . the throwing of a rock yesterday into the state hospital here." Quite in keeping with this pattern was Washington's conclusion that it would support "any provisional government which gave satisfactory evidence of an intention to re-establish constitutional order."

Central to American diplomacy of the twenties was the issue of Germany and Japan. And it was in this area that the government ran into trouble with its partners, the large associations of capital. The snag was to convince the bankers of the validity of the long range view. Hoover, Hughes and Stimson all agreed that it was vital to integrate Germany and Japan into the American community. Thus Hughes opposed the French diplomacy of force on the Rhine, and for his own part initiated the Dawes Plan. But the delegation of so much authority to the financiers backfired in 1931. The depression scared the House of Morgan and it refused to extend further credits to Germany. Stimson "blew up." He angrily told the Morgan representative in Paris that this strengthened France and thereby undercut the American program. Interrupted in the midst of this argument by a trans-Atlantic phone call from Hoover, Stimson explained to the President that "if you want to help the cause you are speaking of you will not do it by calling me up, but by calling Tom Lamont." Stimson then turned back to Lamont's agent in Europe and, using "unregulated language," told the man to abandon his "narrow banking axioms."

Similar difficulties faced the government in dealing with Japan and China. The main problem was to convince Japan, by persuasion, concession, and the delicate use of diplomatic force, to join the United States in an application of its Latin American policy to China. Washington argued that the era of the crude exploitation of, and the exercise of direct political sovereignty over, backward peoples was past. Instead, the interested powers should agree to develop and exercise a system of absentee authority while increasing the productive capacity and administrative efficiency of China. Japan seemed amenable to the proposal, and at the Washington Conference, Secretary Hughes went a great distance to convince Tokyo of American sincerity. Some writers, such as George Frost Kennan and Adolf A. Berle, claim that the United States did not go far enough. This is something of a mystery. For in his efforts to establish "cooperation in the Far East," as Hughes termed it, the Secretary consciously gave Japan "an extraordinarily favorable position."

Perhaps what Kennan and Berle have in mind is the attitude of Thomas Lamont. In contrast to their perspective on Europe, the bankers took an extremely long range view of Asia. Accepting the implications of the Four and Nine Power Treaties, Lamont began to finance Japan's penetration of the mainland. Hughes and Stimson were trapped. They continued to think in terms of American business men taking care of themselves if given an opportunity, and thus strengthening Washington's position in the world community. Hughes wrote Morgan that he hoped the consortium would become an "important instrumentality of our 'open door' policy." But the American members of the banking group refused to antagonize their Japanese and British colleagues, and so vetoed Washington's hope to finance the Chinese Eastern Railway and its efforts to support the Federal Telegraph Company in China.

In this context it is easy to sympathize with Stimson's discomfort when the Japanese Army roared across Manchuria. As he constantly reiterated to the Japanese Ambassador in Washington, Tokyo had come far along the road "of bringing itself into alignment with the methods and opinion of the Western World." Stimson not only wanted to, but did in fact give Japan every chance to continue along that path. So too did President Hoover, whose concern with revolution was so great that he was inclined to view Japanese sovereignty in Manchuria as the best solution. Key men in the State Department shared the President's conclusion.

Stimson's insight was not so limited. He realized that his predecessor, Secretary of State Frank B. Kellogg, had been right: the community of interest that America should seek was with the Chinese. The Secretary acknowledged his error to Senator Borah, who had argued just such a thesis since 1917. Stimson's letter to Borah of February 23, 1932, did not say that America should abandon her isolationism, but rather that she had gone too far with the wrong friends. The long and painful process of America's great awakening had begun. But in the meantime President Hoover's insistence that no move should be made toward the Soviet Union, and that the non-recognition of Manchukuo should be considered as a formula looking toward conciliation, had opened the door to appeasement.

Mythology of Roosevelt, the New Deal, and Beyond

These really are good times, but only a few know it.
Henry Ford *(March 15, 1931)*

In our day these economic truths have been accepted as self-evident.

We have accepted, so to speak, a second Bill of Rights under which a new basis of security and prosperity can be established for all—regardless of station, race, or creed. Among these are: the right to a useful and remunerative job in the industries or shops or farms or mines of the Nation; the right to earn enough to provide adequate food and clothing and recreation; the right of every farmer to raise and sell his products at a return which will give him and his family a decent living; the right of every businessman, large and small, to trade in an atmosphere of freedom from unfair competition and domination by monopolies at home or abroad; the right of every family to a decent home; the right to adequate medical care and the opportunity to achieve and enjoy good health; the right to protection from the economic fears of old age, sickness, accident, and unemployment; the right to a good education.

All of these rights spell security. And after this war is won, we must be prepared to move forward, in the implementation of these rights, to new goals of human happiness and well-being.

America's own rightful place in the world depends in large part upon how fully these and similar rights have been carried into practice for our citizens. For unless there is security here at home there cannot be lasting peace in the world.
Franklin D. Roosevelt, *State of the Union Message* *(January 11, 1944)*

East meets West: Torgau, 1945. [Tass, Sovfoto.]

"Freedom from Want." [Norman Rockwell, *Ours . . . to Fight For: Freedom from Want.* Reproduced from the collections of the Library of Congress.]

East confronts West: Berlin. [Photo by Patrick Gerster.]

Freedom from want? [Courtesy of the Dorothea Lange Collection. © The City of Oakland, The Oakland Museum, 1990.]

*M*uch that was said in the introduction to the preceding section about the receptive climate for myth building during the progressive era might also be applied to the time of Franklin D. Roosevelt. But there were important differences that should be pointed out, particularly because many of the events and decisions of the Roosevelt administration more directly affect present-day America.

Nearly everyone, supporters and detractors alike, agrees that Franklin Delano Roosevelt was more central to his age than either Theodore Roosevelt or Woodrow Wilson had been to theirs. In any assessment of the New Deal, students as well as scholars are compelled to deal with FDR's rather elusive personal style. Indeed, for many this is the key to understanding Roosevelt's unique success. Also, the further one moves to either the conservative or the radical end of the interpretive spectrum, the more clearly focused become the myths of the man and his age. This is true in considering foreign as well as domestic affairs.

After temporary setbacks in dealing with the Depression and following the "quarantine speech" at Chicago in 1937 (in which he said that trade with Fascist Germany, Italy, and Japan should be restricted), Roosevelt slowly came to dominate American foreign policy. Against strong opposition from isolationists, Roosevelt pursued an internationalist course in foreign affairs. His intention became increasingly evident after the outbreak of war in Europe in September 1939. Involvement in the war became a major controversy. Political groups were formed to give voice to the strong feelings on the issue. On the isolationist side, there was the America First Committee; on the internationalist side, there was the Committee to Defend America by Aiding the Allies. The climate of intense disagreement (exemplified by a developing West Coast anti-Japanese hysteria) acted as an incubator for opinions and myths concerning American involvement in the war and the role that Roosevelt played in that involvement. Since then, many of these myths have been incorporated in various historical works on FDR and the entry of the United States into World War II.

FDR's influence, tempered by many myths during the entire length of his presidency, continued beyond his death in 1945. In *The Crucial Decade—and After: America, 1945–1960,* Eric Goldman argues that the economic and social revolution of the New Deal era continued unabated into the 1960s, along with the policies of containment and coexistence that resulted from the period of World War II. Not surprisingly, FDR's successor, Harry Truman, fell victim to the liberal Roosevelt myth. Having alienated several key factions that made up the Roosevelt coalition, Truman overcame predictions of sure defeat to win the presidential election of 1948 and thereby further liberated himself from the shadow of the Roosevelt mythology.

Postwar politics—strongly conditioned by a Cold War mentality, fears of conspiracy, and Communist paranoia—did much to distort the atmosphere and realities of American political culture for decades to come. But even as the postwar era seems to offer a pattern of consistent opinion and rather uniform ideology, the era itself has come in for serious reevaluation, especially the Eisenhower years. To some degree, it seems, Dwight Eisenhower was successful in transcending the mythologies of his time.

Constructing myths about presidents consistently has been a minor industry in America—a recent example being the myths that evolved following the assassination of the popular and promising John F. Kennedy. Of late, however, an era of Kennedy revisionism has ensued. Many of the myths associated with JFK have been reevaluated as growing numbers of Americans have come to question his conduct of, and in, the office of president.

The Great Wall Street Crash

John Kenneth Galbraith

The decade of the so-called Roaring Twenties—the Jazz Age—came to a close (to reverse T. S. Eliot) "not with a whimper but a bang." For in late October 1929 the apparent prosperity of the previous years, which had dazzled Americans with visions of easy riches, collided with economic realities to produce the Great Crash. The impact of the stock market crash would form a new chapter in American mythology: In the words of one historian, "like the Battle of Marathon, the assassination of Julius Caesar, the voyage of Columbus, and the storming of the Bastille, it has entered the realm of mythology and semi-truth, no longer studied as an historical event, but more as a symbol of greater forces and new beginnings." The former Harvard economist John Kenneth Galbraith, sensing the need for clarity of thinking on this historical event, debunks the myth of capitalism's invincibility. Horatio Alger mythology notwithstanding, the nation found itself in a depression because of its refusal to allow income distribution to find its way to the underclasses. The rhetoric of the time continued the chorus of economic clichés regarding "laissez-faire," "rugged individualism," and "free enterprise." It would require the Depression itself to dramatize that emerging economic realities—an interdependent global economy, for example, the workings of which transcended the "economic individual"—were rendering such beliefs mostly mythical, a form of economic nostalgia for a time gone by.

The climactic stock-market crash which launched the Great Depression occurred [better than] 50 years ago . . ., but it has already receded far into the mists of memory. One measure of this is the widespread assumption that there was one day in October 1929 when the great crash occurred. Another is the total absence of agreement as to what day it was. Thus Thursday, October 24, the first day on which panic seized the market, has regularly been cited as Black Thursday. But the professionals always have leaned to the following Monday or Tuesday, when the losses were far greater and when the volume of trading reached its all-time high. In a book explaining the debacle, Professor Irving Fisher of Yale—Professor Fisher, as the acknowledged prophet of the boom, was left with much explaining to do—singled out October 21 as the day of catastrophe. On that day trading was very heavy but the declines relatively

John Kenneth Galbraith, "The Great Wall Street Crash," in *The New Republic* (October 13, 1979). Reprinted by permission of the author.

modest. Others have picked still other days. Not perhaps since the siege of Troy has the chronology of a great event been so uncertain.

As a matter of fact, economic history, even at its most violent, has a much less exciting tempo than military or even political history. Days are rarely important. All of the autumn of 1929 was a terrible time, and all of that year was one of climax. With the invaluable aid of hindsight it is possible to see that for many previous months the stage was being set for the final disaster.

On January 1, 1929, the Coolidge Bull Market was at least four years old. The *New York Times* average of the prices of 25 representative industrial stocks—then a standard reference—had stood at 110 at the beginning of 1924, and had eased up to 135 at the beginning of 1925. At the close of trading on January 2, 1929, it was at 338.35. This climb had been almost uninterrupted. There were very few months when the average did not show an improvement on the month preceding. There had been, in short, a speculative upsurge of unparalleled magnitude and duration.

There were some reasons for thinking that 1929 might be different. For one thing, Herbert Hoover would replace Calvin Coolidge in the White House in March; and in the narrow political spectrum of the day, that meant a modest shift to the left. Coolidge, as Hoover himself said later, knew nothing and cared less about the speculative orgy in which the country was indulging itself. A few days before leaving office, he assured the country that things were "absolutely sound" and that stocks were a good buy at current prices. Moreover, even if Coolidge had wished to act, his instrument would have had to be the Federal Reserve Board, and in his time the possibility of this body's initiating any drastic measures was remarkably slight. Its authority, constitutional and moral, was shared with the powerful Federal Reserve Bank of New York. The chairman of the board, one Daniel R. Crissinger, was a small-town boy from Ohio who had been appointed in the belief that any amiable citizen could be a central banker. His colleagues, with one exception, were later described accurately by Hoover as mediocrities.

In his memoirs, Hoover suggests that by the beginning of 1929 the halting of the stock-market boom had become practically an obsession with him. This was a fairly well-kept secret, for the market hailed his election in November 1928 with the wildest advance to date, and a day or two before he took office in March there was a fine upsurge which was dubbed the "inaugural market." But Hoover did know what was going on. Furthermore, Crissinger had been replaced late in 1927 by Roy A. Young, a more substantial figure. As a result, 1929 promised at least a chance that an effort might be made to restrain the speculation.

But there remained the problem of what could be done—and at what cost. Stocks, overwhelmingly, were being bought on margin. That meant that someone was lending the buyer part of the purchase price. The way for the Federal Reserve to slow stock speculation was to get control of the funds being used to finance it. But the interest rates on these brokers' loans were high for the times. During January 1929, for example, they averaged a shade under seven percent. Seven percent with near-perfect safety and your money available on demand was then a magnificent return. Individuals and especially corporations were finding the market an increasingly attractive outlet for surplus cash, and the Federal Reserve had no obvious way of checking this source of money for speculation.

But in many respects this was a detail. There was the much more inconvenient question of whether any control could be exercised which, if effective, wouldn't bring an awful smash. It is easy enough to burst a bubble. To incise it with a needle so that it subsides gradually is an operation of undoubted delicacy. Collapse and an ensuing depression would be unpleasant for, among others, those who were blamed for bringing them about. This was sensed if not seen.

Yet there was the danger that if the bull market were allowed to go roaring along, eventually there would be an even more violent crack-up. So, early in 1929, the monetary authorities began debating the relative merits of sudden death or a more horrible demise a little later on. Secretary of the Treasury Mellon was passionately for inaction. Governor Young and a part of his Federal Reserve Board were for action, although there was a dispute on the particular controls to be invoked. The issue was never decided, but the knowledge that the debate was going on began to be a source of uneasiness in Wall Street.

Meanwhile the market itself supplied more serious sources of uneasiness. In a market like that of 1929, there are three possible reasons why people buy stocks. One is for the old-fashioned purpose of sharing in the current income of an enterprise. Some eccentrics were undoubtedly so motivated in those days, although in the case of such a speculative favorite as RCA—which, adjusted for split-ups, reached 505 on September 3, 1929, up from 94½ in the preceding 18 months—the desire for immediate income must have been fairly slight. The stock had never paid a dividend. Elsewhere the showing was better. A hundred dollars' worth of shares, which provided an average return of $5.90 in 1921, paid $3.50 in 1929. Yields did not keep pace with market values, but they did not vanish.

Many more people were buying stocks because they had heard that the stock market was a place where people could get rich, and they were righteously persuaded that their right to be rich was as good as the next person's. These were the innocent, although it was also their misfortune to believe— perhaps with some assistance from the customer's man of a brokerage firm— that they were really very wise. These buyers talked of the prospects for Steel, GM, United Corporation, and Blue Ridge with the familiarity of a friend and that unique certainty not of one who knows but of one who doesn't know that he doesn't know.

Finally, some people who were buying stocks knew that a boom was on, but they intended to get out—or even, at a high level of professionalism, to go short—before the crash came. As 1929 wore along, it was this group that became increasingly nervous. The market was making phenomenal advances; one couldn't get out while there were still such gains to be made. But whenever there was upsetting news, the market dropped sharply on large volume. Some *were* getting out.

Thus, in February 1929, when the Federal Reserve Board finally decided to issue a warning in careful financial prose—"a member bank is not within its reasonable claims for rediscount facilities at the Federal Reserve Bank when it borrows for the purpose of making speculative loans"—prices broke sharply. There was a prompt recovery, but in the following month it became known that the Federal Reserve Board was meeting daily on its problem of immediate suicide versus eventual disaster. The market broke again. On March 26, 8,239,000 shares changed hands on the New York Stock Exchange. (Once in the early days of the bull market, it had been said that men might live to see a five-million-share day.) Prices fell precipitately, and call money rates that day went to 20 percent, which meant that anyone who bought General Electric on margin paid interest at the then phenomenal rate of 20 percent per annum for money to buy a security that was yielding around 1.25 percent.

The bubble might have been pricked then and there, but, in an act of historic arrogance, Charles E. Mitchell, chairman of the board of the National City Bank and himself a speculator, put his bank behind the boom. "We feel that we have an obligation which is paramount to any Federal Reserve warning, or anything else, to avert . . . any dangerous crisis in the money market," Mitchell said. The National City Bank let it be known that it was loaning freely in the call market and had more to come if rates got unduly high, i.e., much above 15 percent. The market steadied. By the end of March 26 most of the day's losses had been recovered.

There were further breaks and more nervousness during the next two months. But the Federal Reserve remained quiet and presumably undecided. So there was a brief recovery of confidence, and prices started on their last great zoom. There was no summer lull in Wall Street that year. Each day the market went on to new highs. Not everyone was playing it as the later legend held—the great majority of Americans were then as innocent of knowledge of how to buy a stock as they are today. But subsequent estimates of no great reliability have suggested that as many as a million people were involved in the speculation. During that summer practically all of them made money. Never before or since have so many people so suddenly gotten so wonderfully rich.

On the first of June the *Times* industrial average stood at 342; by the first of July it was 394; on the first of August it was 418; when the market reopened on September 3 after the Labor Day holiday, it reached 452. This was a gain of 110 points—25 percent—in 90 days. The *New York Times* financial section on September 3 ran to 15 full pages. Later in the week it was announced that brokers' loans had reached the remarkable total of $6.35 billion. (In the preceding three months they had been increasing faster than $400 million a month.) But the end was near, although never so far from being in sight.

On September 5 there was a break, and the industrial average fell about

10 points. The nervousness of those who wanted both to stay to the last and get out in time was admirably indicated by the cause of this setback. It followed a statement by one Roger Babson on September 4 that "Sooner or later a crash is coming and it may be terrific." Mr. Babson was a professional forecaster; the drop was promptly labeled the Babson Break. All honor must go to Babson for his historic omniscience, although it deserves to be added that he had been making similar predictions at frequent intervals for four years.

The market was ragged the rest of September and into October. There were days of strength, but there were also days of weakness. Generally speaking, the direction was down. No one wished to believe that the market boom was over. In the arresting terminology of the time—as used in this instance by the *Wall Street Journal*—"Price movements in the main body of stocks continued to display the characteristics of a major advance temporarily halted for technical readjustments." On October 8, from Germany, Charles E. Mitchell of National City Bank announced "Nothing can arrest the upward movement in the United States." A week later, on taking the boat for home, he helpfully added that the market was now "in a healthy condition" and that "values have a sound basis in the general prosperity of our country." During the same week, Irving Fisher announced that stocks had reached a "new high plateau."

On Saturday, October 19, the papers told of a very weak market the day before—there were heavy declines on late trading, and the *Times* industrial average had dropped about seven points. Meanwhile that day's market was also behaving very badly. In the second heaviest Saturday's trading in history, 3,488,100 shares changed hands. At the close the *Times* industrial index was down 12 points.

On Sunday the break was front-page news. The *Times* financial editor— who, to his credit, had never wavered in his conviction that the market had gone insane, suggested that, for the moment at least, "Wall Street seemed to see the reality of things." The news stories featured two other observations which were to become wonderfully familiar in the next fortnight. It was said that at the end of Saturday's trading, an exceptionally large number of margin calls went out (meaning that lenders wanted their money back). And it was predicted that come the following week, "organized support" could definitely be expected for the market.

Monday, October 21, was another poor day. Sales totaled 6,091,870, the third greatest volume in history, and hundreds of thousands throughout the country who were watching the market made a disturbing discovery: there was no way of telling what was happening. The ticker often had fallen behind on big days of the bull market, and one didn't discover until well after the market closed how much richer one had become. But with a falling market things were very different. Now one might be ruined, totally and forever, and not know it. And even if one were not ruined, there was a strong tendency to imagine it. On October 21 the ticker lagged from the opening; by noon it was an hour behind in reporting trades. Not until an hour and 40 minutes after the close of the market did it record the last transaction. Every 10 minutes, prices of selected stocks were printed on the bond ticker, but the wide divergence between these and the prices being reported on the stock tape only added to the uneasiness—and to the growing conviction that it might be best to sell.

This conviction notwithstanding, the market closed well above its low for the day—the net loss on the *Times* industrial average was only about six points—and on Tuesday there was a further though rather shaky gain. Some credit for this improvement possibly should go to Wall Street's two cheeriest seers. On Monday in New York Professor Fisher said that the declines had represented only a "shaking out of the lunatic fringe." He reaffirmed his belief that the prices of stocks still had not caught up with their real value. Among other reasons, Fisher said, the market did not yet reflect the beneficent effects of Prohibition, which had made the American worker "more productive and dependable."

On Tuesday, Charles E. Mitchell dropped anchor with the observation that "the decline had gone too far." (Time and sundry congressional court proceedings were to show that Mr. Mitchell had strong personal reasons for feeling that way.) He added that conditions were "fundamentally sound," that too much attention had been paid to the large volume of brokers' loans, and that the "situation is one which will correct itself if left alone." There was, however, another jarring suggestion from Roger Babson. He recommended selling stocks and buying gold.

By Wednesday, October 23, the effect of this cheer had been dissipated. Instead of further gains there were heavy losses. The opening was quiet enough, but volume soon began to increase. The last hour was quite phenomenal—2,600,000 shares changed hands at rapidly declining prices. The *Times* industrial average for the day dropped from 415 to 384, giving up all of its gains since the end of the previous June. Again the ticker was far behind, and to add to the uncertainty an ice storm in the Middle West caused widespread disruption of communications. Wednesday afternoon and evening thousands of speculators decided to get out while—as they mistakenly supposed—the getting was good. Other thousands were told they would have no choice but to get out unless they posted more collateral, for, as the day's business came to an end, an unprecedented volume of margin calls went out.

Speaking in Washington, even Professor Fisher was fractionally less optimistic. He told a meeting of bankers that "security values *in most instances* were not inflated." But he did not weaken on the unrealized efficiencies of Prohibition. There was one bit of cheer. It was everywhere predicted that, on the morrow, the market would begin to receive "organized support."

Thursday, October 24, is the first of the days which history identified with the panic of 1929. Measured by disorder, fright, and confusion, it deserves to be so regarded. 12,894,650 shares changed hands that day, most of them at prices that shattered the dreams and the hopes of those who had owned them. Of all the mysteries of the stock exchange, there is none so impenetrable as why there should be a buyer for everyone who seeks to sell. October 24, 1929, showed that this arrangement is not inevitable. Often there were no buyers, and only after wide vertical declines could anyone be induced to bid.

The morning was the terrible time. Prices were firm for a little while, but volume was large, and soon prices began to sag. Once again the ticker dropped behind. Prices fell further and faster, and the ticker lagged more and more. By 11 o'clock what had been a market was only a wild scramble to sell. In the crowded board rooms of brokerage houses across the country, the stock ticker told of a frightful collapse. But the selected quotations coming in over the bond ticker also showed that even the values on the stock tape were ancient history. The uncertainty led more and more people to try to sell. Others, no longer able to respond to margin calls, were sold. By 11:30, panic, pure and unqualified, was in control.

Outside the Exchange on Broad Street, a weird roar could be heard. A crowd gathered, and the New York police commissioner dispatched a special police detail to ensure the peace. A workman appeared to accomplish some routine repairs atop one of the high buildings. The multitude, assuming he was a would-be suicide, waited impatiently for him to jump. At 12:30 the visitors' gallery of the Exchange was closed on the wild scenes below. One of the visitors who had just departed was displaying his customary genius for being on hand for history. He was the former British chancellor of the exchequer, Mr. Winston Churchill. It was he in 1925 who returned Britain to a gold standard that substantially overvalued the pound. To help relieve the subsequent strain, the Federal Reserve eased money rates, and, in the conventional though far from reliable view, this is what launched the bull market. There is no record that anyone that day reproached Churchill for the trouble he was causing. It is most unlikely that he reproached himself.

At noon things took a turn for the better. At last came the long-awaited organized support. The heads of the big New York banks—National City, Chase, Guaranty Trust, and Bankers Trust—met with Thomas W. Lamont, the senior partner of the great house of J. P. Morgan at 23 Wall Street. All quickly agreed to come to the support of the market and to pool substantial resources for this purpose. Lamont then met with reporters and, in what was later described as one of the most remarkable understatements of all time, said: "There has been a little distress selling on the Stock Exchange." He added that this passing inconvenience was "due to a technical situation rather than any fundamental cause," and he told the newsmen the situation was "susceptible to betterment."

Meanwhile word had reached the Exchange floor that the bankers were meeting and succor was on the way. These were the nation's most potent financiers. They had not yet been pilloried and maligned by the New Dealers. Prices promptly firmed and rose. Then at 1:30 p.m. Richard Whitney, the vice president of the Exchange and widely known as a floor broker for Morgan, walked jauntily to the post where United States Steel was traded and left an order for 10,000 shares at several points above the current bid. He continued the rounds with this largesse. Confidence was wonderfully revived and the market actually boomed upward. In the last hour, the selling orders which were still flooding in turned it soft again, but the net loss for the day—about 12 points on the *Times* industrial average—was far less than the day before. Some issues, Steel among them, were actually higher on the day's trading.

But this recovery was of distant interest to the tens of thousands who had sold or been sold out during the decline and whose dreams of opulence had gone glimmering along with most of their merchantable possessions. It was after seven that night before the ticker finished recording the day's misfortunes. In the board rooms, speculators who had been sold out since early morning sat silently watching the tape. The habit of months or years, however idle it had now become, could not be broken at once. Then, as the final trades were registered, they made their way out into the gathering night.

In Wall Street itself lights blazed from every office as clerks struggled to come abreast of the day's business. Messengers and board-room boys, caught up in the excitement and untroubled by losses, went skylarking through the streets until the police arrived to quell them. Representatives of 35 of the largest brokers assembled at the offices of Hornblower and Weeks and told the press on departing that the market was "fundamentally sound" and "technically in better condition than it has been in months." The host firm dispatched a market letter which stated that "Commencing with today's trading the market should start laying the foundation for the constructive advance which we believe will characterize 1930." Charles E. Mitchell announced that the trouble was "purely technical" and that "fundamentals remained unimpaired." Senator Carter Glass said the trouble was due to Charles E. Mitchell. Senator Wilson of Indiana attributed the crash to Democratic resistance to a higher tariff.

On Friday and Saturday trading continued heavy but prices, on the whole, were steady. The average was a trifle up on Friday but slid off on Saturday. It was thought that the bankers were able to dispose of most of the securities they had acquired while shoring up the market. Not only were things better, but everyone was clear that it was the banking leaders who had made them so. They had shown both their courage and their power, and the people applauded warmly and generously. Commenting on Friday's market, the *Times* said: "Secure in the knowledge that the most powerful banks in the country stood ready to prevent a recurrence [of panic] the financial community relaxed its anxiety yesterday."

From other sources came statements of reassurance and even self-congratulation. Colonel Leonard Ayres of Cleveland, another prophet of the period, thought no other country could have survived such a crash so well. Walter Teagle, the telephone magnate, said there had been no "fundamental change" in the oil business to justify concern; Charles M. Schwab, the steel magnate, said that the steel business had been making "fundamental progress" toward stability and added that this "fundamentally sound condition" was responsible for the prosperity of the industry; Samuel Vauclain, chairman of the Baldwin Locomotive Works, declared that "fundamentals are sound"; President Hoover said that "The fundamental business of the country, that is production and distribution of commodities, is on a sound and prosperous basis." H. C. Hopson, the head of Associated Gas & Electric, a great utility combine, omitted the standard reference to fundamentals and said it was "undoubtedly beneficial to the business interests of the country to have the gambling type of speculator eliminated." Mr. Hopson, himself a speculator, was eliminated in due course. A Boston investment trust took space in the *Wall Street Journal* to say, "S-T-E-A-D-Y Everybody! Calm thinking is in order. Heed the words of America's greatest bankers." A single dissonant note, though great in portent, went completely unnoticed. Speaking in Poughkeepsie, New York, Governor Franklin D. Roosevelt criticized the "fever of speculation."

On Sunday there were sermons in the New York churches suggesting that a certain measure of divine retribution had been visited on the republic, and that it had not been entirely unmerited. But almost everyone apparently believed that this heavenly knuckle-rapping was over and that speculation could now be resumed in earnest. The papers were full of the prospects for next week's market. Stocks, it was agreed, were cheap again, and accordingly there would be a heavy rush to buy. Numerous stories from the brokerage houses, some of them possibly inspired, told of a fabulous volume of buying orders piling up in anticipation of the opening of the market. In a concerted advertising campaign in Monday's papers, stock-market firms urged the wisdom of buying stocks promptly. On Monday the real disaster began.

Trading on Monday was smaller than on the previous Thursday— 9,212,800 as compared with nearly 13 million—but the sustained drop in prices was far more severe. The *Times* industrial average was down 49 points for the day. General Electric was off 47½; Westinghouse, 34½; Tel. & Tel., 34. Indeed, the decline on this one day was greater than that of all the preceding week of panic. Again a late ticker left everyone in ignorance of what was happening except that it was bad.

At 1:10 there was a momentary respite: the banker Charles E. Mitchell was detected going into Morgan's, and the news ticker carried the magic word. Steel rallied and went from 193½ to 198. But this time Richard Whitney did not appear; "organized support" was not forthcoming. Support, organized or otherwise, could no longer contend with the wild desire to sell. The market weakened again, and in the last hour three million shares changed hands at rapidly declining prices. Mitchell, by later evidence, was going into Morgan's to get a loan for himself.

The bankers assembled once again from 4:30 to 6:30. They were described as having a "philosophical attitude," and they told the press that the situation "retained hopeful features." It was explained at the conclusion that it was no part of the bankers' purpose to maintain any particular level of prices on the market. Their operations were confined to seeing that the market was orderly—that offers would be met by bids at some price and that "air holes," as Mr. Lamont dubbed them, would not be allowed to appear in the market. This was chilling news. To the man who held stock on margin, disaster wore only one face and that was falling prices. He wanted to be saved from disaster. Now he had to comfort himself with the knowledge that his ruin would be accomplished in an orderly and becoming manner.

Tuesday, October 29, was the most devastating day in the history of the New York stock market, and it may have been the most devastating in the history of markets. Selling began at once and in huge volume. The "air holes," which the bankers were supposed to close, opened wide. Repeatedly and in many stocks there was a plethora of selling orders and there were no buyers at all. Once again, of course, the ticker lagged—at the close it was two and a half hours behind. By then 16,410,030 shares were known to have been traded—more than three times the number that had once been considered a fabulously big day. Despite a closing rally on dividend news, the losses were again appalling. The *Times* industrial average was down 43 points, canceling all of the huge gains of the preceding 12 months. Losses on individual issues were far greater. By the end of trading, members were near collapse from strain and fatigue. Office staffs, already near the breaking point, now had to tackle the greatest volume of transactions yet. But now, also, there was no longer the same certainty that things would get better. Perhaps they would go on getting worse.

During the preceding week, the slaughter had been of the innocents. Now it was the well-to-do and the wealthy—the men of affairs and professionals—who were experiencing the egalitarianism long supposed to be the first fruit of avarice. Where the board rooms were crowded the week before, now they were nearly empty. The new victims had facilities for suffering in private. The great bankers met at noon on Tuesday and again in the evening; but there was no suggestion that they were even philosophical. In truth, their prestige had been falling even more disconcertingly than the market. During the day the rumor had swept the Exchange that, of all things, they were busy selling stocks, and Mr. Lamont met the press after the evening session with the trying assignment of denying that this was so. It remained for James J. Walker, mayor of New York, to come up with the only constructive proposal of the day. Addressing an audience of motion picture exhibitors, he asked them to "show pictures that will reinstate courage and hope in the hearts of the people."

On the Exchange itself a strong feeling was developing that courage and hope might best be reinstated if the market were closed and everyone were given a breathing spell. This simple and forthright thought derived impressive further support from the fact that everyone was badly in need of sleep. The difficulty was that the announcement of the closing of the Exchange might simply worsen the panic. At noon on Tuesday the 29th, the members of the Governing Committee left the floor in twos and threes to avoid attracting attention; they met not in the regular room but in the office of the Stock Clearing Corporation below the trading floor. As Richard Whitney—later to go to Sing Sing prison for embezzlement but still the man in charge—described the session, the air quickly became blue with tobacco smoke as the tired and nervous brokers lit cigarettes, stubbed them out, and lit fresh ones. Everyone wanted a respite from the agony. Quite a few firms needed a few hours to ascertain whether they were still solvent.

But caution was on the side of keeping the market open at least until it could be closed on a note of strength and optimism. The decision was made to carry on until things improved. Again the lights blazed all night. In one brokerage house an employee fainted from exhaustion, was revived and put back to work.

Next day those imponderable forces were at work which bring salvation just at the moment when salvation seems impossible. Volume was still enormous, but prices were much better—the *Times* industrial average rose 31 points, and individual issues made excellent gains. Possibly it was the reassurances that accomplished the miracle—in any case, these were forthcoming in volume. On the evening of the 29th, assistant secretary of commerce Julius Klein took to the radio to remind the country that President Hoover had said that the "fundamental business of the country" was sound and prosperous. On Wednesday, Wadill Catchings, the head of the great Goldman, Sachs investment house, announced that general business conditions were "unquestionably fundamentally sound." (The same, it subsequently developed, could not unquestionably be said for companies promoted by Goldman, Sachs. By the time Mr. Sachs himself was called before a Senate Banking Committee hearing on stock market practices in 1932, shares in the Goldman Sachs Trading Corporation, which had been sold to the public for $104 each, were trading, after a two-for-one split, for 1¾.) From Pocantico Hills came the first public statement from John D. Rockefeller in some decades: "Believing that fundamental conditions of the country are sound . . . my son and I have for some days been purchasing sound common stock." Eddie Cantor, a noted comedian (and, as he described himself, victim) of the time, said of the announcement: "Sure, who else had any money left?"

Just before the Rockefeller statement arrived, things looked good enough on the Exchange so that Richard Whitney felt safe in announcing that the market would not open until noon the following day (Thursday) and that on Friday and Saturday it would stay shut. The announcement was greeted by cheers. Nerves were clearly past the breaking point. On La Salle Street in Chicago a boy exploded a firecracker. Like wildfire the rumor spread that gangsters whose margin accounts had been closed out were shooting up the street. Several squads of police arrived to make them take their losses like honest men.

No feature of the Great Crash was more remarkable than the way it passed from climax to anticlimax to destroy again and again the hope that the worst had passed. Even on Wednesday, October 30, the worst was still to come, although henceforth it came more slowly. Day after day during the next two weeks prices fell with monotonous regularity. At the close of trading on October 29, the *Times* industrial average stood at 275. In the rally of the next two days it gained more than 50 points, but by November 13, it was down to 224 for a further net loss of 51 points.

And these levels were wonderful compared with what were to follow. On July 8, 1932, the average of the closing levels of the *Times* industrials was 58.46. This was not much more than the amount by which the average dropped on the single day of October 28, and considerably less than a quarter of the closing values on October 29. By then, of course, business conditions were no longer sound, fundamentally or otherwise.

What might be called the everyday history book tells of the Great Depression of the 1930s which began with the great stock-market crash of 1929. For a long time there was a tendency among sophisticates—professional students of the business cycle in particular—to deny the importance that this attributed to the stock-market crash as a cause of the Depression. The crash was part of the froth rather than the substance of the situation. A depression, it was pointed out, had been in the making since midsummer of 1929, when numerous indexes began to turn down.

In this matter the everyday history is almost certainly right, and in recent times the sophisticated historians have come to agree. The market crash (and, of course, the speculation that set the stage) was of profound importance for what followed. It shrank the supply of investment funds and, at the same time, it shocked the confidence on which investment expenditure depends. The crash also reduced personal expenditures and deeply disrupted international capital flows and international trade. The effect of all this on economic activity was prompt and very real. Nothing else is a fraction so important for explaining the severity of the depression that followed.

Since it was important, the question inevitably arises whether a similar cycle of speculation and collapse could again occur. The simple answer is of course! Laws have been passed to outlaw some of the more egregious behavior which contributed to the big bull market of the 1920s. Nothing has been done about the seminal lunacy that possesses people who see a chance of becoming rich.

The Lengthening Shadow of FDR: An Enduring Myth

William E. Leuchtenburg

In every recent poll taken among historians ranking the performance of past presidents, Franklin Delano Roosevelt invariably ranks as "great"—in company with the likes of George Washington, Andrew Jackson, Abraham Lincoln, and Woodrow Wilson. In the most recent survey, only Lincoln is of higher stature. Not surprisingly, given the fact that Roosevelt is the most recent of the great leaders, subsequent presidential expectations have been rather exclusively drawn in terms of the achievement—ultimately the mythic image—of FDR, idol to professor and public, Democrat and Republican. In the estimation of William E. Leuchtenburg, William Rand Kenan Professor of History at the University of North Carolina, Chapel Hill, the nature of Roosevelt's greatness resides in large measure in his confident enlargement of the power of the presidency and his "leading the nation to accept the responsibilities of world power." Roosevelt's contagious optimistic manner spiritually mobilized the nation to confront challenges of the Depression and World War II. Having an intuitive sense of the new media politics, which would so much define the conduct of national affairs in the decades to come, Roosevelt reshaped the office he occupied—in relation to an attentive public, an expectant press corps, and (at least initially) a charmed Congress—into what is often called the "imperial presidency." To some he was a usurper king whose reign laid the foundations for a questionable extension of executive power. For the great many, however, FDR was a personal hero, a "take-charge guy," an "event-making man."

When the American people got their first look at the entries in the 1988 presidential race, they sensed immediately that not one of the contenders measured up to their highest expectations. The Republican heir apparent was dismissed as a "wimp," and the original Democratic field as the "seven dwarfs." Asked whom in either party they preferred, a huge proportion of respondents replied, "None of the above." And if inquirers has gone on to ask what sort of nominee voters had in mind, not a few would have answered without hesitation, "Franklin Delano Roosevelt."

That sentiment cut across party lines. Predictably more than one Democrat sought to associate himself with his party's four-time winner. At the 1984 Democratic National Convention in San Francisco, Jesse Jackson had drawn a

From "Why the Candidates Still Use FDR as Their Measure" by William E. Leuchtenburg. Reprinted with permission from *American Heritage* magazine (February 1988).

roar of approval when he said that FDR in a wheelchair was better than Ronald Reagan on a horse, and in the 1988 contest Senator Paul Simon of Illinois offered any number of New Deal solutions to contemporary problems. More surprisingly, Franklin Roosevelt has attracted no little favorable comment from Republicans, most conspicuously President Reagan. In his 1980 acceptance address Reagan spoke so warmly of FDR that the *New York Times* editorial the next morning was entitled "Franklin Delano Reagan," and thereafter he rarely missed an opportunity to laud the idol of his opponents.

Indeed, so powerful an impression has FDR left on the office that in the most recent survey of historians, he moved past George Washington to be ranked as the second greatest President in our history, excelled only by the legendary Abraham Lincoln.

This very high rating would have appalled many of the contemporaries of "that megalomaniac cripple in the White House." In the spring of 1937 an American who had been traveling extensively in the Caribbean confided, "During all the time I was gone, if anybody asked me if I wanted any news, my reply was always—'there is only one bit of news I want to hear and that is the death of Franklin D. Roosevelt. If he is not dead you don't have to tell me anything else.' " And at one country club in Connecticut, a historian has noted, "mention of his name was forbidden as a health measure against apoplexy."

Roosevelt, his critics maintained, had shown himself to be a man of no principles. Herbert Hoover called him a "chameleon on plaid," while H. L. Mencken declared, "If he became convinced tomorrow that coming out for cannibalism would get him the votes he so sorely needs, he would begin fattening a missionary in the White House backyard come Wednesday."

This reputation derived in good part from the fact that Roosevelt had campaigned in 1932 on the promise to balance the budget but subsequently asked Congress to appropriate vast sums for relief of the unemployed. Especially embarrassing was the memory of his 1932 address at Forbes Field, home of the Pittsburgh Pirates, in which he denounced Hoover as a profligate spender. The presidential counsel Sam Rosenman recalled how FDR asked him to devise a way to explain this 1932 speech in one he planned to make in his 1936 campaign. After careful consideration, Rosenman had one suggestion: "Deny categorically that you ever made it."

Historians, too, have found fault with FDR. New Left writers have chided him for offering a "profoundly conservative" response to a situation that had the potential for revolutionary change, while commentators of no particular persuasion have criticized him for failing to bring the country out of the Depression short of war, for maneuvering America into World War II (or for not taking the nation to war soon enough), for permitting Jews to perish in Hitler's death camps, and for sanctioning the internment of Japanese-Americans.

Roosevelt has been faulted especially for his failure to develop any grand design. The political scientist C. Herman Pritchett claimed that the New Deal never produced "any consistent social and economic philosophy to give meaning and purpose to its various action programs." Even harsher disapproval has come from Undersecretary of Agriculture Rexford Tugwell, who in many ways admired FDR. "He could have emerged from the orthodox progressive chrysalis and led us into a new world," Tugwell said, but instead, FDR busied himself "planting protective shrubbery on the slopes of a volcano."

Given all this often very bitter censure, both at the time and since, how can one now account for FDR's ranking as the second-greatest President ever? We may readily acknowledge that polls can be deceptive and that historians have been scandalously vague about establishing criteria for "greatness." Yet there are, in fact, significant reasons for Roosevelt's rating, some of them substantial enough to be acknowledged even by skeptics.

To begin with the most obvious, he was President longer than anyone else. Alone of American Presidents he broke the taboo against a third term and served part of a fourth term as well. Shortly after his death the country adopted a constitutional amendment limiting a President to two terms. Motivated in no small part by the desire to deliver a posthumous rebuke to Roosevelt, this amendment has had the ironic consequence of assuring that Franklin Roosevelt will be, so far as we can foresee, the only chief executive who will ever have served more than two terms.

Roosevelt's high place rests, too, on his role in leading the nation to accept the responsibilities of a world power. When he took office, the United States was firmly committed to isolationism; it refused to join either the League of Nations or the World Court. Roosevelt made full use of his executive power to recognize the USSR, craft the good-neighbor policy with Latin America, and, late in his second term, provide aid to the Allies and lead the nation into active involvement in World War II. So far had America come by the end of the Roosevelt era that the Secretary of War, Henry Stimson, was to say that the United States could never again "be an island to herself. No private program and no public policy, in any sector of our national life, can now escape from the compelling fact that if it is not framed with reference to the world, it is framed with perfect futility."

As wartime President, FDR demonstrated his executive leadership by guiding the country through a victorious struggle against the Fascist powers. "He overcame both his own and the nation's isolationist inclination . . .," the historian Robert Divine has concluded. "His role in insuring the downfall of Adolf Hitler is alone enough to earn him a respected place in history."

Whatever his flaws, Roosevelt came to be perceived all over the globe as the leader of the forces of freedom. The British political scientist Sir Isaiah Berlin wrote that in the "leaden thirties, the only light in the darkness was the administration of Mr. Roosevelt . . . in the United States."

For good or ill, also, America first became a major military power during Roosevelt's Presidency. As late as 1939 the U.S. Army ranked eighteenth in the world, and soldiers trained with pieces of cardboard marked "Tank." Under FDR, Congress established peacetime conscription and after Pearl Harbor put millions of men and women in uniform. His long reign also saw the birth of the Pentagon, the military-industrial complex, and the atomic bomb. At the conclusion of FDR's Presidency, one historian has noted, "a Navy superior to the combined fleets of the rest of the world dominated the seven seas; the Air Force commanded greater striking power than that of any other country; and American overseas bases in the . . . Atlantic, the Mediterranean, and the Pacific rimmed the Eurasian continent."

A Light in a Dark Age

But there is an even more important reason for FDR's high ranking: his role in enlarging the presidential office and expanding the realm of the state while leading the American people through the Great Depression.

Roosevelt came to office at a desperate time, in the fourth year of a worldwide depression that raised the gravest doubts about the future of the Western world. "In 1931," commented the British historian Arnold Toynbee, "men and women all over the world were seriously contemplating and frankly discussing the possibility that the Western system of Society might break down and cease to work." And in the summer of 1932, the economist John Maynard Keynes, asked by a journalist whether there had ever been anything before like the Great Depression, replied, "Yes, it was called the Dark Ages, and it lasted four hundred years."

By the time Roosevelt was sworn in, national income had been cut in half and more than fifteen million Americans were unemployed. Every state in the Union had closed its banks or severely restricted their operations, and on the very morning of his inauguration, the New York Stock Exchange had shut down. For many, hope had gone. "Now is the winter of our discontent the chilliest," wrote the editor of *Nation's Business*.

Only a few weeks after Roosevelt took office, the spirit of the country seemed markedly changed. Gone was the torpor of the Hoover years; gone, too, the political paralysis. "The people aren't sure . . . just where they are going," noted one business journal, "but anywhere seems better than where they have been. In the homes, on the streets, in the offices, there is a feeling of hope reborn." Again and again, observers resorted to the imagery of darkness and light to characterize the transformation from the Stygian gloom of Hoover's final winter to the bright springtime of the Hundred Days. People of every political persuasion gave full credit for the revival of confidence to one man: the new President.

In April the Republican senator from California, Hiram Johnson, acknowledged: "The admirable trait in Roosevelt is that he has the guts to try. . . . He does it all with the rarest good nature. . . . We have exchanged for a frown in the White House a smile. Where there were hesitation and vacillation, weighing always the personal political consequences, feebleness, timidity, and duplicity, there are now courage and boldness and real action." On the editorial page of *Forum*, Henry Goddard Leach summed up the nation's nearly unanimous verdict: "We have a leader."

The Temperament of a Leader

The new President had created this impression by a series of actions—delivering his compelling inaugural address, summoning Congress into emergency session, resolving the banking crisis—but even more by his manner. Supremely confident in his own powers, he could imbue others with a similar confidence. Moreover, he had acquired an admirable political education: state senator, junior cabinet officer, his party's vice-presidential nominee, two-term governor of the most populous state in the Union. As the political scientist Richard Neustadt has observed, "Roosevelt, almost alone among our Presidents, had no conception of the office to live up to; he was it. His image of the office was himself-in-office."

FDR's view of himself and his world freed him from anxieties that other men would have found intolerable. Not even the weightiest responsibilities seemed to disturb his serenity. One of his associates said, "He must have been psychoanalyzed by God."

A Washington reporter noted in 1933: "No signs of care are visible to his main visitors or at the press conferences. He is amiable, urbane and apparently untroubled. He appears to have a singularly fortunate faculty for not becoming flustered. Those who talk with him informally in the evenings report that he busies himself with his stamp collection, discussing in an illuminating fashion the affairs of state while he waves his shears in the air."

The commentator Henry Fairlie has remarked: "The innovating spirit . . . was [FDR's] most striking characteristic as a politician. The man who took to the radio like a duck to water was the same man who, in his first campaign for the New York Senate in 1910, hired . . . a two-cylinder red Maxwell, with no windshield or top, to dash through (of all places) Dutchess County; and it was the same man who broke all precedents twenty-two years later when he hired a little plane to take him to Chicago to make his acceptance speech. . . . The willingness to try everything was how Roosevelt governed."

This serenity and venturesomeness were precisely the qualities called for in a national leader in the crisis of the Depression, and the country drew reassurance from FDR's buoyant view of the world. Secretary of Labor Frances Perkins remarked on his feeling that "nothing in human judgment is final. One may courageously take the step that seems right today because it can be modified tomorrow if it does not work well. . . ."

FDR's self-command, gusto, and bonhomie created an extraordinary bond with the American people. Millions of Americans came to view him as one who was intimately concerned with their welfare. In the 1936 campaign he heard people cry out, "He saved my home"; "He gave me a job." In Bridgeport, Connecticut, he rode past signs saying, "Thank God for Roosevelt," and in the Denver freight yards a message in chalk on the side of a boxcar read, "Roosevelt Is My Friend."

He Meets the Press

Roosevelt made conscious use of the media almost from the moment he entered the White House, with his press conferences serving to educate newspaper writers and, through them, the nation on the complex, novel measures he was advocating. He was fond of calling the press meeting room in the White House his "schoolroom," and he often resorted to terms such as *seminar* or, when referring to the budget, *textbook*. When in January 1934 the President invited thirty-five Washington correspondents to his study, he explained his budget message to them "like a football coach going through skull practice with his squad."

FDR's performance at his first press conference as President on March 8, 1933, the journalist Leo Rosten has written, has "become something of a legend in newspaper circles. Mr. Roosevelt was introduced to each correspondent. Many of them he already knew and greeted by name—first name. For each he had a handshake and the Roosevelt smile. When the questioning began, the full virtuosity of the new Chief Executive was demonstrated. Cigarette-holder in mouth at a jaunty angle, he met the reporters on their own grounds. His answers were swift, positive, illuminating. He had exact information at his fingertips. He showed an impressive understanding of public problems and administrative methods. He was lavish in his confidences and 'background information.' He was informal, communicative, gay. When he evaded a question it was done frankly. He was thoroughly at ease. He made no effort to conceal his pleasure in the give and take of the situation."

Jubilant reporters could scarcely believe the transformation in the White House. So hostile had their relations become with FDR's predecessor that Hoover, who was accused of employing the Secret Service to stop leaks and of launching a campaign of "terrorism" to get publishers to fire certain newspapermen, finally abandoned press conferences altogether. Furthermore, Hoover, like Harding and Coolidge before him, had insisted on written questions submitted in advance. But to the delight of the Washington press corps, Roosevelt immediately abolished that requirement and said that questions could be fired at him on the spot. At the end of the first conference, reporters did something they had never done before: they gave the man they were covering a spontaneous round of applause.

The initial euphoria continued long afterward. Roosevelt could sometimes be testy—he told one reporter to go off to a corner and put on a dunce cap—but mostly, especially in the New Deal years of 1933 to 1938, he was jovial and even chummy, in no small part because he regarded himself as a longtime newspaperman, since he had been editor in chief of the *Harvard Crimson*. The first President to appoint an official press secretary, he also made clear that members of the Fourth Estate were socially respectable by throwing a spring garden party for them at the White House.

Above all, FDR proved a never-ending source of news. Jack Bell, who covered the White House for the Associated Press, has written of him: "He talked in headline phrases. He acted, he emoted; he was angry, he was smiling. He was persuasive, he was demanding; he was philosophical, he was elemental. He was sensible, he was unreasonable; he was benevolent, he was malicious. He was satirical, he was soothing; he was funny, he was gloomy. He was exciting. He was human. He was copy."

One columnist wrote afterward, "The doubters among us—and I was one of them—predicted that the free and open conference would last a few weeks and then would be abandoned." But twice a week, with rare exceptions, year after year, the President submitted to the crossfire of interrogation. He left independently minded newspapermen like Raymond Clapper with the conviction that "the administration from President Roosevelt down has little to conceal and is willing to do business with the doors open." If reporters were 60 percent for the New Deal, Clapper reckoned, they were 90 percent for Roosevelt personally.

Some observers have seen in the FDR press conference a quasi-constitutional institution like the question hour in the House of Commons. To a degree, it was. But one should keep in mind that the President had complete control over what he would discuss and what could be published. He used the press conference as a public relations device he could manipulate to his own advantage.

Franklin Roosevelt also was the first Chief Executive to take full advantage of radio as a means of projecting his ideas and personality directly into American homes. When FDR got before a microphone, he appeared, said one critic, to be "talking and toasting marshmallows at the same time." In his first days in office he gave a radio address that was denominated a "fireside chat" because of his intimate, informal delivery that made every American think the President was talking directly to him or her. As the journalist and historian David Halberstam has pointed out: "He was the first great American radio voice. For most Americans of this generation, their first memory of politics would be sitting by a radio and hearing *that* voice, strong, confident, totally at ease. If he was going to speak, the idea of doing something else was unthinkable. If they did not yet have a radio, they walked the requisite several hundred yards to the home of a more fortunate neighbor who did. It was in the most direct sense of government reaching out and touching the citizen, bringing Americans into the political process and focusing their attention on the presidency as the source of good. . . . Most Americans in the previous 160 years had never even seen a President; now almost all of them were hearing him, *in their own homes.* It was literally and figuratively electrifying."

A Teacher for the Nation

By quickening interest in government, Roosevelt became the country's foremost civic educator. One scholar has observed: "Franklin Roosevelt changed the nature of political contests in this country by drawing new groups into active political participation. Compare the political role of labor under the self-imposed handicap of Samuel Gompers' narrow vision with labor's political activism during and since the Roosevelt years. The long-run results were striking: . . . public policy henceforth was written to meet the needs of those who previously had gone unheard."

Roosevelt and his headline-making New Deal especially served to arouse the interest of young people. When Lyndon Johnson learned of FDR's death, he said: " I don't know that I'd ever have come to Congress if it hadn't been for him. But I do know that I got my first desire for public office because of him—and so did thousands of other men all over this country."

FDR's role as civic educator frequently took a decidedly partisan turn, for he proved to be an especially effective party leader. In 1932, in an election that unraveled traditional party ties, he became the first Democrat elected to the White House with a popular majority since Franklin Pierce eighty years before. Yet this heady triumph, reflecting resentment at Hoover more than approval for FDR and the Democrats, might have been short-lived if Roosevelt had not built a constituency of lower-income ethnic voters in the great cities tenuously allied with white voters in the Solid South.

He brought into his administration former Republicans such as Henry Wallace and Harold Ickes; enticed hundreds of thousands of Socialists, such as the future California congressman Jerry Voorhis, to join the Democrats; worked with anti-Tammany leaders like Fiorello La Guardia in New York; backed the independent George Norris against the Democratic party's official nominee in Nebraska; and forged alliances with third parties such as the American Labor party. In 1938 he even attempted, largely unsuccessfully, to "purge" conservative Democrats from the party and in World War II may even have sought to unite liberal Republicans of the Wendell Willkie sort with liberal Democrats in a new party, though the details of that putative arrangement are obscure.

Getting the Laws He Wanted

Roosevelt won such a huge following both for himself and for his party by putting together the most ambitious legislative program in the history of the country, thereby considerably enhancing the role of the President as chief legislator. He was not the first chief executive in this century to adopt that role, but he developed the techniques to a point beyond any to which they had been carried before. He made wide use of the device of special messages, and he accompanied these communications with drafts of proposed bills. He wrote letters to committee chairmen or members of Congress to urge passage of his proposals; summoned the congressional leadership to White House conferences on legislation; used agents like the presidential adviser Tommy Corcoran on Capitol Hill to corral maverick Democrats; and revived the practice of appearing in person before Congress. He made even the hitherto mundane business of bill signing an occasion for political theater; it was he who initiated the custom of giving a presidential pen to a congressional sponsor of legislation as a memento. In the First Hundred Days, Roosevelt adroitly dangled promises of patronage before congressmen, but without delivering on them until he had the legislation he wanted. The result, as one commentator put it, was that "his relations with Congress were to the very end of the session tinged with a shade of expectancy which is the best part of young love."

To the dismay of the Republican leadership, Roosevelt showed himself to be a past master not just at coddling his supporters in Congress but at disarming would-be opponents. The conservative Republican congressman Joseph W. Martin, who had the responsibility of insulating his party members in the House from FDR's charm, complained that the President, "laughing, talking, and poking the air with his long cigarette holder," was so magnetic that he "bamboozled" even members of the opposition. Martin resented that he had to rescue opposition members from the perilous "moon glow."

To be sure, FDR's success with Congress has often been exaggerated. The Congress of the First Hundred Days, it has been said, "did not so much debate the bills it passed . . . as salute them as they went sailing by," but in later years Congress passed the bonus bill over his veto; shelved his "Court-packing" plan; and, on neutrality policy, bound the President like Gulliver. After the enactment of the Fair Labor Standards law in 1938, Roosevelt was unable to win congressional approval of any further New Deal legislation. Moreover, some of the main New Deal measures credited to Roosevelt were proposals originating in Congress that he either outrightly opposed or accepted only at the last moment, such as federal insurance of bank deposits, the Wagner Act, and public housing. In fact, by latter-day standards, his operation on the Hill was primitive. He had no congressional liaison office, and he paid too little attention to rank-and-file members.

Still, Roosevelt's skill as chief legislator is undeniable. A political scientist has stated: "The most dramatic transformation in the relationship between the presidency and Congress occurred during the first two terms of Franklin D. Roosevelt. FDR changed the power ratio between Congress and the White House, publicly taking it upon himself to act as the leader of Congress at a time of deepening crisis in the nation. More than any other president, FDR established the model of the most powerful legislative presidency on which the public's expectations still are anchored."

As one aspect of his function as chief legislator, Roosevelt broke all records in making use of the veto power. By the end of his second term, his vetoes already represented more than 30 percent of all the measures disallowed by Presidents since 1792. According to one credible tale, FDR used to ask his aides to look out for a piece of legislation he could veto, in order to remind Congress that it was being watched.

So far did Roosevelt plumb the potentialities of the chief executive as legislative leader that by the end of his first term, the columnist Raymond Clapper was writing, "It is scarcely an exaggeration to say that the President, although not a member of Congress, has become almost the equivalent of the prime minister of the British system, because he is both executive and the guiding hand of the legislative branch."

In 1938, in his annual message to Congress, Roosevelt made his philosophy about the duty of the state still more explicit: "Government has a final responsibility for the well-being of its citizenship. If private co-operative endeavor fails to provide work for willing hands and relief for the unfortunate, those suffering hardship from no fault of their own have a right to call upon the Government for aid; and a government worthy of its name must make fitting response."

Starting in the electrifying First Hundred Days of 1933, Roosevelt brought the welfare state to America, years after it had come to other lands. He moved beyond the notion that "rights" embodied only guarantees against denial of freedom, to the conception that government also has an obligation to assure certain economic essentials. In his State of the Union message of January 1944, he declared: "This Republic had its beginning, and grew to its present strength, under the protection of certain inalienable political rights— among them the right of free speech, free press, free worship, trial by jury, freedom from unreasonable searches and seizures. . . .

"As our Nation has grown in size and stature, however—as our industrial economy expanded—these political rights proved inadequate to assure us equality in the pursuit of happiness.

"We have come to a clear realization of the fact that true individual freedom cannot exist without economic security and independence. 'Necessitous men are not free men.' People who are hungry and out of a job are the stuff of which dictatorships are made.

"In our day these economic truths have become accepted as self-evident. We have accepted, so to speak, a second Bill of Rights under which a new basis of security and prosperity can be established for all—regardless of station, race, or creed."

In expanding the realm of the state, Roosevelt demanded that business recognize the superior authority of the government in Washington. At the time, that was shocking doctrine. In the pre–New Deal period, government often had been the handmaiden of business, and many Presidents had shared the values of businessmen. But FDR clearly did not. Consequently the national government in the 1930s came to supervise the stock market, establish a central banking system monitored from Washington, and regulate a range of business activities that had hitherto been regarded as private.

As a result of these measures, Roosevelt was frequently referred to as the "great economic emancipator" (or, conversely, as a traitor to his class), but his real contributions, as the historian James MacGregor Burns has said, were "a willingness to take charge, a faith in the people, and an acceptance of the responsibility of the federal government to act."

After a historic confrontation with the Supreme Court, Roosevelt secured the legitimization of this enormous increase in the growth of the state. As a consequence, not once since 1936 has the Court invalidated any significant statute regulating the economy.

FDR: Administrator

Roosevelt quickly learned that enacting a program was one thing; getting it carried out was something altogether different. He once complained: "The Treasury is so large and far-flung and ingrained in its practices that I find it almost impossible to get the action and results I want. . . . But the Treasury is not to be compared with the State Department. You should go through the experience of trying to get any changes in the thinking, policy, and action of the career diplomats and then you'd know what a real problem was. But the Treasury and the State Department put together are nothing compared with the Na-a-vy. The admirals are really something to cope with—and I should know. To change something in the Na-a-vy is like punching a feather bed. You punch it with your right and you punch it with your left until you are finally exhausted, and then you find the damn bed just as it was before you started punching."

To overcome resistance to his policies in the old-line departments, Roosevelt resorted to the creation of emergency agencies. "We have new and complex problems," he once said, "Why not establish a new agency to take over the new duty rather than saddle it on an old institution?"

Roosevelt also departed from orthodoxy in another way. In flat defiance of the cardinal rule of public administration textbooks—that every administrator ought to appear on a chart with a clearly stated assignment—the President not only deliberately disarranged spheres of authority but appointed men of clashing attitudes and temperaments. The historian Arthur Schlesinger, Jr., has maintained: "His favorite technique was to keep grants of authority incomplete, jurisdictions uncertain, charters overlapping. The result of this competitive theory of administration was often confusion and exasperation on the operating level; but no other method could so reliably insure that in a large bureaucracy filled with ambitious men eager for power the decisions, and the power to make them, would remain with the President."

To ensure trustworthy information, Roosevelt relied on a congeries of informants and personal envoys. Though there were times when one man had an especially close relationship to him—Louis Howe early in the New Deal, Harry Hopkins in the war years—Roosevelt never had a chief of staff, and no single individual was ever permitted to take the place of what one historian called the "countless lieutenants and supporters" who served "virtually as roving ambassadors collecting intelligence through the Executive Branch," often unaware that more than one man had the same assignment. "He would call you in, and he'd ask you to get the story on some complicated business," one of FDR's aides later said, "and you'd come back after a couple of days of hard labor and present the juicy morsel you'd uncovered under a stone somewhere, and *then* you'd find out he knew all about it, along with something else you *didn't* know."

So evident were the costs of FDR's competitive style—not only bruised feelings but, at times, a want of coherence in policy—and so harum-scarum did his methods seem, that it became commonplace to speak of Roosevelt as a poor administrator. A British analyst has commented that though the "mishmash" Roosevelt put together was "inspired," it resulted not in a "true bureaucracy" but in "an ill-organized flock of agencies with the sheep dogs in the White House snapping at their heels as the President whistled the signals."

Not a few commentators, though, have concluded that Roosevelt was a superior administrator. They point out that he vastly improved staffing of the Presidency and that he broke new ground when he assigned Henry Wallace to chair a series of wartime agencies, for no Vice-President had ever held administrative responsibilities before. Granted, there was no end of friction between subordinates such as Hopkins and Ickes, or Cordell Hull and Sumner Welles, but Wallace once observed, in a rare witticism, that FDR "could keep all the balls in the air without losing his own."

Furthermore, his admirers maintain, if the test of a great administrator is whether he can inspire devotion in his subordinates, FDR passes with flying colors. Even Ickes, the most conspicuous grumbler of the Roosevelt circle, noted in his diary, "You go into Cabinet meetings tired and discouraged and out of sorts and the President puts new life into you. You come out like a fighting cock."

An even better test of an administrator is whether he can recruit exceptional talent, and Roosevelt broke new ground by giving an unprecedented opportunity to a new corps of officials: the university-trained experts. Save for a brief period in World War I, professors had not had much of a place in Washington, but in his 1932 presidential campaign FDR enlisted several academic advisers, most of them from Columbia University, to offer their thoughts and to test his own ideas. The press called this group the Brain Trust. During the First Hundred Days of 1933, droves of professors, inspired by that example, descended on Washington to take part in the New Deal. So, too, did their students—young attorneys fresh out of law school and social scientists with recent graduate degrees who received an unprecedented open-arms reception from the federal government.

The sudden change of personnel was discountenanced by the President's critics, not least H. L. Mencken. "You Brain Trusters," he complained, "were hauled suddenly out of a bare, smelly classroom, wherein the razzberries of sophomores had been your only music, and thrown into a place of power and glory almost befitting Caligula, Napoleon I, or J. Pierpont Morgan, with whole herds of Washington correspondents crowding up to take down your every wheeze."

Roosevelt had such success in recruiting this new cadre of administrators because of his openness to groups that had long been discriminated against. Before the New Deal, the government had largely been the domain of a single element: white Anglo-Saxon Protestants. Under FDR, that situation altered perceptibly, with the change symbolized by the most famous team of FDR's advisers: Tommy Corcoran and Ben Cohen, the Irish Catholic and the Jew. Nor did ethnic diversity end there. Though some patterns of racial discrimination persisted, the President appointed enough blacks to high places in the government to permit the formation of what was called the "black cabinet."

For the first time, also, women received more than token recognition. In appointing Frances Perkins Secretary of Labor, Roosevelt named the first woman ever chosen for a cabinet post. He also selected the first female envoy and the first woman judge of the U.S. Circuit Court of Appeals. As First Lady, Mrs. Roosevelt, in particular, epitomized the new impact of women on public affairs. One of the original Brain Trusters, Rexford Tugwell, has written, "No one who ever saw Eleanor Roosevelt sit down facing her husband, and . . . say to him, 'Franklin, I think you should' . . . or, 'Franklin, surely you will not' . . . will ever forget the experience." She became, as one columnist said, "Cabinet Minister without portfolio—the most influential woman of our times."

In addition to attracting hitherto neglected talent to government service, Roosevelt, for all his idiosyncratic style, also made significant institutional changes. For instance, by an executive order of 1939, he moved several agencies, notably the Bureau of the Budget, under the wing of the White House and provided for a cadre of presidential assistants. This Executive Order 8248 has been called a "nearly unnoticed but none the less epoch-making event in the history of American institutions" and "perhaps the most important single step in the institutionalization of the Presidency."

Harold Smith, who served in the pre-war era and throughout the war years as FDR's budget director, later reflected: "When I worked with Roosevelt—for six years—I thought as did many others that he was a very erratic administrator. But now, when I look back, I can really begin to see the size of his programs. They were by far the largest and most complex programs that any President ever put through. People like me who had the responsibility of watching the pennies could only see the five or six or seven per cent of the programs that went wrong, through inefficient organization or direction. But now I can see in perspective the ninety-three or -four or -five percent that went right—including the winning of the biggest war in history—because of unbelievably skillful organization and direction. . . . Now, I think I'd say that Roosevelt must have been one of the greatest geniuses as an administrator that ever lived. What we couldn't appreciate at the time was the fact that he was a real *artist* in government."

It has become commonplace, even among Roosevelt's admirers, to view the President as an intellectual lightweight. He read few books, and these not very seriously. "He was neither a philosopher, like Jefferson, nor a student of government, like Wilson, the two Presidents he most admired," one writer has said. He had small talent for abstract reasoning, although perhaps no less than most men in public life. He loved brilliant people, commented one of his former aides, but not profound ones. The Brain Trustee Raymond Moley has observed that a picture of Teddy Roosevelt, "regaling a group of his friends with judgments on Goya, Flaubert, Dickens, and Jung, and discussions of Louis the Fat or the number of men at arms seasick in the fleet of Medina Sidonia—this could never be mistaken for one of Franklin Roosevelt. F.D.R.'s interests have always been more circumscribed. His moments of relaxation are given over exclusively to simpler pleasures—to the stamp album, to the Currier and Ives naval prints, to a movie or to good-humored horseplay."

Roosevelt kept himself informed not by applied study but by observation and conversation, and his particular qualities of mind served him reasonably well in the thirties. True, he was not well versed in economic theory, but had he accepted the greater part of what went for economic wisdom in 1932, he would have been badly misguided. Furthermore, contrary to the general notion, he knew far more about economic matters—utilities regulation, agriculture, banking, corporate structure, public finance—than was usually recognized.

He impressed almost everyone who worked with him with his knowledge of detail and, more important, with his grasp of the interrelationship of the larger aspects of public policy. "Never, at least since Jefferson," a prominent jurist wrote Justice Brandeis in 1937, "have we had a President of such constructive mind as Roosevelt."

The First Imperial President

Indeed, so manifest has been FDR's mastery of the affairs of state and so palpable his impact on the office as chief administrator, chief legislator, and tribune of the people that in recent years a separate, and disturbing, line of inquiry has surfaced: Does the imperial Presidency have its roots in the 1930s, and is FDR the godfather of Watergate? For four decades much of the controversy over the New Deal centered on the issue of whether Roosevelt had done enough. Abruptly, during the Watergate crisis, the obverse question was raised: Had he done too much? Had there been excessive aggrandizement of the executive office under FDR?

The notion that the origins of Watergate lie in the age of Roosevelt has a certain plausibility. In the First Hundred Days of 1933, Roosevelt initiated an enormous expansion of the national government with proliferating alphabet agencies lodged under the executive wing. Vast powers were delegated to presidential appointees with little or no congressional oversight. In foreign affairs Roosevelt bent the law in order to speed aid to the Allies, and in World War II he cut a wide swath in exercising his prerogatives. FDR was the first and only President to break the barrier against election to a third term, and for good measure he won a fourth term too. Only death cut short his protracted reign.

Those captivated by the historical antecedents of the Watergate era allege that Roosevelt showed no more sensitivity about Congress than did Nixon. When Roosevelt was asked in 1931 how much authority he expected Congress to grant him when he became President, he snapped, "Plenty." In office he ran into so much conflict with the legislators that on one occasion he said he would like to turn sixteen lions loose on them. But, it was objected, the lions might make a mistake. "Not if they stayed there long enough." Roosevelt answered.

Many have found Roosevelt's behavior on the eve of America's intervention in World War II especially reprehensible. Senator J. William Fulbright accused Roosevelt of having "usurped the treaty power of the Senate" and of having "circumvented the war powers of the Congress." On shaky statutory authority the President, six months before Pearl Harbor, used federal power to end strikes, most notably in sending troops to occupy the strikebound North American Aviation plant in California, his detractors assert. In this era, too, they point out, Roosevelt dispatched American forces to occupy Iceland and Greenland, provided convoys of vessels carrying arms to Britain, and ordered U.S. destroyers to shoot Nazi U-boats on sight, all acts that invaded Congress's war-making authority.

After the United States entered the war, Roosevelt raised the ire of his critics once more by his audacious Labor Day message of 1942, "one of the strangest episodes in the history of the presidency." In a bold—many thought brazen—assertion of inherent executive prerogative, Roosevelt, in demanding an effective price-and-wage-control statute, sent a message to Congress on September 7, 1942, saying: "I ask the Congress to take . . . action by the first of October. Inaction on your part by that date will leave me with an inescapable responsibility to the people of this country to see to it that the war effort is no longer imperiled by threat of economic chaos.

"In the event that the Congress should fail to act, and act adequately, I shall accept the responsibility, and I will act. . . .

"The President has the powers, under the Constitution and under Congressional acts, to take measures necessary to avert a disaster which would interfere with the winning of the war. . . .

"The American people can be sure that I will use my powers with a full sense of my responsibility to the Constitution and to my country. The American people can also be sure that I shall not hesitate to use every power vested in me to accomplish the defeat of our enemies in any part of the world where our own safety demands such a defeat.

"When the war is won, the powers under which I act automatically revert to the people—to whom they belong."

Congress quickly fell into line, and Roosevelt never had to make use of this threat.

It has also been contended that Nixon's overweening privy councillors wielded their inordinate power as a consequence of a reform brought about by Roosevelt. The 1937 report of the President's Committee on Administration Management called for staffing the executive office with administrative assistants "possessed of . . . a passion for anonymity." That job description sounded tailor-made for the faceless men around Nixon, for Haldeman and Ehrlichman seemed so indistinguishable that they were likened to Rosencrantz and Guildenstern.

Yet the parallels between Roosevelt and Nixon need to be set against the dissimilarities. "To Roosevelt, the communications of a President had to be . . . lively, intimate, and open," the journalist and Republican speech writer Emmet Hughes has observed. "He practiced an almost promiscuous curiosity." In marked contrast with the obsessionally reclusive Nixon regime, the New Deal government went out of its way to learn what the nation was thinking and to open itself to questioning. Each morning the President and other top officials found a digest of clippings from some 750 newspapers, many of them hostile, on their desks, and before Roosevelt turned in for the night, he went through a bedtime folder of letters from ordinary citizens. During the First Hundred Days he urged the press to offer criticism so that he might avoid missteps, and then and later he solicited everyone from old friends to chance acquaintances outside the government to provide information that would serve as a check on what his White House lieutenants were telling him.

Roosevelt differed from Nixon, too, in creating a heterogeneous administration and encouraging dissenting voices within the government. "What impresses me most vividly about the men around Roosevelt," wrote the historian

Clinton Rossiter, "is the number of flinty no-sayers who served him, loyally but not obsequiously."

Furthermore, even in the crisis of the Second World War, Roosevelt most often acted within constitutional bounds, and any transgressions have to be placed within the context of the dire challenge raised by Hitler and his confederates. Winston Churchill was to tell the House of Commons: "Of Roosevelt . . . it must be said that had he not acted when he did, in the way he did, had he not . . . resolved to give aid to Britain, and to Europe in the supreme crisis through which we have passed, a hideous fate might well have overwhelmed mankind and made its whole future for centuries sink into shame and ruin."

Such defenses of Roosevelt, however impressive, fall short of being fully persuasive. As well disposed a commentator as Schlesinger has said that FDR, "though his better instincts generally won out in the end, was a flawed, willful and, with time, increasingly arbitrary man." Unhappily, of FDR's many legacies, one is a certain lack of appropriate restraint with respect to the exercise of executive power.

What If FDR Had Been Assassinated?

The historian confronts one final, and quite different, question: How much of an innovator was Roosevelt? Both admirers and detractors have questioned whether FDR's methods were as original as they have commonly been regarded. Some skeptics have even asked, "Would not all of the changes from 1933 to 1945 have happened if there had been no Roosevelt, if someone else had been President?" Certainly trends toward the centralization of power in Washington and the White House were in motion well before 1933.

FDR himself always refused to answer what he called "iffy" questions, but this iffy question—would everything have been the same if someone else had been in the White House?—invites a reply, for it came very close to being a reality. In February 1933, a few weeks before Roosevelt was to take office, he ended a fishing cruise by coming to Bay Front Park in Miami. That night an unemployed bricklayer, Giuseppe Zangara, fired a gun at him from point-blank range, but the wife of a Miami physician deflected the assassin's arm just enough so that the bullets missed the President-elect and instead struck the mayor of Chicago, fatally wounding him. Suppose he had not been jostled and the bullets had found their mark. Would our history have been different if John Nance Garner rather than FDR had been President? No doubt some of the New Deal would have taken place anyway, as a response to the Great Depression. Yet it seems inconceivable that many of the more imaginative features of the Roosevelt years—for example, the Federal Arts Project—would have come under Garner, or that the conduct of foreign affairs would have followed the same course, or that the institution of the Presidency would have been so greatly affected. As the political scientist Fred Greenstein has observed, "Crisis was a necessary but far from sufficient condition for the modern presidency that began to evolve under Roosevelt."

The conclusion is one with which most scholars would agree: that Franklin Roosevelt was, to use the philosopher Sidney Hook's terminology, an "event-making man" who not only was shaped by but also shaped his age. He comprehended both the opportunity that the Great Depression offered to alter the direction of American politics and the menace Hitler posed to the nation, and as a consequence of both perceptions, America, and indeed the world, differed markedly in 1945 from what it had been in 1933, to no small degree because of his actions.

Roosevelt is one of the few American Presidents who loom large not just in the history of the United States but in the history of the world. The economist John Kenneth Galbraith has spoken of the "Bismarck–Lloyd George–Roosevelt Revolution," and Lloyd George himself called FDR the "greatest reforming statesman of the age."

Setting the Standard

Because Roosevelt "discovered in his office possibilities of leadership which even Lincoln had ignored," wrote the Oxford don Herbert Nicholas, it is hardly surprising that he continues to be the standard by which American Presidents, more than forty years after his death, continue to be measured. When the stock market slumped in the fall of 1987, the White House correspondent of the *Washington Post*, Lou Cannon, wrote a column that appeared under the headline REAGAN SHOULD EMULATE FDR, NOT HOOVER. Cannon, noting that "President Reagan has spent much of his public career emulating the style and cheerful confidence of his first political hero, Franklin D. Roosevelt," maintained that in dealing with the financial crisis, Reagan could "dodge the legacy of Roosevelt's luckless predecessor, Herbert Hoover," only "if he is willing to behave like FDR."

Even in an era when the country is said to have moved in a more conservative direction and the FDR coalition no longer is as potent as it once was, the memory of Franklin Roosevelt is still green. As the political scientist Thomas E. Cronin has observed, "With the New Deal Presidency firmly fixed in memory . . . we now expect our Presidents to be vigorous and moral leaders, who can steel our moral will, move the country forward, bring about dramatic and swift policy changes, and slay the dragons of crisis. An FDR halo effect has measurably shaped public attitudes toward the Presidency, persisting even today. . . . So embellished are some of our expectations that we virtually push . . . candidates into poses akin to the second coming of FDR."

The New Deal

Paul K. Conkin

Even before Franklin D. Roosevelt's death in April 1945, assessment of his New Deal was already well under way. Viewpoints and opinions were expressed on subjects ranging from Roosevelt's personality to the legitimacy of New Deal legislation. Many politicians, citizens, and historians then and since have volunteered their commentary on the meaning of the New Deal for America. Predictably, interpretations have differed widely, creating many myths in the process. While it is traditional to see the New Deal as fundamentally liberal and democratic, some historians questioned the alleged "revolutionary" nature of FDR's programs. One of these historians, Professor Paul K. Conkin of Vanderbilt University, finds the conventional image of "Roosevelt as radical" mostly legend. In seeking an evenhanded assessment of the Age of Roosevelt and the New Deal, he fails to find evidence that New Deal legislation in any appreciable way destroyed such cherished American ideals as free enterprise, individual initiative, or laissez-faire capitalism. Though the hero-president succeeded in giving America a "transfusion of courage," his programs in the long run failed to bring economic recovery, did little to end poverty, largely ignored the plight of minorities, and in general brought little significant change to American society. The New Deal, in short, was conservative in its intent and its outcome.

Today only a small minority of Americans remember Franklin Roosevelt, at least with more than vague images of childhood. Unswayed by his vital presence, ever less impressed by his recorded speeches, unmoved by his increasingly dated political concerns, young Americans are baffled by the continued passion of their parents or grandparents, by the subdued fervor of professors, by all oldsters who still dare confess their love or who ever yet vent their hate. They note the touch of reverence in the books of Arthur M. Schlesinger, Jr., the adulation of an aged or departed court—Rosenman, Tully, Tugwell, Perkins, Morgenthau. They also note the last echoes of bitterness from right-wing critics, who continue to identify an almost unbearably conventional Roosevelt with both domestic and foreign treason. Surely the sympathetic portraits are more revealing. Hate is a poor vehicle for communicating personality. But even the best portraits, conceived in love, often seem unlovely to another generation.

Roosevelt, as president, gave millions of Americans a transfusion of courage. They still remember. From his confidence, his optimism, they gleaned bits of hope in times of trouble and confusion. This was Roosevelt's only unal-loyed success as president. It was a pervasive aspect of his administration, yet tied to no policies and no programs. It was the magic of a man, based as much on illusion as on reality. There was much to fear in 1933, as there is today. Only fools or gods believed otherwise.

. . . The New Deal, as a varied series of legislative acts and executive orders dealing either with the problems of depression or with problems created or aggravated by depression, lasted only five years. Most of the important legislation came in brief spurts in 1933, 1935, and, least important, in 1938. But the volume of important legislation so exceeded any earlier precedents, so overwhelmed the immediate capacity for full comprehension, that even today no one can more than begin to make sense out of the whole.

Most New Deal legislation was, in a broad sense, economic. The early legislation was directed at early economic recovery. Some of it, as well as much later legislation, dealt directly with the overall structure of our market system and with the relationship of the federal government to this system. After 1934 the most significant New Deal measures dealt more directly with the immediate economic needs of individuals, families, or exploited groups. These efforts failed to gain complete recovery but significantly modified the American economy. After the New Deal innovations, major producers enjoyed more security in their property, more certainty of profits, less vulnerability to economic cycles, and both more federal subsidies and more extensive federal regulation. Laborers had clearer rights to organize unions and gained new polit-ical leverage in the Democratic party. Finally, new welfare policies guaranteed at least a minimum of subsistence for many people excluded from, or unable to compete effectively for, the benefits of a corporate and highly centralized system of production.

By habit, historians often divide the New Deal into two parts. The identi-fication of a second New Deal goes back to contemporary newspaper articles, which noted a policy shift in 1935 toward welfare legislation and a divisive class appeal. Some major changes did occur in 1935, but they overlay continu-ities in agricultural policy and in resource management. Also, the crucial Court-packing issue in 1937, and other Roosevelt efforts to attain a more di-rectly responsive democracy, might even lend credence to a third New Deal. But all such categories have an arbitrary aspect and are justified only by their usefulness.

In 1932 Roosevelt asked for only one clear mandate—bold action. In what seemed a terribly dangerous and callous demagoguery to an exasperated Hoo-ver, an unseasoned immaturity to commentators, Roosevelt refused to use his campaign to chart a coherent economic program, with all its demands and costs and promised rewards. In many cases he could not. On the central prob-lem of recovery he was lost, although the outlines of the National Recovery Administration (NRA) and the Agricultural Adjustment Administration (AAA) were already forming. But even in areas where his commitments were firm, he preferred general to specific recommendations and refused to join Hoover in a serious dialogue either on the causes of the depression or on basic

American ideals. He balanced suggestive speeches on forgotten men, concert of interests, planning of production and distribution, administered resources, and restored purchasing power with traditional pledges of a lower budget and complete fiscal integrity. Most of the time he simply berated the Hoover administration, condemned Republican mistakes, or promised to drive the evil money-changers from the temple. His concealed pack seemed to be full of aces, with something for almost everyone but the financiers. Even his devils were vague enough to be almost empty. At times every ambiguous label of the American political repertoire seemed to fit—left or right, liberal or conservative, socialist or capitalist, individualist or collectivist. His technique proved a political success. Even much of the vagueness, much of the ambiguity, was unavoidable. It was Roosevelt, an unbeatable Roosevelt, at work. But, of course, only some of the cards could be played. Many newly aroused hopes could never be fulfilled.

The overwhelming concern of almost everyone in 1933 was recovery, the most attractive but elusive god of the thirties. This was Roosevelt's clearest commitment. If he had quickly attained this goal much of the later New Deal, including the relief and welfare programs, would have seemed unnecessary. For this reason the NRA, with its permissive monopolies in each industry, its elaborate code system, and its fanfare and promotional excesses, was the most important agency established during the famous hundred-day legislative session of 1933. Complementing this was a complex agricultural act, which established the AAA and inaugurated several lasting programs looking toward both recovery and structural changes. These two efforts represented Roosevelt's earliest response to unprecedented economic maladies which he blamed on Hoover and the Republican party.

. . . The legislative climax of 1935 preceded the political climax of the New Deal in 1936. But again, as in 1932, Roosevelt won no mandate for specific new programs. Then, in the Court fight and the new depression, both in 1937, he lost much of his political leverage. By 1938 he was frustrated in his domestic policies and imprisoned by neutrality legislation in his early ventures into international diplomacy. After a desperate attempt at party realignment, he began buying congressional help in foreign policy at the expense of further domestic innovation. . . .

The New Deal stopped growing. It did not disappear. A subsidized, regulated welfare capitalism still stands . . . as the core of American domestic policy. The United States has neither moved beyond it nor tried other alternatives, despite the varied and often confused protest movements of the sixties. At best, subsequent presidents have patched a few holes, repaired a few loose shingles, and added some new rooms to the welfare state. Thus the changes of the thirties were not only numerous but prophetic, setting the themes for subsequent political discourse. The welfare measures—social security, labor protection, housing—have all been expanded. None has been repudiated. Both conservation and advisory types of planning have remained as generally accepted ideals, however compromised in practice. Whatever the internal inequities, agriculture, our greatest economic success story, still functions under a subsidized price system and, when needed, production controls. Large business enterprise has learned to accept, if not to love, the protective and only mildly restrictive role of government in maintaining growth and high profits. Likewise, organized labor has shrugged off its earlier militancy and, like a happy but protected lamb, finally lain down beside the business lion.

The same continuity is evident at the political level. Whatever the limitations of Roosevelt, America's political parties have not discovered or created another political leader who could tear away, with the wisdom or the foolishness of a child, so many traditional articles of faith, and thus open up so many pregnant possibilities. Instead, many of his successors have turned fragile New Deal policies into new, binding articles of faith. None has been able to step into the inviting flux, the confused and discordant flux of New Deal policies, and provide what Roosevelt so often lacked—a mature comprehension of complexity, a scholar's ability to make clear and careful distinctions, and a teacher's ability to lift the level of popular understanding.

Within the one inescapable context of the thirties—the need for economic growth—the New Deal was a short-run failure, but it did initiate changes that led to long-run success. It began the final maturation of our economic system, and at least pointed toward the political economy most capable of maximizing production, consumption, profits, and jobs. We are as yet only beginning to exploit the full potential of government credit, incentives, and subsidies, even as we glimpse the sometimes disturbing promise of advertising, automation, and more careful political indoctrination, and even as we finally begin to appreciate some of the unanticipated social costs of unending economic growth.

To emphasize the eventual economic results of New Deal policies is not to evaluate the New Deal as a whole. Almost no one in the New Deal, almost no one in the thirties, even dared predict such long-term economic gains. But, superb irony, few New Dealers expected quite so little in other areas. The fervent New Deal bureaucrats dreamed of a much greater level of social justice, of a truer community, than the United States has as yet achieved. They, of course, wanted more production and more jobs, but they also wanted everyone to have a sense of meaningful involvement and worth. They wanted everyone to be able to consume more, but desired consumption not as a balm of meaninglessness but as a necessary adjunct of a sense of real achievement and fulfillment. They wanted industrial growth and even restored profits, not as ends but as corollaries of widespread opportunities for creative and socially beneficial enterprise.

As these more idealistic New Dealers grew older, they often became tragic figures, seemingly out of touch with things. They looked back in nostalgia to what they had dreamed, and what they had all shared, and what they had longed for. The prosperous but callous fifties seemed a mockery. They talked of how Roosevelt, had he lived, would at last have led them into the kingdom. Like lonely and unneeded soldiers, they cried aloud for their old commander and for the old crusade. If anything seemed clear to them, it was that their dreams and hopes had been betrayed. Instead of responding to the greater efficiency, the accelerating growth, even the new welfare measures of the sixties, they looked on sadly, as if the substance, the moral heart, had been removed from things.

For some of the most perceptive social critics of the thirties, for an Edmund Wilson or a John Dewey, the New Deal was not a promise betrayed; it was essentially misdirected from the beginning. It began and ended with conventional or oversimplified half-answers, answers which the more alienated, more sensitive, and more analytic intellectuals all too easily repudiated. But the more radical critics, despite the early hopes of someone like Tugwell, had no pathway to power. In fact, they can never attain power in a democracy unless conditions produce a passive resignation on the part of citizens, a willingness to relinquish responsibility to angry but largely incomprehensible prophets. In a working democracy the penetrating critic, like a lonely Jeremiah, must teach and often suffer. He cannot dictate. Neither can he win elections. His ringing voice must be heard from the lectern and pulpit. He will never master the soothing art of the fireside—and should not. He is too honest and too clearheaded.

For the historian, every judgment and every evaluation of the past has to be tinged with a pinch of compassion, a sense of the beauty and nobility present even in the frustration of honest hopes and humane ideals. He sees that, from almost any valuative perspective, the thirties could have brought so much more, but also so much worse, than the New Deal. No diverse political movement, responding to multiple pressures, can come close to matching the expectations of any sensitive social critic. The limiting political context has to be understood—the safeguards and impediments of our political system, Roosevelt's intellectual limitations, and most of all the economic ignorance and philosophic immaturity of the American electorate. The plausible alternatives to the New Deal are not easily suggested, particularly if one considers all the confining and limiting circumstances.

From almost any perspective, the New Deal solved a few problems, ameliorated others, obscured many, and created unanticipated new ones. This is about all our political system can generate, even in crisis. If the people knew better and chose better, if they shared similar goals, there would be few crises anyway. If they must know better to have better, then our conventional politics is no answer, except as a perennial interim accommodation with incompatible goals and with ignorance. Even this permits more thorough criticism its long day of persuasion and education.

Only with trepidation will the student of history try to judge the results of the New Deal. He will not do it with a sense of heartless criticism. Not only would it be unfair, but too much is involved. But judge he must, not to whip the past but to use it. For so much that originated or at least matured in the policies of the Roosevelt administration lives on in our present institutions. Thus his rightful criticism is directed at himself, his country, his institutions, his age. If so directed, his evaluation must be just, thorough, and honest; otherwise, he practices only self-deceit.

Pearl Harbor and the Yellow Peril

Roger Daniels

Wartime is generally a time of heightened mythologies. This is particularly true of racial and ethnic mythologies, and most particularly true of those involving the enemy—without and within. Add to this mix an exaggerated partriotism fueled by a concerted propaganda effort and the ever-present human susceptibility to fear-mongering, and the stage is set. Here, Roger Daniels of the State University of New York, Fredonia, deals with a clear example—the internment of West Coast Japanese Americans during World War II. The Japanese-as-"Yellow Peril" idea had been developing for over fifty years prior to 1941, and it even proved divisive between the Issei (first-generation) and the Nisei (second-generation) Japanese-Americans within the West Coast community by the 1930s. Pearl Harbor was the spark that set off the tinder nationally. Without any real proof and against the best instincts and judgments of many American leaders, including FDR, the the spread of prejudice accelerated, and as a result over 100,000 West Coast Japanese Americans—both Issei and Nisei—were interned. The basic American tenet of equal protection under the law became instant myth for these Americans. Success in the war, the absence of depredations caused by the "Yellow Peril," and the patriotism and valor shown by Japanese Americans such as those who served in the 442nd Regimental Combat Team in Italy (the most highly decorated unit in all of American military history) finally lessened the collective national fear even before war's end. Official admission of guilt and token restitution came slowly, in some cases even reluctantly. This historical example of the destructive power of myth-run-amok remains. In the words of Eugene V. Rostow, "a great principle was never lost so casually."

If the attack on Pearl Harbor came as a devastating shock to most Americans, for those of Japanese ancestry it was like a nightmare come true. Throughout the 1930s the Nisei generation dreaded the possibility of a war between the United States and Japan; although some in both the Japanese and American communities fostered the illusion that the emerging Nisei generation could help bridge the gap between the rival Pacific powers, most Nisei, at least, understood that this was a chimera. As early as 1937 Nisei gloom about the future predominated. One Nisei spoke prophetically about what might happen to Japanese Americans in a Pacific war. Rhetorically he asked his fellow Nisei students at the University of California:

> . . . what are we going to do if war does break out between United States and Japan? . . . In common language we can say "we're sunk." Even if the Nisei wanted to fight for America, what chances? Not a chance! . . . our properties would be confiscated and most likely [we would be] herded into prison camps— perhaps we would be slaughtered on the spot.[1]

As tensions increased, so did Nisei anxieties; and in their anxiety some Nisei tried to accentuate their loyalty and Americanism by disparaging the generation of their fathers. Newspaper editor Togo Tanaka, for example, speaking to a college group in early 1941, insisted that the Nisei must face what he called "the question of loyalty" and assumed that since the Issei were "more or less tumbleweeds with one foot in America and one foot in Japan," real loyalty to America could be found only in his own generation. A Los Angeles Nisei jeweler expressed similar doubts later the same year. After explaining to a Los Angeles *Times* columnist that many if not most of the older generation were pro-Japanese rather than pro-American, he expressed his own generation's fears. "We talk of almost nothing but this great crisis. We don't know what's going to happen. Sometimes we only look for a concentration camp."[2]

While the attention of Japanese Americans was focused on the Pacific, most other Americans gave primary consideration to Europe, where in September 1939 World War II had broken out. Hitler's amazing blitzkrieg against the west in the spring of 1940—which overran, in quick succession, Denmark and Norway and then Holland, Belgium, Luxembourg, and France—caused the United States to accelerate its defense program and institute the first peacetime draft in its history. Stories, now known to be wildly exaggerated, told of so-called fifth column and espionage activities, created much concern about the loyalty of aliens, particularly German-born aliens, some 40,000 of whom were organized into the overtly pro-Nazi German-American Bund. As a component part of the defense program, Congress passed, in 1940, an Alien Registration Act, which required the registration and fingerprinting of all aliens over fourteen years of age. In addition, as we now know, the Department of Justice, working through the Federal Bureau of Investigation, was compiling a relatively modest list of dangerous or subversive aliens—Germans, Italians, and Japanese—who were to be arrested or interned at the outbreak of war with their country. The commendable restraint of the Department of Justice's plans was due, first of all, to the liberal nature of the New Deal. The Attorney General, Francis Biddle, was clearly a civil libertarian, as befitted a former law clerk of Oliver Wendell Holmes, Jr.

Elsewhere in the government however, misgivings about possible fifth column and sabotage activity, particularly by Japanese, were strongly felt. For example, one congressman, John D. Dingell (D-Mich.), wrote the President to suggest that Japanese in the United States and Hawaii be used as hostages to ensure good behavior by Japan. In August 1941, shortly after Japanese assets in the United States were frozen and the Japanese made it difficult for some one hundred Americans to leave Japan, Dingell suggested that as a reprisal the United States should "cause the forceful detention or imprisonment in a concentration camp of ten thousand alien Japanese in Hawaii. . . . It would be well to remind Japan," he continued, "that there are perhaps one hundred fifty thousand additional alien Japanese in the United States who [can] be held in a reprisal reserve."[3]

And, in the White House itself, concern was evidenced. Franklin Roosevelt, highly distrustful of official reports and always anxious to have independent checks on the bureaucracy, set up an independent "intelligence" operation, run by John Franklin Carter. Carter, who as the "Unofficial Observer" and "Jay Franklin" had written some of the most brilliant New Deal journalism and would later serve as an adviser to President Harry S Truman and Governer Thomas E. Dewey, used newspapermen friends to make special reports. In early November he received a report on the West Coast Japanese from Curtis B. Munson. His report stressed the loyalty of the overwhelming majority, and he understood that even most of the disloyal Japanese Americans hoped that "by remaining quiet they [could] avoid concentration camps or irresponsible mobs." Munson was, however, "horrified" to observe that

> dams, bridges, harbors, power stations etc., are wholly unguarded. The harbor of San Pedro [Los Angeles' port] could be razed by fire completely by four men with hand grenades and a little study in one night. Dams could be blown and half of lower California could actually die of thirst. . . . One railway bridge at the exit from the mountains in some cases could tie up three or four main railroads.[4]

Munson felt that despite the loyalty or quiescence of the majority, this situation represented a real threat because "there are still Japanese in the United States who will tie dynamite around their waist and make a human bomb out of themselves."[5] This imaginary threat apparently worried thc President too, for he immediately sent the memo on to Secretary of War Henry L. Stimson, specifically calling his attention to Munson's warnings about sabotage. In early December, Army Intelligence drafted a reply (which in the confusion following Pearl Harbor was never sent) arguing, quite correctly as it turned out, that "widespread sabotage by Japanese is not expected . . . identification of dangerous Japanese on the West Coast is reasonably complete."[6] Although neither of these or other similar proposals and warnings was acted upon before the attack on Pearl Harbor, the mere fact that they were suggested and received consideration in the very highest governmental circles indicates the degree to which Americans were willing to believe almost anything about the Japanese. This belief, in turn, can be understood only if one takes into account the half century of agitation and prophecy about the coming American-Japanese war and the dangers of the United States being overwhelmed by waves of yellow soldiers aided by alien enemies within the gates.

This irrational fear of Oriental conquest, with its racist and sex-fantasy overtones, can be most conveniently described as the "yellow peril," a term probably first used by German Kaiser Wilhelm II about 1895. As is so often the case, the phenomenon existed long before the name. Between 1880 and 1882 three obscure California publicists produced works describing the successful invasion and conquest of the United States by hordes of Chinese. These works were undoubtedly concocted to stimulate and profit from the initial campaign for Chinese exclusion, successfully consummated in 1882. There is no evidence that they were taken seriously by any significant number of people; in that period, after all, China was a victim, not a predator. But, by the end of the century, a potential predator had appeared; in 1894 formerly isolated and backward Japan won its first modern naval battle, defeating the Chinese off the Yalu River. The very next year, that prince of Jingoes, Henry Cabot Lodge, then a Republican congressman from Massachusetts, warned Congress that the Japanese "understand the future . . . they have just whipped somebody, and they are in a state of mind when they think that they can whip anybody." In 1898, during the discussion of the American annexation of Hawaii, Senator Cushman K. Davis (R-Minn.), chairman of the Senate Foreign Relations Committee, warned his colleagues that the mild controversy with Japan over Hawaii was merely "the preliminary skirmish in the great coming struggle between" East and West.

These still nascent fears about Japan were greatly stimulated when the Japanese badly defeated Russia in the war of 1904–1905, the first triumph of Asians over Europeans in modern times. The shots fired at Mukden and in the Strait of Tsushima were truly shots heard round the world. Throughout Asia the Japanese victory undoubtedly stimulated nationalism and resistance to colonialism; in Europe, and particularly in the United States, it greatly stimulated fears of conquest by Asia. Shortly after the end of that war the "yellow peril" was adopted by its most significant American disseminator, newspaper mogul William Randolph Hearst. Although the theme of possible Japanese attack had been initiated by a rival paper, the San Francisco *Chronicle*, it was Hearst's San Francisco *Examiner*, as well as the rest of his chain, which made the theme of danger from Asia uniquely its own. Although there are earlier scattered references to the external Japanese threat, the real opening salvo of what the chain later called its thirty-five-year war with Japan began in the *Examiner* on December 20, 1906. Its front page that day proclaimed

JAPAN SOUNDS OUR COASTS
Brown Men Have
Maps and Could
Land Easily

The next year the Hearst papers printed the first full-scale account of a Pacific war between the United States and Japan. Richmond Pearson Hobson, who had translated an inept but heroic exploit in the Spanish-American War into a seat in Congress (he was an Alabama Democrat), was the author of the two-part Sunday Supplement fantasy. Under the headline JAPAN MAY SEIZE THE PACIFIC COAST, Hobson wrote, "The Yellow Peril is here." Unless a really big navy were built, Hobson calculated, an army of "1,207,700 men could conquer the Pacific Coast." He predicted that Japan would soon conquer China and thus "command the military resources of the whole yellow race."

An even more elaborate military fantasy—or rather a series of fantasies—was concocted by "General" Homer Lea. Lea was a Sinophile who served as a military adviser to Sun Yat-sen. There is no evidence, despite the claims of naïve publicists, that he ever commanded troops in battle. His most important literary work, *The Valor of Ignorance,* was published in 1909 and reissued, with an effusive introduction by Clare Booth Luce, shortly after Pearl Harbor. It foretold, in great detail, a Japanese conquest of the Philippine Islands, quickly followed by a landing on the Pacific Coast and the occupation of California, Oregon, and Washington. Lea, who felt that only professional armies could fight, insisted that the small American army would be no match for the Japanese. In florid prose, he described the results of this conquest.

> Not months, but years, must elapse before armies equal to the Japanese are able to pass in parade. These must then make their way over deserts such as no armies have ever heretofore crossed; scale the entrenched and stupendous heights that form the redoubts of the desert moats; attempting, in the valor of their ignorance, the militarily impossible; turning mountain gorges into the ossuaries of their dead, and burdening the desert winds with the spirits of their slain. The repulsed and distracted forces to scatter, as heretofore, dissension throughout the Union, breed rebellions, class and sectional insurrections, until this heterogenous Republic, in its principles, shall disintegrate, and again into the palm of re-established monarchy pay the toll of its vanity and its scorn.

Hearst, Hobson, and Lea were all essentially conservative, social Darwinistic racists. But the yellow peril was popular on the left as well. The English Fabian Socialist H. G. Wells, perhaps the greatest English-speaking science fiction writer, is best known for his fantasy about a Martian invasion. But in his *War in the Air* (1908) Orientals rather than Martians were the bogeymen. In the novel Wells rather accurately predicts World War I, and has the United States, France, and Great Britain locked in a death struggle with Germany. Then, without warning, Japan and China indiscriminately attack the white powers almost destroying civilization in the process. A character comments, "the Yellow Peril was a peril after all."

Even during World War I, when Japan fought Germany, anti-Japanese military propaganda did not cease; the publication of the infamous Zimmermann telegram of early 1917 which proposed a German-Mexican-Japanese alliance against the United States further inflamed American, and particularly Pacific Coast, feeling, even though Japan, interested in annexations in the Pacific and on the East Asian Mainland, clearly wanted to have nothing to do with it. During and after the war a number of anti-Japanese movies, which often showed the Japanese actually invading or planning to invade the United States, were produced and shown in theaters throughout the country; some of the most noxious were made by the motion picture arm of the Hearst communications empire. Sunday supplements and cheap pulp magazines featured the "yellow peril" theme throughout the 1920s and 1930s and a mere inventory of "yellow peril" titles would cover many pages. It is impossible, of course, to judge with any accuracy the impact or influence of this propaganda, but it seems clear that well before the actual coming of war a considerable proportion of the American public had been conditioned not only to the probability of a Pacific war with Japan—that was, after all, a geopolitical fact of twentieth-century civilization—but also to the proposition that this war would involve an invasion of the continental United States in which Japanese residents and secret agents would provide the spearhead of the attack. After war came at Pearl Harbor and for years thereafter many Japanophobes insisted that, to use Wells's phrase, "the Yellow Peril was a peril after all," but this is to misunderstand completely Japan's intentions and capabilities during the Great Pacific War. The Japanese military planners never contemplated an invasion of the continental United States, and, even had they done so, the logistical problems were obviously beyond Japan's capacity as a nation. But, often in history, what men believe to be true is more important than the truth itself because the mistaken belief becomes a basis for action. These two factors—the long racist and anti-Oriental tradition plus the widely believed "yellow peril" fantasy—when triggered by the traumatic mechanism provided by the attack on Pearl Harbor, were the necessary preconditions for America's concentration camps. But beliefs, even widely held beliefs, are not always translated into action. We must now discover how this particular set of beliefs—the inherent and genetic disloyalty of individual Japanese plus the threat of an imminent Japanese invasion—produced public policy and action, the mass removal and incarceration of the West Coast Japanese Americans.[7]

As is well known, despite decades of propaganda and apprehension about a Pacific war, the reality, the dawn attack at Pearl Harbor on Sunday, December 7, 1941, came as a stunning surprise to most Americans. Throughout the nation the typical reaction was disbelief, followed by a determination to close ranks and avenge a disastrous defeat. Faced with the fact of attack, the American people entered the war with perhaps more unity than has existed before or since. But if a calm determination to get on with the job typified the national mood, the mood of the Pacific Coast was nervous and trigger-happy, if not hysterical. A thousand movies and stories and reminiscences have recorded the solemnity with which the nation reacted to that "day of infamy" in 1941. Yet, at Gilmore Field, in Los Angeles, 18,000 spectators at a minor league professional football game between the Hollywood Bears and the Columbus Bulldogs "jumped to their feet and cheered wildly when the public address system announced that a state of war existed between Japan and the United States."

The state's leading paper, the Los Angeles *Times* (Dec. 8, 1941), quickly announced that California was "a zone of danger" and invoked the ancient vigilante tradition of the West by calling for alert, keen-eyed civilians [who could be] of yeoman service in cooperating with the military authorities against spies, saboteurs and fifth columnists. We have thousands of Japanese here.... Some, perhaps many, are ... good Americans. What the rest may be we do not know, nor can we take a chance in the light of yesterday's demonstration that treachery and double-dealing are major Japanese weapons.

Day after day, throughout December, January, February, and March, almost the entire Pacific Coast press (of which the *Times* was a relatively restrained example) spewed forth racial venom against all Japanese. The term Jap, of course, was standard usage. Japanese, alien and native-born, were also "Nips," "yellow men," "Mad dogs," and "yellow vermin," to name only a few of the choicer epithets. *Times* columnist Ed Ainsworth cautioned his readers "to be careful to differentiate between races. The Chinese and Koreans both hate the Japs more than we do. . . . Be sure of nationality before you are rude to anybody." (*Life* Magazine soon rang some changes on this theme for a national audience with an article—illustrated by comic strip artist Milton Caniff, creator of *Terry and the Pirates* and, later, *Steve Canyon*—which purported to explain how to tell "Japs" from other Asian nationalities.) The sports pages, too, furnished their share of abuse. Just after a series of murderous and sometimes fatal attacks on Japanese residents by Filipinos, one sports page feature was headlined FILIPINO BOXERS NOTED FOR COURAGE, VALOR.

Newspaper columnists, as always, were quick to suggest what public policy should be. Lee Shippey, a Los Angeles writer who often stressed that *some* Japanese were all right, prophetically suggested a solution to California's Japanese problem. He proposed the establishment of "a number of big, closely guarded, closely watched truck farms on which Japanese-Americans could earn a living and assure us a steady supply of vegetables." If a Nazi had suggested doing this with Poles, Shippey, a liberal, undoubtedly would have called it a slave labor camp. But the palm for *Schrecklichkeit* must go to Westbrook Pegler, a major outlet of what Oswald Garrison Villard once called "the sewer system of American journalism." Taking time off from his vendettas with Eleanor Roosevelt and the American labor movement, Pegler proposed, on December 9, that every time the Axis murdered hostages, the United States should retaliate by raising them "100 victims selected out of [our] concentration camps," which Pegler assumed would be set up for subversive Germans and Italians and "alien Japanese."

Examples of newspaper incitement to racial violence appeared daily (some radio commentators were even worse). In addition, during the period that the Japanese Americans were still at large, the press literally abounded with stories and, above all, headlines, which made the already nervous general public believe that military or paramilitary Japanese activists were all around them. None of these stories had any basis in fact; amazingly, there was not one demonstrable incident of sabotage committed by a Japanese American, alien or native-born, during the entire war. Here are a few representative headlines.

JAP BOAT FLASHES MESSAGE ASHORE

ENEMY PLANES SIGHTED OVER CALIFORNIA COAST

TWO JAPANESE WITH MAPS AND ALIEN LITERATURE SEIZED

JAP AND CAMERA HELD IN BAY CITY

VEGETABLES FOUND FREE OF POISON

CAPS ON JAPANESE TOMATO PLANTS POINT TO AIR BASE

JAPANESE HERE SENT VITAL DATA TO TOKYO

CHINESE ABLE TO SPOT JAP

MAP REVEALS JAP MENACE

NETWORK OF ALIEN FARMS COVERS STRATEGIC DEFENSE AREAS OVER SOUTHLAND

JAPS PLAN COAST ATTACK IN APRIL WARNS CHIEF OF KOREAN SPY BAND[8]

In short, any reading of the wartime Pacific Coast press—or for that matter viewing the wartime movies that still pollute our television channels—shows clearly that, although a distinction was continually being made between "good" and "bad" Germans (a welcome change from World War I), few distinctions were ever made between Japanese. The evil deeds of Hitler's Germany were the deeds of bad men; the evil deeds of Tojo and Hirohito's Japan were the deeds of a bad race. While the press was throwing fuel on the fires of racial animosity, other faggots were contributed by politicians, federal officials, and, above all, the military. The governor of California, Culbert L. Olson, a liberal Democrat, had insisted, before Pearl Harbor, that Japanese Americans should enjoy all their rights and privileges even if war with Japan came, and correctly pointed out that equal protection under the law was a "basic tenet" of American government. But Olson's constitutional scruples were a casualty of Pearl Harbor: on December 8, the governor told the press that he was thinking of ordering all Japanese, alien and citizen, to observe house arrest "to avoid riot and disturbance."[9]

The Department of Justice, working through the FBI and calling on local law enforcement officials for assistance and detention, began roundups of what it considered "dangerous" enemy aliens. Throughout the nation this initial roundup involved about 3000 persons, half of whom were Japanese. (All but a handful of these lived on the Pacific Coast.) In other words the federal officials responsible for counterespionage thought that some 1500 persons of Japanese ancestry, slightly more than 1 percent of the nation's Japanese population, constituted some kind of threat to the nation. Those arrested, often in the dead of night, were almost universally of the immigrant, or Issei, generation, and thus, no matter how long they had lived here, "enemy aliens" in law. (It must be kept in mind that American law prohibited the naturalization of Asians.) Those arrested were community leaders, since the government, acting as it so often does on the theory of guilt by association, automatically hauled in the officers and leading lights of a number of Japanese organizations and religious groups. Many of these people were surely "rooting" for the Emperor rather than the President and thus technically subversive, but most of them were rather elderly and inoffensive gentlemen and not a threat to anything. This limited internment, however, was a not too discreditable performance for a government security agency, but it must be noted that even at this restrained level the government acted much more harshly, in terms of numbers interned, toward Japanese nationals than toward German nationals (most known members of the German-American Bund were left at liberty), and more harshly toward Germans than to Italians. It should also be noted, however, that more than a few young Nisei leaders applauded this early roundup and contrasted their own loyalty to the presumed disloyalty of many of the leaders of the older generation.

In addition to the selective roundup of enemy aliens, the Justice Department almost immediately announced the sealing off of the Mexican and Canadian borders to "all persons of Japanese ancestry, whether citizen or alien." Thus, by December 8, that branch of the federal government particularly charged with protecting the rights of citizens was willing to single out one ethnic group for invidious treatment. Other national civilian officials discriminated in other ways. Fiorello La Guardia, an outstanding liberal who was for a time director of the Office of Civilian Defense as well as mayor of New York, pointedly omitted mention of the Japanese in two public statements calling for decent treatment for enemy aliens and suggesting that alien Germans and Italians be presumed loyal until proved otherwise. By implication, at least, Japanese were to be presumed disloyal. Seventeen years earlier La Guardia had been one of three congressmen who dared to speak in favor of continuing Japanese immigration, but in December 1941 he could find nothing good to say about any Japanese.

Even more damaging were the mendacious statements of Frank Knox, Roosevelt's Republican Secretary of the Navy. On December 15 Secretary Knox held a press conference in Los Angeles on his return from a quick inspection of the damage at Pearl Harbor. As this was the first detailed report of the damage there, his remarks were front-page news all across the nation. Knox spoke of "treachery" in Hawaii and insisted that much of the disaster was caused by "the most effective fifth column work that's come out of this war, except in Norway."[10] The disaster at Pearl Harbor, as is now generally acknowledged, was caused largely by the unpreparedness and incompetence of the local military commanders, as Knox already knew. (The orders for the relief of Admiral Kimmel were already being drawn up.) But the secretary, who, as we shall see, harbored deep-felt anti-Japanese prejudices, probably did not want the people to lose faith in their Navy, so the Japanese population of Hawaii—and indirectly all Japanese Americans—was made the scapegoat on which to hang the big lie. (Knox, it should be remarked, as a Chicago newspaper publisher in civilian life, had a professional understanding of these matters.)

But the truly crucial role was played by the other service, the United States Army. The key individual, initially, at least, was John L. De Witt, in

1941 a lieutenant general and commander of the Western Defense Command and the 4th Army, both headquartered at San Francisco's Presidio. Despite these warlike titles, De Witt, who was sixty-one years old and would be retired before the war's end, was essentially an administrator in uniform, a staff officer who had specialized in supply and had practically nothing to do with combat during his whole Army career. Even before Pearl Harbor, De Witt had shown himself to be prejudiced against Japanese Americans. In March 1941, for example, he found it necessary to complain to Major General William G. Bryden, the Army's Deputy Chief of Staff, that "a couple of Japs" who had been drafted into the Army were "going around taking pictures." He and Bryden agreed to "just have it happen naturally that Japs are sent to Infantry units," rather than to sensitive headquarters or coast defense installations. De Witt's prejudices, in fact, extended all along the color line. When he discovered that some of the troops being sent to him as reinforcements after Pearl Harbor were Negro, he protested to the Army's chief of classification and assignment that

> you're filling too many colored troops up on the West Coast. . . . there will be a great deal of public reaction out here due to the Jap situation. They feel they've got enough black skinned people around them as it is. Filipinos and Japanese. . . . I'd rather have a white regiment. . . .[11]

Serving under De Witt, in December 1941, as the corps commander in charge of the defense of Southern California, was a real fighting man, the then Major General Joseph W. Stilwell, the famed "Vinegar Joe" of the heartbreaking Burma campaigns. His diary of those days, kept in pencil in a shirt-pocket notebook, gives an accurate and pungent picture of the hysteria and indecisiveness that prevailed at De Witt's headquarters and on the Coast generally.

> *Dec. 8*
> Sunday night "air raid" at San Francisco . . . Fourth Army kind of jittery.
> *Dec. 9*
> . . . Fleet of thirty-four [Japanese] ships between San Francisco and Los Angeles. Later—not authentic.
> *Dec. 11*
> [Phone call from 4th Army] "The main Japanese fleet is 164 miles off San Francisco." I believed it, like a damn fool. . . .
>> Of course [4th Army] passed the buck on this report. They had it from a "usually reliable source," but they should never have put it out without check.
> *Dec. 13*
> Not content with the above blah, [4th] Army pulled another at ten-thirty today. "Reliable information that attack on Los Angeles is imminent. A general alarm being considered. . . ." What jackass would send a general alarm [which would have meant warning all civilians to leave the area including the workers in the vital Southern California aircraft industry] under the circumstances. The [4th] Army G–2 [Intelligence] is just another amateur, like all the rest of the staff. Rule: the higher the headquarters, the more important is *calm*.[12]

Stilwell's low opinion of General De Witt was apparently shared by others within the Army; shortly after Vinegar Joe's transfer to Washington just before Christmas, he noted that Lieutenant General Lesley J. McNair, Deputy Commander, Army Ground Forces, had told him that "De Witt has gone crazy and requires ten refusals before he realizes it is 'No.' "[13] De Witt, it must be understood, was a cautious, conservative officer in the twilight of his career. He saw, throughout the Army, younger men being promoted into key posts; his contemporary, Lieutenant General Walter C. Short, the Army commander in Hawaii, was in disgrace. With misplaced concreteness De Witt apparently decided that there would be no Pearl Harbors on the West Coast. It is interesting to note that the cautious De Witt, in safe San Francisco, was more alarmed by the famous "war warning" telegram of November 27 than was Short in exposed Honolulu, and had the former been the Hawaiian commander, the Army, at least, might have been in a more advanced state of readiness. But after Pearl Harbor, caution turned into funk; no one who reads the transcripts of De Witt's telephone conversations with Washington or examines his staff correspondence can avoid the conclusion that his was a headquarters at which confusion rather than calm reigned, and that the confusion was greatest at the very top.

It was in this panic-ridden, amateurish Western Defense Command atmosphere that some of the most crucial decisions about the evacuation of the Japanese Americans were made. Before examining them, however, it should be made clear that the nearest Japanese aircraft during most of December were attacking Wake Island, more than 5000 miles west of San Francisco, and any major Japanese surface vessels or troops were even farther away. In fact, elements of the Luftwaffe over the North Atlantic were actually closer to California than any Japanese planes. California and the West Coast of the continental United States were in no way seriously threatened by the Japanese military. This finding does not represent just the hindsight of the military historian; the high command of the American army realized it at the time. Official estimates of Japanese capabilities made late in December concluded correctly that a large-scale invasion was beyond the capacity of the Japanese military but that a hit-and-run raid somewhere along the West Coast was possible.

In the days just after Pearl Harbor there was no concerted plan for mass incarceration. As evidence of this, on December 9 General Brehon Somervell, the Army's G–4 (Supply), ordered the construction of "facilities for the internment of alien enemies and other prisoners of war"; the three facilities authorized within De Witt's Western Defense Command had a total capacity of less than 2000, a figure consistent with the number of enemy aliens the FBI was in the process of rounding up.[14] But De Witt and his nervous headquarters staff, ready to believe anything, soon began to pressure Washington for more drastic action against the presumably dangerous enemies in their midst.

The first proposal by the Army for any kind of mass evacuation of Japanese Americans was brought forward at a De Witt staff conference in San Francisco on the evening of December 10. In the language of a staff memo, the meeting considered "certain questions relative to the problem of apprehension, segregation and detention of Japanese in the San Francisco Bay Area." The initial cause of the meeting seems to have been a report from an unidentified Treasury Department official asserting that 20,000 Japanese in the Bay Area were ready for organized action. Apparently plans for a mass roundup were drawn up locally, and approved by General Benedict, the commander of the area, but the whole thing was squelched by Nat Pieper, head of the San Francisco office of the FBI, who laughed it off as "the wild imaginings" of a former FBI man whom he had fired. The imaginings were pretty wild; the figure of 20,000 slightly exceeded the total number of Japanese men, women, and children in the Bay Area. But wild or not, De Witt's subordinate reported the matter to Washington with the recommendation that "plans be made for large-scale internment." Then on December 19 General De Witt officially recommended "that action be initiated at the earliest practicable date to collect all alien subjects fourteen years of age and over, of enemy nations and remove them" to the interior of the United States and hold them "under restraint after removal" to prevent their surreptitious return.[15] (The age limit was apparently derived from the federal statutes on wartime internment, but those statutes, it should be noted, specified males only.)

De Witt was soon in touch with the Army's Provost Marshal General, Allen W. Gullion, who would prove to be a key figure in the decision to relocate the Japanese Americans. Gullion, the Army's top cop, had previously served as Judge Advocate General, the highest legal office within the Army. He was a service intellectual who had once read a paper to an International Congress of Judicial Experts on the "present state of international law regarding the protection of civilians from the new war technics." But, since at least mid-1940, he had been concerned with the problem of legally exercising military control over civilians in wartime. Shortly after the fall of France, Army Intelligence took the position that fifth column activities had been so successful in the European war in creating an internal as well as an external military front that the military "will actually have to control, through their Provost Marshal Generals, local forces, largely police" and that "the Military would certainly have to provide for the arrest and temporary holding of a large number of suspects," alien and citizen.

Gullion, as Judge Advocate General, gave his official opinion that within the United States, outside any zone of actual combat and where the civil courts were functioning, the "Military . . . does not have jurisdiction to participate in the arrest and temporary holding of civilians who are citizens of the United States." He did indicate, however, that if federal troops were in actual control (he had martial law in mind), jurisdiction over citizen civilians might be exercised.[16] Although martial law was never declared on the Pacific Coast, Chief of Staff George C. Marshall did declare the region a "Theater of Operations" on December 11. This declaration, which was not made with the Japanese Americans in mind, created the legal fiction that the Coast was a war zone and would provide first the Army and then the courts with an excuse for placing entirely blameless civilian citizens under military control.

By December 22 Provost Marshal General Gullion, like any good bureaucrat, began a campaign to enlarge the scope of his own activities, an activity usually known as empire building. He formally requested the Secretary of War to press for the transfer of responsibility for conduct of the enemy alien program from the Department of Justice to the War Department. This recommendation found no positive response in Stimson's office, and four days later Gullion was on the telephone trying to get General De Witt to recommend a mass roundup of all Japanese, alien and citizen. Gullion told the Western Defense commander that he had just been visited by a representative of the Los Angeles Chamber of Commerce urging that all Japanese in the Los Angeles area be incarcerated. De Witt, who would blow hot and cold, was, on December 26, opposed. He told Gullion that

> I'm very doubtful that it would be common sense procedure to try and intern 117,000 Japanese in this theater. . . . An American citizen, after all, is an American citizen. And while they all may not be loyal, I think we can weed the disloyal out of the loyal and lock them up if necessary.[17]

De Witt was also opposed, on December 26, to military, as opposed to civilian, control over enemy aliens. "It would be better," he told Gullion, if "this thing worked through the civil channels."[18]

While these discussions and speculations were going on all about them, the West Coast Japanese in general and the citizen Nisei in particular were desperately trying to establish their loyalty. Many Japanese communities on the Coast were so demoralized by the coming of war that little collective action was taken, especially in the first weeks after Pearl Harbor. But in Los Angeles, the major mainland center of Japanese population, frantic and often pitiful activity took place. Most of this activity revolved around the Japanese American Citizens League, an organization, by definition, closed to Issei, except for the handful who achieved citizenship because of their service in the United States armed forces during World War I. Immediately following Pearl Harbor the Japanese American Citizens League (JACL) wired the President, affirming their loyalty; the White House had the State Department, the arm of government usually used to communicate with foreigners, coolly respond by letter that "your desire to cooperate has been carefully noted." On December 9 the JACL Anti-Axis Committee decided to take no contributions, in either time or money, from noncitizens, and later, when special travel regulations inhibited the movement of aliens, it decided not to help Issei "in securing travel permits or [giving] information in that regard." In addition, Nisei leaders repeatedly called on one generation to inform on the other.

On the very evening of Pearl Harbor, editor Togo Tanaka went on station KHTR, Los Angeles, and told his fellow Nisei:

> As Americans we now function as counterespionage. Any act or word prejudicial to the United States committed by any Japanese must be warned and reported to the F.B.I., Naval Intelligence, Sheriff's Office, and local police. . . .

Before the end of the week the Los Angeles Nisei had set up a formal Committee on Intelligence and had regular liaison established with the FBI.[19] These patriotic activities never uncovered any real sabotage or espionage, because there was none to uncover. Nor did it provide the protective coloration that the Nisei hoped it would; race, not loyalty or citizenship, was the criterion for evacuation. It did, however, widen the gap between the generations, and would be a major cause of bitterness and violence after the evacuation took place.

Notes

1. *Campanile Review* (Berkeley), Fall, 1937.
2. Tom Treanor, "The Home Front," Los Angeles *Times*, August 6, 1941.
3. Dingell to FDR, August 18, 1941, Franklin D. Roosevelt Library, Hyde Park, Official File 197.
4. Munson's Report enclosed in Memo, FDR-Stimson, November 8, 1941, Franklin D. Roosevelt Library, Hyde Park, "Stimson Folder."
5. *Ibid.*
6. Stetson Conn, "Notes," Office, Chief of Military History, U.S. Army. Illuminating but fragmentary details of the Carter intelligence operations may be found in the Carter Mss., University of Wyoming.
7. For a fuller treatment of the "yellow peril," see Roger Daniels, *The Politics of Prejudice* (Berkeley and Los Angeles: University of California Press, 1962), pp. 65–78.
8. Headlines and quotations from the Los Angeles *Times*, December 8, 1941–February 23, 1942, *passim*; similar material may be found in almost any West Coast paper for the period.
9. Robert E. Burke, *Olson's New Deal for California* (Berkeley and Los Angeles: University of California Press, 1953), p. 201.
10. Knox Press conference transcript, December 15, 1941, Knox Collection, Office of Naval History, Washington Navy Yard.
11. Telephone conversations: De Witt to Bryden, March 13, 1941, Office, Chief of Staff Binder #11; De Witt and General Green, January 31, 1942, Office, Chief of Staff Binder #2, both from Stetson Conn, "Notes."
12. Theodore H. White, ed., *The Stilwell Papers* (New York: William Sloane Associates, 1948), pp. 3–23; and Stilwell Diaries, The Hoover Institution.
13. *Ibid.*
14. General Somervell, Memo for the Adjutant General, "Construction of Facilities for the Internment of Alien Enemies. . .," December 9, 1941, Adjutant General's Office 14.311, National Archives.
15. Stetson Conn, "Japanese Evacuation from the West Coast," pp. 116–18, in Stetson Conn, Rose C. Engleman, and Byron Fairchild, *United States Army in World War II: The Western Hemisphere: Guarding the United States and Its Outposts* (Washington: Government Printing Office, 1964).
16. Memo, Gullion to Assistant Chief of Staff (G–1), "Internment of Enemy Aliens," August 12, 1940, JAG 383.01, National Archives.
17. Stetson Conn et al., *United States Army in World War II . . ., loc. cit.*
18. *Ibid.*
19. Minutes of the Japanese American Citizens League Anti-Axis Committee, John Anson Ford Mss., Box 64, Huntington Library.

American Entry into World War II: A Historiographical Appraisal

Wayne S. Cole

The crisis of a war experience seems to have the peculiar quality of heightening a society's ever-present inclination to passion and prejudice while simultaneously clouding the sensibilities and intellectual precision of historians. To Wayne S. Cole of the University of Maryland, this merging of image and emotion is particularly characteristic of the volatile circumstances surrounding American involvement in World War II. Through a discussion of the diverse "schools" of historical thought concerning American entry into the war, Cole suggests the limitations of historical interpretation and the inherent difficulty in determining what constitutes historical "truth." This article was originally published only a little more than fifteen years after Pearl Harbor and only a dozen years after the death of President Roosevelt. Many of the important research gaps that Professor Cole notes have since been filled. For example, the *Foreign Relations* series, which is being published in installments, now documents the years through the late 1950s and may elicit further reinterpretation.

The aggressive expansion of the Axis powers in Europe and Asia in the 1930's aroused an impassioned debate on American foreign policy. "Isolationists" contended with "interventionists" over the policies adopted by the Roosevelt administration. Though few, if any, of the so-called isolationists wanted literally to isolate the United States from the rest of the world, they joined in opposition to what seemed the major trend in foreign affairs under President Roosevelt. A second phase in the dispute over policy was inaugurated by the attack on Pearl Harbor on December 7, 1941, for with that event the old quarrels became academic. But the policies of the Roosevelt administration continued as the core of dispute between two schools of historians who launched their own war of words over the background of America's entry into war. In the years after 1941 the "internationalist" writers were met by the "revisionists"—the latter term now used almost universally to describe the historians who have written critically of Roosevelt's pre–Pearl Harbor foreign policies and of American entry into World War II. Since the controversy is a continuing

From "American Entry into World War II: A Historiographical Appraisal," by Wayne S. Cole, in *Mississippi Valley Historical Review* (March 1957). Reprinted without footnotes by permission of the publisher and author.

one, and because the books and articles on the subject have grown to confusing proportions, some orientation is necessary both for the reader who must work his way through the published historical materials and for those attracted to the problem as a field for further research and writing.

Histories of American entry into World War II published during the war defended the pre–Pearl Harbor policies of the Roosevelt administration. Forrest Davis and Ernest K. Lindley had close ties with the administration which enabled them to obtain important data for their volume, *How War Came.* Walter Johnson's book, *The Battle Against Isolation,* published in 1944, was a study of the most powerful interventionist pressure groups before Pearl Harbor. Johnson, unlike some later writers, based his study upon previously unused manuscripts—principally the William Allen White papers. In the same year Dexter Perkins provided a concise survey in *America and Two Wars.* The authors of these books shared and endorsed most of the assumptions and convictions of the interventionists and the Roosevelt administration on foreign affairs. The emotional atmosphere of the war years, the necessity for unity in the prosecution of the war, and the inadequacy of available source materials combined to prevent any serious challenge to the pro-Roosevelt interpretation during the war. Pamphlets by John T. Flynn, published in 1944 and 1945, advanced the revisionist point of view, but they received relatively little attention.

During and since World War II growing quantities of raw materials for historical research and interpretation on the subject have been published and made available to scholars. The United States government published special sets of documents related to American entry into the war, beginning with the publication in 1943 of *Peace and War: United States Foreign Policy, 1931–1941.* In addition, the regular *Foreign Relations* series is now being brought close to Pearl Harbor. Military leaders and civilians associated with the Roosevelt administration published personal accounts. Among Americans whose memoirs or letters have been published in full or in part are Raymond Moley, William E. Dodd, Joseph E. Davies, Sumner Welles, Frances Perkins, John G. Winant, Henry Morgenthau, Jr., Henry L. Stimson, Cordell Hull, James A. Farley, Sherman Miles, Eleanor Roosevelt, William D. Leahy, Samuel I. Rosenman, Joseph C. Grew, Ernest J. King, Harold L. Ickes, Husband E. Kimmel, and Jay P. Moffat. Several key figures thus far have not published memoirs—including George C. Marshall, Harold R. Stark, Walter C. Short, Frank Knox, and President Roosevelt. Edited volumes of Roosevelt's speeches, press conferences, and personal letters, however, have been published. Documents, testimony, and reports of the several Pearl Harbor investigations were made available with the publication in 1946 of a total of forty volumes covering the work of the Joint Congressional Committee on the Investigation of the Pearl Harbor Attack. The war crimes trials in Nuremberg and the Far East added pertinent documents and testimony. Documents on British and German foreign policy before the war have been published. Memoirs of leaders of European states were printed, containing much information of value for an understanding and analysis of American policies. The volumes by Winston Churchill and Count

Ciano's diaries are two important examples. And gradually in recent years historians have obtained increased opportunities for research in unpublished manuscripts.

Most of the histories published from 1947 to 1950 on American entry into World War II were based almost exclusively on published sources—particularly on the volumes growing out of the Pearl Harbor investigations and on the memoirs of Hull, Stimson, and others. Most of these early books followed the lead of either the majority (pro-Roosevelt) or the minority (anti-Roosevelt) report of the congressional investigation committee. Among the volumes of this sort defending Roosevelt's foreign policies were *This Is Pearl*, by *Walter Millis*, and *Roosevelt, from Munich to Pearl Harbor*, by Basil Rauch. Revisionist volumes, based largely on published sources, included *Pearl Harbor*, by George Morgenstern; *President Roosevelt and the Coming of the War, 1941*, by Charles A. Beard; *America's Second Crusade*, by William Henry Chamberlin; *Design for War*, by Frederic R. Sanborn, published in 1951; and *The Final Secret of Pearl Harbor*, by Robert A. Theobald, published in 1954.

Gradually in the late 1940's and early 1950's scholars began to expand into new frontiers by research in unpublished manuscripts. Most of this group wrote from points of view sympathetic with the policies followed by the American government before Pearl Harbor. Robert E. Sherwood used the files of Harry Hopkins as the basis for his Pulitzer-prize-winning *Roosevelt and Hopkins*, published in 1948. *The Battle of the Atlantic* and *The Rising Sun in the Pacific*, by Samuel Eliot Morison, traced the naval side of the background of American entry into the war. *Chief of Staff: Prewar Plans and Preparations*, by Mark S. Watson, analyzed the role of the Army. Herbert Feis' study of American relations with Japan, entitled *The Road to Pearl Harbor*, was based on more extensive research than earlier volumes on that subject. The culmination of the internationalist interpretation came with the publication in 1952 and 1953 of the two-volume work by William L. Langer and S. Everett Gleason under the general title of *The World Crisis and American Foreign Policy*. This massive study, covering the years from 1937 to 1941, was sponsored and financed by the Council on Foreign Relations and the Rockefeller Foundation. These volumes were based not only on published materials but also on extensive research in the records of the Department of State and in the material at the Franklin D. Roosevelt Library at Hyde Park. Since the publication of the Langer-Gleason work, the most recent book written from this same general point of view is *The Passing of American Neutrality, 1937–1941*, by Donald F. Drummond, published in 1955. On the revisionist side, Charles Callan Tansill, after research comparable to that of Langer and Gleason, published his *Back Door to War* in 1952. Harry Elmer Barnes, who had published several pamphlets on the subject earlier, edited a volume called *Perpetual War for Perpetual Peace* that included essays written by most major revisionists. Richard N. Current's critical study, *Secretary Stimson*, was published in 1954. In addition, other books and numerous articles have appeared, particularly since 1950, on specialized aspects of the subject.

The interpretative controversies among historians concerning American entry into World War II are in part a direct extension of the pre–Pearl Harbor debate between interventionists and non-interventionists. Writers of history have not only dealt with the same basic subject and issues, but have also used the same arguments, made the same fundamental assumptions, and advanced similar hypotheses. For most major hypotheses advanced by postwar historians, counterparts could be found in the writings and speeches of prewar interventionists and non-interventionists. Furthermore, the debate among historians aroused some of the same emotional heat, the same ideological dogmatism, the same intolerance of conflicting views, and the same black-and-white portraits—on both sides—as were aroused in the "Great Debate" before Pearl Harbor. There are exceptions, of course, but there were also exceptions before Pearl Harbor.

In many instances the individuals who have written scholarly histories on the subject were involved directly (sometimes prominently) in the pre–Pearl Harbor foreign policy debate—and on the same side that they are now defending in their histories. There is no evidence that any of these writers was persuaded to change his basic point of view as the result of historical research after the war. It is true, of course, that Walter Millis' *Road to War*, published in 1935, was a major revisionist interpretation of American entry into World War I. Millis, however, was on the editorial staff of the interventionist New York *Herald Tribune*, and by 1939 he publicly endorsed the interventionist position. In June, 1940, he signed a petition urging an American declaration of war on Nazi Germany. In 1941 he was a sponsor of the Fight for Freedom Committee—a major pressure group advocating full United States participation in the war against the Axis. Robert E. Sherwood's Pulitzer-prize-winning play, *Idiot's Delight*, with its arraignment of war and war passions, undoubtedly aroused pacifist and non-interventionist emotions. By 1939–1941, however, Sherwood was an interventionist. He actively and prominently supported William Allen White's Committee to Defend America by Aiding the Allies. Harry Hopkins assured himself of the vigor of Sherwood's interventionist views before he added the playwright to President Roosevelt's speech-writing staff in 1940.

Barnes and Tansill refer to the internationalist writers as "Court Historians." One need not endorse the sinister implications of this sobriquet. Many internationalist writers, however, did have sympathetic personal ties and friendships with key figures in the events they described in their histories. Several of them have held important government positions in the administration whose foreign policies they were analyzing and evaluating. Ernest K. Lindley's personal friendship with President Roosevelt and other key administration figures enabled him to obtain special interviews and inside information for the preparation of his sympathetic volume. Robert E. Sherwood assisted President Roosevelt with the writing of his speeches from 1940 until the President's death in 1945. Herbert Feis was an economic adviser in the Department of State from 1931 to 1943 and was special consultant to the Secretary of War from 1944 to 1946. William L. Langer from 1941 to 1946 held various positions in the Office of Coordinator of Information, the Office of Strategic Services, and the Department of State. He served the Central Intelligence Agency in 1950–1951. S. Everett Gleason was with the Office of Strategic Services from 1943 to 1945 and the Department of State in 1945. He has served as deputy executive secretary to the National Security Council since 1950. Samuel Eliot Morison was commissioned in the naval reserve with the sole duty of preparing the history of United States naval operations in World War II. He rose to the rank of rear admiral by the time he retired in 1951. Mark S. Watson's book is a part of the official history of the Army in World War II. None of the major revisionist writers, on the contrary, held important administrative positions under either President Roosevelt or President Truman.

All revisionists for whom specific evidence is available adhered to the non-interventionist position before Pearl Harbor. Charles A. Beard's prewar "Continentalism" as expressed in such books as *The Open Door at Home* and *A Foreign Policy for America* is well known. He publicly endorsed (but did not join) the America First Committee, the leading non-interventionist pressure group before Pearl Harbor. He also testified against Lend-Lease before the Senate Foreign Relations Committee. Harry Elmer Barnes, one of the leading and more uncompromising revisionists regarding the origins of World War I, spoke at meetings of the America First Committee in 1941. Charles C. Tansill in 1938 published the best of the revisionist studies of American entry into World War I. George Morgenstern joined the editorial staff of the non-interventionist Chicago *Tribune* in 1941. For revisionist as well as internationalist it is possible to discern a continuity in viewpoint, extending from the pre– to the post–Pearl Harbor period.

Any brief summaries of the revisionist and internationalist interpretations of American entry into World War II can at best be no more than simplified versions of detailed and complicated accounts. It is necessary in presenting such a summary to pass over countless important details and individual variations in interpretation. There is, nevertheless, a wide area of agreement among writers on each side of the interpretative controversy.

Internationalist writers, looking back to the days before Pearl Harbor, view the Axis powers as extremely serious threats to American security and interests. They point to the strength and speed of the Axis forces which by the middle of 1940 had rolled over Austria, Czechoslovakia, Poland, Denmark, Norway, the Netherlands, Luxemburg, Belgium, and France. Britain alone was successfully resisting Nazi assaults on her home islands. By May, 1941, Hitler was in control of the Balkan Peninsula and was threatening the Middle East. Most authorities at the time expected the Soviet Union to fall quickly after Hitler's *Blitzkrieg* was turned against Russia on June 22, 1941. Axis successes in North Africa raised fears that control of that continent might prove a steppingstone to the Western Hemisphere. In the meantime Japan took advantage of the European crises to step up her aggressive campaigns in Asia.

According to the internationalist interpretation, President Roosevelt believed the United States could most effectively increase the possibility of peace in the 1930's by using its power to discourage potential aggressors from provoking war. In this aim, however, he was handicapped by the "isolationist" attitude of the American people and particularly by the powerful opposition in Congress. After war began in Asia and in Europe, according to this interpretation, the President hoped to prevent the United States from becoming involved in the hostilities—providing that could be accomplished without sacrificing American security, vital interests, and principles.

President Roosevelt and his major advisers believed that aggression by Germany and Italy in Europe constituted a more serious threat to American security than did Japanese actions in the Far East. In general, internationalist writers follow the administration view that the defeat of Nazi Germany and Fascist Italy was essential to American peace and security. Like the Roosevelt administration, most of these writers tend to rule out a negotiated peace as a possible acceptable alternative in Europe—particularly after the fall of France. President Roosevelt hoped that his policy of extending aid short of war to the victims of Axis aggression in Europe would prevent the defeat of Great Britain, contribute to the essential defeat of the Axis powers, and thereby enable the United States to maintain both its peace and its security. Among the many steps taken by the Roosevelt administration to aid the victims of aggression in Europe were repeal of the arms embargo, the destroyer deal, Lend-Lease, the Atlantic patrol system, occupation of Iceland, the shoot-on-sight policy, arming of American merchant ships, and permitting the use of those ships to transport goods directly to England.

According to the internationalist interpretation, Roosevelt and Hull wanted to prevent war between the United States and Japan—in part because such a war would interfere with the main task of defeating Hitler. They believed that the best way to preserve American peace and security in the Pacific was to take steps short of war to check Japanese aggression. Among American actions of this sort were the "moral embargo," the termination of the commercial treaty with Japan, various forms of aid to Chiang Kai-shek, keeping the American fleet at Pearl Harbor, and freezing Japanese assets in the United States. The United States was eager to seek a peaceful settlement with Japan—providing such a settlement would not jeopardize American security and principles, and providing it would not require the United States to abandon China, Britain, France, and the Netherlands in the Pacific. As it became increasingly apparent that compromise was impossible on terms acceptable to both countries, the Roosevelt administration tried to delay war to gain time for military preparations.

With regard to the European theater as well as the Pacific, there were distinct variations in the views of administration leaders before Pearl Harbor about implementing American policies and presenting them to the American people. Cordell Hull, hoping to avoid war and fearful of non-interventionist opposition, generally advised caution. He favored limiting action to steps short of war and he explained each step in terms of peace, security, and international morality. Henry L. Stimson, Frank Knox, Henry Morgenthau, Jr., and others were critical of the indirect and step-at-a-time approach. They early came to believe that aid short of war would not be sufficient to insure the defeat of the Axis and they urged the President to take more vigorous action against the agressors. Stimson believed the American people would support the President in a declaration of war even before Pearl Harbor. Of a different temperament, President Roosevelt, like Hull, was fearful of arousing effective public opposition to his policies and adhered to the step-at-a-time, short-of-war approach.

Internationalist interpretations tend to reflect these variations in attitudes among prewar interventionists. Feis treats Hull with considerable respect. Rauch's interpretation is similar to that advanced by Hull, though the hero in Rauch's book is definitely President Roosevelt. A number of writers, like Davis, Lindley, Millis, and Sherwood, generally feel that in view of conditions then existing President Roosevelt's decisions and methods on foreign policy matters were wise and sound at most crucial points before Pearl Harbor. Dexter Perkins has emphasized that Roosevelt's actions to check the Axis in Europe short of war reflected and expressed the desires of the majority of the American people. Langer and Gleason are sympathetic with the more direct and vigorous approach urged by Stimson—particularly as applied to the European theater. They believe that Roosevelt overestimated the strength of the opposition to his policies among the American people.

Writers of the internationalist school find the fundamental causes for American involvement in the war in developments in other parts of the world—beyond the American power to control by 1941. They do not find the explanation within the United States—except in so far as non-interventionist opposition inhibited administration actions that might have prevented the war from beginning or from reaching such a critical stage. Nearly all internationalist histories are highly critical of the opponents of Roosevelt's foreign policies. Needless to say, they all deny that President Roosevelt wanted to get the United States into war. They are convinced that the Japanese attack on Pearl Harbor was a genuine surprise to the members of the Roosevelt administration. These leaders knew that Japanese armed forces were under way and that war was imminent, but they expected the blows to fall in the southwest Pacific. In that event, administration leaders believed the United States would have to fight—though they were worried about the reaction of the American people to a declaration of war on Japan if American territory were not attacked. In so far as there was any American responsibility for the disaster at Pearl Harbor most internationalist writers blame the military commanders in Hawaii—Admiral Husband E. Kimmel and General Walter C. Short. None of them believe that there were any alternatives available to President Roosevelt by 1940–1941 which could have prevented American involvement in World War II without sacrificing American security and principles.

Revisionists have formed an entirely different estimate of Roosevelt's role and policies. Most of the revisionist interpretation can be summarized under four major headings. First, revisionists believe the Axis powers did not (or, need not—if the United States had followed wiser policies) constitute a serious threat to American security and vital interests. Second, they contend that President Roosevelt followed policies that he knew (or should have known) would lead to war in Asia and Europe and would involve the United States in those wars. Third, while leading the nation to war, the President

302 MYTHOLOGY OF ROOSEVELT, THE NEW DEAL, AND BEYOND

deceived the American people by telling them he was working for peace. And fourth, revisionists maintain that American policies before and during World War II contributed to the rise of a much more serious threat to peace and security—Communist Russia and her satellites.

In striking contrast to the internationalist interpretation, the revisionists minimize or reject the idea that the Axis powers constituted a threat to American security. They point out that Hitler had no concrete plans for attacking the Western Hemisphere. They portray the Japanese attack on Pearl Harbor as an action provoked by American restrictions that threatened Japanese security and vital interests. In so far as revisionists concede the reality of an Axis threat to the United States, they believe it was caused largely by American short-sighted and provocative policies. Like non-interventionists before Pearl Harbor, the revisionists maintain that the issue was not primarily security but instead was war or peace. And revisionists hold that the United States government had the power to choose for itself whether it would or would not enter the war. Thus, in contrast to internationalists, the revisionists find the explanation for American entry into World War II primarily within the United States rather than in the actions of nations in other parts of the world. In seeking the explanation within the United States, they focus their attention almost exclusively upon administration and military leaders—and particularly upon President Roosevelt.

Some revisionist historians believe that the Roosevelt foreign policies helped to provoke and prolong war in Asia and Europe. They interpret Roosevelt's steps to aid Britain short of war as actually steps *to* war. Opinions of revisionists vary on the question of whether Roosevelt deliberately meant these as steps to war. In any event, they contend, these actions did not provoke Hitler into war against the United States; and the shooting incidents that occurred in the Atlantic did not arouse American enthusiasm for entering the European war.

Instead, according to most revisionist writers, the Roosevelt administration got the United States into war through the Asiatic "back door" by provoking the Japanese attack on Pearl Harbor. This was accomplished by increasing pressures on Japan while refusing any compromise that the Japanese could accept. The decisive economic pressure in 1941 was exerted through the curtailment of oil shipments, and the key issue on which compromise proved impossible was China. The freezing of Japanese assets in the United States on July 26, 1941, accompanied by parallel action by the British and Dutch, virtually terminated American trade with Japan. This was particularly serious in cutting Japan off from her essential oil supplies. On August 17, 1941, at the suggestion of Churchill, President Roosevelt presented a formal and vigorous warning to the Japanese against further expansion. The President then rejected Premier Konoye's proposal for a personal meeting between the two leaders. Then, Secretary of State Hull, after objections from China and Britain, abandoned the idea of proposing a *modus vivendi*. Instead, on November 26, Hull (though aware that time was running out) submitted a ten-point program to Japan—including the demand that the Japanese withdraw from China and

Indo-China. This proposal (which revisionists generally call an "ultimatum") was so extreme that Hull knew in advance that Japan would not accept it. According to most revisionists these and other actions by the Roosevelt administration (out of either design or blunder) provoked war with Japan. The United States confronted Japan with the alternatives of backing down or fighting. With oil reserves falling dangerously low, and believing that their vital interests and security were at stake, the Japanese chose to fight.

Through all of this, according to the revisionists, President Roosevelt deceived the American people concerning his policies and objectives in foreign affairs. Revisionists maintain that Roosevelt publicly committed his administration to a policy of peace while secretly leading the nation to war—a war that these writers consider contrary to national interests and contrary to the desires of 80 percent of the American people. The most famous expression of this thesis is in Beard's last book and particularly in his final chapter.

Most revisionists maintain that administration and military leaders in Washington gave inadequate, ambiguous, and belated warnings to the commanders in Hawaii and withheld essential information from them. According to their contention, officials in Washington had sufficient information—including that obtained by breaking the Japanese secret diplomatic code—to anticipate an early Japanese attack. Futhermore, most of the revisionists believe that data at the disposal of leaders in Washington were sufficient (if properly analyzed) to have warned of a possible attack on Pearl Harbor. After Pearl Harbor, they say, the administration attempted unjustly to make General Short and Admiral Kimmel, the commanders in Hawaii, scapegoats for the tragedy. Instead of blaming the commanders in Hawaii, the revisionists place the main responsibility upon civilian and military leaders in Washington—including Marshall, Stark, Stimson, Knox, and particularly President Roosevelt. Tansill phrased the idea of Washington responsibility for the war most starkly when he wrote: "It seems quite possible that the Far Eastern Military Tribunal brought to trial the wrong persons. It might have been better if the tribunal had held its sessions in Washington." On this, as on other phases of the subject, some revisionists, including Beard, Current, and William L. Neumann, write in more restrained and qualified terms than either Tansill or Barnes.

Finally, the revisionists insist that the Roosevelt foreign policies failed to serve American national interests. If, as Roosevelt and Hull contended, American aid to the victims of aggression was designed to keep America out of war, these policies obviously failed. If the Roosevelt policies were designed to protect American security, they were, according to revisionists, of questionable success. By helping to crush Germany and Japan the United States removed two major barriers to Soviet expansion and created power vacuums and chaos which contributed to the rise of the Soviet Union to world power and to the resultant explosive Cold War situation. China, which was considered too vital to compromise in 1941, is now in Communist hands—in part, some revisionists say, because of Roosevelt's policies before and during World War II. Revisionists maintain in general that American involvement left the United States less secure, more burdened by debts and taxes, more laden with the necessity of maintaining huge armed forces than ever before in American history. Some revisionists predict that unless the United States returns to a policy of "continentalism" the nation may be headed for the nightmare described by George Orwell in *Nineteen Eighty-Four*, and toward World War III.

It is probable that the reception accorded the revisionist or the internationalist interpretation has been affected as much by the climate of thought and the international developments since Pearl Harbor as by the specific evidence and reasoning relied upon by historians. Emotional, ideological, political, economic, and military conditions from 1942 to 1950 contributed to a widespread acceptance of the internationalist interpretation. The historian who conformed to prevailing modes of thought in the profession did not seriously question the pro-Roosevelt interpretation of American entry into World War II. Revisionist hypotheses were viewed for the most part as biased and unsound. Critical references to the Beard group were in vogue.

With the breakdown of bipartisanship around 1950, the beginning of a new "Great Debate," the development of neo-isolationism of the Hoover-Taft-Knowland variety, and the Republican campaign of 1952, revisionist interpretations found a somewhat more receptive environment. The Cold War tensions and insecurity encouraged the conviction that American entry into World War II had some aftereffects dangerous to American security. These developments were supplemented by a growth of political, economic, and intellectual conservatism that encouraged a more critical attitude toward Roosevelt's prewar domestic policies as well as his actions in foreign affairs. Revisionist volumes and articles were published in increasing numbers. Although most historians continued to express themselves sympathetically toward Roosevelt's foreign policies before Pearl Harbor, there was a more widespread inclination to question specific features of the internationalist interpretation. Internationalist historians, such as Feis, or Langer and Gleason, phrased their accounts in moderate, restrained, and qualified terms. At the same time some revisionist historians became less defensive and more positive in their phrasing. But the neo-isolationism of the early 1950's did not win the dominant position in popular thought or national policies. And revisionist interpretations still failed to gain a really large following among American historians. It well may be that the future attitudes of many historians and of the American people toward American entry into World War II will be shaped as much by the future course of the United States as by the evidence uncovered by historical research.

Historians need not speak disparagingly, however, of the results of their inquiries during a period of only fifteen years on the subject of American entry into World War II. A prodigious amount of research has been accomplished. The diplomatic and military phases have been examined with striking thoroughness within the limits of available sources. Important beginnings have been made in the study of other aspects of the subject. Both revisionist and internationalist writers have advanced provocative and stimulating interpretations and have buttressed them with impressive documentation.

Despite these major accomplishments, there are important deficiencies and much work remains. Individuals will vary widely in their evaluations of what has been done and what remains to be done, but many of the criticisms of existing studies (criticisms which suggest possible directions for future efforts) may be analyzed under two major headings. In the first place, the narrow focus of most publications has left major areas almost untouched by serious historical research. Secondly—though the problem is probably incapable of final solution—there is need for a serious re-examination of the role and limitations of historical interpretation.

When measured by the standards of the "actualities" of pre–Pearl Harbor events, the scope and depth of available publications on American entry into World War II have been quite narrow in terms of time covered, subject matter, and source materials. Only a few books dealing specifically with this subject put it in the time context of the two World Wars. The volumes by Perkins, Chamberlin, Tansill, and Barnes all have this merit. Most studies of American entry into World War II, however, begin with 1940 or 1937. This point of departure is defensible if the scholar remains sensitively aware that he is examining only a tiny segment of the path that led to Pearl Harbor. Many historians, however, write almost as though the years from 1937 through 1941 were separated from and uninfluenced by earlier developments. For example, from a study of most available volumes a reader would not learn that these years were preceded by a devastating world depression with jolting economic, social, ideological, emotional, political, and power consequences that influenced the course of nations to December 7, 1941. Despite many important volumes and articles now available, there is much need for substantial research on foreign affairs in the years from 1921 to 1937. And a more meaningful perspective might be obtained if the subject were put in the broader context of the long-term but changing power relationships, industrialization of the world, the rise of the common man, and the development of secular ideologies designed to explain the mysteries of social, economic, and political changes whose ultimate form can only be dimly and imperfectly perceived.

Most published volumes are concerned largely with diplomatic, military, and some political aspects of the subject. The authors trace in intricate detail the policy planning, the minutiae of diplomatic exchanges, and the reactions of statesmen to the developments abroad. These phases are of major importance. They do not, however, constitute the whole story nor necessarily the most meaningful part. Economic, social, psychological, ethnic, religious, and political conditions that help to give direction and meaning to the diplomacy have been inadequately and imprecisely studied.

Political influences have been given much attention. Even the political analyses, however, often leave much to be desired when the subject is American entry into World War II. A good many historians on both sides have followed the almost standard procedure of charging individuals whose foreign policy views they do not like with partisan political motives. Writers on both sides often seem blind to political influences among those with whom they sympathize. Political analysts also have directed their attention largely to the top administration, military, and diplomatic officials. There has been relatively little serious study of the influence of individual congressmen and of state political organizations on the nation's foreign policies before Pearl Harbor. Furthermore, most references to political figures—even the prominent administration leaders—are of a two-dimensional variety. There is need for thorough biographies of scores of individuals. Frank Freidel's excellent biography of Franklin D. Roosevelt, now being published, suggests the sort of work needed on countless other figures in the story. Some important beginnings have been made, too, in studying sectional variations, but this subject has by no means been exhausted.

One need not be an economic determinist to be disturbed by the neglect of economic influences in existing histories of American entry into World War II. How did foreign policies affect those groups of persons who shared a particular economic interest? How did such effects influence the attitude of those groups toward foreign policy? What influence did those groups exert on policy making? Articles by John W. Masland and Roland N. Stromberg provide important beginnings on this phase of the subject, but much more remains to be done.

Samuel Lubell and John Norman have published studies on the foreign policy attitudes of German-Americans and Italian-Americans. There is need, however, for additional research on the role of numerous ethnic and religious groups in the history of American foreign affairs before Pearl Harbor. Volumes have been published on such pressure groups as the Committee to Defend America by Aiding the Allies, the Fight for Freedom Committee, the America First Committee, and the American Legion. But studies are needed on the attitudes and influence of countless other organized pressure groups of all sorts on American foreign policies before Pearl Harbor. Several books and articles have analyzed the non-interventionists and interventionists—but neither of these groups has by any means been exhausted as a field for constructive historical research.

There has been almost no serious research on the influence of psychological and emotional factors. Both revisionists and internationalists write almost as though the actions of the key figures could all be explained in intellectual and rational terms. It is conceivable that historians could learn as much about American entry into World War II by studying the psychological and emotional make-up of the individuals involved, as by studying the phrasing of the diplomatic dispatches and state papers. Ralph K. White, Harold Lavine, and James Wechsler have published suggestive studies on the role of propaganda in pre-Pearl Harbor developments, but for the most part the role of psychological influences on the attitudes of the American people and of American statesmen has scarcely been touched.

Results of the limited research on these non-diplomatic influences have seldom been integrated into the major works. Thomas A. Bailey's interpretative survey, *The Man in the Street*, contains more data on these phases of the subject than do any of the major volumes on American entry into World War II. But his study is suggestive rather than definitive.

In addition to the narrowness of approach with regard to time span and subject matter, there has been a narrowness in terms of the source materials used. If the focus of the subject matter is to be broadened as suggested in this article, historians will have to demonstrate a high degree of ingenuity in tapping additional source materials—including manuscripts in private hands. This appeal for greater breadth and depth is not meant to disparage the work thus far completed. But much of great importance remains to be done by scholars on the subject of American involvement in the war.

Montaigne's assertion that "nothing is so firmly believed as what we least know" suggests a second deficiency in most major volumes on American entry into World War II. The most heated controversies among historians do not center on those matters for which the facts and truth can be determined with greatest certainty. The interpretative controversies, on the contrary, rage over questions about which the historian is least able to determine truth. Despite the thousands of documents and tons of manuscripts, the written record and the physical remains constitute only a tiny fraction of the reality of America's course toward World War II—and these remains do not necessarily represent the "truth."

With the relatively inexact methods and incomplete data at his command, even the finest historian can often make only semi-informed guesses concerning motives, causes, and wisdom of pre–Pearl Harbor decisions. As Herbert Butterfield phrased it, the historian "can never quite carry his enquiries to that innermost region where the final play of motive and the point of responsibility can be decided. . . . He does not study human nature, therefore, in the way that an omniscient deity might observe it, with an eye that pierces our unspoken intentions, our thick folds of insincerity and the motives that we hardly avow to ourselves." The historian can determine that certain events preceded American entry into World War II and he may find circumstantial evidence suggesting possible causal relationships. But he cannot conduct controlled experiments to measure with any degree of certainty the causal significance of antecedent developments and incidents. Furthermore, these various interpretations of individual historians are based upon different opinions concerning the wisdom of possible pre–Pearl Harbor policies as judged in terms of certain criteria, such as world peace and security, American peace and security, economic order and prosperity, and freedom and democracy. As Sumner Welles phrased it, "The wisdom of any foreign policy can generally be determined only by its results." But in order to measure this wisdom, the results of policies that were actually followed would have to be compared with the results of possible alternative policies that were not followed. It is, of course, impossible to run controlled experiments to determine what would have happened if alternative policies had been followed. Furthermore, the possible alternatives were not necessarily of the simple "either/or" variety. The path to Pearl Harbor was filled with millions of decisions, great and small, each based upon other decisions which preceded it. There were countless forks in the road that led to Pearl Harbor. And no historian can know for certain what lay at the end of the paths that were not followed.

Writers on both sides, of course, are conscious of limitations inherent in historical interpretation. All of them qualify their generalizations with references to the inadequacy of their sources. But they recognize the limitations more clearly when referring to interpretations with which they do not agree. Sanborn, a revisionist, wrote that the internationalists' "first line of defense has always rested and still rests upon a foundation blended of faith, emotion, and hypothesis." Dexter Perkins, on the other side, has written that revisionism is "shot through with passion and prejudice. . . . It also rests upon hypotheses which . . . cannot be demonstrated." To a certain extent both Sanborn and Perkins are correct. But their generalizations apply in varying degree to books on *both* sides in the interpretative controversy.

Probably no one would want the historian to refrain from interpreting the course of events simply because he cannot scientifically prove the truth of his interpretations. The historian could not avoid some degree of interpretation even if he tried. Inadequate though his analyses may be, who is better qualified to perform the function? Both revisionist and internationalist historians have a responsibility to attempt to explain American entry into World War II as they understand it.

Nevertheless, considering the incompleteness and inexactness of their knowledge and understanding, historians do not seem justified in the cavalier, dogmatic tone that they so frequently use. They base their interpretations in part on a personal faith in the wisdom of the policies they support. Like devout believers in less secular faiths, writers on both sides tend to be intolerant of conflicting beliefs. This may not be true of all writers on the subject, but it does apply in varying degree to many on both sides. Historians need to emphasize the limits of their knowledge as well as the expansiveness of it. There is need for more awareness of the tentative nature of human inquiry, for self-criticism and the humility of an Albert Einstein, rather than the positive, dogmatic self-righteousness of the propagandist. Perhaps in the furious twentieth-century struggle for men's minds there can be no real place for moderation and restraint—even in historical interpretation. Numerous critics, however, both here and abroad, are fearful of the immaturity of American attitudes toward international affairs. If the historian is sensitive to the many-sided complexities of issues and demonstrates intellectual humility and ideological tolerance, perhaps others, influenced by his example, may be less inclined to grasp at simplified, crusading, utopian theories regarding contemporary international affairs.

The Liberals, Truman, and FDR as Symbol and Myth

Alonzo L. Hamby

Alonzo L. Hamby of Ohio University notes the important mythic qualities that conditioned Democratic politics as America witnessed the passing of the hero-president Franklin D. Roosevelt and the assumption of presidential power by his successor, Harry S. Truman. The tradition bequeathed from the Roosevelt to the Truman administration, says Professor Hamby, was one replete with symbol and myth. The unique charisma of FDR, as transformed into an equally unique source of inspiration by American liberals, cast a mythic shadow of skepticism over Truman's first administration. As Hamby perceives it, "the FDR mythology . . . added an emotional and subjective element to the liberal attitude." In the end, Truman's redemption would only be achieved through his upsct victory over Thomas E. Dewey in the presidential election of 1948.

We cannot think of President Roosevelt as one who is gone. He is here. Every hope, yes, the peace of the world, requires his constant spiritual presence. . . .

   How we miss him. Hardly a domestic problem or an international situation today but what we say "Oh, if F.D.R. were only here."

Fiorello La Guardia,
January 26, 1947,
WJZ radio script

With these words, spoken twenty-one months after Franklin D. Roosevelt's death, Fiorello La Guardia eloquently demonstrated a sense of loss and aimlessness which many liberals felt. The liberals, those middle-class reformers often described as "intellectuals," were held together by a body of well-articulated principles—equal opportunity, economic security, racial equality, international economic development, and the support of democratic forces abroad—but their sense of identity, as is the case with any social movement, depended also upon a mythology which gave inner inspiration, provided symbols for outer persuasion, and did much to determine their perceptions of reality. In the years immediately after World War II, the liberal mythology was built around the memory of Franklin D. Roosevelt and the New Deal.

   His death left the liberal movement in a state of crisis. His personality

From "The Liberals, Truman, and FDR as Symbol and Myth," by Alonzo L. Hamby, in *Journal of American History*, 56 (March 1970), pp. 859–867. Copyright © 1970 Organization of American Historians. Reprinted by permission.

had given the liberals unity as well as inspiration; Harry S. Truman could provide neither. Moreover, the ambiguity of FDR's legacy in foreign affairs left no sure guidelines in a chaotic and swiftly changing international situation. What followed was a period of demoralization and division among liberals, which is entirely understandable only if one grasps the importance of the myths and symbols that developed out of the memory of FDR.

Truman's lack of Rooseveltian qualities almost immediately distressed liberals. FDR had been sophisticated and cosmopolitan; Truman came from the small-town, Midwestern middle class. His cultural heritage, the *New Republic* commented, was not "too well attuned to the future of a world in depression, war, and revolution." FDR, the liberals believed, had been essentially an independent reformer; Truman was a party regular who had been associated with the notorious Pendergast machine. The liberals, somewhat mistakenly, thought of Franklin D. Roosevelt as an overpowering mass leader who could put a reform program through Congress by mobilizing public opinion. In contrast, Truman seemed weak and ineffective. The nation, commented *New Republic* columnist "T.R.B." in the spring of 1946, was "listening for a clarion call, but maybe the man who could give it is dead."

At least as disturbing as Truman's personal qualities was the steady departure from the administration of men who had been associated with the New Deal years and their displacement by the mediocre "cronies" whom the President seemed to find congenial. Truman had been in office only six weeks when a California liberal commented privately: "You get this stuff every place you turn: 'Truman is a nice man, but no superman; he is surrounded by a bunch of "regular" party hacks who are going to drive every decent person out of important administrative positions.' "

In 1945 and 1946, one New Dealer after another left the government, some voluntarily, some in anger. William H. Davis, head of the Office of Economic Stabilization, was arbitrarily fired. Robert Nathan, the deputy director of the Office of War Mobilization and Reconversion, resigned after he found himself unable to work or even communicate with his new chief, Truman's close friend, John Snyder. Samuel I. Rosenman, Franklin D. Roosevelt's close lieutenant, returned to private law practice. Harold Ickes, Secretary of the Interior, stormed out of the administration, outraged by Truman's effort to appoint Edwin Pauley, a California oil company executive, as undersecretary of the navy. Chester Bowles, the foremost champion of price controls, resigned in mid-1946 after, though not because of, policy disagreements with Snyder. And, in September 1946, Truman fired the most important of all the New Dealers, Henry Wallace, after a fundamental foreign-policy disagreement.

With each departure or dispute apprehension among liberals increased. "I have kept my confidence in [Truman's] integrity of purpose," Californian Bartley Crum wrote to Rosenman. "You can understand, however, that each resignation—top-side—makes the task of convincing others more difficult. It makes, in brief, for dissolution of the coalition of progressive forces." By the time Wallace was fired, the Chicago *Sun* felt that "the New Deal, as a driving force, is dead within the Truman administration."

There also was talk of a massive exodus of liberals from the government. "Hundreds on the lower levels have slipped out unnoticed . . .," wrote labor journalist Henry Zon, "and thousands of others are eyeing the door." Zon was probably exaggerating, but many did leave Washington. The "Truman climate" was not congenial to the bright, idealistic young lawyers who had come into the Roosevelt administration. As Zon remarked, it seemed more important to have a connection with Truman's old army outfit than with Felix Frankfurter. "Who wants to work in a set-up where you have to go through this forward-wall of politicians?" asked a disillusioned liberal within the administration, adding: "Even FDR's bad appointments were first-team." By late 1946, the New York *Post* was attributing the administration defeat in the congressional elections to the fact that: "The men who gave the New Deal its vitality have been brushed out of Washington."

Actually, many who left government service in 1945 and 1946—including Harry Hopkins, Rosenman, and Bowles—had no desire to repudiate Truman. They simply were physically and financially exhausted by arduous wartime jobs. Yet, as the astute journalist Cabell Phillips observed, they were more willing to leave an administration headed by Truman. Franklin D. Roosevelt had been a "spiritual anchor" holding them to their positions; Truman could play no such role.

Nor could Truman replace FDR as a source of inspiration who could unify the liberals. The fate of liberalism had been bound up to a remarkable extent with Franklin D. Roosevelt's personal fortunes. His talent as a political leader and manipulator had made it largely unnecessary for the liberals to do much of the day-to-day work of politics—the vital jobs of organizing and campaigning. His death left the liberal movement in disarray.

During World War II, the liberals had groped toward the objective of establishing a power base independent of the Roosevelt charisma. In 1941, some founded the Union for Democratic Action (UDA); but, despite the prestige of such leaders as Reinhold Niebuhr and Eleanor Roosevelt, it remained a weak little group tottering on the edge of bankruptcy. In 1944, the Congress of Industrial Organizations, as part of its ambitious political program, set up the National Citizens Political Action Committee; and at about the same time an impressive group of writers, artists, actors, directors, producers, and scientists formed the Independent Citizens Committee of the Arts, Sciences, and Professions. These organizations worked primarily for a common objective—the support of FDR—but it is questionable that many of their members looked beyond the Roosevelt era. Only a few liberals, most notably James Loeb, Jr., of UDA, sought to establish the attitudes and organizational base which would allow the liberal movement to transcend its dependence upon FDR. Franklin D. Roosevelt's sudden death cut their efforts short.

In 1946, as disillusion with Truman deepened and as the liberal movement suffered repeated defeats, many liberals felt that the memory of Franklin D. Roosevelt presented the best hope for the revival of their cause. John L. Nichols, a transportation consultant with an interest in Democratic politics, proposed an elaborate system of National Roosevelt Clubs in order to resuscitate the spirit of the New Deal and identify it with the Democratic party. Some important liberal politicians—Claude Pepper, Bowles, and Oscar Chapman—planned a national pressure group tentatively called the Roosevelt Forum. Both schemes proceeded from the assumption that Truman had rejected the New Deal. A memorandum outlining the ambitious plans for the Roosevelt Forum asserted that popular dissatisfaction with the Truman administration stemmed from "the fact that the leadership of the Democratic Party has turned away from the Roosevelt program and policies." Neither plan reached fruition because of the hostility of the Democratic National Committee and the intense activity underway on other fronts to rebuild the liberal movement.

At the end of 1946, the National Citizens Political Action Committee and the Independent Citizens Committee of the Arts, Sciences, and Professions merged to become the Progressive Citizens of America (PCA), which was under Wallace's informal leadership. Just a few days later, a greatly expanded Union for Democratic Action became the Americans for Democratic Action (ADA). It soon was apparent that these two new liberal organizations were involved in an irreconcilable conflict, despite the fact that both passionately identified with FDR. The struggle between PCA and ADA was the result of an argument among liberals about the nature of the Cold War. The argument demonstrated that, in some respects, the Roosevelt legacy was too hazy and ambiguous to serve as a sure guide for liberals and that it could not serve as a basis for liberal unity.

As the wartime alliance began to disintegrate, virtually all liberals assumed that FDR had developed the correct formula for dealing with the Soviet Union, but they differed in their interpretations of that formula. One group—probably a majority of the liberals until the announcement of the Marshall Plan and the shock of the Communist coup in Czechoslovakia—felt that FDR, by one means or another, would have preserved Big Three unity and that the Truman administration had junked FDR's foreign policies just as it had abandoned the Roosevelt heritage in domestic politics.

As early as December 1945, the Independent Citizens Committee, at a New York "crisis meeting," adopted a resolution asserting that the Truman administration was "departing from the tested and successful foreign policy of the late President Roosevelt." A few months later, the Win-the-Peace Conference, a gathering of diverse liberals and leftists reminiscent of the Popular Front, met in Washington and reasserted this position. Speakers combined criticism of Truman with eulogies of Franklin D. Roosevelt; FDR's picture was on the front page of the program; and large portraits of him dominated the meeting hall.

At about the same time, the first anniversary of Franklin D. Roosevelt's death, the widely read liberal columnist Samuel Grafton insisted that FDR could have prevented the Cold War:

> [I]t is because he is gone that the West, squealing legalisms, is now forlornly on the defensive, whereas if he had lived, blessed bad lawyer that he was, we might now be trying for a new level of international understanding.

For he, more than any other, was the coalition, he, could deal with Mr. Churchill as a country squire, and with Mr. Stalin as a commoner. Somehow, in him, the two currents had met, but not in a whirlpool; and the fact that these two contrary streams could produce a man so much at peace with himself and at ease with his world, made hope feasible for others.

In mid-1946, Elliott Roosevelt's *As He Saw It* seemed to confirm this viewpoint. Depicting his father as a determined opponent of British imperialism and a dedicated believer in Soviet-American friendship, Elliott Roosevelt asserted that FDR had forged a successful relationship with Joseph Stalin in the joint battle against fascism and reaction. FDR had listened to both sides and had established himself as an honest broker. But now the United States was blindly backing the British imperialists, and "a small group of willful men in London and Washington are anxious to create and foster an atmosphere of war hatred against the Russians. . . ."

Jonathan Daniels, a liberal southerner who had served as a presidential assistant throughout the war, expressed his agreement: "Nothing is so obvious as that the warm, human, smiling, face-to-face dealings Roosevelt made famous and effective have disappeared." Truman was a man of good intentions, but he had been pushed toward a break with FDR's foreign policies by state department reactionaries, conservative publishers, "Irish politicians and Claghorn senators." "He was—and I believe is—eager to fulfill the hopes Roosevelt delivered to him. But Mr. Truman is not Roosevelt."

In the fall of 1946, a wide and representative assembly of liberals, the Conference of Progressives, met in Chicago. Its foreign policy resolutions urged "a swift return to the progressive global thinking of Franklin Roosevelt," specifically the "recapture" of the Big Three unity which FDR had forged. The Conference also adopted a resolution of greeting to Wallace, who had just been ejected from the cabinet: "Carry on with confidence that you have the support of the millions upon millions of Americans who believe in the program of Franklin Delano Roosevelt."

Wallace himself constantly invoked the name of FDR and the symbols connected with it. Under his direction, the *New Republic* began a series of articles calling for "A New Deal With Russia." "Where are the millions who supported Roosevelt's ideals?" he asked, as he attempted to rally the liberal movement behind him. As he traveled around the country, large crowds actually paid admission to hear him, a phenomenon which the New York *Post* reluctantly conceded was "an eloquent demonstration of the widespread thirst for affirmative idealism in public life; a thirst which has been virtually unslaked since the death of President Franklin Delano Roosevelt."

Wallace's liberal opponents, however, drew upon their own version of the Roosevelt mythology and were equally convinced that they represented the Roosevelt heritage. Important policy differences were involved in the liberal split, but they were differences which could exist largely because the Roosevelt legacy in foreign policy was so vague. The argument, therefore, was also a dispute over which side could rightly invoke the name and symbolism of FDR. Adolf A. Berle, Jr., the old New Dealer and a leader of the New York

Liberal party, asserted, for example, not that FDR had been wrong or unrealistic in his attitudes toward the Russians, but rather that Elliott Roosevelt had reported these attitudes incorrectly—"a passionate perversion of the truth," he wrote indignantly. ADA stressed its connections with Rooseveltian symbols. Many of ADA's leading members had come to prominence under the New Deal and men like Leon Henderson, Bowles, Paul Porter, William Davis, Isador Lubin, Benjamin V. Cohen, and Elmer Davis, among others laid claim to the FDR aura. Moreover, Franklin D. Roosevelt, Jr., then a dynamic young politician of considerable ability, was, no doubt because of the memory of his father, ADA's foremost attraction as a speaker. Even more valuable was the membership of Eleanor Roosevelt. She was an asset so great that, shortly after ADA was established, Wallace attempted to minimize her affiliation, and ADA leadership responded with a sharp rebuke. After such an incident, an uninformed observer might well have wondered whether the liberal debate was about questions of substance and national interest or simply an argument over which side possessed the best claim to the memory of FDR.

There was, of course, more to liberal politics in the early postwar years than the memory of FDR, but liberal rhetoric and political perceptions were dominated to a remarkable extent by symbol and myth. Criticisms of Truman, for example, were almost invariably expressed in terms of a comparison with Franklin D. Roosevelt. The implication seemed to be that if Truman "departed" from a "Roosevelt policy," the departure had to be bad. If Truman's style was unlike Roosevelt's, then Truman could not be a liberal leader. Truman's policies might be discussed rationally; the FDR mythology, however, added an emotional and subjective element to the liberal attitude. Criticism became alienation. By 1948, there was little substantive policy difference between Truman and ADA liberals; yet ADA led a vain effort to replace the President with either Dwight D. Eisenhower or William O. Douglas. One reason was the belief that Truman would be a weak candidate, but also important was a quest for Rooseveltian charisma. Douglas, a vigorous New Dealer, was the special favorite of the liberals, although few of them believed that he could win the election. As one ADA member put it, "we would rather lose with Douglas than lose with Truman."

Moreover, it is difficult to imagine a major split among liberals on foreign policy had FDR lived. As it was, both factions argued that they were following the guidelines he had left. They seemed to assume that his course necessarily would have been the right one and that the conduct of foreign relations was primarily a matter of somehow discovering what he would have done. If both sides drew inspiration from their identification with him, they also had demonstrated that his memory could not serve as the unifying force which the liberals needed.

In 1947 and 1948, Truman at least partially provided leadership for the liberals by making the Marshall Plan the keystone of American foreign policy, vetoing the Taft-Hartley bill, advocating a comprehensive civil rights program, and striking blow after blow at the reactionary Eightieth Congress. As the presidential campaign began, an editorial cartoon in the New York *Star* depicted

Truman as a battered but undefeated figure holding aloft the flickering "Liberal Torch of F.D.R."

Truman's unexpected victory largely resolved the liberal division on foreign policy and won him a large degree of acceptance within the liberal movement. "This election clearly is a victory for the progressive principles and policies of Franklin D. Roosevelt," noted the St. Louis *Post-Dispatch.* "The New Deal and the Democratic Party did not die with their great champion," observed the New York *Post.* Truman, said Elmer Davis, "made a New Deal campaign and won a New Deal victory; at this moment he has made himself the successor to Roosevelt." Truman had not eclipsed the memory of FDR; he had succeeded in identifying himself with it. As a result, for the first time since April 1945, a majority of the liberals could feel that they had a leader in the White House.

Postwar America: Distorted Realities

Athan Theoharis

As tensions increased between the Communist and free worlds in the years after World War II in international arenas such as Eastern Europe and Korea, a relatively obscure U.S. senator from Appleton, Wisconsin, began a crusade designed to purge America of an imagined Communist conspiracy. In a famous Lincoln Day speech in Wheeling, West Virginia, in February of 1950, Senator Joseph R. McCarthy began his campaign to save America from Communism by declaring that the State Department was "infested" with disloyal conspirators. Before his censure by his Senate colleagues in December 1954 for conduct "contrary to senatorial traditions," he succeeded in casting suspicion on the character and patriotism of numerous Americans through a series of unsubstantiated charges, which one historian has called "multiple untruths." The McCarthy phenomenon, however, as seen by Professor Athan Theoharis of Marquette University, should not be dismissed as the product of one strangely disturbed mind. McCarthy found a basis for his rise to fame in the mythic Cold War atmosphere that many Americans, including President Truman, had done so much to create and perpetuate. The fantasy, illusion, and mass deception of the Cold War environment abroad inevitably influenced the direction of American politics at home—for example, the outcome of the 1952 presidential election. McCarthyism began to decline only as a result of its empty criticisms of the Eisenhower Republican administration.

In the early 1950's Joseph R. McCarthy, junior senator from Wisconsin, came to dominate American politics and to symbolize the phenomenon now called "McCarthyism." Relying on charges of "Communists in government" and accusing American leaders of being "soft toward Communism," Senator McCarthy and his followers attributed America's Cold War problems to subversive influence in the formulation of United States government policy. Their objective was not simply to remove that influence and alter the direction of United States policy but to discredit the administrations of Franklin D. Roosevelt and Harry S. Truman and, indirectly, the reform measures associated with the New Deal and Fair Deal. McCarthyism was not, however, an overtly conservative—that is, an antireformist—political movement. It drew its strength from popular concerns over national security, fears of internal subversion, and the people's underlying frustration with the costs and complexity of the Cold War.

McCarthyism offered no program to insure security. Instead, its approach, almost wholly negative, involved an emotional reaction to Cold War problems, chiefly an explanation of "conspiracy" for complex issues, that was attractive because it was simplistic. McCarthy's charges of Communist influence in fact paralleled, in an exaggerated way, the popular obsession with national security that arose after World War II. The Truman administration committed itself to victory over Communism and to safeguarding the nation from external and internal threats; the rhetoric of McCarthyism was in this sense well within the framework of Cold War politics. The senator and the administration differed not so much over ends as over means and emphasis.

McCarthyism perceived subversives in Washington, not Soviet power or strategic realities, as the major obstacle to achieving "victory over Communism." This focus on internal subversion distinguished the senator and his followers from Cold Warriors within the Truman administration as well as from earlier conservative critics of the New Deal.

Since the 1930's congressional conservatives had sought to discredit FDR's policies by charging Communist influence was behind them. After World War II, and especially in dramatic, well-staged and well-publicized hearings during 1947 and 1948, the House Committee on Un-American Activities reiterated these charges. During the 1950's McCarthy and his conservative congressional supporters focused on national security rather than political reform. With the postwar confrontation between Russia and the West as a backdrop, they assailed the administration's loyalty program as well as its foreign policy. The administration's security measures, they charged, were inadequate because the administration itself was sympathetic toward Communism or ignorant of its threat. Foreign policy was a failure because pro-Soviet or disloyal employees in the State Department and elsewhere had helped to formulate and execute it.

In the political climate produced by these charges, the Truman administration found it impossible to use its own anti-Communist record to advantage, or make political capital out of the fact that McCarthy's followers had often failed to support such measures as NATO, the Truman Doctrine, and universal military training. As fiscal conservatives, isolationists, and opponents of a strong executive, during the period 1945 through 1949 they had dissented from the Truman administration's attempts to contain Communism. Their anticommunism relied on verbal bluff, not military power. Their earlier concern over subversion had centered not on foreign espionage or sabotage but on what they believed to be the un-Americanism of domestic dissenters. Yet Truman's efforts to discredit McCarthy and his followers proved unconvincing and, ironically, even counterproductive.

In point of fact, as I argue in the pages that follow, McCarthyism derived its effectiveness from (1) the changed political climate that came with the intensification of the Cold War, and (2) President Truman's loss of credibility. The Cold War created the context, and Truman's rhetoric and leadership the political vacuum, that made the charges and appeals of McCarthyism not merely viable but persuasive to a great many Americans. Truman's loss of credibility stemmed partly from the nature of his rhetoric and the priority of his policies, and partly from the way he responded to McCarthyite charges. His difficulties were reinforced by a series of events at home and abroad in 1949 and 1950 which, seemingly, confirmed the existence of a subversive threat.

McCarthyism, then, was no aberration. It was a political movement in touch with the major concerns of Cold War politics. Its emergence dramatized the connection between foreign policy and domestic politics—specifically the way in which a suspicious, militaristic approach to foreign policy, emphasizing the subversive character of the Soviet threat, substantively altered the domestic political climate. The intensification of the Cold War, both because of the U.S.-Soviet conflict and Truman's rhetoric, changed national priorities and values, and in so doing created a distinctly conservative mood whose primary commitment was to absolute security and the status quo. . . .

Ascribing the nation's problems (both domestic and international) to the existence of "Communists in government," McCarthyites simultaneously stimulated and derived support from the popular belief that national security was truly being threatened—and would continue to be theatened—unless a more resourceful approach than the Truman administration's was adopted. Indeed, by 1950 many Americans had come to believe that (1) the Soviet Union had a definite strategy for the eventual communization of the world; (2) Soviet actions directly threatened the security of the United States; (3) that threat could assume the form of direct aggression or internal subversion; (4) the basic impetus to any revolutionary or radical political change was a Moscow-directed Communist conspiracy; (5) superior military power was essential to achieving peace and security; (6) a diplomacy of compromise and concession was in effect a form of appeasement and betrayal; (7) American objectives were altruistic and humanitarian; (8) the United States—because omnipotent—could shape the world to conform to American ideals and principles; (9) the God-fearing United States had to triumph over godless Communism; (10) international options were clear-cut and definable in terms of good versus evil; (11) the U.S. confrontation with the Soviet Union demanded not only the containment of Soviet expansion but the liberation of "enslaved peoples"; and (12) Communist leaders, whether in the Soviet Union, Eastern Europe, or China, lacked a popular base of support and were thus able to remain in power only through terror and subversion.

By 1950 these beliefs had strengthened popular demands for victory over Communism at home and abroad. Many Americans also believed that foreign policy could not be effective unless Communist infiltration of the government was prevented by a strong internal-security program. Thus the themes of "Communists in government" and "softness toward Communism," though they reflected different concerns and fears, were directly linked in the public mind: victory abroad could not be secured without victory at home; a dynamic foreign policy necessitated a rigorous internal-security program.

Popular fears about threats to American national security were far indeed from being endemic in the United States at the end of World War II. In 1945, according to opinion polls, most Americans believed that a durable peace required the continuation of Allied cooperation; thus they welcomed the Yalta Conference as a means of achieving that objective. Majority opinion supported Roosevelt's efforts to promote mutual trust and understanding with the Soviet Union; it recognized the necessity for compromise and appreciated the inevitable differences in purposes between the "democracies" of the United States, the Soviet Union, and Great Britain. In 1945 most Americans considered the Soviet Union to be not the Anti-Christ but a Great Power having legitimate security aims which sometimes conflicted with those of the United States. Most differences between the United States and the Soviet Union were considered resolvable through international conferences—particularly conferences involving the Big Three—and required diplomatic compromise, not military confrontation.

In line with these views, a popular distrust of the military prevailed. This distrust was reflected in support for limiting the role of the military in the control and development of atomic energy, demands for immediate demobilization of troops, and opposition to peacetime conscription. While appreciating the limits of American military power, many citizens also recognized the important role that anti-Nazi resistance forces and British and Soviet troops had played in the ultimate Allied victory over the Axis powers.

In short, majority opinion in America believed in neither the omniscience nor the omnipotence of the United States; peace and security depended on continued American cooperation with other nations, whether major or minor powers. Finally, most Americans demanded that the administration pursue an internationalist foreign policy—multilaterally rather than unilaterally run. They considered economic problems the basis of threats to world peace, and felt that these could be settled through aid and negotiation.

By 1950 a dramatic shift in this outlook had taken place, and it contributed to the emergence of McCarthyism. It was a reaction that differed considerably from the conservative reaction following World War I. The earlier Red Scare [in 1919–1920] had been a direct product of the passions and fears wrought by American involvement in the war, and represented a distinct domestic political conservatism. In contrast, McCarthyism was not directly a product of the war, since it appeared not in 1945 but in 1950, nor was its thrust overtly antiprogressive. Instead it was the product of the Cold War confrontation between the United States and the Soviet Union and the resulting obsession on the part of Americans with national security. Because this confrontation was viewed not in terms of power politics but in distinctly moralistic terms, it led to no less than an oversimplified belief in the possibility of, indeed demand for, victory over the Soviet Anti-Christ.

This change in national opinion was in great part shaped by the rhetoric of the Truman administration. In the period 1945–1949—that is, before Senator McCarthy's Wheeling speech—the Truman administration conducted foreign policy debate along narrowly anti-Communist lines. To secure support for its containment policy, from 1947 through 1949 administration rhetoric vastly oversimplified the choices confronting the nation; it also characterized international change in terms of crisis and national security. Indeed, the administration's anti-Communist rhetoric, the thrust of its appeals both before and after McCarthy's Wheeling speech, did not differ substantively from that of McCarthy and his conservative congressional supporters.

After 1945 the Truman administration had gradually, yet distinctly, renounced the priorities of the Roosevelt administration. The bases for this shift are to be found in two dominant strains of Truman's thought: a deep distrust of Soviet objectives, and a belief in the importance of military superiority. In contrast to Roosevelt's sophisticated international approach, which relied on negotiation and détente, Truman's outlook—an outlook shaped by his World War I experience, his active participation in the American Legion, and his antipathy to the isolationism and antimilitarism of the 1930s—was based on the primacy of power in international politics. Although an avowed internationalist and advocate of peace, Truman believed that peace could best be secured through military deterrence and alliances. Unlike Roosevelt, whose distrust of the Soviet Union was mitigated by an expediential wartime alliance and an appreciation that Soviet involvement in Eastern Europe was as legitimate a security objective as United States involvement in Latin America, Truman felt that Soviet expansion merely confirmed the Soviet leaders' perfidy and imperialistic intentions, and thus must be averted.

Accordingly, Truman's "internationalism" assumed a unilateral form in which American national interests became the sole foundation for cooperation and peace. More importantly, in 1945, and increasingly after 1948, the administration tended to subordinate traditional diplomatic or economic options to its overriding commitment to attaining superior military power. In contrast to Roosevelt's view that disagreement, even conflict, between the United States and the Soviet Union was inevitable—and possibly even salutary, insuring a diverse world order—Truman made his administration's long-term goal the achievement of "freedom" and "democracy" for the peoples of Eastern Europe, the Soviet Union, China, and the underdeveloped world. He characterized the U.S.-Soviet conflict in moralistic terms, seeing America's role as a "mission," and redefining "appeasement" to mean the failure of the United States to confront revolutionary or disruptive change head-on. A sense of American omnipotence, the belief that the United States could impose its will on the postwar world, was behind the Truman administration's rhetoric on foreign policy.

Yet this shift away from Roosevelt's foreign policy developed gradually. The 1952 priorities of the Truman administration differed radically from its 1945 priorities. This shift resulted in part from Soviet actions in Eastern Europe and the United Nations, in part from the administration's reassessment of basic foreign policy questions. What would have been politically feasible in 1945 had become politically impossible by 1952, for by then the administration, trapped in its own rhetoric, could no longer even suggest that any Soviet interest in peace or negotiation was valid. . . .

By 1951 Truman's hotted-up rhetoric had caused a loss of credibility in his administration. On the one hand, the administration repeatedly emphasized the gravity of the crisis posed by Soviet subversion and expansionism and expressed confidence in eventual success if the American public only possessed the necessary will and purpose to carry out Truman's policies. All the while it continued to characterize the U.S.-Soviet opposition as a confrontation between American Christian selflessness and Communist atheistic expansionism. On the other hand, quite apart from the forcefulness of its rhetoric, the administration was actually pursuing a policy of restraint in its use of military power, conducting its military operations within firm strategic guidelines. In point of fact, American military potential, particularly nuclear weapons, was by no means fully utilized in Korea: the air war was limited to the Korean peninsula, and Chinese Nationalist troops were confined to Formosa. Nor did the administration use either potential military resources or diplomatic pressure to effect the liberation of the "satellite" peoples. The Chinese Nationalists were prevented from attempting to free the mainland Chinese; Eastern European exiles were neither encouraged nor supplied with weapons; and, despite Soviet violations, the administration opposed congressional efforts to repudiate the Yalta agreements.

These military and political restrictions were inconsistent with the total war against Communism which the administration advertised in its rhetoric, and they were in direct contradiction to its projection of what would come about if Soviet subversion were not vigorously confronted. Indeed, if the Soviet threat was worldwide, if world peace and the very liberties of the American people were ultimately threatened by the Korean conflict—and the Truman administration had repeatedly said as much—then nothing less than the full use of American military might in Korea was required. Thus, to countenance military and political restraint, as Truman and his administration clearly did, seemed to be either a misunderstanding of the seriousness of the Communist threat to American security or a dereliction of duty. To argue that restraint was necessary to prevent the escalation of Korea into a world war seemed to reflect a staggering ignorance of the Soviet Union's basic intention—as Truman had time and again declared it to be—of utterly destroying Western Christian democracy.

The inconsistencies between the Truman administration's go-for-broke rhetoric and its cautious military response in Korea paved the way for the success of Joseph McCarthy and his followers. The moralistic and defensive tenor of administration rhetoric, its stress on the American "mission," its emphasis on national security, and its strained definition of Communist subversion—all served to create a climate in which such terms as "sell-out," "betrayal," "liberation," and "victory" could be successfully used by the McCarthyites against the Truman administration. By exploiting the inconsistencies between administration rhetoric and response, McCarthy and other congressional conservatives were able to "explain" that the real Soviet threat to the national security was internal subversion. They thereby capitalized on both fears of a third world war and doubts about the administration's methods and intentions in foreign affairs.

The McCarthyites never did, nor were they required to, formulate an alternative course to Truman's. Instead, because of the inconsistency between administration rhetoric and response, they were able to concentrate on criticizing past administration policy decisions and personnel. Because the administration had set an American peace as its rhetorical goal, the McCarthyites could blame the "failure" to achieve that peace on either the administration's ignorance of the threat of Communism, or its lax security procedures which enabled Communists and their sympathizers to infiltrate the government and help bring about pro-Soviet policies. Although this critique was simplistic, conspiratorial at its base, and rather sleazily moralistic it nonetheless neatly used administration rhetoric to condemn administration policy. Through its own rhetoric, the Truman administration had closed the vicious circle on itself. All the McCarthyites had to do was chase around it. . . .

The specifically anti-Communist crusade led by the junior senator from Wisconsin and called McCarthyism in the end turned out to be an ephemeral phenomenon. In large part it was the direct product of the inception of the Cold War and the presidency of Harry S. Truman. When the Eisenhower administration came into office it continued, or at any rate neglected to change, many of those Truman administration policies which McCarthy and his conservative congressional supporters had specifically opposed. Consistency as well as political expediency required that McCarthy and his supporters also denounce the Eisenhower administration. But doing so ultimately undermined their former image of disinterested patriotism; for the nature of their critique reflected less consistency than concern over the loss of a good campaign issue. In stridently attacking their own Republican administration, they inadvertently identified themselves as reactionaries, and thereby disclosed their real character—formerly masked by the announced goal of preserving the national security—as a self-interested, anti–New Deal minority.

This is not to say that the Eisenhower administration ever formally repudiated Senator McCarthy and his conservative adherents, though after 1952 it challenged, if only indirectly, the McCarthyite influence by advancing measures which tacitly repudiated its earlier tolerance of McCarthyism. During the 1952 presidential campaign, Eisenhower and his supporters had found it politically expedient to accept McCarthy's charges of "treason and betrayal" in high places. If for no other reason, not to have done so would have indirectly affirmed the Truman administration's consistent contention between 1950 and 1952 that McCarthy and his conservative congressional supporters were irresponsible, their criticism both inimical to the national interest and wholly partisan in motivation. . . .

In the final analysis, McCarthyite criticisms of the Eisenhower administration, which were essentially a repetition of the tactics and charges directed at the more vulnerable Truman administration, were counterproductive. By attacking Eisenhower, McCarthy and other conservative congressmen overstepped the bounds of their popular support. The public did not mistrust Eisenhower as it had Truman, and certainly not in the early years of his administration when McCarthy unwisely launched his attack. Eisenhower's tremendous popularity, the absence of any dramatic evidence of personnel disloyalty in his administration, and the public's gradual if reluctant acceptance of the possibility of negotiating with the Soviet Union had by 1955 rendered McCarthy's and the McCarthyites' tactics ineffective—if not offensive. In fact, McCarthyite attacks on the Eisenhower administration only enhanced the administration's standing with the public. In contrast to McCarthy's frenzied tone and shotgun charges—particularly in the Army hearings of 1954, his Waterloo—the administration appeared a veritable repository of reason and moderation.

Eisenhower was not Truman, and it was Truman and such Cold War liberals as Acheson and McGrath who, by heightening popular fears of communism and raising distrust about executive priorities and methods, had helped to create the phenomenon of McCarthyism. Eisenhower's election and his subsequent foreign policy decisions reduced the effectiveness of McCarthyite charges and dramatically, though unintentionally, revealed McCarthyism to be an irresponsible force in American politics. McCarthy's former image of objectivity was thereby destroyed. Yet to the extent that absolute security and containment remained basic objectives of United States policy, post-1955 foreign policy debate remained narrowly circumscribed. In that sense, the tactics of Joseph McCarthy and his supporters of pointing out guilt by association and charging leaders with being "soft on communism" continued to be an essential part of national politics. The immediate and direct impact of McCarthyism might have been reduced, but even today it lingers on as a conservative force in American political life.

The Ike Age:
The Revisionist View of Eisenhower

Stephen E. Ambrose

In many ways, Dwight Eisenhower's years in the White House (1953–1961)
revitalized old brands of American mythology. There was a renewed commitment,
for example, to the economic legend that an unbalanced budget would bring financial
ruin to America—even though Eisenhower succeeded in balancing the budget in only
two of his eight years as president. Ike's years in office also witnessed a reemphasis
of the sacred American belief that the public affairs of the nation could only reputably
be handled by those with a business background or predisposition—as stated by a
contemporary cabinet member, "What's good for General Motors is good for
America." With the assistance of historical hindsight, however, certain elements of
the Eisenhower era appear to deserve praise. The stereotyped image of the army
general–president as a conservative leader with few redeeming qualities is well on
its way toward being revised. Though many do not share all his conclusions, Ike's
biographer Stephen E. Ambrose of the University of New Orleans is in the vanguard
of Eisenhower revisionism, citing Eisenhower's standing relative to subsequent
presidents, his ending of the Korean conflict, his refusal to engage the United States
more deeply in Southeast Asia, and his control of the arms race. Rather than simply
being seen as an amiable and none-too-assertive public figure, a "captive hero" who
delegated responsibility to subordinates while he himself read Westerns and played
golf, Eisenhower needs to be seen as a president of real achievement—one having
carefully conceived policies and firm leadership skills.

Since Andrew Jackson left the White House in 1837, 33 men have served as
president of the United States. Of that number, only four have managed to
serve eight consecutive years in the office—Ulysses Grant, Woodrow Wilson,
Franklin Roosevelt, and Dwight Eisenhower. Of these four, only two were also
world figures in a field outside politics—Grant and Eisenhower—and only two
had a higher reputation and broader popularity when they left office than when
they entered—Roosevelt and Eisenhower.

Given this record of success, and the relative failure of Ike's successors,

From "The Ike Age: The Revisionist View of Eisenhower," by Stephen E. Ambrose, in *The New
Republic* (May 9, 1981), pp. 26–28 and 30–34. Reprinted by permission of *The New Republic*, ©
1981, The New Republic, Inc.

it is no wonder that there is an Eisenhower revival going on, or that President Reagan and his staff . . . attempt[ed] to present themselves as the Eisenhower administration resurrected. Another major reason for the curent Eisenhower boom is nostalgia for the 1950s—a decade of peace with prosperity, a 1.5 percent annual inflation rate, self-sufficiency in oil and other precious goods, balanced budgets, and domestic tranquility. Eisenhower "revisionism," now proceeding at full speed, gives Ike himself much of the credit for these accomplishments.

The reassessment of Eisenhower is based on a multitude of new sources, as well as new perspectives, which have become available only in the past few years. The most important of these is Ike's private diary, which he kept on a haphazard basis from the late 1930s to his death in 1969. Other sources include his extensive private correspondence with his old military and new big business friends, his telephone conversations (which he had taped or summarized by his secretary, who listened in surreptitiously), minutes of meetings of the cabinet and of the National Security Council, and the extensive diary of his press secretary, the late James Hagerty. Study of these documents has changed the predominant scholarly view of Eisenhower from, in the words of the leading revisionist, political scientist Frcd Greenstein of Princeton, one of "an aging hero who reigned more than he ruled and who lacked the energy, motivation, and political skill to have a significant impact on events," to a view of Ike as "politically astute and informed, actively engaged in putting his personal stamp on public policy, [who] applied a carefully thought-out conception of leadership to the conduct of his presidency."

The revisionist portrait of Ike contains many new features. Far from being a "part-time" president who preferred the golf course to the Oval Office, he worked an exhausting schedule, reading more and carrying on a wider correspondence than appeared at the time. Instead of the "captive hero" who was a tool of the millionaires in his cabinet, Ike made a major effort to convince the Republican right wing to accept the New Deal reforms, an internationalist foreign policy, and the need to modernize and liberalize the Republican party. Rather than ducking the controversial issue of Joseph McCarthy, Eisenhower strove to discredit the senator. Ike's failure to issue a public endorsement of *Brown v. Topeka* was not based on any fundamental disagreement with the Warren Court's ruling, but rather on his understanding of the separation, the balance, of powers in the U.S. government—he agreed with the decision, it turns out, and was a Warren supporter. Nor was Ike a tongue-tied general of terrible syntax; he was a careful speaker and an excellent writer who confused his audiences only when he wanted to do so.

Most of all, the revisionists give Eisenhower high marks for ending the Korean War, staying out of Vietnam, and keeping the peace elsewhere. They argue that these achievements were neither accidental nor lucky, but rather the result of carefully conceived policies and firm leadership at the top. The revisionists also praise Ike for holding down defense costs, a key factor in restraining inflation while maintaining prosperity.

Altogether, the "new" Ike is an appealing figure, not only for his famous grin and winning personality, but also because he wisely guided us through perilous times.

"The bland leading the bland." So the nightclub comics characterized the Eisenhower administration. Much of the blandness came from Ike's refusal to say, in public, anything negative about his fellow politicians. His lifelong rule was to refuse to discuss personalities. But in the privacy of his diary, parts of which have just been published with an excellent introduction by Robert H. Ferrell (*The Eisenhower Diaries*, W. W. Norton), he could be sarcastic, slashing, and bitter.

In 1953, when Ike was president and his old colleague from the war, Winston Churchill, was prime minister, the two met in Bermuda. Churchill, according to Ike,

> has developed an almost childlike faith that all of the answers to world problems are to be found merely in British-American partnership. . . . He is trying to relive the days of World War II. In those days he had the enjoyable feeling that he and our president were sitting on some rather Olympian platform . . . and directing world affairs. Even if this picture were an accurate one of those days, it would have no application to the present. But it was only partially true, even then, as many of us who . . . had to work out the solutions for nasty local problems are well aware.

That realistic sense of the importance of any one individual, even a Churchill or a Roosevelt, was basic to Eisenhower's thought. Back in 1942, with reference to MacArthur, Ike scribbled in his diary that in modern war, "no one person can be a Napoleon or a Caesar." What was required was teamwork and cooperation.

Although Lyndon Johnson, John F. Kennedy, Hubert Humphrey, and other Democratic senators of the 1950s catch hell from time to time in Ike's diary, he reserved his most heartfelt blasts for the Republicans (he never expected much from the Democrats anyway). Thus, Ike wrote of Senator William Knowland of California, "In his case there seems to be no final answer to the question 'How stupid can you get?' " In *Eisenhower the President* (Prentice-Hall), William Bragg Ewald Jr., a former Eisenhower speechwriter, records that when Republicans urged Ike to convince Nelson Rockefeller to take the second place on a 1960 ticket with Richard Nixon, Ike did so, rather half-heartedly, and then reported on Rockefeller: "He is no philosophical genius. It is pretty hard to get him in and tell him something of his duty. He has a personal ambition that is overwhelming." Eisenhower told Nixon that the only way to persuade Rockefeller to run for the vice presidency was for Nixon to promise to step aside in Rockefeller's favor in 1964.

Ike didn't like "politics," and he positively disliked "politicians." The behind-the-scenes compromises, the swapping of votes for pork-barrel purposes, the willingness to abandon conviction in order to be on the popular side all nearly drove him to distraction. His favorite constitutional reform was to limit congressional terms to two for the Senate and three or four for the House, in order to eliminate the professional politician from American life.

Nor did Ike much like the press. "The members of this group," he wrote in his diary, "are far from being as important as they themselves consider," but he did recognize that "they have a sufficient importance . . . in the eyes of the average Washington officeholder to insure that much government time is consumed in courting favor with them and in dressing up ideas and programs so that they look as saleable as possible." Reporters, Ike wrote, "have little sense of humor and, because of this, they deal in negative criticism rather than in any attempt toward constructive helpfulness." (Murray Kempton, in some ways the first Eisenhower revisionist, recalled how journalists had ridiculed Ike's amiability in the 1950s, while the president actually had intelligently confused and hoodwinked them. Kempton decided that Eisenhower was a cunning politician whose purpose was "never to be seen in what he did.")

The people Ike did like, aside from his millionaire friends, were those men who in his view rose above politics, including Milton Eisenhower, Robert Anderson, and Earl Warren. Of Milton, Ike wrote in 1953, "I believe him to be the most knowledgeable and widely informed of all the people with whom I deal. . . . So far as I am concerned, he is at this moment the most highly qualified man in the United States to be president. This most emphatically makes no exception of me. . . ." Had he not shrunk from exposing Milton to a charge of benefiting from nepotism, Ike would have made his younger brother a member of his cabinet.

In 1966, during an interview in Eisenhower's Gettysburg office, I asked him who was the most intelligent man he had ever met, expecting a long pause while he ran such names as Marshall, Roosevelt, de Gaulle, Churchill, Truman, or Khrushchev through his mind. But Ike never hesitated: "Robert Anderson," he said emphatically. Anderson, a Texan and a Democrat, served Ike in various capacities, including secretary of the navy and secretary of the treasury. Now Ewald reveals for the first time that Eisenhower offered Anderson the second spot on the Republican ticket for 1956 and wanted Anderson to be his successor. Anderson turned down the president because he thought the offer was politically unrealistic.

Which inevitably brings up the subject of Richard Nixon. Eisenhower's relations with Nixon have long been a puzzle. Ike tried to get Nixon to resign during the 1952 campaign, but Nixon saved himself with the Checkers speech. In 1956 Ike attempted to maneuver Nixon off the ticket by offering him a high-level cabinet post, but Nixon dug in his heels and used his connections with the right wing of the party to stay in place. And in 1960, Ike's campaign speeches for Nixon were distinctly unenthusiastic. Still, Eisenhower and Nixon never severed their ties. Ike stuck with Nixon throughout his life. He often remarked that Nixon's defeat by Kennedy was one of his greatest disappointments. And, of course, his grandson married one of Nixon's daughters. Sad to say, neither the diary nor the private correspondence offers any insights into Eisenhower's gut feelings toward Nixon. The relationship between the two men remains a puzzle.

Some writers used to say the same about the Eisenhower–Earl Warren relationship, but thanks to Ike's diary, Ewald's book, and the correspondence, we now have a better understanding of Eisenhower's feelings toward Warren personally, and toward his Court. In December 1955, Jim Hagerty suggested that if Ike could not run for a second term for reasons of health, Warren might make a good nominee. "Not a chance," Ike snapped back, "and I'll tell you why. I know that the Chief Justice is very happy right where he is. He wants to go down in history as a great Chief Justice, and he certainly is becoming one. He is dedicated to the Court and is getting the Court back on its feet and back in respectable standing again."

Eisenhower and Warren were never friends; as Ewald writes, "For more than seven years they sat, each on his eminence, at opposite ends of Pennsylvania Avenue, by far the two most towering figures in Washington, each playing out a noble role, in tragic inevitable estrangement." And he quotes Attorney General Herbert Brownell as saying, "Both Eisenhower and Warren were very reserved men. If you'd try to put your arm around either of them, he'd remember it for sixty days."

Ike had a great deal of difficulty with *Brown v. Topeka*, but more because of his temperament than for any racist reasons. He was always an evolutionist who wanted to move forward through agreement and compromise, not command and force. Ike much preferred consensus to conflict. Yet Ewald argues that he privately recognized the necessity and justice of *Brown v. Topeka*. Even had that not been so, he would have supported the Court, because—as he carefully explained to one of his oldest and closest friends, Sweed Hazlett, in a private letter—"I hold to the basic purpose. There must be respect for the Constitution—which means the Supreme Court's interpretation of the Constitution—or we shall have chaos. This I believe with all my heart—and shall always act accordingly."

Precisely because of that feeling, Eisenhower never made a public declaration of support for the *Brown v. Topeka* decision, despite the pleas of liberals, intellectuals, and many members of the White House staff that he do so. He felt that once the Supreme Court had spoken, the president had no right to second-guess nor any duty to support the decision. The law was the law. That Ike was always ready to uphold the law, he demonstrated decisively when he sent the U.S. Army into Little Rock in 1957 to enforce court-ordered desegregation.

Despite his respect for Warren and the Court, when I asked Eisenhower in 1965 what was his biggest mistake, he replied heatedly, "The appointment of that S.O.B. Earl Warren." Shocked, I replied, "General, I always thought that was your best appointment." "Let's not talk about it," he responded, and we did not. Now that I have seen the flattering and thoughtful references to Warren in the diary, I can only conclude that Eisenhower's anger at Warren was the result of the criminal rights cases of the early 1960s, not the desegregation decisions of the 1950s.

As everyone knows, Ike also refused publicly to condemn Senator McCarthy, again despite the pleas of many of his own people, including his most trusted adviser, Milton. Ike told Milton, "I will not get into a pissing contest with that skunk."

The revisionists now tell us that the president was working behind the scenes, using the "hidden hand" to encourage peaceful desegregation and to censure McCarthy. He helped Attorney General Brownell prepare a brief from the Justice Department for the Court on *Brown v. Topeka* that attacked the constitutionality of segregation in the schools. As for McCarthy, Greenstein writes that Eisenhower,

> working most closely with Press Secretary Hagerty, conducted a virtual day-to-day campaign via the media and congressional allies to end McCarthy's political effectiveness. The overall strategy was to avoid *direct mention* of McCarthy in the president's public statements, lest McCarthy win sympathy as a spunky David battling against the presidential Goliath. Instead Eisenhower systematically condemned the *types* of actions in which McCarthy engaged.

Eisenhower revisionism is full of nostalgia for the 1950s, and it is certainly true that if you were white, male, and middle class or better, it was the best decade of the century. The 1950s saw peace and prosperity, no riots, relatively high employment, a growing GNP, virtually no inflation, no arms race, no great reforms, no great changes, low taxes, little government regulation of industry or commerce, and a president who was trusted and admired. Politics were middle-of-the-road—Eisenhower was the least partisan president of the century. In an essay entitled "Good-By to the 'Fifties—and Good Riddance," historian Eric Goldman called the Eisenhower years possibly "the dullest and dreariest in all our history." After the turmoil of the 1960s and 1970s—war, inflation, riots, higher taxes, an arms race, all accompanied by a startling growth in the size, cost, and scope of the federal government—many Americans may find the dullness and dreariness of the 1950s appealing.

Next to peace, the most appealing fact was the 1.5 percent inflation rate. The revisionists claim that Ike deserved much of the credit for that accomplishment because of his insistence on a balanced budget (which he actually achieved only twice, but he did hold down the deficits). Ike kept down the costs by refusing to expand the New Deal welfare services—to the disgruntlement of the Republican right wing, he was equally firm about refusing to dismantle the New Deal programs—and, far more important, by holding down defense spending.

This was, indeed, Ike's special triumph. He feared that an arms race with the Soviet union would lead to uncontrollable inflation and eventually bankrupt the United States, without providing any additional security. In Ike's view, the more bombs and missiles we built, the less secure we would be, not just because of the economic impact, but because the more bombs we built, the more the Soviets would build. In short, Ike's fundamental strategy was based on his recognition that in nuclear warfare, there is no defense and can be no winner. In that situation, one did not need to be superior to the enemy in order to deter him.

The Democrats, led by Senator John F. Kennedy, criticized Ike for putting a balanced budget ahead of national defense. They accused him of allowing a "bomber gap" and, later, a "missile gap" to develop, and spoke of the need to "get America moving again." Nelson Rockefeller and Richard Nixon added to the hue and cry during the 1960 campaign, when they promised to expand defense spending. But as long as Eisenhower was president, there was no arms race. Neither the politicians nor the military-industrial complex could persuade Eisenhower to spend more money on the military. Inheriting a $50 billion defense budget from Truman, he reduced it to $40 billion and held it there for the eight years of his tenure.

Holding down defense costs was a long-standing theme of Ike's. As early as December 1945, just after he replaced George Marshall as army chief of staff, he jotted in his diary, "I'm astounded and appalled at the size and scope of plans the staff sees as necessary to maintain our security position now and in the future." And in 1951, before he became a candidate, he wrote in his diary that if the Congress and military could not be restrained about "this armament business, we will go broke and still have inefficient defenses."

President Eisenhower was unassailable on the subject. As one senator complained, "How in hell can I argue with Ike Eisenhower on a military matter?" But as Ike wrote in 1956 to his friend Hazlett, "Some day there is going to be a man sitting in my present chair who has not been raised in the military services and who will have little understanding of where slashes in their estimates can be made with little or no damage. If that should happen while we still have the state of tension that now exists in the world, I shudder to think of what could happen in this country."

One reason why Ike was able to reduce the military in a time of great tension was his intimate knowledge of the Soviet military situation. From 1956 on, he directed a series of flights by the U-2 spy plane over the Soviet Union. He had personally taken the lead in getting the U-2 program started, and he kept a tight personal control over the flights—he gave his approval to the individual flights only after a thorough briefing on where in the USSR the planes were going and what the CIA wanted to discover. Here too the revisionists have shown that the contemporary feeling, especially after Francis Gary Powers was shot down in 1960, that Ike was not in charge and hardly knew what was going on inside his own government is altogether wrong. He was absolutely in charge, not only of broad policy on the use of the U-2, but of implementing details as well.

The major factor in Eisenhower's ability to restrain defense spending was keeping the peace. His record here is clear and impressive—he signed an armistice in Korea less than half a year after taking office, stayed out of Vietnam, and managed to avoid war despite such crisis situations as Hungary and the Suez, Quemoy and Matsu, Berlin and Cuba. The revisionists insist that the credit must go to Ike, and they equally insist that Eisenhower, not Secretary of State John Foster Dulles, was in command of American foreign policy in the 1950s. Dulles, says Greenstein, "was assigned the 'get tough' side of foreign-policy enunciation, thus placating the fervently anti-Communist wing of the Republican party." Ike, meanwhile, appeared to be above the battle, while actually directing it on a day-to-day basis.

"In essence, Eisenhower used Dulles." So writes Robert Divine, one of America's leading diplomatic historians, in his provocative new book, *Eisen-*

hower and the Cold War (Oxford University Press). Divine concludes that "far from being the do-nothing President of legend, Ike was skillful and active in directing American foreign policy." All the revisionists agree that the contemporary idea that Dulles led Ike by the nose was a myth that Eisenhower himself did the most to encourage. Nevertheless, Eisenhower did have a high opinion of his secretary of state. Divine quotes Ike's comment to Emmet Hughes on Dulles: "There's only one man I know who has seen *more* of the world and talked with more people and *knows* more than he does—and that's me."

The quotation illustrates another often overlooked Eisenhower characteristic—his immense self-confidence. He had worked with some of the great men of the century—Churchill, Roosevelt, Stalin, de Gaulle, Montgomery, and many others—long before he became president. His diary entry for the day after his inauguration speaks to the point: "My first day at the president's desk. Plenty of worries and difficult problems. But such has been my portion for a long time—the result is that this just seems (today) like a continuation of all I've been doing since July 1941—even before that."

Ike's vast experience in war and peace made him confident in crises. People naturally looked to him for leadership. No matter how serious the crisis seemed to be, Ike rarely got flustered. During a war scare in the Formosa Straits in 1955, he wrote in his diary, "I have so often been through these periods of strain that I have become accustomed to the fact that most of the calamities that we anticipate really never occur."

Ike's self-confidence was so great that, Greenstein writes, he had "neither a need nor a desire" to capture headlines. "He employed his skills to achieve his ends by inconspicuous means." In foreign policy, this meant he did not issue strident warnings, did not—in public—threaten Russia or China with specific reprisals for specific actions. Instead, he retained his room for maneuver by deliberately spreading confusion. He did not care if editorial writers criticized him for jumbled syntax; he wanted to keep possible opponents guessing, and he did. For example, when asked at a March 1955 press conference if he would use atomic bombs to defend Quemoy and Matsu, he replied:

> Every war is going to astonish you in the way it occurred, and in the way it is carried out. So that for a man to predict, particularly if he has the responsibility for making the decision, to predict what he is going to use, how he is going to do it, would I think exhibit his ignorance of war; that is what I believe.

As he intended, the Chinese found such statements inscrutable, as they had in Korea two years earlier. When truce talks in Korea reached an impasse in mid-May 1953, Ike put the pressure on the Chinese, hinting to them that the United States might use atomic weapons if a truce could not be arranged, and backing this up by transferring atomic warheads to American bases in Okinawa. The Chinese then accepted a truce. As Divine writes, "Perhaps the best testimony to the shrewdness of the President's policy is the impossibility of telling even now whether or not he was bluffing."

Nearly all observers agree that one of Ike's greatest accomplishments was staying out of Vietnam in the face of intense pressure from his closest advisers to save the French position there or, after July 1954, to go in alone to defeat Ho Chi Minh. Ike was never tempted. As early as March 1951 he wrote in his diary, "I'm convinced that no military victory is possible in that kind of theater." And in a first draft of his memoirs, written in 1963 but not published until 1981 by Ewald, Ike wrote·

> The jungles of Indochina would have swallowed up division after division of United States troops, who, unaccustomed to this kind of warfare, would have sustained heavy casualties until they had learned to live in a new environment. Furthermore, the presence of ever more numbers of white men in uniform probably would have aggravated rather than assuaged Asiatic resentments.

That was hardheaded military reasoning by General Eisenhower. But President Eisenhower stayed out of Vietnam as much for moral as for military reasons. When the Joint Chiefs suggested to him in 1954 that the United States use an atomic bomb against the Vietminh around Dien Bien Phu, the president said he would not be a party to using that "terrible thing" against Asians for the second time in less than a decade. And in another previously unpublished draft of his memoirs, he wrote:

> The strongest reason of all for the United States refusal to [intervene] is that fact that among all the powerful nations of the world the United States is the only one with a tradition of anti-colonialism. . . . The standing of the United States as the most powerful of the anti-colonial powers is an asset of incalculable value to the Free World. . . . Thus it is that the moral position of the United States was more to be guarded than the Tonkin Delta, indeed than all of Indochina.

Ike's international outlook, already well known, is highlighted by the new documents. He believed that the bonds that tied Western Europe and the United States together were so tight that the fate of one was the fate of the other. In May 1947, one year before the Marshall Plan, he wrote in his diary, in reference to Western Europe:

> I personally believe that the best thing we could now do would be to post 5 billion to the credit of the secretary of state and tell him to use it to support democratic movements wherever our vital interests indicate. Money should be used to promote possibilities of self-sustaining economies, not merely to prevent immediate starvation.

Ike also anticipated Kennedy's Alliance for Progress. Historian Burton Kaufman, in the narrowest but perhaps most important study reviewed here, *Trade and Aid: Eisenhower's Foreign Economic Policy* (Johns Hopkins University Press), concludes: "Not only did Eisenhower reorient the mutual security program away from military and toward economic assistance, he was also the first president to alter the geographical direction of American foreign aid toward the developing world." After an exhaustive examination, Kaufman also gives Ike high marks for resisting Nelson Rockefeller and others who wanted the president to encourage private investment overseas through tax breaks, while reducing or eliminating all forms of public foreign aid. Kaufman's basic theme is "the transition of a foreign economic program based on the concept of 'trade not aid' when Eisenhower took office to one predicated on the principle of 'trade and aid,' with the emphasis clearly on the flow of public capital abroad, by the time he left the White House."

That Ike himself was in charge of this transition, Kaufman leaves no doubt. That Kaufman likes Ike is equally clear: the foreign aid and trade program, Kaufman writes, "demonstrates the quality and character of Eisenhower's intellect and the cogency and forcefulness of his arguments in defense of administration policy. Finally, it emphasizes Eisenhower's flexibility as president and his capacity to alter his views in response to changing world conditions."

Kaufman, however, is critical of Ike on a number of points. Eisenhower himself, it turns out, could be as hypocritical as the "politicians" he scorned. In his speeches, Ike espoused the principles of free trade with sincerity and conviction; in his actions, he supported a protectionist agricultural policy and made broad concessions to the protectionist forces in Congress. Kaufman reaches the conclusion that "he often retreated on trade and tariff matters; he gave up the struggle with hardly a whimper."

And, as Blanche Wiesen Cook, another of the new Eisenhower scholars (but no revisionist), points out in *The Declassified Eisenhower* (Doubleday), Ike's vision of a peaceful world was based on a sophisticated version of Henry Luce's "American Century." Cook argues that Eisenhower's "blueprint . . . involved a determination to pursue political warfare, psychological warfare, and economic warfare everywhere and at all times." Under Ike's direction, she writes, the CIA and other branches of the government "ended all pretentions about territorial integrity, national sovereignty and international law. Covert operatives were everywhere, and they were active. From bribery to assassination, no activity was unacceptable short of nuclear war."

Cook does stress the importance of Eisenhower's stance against general war and his opposition to an arms race, but insists that these positions have to be placed in context, a context that includes the CIA-inspired and -led governmental overthrows in Iran and Guatemala, covert operations of all types in Vietnam and Eastern Europe, and assassination attempts against political leaders in the Congo and Cuba. Returning to an earlier view of Ike, Cook regards him as a "captive hero," the "chosen instrument" of the leaders of the great multinational corporations "to fight for the world they wanted."

One does not have to accept Cook's "captive hero" view to realize that it may indeed be time, as Kaufman indicates, to blow the whistle on Eisenhower revisionism. Ike had his shortcomings and he suffered serious setbacks. For all his openness to new ideas, he was rigid and dogmatic in his anti-communism. The darker side of Eisenhower's refusal to condemn McCarthy was that Ike himself agreed with the senator on the nature, if not the extent, of the problem, and he shared the senator's goals, if not his methods. After his first year in office, Ike made a list of his major accomplishments to date. Peace in Korea was first, the new defense policy second. Third on the list: "The highest security standards are being insisted upon for those employed in government service," a bland way of saying that under his direction, the Civil Service Commission had fired 2,611 "security risks" and reported that 4,315 other government workers had resigned when they learned they were under investigation. That was the true "hidden hand" at work, and the true difference between Ike and McCarthy—Ike got rid of Communists and fellow travelers (and many liberals) quietly and effectively, while McCarthy, for all his noise, accomplished nothing.

Thus, no matter how thoroughly the revisionists document Ike's opposition to McCarthy personally or his support for Warren, it remains true that his failure to speak out directly on McCarthy encouraged the witch hunters, just as his failure to speak out directly on the *Brown v. Topeka* decision encouraged the segregationists. The old general never admitted that it was impossible for him to be truly above the battle, never seemed to understand that the president is inevitably a part of the battle, so much so that his inaction can have as great an impact as his action.

With McCarthy and *Brown v. Topeka* in mind, there is a sad quality to the following Eisenhower diary passage, written in January 1954, about a number of Republican senators whom Ike was criticizing for being more inclined to trade votes than to provide clear leaderhip:

> They do not seem to realize when there arrives that moment at which soft speaking should be abandoned and a fight to the end undertaken. Any man who hopes to exercise leadership must be ready to meet this requirement face to face when it arises; unless he is ready to fight when necessary, people will finally begin to ignore him.

One of Ike's greatest disappointments was his failure to liberalize and modernize the Republican party, in order to make it the majority party in the United States. "The Republican party must be known as a progressive organization or it is sunk," he wrote in his diary in November 1954. "I believe this so emphatically that far from appeasing or reasoning with the dyed-in-the-wool reactionary fringe, we should completely ignore it and when necessary, repudiate it." Responding to cries of "impeach Earl Warren," Ike wrote in his diary, "If the Republicans as a body should try to repudiate him, I shall leave the Republican Party and try to organize an intelligent group of independents, however small." He was always threatening to break with the Republican party, or at least rename it; in March 1954, he told Hagerty, "You know, what we ought to do is get a word to put ahead of Republican—something like 'new' or 'modern' or something. We just can't work with fellows like McCarthy, Bricker, Jenner and that bunch."

A favorite revisionist quotation, which is used to show Ike's political astuteness, comes from a 1954 letter to his brother Edgar:

> Should any political party attempt to abolish social security and eliminate labor laws and farm programs, you would not hear of that party again in our political history. There is a tiny splinter group, of course, that believes that you can do these things. Among them are H. L. Hunt, a few other Texas oil millionaires,

and an occasional politician and businessman from other areas. Their number is negligible and they are stupid.

Good enough, but a critic would be quick to point out that Ike's "tiny splinter group" managed to play a large role in the nominations of Barry Goldwater, Richard Nixon, and Ronald Reagan. In short, although Ike saw great dangers to the right in the Republican party, he did little to counter the reactionary influence in his own organization. Franklin Roosevelt did a far better job of curbing the left wing in the Democratic party, and generally in building his party, than anything Ike did for the Republicans. . . .

Shortly after Ike left office, a group of leading American historians was asked to rate the presidents. Ike came in near the bottom of the poll. That result was primarily a reflection of how enamored the professors were with FDR and Harry Truman. Today, those same historians would compare Ike with his successors rather than his predecessors and place him in the top ten, if not the top five, of all our presidents. No matter how much one qualifies that record by pointing to this or that shortcoming or failure of the Eisenhower administration, it remains an enviable record. No wonder the people like Ike.

JFK: How Good a President?

Lance Morrow

The assassination of President John F. Kennedy and the distinct aura of its emotional aftermath provide the historian a ready example of the interrelationship and intersection of political reality and social mythology. The tragic circumstances of Kennedy's death, the dramatic media coverage of the nation's traumatic response, and the Kennedy mystique of youthfulness, élan, and optimism did much, at least initially, to fashion a "stained-glass image" of JFK. As here reported by essayist Lance Morrow, however, the glistening Kennedy image has come in for recent revision. When viewed with the growing advantage of hindsight and objectivity, Kennedy's aggressive idealism seems to have been both episodic and at times misdirected. His unquestionable style often failed to yield enduring results. His record on such matters as civil rights, foreign policy, and legislative leadership was decidedly uneven, even though he must be credited with rekindling the flames of expectation. Conclusive judgment on the foreshortened Kennedy presidency rests in great measure on whether one attends most to rhetoric or reality, to personality or performance. The myth and reality of the Kennedy legacy remain most difficult to assess.

In an essay on Napoleon, Ralph Waldo Emerson wrote, "He was no saint—to use his word, 'no capuchin,' and he is no hero, in the high sense." Napoleon had fulfilled an earthly career, at any rate. His life went the full trajectory. One could study the line of it and know, for better and worse, what the man was, and did, and could do. He inhabited his life. He completed it. He passed through it to the end of its possibilities.

John Kennedy's bright trajectory ended in midpassage, severed in that glaring Friday noontime in Dallas. The moment . . . when one learned the news became precisely fixed in the memory, the mind stopping like a clock just then. It is Kennedy's deathday, not his birthday, that we observe. History abruptly left off, and after the shock had begun to pass, the mythmaking began—the mind haunted by the hypothetical, by what might have been.

And the myth overwhelmed conventional judgment, as if some wonderful song prevented the hall from hearing the recording secretary read the minutes of the last meeting, or the minutes of a thousand days. Today, Kennedy still occupies an unusual place in the national psyche. His presence there in the memory, in the interior temple, remains powerful, disproportionate to his substantive accomplishments. He probably was not President long enough to be judged by the customary standards.

Kennedy had his obvious accomplishments. Merely by arriving at the White House, he had destroyed forever one religious issue in American politics. When Edmund Muskie ran for the Democratic presidential nomination in 1972, his Catholicism was only a minor biographical detail. Kennedy presided over a change of political generations in America, and did it with brilliant style. He brought youth and idealism and accomplishment and élan and a sometimes boorish and clannish elitism to Washington. He refreshed the town with a conviction that the world could be changed, that the improvisational intelligence could do wonderful things. Such almost ruthless optimism had its sinister side, a moral complacency and dismissive arrogance that expressed itself when the American élan went venturing into Viet Nam. But Kennedy, when he died, was also veering away from the cold war. He made an eloquently conciliatory speech at American University in June 1963, and he accomplished the limited test-ban treaty. He had many plans, for Medicare, for civil rights, for other projects.

But after November 22, the record simply went blank. An anguished and fascinating process of canonization ensued. The television networks focused their gaze on the story almost continuously from Parkland Memorial Hospital to Arlington National Cemetery, as if in professional tribute to the first President who understood the medium and performed perfectly in it. In sanctifying his memory, videotape became Kennedy's Parson Weems. The reality of what the nation had lost was preserved with unprecedented, unthinkable vividness: his holographic ghost moving and talking inside every television set, that American dreamboat campaigning through the primaries among leaping and squealing adolescent girls, the snow-dazzled Inaugural ceremony, the wonderfully witty press conferences replayed endlessly, the children, the family, the one brief shining moment shown shining again and again in counterpoint with the Book Depository and the shots, and riderless Black Jack fighting the bridle, and the window, the little boy saluting, and the long mahogany box in the Rotunda—the protagonist and the irretrievable mystery of the piece. The death of John F. Kennedy became a participatory American tragedy, a drama both global and intensely intimate.

The event eerily fused, for a moment, the normally dissociated dimensions of public life and private life. And so Americans felt Kennedy's death in a deeply personal way: they, and he, were swept into a third dimension, the mythic. The ancient Greeks thought that gods and goddesses came down and walked among them and befriended them or betrayed them. The drama 20 years ago—bright young life and light and grace and death all compounded by the bardic camera—turned Kennedy into a kind of American god.

In any case, for a long time, some thought forever, it seemed almost impossible to look objectively at the man and his presidency, to see what he had done and left undone. Not long after the assassination, Journalist Gerald W.

Johnson wrote, "Already it has happened to two of the 35 men who have held the presidency, rendering them incapable of analysis by the instruments of scholarship; and now Washington, the godlike, and Lincoln, the saintly, have been joined by Kennedy, the young chevalier."

. . . It is fascinating, though complicated, that the youngest elected President, who occupied the White House for the shortest (elected) term since Warren Harding—and who had a problematic tenure, very much a learning process and a mixed bag of one fiasco and many missteps and some accomplishments—should be thus elevated, by the force of his presence, his vivid charm, to the company of the greatest Presidents, as if the inspirational power of personality were enough for greatness. Perhaps it is. Many Americans make the association. Yet what sways them is in some sense the strange coercive power of the martyr, Kennedy's great vitality turned inside out. He came to have a higher reputation in death than he enjoyed in life. And in a bizarre way he even accomplished more in death than in life. In the atmosphere of grief and remorse after the assassination, Lyndon Johnson pushed through Congress much of Kennedy's program, and more: Medicare, civil rights and the other bills that came to form Johnson's Great Society.

Three million visitors still come to his grave at Arlington every year. Although fewer photographs of Kennedy are enshrined in bars and barbershops and living rooms around the U.S. than there once were, they can still be found in huts all over the Third World: an image of an American President, dead for 20 [plus] years, a symbol—but of what exactly? Mostly of a kind of hope, the possibility of change, and the usually unthinkable idea that government leadership might intercede to do people some good.

Is it possible now, at a remove of 20 [plus] years, to detach Kennedy's presidency from the magic and to judge it with the cold rationality that Kennedy tried to bring to bear upon his world? Or is the myth, the sense of hope and the lift he gave thereby, a central accomplishment of his presidency? W.B. Yeats wrote, "How can we know the dancer from the dance?"

Kennedy would have found the solemnity and mythmaking amusing, and hopelessly overdone. His intellectual style was sardonic and self-aware: wonderful lights of satire played across it. If he sometimes labored hard at being a hero, or *seeming* a hero (before his election in 1960, he listened intently to recordings of Winston Churchill's speeches, picking up the grand rhythms of the language), he knew the limitations of everything, including himself. His instruments were sensitive to the bogus. He might even have had some mordant crack to make about that Eternal Flame.

As the years have passed, Kennedy has been inevitably caught up in the pattern of idolatry and revisionism. All presidential reputations ride up or down upon wind currents of intellectual fashion and subsequent history, the perspective of the present constantly altering interpretations of the past.

First the murdered President became saint and martyr. But then the '60s arrived in earnest. In a study of tragedy, Critic George Steiner wrote, "The fall of great personages from high places *(casus virorum illustrium)* gave to medieval politics their festive and brutal character." The real '60s began on the afternoon of November 22, 1963, and they turned festive and brutal too. It came to seem that Kennedy's murder opened some malign trap door in American culture, and the wild bats flapped out. His assassination became the prototype in a series of public murders: Malcolm X, Martin Luther King Jr., Robert Kennedy. His death prefigured all the deaths of the young in Viet Nam.

The '60s eventually turned on Kennedy. The protests and violent changes of the time jarred loose and shattered fundamental premises of American life and power. From the perspective of Viet Nam in the late '60s, some of Kennedy's rhetoric sounded incautious, jingoistic and dangerous. The Arthurian knight talked about building bomb shelters. The extravagance of all that the hagiologists claimed for him now seemed to make him a fraud. His performance on civil rights came to seem tepid and reluctant and excessively political. Stories about his vigorous sex life, including an alleged affair with the girlfriend of a Mafia don, brought into question not only his private morals but his common sense. At last, the revisionists wondered whether his presidency belonged more to the history of publicity and hype than to the history of political leadership.

Presidential reputations are always fluid. Dwight Eisenhower, for example, was regarded during the '60s as a somewhat vague golfer with a tendency to blunder into sand traps when attempting a complicated English sentence. Now he is enjoying a rehabilitation. His watch was essentially peaceful and prudent, his revisionists say.

At the end of his terms, though, Ike seemed archaic and gray. The virile young man in top hat who rode with him down Pennsylvania Avenue in 1961 had promised to "get the country moving again." That bright Inauguration Day, Kennedy brought Robert Frost to read a special poem for the occasion. The glare of sun on new-fallen snow blinded the aged poet, and so he recited another poem from memory. The poem he had not read that day contained these lines for the Kennedy era:

> It makes the prophet in us all presage
> The glory of a next Augustan age
> Of a power leading from its strength and pride,
> Of young ambition eager to be tried,
> Firm in our free beliefs without dismay,
> In any game the nations want to play.
> A golden age of poetry and power
> Of which this noonday's the beginning hour.

Frost had caught just the spirit of the venture, with a confidence about the uses of power and ambition that now seems amazing. Kennedy took office with extraordinary energy and the highest hopes. He seemed in some ways the perfect American. As Historian Doris Kearns Goodwin points out, he exemplified two usually contradictory strains in American tradition. One is the immigrant experience, the old American story of the luckless or disfavored or dispossessed who came from Europe and struggled in the New World. Rooted in that experience is the glorification of the common man and the desire for a common-man presidency, a celebration of the ordinary. The other strain is the American longing for an aristocracy, the buried dynastic, monarchical urge. "Jack is the first Irish Brahmin," said Paul Dever, a former Massachusetts Governor. He had both Harvard and Honey Fitz in him. He was an intellectual who could devastate any woman in the room and devour *Melbourne* in a speed reader's blitz and curse like the sailor that he also was.

Kennedy's critics sometimes wondered whether he was animated by a larger, substantive vision of what he would like America to become, or simply by a substantive vision of what he wanted Jack Kennedy to become. His rhetoric was full of verbs of motion and change, but his idea of what America ought to be—other than wanting it to be an excellent place in all ways, not a bad vision to entertain—was often murky, crisscrossed by his own ambivalent impulses. When Kennedy came to the White House, his main previous administrative experience was running a PT boat. He had a great deal to learn.

One New Frontiersman who became a minor patron saint of the Kennedy revisionists was Chester Bowles, the career diplomat. He thought that he had located a central problem with the Kennedy Administration. He feared that it deliberately, almost scornfully detached pragmatic considerations from a larger moral context. To discuss the morality of actions was evidence of softness, and intellectuals with power in their hands cannot bear to be thought soft. Everyone carried the Munich model around in his head. One talked in laconic codes, a masculine shorthand; one did not, like Adlai Stevenson, deliver fluty soliloquies about the morality of an act. After the Bay of Pigs, Bowles wrote: "The Cuban fiasco demonstrates how far astray a man as brilliant and well-intentioned as President Kennedy can go who lacks a basic moral reference point."

Kennedy's Inaugural Address bristled with a certain amount of cold war rhetoric, tricked up in reversible-raincoat prose ("Let us never negotiate out of fear. But let us never fear to negotiate"). To a nation reading it from the far side of the Viet Nam War, the most alarming passage was the one in which Kennedy promised to "pay any price . . . to assure the survival . . . of liberty." The revisionists have always seen that line as a précis of the mentality that brought on the war. But both Arthur M. Schlesinger Jr. and Theodore Sorensen reject the notion that the Inaugural speech was a prelude to cowboy interventionism. "It was," says Schlesinger, "in part an overreaction to a speech two weeks earlier by Khrushchev that was read in Washington as being very truculent." Sorensen, who drafted the text, insists, "The speech isn't as bellicose as the revisionists have made it. It was really a call to negotiation. But he knew you didn't get there with just appeals to the other side's good will."

One of the central dramas of the brief Kennedy Administration was his passage from a sometimes indiscriminate anti-Communist hard line to a deepening awareness of the real dangers of nuclear war. It did not help Kennedy in his passage that he assembled a staff of war-hawk anti-Communist intellectuals (McGeorge Bundy, Walt Rostow and Robert McNamara, for example) who were brilliantly nimble and self-confident and often disastrously wrong about what counted most. They could be overbearing men, and curiously disconnected from the realities of American life. Once, after Vice President Johnson talked wonderingly of all the brilliant characters Kennedy had brought into the White House, House Speaker Sam Rayburn remarked to him, "Well, Lyndon, they must be just as intelligent as you say. But I'd feel a helluva lot better if just one of them had ever run for sheriff."

Kennedy's team of White House men, according to Historian Joan Hoff-Wilson, began the pattern in which Congress and the federal bureaucracies became adversaries of the White House rather than partners. "That kind of privatization and centralization of power in and around the White House clearly begins with Kennedy," says Hoff-Wilson. For men who put such a premium on brains and information, the elite around Kennedy sometimes seemed either exceptionally naive (about the Bay of Pigs, for example) or ignorant (about Vietnamese history and culture). Some of the same men stayed on with Johnson, and presided over the escalation of what became in some ways the nation's hardest war.

The Bay of Pigs fiasco, however, came early. Kennedy had inherited the plan from the Eisenhower Administration, which, according to Arkansas Senator J. William Fulbright, had already sunk $40 million into the training of a band of Cuban exiles who were supposed to sweep ashore in Cuba, join forces with the grateful, disenchanted islanders and dislodge Fidel Castro. Kennedy was skeptical of the idea, but allowed himself to be talked into it by men who seemed so sure of what they were doing. The mission, of course, was an utter disaster, and it taught Kennedy several important lessons. One was that truculently self-confident experts, such as generals and CIA men, can be ludicrously wrong. After the Bay of Pigs, according to his special counsel, Theodore Sorensen, Kennedy came to mistrust military solutions.

The botched invasion also revealed an attractive trait in Kennedy: an openness and candor, and a freedom from that neurotic, squirming evasiveness, the deflected gaze or outright mendacity, that one came to expect from one or two subsequent occupants of the White House. Kennedy made no effort to escape blame for the folly, to cover it up or excuse it. We made a terrible mistake, he said. Let's go on from here.

As an administrator, Kennedy was intense, but also casual about the forms—improvisational, never rigid. Eisenhower favored a formal chain of command, with orderly, predictable structures. Kennedy's mind was extremely orderly, but his techniques in office were sometimes heterodox and unexpected. They might have struck an outsider as being somewhat chaotic. He constantly bypassed the chain of command. He telephoned Assistant Secretaries or lesser military officers in order to seek information he needed. His press secretary, Pierre Salinger, once remarked that the back door of the White House always seemed more open than the front door. He understood the dynamics of meetings, and sometimes mistrusted them as a way of doing business. He thought that his presence might intimidate people. He liked to get information orally, in small groups or one-to-one, or else in memos from those people he trusted and admired—his brother Bobby and Arthur M. Schlesinger Jr., for example, or John Kenneth Galbraith, whose elegantly intelligent reports he always enjoyed reading. Kennedy detested long, tiresome memos from the bureaucracy. He complained that the functionaries at the State Department were incapable of getting to the point, to the essence, in their reports.

He did not keep rigid office hours. If he wanted to take a little more time in the morning to play with Caroline in the family quarters of the White House, he did so. He had a sort of seigneurial ease about the day's routines. When he went for a swim, when he had people to dinner, when he went away for weekends at Hyannis Port, the world he thought about and tried to control was always there with him. It also kept him up late on many nights.

Kennedy's tenure was littered with messy crises—in Laos, Cuba, the Congo, Latin America, Algeria, Viet Nam and Berlin—and his record in dealing with them is decidedly uneven. Revisionists like to say that Kennedy was a cold warrior who sought confrontation, but in the early '60s, the Soviets busied themselves around the world in ways that no American President could ignore.

Too quickly after the Bay of Pigs, Kennedy went to Vienna for a summit with Nikita Khrushchev, who, judging Kennedy to be callow and inexperienced, ranted and bullied. Khrushchev followed the meeting by building the Berlin Wall and then, within a month, interrupting the informal moratorium on nuclear testing in the atmosphere.

Kennedy's strategy in world affairs was a mixture of gestures. The founder of the Alliance for Progress and the Peace Corps, those aggressively idealistic enterprises, could be by turns imperial, bold and assertive, and restrained. He learned eventually to define American interests and hold firmly to the line he had drawn, as he did in the Berlin crisis and, most notably, in the Cuban missile crisis. The Bay of Pigs had taught him caution and the exploration of options.

The missile crisis, more than any other single event of his presidency, demonstrated the way in which Kennedy matured in the office, the way in which he could master complexities of process, could orchestrate alternatives. He had learned to wait and to question. The Bay of Pigs had instructed him to rely more on his own internal deliberations and less on the hormonal instincts of his military intelligence advisers. During those 13 days in October 1962, the world held its breath; it waited in a real sweat of nuclear panic. Never, before or since, has global annihilation seemed a more immediate possibility. Kennedy rejected the idea of direct strikes against the offensive missile sites that the Soviets were installing in Cuba. Working in the extraordinary partnership that he had developed with his brother Bobby, the President imposed a naval quarantine on Cuba and allowed Khrushchev time to consider. When the Soviets sent two somewhat contradictory replies to his ultimatum, one hard and one more accommodating, Kennedy simply ignored the hard message and replied to the softer one. It worked. Khrushchev blinked, and in the memorable denouement, the Soviet ships turned and steamed away from Cuba. Says

Harvard Political Scientist Richard Neustadt: "The Administration set a new standard of prudence in dealing with the Soviet Union. The standard of prudence, the hard thought given about the crisis as the Soviets would see it, thus giving our opponent as much room as possible—these were a model of presidential conduct."

But there were deep contradictions in Kennedy's foreign policy, conflicts in which an old view of the world and an emerging view competed with each other. Part of him retained the mentality of the cold war, a kind of Dulles-like brinkmanship. At the same time, a succession of crises convinced him that a new course was necessary. At American University he declared, "What kind of peace do we seek? Not a *Pax Americana* enforced on the world by American weapons of war. Not the peace of the grave or the security of the slave . . . not merely peace for Americans but peace for all men and women—not merely peace in our time, but peace for all time . . . Let us re-examine our attitude toward the cold war, remembering that we are not engaged in a debate . . . We must deal with the world as it is." It was the American University speech that began the long process of détente between the U.S. and the Soviet Union. Ironically, the man who brought Kennedy's policy to its fullest bloom was Richard Nixon.

And yet Kennedy would ask for nearly 1,000 new ICBMs for the American nuclear arsenal, which eventually triggered what has become the greatest arms race in history. He acquiesced in the overthrow of the Diem government in South Viet Nam in 1963. And he ordered 16,000 American troops into the country.

Would Kennedy have become involved in Viet Nam to the extent that Johnson eventually did? The answer is unknowable. Many Kennedy loyalists think not, though their opinion is not disinterested. They point out that Kennedy was eminently a pragmatist; he would have seen the morass that lay in wait. Kennedy was a superbly self-assured man. He had already proved himself in war and had no need to do so again. With his keen sense of public relations, his loyalists believe, with his knowledge of the uses of the media, he would simply have decided that Viet Nam was not worth the dreadful publicity, which is not a very principled notion to put hypothetically into Kennedy's mind, but still a plausible one.

At home, as abroad, Kennedy's performance was mixed. He was a fiscal conservative. The economy was robust during his thousand days. Economic growth averaged 5.6% annually. Unemployment came down by almost two percentage points from the nearly 8% level when he took office. Inflation held at a prelapsarian 1.2%.

The central problem was confrontation between blacks and whites. Kennedy's approach to civil rights at the beginning of his term was slow and inattentive. Writes Schlesinger in the current *New Republic:* "If anyone had asked Kennedy in 1960 how he really felt about civil rights, he might have answered something like this: 'Yes, of course, we must achieve racial justice in this country, and we will; but it is an explosive question, so let us go about it prudently.' Like most other white politicians, he underestimated the moral passion behind the movement. The protests of the Freedom Riders on the eve of his departure for the 1961 meeting with Khrushchev irritated him."

He appointed some Southern judges who proved to be outright racists. But the civil rights movement was becoming an urgent presence in the nation; it demanded Kennedy's attention. He was not a leader on this subject, not for a long time, but was led by events and historical pressures and by figures like Martin Luther King Jr.

The South was filled with agitation and change. There were riots at the all-white University of Mississippi when a black man named James Meredith tried to enroll. Two people were killed. Kennedy was forced to call out federal troops to install Meredith in the university. In Birmingham, Public Safety Commissioner Theophilus Eugene ("Bull") Connor turned loose police dogs upon a march led by King. The news photographs of that spectacle—the fire hoses and the snapping dogs and the beefy Southern lawmen—outraged Americans and turned the public mood. In the spring of 1963 there were 2,000 civil rights demonstrations in more than 300 cities. Kennedy now faced the civil rights cause directly. "We are confronted primarily with a moral issue," he said. "It is as old as the Scriptures and is as clear as the American Constitution." Eight days later he sent Congress a civil rights bill that would assure equal access to public accommodations and fight discrimination in schools and jobs and at the polls.

But as in foreign policy, Kennedy's performance was somehow deflected, inconsistent. While pronouncing civil rights to be a moral issue, he acquiesced in an FBI investigation of King. FBI Director J. Edgar Hoover, for decades the lord of his own almost independent principality within the American Government, said that King was associating with Communists. Kennedy and his brother Bobby, then Attorney General, allowed the wiretaps of King 1) to clear King's name and thus disarm Hoover, 2) to see for themselves whether Hoover's suspicions were correct, or 3) both. They did not, however, authorize the bugging that amounted to a much broader invasion of King's privacy.

Kennedy died before his civil rights bill could become law. His relations with Congress were not good, one of his failures as a leader. His program also suffered because he lacked a working majority on the Hill. Eventually President Johnson, that consummate creature of the Congress, obtained a comfortably functional Democratic majority in 1964. Johnson pushed through the Civil Rights Act of 1964 and the 1965 Voting Rights Act. His Great Society went well beyond what Kennedy envisioned. "He's done," wrote Walter Lippmann in April 1964, "what President Kennedy could not have done had he lived."

Kennedy all along had calculated that his first term would be a period for developing programs, for sowing seeds that a second term would allow him to bring to fruition. He might have run a modified version of the Great Society much more successfully than Johnson did, without the middle-class entitlements and the immense and inflationary burden upon the economy.

It is sometimes difficult to know whether Kennedy was visionary or simply a rhetorician. He did have a high sense of adventure, which he combined with patriotism in the launching of his plan to put a man on the moon and thereby repay the Soviets for the technological humiliations of Sputnik. He did imagine a better America, a fairer place, a more excellent place. He even believed that it was part of his task as President to lift American culture. He and his wife Jacqueline brought Pablo Casals and Igor Stravinsky and Bach and Mozart to the White House. His own taste may have run more toward Sinatra or Broadway musicals, but Kennedy believed that it was his duty to endorse the excellent in all things, to be a leader in matters of civilization. That was a novel notion in American politics, novel at least since the days of Thomas Jefferson.

A judgment of Kennedy's presidential performance inevitably ends in a perplexity of conditional clauses. If he had lived and been elected to a second term, Kennedy would have become, at age 50 or so, a world leader, with unprecedented moral authority. Perhaps. One of Kennedy's strongest qualities was his capacity to learn from experience, to grow. His first six months in office were nearly a disaster. But by 1963 he was far maturer, riper, smarter, still passionate, but seasoned. It is interesting to wonder what his second Inaugural Address would have sounded like. It would almost surely not have reverberated with the grandiloquent bluster that one heard in the first.

It is possible, in any case, that the manner of Kennedy's leaving the office, his assassination, much more profoundly affected the course of America than anything he did while he was in the White House. There was a kind of dual effect: his death enacted his legislative program and at the same time seemed to let loose monsters, to unhinge the nation in some deep way that sent it reeling down a road toward riots and war and assassinations and Watergate.

One Kennedy revisionist, Garry Wills, argues that the extraordinary glamour and heightened expectations that Kennedy brought to the office have crippled all of his successors. They cannot compete with such a powerful myth. It is equally possible, of course, that Kennedy's successors simply do not measure up. Kennedy's was a mind with all of its windows open and a clear light passing through it. That has not been true of anyone who has sat in the place since.

Robert K. Murray of Pennsylvania State University has surveyed 1,000 Ph.D. historians as part of a study on how such authorities assess American Presidents. The 1,000 rated Kennedy 13th, in the middle of the "above average" category. Those considered great: Abraham Lincoln, Franklin Roosevelt, George Washington, Thomas Jefferson. Near great: Theodore Roosevelt, Woodrow Wilson, Andrew Jackson, Harry Truman. Above average: John Adams, Lyndon Johnson, James K. Polk, John Kennedy, James Madison, James Monroe, John Quincy Adams, Grover Cleveland.

The fact is that Kennedy was in the White House so short a time that he almost cannot be judged against other Presidents. The first twelve or eighteen months of any presidency are a learning period during which the man in the Oval Office must get his bearings and put his Administration in place for the work he hopes to accomplish. That would not have given Kennedy—elected in a squeaker, with no clear mandate and no working majority in Congress—much time to prove himself.

American political moods run in cycles. Periods of activity and reform, of idealism and change, alternate with more quiescent, complacent, even cynical times. Schlesinger believes that the activist cycle comes around every 30 years or so. Thus the era of Teddy Roosevelt at the turn of the century, then the New Deal beginning in 1933, then Kennedy in 1961. By Schlesinger's hopeful calculation, the U.S. will be ripe for another time of idealism and political innovation toward the end of this decade.

The wave of negative revisionism about Kennedy may now be receding. But the myth of John Kennedy will undoubtedly outlive the substance of what he achieved. History will remember not so much what he did as what he was, a memory kept in some vault of the national imagination. In the end, the American appreciation of Kennedy may come to be not political but aesthetic, and vaguely religious.

V

Myths of Modern America

MYTHOLOGY—*The body of a primitive people's beliefs concerning its origin, early history, heroes, deities and so forth, as distinguished from the true accounts which it invents later.*
Ambrose Bierce, *The Devil's Dictionary*

MYTH—*A coherent set of beliefs or attitudes which shape perceptions and organizations of chaotic information.*
Merrill Skaggs

America, please wake up and listen to your poor, who are too honest to lie, too proud and tired to cry.
John C. Johnson, *Principal, J. J. McClain High School, Holmes County, Mississippi*

We who are privileged to be Americans have had a rendezvous with destiny since the moment, back in 1630, when John Winthrop, standing on the deck of the tiny Arbella *off the Massachusetts coast, told his little band of Pilgrims [sic], 'We shall be as a City upon a hill'."*
Ronald Reagan *(1976)*

347

[Reprinted from *Images of Our Times* by Harry Lebelson, copyright 1971, by permission of the publisher, Horizon Press, New York.]

[Bruce Davidson, Magnum Photos, Inc.]

*T*o assure the intellectual integrity of one's society, it is necessary continually to think anew. The familiar must be reexamined in the interest of achieving greater dimensions of clarity and understanding. Accepting this, and the axiom that the time for historical reinterpretation is always *now,* historians have continually renewed their inquiry into both the high contours and the nuances of the American past. The previous sections have, it is hoped, demonstrated that myth is an important ingredient in the American experience. For that very reason, however, a growing consensus seems to suggest that America can no longer find historical sanction for either the enchantment that surrounds much of the nation's past or the heroic stature enjoyed by many of its participants. Yet, somewhat ironically, the previous selections have sought to argue that myth supplies much of the inner logic of American history.

At this juncture, it would be well to keep in mind the warning of the American historian Carl Becker, who in his essay "Everyman His Own Historian" observed, "We are apt to think of the past as dead, the future as nonexistent, the present alone as real." Of course no such easy distinctions can be made. The past is prologue; it underscores the present and conditions the future. Therefore, it would seem wise to become attuned to the continuation of myth within America's present cultural, social, and political context.

The dominant perspective of this book—the persistence of myth in America history—seems especially logical and appropriate when juxtaposed with some relevant features of America's more recent condition. Convinced that important mythical discrepancies existed in the nation's past experience, one more naturally comes to see American attitudes toward Vietnam, Watergate, women, minorities, and America's global status as shaped in accordance with myth. Mythmaking is today an ongoing enterprise of the American mind, as prolific as the current issues of a dynamic society.

Myth, then, has decided importance to contemporary American society, for individually and collectively people are selective in what they wish to remember concerning their past. Even though myth operates universally and diversely, Americans seem to have found the material for their myths nearer at hand than have older and more traditional societies. Thus do Americans continue to base their behavior and policies on distorted facts and, hence, questionable conclusions. It can be argued as well, however, as the concluding article does, that American myth needs selectively and creatively to be revivified, an activity constituting a new cultural agenda for the nation. For paradoxically, as an important dimension of human existence, myth is at once the process by which human beings order their world and the entity that serves to perpetuate their grandest illusions. As the late American poet Robert Penn Warren once pointedly observed, "The dream is a lie, but the dreaming is true." Thus, the question remains valid for historians and Becker's "everyman" alike: What is myth and what is reality—yesterday, today, and in the future?

Image and Reality in Indochina

Harrison E. Salisbury

The idea of myth implies that it is instructive to study the differences between reality on the one hand and the way in which most people see that reality on the other. In the judgment of Harrison E. Salisbury, former managing editor of the *New York Times* and foreign policy specialist, this is the proper approach to the nature and goals of United States policy in Indochina. The interplay between myth and reality as it affected America's Vietnam policy, says Salisbury, began even before U.S. involvement in the Second World War. It has continued unabated ever since. A dimension of complexity was added, however, in that the mythic images underwent constant change and were common to all parties concerned.

Re-examining the thirty and more years since Indochina entered the agenda of world problems one is struck constantly by the curious mirages, the discordance between image and reality which seem to persist not only in American perceptions of Indochina but in the evaluations by other great powers and the Indochinese themselves of the actual nature and goals of U.S. policy.

We are all familiar with the "mirror image" phenomenon in which two rival powers tend to see each other in somewhat similar turns of threat, each mirroring the other's fears and expectations, thus often giving rise to self-fulfilling prophecies. The Indochina phenomenon is different. It lies in a distortion of perception in which one, two or more powers see a different sequence of events as being in progress, each one of these images having little or no resemblance to reality or to the image in the consciousness of the other powers. It strikingly reminds one of the classic Japanese story of Rashomon. An event, a series of events takes place. But exactly what were these events? To each participant it seems that a different thing has happened. We see the tragedy through the eyes of one participant after the other. Each vision is so different, so contradictory, that in the end we can never be certain of what it is that has actually transpired.

So it is with Indochina. I think that it is this diverse interplay of myth and reality, this inability at almost any given moment to find common understanding not only of motivation but of the nature of current evolutions which has placed resolution of the Indochina problem almost beyond the reach of even the most skillful diplomats.

For the United States this process began long, long ago. Even before our entry into World War II, President Roosevelt was expressing to Admiral Leahy, our ambassador to Vichy, the essence of what came to be an *idée fixe*—that French colonial policy in Indochina (and to a lesser extent that of the Dutch in the East Indies and the British in Southeast Asia) was "responsible" for the aggressions of the Japanese. Indeed, later, FDR went so far as to blame the whole war in the Pacific on the colonial powers and, specifically, on the French. He advised Leahy on July 29, 1941, that "if Japan wins Japan gets Indochina—if the Allies win *we* would" take it over. It is not likely that he contemplated an actual "U.S. takeover." More probably, he had in mind some kind of international supervision in which the United States would play a leading role.

It was the President's confused view that France and French policy in Indochina were "responsible" for Japan's aggression and that France must therefore be penalized, and specifically, that for this reason Indochina must never go back to the French. The President's position hardened with the years. He advanced it at the wartime meetings with Churchill and Stalin, winning mild, *pro forma* support from Stalin (who never displayed the slightest interest in this portion of the world) and indignation on the part of Churchill, who was always aroused by Roosevelt's stubborn desire to liquidate colonial empires.

Probably the acme of Rooseveltian schemes for Indochina (of course, by this time under the vicious occupation of the Japanese) was a proposal conveyed to Chiang Kai-shek through Vice President Wallace during his 1944 mission to Chungking in which he offered China a "trusteeship" over Indochina on the grounds that, after all, the Indochinese and the Chinese were "the same kind of people."

If Mr. Roosevelt's thesis that French conduct in Indochina put the Japanese on the road to Pearl Harbor was dubious, his assumption of communality between the peoples of Indochina and those of China displayed an even more profound distortion of reality, both ethnic and historic. Probably the most striking fact about the Indochinese (be they Vietnamese, Cambodians, Laotians or Montagnards) is their ethnic differentiation from the Han Chinese, the two thousand years of intermittent war and struggle between the Indochinese and the Chinese and the implacable hostility and fear with which most Indochinese regard the Chinese. It is no accident that the first visit of every foreigner coming to Hanoi is to the Museum of the Revolution where he is shown the historic record of the endless wars with the Chinese, combat that started at a time when the Vietnamese occupied areas of what is now South China, and is made acquainted with the national and folk heroes of Vietnam, all of them winning their fame in victories over the hated Chinese.

Fortunately, Chiang Kai-shek possessed a keener grasp of reality than FDR. He rejected Roosevelt's offer. There is no record as to what he thought the American motive might be but it would have been natural for him to think that the President was trying to stir up trouble for China in Southeast Asia.

Thus the situation stood at the time of FDR's death in April 1945. Because of his repeated insistence, the French were not permitted to participate in the liberation of Indochina. Under plans made before the President's death the Chinese accepted the Japanese surrender in the north and the British in the south.

This early episode makes plain that major illusions as to the nature of Indochina lay largely on the American side, that is, specifically, in President Roosevelt's mind. But another small yet significant episode involving Indochina and the United States was in the process of taking shape. A close and increasingly warm and friendly liaison had been established in Indochina between special U.S. forces (specifically, OSS teams) and the Vietminh, the nationalist Vietnamese movement, then led by Ho Chi Minh. These relations have sometimes been characterized in recent years in a rather sentimental way, as if they were compounded simply of goodwill and good feeling between the OSS team, on the one hand, and Ho, on the other. That genuine mutual regard existed on both sides there can be no doubt. When Ho in September 1945 proclaimed the new Republic of Vietnam he modelled his declaration on the U.S. Declaration of Independence, actually requesting of the OSS men a copy of the Declaration in order to copy its language in his draft. None of the OSS officers possessed a copy. None the less, the Vietnamese declaration begins: "All men are created equal. They are endowed by their Creator with certain inalienable rights, among these are Life, Liberty and the Pursuit of Happiness. . . ." At about the same time a delegation of Vietminh ladies called at the OSS Mission in Hanoi, asking to be put in touch with their sister American organization, the Daughters of the American Revolution. There is no record as to what, if anything, resulted from this bizarre effort.

The Americans saw in these relations a "natural" affinity between themselves and Ho's Vietminh. What did Ho see? Did he and his associates feel a kinship between their movement, their independence, their revolution and that of America? There was some such feeling, and even in his last years when deeply engaged in warfare with the United States Ho occasionally spoke with nostalgia of the State of Liberty (which he had seen as a young seaman) and of the principles of the American Constitution. But underlying this was something, of course, far more fundamental, as Ho's policy clearly revealed. In 1945 Ho had three major antagonists: the Japanese, who were being expelled from Indochina and who, presumably, would not soon again endanger the region; the French, who were only too eager to resume their colonial overlordship; and the Chinese, whom geography and history had made Indochina's traditional enemy.

What more natural, then, than that Ho hoped to get a distant and presumably disinterested but important power involved as Indochina's chief protector? This would prevent the return of France and would hold the Chinese at bay. This was the classic policy of the weak power. It was the device which Turkey employed during its long years as "the sick man of Europe."

That, in fact, Ho was actually following the policy of the "lesser evil" quickly became apparent. When, after Roosevelt's death, U.S. policy changed, and the way was opened for France's return, Ho did not turn to the Chinese as a "protecting power" (as FDR might have expected). Rather, he sought to make a deal with the French and successfully concluded one which the French promptly violated. Anything, thus, rather than be thrust into the nearby Asian but dangerous arms of the Chinese. Even as the war with the French quickened Ho did not turn to China. The Vietminh fought on their own. Only after the emergence of Mao's communist régime, that is, after—considerably after—1949, did Ho approach China and even then on a carefully limited and circumscribed basis.

This ancient history is useful as a benchmark in analyzing later development of great-power policy *vis-à-vis* Indochina. It shows the United States frequently misjudging the reality in Indochina. It shows Indochina misjudging the United States as well. It also shows marked realism—and antagonism—between Indochina and China and profound lack of interest in the whole region on the part of the Soviet Union.

Between 1945 and 1950 France was the principal outside power engaged in Indochina. U.S. interest was minimal. So was that of the Soviet Union. China, wracked by the great struggle of nationalists versus communists, had neither time nor inclination for affairs beyond its frontiers.

It was the success of the communist Chinese Revolution and the steadily deteriorating position of the French which finally brought Indochina back into American focus—but a focus which was probably more distorted than it had ever been before or was likely to be in the future.

From 1949 onward the official American perception of Indochina cannot be separated from the U.S. overview of the communist world and, specifically, of the Chinese Revolution. Mao's success was seen initially as a Chinese victory in a Chinese civil war. But this image quickly was to change. The signature of the Sino-Soviet Alliance, February 14, 1950, after a long visit to Moscow by Mao, was widely interpreted in and out of the U.S. government as primary evidence that the Kremlin had "put over" the Chinese Revolution and now dominated Peking.

As Senator McCarthy said on March 30, 1950: "It was not Chinese democracy under Mao that conquered China as Acheson, Lattimore and Jessup contended. Soviet Russia conquered China, and an important ally of this conqueror was the small left-wing element in our Department of State."

Or as Dean Rusk put it a year later, May 18, 1951: "We do not recognize the authorities in Peiping for what they pretend to be. The Peiping régime may be a colonial Russian government—a Slavic Manchukuo on a larger scale. It is not the Government of China. It does not pass the first test. It is not Chinese."

It was not necessary for Dean Acheson and President Truman to share this view in toto (although they may have moved very far in this direction by mid-spring 1950) for them to agree on May 8, 1950, to advance $10,000,000 in credits to France for the support of the Bao Dai régime which was opposing Ho's Vietminh. By this time Acheson had been persuaded that the Kremlin was directing the Vietminh operations in Indochina.

The date of May 8, 1950, is an important one. Ordinarily it is assumed that the U.S. involvement in Vietnam occurred *after* Korea, that is in June

1950. In reality we had already begun to edge into Indochina *before* Korea under the perceived image of a united, powerful communist challenge, directed in Moscow and remarkably reinforced by the "puppet" régime in Peking.

What was the reality of China and the communist world at that moment?

We now know it was far, far different. Mao Tse-tung arrived in Moscow in early December 1949, having officially proclaimed his régime on October 1, 1949. The treaty with Stalin was signed nearly two months later, February 14, 1950. There was much evidence at that time (and even earlier) suggesting that Sino-Soviet relations were neither so close nor so warm as each party sought to indicate. But it was only after the open breach of the two powers and the polemics beginning in 1961 that Nikita Khrushchev revealed the reality—that China and Russia almost came to a parting of the ways in the very period when the world, and America in particular, concluded they were almost one and the same thing. Mao was so outraged by Stalin's "great power chauvinism," his insistence upon quasi-colonial agreements for the exploitation of China's natural resources, his determination to regain Russia's traditional economic and military posture in North China and Manchuria (and especially, the Dairen and Port Arthur bases) that Mao almost broke off talks. The two powers were held together only by their perception of the overwhelming danger of U.S. aggression.

The inference is clear that had President Truman and Secretary Acheson persisted in the policy which was almost surely their intention in the autumn of 1949, after Mao's October 1 proclamation and before his arrival in Moscow in December—that is, to move toward the recognition of the new Peking régime—this act alone would have been sufficient to derail the alliance of the two communist states and set China on the path of a far different course in world affairs.

Thus, by mid-spring 1950 America perceived a singular unity and direction of a Muscovite communist menace in Asia (which, in fact, did not exist). What of the perceptions in Peking of Russia and in Moscow of Peking?

There is substantial evidence to indicate that Stalin, at least, envisaged Mao as much more of an immediate and direct threat than, perhaps, Mao saw Stalin. I support that conclusion with what I readily confess is a somewhat unorthodox hypothesis concerning the cause and origin of the Korean War. I believe the war was instigated by Stalin but that his target was not, as is supposed, the United States but actually communist China.

In general terms, we know that Stalin placed very little confidence in any foreign communist leaders, including those he had named himself. The long record of hostile relations between the Chinese Party and Stalin and the emergence of Mao with a program and a strategy almost diametrically opposed to Stalin's (Mao, of course, was repeatedly reprimanded and even expelled from the Central Committee and the party for his deviations) in itself would be strong evidence for Stalinist hostility. The years 1949 and 1950 were those of extreme paranoia on Stalin's part, so far as foreign parties were concerned, touched off by Tito's defiant break. These were the years when Stalin and his secret police put in motion the purges of the East European parties, eliminating the old wheelhorses and replacing them with even more handpicked police nominees. There was nothing in the emergence and success of Mao and his movement calculated to quiet Stalin's nerves. In Moscow he purged at least two suspected Maoists, Mikhail Borodin and Anna Louise Strong.

Moreover, there is compelling evidence that even before Mao proclaimed his régime Stalin had secretly begun to construct an apparatus in China, to be used for his own purposes when the time came. His vehicle was a Chinese Party official named Kao Kang who emerged in early 1949 as the leader of the special Northeastern Autonomous region. As early as June and July of 1949 Kao Kang had been to Moscow and had signed special direct economic and other agreements. His relations with Moscow were extremely close, quite independent of Peking, and he was the virtual master of the most important industrial area of China. After Stalin's death convincing evidence came to light that Kao Kang was, in fact, Stalin's agent. He committed suicide and was charged by the Chinese with having been a traitor and with having plotted to turn Manchuria into a separate "kingdom." No public mention of whom he may have plotted with. The only plausible partner, of course, was Stalin, with whom he had so often conferred.

Premier Tsedenbal of Outer Mongolia has told me that one of Mao's first acts on coming to power was a request to Stalin for the return of Chinese suzerainty of Outer Mongolia. Stalin refused this request and tightened his control of this strategic area with its 1,500-mile frontier on China under his most reliable ally, the then party chief Choibalsan. He also improved Soviet military positions in Manchuria and North China by the terms of the 1950 treaty.

In the reality of the Soviet position *vis-à-vis* China the Korean venture assumes a radically new light. Acheson on January 12, 1950, speaking to the National Press Club in Washington, had drawn the U.S. defense line in the Pacific from Alaska and the Aleutians to Japan to the Ryukyus (Okinawa) and south to the Philippines. He did not mention Korea in this context. There were other similar statements (including one the year before by MacArthur), but the Acheson declaration was the most important. It was specific, detailed, calculated. There could be no reason for the omission of Korea (although Acheson continued to argue otherwise), except that it was not, in fact, on the U.S. defense perimeter.

The United States and Russia had withdrawn their occupation forces from South and North Korea respectively. I think it is reasonable to assume that Stalin felt he could take Washington's word—that we did not feel obligated to rise to the defense of South Korea.

This, then, unexpectedly presented him with a tempting possibility: if he could overrun all of Korea he would, in fact (although Mao, ignorant of the secret Stalin-Kao Kang relationship, could not be aware of this), be able to dominate Peking from positions in Mongolia, Manchuria and Korea. He would possess the power to deal with Mao as he once said he would with Tito ("I'll shake my little finger and Tito will fall").

Khrushchev in his new volume of reminiscences depicts Kim Il-sung as coming to Moscow and asking permission to attack the South—permission which Stalin gave. If this hypothesis is correct, Stalin triggered the Korean War on the basis of a mistaken image of the U.S. position. He anticipated noninterference. He got, instead, massive intervention under the auspices of the United Nations.

But if Stalin's image of the U.S. position was distorted, the U.S. image of Korea, Russia and China was equally distorted. Whatever the inner convictions of President Truman and Secretary Acheson may have been regarding the instigator of the conflict, they treated it as one, basically, of Chinese aggression. Moscow was asked to use its good offices in Pyongyang and Peking to persuade Kim Il-sung to withdraw. The U.S. response, outside of Korea, was entirely directed against the image of imminent Chinese aggression. The President not only ordered General MacArthur to take up Korea's defense. He gave Chiang Kai-shek the pledge specifically denied him in October 1949, an immediate defense blanket. He sent the Seventh Fleet into the Formosa Straits to bar an attack by communist China. He rushed military aid to the Philippines and sent (fateful move!) a military mission to aid the beleaguered French in Indochina.

Now, as can quite readily be determined today, there was no Chinese connection whatever with the Korean attack. There is every indication that Peking was as startled as Washington. The North Korean forces were armed and trained by the Russians. The Chinese had no part in that whatever. Kim Il-sung was a chosen Soviet agent for North Korea, trained by and devoted to Moscow. While the Soviet armed forces had left Korea in January 1949, Soviet specialists remained in all branches of the Korean military and government. The Chinese did not even send a diplomatic mission to North Korea until August 1950, two months after the attack occurred.

Of course, the hypothesis may be mistaken. Stalin may have given Mao some warning. But Mao's attention was deeply occupied at that time with the consolidation of his régime. He was busy with the absorption of Tibet and myriad other problems. His principal forward objective was Formosa, not Korea, and the Korean attack effectively put Formosa beyond his reach by the interposition of the U.S. fleet.

It is likely that Mao regarded the Korean move as a reckless Soviet gamble which confronted China with critical problems and serious dangers. If so, his analysis would have been fairly accurate, as the events of September and October 1950, the threat to the Yalu and the massive Chinese intervention, were to show. By this time, Stalin could see that his perception of U.S. policy had been grossly distorted and was probably quite willing to settle for as deep and complex an entanglement between the United States and China as could be produced. If his gambit for getting a stranglehold around Peking had failed, at least he had succeeded in embroiling two of his major antagonists.

However the Chinese may have perceived Soviet motivations in 1950, they have in recent years on several occasions informally cited the Korean War as a deliberate Soviet provocation, designed to embroil them with the United

States. Certainly by the time that MacArthur approached the Yalu the Chinese had concluded that the American operations in Korea were only a springboard for an assault upon China and a reopening of the U.S. intervention which had come to a close with the departure of Chiang Kai-shek from the mainland.

Here, to be sure, the Chinese deluded themselves. While there clearly was MacArthurian enthusiasm for going into China, President Truman dramatically demonstrated a bit later that he had absolutely no intention of broadening the Korean engagement into a continental war with China.

What of events in Indochina?

Here again reality was quite different from the perceptions of most of the participants. Ho had appealed for recognition of his régime on January 14, 1950. The Chinese granted recognition January 18, the Russians not until January 30. But neither of the major communist powers sent any formal missions to North Vietnam until after the 1954 ceasefire. Nor, in the opinion of the late Bernard Fall, did any direct connections exist with the Soviet Union until that time. Indeed, in his opinion Hanoi's principal communist party link up to 1954 was with the French Communist Party, not the Russian, not the Chinese, further evidence of the cautious effort of the Vietnamese to avoid falling under domination of a force which might control them.

In contrast to this reality there is abundant evidence that Secretary of State Dulles fully shared the perception of President Truman and Secretary Acheson (from June 1950 onwards) that Indochina was, in essence, merely the southern sector of a common front against China which extended from North Korea southward in a long curving arc. The truce in Korea did not shake the Dulles concept nor, in fact, did the Geneva agreement of 1954 which was designed to end the Indochina fighting. It is true that by this time, and particularly in the preparations of the Dien Bien Phu trap sprung against the French, Ho and General Giap were receiving a measure of cooperation from the Chinese, particularly in the form of rice to feed the besieging forces and the arms which were transported, broken down into loads carried by men and mules, some 1,500 miles from China.

But neither then nor later was it true, as Dulles and many U.S. policymakers supposed, that Ho was a "puppet" of Peking or that Peking was a "puppet" of Moscow. Khrushchev's remembrances cast some, not necessarily clarifying, light on this relationship. He asserts that the Chinese believed that Ho's jig was up at the time of Dien Bien Phu, that the Vietminh had come to the end of the road—an analysis which would indicate that the Chinese were not in close touch with the real situation and the Russians in even less touch. He also recalls telling his colleagues on his return from his first visit with Mao in Peking in November 1954 that "conflict is inevitable" with the Chinese.

Perhaps at no time did distortion and misperception over Indochina rise higher than in the 1965–66 period when U.S. air and ground action was constantly escalating to heights undreamed of earlier. By this time, to be sure, Hanoi had established close relationships with both Moscow and Peking. An estimated one billion dollars in aid had flowed into North Vietnam by the time of the Sino-Soviet break, roughly two-thirds Chinese and one-third Russian. In the subsequent years the totals were carefully balanced and probably the net contribution of the Soviet Union plus that of her East European allies more than equalled that of China. None the less, as anyone in a position to observe Hanoi closely could testify, North Vietnam had in no sense fallen under the domination of either of the great communist powers. In fact, Hanoi's role was one of constant, careful balancing between the two because hostility between Russia and China was so intense that the slightest act of favoritism was magnified and could—indeed, often did—result in reprisals by the affronted power, usually China.

It is not possible to reconstruct a unified American image of Vietnam at that time. Sometimes, Washington seemed to regard Hanoi as an instrument of Chinese policy, sometimes (particularly when trying to get Moscow to intercede in our behalf) as an instrument of Soviet policy, sometimes—ignoring the obvious evidence of Sino-Soviet hostility—as an instrument of the "international communist conspiracy" and even, occasionally, as an intransigent native communist movement seeking to "humiliate" the United States.

The view of the United States held in Hanoi at this time, as I was able to establish in conversations with Hanoi officials in December 1966 and January 1967, was much more in the image of the French than of the American reality. It was generally asserted and assumed that the United States simply wished to replace France as the exploiting colonial power in Indochina and that we had mounted the huge war effort for the benefit of capitalists who wished to exploit the enormous natural resources of Vietnam. When I rejoined that there was really nothing in the way of assets or resources in Vietnam which the United States coveted, my comment was regarded as both unfriendly and naive.

The Chinese image of the United States at that time was entirely different. The Chinese (as they told me) saw the U.S. escalation as the opening move in preparation for an all-out assault on China itself, an operation in which the United States was said to be collaborating closely with Moscow. Indochina was merely needed as a *place d'armes,* a springboard for the U.S. attack. It was expected that we would use nuclear arms, and a frequent justification given for the Red Guard and cultural revolution movement which was launched in mid-1966 was that it was designed to prepare, harden and "blood" the youth of China for the tremendous hardships of war with the United States which lay just ahead.

Peking's fear that Moscow was conniving with the United States in Vietnam was matched by fears expressed in Moscow that the Chinese, in some manner, would turn the Vietnamese war in a direction which would embroil the United States and the Soviet Union. It was fear of such possibilities which spurred Moscow, occasionally, to lend some assistance to the United States in exploring possible ways toward peace in Vietnam.

By 1969, it should be noted, the Chinese had moved away from their image of Vietnam as an American springboard for attack on China and, indeed, gradually were tending to abandon the theory of U.S.-U.S.S.R. collaboration against Peking. By this time both China and the Soviet Union tended to view Vietnam not so much in terms of U.S.-Vietnamese confrontation but as a "front" in their own ever-widening confrontation. Thus, China had opposed negotiations between the United States and Hanoi which finally opened in Paris in January 1969, to a substantial extent because of fear that this might move the United States and the U.S.S.R. closer to détente. Moscow generally favored negotiations because the end of the war in Indochina would be a blow to the Chinese communist propaganda line, directed toward Asian communist movements, of a continuous and constantly widening revolutionary movement of backward countries against more advanced ones.

The wide difference between the image of Indochina as viewed by Peking and by Moscow was spectacularly demonstrated in the Cambodian events of 1970. Peking seized upon the coup against Sihanouk to sponsor a summit meeting of Indochinese movements—Sihanouk for Cambodia, Prince Souphanouvong for Laos, Premier Pham Van Dong of North Vietnam and representatives of the Provisional Revolutionary Government of South Vietnam. With Chinese sponsorship, all the forces opposed to the United States in Indochina formed a "united front," dedicated to the principle of a common struggle and unified peace negotiation. The Russians, excluded from the China-sponsored meeting, studiously snubbed Sihanouk, maintained relations with the Lon Nol government (and insisted that their satellites do the same) and blamed the Chinese for the U.S. action in Cambodia (and in Vietnam) on the grounds that China had refused to form a "united front" against U.S. aggression.

I think enough instances have been presented (although there are many more which might be noted) to establish the thesis that the image of Indochina not only varies widely from one power to another but also from one period to another. The same is true of the images which the involved powers have of each other's actions and motivations. Rarely at any time do these perceptions coincide; almost equally rarely do they coincide with what, in retrospect, the objective truth is seen to be.

Watergate and the Myth of the Presidency

Theodore H. White

The era of national self-deception in Vietnam had not yet ended when Richard M. Nixon, sporting a "New Nixon" image, was inaugurated president of the United States in January 1969. During his first term in the White House, he rejected a past built on largely fanciful suspicions of Communism to achieve important breakthroughs in détente with the Soviet Union and a deescalation of the crusade against Communism in Southeast Asia. Even as Nixon swept to a second term with a victory over George McGovern in the presidential campaign of 1972, however, the nation was slowly becoming aware of another pattern of deception, mythmaking, and government-by-lying, which facts would finally disclose had been and continued to be a presidential disease. Watergate, the series of events that began in an abortive attempt to burglarize the Democratic National Committee headquarters in Washington's Watergate Hotel, was destined to lay bare the Nixon administration's talent for evasion, misrepresentation, and myth manipulation. In the opinion of the late president-watcher and free-lance historian Theodore H. White, as the facts of Watergate were gradually revealed Americans began to see more clearly that the image of the presidency had been used as a cover for unethical and often illegal activities. What Richard Nixon relied on most heavily before his fall from power was the "myth of the presidency"—the impression of honesty, credibility, and sincerity that through history had come to surround the Oval Office.

The true crime of Richard Nixon was simple: he destroyed the myth that binds America together, and for this he was driven from power.

The myth he broke was critical—that somewhere in American life there is at least one man who stands for law, the president. That faith surmounts all daily cynicism, all evidence or suspicion of wrongdoing by lesser leaders, all corruptions, all vulgarities, all the ugly compromises of daily striving and ambition. That faith holds that all men are equal before the law and protected by it; and that no matter how the faith may be betrayed elsewhere, at one particular point—the presidency—justice will be done beyond prejudice, beyond rancor, beyond the possibility of a fix. It was that faith that Richard Nixon broke, betraying those who voted for him even more than those who voted against him.

All civilizations rest on myths, but in America myths have exceptional meaning. A myth is a way of pulling together the raw and contradictory evidence of life as it is known in any age. It lets people make patterns in their own lives, within the larger patterns. Primitive people saw the forces at work as sun gods, moon gods, war gods, and prayed to them. Judaic civilization rested on the belief in the One Almighty, and Roman civilization on the myth of the republic. So, too, did later states and civilizations rest on myths—whether of the mandate of Heaven (as in China), or on the divinity of kings (as in medieval Europe), or on the Hegelian dialectic (as in the Marxist states of our times).

There is, however, an absolutely vital political difference between the mythology of other nations and the mythology of America. Other states may fall or endure; they may change or refresh their governing myths. But Frenchmen will always remain Frenchmen, Russians will be Russians, Germans remain Germans, and Englishmen—Englishmen. Nationhood descends from ancestral loins. One can easily contemplate the British Royal Navy becoming the People's Royal Navy, its remaining salts cheering alike for Comrades Horatio Nelson, Francis Drake, and Wat Tyler. But America is different. It is the only peaceful multiracial civilization in the world. Its people come of such diverse heritages of religion, tongue, habit, fatherhood, color, and folk song that if America did not exist it would be impossible to imagine that such a gathering of alien strains could ever behave like a nation. Such a stewpot civilization might be possible for city-states—a Tangier, a Singapore, a Trieste. But for so mixed a society to extend over a continent, to master the most complicated industrial structure the world has ever known, to create a state that has spread its power all around the globe—that would be impossible unless its people were bound together by a common faith. Take away that faith, and America would be a sad geographical expression where whites killed blacks, blacks killed whites; where Protestants, Catholics, Jews made of their cities a constellation of Belfasts; where each community within the whole would harden into jangling, clashing contentions of prejudices and interests that could be governed only by police.

Politics in America is the binding secular religion; and that religion begins with the founding faith of the Declaration of Independence, "We hold these truths to be self-evident, that all men are created equal, that they are endowed by their creator with certain unalienable rights, that among these are life, liberty, and the pursuit of happiness."

These words were written by men who had taken the best ideas of their English-speaking heritage and made them universal. Such language was almost incomprehensible to the non-English-speaking peoples who were drawn to America later in ever growing numbers seeking the promise. But the ideas were compelling, and still compel. The ideas could be couched in inflammatory political phrases: "No taxation without representation" or "Give me liberty or give me death." They could be robed in legal phrases, or juridical admonitions against illegal search and seizure; guarantees of right to trial; guarantees of freedom of assembly, free speech, free press, and, for the first time in history, the guarantee that the state would support no "establishment of religion." Most important of all, the original political myths promised "equal justice under law" and its consort, "due process of law." Though the strangers who came here to become Americans could not read the notes, the melody of those phrases gripped them.

Of all the political myths out of which the republic was born, however, none was more hopeful than the crowning myth of the presidency—that the people, in their shared wisdom, would be able to choose the best man to lead them. From this came a derivative myth—that the presidency, the supreme office, would make noble any man who held its responsibility. The office would burn the dross from his character; his duties would, by their very weight, make him a superior man, fit to sustain the burden of the law, wise and enduring enough to resist the clash of all selfish interests.

That myth held for almost two centuries. A man of limited experience like George Washington was transformed, almost magically, into one of the great creative architects of politics, fashioning a state and an administration out of nothing, a work of governmental art equal to that of a Lenin or a Mao. An ambitious politician like Abraham Lincoln of Illinois could, in the crucible of the presidency, be refined to a nobility of purpose and a compassion that hallow his name. A snob like Franklin D. Roosevelt and his missionary wife, Eleanor, could find in themselves and give to their country a warmth, a humanity, a charity that make them universal symbols of mercy and strength.

Within all the myths, thus, the myth of the presidency was crucial in the action against Richard Nixon. Many stupid, hypocritical, and limited men had reached that office. But all, when publicly summoned to give witness, chose to honor the legends—or, if they had to break with them, broke only to meet a national emergency.

Richard Nixon behaved otherwise. His lawlessness exploded the legends. He left a nation, approaching the 200th anniversary of its glorious independence, with a president and a vice-president neither of whom had been chosen by the people. The faith was shattered; and being shattered, it was to leave American politics more fluid and confused than ever since the Civil War.

Richard Nixon's legacy is best understood as a set of questions—questions that reach back for years, that reach forward for decades, questions about ourselves and what we seek from government.

The simplest set of questions can be embraced and answered in the formula of popular detective stories: Who did it?

Like any popular detective story, this is a story of bungling criminals. It begins with the circumstance, very difficult for Richard Nixon's enemies to accept, that most of the top men involved were devout patriots, convinced that what they were doing was best for their country. Men like Ehrlichman, Haldeman, Krogh were true believers in the purpose of America as they saw it, and sought nothing for themselves. Indeed, their self-righteousness made them far more frightening than men like John Mitchell, who was a rogue of a recognizable type, a cynic of fading health and energy who saw the crimes coming and failed to act. Beneath came all the others, men of little patriotism and no principle, as self-seeking as their enemies saw them—the hustlers, the bullies and all the crawling creatures of the underground, men set in motion by nothing more than ambition, and whose authority came from the self-righteous moralists at the top.

They entered into government, all of them, with no greater knowledge of how power works than the intrigues of the political antechambers and the folklore of advance men—and were quickly off into a dark land.

They were tantalized by the temptations of power, particularly the abuses of it they had found in Washington after the departure of Lyndon Johnson. Too many of the subordinate instruments of intelligence of the American government—the CIA, the FBI, the defense intelligence agencies—had crossed the threshold of law years before. They were there to be used. The clumsy break-in at Democratic headquarters in 1972 by Nixon men was technically criminal but of no uglier morality than the spying at Barry Goldwater's headquarters which Howard Hunt of the CIA had supervised for Lyndon Johnson in 1964. Their penchant for wire-tapping must certainly have been stimulated by the wire-tapping authorized by Johnson against the Nixon campaign of 1968. Their little early illegalities must have come naturally—and must have seemed only a step beyond those of their predecessors.

Still, there was nothing inevitable about the ultimate Nixon tragedy as the affair took root in early 1969 and 1970. But the political leaders of the Nixon administration, though they were experts at administration and professionals in politics, were amateurs in government.

They could not understand the essential balance there must always be in large affairs between cynicism and suspicion on the one hand and faith and truth on the other. A naïve politician gets nowhere—he flounders in passion, manipulation, prejudice, greed, interests. A successful politician must, inescapably, be something of a hypocrite, promising all to all, knowing that, if elected, he must inevitably sacrifice the interests of some for others. But a man in government must know when to choose trust and faith over political need. If exposure of his acts threatens to contradict his words, he must renounce his acts and keep his word, because the people must trust his words at whatever cost—or he cannot govern. In the presidency, *a fortiori*, where the words are the words of the high priest, it is essential to recognize the moment for truth.

That moment came first, for Richard Nixon, on June 20th, 1972, when he and Haldeman discussed the lawless break-in at Watergate during the previous weekend. The lost clue in the detective-story "whodunit" still remains the deliberate erasure of eighteen and a half minutes of that morning's conversation. Did they recognize the difference between what the partisan politics of the campaign required and what the responsibility of the presidency required? Did they measure the extent of their gamble? No one but Nixon can know who erased that tape later, or for what reason. But the two top men of the administration—Nixon and Haldeman—must at least have exchanged surmises as to how the break-in came about and what they should do about it. The extent, if any, of their first recognition of responsibility is forever lost. By

June 23rd, however, three days later, came a clear act of obstruction of justice—the attempt to use the CIA to halt the FBI's investigation of the crime. Straining as hard as imagination permitted, and if one drew on no other evidence, one could persuade one's self from the transcript of that conversation that here were two malicious politicians simply playing dirty tricks without any awareness of what government is supposed to mean.

There was as yet nothing inevitable about the great explosion to come. For the first weeks after the burglary, it was possible for the president to purge himself simply by calling for or permitting the indictment of two men, John Mitchell and Jeb Magruder. Nixon would have had to butcher these two aides; this would have been painful. But as president he would have been faithfully executing the law and so would have retained his presidency—and with it the power, as a politician, to pardon later those who had served him fervently but neither wisely nor well. Indeed, in those early weeks, before John Mitchell committed perjury, it would have been difficult for even the most effective prosecutor to have persuaded a District of Columbia jury that the nodding acquiescence of the faltering old man was in fact complicity in crime, or participation in a conspiracy. But Mitchell's reputation would have had to be sacrificed and with it his dignity, for he would then have been exposed as a fool. And Magruder's freedom would have had to be sacrificed, for he was then already a criminal.

By the time of the election of 1972, however, too much more had happened, with or without the president's knowledge, for him to have satisfied the law without sacrificing not only Mitchell and Magruder but also his personal lawyer, Kalmbach, his official lawyer, John Dean, and probably his personal aides, Haldeman and Ehrlichman. Of their precise complicities in coverup the president was either unwitting or could make himself appear to have been unwitting. His lying had already begun—tentatively but undeniably.

By early April of 1973, he could no longer even make himself appear unwitting. In March he had come under blackmail and had begun to learn all the details of the bungled coverup. This pained his neat mind, for the coverup was grotesquely mismanaged, hilariously inefficient, his white-collar managers proving themselves hideously incompetent at what Mafiosi could do skillfully. Not only that: by April, 1973, the news system had the story in raw outline, by May in detail, and by midsummer the Ervin Committee had put face, flesh, and voice to the drama in public. Yet Nixon persisted in concealment. And it was his persistence in the coverup that gave the motor energy to the charges of obstruction of justice, Article I of impeachment.

This persistence in the coverup led, however, to drama of a greater order—the search for evidence. And when the evidence, the tapes, and the internal White House memoranda began to unfold, they revealed a more shattering hidden story: that of abuse of power. In that story, quickly or slowly, everyone interested in American politics began to see the fundamental threat—the threat to the future, the threat that moved the most thoughtful members of the Judiciary Committee to vote for Nixon's impeachment. If such practices had occurred before, they had occurred secretly. Now they were public. If they were to be accepted publicly and not repudiated, then all future presidents would be free to break the same laws Nixon had broken.

The challenge to the myth was open. If the Judiciary Committee did not act, the office of the president would be transformed. And then there would be no faith, no real strength in America, no compelling reason for men to stand and fight or die in jungles or in air, nor even to behave decently to one another as law-abiding citizens.

From mid-April of 1973 to his end in 1974, the president lied; lied again; continued to lie; and his lying not only fueled the anger of those who were on his trail, but slowly, irreversibly, corroded the faith of Americans in that president's honor. He knew what he was doing, for he consciously relied on the mystique of the presidency to carry him through what lay ahead. Very little in all the transcripts of his conversations is more poignant than an interchange in one of the last recorded with Bob Haldeman—a telephone conversation on April 25th, 1973, when their front of deception was being broken, but hope still lived. "Bring it out and fight it out and it'll be a bloody god-damned thing," said Nixon to Haldeman that day as they recognized how damning John Dean's testimony might be. But, admitting that the fight would be "rough as a cob," Nixon continued, "we'll survive. . . . Despite all the polls and all the rest, I think there's still a hell of lot of people out there, and from what I've seen they're—you know, they, they want to believe, that's the point, isn't it?"

If Nixon had committed a historic crime—treason, or accepting graft, or knowingly warping American national policy for personal or partisan ends—the detective story would suffice. Its answer to the question is that the criminals were caught because they were bunglers.

But the initial crime was so commonplace; and Nixon might have erased it so easily by acting as presidents must act against lawbreakers; and he compounded that crime so casually into the coverup and disaster, that another set of questions presses on—not how the criminals were caught, but why Nixon did what he was caught doing.

"Why?" is a political question and one that will overhang American politics for years to come. Nixon was not a stupid man. What did he think he was defending beyond his own skin and reputation?

To get at the political answer, one must discard the criminal-story approach and approach the facts as a political detective story.

Many clues mislead or confuse, as in all detective stories. There is, for example, the almost absurd love of money which underlay so much of Richard Nixon's behavior—his use, for example, of government purse and government facilities to give him the comforts which many poor men can only imagine. But other presidents—Eisenhower and Johnson, too—had shared this absurd love of money. Nixon's personal avarice turned out to be irrelevant—no one bought, bribed, or paid either the president or any of those closest to him for favors which personally enriched them. There is the bizarre shakedown of great corporations and industrialists organized by his campaign financers—but his operators were acting not out of personal greed but out of managerial zeal and competitive instinct, tracking down the same big game of fat cats their rivals hunted, only with more enthusiasm, lawlessness, and efficiency than ever before. And there is no record of any such corporation or contributors' group, from ITT to the milk producers, having succeeded in buying favor from the Nixon administration or its agencies remotely comparable to the secret lease in 1922 of Naval oil reserves at Elk Hills and Teapot Dome by Edward L. Doheny and Harry F. Sinclair, who "loaned" or paid $100,000 and $223,000 respectively to Secretary of the Interior Albert B. Fall. There are all sorts of other clues and facts, from the bloody (like the bombing of Cambodia) to the technical (like the impoundment of funds). But they, too, lead one off the trail.

To trace the answers to the question of "Why?" one must accept the political reality that Richard Nixon and his men were, for the first time in American politics since 1860, carrying on an ideological war. Because they felt their purpose was high and necessary and the purpose of their enemies dangerous or immoral, he and his men believed that the laws did not bind them—or that the laws could legitimately be bent.

Again one must go back to a set of American myths to explain the intensity of the ideological war that began in the decade of the sixties—the war simplifiers see as the struggle over "government controls."

Wrapped around the original political myths of America—of liberty, of equality, of a government-of-laws-not-men—had been a culture, long since demolished, with a set of social myths now twisted by time and Talmudic exegesis into the rigid political dogmas of today.

The old social myths rested on the underbracing belief that a free citizen was able to control his own future by his own efforts. In the original American community of farmers 200 years ago, when rich and fertile land spread unplowed beyond the Alleghenies, it was considered a matter of gumption and go, of thrift and diligence and planning, whether a man made it or did not. Accident, or drought, or a bad harvest might prevent him from reaping what he sowed—but next year might bring better luck. Government was the town meeting, which built roads to the city to sell the harvest, or, on a federal scale, opened roads over the Alleghenies to the fertile loam of the Midwest. But in corporate America, since the turn of the twentieth century, fewer and fewer men have been able to control their own future by their own efforts—except lucky speculators or the very rich who controlled their family future by wisely sheltering the fortunes that came down to them from their fathers. Now, in a present-day America, everyone was locked up—in corporations, in unions, in organizations, in schools, in draft boards, in the tax net—and group leverage was the thing. Nixon and his men believed in the old social myths and the old culture; his adversaries believed in mobilizing group leverage to compel the federal government to do their will or protect their future. Nixon and his men believed in no free rides. His adversaries believed that government must provide the ride. Translated into practical politics, the old social myths gave no guidance on how you provided jobs or security for all in an industrial society, how you made sure the paycheck would stretch with inflationary prices, how you protected people in old age when there was no hearth to warm them, no village green where they could sit and sun, no family to nurse them.

The old myths extolled self-government. In a beautiful political symmetry, the states and the federal government originally agreed that each had separate responsibilities, and after that, the states worked out the powers of counties, villages, towns, cities, giving them large subordinate responsibilities. But in practice, by the 1960's, the heart of the problem lay in the cities and suburbs—how you moved resources down to local governments so they could meet their local responsibilities; and secondly, whether the federal government would or should insist that local governments adjust to the national cultural requirements of the day.

But the most deceptive inherited social myth was of American power. The virulence of that myth was fresh—and rested on the fleeting dominance of American arms as they spread triumphant over the entire globe in 1945, when, from the Golden Gate to Karachi, from the rim of the Atlantic all the way to the Middle East, no plane flew the globe except under the surveillance or with the permission of American might. Americans fight their wars with a singular moral ferocity that is the terror of their enemies; strangers who see the American planes winging in overhead must regard them as the Christian world regarded the Arab horsemen of the seventh and eighth centuries. Not only that—Americans were accustomed to carry this moral ferocity into home politics while they fought their wars, ostracizing entire social groups, choking free discussion at home, seeking enemies hidden among themselves, granting autocratic powers to the president, who must command the war effort. What had happened, however, by the sixties, was that the myth of American power had been substantially eroded by the revolutions of the postwar world. Americans were confronted with a new reality—they were engaged in the first major war that they would not win. By the time Nixon came to power, that realization had split the country at every level, and resentment at the waste and killing in Vietnam had spilled out into the street in sputtering violence and frightening bloodshed.

Nixon had, to be sure, recognized the erosion of American power abroad. As soon as he was inaugurated in 1969, he had begun to liquidate the war in Vietnam, the first strategic retreat of American arms since George Washington yielded the cities of the Atlantic seaboard to the British. But he clung to the old doctrine that the president must command this retreat, that the president alone could make the decisions and arrange the timing for a withdrawal from Asia that would bring peace with honor. Those who opposed him, whether in the streets or in the news system, he would treat with the moral ferocity of previously sanctioned wars. He had come out of one war a veteran; moved up in politics at the time of the Korean War, at the height of the anti-Red hysteria of the late forties and early fifties. He had won his first national fame by trapping Alger Hiss. Hiss, a trusted officer of the State Department, had been dealing with Whittaker Chambers, a member of the Communist conspiracy. Of his role in that case Nixon made the first chapter of his book, *Six Crises*— and he would never forget, nor let his closest aides forget, about Alger Hiss. For him and for them, the enemies of America were present as much within the government as overseas. His distrust of the servants of government began then, and continued to the end. The idea of ever-present conspiracy blurred and merged always in his political thinking with the political issues which his ideological enemies thrust at him.

The real domestic political issues had been growing increasingly divisive for years before Nixon came to power: How could the cities be helped to meet their responsibilities? How far should the Federal government go in support of education? At what price to the whites must the needs of the blacks be met? How should the government go about making a national welfare system reasonable? What price must be paid to clean the environment of pollution that all recognized as a menace? Here, in modern politics, very few of the old social myths helped either explain or shape the new realities that demanded confrontation.

And one divisive question above all was tearing at America when Nixon came to power: What right did the government have to conscript American men to kill people in other countries in order to save those countries?

The political detective story of Nixon's crime begins there—with his belief that he, as president, was sole custodian of America's power. The Nixon men saw themselves as waging war in Vietnam to make peace. They had no doubt that national security required them to carry on that war by all means possible until peace with honor had been won. If the end was good, then the means, however brutal, must also be good. And from this concept of the president's authority came most of the early illegalities, the buggings, the wire taps, the surveillances, the minor crimes. Until finally the president's men saw no distinction between ends and means, and they were making war not just in Vietnam but all across the home front, too. All the disputes over home issues, as well as foreign issues, were sucked into the vortex of ideological war; and, as in war, victory became the only goal and the means savage.

But the political story does not quite answer the "Why?" or explain the particular ferocity of behavior of the men at the White House.

To explain the venom and hatred of their struggle, one must add one more condition—the change of culture that was taking place all over America of the sixties. All great political conflicts, everywhere, are underlain by a struggle of cultures, as men begin to see their places in the world differently, as their "consciousness" is "raised" to new perceptions and indignations. And the political struggle of the sixties and the early seventies was taking place at just such a moment of cultural upheaval. The Nixon men were men of the embattled old culture. As such, they believed the new culture was not only undermining the authority of their president to make war-and-peace, but striking into the homes, families, and schools, too. It was undermining the values with which they had grown up and still held dear. The beardies and the longhairs, the bikini-clad and miniskirted merged in their minds with the rioters, the street demonstrators, the draft-card burners, the sex revolutionaries. They had no great literate spokesmen to speak for their side; but as politicians and manipulators they could fight back by the code of the jungle.

This conflict of the two cultures far surpassed in emotion the traditional

American political struggle between "conservatives" and "liberals." Both cultures now shared only one word, "freedom," which came down from the original political myths. But that word, as it always had, concealed the practical conundrum—one man's total freedom meant curtailing some other man's freedom. The prosperity of the sixties had incubated so many experiments, so many dreams, had opened so many avenues for self-exploration that now the concept of individual liberty or community responsibility carried totally different meanings on different lips. There were the people of the old culture who still felt no one should be allowed to threaten close-knit family life; who felt a choke in their throats when the flag passed by; who felt the Bible was an externally true code of morals which teachers ought to be free to read in class; who felt that neatness in dress, diligence in work, neighborliness were visible indexes of good citizenship. But others of the new culture, just as sincere, believed that good family life required free choice in or out of wedlock, that the responsibility of parenthood or personal behavior patterns was theirs alone to decide. A new Babbitry of permissiveness confronted an old Babbitry of conformity.

The two cultures clashed in every form of expression—in language, in costume, in slogans. They clashed, as political issues between them hardened, over such trivia as pornography and homosexuality. They clashed over much more important matters—civil rights, "law-and-order," safety in the streets, drug abuse, the dignity of women.

Claiming for themselves the undeniable right to lead their own lives and to direct their children's lives as they wanted, the spokesmen of the new culture paradoxically insisted on ever-widening intervention by the government in other people's lives—to tell other people where to send their children to school, where and how to build their homes, where and how to dispose of their wastes. The old culture insisted that such social controls were dangerous—but it also insisted, as paradoxically as its adversaries, the government must have the right to send men to die in an illegal war, that police must have the right to raid without court warrant the homes of anyone suspected of hiding narcotics.

The line of clash between the two cultures ran through families as well as communities. Fathers against sons, mothers against daughters, students against teachers, arguing over such matters as dress and manners and morals and sex and drugs and rioting. Bob Haldeman wore his hair crew-cut, his son wore his hair shoulder-length. Within families, within communities, much of the clash could be translated as the natural clash between generations—most fathers and mothers have revolted at some point against their own parents. Long-hairs and short-hairs, beardless and bearded have succeeded each other in those generations of American heroes whose portraits hang in schoolrooms and the corridors of the Capitol. But now this clash of culture and personal values was taking place at the same time as the political clash over the hard issues. And the two multiplied each other emotionally and politically, to conceal the intricate, complex, true problems of American government—What must be changed in this industrial society where the old social myths no longer held? How fast the change? How much control was needed? Who would control? Who must pay? Who must get hurt?

One must see all three wars—the war abroad, the ideological war, the cultural war—as intersecting in the agony of an unstable personality in order to answer the personal "Why?" of Richard Nixon's collapse.

Unless one is satisfied that Nixon is a total hypocrite, a man of unrelieved brutishness, one must ask how he could stomach what he authorized and learned about his administration and its underground. And the answer can come only by imagining that here was a man who could not, in his waking moments, acknowledge the man he recognized in his own nightmares—the outsider, the loner, the loser.

Throughout his career, except for a few brief years in 1971 and 1972, that had been his inner role—the outsider, the loser. "They" were against him, always, from the rich boys of Whittier College to the hostile establishment that sneered at his presidency. His authority as president was being challenged by the news system, the rioters, the Congress, the intellectuals. The culture, the manners, the credos of his lonely life of striving were being wiped out by the fashions of the new culture. Nixon could deal masterfully with Russians, Chinese, Arabs of the Middle East by the old set rules of power. But at home the rules were being changed against him, and he was losing. Losers play dirty; he, too, would change the rules. His ruthlessness, vengefulness, nastiness were the characteristics of a man who has seen himself as underdog for so long that he cannot distinguish between real and fancied enemies, a man who does not really care whom he clashes with or hurts when pressed, who cannot accept or understand when or what he has won. Thus, then, the portrait of a man who saw himself at Thermopylae or Masada.

Over and over again, as one reads the transcripts of his inner thoughts from the tape recordings, one sees he did consider such matters as honor and faith, and even thought of himself as honorable and faithful. But then he came down, knowingly, against honor, against faith. Cornered by history, he seemed to be defending all at once the authority of the presidency, his cultural values, his confederates—and his own skin.

And always, in the crisis, he reacted as the cornered loser. He could not shake that characteristic—which made of the election of 1972 not only a political paradox but a personal paradox: the loser had won—and won by such a margin as to unsettle even more stable personalities. He had won so largely that he could misread his victory. It was a victory for his ideas and politics. But he saw it as personal, as a loner. It was not simply an election he had won; he had conquered a land; its citizens were the occupied and he could toy with law as he wished, however much a hostile Congress, the news system, or intellectuals protested.

Yet even those who had voted for him in 1972 thought otherwise.

Not Separate; Not Equal

Carol Ruth Berkin

Myths concerning the role of women in American society—myths based on sexual attitudes, gender roles, and cultural mores—are being challenged vigorously. No longer is it acceptable to view women as the "second sex." Women have in many important respects overcome a historical legacy fashioned by social practice, literature, religion, mythology, and folklore that consistently cast them in the role of inferior, submissive—yet of course highly respected—creatures. This evolution of new attitudes toward women, this redefinition of gender roles and reconfiguration of social mythology, has been especially pronounced since the passage of the Nineteenth Amendment in 1920. While constituting a cultural revolution of the first magnitude, concludes Carol Ruth Berkin, Professor of History at Baruch College, City University of New York, the women's movement in the twentieth century has enjoyed both significant triumphs and a good many Pyrrhic victories. While American society has taken on a new complexion, much of the tyranny of past thinking and practice regarding women remains. Faced with a "confusion of choices," women have sought to shape a new set of realities even as apparent employment gains won in World War I, for example, proved illusory. The postsuffrage sexual revolution was "more doubtful than real," and today the often contradictory practicalities of being both career woman and "professional wife" have proved difficult to resolve. True egalitarianism—the movement's ultimate objective—has been thus far an elusive dream.

If the movement for suffrage has always excited the interest of historians, the apparent disintegration of the women's movement after the passage of the Nineteenth Amendment has disturbed and puzzled them. In dozens of different ways, historians have echoed the sentiments of reformers like Jane Addams and Charlotte Perkins Gilman, asking, "What happened to feminism in the 1920s?"

What Happened to Feminism?

The question is both legitimate and vital. Yet strangely, even historians who view themselves as sympathetic to feminism have sought to answer it by a sometimes merciless dissection of the movement itself. The result has been the isolation of a social movement from the larger context in which, perforce,

From *Women of America: A History*, ed. Carol Ruth Berkin and Mary Beth Norton. Copyright © 1979 by Houghton Mifflin Company. Used with permission.

it operated, and an internal exploration that seriously distorts the complex relationship between the women's movement and American society.

The approach does have its ironies. It is surely an ironic compliment to the feminist minority that, in laying the blame for the unfinished revolution on their shoulders, historians have invested these women with the very control over events and over their own destinies that they had long been seeking. But we must take care to look for cause and effect in their proper place, even if it diminishes our confidence in the power of a determined minority.

It was true that suffrage marked a watershed for the women's movement—if not for women. It is also true that there were many clear signs that feminism, in its most heralded victory, had somehow gone astray. Suffrage, once a practical goal among many, had come to be seen as the struggle itself. Perhaps this was inevitable, for the efforts and energies involved in the campaign tended to escalate and elevate the importance of the vote. Perhaps, in this insistence that the vote would be the universal panacea, we see the wishful thinking of women who were themselves in conflict over their personal and social identities. Yet the ballot, and the campaign for it, should not be dismissed as a symbol become an albatross. The vote could be a powerful tool for social change if wielded with skill and precision and with excellent timing.

But it was the *ifs* that proved overwhelming: if American women could be organized, quickly, into a conscious voting bloc; if a structure could be created for and by women so that they could communicate, debate, and resolve political questions as a first step toward united political action; if effective mechanisms could be found to influence the existing major party structures; and finally, if the political atmosphere in the nation was such that the political agenda could be turned to women's issues in order to bring them to a vote at all. Not surprisingly, the loose coalition known as the women's movement was no more successful in turning suffrage into a force for social change than labor or the blacks would prove to be.

This does not deny that there were also major internal weaknesses in the feminist movement. Participating women's groups—varying from pacifists to radical feminists to social reformers—could not agree on new priorities. The coalition around suffrage crumbled as old, suppressed, and unresolved differences reemerged; what, after all, did women want?

Unfortunately, the confusion of choices they faced were largely negative, not positive, choices. The question was what to struggle for next: economic equality, psychological liberation, educational reform, unionization, an end to legal discrimination? Should the priorities be women's issues or social reform in general? And, which women did the activists now represent? Womanhood was woven into the complex fabric of class, region, religion, race—a common strand that could not be pulled with the ease it occasionally seemed to promise.

The leadership was divided and uncertain about what feminism even meant. After so many years, feminism could not be defined in ways that satisfied all. The radical interpretation, an inheritance from nineteenth-century thinkers like Gilman, challenged home and family structure in ways that many reformist women could not accept. Yet no new definition was forthcoming. These women could not provide models for the mass of middle- and working-class white women, for they were themselves without a clear vision of what the modern woman and her movement should be. The consequence of this confusion was a decentralization, a return by many to discrete arenas of struggle, and a new generation of younger women who could respond to the multiple image before them by selecting bits and pieces from it to build their own identities. The middle-class flapper was, in that sense, a true child of feminism. For one thread of the women's movement had stressed acceptance as an individual as a measure of equality. The boundaries between individuality and self-absorption could be hazy; the sexual self could be viewed as the individual self; and the pursuit of individual happiness was, after all, part of America's most cherished ideological baggage.

But the inability of women activists to select and define new goals was not the major problem they faced. Even had they been able to repeat the extraordinary and difficult task of coalition they had just seen end in victory, there were concrete signs that the social and political milieu in which they operated as a minority was hostile to further reform. Historians of the 1920s give abundant evidence that this was not a decade hospitable to reform. In 1919 the Palmer raids disrupted and frightened radical labor and socialist organizations. In the twenties, a conservative Supreme Court threatened to reverse the few gains made by women and other workers toward minimum wages and maximum hours. A decade of presidents without obligations to reform factions meant that no White House support (with its legitimation of issues) could be expected. Open hostility to reform groups grew during the postwar era, and feminism, like labor organizations, was labeled foreign, dangerous, un-American. Jane Addams, it was rumored, was a Communist.

The Successful Woman's Revolution: Myths and Realities

Perhaps most frustrating for those who remained feminists was the public insistence, by means of the media, that equality had, after all, been achieved. The popular media treated liberation as a fait accompli, and, with a style both self-congratulatory and breathless, heralded the flapper as living proof of the revolution completed. Modern women were no longer restricted by archaic codes of dress or behavior; they smoked in public, exposed their knees, and spoke openly of sex and sexuality. They could now choose freely between a career or marriage. And, though it was conceded that the two options could not be integrated, either choice was sure to prove exciting and fulfilling. The new marriage and the new motherhood, detailed in guides like John Watson's *Psychological Care of Infant and Child,* had transformed the domestic world into a challenging life career. The woman question had, in short, been answered to every sensible American's satisfaction.

The realities of the 1920s and 1930s did not confirm this view. Mere jobs, rather than exciting careers, were not so easy to find. Access on any level to the job market, which had risen so dramatically in the first decade of the century, now seemed frozen; 23 percent of the labor force were women in 1920; 24 percent were women a decade later. The apparent employment gains won in World War I proved more illusory than real. War mobilization had not provided new workers with jobs, but new jobs for old workers; women in menial and unskilled factory jobs had been promoted to better positions during the war emergency. But their wages remained discriminatory and their promotions proved temporary.

With the armistice, women were driven out of these slots in order to restore men to their civilian occupations. The discrimination was entirely egalitarian: Women streetcar conductors and women judges were removed with the same dispatch. The same equality of treatment appeared for those who managed to remain employed; for them all, wage differentials were a constant. Among middle-class teachers, women performed their classroom tasks for 1,394 dollars a year in 1939, while men earned 1,953 dollars for the same duties. Among the working class, the differential in wages for men and women actually rose from 6.3 cents an hour in 1923 to 10.2 cents in 1929.

Those women who did find jobs in the peacetime era were clustered in the ranks of unskilled labor. Fifty-seven percent of all working women were black and foreign-born and worked as domestic servants or garment industry laborers. And, middle-class women soon discovered that training for a career and actually having one were not equally attainable goals. The doors of academia had opened wide to female students but not to female professors: One-third of all graduate degrees were awarded to women in the 1930s, but women constituted only 4 percent of the full professors at American universities. Even acquiring the skills of prestigious professions proved difficult, for medical schools and law schools established quotas as rigid as 5 percent until 1945.[1]

Few, if any, of these depressing realities were susceptible to modification by the ballot just won. The battlefields were too diverse, ranging from the courts to the conference rooms of the American Federation of Labor, where leaders decided women were not worth the effort to organize. Without unionization, without favorable new government policy or enforcement of old policy, without a political machine to force change, and with a diffused consciousness among their own ranks, women remained during these decades the cheapest, most flexible, and least demanding labor force in the country.

Even the sexual revolution of the postsuffrage era was more doubtful than real. The acceptance of a notion that women too had sexual drives was surely important, but a woman defined by her sexuality remained a woman defined by her sex. And, somehow, the new search for sexual satisfaction seemed to lead where the old denials of sexual drives had also led: to marriage, a family, and total responsibility for child and home care. An old set of obligations was now presented to women as a new profession; women's colleges like Barnard and Bryn Mawr rededicated themselves to producing the educated wife and the educated mother.

The Depression decade brought an end to the romantic imagery of flapper and bowdlerized Freudianism. As jobs grew scarce, complaints against working women grew frequent. The old, persistent notion that women worked for "pin money" while men worked to support their families led many to argue that one more unemployed woman meant one more working man. In 26 states, bills were introduced to prohibit married women from working. In fact, because women were confined largely to domestic service and menial factory jobs, their employment was never competitive with men.

The new Democratic administration of 1933 did seem, however, to promise improved circumstances for American working women. Women became visible in the federal government, called to Washington as members of a bureaucracy once closed to them by rule and custom. The reversal of fortune was a logical product of Roosevelt's reform agenda, with its many relief and welfare agencies. The male agency heads needed experienced social workers to implement their programs, and social work, from the earliest pioneer days of Jane Addams, was a woman's profession.

More important than this sudden visibility were the legislative gains made during the New Deal period. Reforms like the Social Security Act of 1935, which provided federal money for programs in maternal and pediatric care, and the Fair Labor Standards Act of 1938, which established at last a maximum hour–minimum wage standard for all workers in interstate commerce, benefitted a broad spectrum of American women. For working-class women in the unskilled labor force, the New Deal's nurturing of labor organizations meant the first welcoming into the union structure through the Congress of Industrial Organizations' (CIO) activities.

These gains, important as they were, were limited; enforcement often fell short of pronouncement. Wherever industries could negotiate terms on an individual basis, they seemed able to win government approval for differential wage scales. The New Deal was willing to give women an old deal when the Friday paychecks came around.

The depth and durability of an automatic discrimination by sex in treatment and in expectation seemed best illustrated in the New Deal Youth Programs. Young men in Franklin D. Roosevelt's Civilian Conservation Corps received a regular salary; young women in Eleanor Roosevelt's retraining program received maintenance and a small allowance.

In the popular and prescriptive literature of the 1920s and even in the 1930s, the potential contradictions of the two dominant images, career woman and professional wife and mother, went largely unnoticed. The tensions did not become apparent because, in reality, the experience of work and of marriage rarely coincided. Neither experience conformed to the exaggerated idealized models, but women did live out the two options in their imperfect forms sequentially rather than simultaneously, if they experienced both at all. The fact was that women with genuine professional careers remained unmarried; only 12.2 percent of all professional women were married in 1920, and 75 percent of all women earning the Ph.D. degree were single in 1924.

The average middle-class woman worked only when she was young and single. As a wife and mother she lived within the domestic circle. Only among the poor whites and the black population did the problems of integrating the demands of the domestic role and the worker's role emerge. And, whatever their resolution to the conflicting roles and the accommodations made in family structure, they were not likely to be trendsetters in a society whose idealizations and legitimized norms filtered downward, never up. The isolation of these immigrant and black women, physically and emotionally, from the middle classes further assured that they would have no impact on American models of womanhood. Until the majority of white American women experienced a conflict between traditional sex-role expectations and the new demands of work outside the house, the "woman problem" would remain officially solved.

The Impact of World War II

Seen in this light, World War II acquires a new primacy in the history of women. As several recent historians have pointed out, the mobilization of women in the war effort changed American reality, even if American sex-role definitions lagged far behind. This very gap between reality and the available interpretation of it may have spurred the social consciousness we associate with the rebirth of feminism in the 1960s.

The war mobilization brought six million women into the labor force—women working outside the home for the first time. The government, now seeking to overcome the very traditional prejudices against working married women that it had long supported, tapped the nation's greatest reserve labor source by propaganda campaigns, by the suspension of protective legislation that had locked women out of skilled work and its higher salaries, and by the establishment of federally funded day care centers. Within five years the percentage of women in the work force rose from 25 percent (1940) to 36 percent (1945). And these women were to be found in heavy industry; "Rosie the Riveter" was a factory worker, not a clerk or a domestic. But a peacetime economy shifted government priorities once again. The problem was to avoid massive unemployment after the war, and to government policy makers, unemployed was a male adjective. Women had to be taken off the job so soldiers could return to their rightful places in the civilian economy.

Women, however, proved resistant. An overwhelming majority wanted to remain in the labor force not the labor reserve. Eighty percent of these working women, especially those black women for whom factory work meant upward mobility from domestic service, tried to keep their jobs. Most were unsuccessful: Layoffs, demotions in rank and pay, outright firings, all eliminated women from their wartime positions. Within less than two years, women were reduced from 25 percent to 7.5 percent of American auto workers.[2] The government assisted women's early retirement by cutting off federal funds for day care in 1946.

But a return to a nostalgic prewar "normalcy" was not to be effected. Although Rosies no longer riveted, many did continue to bring home a paycheck. Increasing bureaucracies shifted labor needs after the war, and the new worker—the office worker—was an excellent slot for the middle-class white woman. What seemed to trouble most of their critics was that these postwar working women included many wives and mothers. In the literature of the day a new reinterpretation of American social ills began to focus on this entrance of housewives into the job market. Philip Wylie's *Generation of Vipers* was typical, and virulent; his analysis pointed that finger at working wives as emasculating, life-sapping vipers, wrecking American morals and culture, rather than as life-giving women. The unnatural woman who deserted her home and family was the new American villain.

Soon all the problems of the modern society—war, economic depression, juvenile delinquency—were attributed to women's absence from the home. These new women were self-wreckers as well as home-wreckers, for movement into the masculine sphere was creating a new, neurotic woman. The fury of this attack by popular Jeremiahs and academic doomsayers may bespeak the certainty of the social change they abhorred. But if the literature did not alter women's steady integration into the work force, it must surely have added a conscious biting edge to the doubts of women fearful that adding new roles might well make them unable to fulfill the old.

If anything, young women of the postwar era seemed more firmly committed to marriage and family. They did not need glossy magazines to extol the virtues of suburban life and large families; the reality was that 60 percent of young women were dropping out of college to marry and start a family.[3] At no time in the twentieth century were the contradictions in the American woman's life more striking than in the 1950s: An invisible black and immigrant minority continued to work without critics showing any concern over their femininity; white middle-class girls were marrying younger than their grandmothers had done; feminism as a conscious ideology was moribund; yet, more women were working outside the home than ever before.

The pattern was not so crazy-quilt, however. Early marriage and a longer life expectancy for middle-class women were the ironic contributing factors to an increase in working wives. Married at 20, finished with childbearing at 26, these women could expect 20 years of adult life without child-rearing duties. Such women were perfectly suited to the job market demands. What employers wanted—now that the once vast immigrant labor pool was a thing of the past and young single women were growing ever rarer—was a supply of cheap, undemanding white-collar labor, with no career ambitions, willing to work part-time at wages kept low by the absence of unions and the low expectations of the workers themselves.

The jobs were there, in short. But what motivated these women to take them? It has been argued that the steady rise of married women who entered the job market was a definitive sign of trouble in suburban paradise and the sexual division of spheres it symbolized. This hypothesis, most dramatically put forward by feminist Betty Friedan, has been sympathetically received by many, but not yet subjected to historical study.[4] A second motivation could be suggested: income. The standard of living the middle-class family sought required dual earnings; amid the inflation and rising expectations of the postwar era, a woman's income was not pin money, but the necessary contribution to sustaining middle-class existence. Providing education, social opportunities, superior medical care for the children became a mothering duty best fulfilled at the typewriter or file-clerk desk.

Was the suburb a trap? On this point, feminist desires to legitimate their demands for new opportunities in the masculine sphere may have misled us. Surely the variety of responses to any role, and the creative ways in which it is given depth and dimension, are evident in women's lives as well as men's in the twentieth century. Volunteer work, participation in a network of women's clubs and organizations, the satisfaction of a familiar life—these may well be realities on a par with the social isolation of the suburb, the pleasures of adult companionship in the work situation, and the sense of emptiness Friedan found in the women she studied. This much is sure: The percentage of married women in the work force rose from 15 percent in 1940 to 30 percent in 1960. And this, despite the fact that ideology lagged behind social change: The increase in married women in the work force preceded the social imprimatur that granted wives the right to work once their mothering chores had ended.

That more women worked does not imply that their place in the competitive job market improved. They met with discriminatory wages, segregation into sex-defined occupations, and little opportunity for advancement. Further, the women of this transitional era were subject to a double jeopardy: Exploited in a job market they needed to enter and whose conditions they could not control, they were also operating in a system that had made no adjustments in the traditional monopoly of duties women faced in the home. Women could, it seemed, enter the male sphere and be women; but the role definition for men held no such reciprocal flexibility. Nothing symbolized the circumstances of the postwar woman more, perhaps, than the evolution of the secretarial position. Here the family homemaker could be the office homemaker as well. A threat to neither boss nor husband, the wife-secretary was welcome to their worlds.

The Second Feminist Movement

In the 1960s a new feminist movement emerged. Room for the feminist movement to develop was provided by a decade of political leadership either personally liberal or dependent in some degree on liberal coalitions within the parties or voting constituencies. The sophisticated concentration on the legal system by other reform coalitions had created a social atmosphere in which feminism could again organize itself. As a movement, its roots lay in that reform cluster of the 1960s—civil rights, student radicalism, the antiwar protest. From participation in these, young women acquired the organizational skills and experience needed to lobby for their own interests.

Many middle-class young women claimed to have discovered their feminism in the sexist atmosphere of these reform movements. This awareness requires our further examination; its relationship to activism may be more, or less, than it has appeared superficially to be. The mothers of these younger activists were not lacking in organizational skills; church-related organizations, work experience as well, made available to at least a sizable minority of American middle-class women the skills needed to operate organizations like those emerging in the late sixties. What prevented them from organizing?

An awareness that the job market was discriminatory could not have been lacking. But a translation of awareness of discrimination into activism was missing. That their daughters made that step, not in relation to their real economic circumstances, but in political activities reminiscent of social feminism—in the struggle for peace, black rights, and the transformation of the society—must be reckoned with. The need for an examination of mother-daughter relationships during the 1950s and 1960s presents itself for feminist scholars and the scholars of feminism.

What seemed to be true is that, if the origins of the movement as a movement lay in the reforms of the 1960s, the changed world of women in which it found itself was at least equally important to its growth and sustenance. By the 1960s a generation with working mothers had role models, no matter how modest, for self-reliance and self-esteem; better and more education had created an articulate, overtrained, and underemployed pool of talents; effective and legal birth control and a widespread belief in a population crisis made motherhood a choice rather than an inevitable product of marriage; and an increasing number of single and divorced women found their middle-class sense of rights and privileges contrasting sharply with their poverty-level economic options. Thus the women's movement was anchored even in the lives of women who refused to identify with it.

The Future of American Women

Today, because the majority of white women have left the exclusivity of the domestic sphere, the "woman problem" has become a pervasive one. Its definition is still not entirely clear, but, like the feminism of Gilman and Stanton, its core seems to be egalitarianism. Whether it will be resolved in an egalitarian manner is, however, not known. This is not the only outcome; other options and forms of accommodation do exist.

Modern feminism struggles in three arenas: the job market and the likelihood of equal access and mobility within it, the private sphere of home and family and the redistribution of roles in it, and the psychosocial sphere, in which the image and self-image of both sexes require major readjustments before equality is a possibility. Logically the arenas overlap. But the problem for feminists is that progress or setback can be uneven in each or in any combination; social policy makers may choose to see these arenas as discrete, each with its own degree of egalitarian or nonegalitarian accommodation. Feminist goals, in short, may be granted legitimacy in one arena but not in another.

Legal victories for egalitarianism were won in the early 1960s, when civil rights legislation laid a new basis for feminist demands, and in 1972, when the Federal Education Act banned sex discrimination in higher education. In 1973 the Supreme Court ruled abortion a private decision; that same year Congress submitted the Equal Rights Amendment (ERA) for ratification. But enforcement is not always vigorous enough to transform the models *de jure* into conditions *de facto*. Significantly, the necessary apparatus to allow freedom from child care to women who wish it does not yet exist. A rational system of day care centers is resisted by policy makers who still insist on maintenance of conservative notions of the family. Public support—male and female—for the transformation of family chores and family organization is far from unanimous.

Politically, the seventies seem less promising than the sixties. The vitality of a women's movement capable of articulating, and pressuring for, reforms is uncertain. Within the movement there remain the difficulties of forging strong political alliances across class lines and racial-ethnic divisions. The growth in the last decades of a new female labor pool composed of legal and illegal immigrants from racial and ethnic groups outside the traditional European-African identifications presents old problems with new faces. These Oriental and Hispanic women workers in the garment industry and in our factories cannot be "invisible" to the eye of the women's movement. Externally, the recessions of the 1970s, the clear shift to the center of liberal factions within the major parties, and the rise of organized antifeminist forces suggest an antireform atmosphere similar to that of the 1920s.

The high morale and the spirit of cooperation shown at the Houston Convention in 1977 must be balanced by the fact that the ERA has not yet been ratified and is in danger of failing, and by the likelihood that abortion may become a ballot-box decision. The insistence that full equality is not a priority or a necessity because many women do not want to exercise it has had an impact even upon historians writing in the field. The notion that equality should be resolved by an appeal to numbers is all too much a part of American tradition; oddly, few defenders of feminist goals have pointed out that should the same criteria apply to other rights, American suffrage itself would have been repealed years ago in the face of repeated voter apathy.

Finally, the fact is that even if the integration of women into the work force continues, this need not mean economic equality. Thus far, it has not. The percentage of women in the professions has actually decreased since 1940 and the differential between male and female wages has increased 8 percent since 1959. In 1970, the average woman college graduate could still expect a smaller annual income than the man with an elementary school education. Poverty among women has increased; in 1959, 26 percent of the total poor were female, but in 1968, that figure was 41 percent.[5]

The future of American women is not yet clear. Modern feminism has increased women's consciousness of inequality and has indicated the areas in which that inequality is buttressed by law, custom, and sexual stereotyping. But because more women know what they want, this does not mean they will get it.

Notes

1. The figures used above are drawn from two secondary sources: William Chafe, *The American Woman: Her Changing Social, Economic and Political Role, 1920–1970,* Oxford University Press, New York, 1972, pp. 48–65; Lois Banner, *Women in Modern America: A Brief History,* Harcourt Brace Jovanovich, New York, 1974, pp. 155–161.

2. Chafe, *The American Woman*, p. 180.
3. Banner, *Women in Modern America*, p. 218.
4. Betty Friedan, *The Feminine Mystique*, Norton, New York, 1963.
5. Banner, *Women in Modern America*, pp. 237–238.

Martin Luther King, Jr.: Charismatic Leadership in a Mass Struggle

Clayborne Carson

The plight of black Americans historically has been that of the "invisible man." Kept "down on the plantation" early in the history of the republic and more recently segregated and ghettoized socially, politically, economically, and educationally, blacks have been systematically stereotyped, caricatured, mythologized, disenfranchised, discriminated against—not to exclude lynched—by a society claiming to subscribe to principles of freedom, equality, and opportunity. Called by some the Second Reconstruction, the modern civil rights movement has sought to redress past wrongs, to set racial mythology aside, and to shame American society into recognizing the faulty alignment between the nation's declared values and its legal and factual affection for racism. A critical agent in beginning this process of change was the charismatic leader the Reverend Martin Luther King, Jr. But even while recognition of Dr. King's greatness is secure, argues Clayborne Carson, Professor of History at Stanford University and a director of the Martin Luther King, Jr., Center for Nonviolent Social Change, the matter of his historical significance needs yet to be defined. Particularly challenging in this regard is an already emergent "King myth" built around his legendary reputation. Certain important correctives to King's "didactic legend"—for example, to tie him to black traditions and institutions and to assess better his relationship to the civil rights movement in its many local manifestations—need to be made before what can approximate a final judgment is possible.

The legislation to establish Martin Luther King, Jr.'s birthday as a federal holiday provided official recognition of King's greatness, but it remains the responsibility of those of us who study and carry on King's work to define his historical significance. Rather than engaging in officially approved nostalgia, our remembrance of King should reflect the reality of his complex and multifaceted life. Biographers, theologians, political scientists, sociologists, social psychologists, and historians have given us a sizable literature of King's place in the Afro-American protest tradition, his role in the modern black freedom struggle, and his eclectic ideas regarding nonviolent activism. Although King scholars may benefit from and may stimulate the popular interest in King generated by the national holiday, many will find themselves uneasy participants in annual observances to honor an innocuous, carefully cultivated image of King as a black heroic figure.

The King depicted in serious scholarly works is far too interesting to be encased in such a didactic legend. King was a controversial leader who challenged authority and who once applauded what he called "creative maladjusted nonconformity."[1] He should not be transformed into a simplistic image designed to offend no one—a black counterpart to the static, heroic myths that have embalmed George Washington as the Father of His Country and Abraham Lincoln as the Great Emancipator.

One aspect of the emerging King myth has been the depiction of him in the mass media, not only as the preeminent leader of the civil rights movement, but also as the initiator and sole indispensable element in the southern black struggles of the 1950s and 1960s. As in other historical myths, a Great Man is seen as the decisive factor in the process of social change, and the unique qualities of a leader are used to explain major historical events. The King myth departs from historical reality because it attributes too much to King's exceptional qualities as a leader and too little to the impersonal, large-scale social factors that made it possible for King to display his singular abilities on a national stage. Because the myth emphasizes the individual at the expense of the black movement, it not only exaggerates King's historical importance but also distorts his actual, considerable contribution to the movement.

A major example of this distortion has been the tendency to see King as a charismatic figure who single-handedly directed the course of the civil rights movement through the force of his oratory. The charismatic label, however, does not adequately define King's role in the southern black struggle. The term *charisma* has traditionally been used to describe the godlike, magical qualities possessed by certain leaders. Connotations of the term have changed, of course, over the years. In our more secular age, it has lost many of its religious connotations and now refers to a wide range of leadership styles that involve the capacity to inspire—usually through oratory—emotional bonds between leaders and followers. Arguing that King was not a charismatic leader, in the broadest sense of the term, becomes somewhat akin to arguing that he was not a Christian, but emphasis on King's charisma obscures other important aspects of his role in the black movement. To be sure, King's oratory was exceptional and many people saw King as a divinely inspired leader, but King did not receive and did not want the kind of unquestioning support that is often associated with charismatic leaders. Movement activists instead saw him as the most prominent among many outstanding movement strategists, tacticians, ideologues, and institutional leaders.

King undoubtedly recognized that charisma was one of many leadership qualities at his disposal, but he also recognized that charisma was not a sufficient basis for leadership in a modern political movement enlisting numerous self-reliant leaders. Moreover, he rejected aspects of the charismatic model that conflicted with his sense of his own limitations. Rather than exhibiting unwavering confidence in his power and wisdom, King was a leader full of self-doubts, keenly aware of his own limitations and human weaknesses. He was at times reluctant to take on the responsibilities suddenly and unexpectedly thrust upon him. During the Montgomery bus boycott, for example, when he worried about threats to his life and to the lives of his wife and child, he was overcome with fear rather than confident and secure in his leadership role. He was able to carry on only after acquiring an enduring understanding of his dependence on a personal God who promised never to leave him alone.[2]

Moreover, emphasis on King's charisma conveys the misleading notion of a movement held together by spellbinding speeches and blind faith rather than by a complex blend of rational and emotional bonds. King's charisma did not place him above criticism. Indeed, he was never able to gain mass support for his notion of nonviolent struggle as a way of life, rather than simply a tactic. Instead of viewing himself as the embodiment of widely held Afro-American racial values, he willingly risked his popularity among blacks through his steadfast advocacy of nonviolent strategies to achieve radical social change.

He was a profound and provocative public speaker as well as an emotionally powerful one. Only those unfamiliar with the Afro-American clergy would assume that his oratorical skills were unique, but King set himself apart from other black preachers through his use of traditional black Christian idiom to advocate unconventional political ideas. Early in his life King became disillusioned with the unbridled emotionalism associated with his father's religious fundamentalism, and, as a thirteen-year-old, he questioned the bodily resurrection of Jesus in his Sunday school class.[3] His subsequent search for an intellectually satisfying religious faith conflicted with the emphasis on the emotional expressiveness that pervades evangelical religion. His preaching manner was rooted in the traditions of the black church, while his subject matter, which often reflected his wide-ranging philosophical interests, distinguished him from other preachers who relied on rhetorical devices that manipulated the emotions of listeners. King used charisma as a tool for mobilizing black communities, but he always used it in the context of other forms of intellectual and political leadership suited to a movement containing many strong leaders.

Recently, scholars have begun to examine the black struggle as a locally based mass movement, rather than simply a reform movement led by national civil rights leaders.[4] The new orientation in scholarship indicates that King's role was different from that suggested in King-centered biographies and journalistic accounts.[5] King was certainly not the only significant leader of the civil rights movement, for sustained protest movements arose in many southern communities in which King had little or no direct involvement.

In Montgomery, for example, local black leaders such as E. D. Nixon, Rosa Parks, and Jo Ann Robinson started the bus boycott before King became the leader of the Montgomery Improvement Association. Thus, although King inspired blacks in Montgomery and black residents recognized that they were fortunate to have such a spokesperson, talented local leaders other than King played decisive roles in initiating and sustaining the boycott movement.

Similarly, the black students who initiated the 1960 lunch counter sit-ins admired King, but they did not wait for him to act before launching their own movement. The sit-in leaders who founded the Student Nonviolent Coordinating Committee (SNCC) became increasingly critical of King's leadership style, linking it to the feelings of dependency that often characterize the followers of charismatic leaders.[6] The essence of SNCC's approach to community organizing was to instill in local residents the confidence that they could lead their own struggles. A SNCC organizer failed if local residents became dependent on his or her presence; as the organizers put it, their job was to work themselves out of a job. Though King influenced the struggles that took place in the Black Belt regions of Mississippi, Alabama, and Georgia, those movements were also guided by self-reliant local leaders who occasionally called on King's oratorical skills to galvanize black protestors at mass meetings while refusing to depend on his presence.

If King had never lived, the black struggle would have followed a course of development similar to the one it did. The Montgomery bus boycott would have occurred, because King did not initiate it. Black students probably would have rebelled—even without King as a role model—for they had sources of tactical and ideological inspiration besides King. Mass activism in southern cities and voting rights efforts in the deep South were outgrowths of large-scale social and political forces, rather than simply consequences of the actions of a single leader. Though perhaps not as quickly and certainly not as peacefully nor with as universal a significance, the black movement would probably have achieved its major legislative victories without King's leadership, for the southern Jim Crow system was a regional anachronism, and the forces that undermined it were inexorable.

To what extent, then, did King's presence affect the movement? Answering that question requires us to look beyond the usual portrayal of the black struggle. Rather than seeing an amorphous mass of discontented blacks acting out strategies determined by a small group of leaders, we would recognize King as a major example of the local black leadership that emerged as black communities mobilized for sustained struggles. If not as dominant a figure as sometimes portrayed, the historical King was nevertheless a remarkable leader who acquired the respect and support of self-confident, grass-roots leaders, some of whom possessed charismatic qualities of their own. Directing attention to the other leaders who initiated and emerged from those struggles should not detract from our conception of King's historical significance; such movement-oriented research reveals King as a leader who stood out in a forest of tall trees.

King's major public speeches—particularly the "I Have a Dream" speech—have received much attention, but his exemplary qualities were also displayed in countless strategy sessions with other activists and in meetings with government officials. King's success as a leader was based on his intellectual and moral cogency and his skill as a conciliator among movement activists who refused to be simply King's "followers" or "lieutenants."

The success of the black movement required the mobilization of black communities as well as the transformation of attitudes in the surrounding society, and King's wide range of skills and attributes prepared him to meet the internal as well as the external demands of the movement. King understood the black world from a privileged position, having grown up in a stable family within a major black urban community; yet he also learned how to speak persuasively to the surrounding white world. Alone among the major civil rights leaders of his time, King could not only articulate black concerns to white audiences, but could also mobilize blacks through his day-to-day involvement in black community institutions and through his access to the regional institutional network of the black church. His advocacy of nonviolent activism gave the black movement invaluable positive press coverage, but his effectiveness as a protest leader derived mainly from his ability to mobilize black community resources.

Analyses of the southern movement that emphasize its nonrational aspects and expressive functions over its political character explain the black struggle as an emotional outburst by discontented blacks, rather than recognizing that the movement's strength and durability came from its mobilization of black community institutions, financial resources, and grass-roots leaders.[7] The values of southern blacks were profoundly and permanently transformed not only by King, but also by involvement in sustained protest activity and community-organizing efforts, through thousands of mass meetings, workshops, citizenship classes, freedom schools, and informal discussions. Rather than merely accepting guidance from above, southern blacks were resocialized as a result of their movement experiences.

Although the literature of the black struggle has traditionally paid little attention to the intellectual content of black politics, movement activists of the 1960s made a profound, though often ignored, contribution to political thinking. King may have been born with rare potential, but his most significant leadership attributes were related to his immersion in, and contribution to, the intellectual ferment that has always been an essential part of Afro-American freedom struggles. Those who have written about King have too often assumed that his most important ideas were derived from outside the black struggle—from his academic training, his philosophical readings, or his acquaintance with Gandhian ideas. Scholars are only beginning to recognize the extent to which his attitudes and those of many other activists, white and black, were transformed through their involvement in a movement in which ideas disseminated from the bottom up as well as from the top down.

Although my assessment of King's role in the black struggles of his time reduces him to human scale, it also increases the possibility that others may recognize his qualities in themselves. Idolizing King lessens one's ability to exhibit some of his best attributes or, worse, encourages one to become a debunker, emphasizing King's flaws in order to lessen the inclination to exhibit his virtues. King himself undoubtedly feared that some who admired him would place too much faith in his ability to offer guidance and to overcome resistance, for he often publicly acknowledged his own limitations and mortality. Near the end of his life, King expressed his certainty that black people would reach the Promised Land whether or not he was with them. His faith was based on an awareness of the qualities that he knew he shared with all people. When he suggested his own epitaph, he asked not to be remembered for his exceptional achievements—his Nobel Prize and other awards, his academic accomplishments; instead, he wanted to be remembered for giving his life to serve others, for trying to be right on the war question, for trying to feed the hungry and clothe the naked, for trying to love and serve humanity. "I want you to say that I tried to love and serve humanity."[8] Those aspects of King's life did not require charisma or other superhuman abilities.

If King were alive today, he would doubtless encourage those who celebrate his life to recognize their responsibility to struggle as he did for a more just and peaceful world. He would prefer that the black movement be remembered not only as the scene of his own achievements, but also as a setting that brought out extraordinary qualities in many people. If he were to return, his oratory would be unsettling and intellectually challenging rather than remembered diction and cadences. He would probably be the unpopular social critic he was on the eve of the Poor People's Campaign rather than the object of national homage he became after his death. His basic message would be the same as it was when he was alive, for he did not bend with the changing political winds. He would talk of ending poverty and war and of building a just social order that would avoid the pitfalls of competitive capitalism and repressive communism. He would give scant comfort to those who condition their activism upon the appearance of another King, for he recognized the extent to which he was a product of the movement that called him to leadership.

The notion that appearances by Great Men (or Great Women) are necessary preconditions for the emergence of major movements for social changes reflects not only a poor understanding of history, but also a pessimistic view of the possibilities for future social change. Waiting for the Messiah is a human weakness that is unlikely to be rewarded more than once in a millennium. Studies of King's life offer support for an alternative optimistic belief that ordinary people can collectively improve their lives. Such studies demonstrate the capacity of social movements to transform participants for the better and to create leaders worthy of their followers.

Notes

1. Martin Luther King, Jr., speech at the University of California, Berkeley, tape recording, May 17, 1967, Martin Luther King, Jr., Papers Project (Stanford University, Stanford, Calif.).
2. Martin Luther King, Jr., described this episode, which occurred on the evening of January 27, 1956, in a remarkable speech delivered in September 1966. It is available on a phonograph record: "Dr. King's Entrance into the Civil Rights Movement," *Martin Luther King., Jr.: In Search of Freedom* (Mercury SR 61170).

3. Martin Luther King, Jr., "An Autobiography of Religious Development" (c. 1950), Martin Luther King, Jr., Papers (Mugar Library, Boston University). In this paper, written for a college class, King commented: "I guess I accepted Biblical studies uncritically until I was about twelve years old. But this uncritical attitude could not last long, for it was contrary to the very nature of my being."

4. The new orientation is evident in William H. Chafe, *Civilities and Civil Rights: Greensboro, North Carolina, and the Black Struggle for Equality* (New York, 1980); David R. Colburn, *Racial Change and Community Crisis: St. Augustine, Florida, 1877–1980* (New York, 1985); Robert J. Norrell, *Reaping the Whirlwind: The Civil Rights Movement in Tuskegee* (New York, 1985); and John R. Salter, *Jackson, Mississippi: An American Chronicle of Struggle and Schism* (Hicksville, N.Y. 1979).

5. The tendency to view the struggle from King's perspective is evident in the most thoroughly researched of the King biographies, despite the fact that the book concludes with Ella Baker's assessment: "The movement made Martin rather than Martin making the movement." See David J. Garrow, *Bearing the Cross: Martin Luther King, Jr., and the Southern Christian Leadership Conference* (New York, 1986), esp. 625. See also David L. Lewis, *King: A Biography* (Urbana, 1978); Stephen B. Oates, *Let the Trumpet Sound* (New York, 1982); and Adam Fairclough, *To Redeem the Soul of America: The Southern Christian Leadership Conference and Martin Luther King, Jr.* (Athens, 1987).

6. See Clayborne Carson, *In Struggle: SNCC and the Black Awakening of the 1960s* (Cambridge, Mass., 1981); and Howard Zinn, *SNCC: The New Abolitionists* (Boston, 1965).

7. For incisive critiques of traditional psychological and sociological analyses of the modern black struggle, see Doug McAdam, *Political Process and the Development of Black Insurgency, 1930–1970* (Chicago, 1982); and Aldon D. Morris, *Origins of the Civil Rights Movement: Black Communities Organizing for Change* (New York, 1984).

8. James M. Washington, ed., *A Testament of Hope: The Essential Writings of Martin Luther King, Jr.* (San Francisco, 1986), 267.

Indian Life: Transforming an American Myth

William W. Savage, Jr.

It is only recently that a measure of greater awareness, a new consciousness, has begun to arise regarding a glaring omission from the nation's history—an adequate incorporation and assessment of the American Indian, the so-called vanishing American. Until the present, any measure of understanding seldom has transcended the myth of the Indian as either Bloodthirsty Savage or Noble Red Man. In the hope of transforming such persistent American mythology, Professor William W. Savage, Jr., of the University of Oklahoma discusses the images and forces that have worked to obscure the first Americans. Attempting to arouse a greater measure of sensitivity to the complexity and distinctiveness of the Indian past, Savage explores especially the images of the Indian in popular culture, from travel narratives through the film era. These representations collectively attest to the fundamental ambiguity of a nation simultaneously preoccupied with, and culturally estranged from, its aboriginal peoples. Given the dialectical nature of enduring cultural stereotypes, American Indians have been a perpetual anomaly and embarrassment to white America; their position within, outside, or at the margins of American society constitutes a continuing national dilemma.

The Indian occupies a unique position in the American popular mind. It is not a position that is easily defined, because its historical antecedents lie in the ambiguity with which Americans have customarily contemplated Indians. Thus, "the Indian"—a myth, a conceptual monolith, a stereotypical composite of all Indians about which more will be said later—appears in American culture in a series of paired images: he is both a noble savage and a brute, a bearer of gifts and a bloodthirsty killer of women and children, a teacher without whose help survival is impossible and a ward incapable of survival without public or private assistance. Such are the renditions of Americans who have always believed that they should come to some conclusion about Indians but who have been equally uncertain how to go about it, a dilemma reflected in three hundred years of American popular culture.

The first ambiguous response to Indians belonged to Christopher Columbus, their discoverer and the man who misnamed them. Struggling to define for his employers just who and what these aborigines were, he described them as being "neither black nor white." That left considerable room for speculation, as did Columbus' observation that Indians would make fine subjects for his majesties and that some could be converted to Christianity. Those who clung to idolatrous ways, he noted, would be suitable slaves.

Europeans, who knew little about Indians except that they existed, craved more information. It was amply provided in extravagant and largely fictional travel narratives, accounts belonging to a literary genre designed to entertain and inform, with emphasis on the former rather than the latter. Travel narratives fired the fantasies of Europeans for a hundred years after Columbus with tales of wild and brutish men who inhabited the New World. The first English colonists, having had a steady diet of such fables and possessing no reliable information, knew at least that Indians were something with which to reckon, and so they came armed, built forts, and organized militia.

On the other hand, the colonists were strangers in the Indians' environment, and, to make their way, they learned what they could of Indian survival techniques and to an extent copied Indian life styles. Later, as the number of colonists grew and as European nations established patterns of expansion in North America, Indians became socially, politically, and economically expendable; thus they were systematically driven from land desired by white settlers and were confined to areas considered by whites to be uninhabitable. The mode of their secular existence was called into question, and the economic bases of their various cultures were destroyed. And, if that were not enough, their spiritual lives were deemed unacceptable to the white majority, and they were beset by missionaries of all persuasions. When all other forms of exploitation had run their course, Indians were utilized by white society as entertainment, which was, after all, precisely the use to which they had been put in the travel narratives.

The history of Indian-white relations in North America, involving diverse European nationalities and equally diverse aboriginal cultures, is complex and merits more than brief consideration. But the point here is this: it is a history that has given rise to potent ideas concerning the ways in which disparate peoples view each other. From that history, or from an imperfect understanding of it, Americans acquired their mythic "Indian," their conceptual monolith—a painted horseman who dwells in tipis; wears feathers in his hair; is given to guttural speech and terrifying war cries; is crafty, wise, sly, and violent; and stands in opposition to that fixture of American popular culture the cowboy. Additionally, the ways in which Americans have stereotyped Indians indicate the presence of something approaching a monumental preoccupation with Indian life. Whatever parallels one finds between the history of Indian-white relations and the patterns of culture contact on frontiers other than North America, it is certain that nowhere else is there a comparable popular preoccupation with the details of aboriginal society and culture manifested by the dominant population. Nowhere else did numbers of whites run away to live with the aborigines, and nowhere else do the vestiges of aboriginal life enjoy such popularity.

From the very beginning, Anglo-Americans ran away to the Indians. In the eighteenth century the phenomenon was sufficiently common to prompt Hector St. John de Crèvecoeur to wonder why there was no corresponding migration by Indians wishing to become "civilized Europeans" and, further, what would become of the whites who became Indians. "It will be worthy of observation," he mused,

> to see whether those who are now with the Indians will ever return and submit themselves to the yoke of European society; or whether they will carefully cherish their knowledge and industry and gather themselves on some fertile spot in the interior parts of the continent; or whether that easy, desultory life so peculiar to the Indians will attract their attention and destroy their ancient inclinations. I rather think that the latter will preponderate, for you cannot possibly conceive the singular charm, the indescribable propensity which Europeans are apt to conceive and imbibe in a very short time for this vagrant life; a life which we civilized people are apt to represent to ourselves as the most ignoble, the most irksome of any. Upon a nearer inspection 'tis far from being so disgusting.

A good many Spanish conquistadores and no less a personage than Captain John Smith had discovered that a portion of the Indian population was female, and that fact accounted for some of the attraction the wilderness had for whites. Longfellow's Hiawatha spoke for the nobility of it all, and James Fenimore Cooper publicized the masculine friendships that waited in the woods, rivaling, in time, the message of Nathaniel Hawthorne's Roger Chillingworth, that life among the Indians was not conducive to good mental health. Chillingworth, of course, had been captured by Indians and so represented another perspective. But if whites contemplated abandoning civilization for Indian ways, they also demonstrated an abiding interest in accounts of the lives of those forced to cohabit with aborigines. Captivity narratives—written or dictated by whites who had been captured by Indians and who subsequently were released or escaped—were enormously popular in the colonial period, and the captivity theme has endured in American popular culture to the twentieth century.

Life among the Indians, whether forced or voluntary, contributed to the ambiguity of white feelings about Indians. The frontier—and the frontier was defined in terms of proximity to Indians—was at once a place to which one might flee to escape from the pressures of civilization and a place where danger lurked behind every rock and tree. There white men might find either sanctuary or death—or, for the religious, salvation in one guise or another. Conflicting images struggled for acceptance, but the contest was not confined to an intellectual plane, and when the economic realities of frontier living manifested themselves, the negative image, wherein devils and danger resided, began to dominate white thinking.

In the colonial period nations measured wealth and power by the amount of territory each controlled. The emergence of the new American nation after 1776 altered that perception only slightly. The thirteen former colonies had debts to pay—the creditors most often being their own citizens—and no money with which to pay them. To the federal and state governments land was money, and debts were paid in land, or the land was sold to private individuals or companies to generate revenue. But if whites were to occupy land, the Indians must first be removed from it, and so whites developed a series of images of Indians and Indian life useful in justifying wholesale dispossession.

The justifying images were, of course, wholly negative with regard to the portrayal of the Indian as a human being. The bloodthirsty brute of the travel narratives was resurrected and amplified in captivity narratives and journalistic pronouncements and, later, in dime novels. To justify the acquisition of territory, Anglo-Americans had to reconcile their economic motives with their ethical and moral responsibilites, a feat accomplished by recourse to law (something that Indians did not "understand") and by defining Indians as less than human. If Indians were not human—and their failure or refusal to comprehend white law proved to whites that they could not reason—then they were mere animals, and the land on which they lived was, by definition, uninhabited. God had told man, whites recalled, to subdue the earth and hold dominion over the beasts of the earth. Indians were not men but animals, and killing them was as good a way as any to hold dominion. Those were widespread beliefs and, to judge from the efficiency with which whites confined, incarcerated, and slaughtered Indians, they provided the necessary philosophical underpinning for white expansion. But, widespread or not, they were not unanimously held, and the romantic myth of the noble savage survived, through one medium or another, thanks largely to the efforts of liberal reformers who opposed harsh treatment of Indians.

The negative stereotype endured after it no longer had any political utility. Even before the last Indian attempt at resistance was broken at Wounded Knee in 1890, entrepreneurs found that the image of a fierce aborigine had a certain appeal to eastern and European audiences. In 1885, William F. Cody, who capitalized on his reputation as a frontiersman by exporting western characters for eastern consumption (it was he who had made a hero of the lowly cowboy), hired the storied Sitting Bull for Buffalo Bill's Wild West for $50 a week and a bonus of $125. Cody favored Sioux employees because people had heard of their tribe and because they were colorful, which is to say that they rode horses and wore feathers. Apaches, of whom people had also heard, were drab by contrast, which is to say that they managed life with few horses and fewer feathers. This use of Indians as picturesque entertainment continued a long literary tradition and established patterns that would be extended yet further by the visual media of the twentieth century. Sight and sound were the Indians' stock in trade in extravaganzas like Cody's, and it is perhaps to Cody's credit that he employed the genuine articles. Motion-picture directors, after all, quickly discovered that anyone could portray an Indian if he could ride and avoid allergic reactions to paint and plumage.

The road shows of Buffalo Bill, Pawnee Bill, Colonel Frederic T. Cummins, and others were popular until well into the twentieth century, as were various traveling medicine shows featuring Indians. These spectacles originally capitalized on the image of the Indian as a teacher—in this case a specialist in the medicinal use of herbs—an image that quacks had been exploiting in America since at least the eighteenth century. But at the end of the nineteenth, when the Indian acquired the status of a curiosity in the East, and in the twentieth, when nostalgia for the vanishing wilderness enjoyed the vogue that gave rise to Tarzan and the National Park Service, Indian medicine shows enjoyed something of a revival in popularity. It is axiomatic that authenticity of heritage (or anything else) was not a prerequisite for selling placebos, but, whereas Cody and the Wild West show promoters had stressed the genuineness of their product, the medicine merchants made only feeble attempts at verisimilitude. There were Indians who spoke with foreign accents and Indians who claimed to be champion cowboys; and each Indian woman was a princess, each man a chief. Whether or not these people were Indians at all often seemed to be of secondary importance. It is doubtful, for example, that the audiences in the 1930's that saw Chief Sweetwater, of Harry B. Cody's Dr. Michael All-Herb and Health Institute of Chicago, cared one whit about the first item in the ballyhoo that billed him as a "full-blooded Sioux Indian, escape artist and aërial daredevil." The legacy of the medicine shows to the concept of Indians-as-entertainment was that anyone who looked like an Indian could be an Indian, because anybody could act like one. Motion-picture directors would discover that, too.

Traveling shows and popular fiction kept the stereotyped Indian before the public until motion pictures could continue the tradition. But the movie Indian required time to develop, owing to the initial limitations of the film medium. The stereotype owed much to sight and sound, but in silent films the Indian could only be picturesque. Hooves could not thunder, Indians could not whoop, and victims could not scream—obvious handicaps for purveyors of popular entertainment. Still, the public wanted Indians, and it got what it wanted. Indian films were abundant in the silent era, and for the most part they marked a return to the romantic myth of the noble savage. They were melodramatic love stories set in bucolic environs, featuring Indian maidens enamored of white men, mixed-blood men enamored of white women, and vice versa, and so forth. The titles told all, as suggested by the following partial list of films with Indian themes made during 1910: *An Indian's Gratitude, Indian Blood, Indian Girl's Awakening, The Indian Girl's Romance, An Indian Maiden's Choice, Indian Pete's Gratitude, Stolen by Indians, Her Indian Mother, The Indian and the Cowgirl, His Indian Bride, The Indian and the Maid, Elder Alden's Indian Ward, The Way of the Red Man, The Red Girl and the Child, Red Eagle's Love Affair, Red Wing's Constancy, White-Doe's Loves,* and *Iron Arm's Remorse.* Of all the Indian films of 1910, thirteen concerned Indians who did good deeds and thereby reversed social opinion in their favor, six were all-Indian love stories, seven dealt with the love of an Indian woman for a white man, and three explored the love of an Indian man for a white woman. There was one film about Indian lust and another about white lust, and four treated the subject of intermarriage between white men and Indian women. These films far outnumbered those dealing with violent themes.

The sound era, which began in 1927, changed things yet again, and the negative stereotype returned with a vengeance. Screaming savages were everywhere, burning, pillaging, raping, scalping, and generally being picturesque.

They were a necessary ingredient in western action films—as necessary as horses, guns, wagons, or forts. They were, in short, props, and their function was to expire (as picturesquely as possible) as a consequence of being plugged by white soldiers, cowboys, settlers, miners, hunters, stagecoach passengers, or whatever. The Indian was to be a target, not a dramatic character, and Hollywood had every expectation that such an assignment would serve to entertain as well as enlighten white audiences. Consider for a moment Paramount's 1939 release *Geronimo*, directed by Paul H. Sloane and starring Preston Foster, Ellen Drew, and Andy Devine. The title role belonged to Cherokee actor Victor Daniels, whose stage name was Chief Thundercloud, but he received no billing under either name. He was to be a prop, not an actor, and his face was cosmetically altered to enhance whatever he could effect in the way of an evil expression. The idea was to exploit the negative stereotype, and the promotional suggestions distributed by Paramount to theater managers left no doubt about the studio's intentions. "Your community," the managers were told,

> can probably produce one or two old veterans who fought in some of the Indian wars. Find them and enlist their aid in selling "Geronimo!" Get their reactions and quote them in advance advertising. Try to plant a local [newspaper] feature story based on the experiences of the veterans and be sure to have them refer prominently to Geronimo as the most brutal savage of them all.[18]

Delmer Daves' *Broken Arrow*, released in 1950, has generally been acknowledged as the first modern film to portray Indians sympathetically and to suggest that Indian life was a valid alternative to existence in white society. The role of Cochise, the reasonable Apache, was played by a white, Jeff Chandler, while that of the malevolent Geronimo went to Indian actor Jay Silverheels. One is tempted to say that Hollywood's rule of thumb in westerns seemed to be, "The only bad Indian is a real Indian," but, whatever the case, it does not appear that *Broken Arrow* had much immediate impact on the ways in which Indians were portrayed in American films. A large number of Indian films concerned confrontations between aborigines and the army, and *Broken Arrow* did nothing to lessen the popularity of such fare. Between 1951 and 1970 at least eighty-six Indians-versus-army films appeared, twelve of them coming within a year of *Broken Arrow*. Titles such as *Tomahawk*, *Slaughter Trail*, *Warpath*, *War Paint*, *Massacre Canyon*, *War Arrow*, *Flaming Frontier*, and *Blood on the Arrow* continued to sell popcorn to audiences that, ironically, had forgotten the origin of that particular delicacy.

And who were the movie Indians? They were actors who looked the part, which most often meant actors who could represent evil personified. Many came from the horror films (Bela Lugosi, Boris Karloff, Lon Chaney, Jr.), and many were professional cinematic heavies (Sheldon Leonard, Bruce Cabot, Claude Akins, Lee Van Cleef, Charles Bronson, Neville Brand, Anthony Caruso), while some were simply journeymen who specialized in portraying virtually every ethnic type (Akim Tamiroff, J. Carrol Naish). Others were comedians, for those occasions when funny and/or drunken Indians were required (Buddy Hackett, Joey Bishop), and still others were cowboy heroes, for those occasions when audience sympathy was a necessary ingredient (Audie Murphy, Guy Madison, John Wayne, Chuck Connors). There have been former Tarzans (Buster Crabbe, Lex Barker), part-time Lone Rangers (Clayton Moore), and pop singers (Elvis Presley). There have been Latin actors (Gilbert Roland, Ricardo Montalban), Japanese actors (Sessue Hayakawa), and black actors (Woody Strode). And there have been the women, beautiful, silent, and seductive (Nancy Kwan, Loretta Young, Katherine Ross, Debra Paget, Donna Reed, Jennifer Jones, Cyd Charisse, Daliah Lavi, Audrey Hepburn), to say nothing of the children, who grew up to be something else (Robert Blake, Dickie Moore). The few Indian actors (Victor Daniels, Jay Silverheels, X Brands, Eddie Little Sky, Chief Yowlachie, Dan George, Will Sampson, Iron Eyes Cody) have been all but lost in that parade of wigs, contact lenses, and body paint. The real Indians remain in the background, and to that extent art imitates life.

Other media have elaborated upon the Indian stereotype. Radio contributed the Lone Ranger's faithful Indian companion, Tonto. Tonto's voice belonged to John Todd, an elderly Shakespearean actor who knew the parts so well that he often slept through the broadcasts, awaking only to emit guttural responses at the appropriate times. And there was Straight Arrow, an articulate Indian hero of sorts who always masqueraded as a white rancher until trouble arose. The character was the brainchild of an advertising agency in search of something for Nabisco to sponsor. Television cast Lebanese actor Michael Ansara as Cochise in its version of *Broken Arrow*, presented singer Ed Ames of the Ames Brothers as an educated Indian sidekick of Fess Parker in *Daniel Boone*, and aired, among other things, a contemporary series, *Hawk*, about an Indian detective in New York, with Burt Reynolds in the title role.

Popular fiction continues to offer the public Navajo detectives, fierce Apaches, and ruthless squawmen. Humorous novels about modern Indians waging spectacular but often ineffectual war against the federal government also have enjoyed a certain vogue, but in the presentation of "funny" Indians newspaper comic strips have no equal. If films have taught that Indians are stoical, ruthless, cunning, and amoral, the western comic strips have demonstrated that these qualities and virtually every aspect of Indian culture are downright laughable. Tom K. Ryan's *Tumbleweeds* is perhaps the best known of the western strips, and Ryan's Indians are outrageous indeed. Their names are Green Gills, Bucolic Buffalo, Limpid Lizard, Hulking Hawk, Fetid Fox, Vericose Viper, Squalid Squirrel, and Effervescent Elk, and they sharpen their skills each year during Sneaky Week, passing the rest of the time vying for the coveted black feather, which designates the Indian of the Month. They admit to being desert dwellers, and they wear feathers and breechcloths (the chief wears a blanket) and live in tipis, but they have no horses. In one episode they are visited by a woodlands Indian from the East who has lost his way because he had one too many for the road. They believe that the canoe he carries on his head is a hat. He has a Mohawk haircut with a feather in it, he wears an earring, and his name is Punkutunkus, son of Kookoonookus. Ryan's Indians are inept to a fault (they are forever unable to deceive Tumbleweeds, the cowboy whose name the strip carries), but they are surpassed in that by Colonel

Fluster and the men of Fort Ridiculous. Thus they have at least something in their favor, although the humor they evoke succeeds largely because of the reader's awareness of, and familiarity with, Indian stereotypes; and ultimately Ryan's strip functions to confirm many of those stereotypes.

The question inevitably arises whether or not such portrayals of Indians are racially inspired. There is no thorough study of the relationship between race thinking and the history of Indian-white contact, but it seems safe to say that, while elements of racism may be present in that history, white stereotypes of Indians are cultural rather than racial responses. That race was never a significant issue is reflected in the volume of white commentary to the effect that Indians could be assimilated by the dominant population. And it is true that most observers emphasized cultural differences between Indians and whites. Although those differences often provided an excuse for white discrimination against Indians, the fact of discrimination does not in itself justify a conclusion of race prejudice. Whites who lived with Indians, or those who lived like Indians, were subject to the same discrimination. Skin color was less effective as a means of social categorization than were dietary habits, mode of dress, religious practices, and the like. Indian stereotypes developed in part because they were useful in justifying the dispossession of the aborigines, not because they were required to keep social distance between the two races. Moreover, it is doubtful that stereotypes could have functioned effectively to that end in frontier situations, particularly in view of the fact that, of the two groups, the Indians seemed most concerned about describing geographical boundaries between themselves and white populations.

These, then, were the uses to which whites put their images of Indians: First, after initial contact, the Indian was a curiosity, then an entertainment. Thereafter he was made noble by whites who required his cooperation and a beast by those secure enough to survive without his help and, beyond that, to take what he had. Then, when his numbers were diminished and he was far removed from the white population, he became again a curiosity and an entertainment. Today, his numbers replenished and his isolation ended, he is still to whites curious and entertaining, largely because, in the context afforded by the dominant society, he has no social utility—not as an Indian, not as a representative of another culture. That which is entertaining is otherwise useless, and so it was in the beginning. . . .

The Chicano Image and the Myth of Aztlán Rediscovered

John R. Chávez

Mexican Americans—or, as they would prefer to be called out of a new sense of cultural pride, "Chicanos"—today are the nation's second largest and fastest-growing minority. Their greater visibility dates largely from the political and cultural maelstrom of the 1960s. In that decade, both nonwhites worldwide during the decolonization period and nonwhite minorities in America began to assert a cultural independence calculated to free them from the control of Western and American myths, respectively. For Chicanos, this development represented a special opportunity to reattach themselves to their origins and cultural traditions. What they rediscovered and revivified—the "myth of Aztlán"—was of great value, says Professor John R. Chávez of Texas A&M University. With their ancient, mythic past providing inspiration, Chicanos reclaimed their history in terms of an Aztec legend, which spoke of ancestral roots in Indian prehistory—an Aztec Eden—when their earliest forebears had inhabited and prevailed in what only later came to be designated the Southwest borderlands. Feeling a new sense of entitlement to the region inspired by the Aztlán myth, Chicano political efforts such as César Chávez's farm workers' strikes in California, Reies López Tijerina's land grant struggles in New Mexico, and Rodolfo Gonzales's community efforts in Denver all found special energy and validity in terms of this newly rediscovered "usable past." While the myth of Aztlán, now expressed in terms of Chicano desire to recover a larger measure of control, has not been fulfilled, the power of myth is once again made manifest and continues to persist.

During the middle and late 1960s, the political situation in the United States developed into a crisis that permitted a resurgence of the image of the lost land. The myths of the Spanish Southwest and the American Southwest, which the Mexicans of the region had accepted for much of the twentieth century, were suddenly set aside. During that period when so many myths were being reexamined by U.S. society in general, many Mexican-Americans found it possible to challenge the images of themselves and their region that had been imposed by the Anglo majority. The shattering effect that the civil rights and the antiwar movements had on the Anglo self-image led many Mexican-Americans to believe that their attempts to be like Anglos were against their own interests. They began to feel that perhaps they had more in common with blacks and even the Vietnamese than with the dominant Anglo-Americans. Reviewing their own socioeconomic position after two decades of "Americanization," Mexican-Americans found themselves lower even than blacks in income, housing, and education. Though they were not as discriminated against or segregated as blacks, Mexican-Americans realized that they had in no way become the equals of Anglos. In searching for the causes, the view that all "immigrant" groups initially experienced such problems seemed to explain less and less, for by 1960, 81 percent of Mexicans in the Southwest were United States–born. Furthermore, the condition of longtime residents in New Mexico and Texas was no better and often worse than that of other Mexican-Americans.

The nationalist movements of such peoples as the Vietnamese and the Cubans inspired a significant number of Mexican-Americans to reexamine their own condition through history and conclude that they too had been the victims of U.S. imperialism. As a result, the nineteenth- and early twentieth-century image of the Southwest as lost and of themselves as dispossessed reemerged from the collective unconscious of the region's Mexicans. . . . [T]hat image had persisted, largely because of the intense Mexican nationalism that radiated from across the border, but in the 1960s it was reasserted and reshaped under the influence of contemporary ideas. Increasingly after World War II the former colonies of the world gained political independence and established nonwhite rule. Nonwhites sought to reestablish pride in their own racial backgrounds to combat the feelings of inferiority that colonialism had imposed. In the United States this phenomenon manifested itself in calls for black pride and black power, and also in cries for Chicano pride and Chicano power. The use of the term "Chicano," derived from *mexicano* and formerly used disparagingly in referring to lower-class Mexican-Americans, signified a renewed pride in the Indian and mestizo poor who had built so much of the Southwest during the Spanish and Anglo colonizations. While investigating the past of their indigenous ancestors in the Southwest, activist Chicanos rediscovered the myth of Aztlán and adapted it to their own time.

After gaining independence from Spain and again after the revolution of 1910, Mexicans had turned to their ancient past for inspiration. It is no surprise that Chicano activists did the same thing during the radical 1960s, especially given the example of contemporary nationalist movements. In the ancient myth of Aztlán, activists found a tie between their homeland and Mexican culture that antedated the Republic of Mexico, the Spanish exploration of the borderlands, and even Tenochtitlán (Mexico City) itself. As we have seen, ancient Aztec legends, recorded in the chronicles of the sixteenth and seventeenth centuries, recounted that before founding Tenochtitlán the Aztecs had journeyed from a wondrous place to the north called "Aztlán." Since this place of origin, according to some of the chroniclers, was located in what is now the Southwest, Chicano activists reapplied the term to the region, reclaiming the land on the basis of their Indian ancestry. And although the preponderance of evidence indicates that the Aztlán of the Aztecs was actually within present Mexico, the activists' use of the term had merit. While the Aztlán whence the Aztecs departed for Tenochtitlán was probably in the present Mexican state of Nayarit, anthropological studies suggest that the distant ancestors of the Aztecs centuries prior to settling in Nayarit had inhabited and migrated through the Southwest. Thus, on the basis of Indian prehistory, Chicanos had a claim to the region, a claim stronger than any based only on the relatively brief history of Spanish settlement in the borderlands.

Since Aztlán had been the Aztec equivalent of Eden and Utopia, activists converted that ancient idealized landscape into an ideal of a modern homeland where they hoped to help fulfill their people's political, economic, and cultural destiny. Therefore, though "Aztlán" came to refer in a concrete sense to the Southwest, it also applied to any place north of Mexico where Chicanos hoped to fulfill their collective aspirations. These aspirations in the 1960s, it turned out, were more or less the same hopes Southwest Mexicans had had since the Treaty of Guadalupe Hidalgo. Chicanos sought bilingual/bicultural education, just representation in the government, justice in the courts, fair treatment from the police and the military, a decent standard of living, and ultimately that which controlled the possibilities of all their other aspirations—their share of the means of production, for this, intellectuals at least now believed, was what the Anglo conquest had fundamentally denied Southwest Mexicans. The northern homeland had been lost militarily and politically in the 1840s; the economic loss had come in subsequent decades with the usurpation of individually and communally owned lands that produced the wealth of the region. During Mexican rule the wealth of the land had been largely agricultural, but later the land of the Southwest had also given forth gold, silver, copper, coal, oil, uranium, and innumerable other products that enriched the Anglos but left Mexicans impoverished. In this respect, Chicanos increasingly saw a parallel between themselves and the native peoples of other colonized lands: all had been conquered, all had been reduced to menial labor, and all had been used to extract the natural bounty of their own land for the benefit of the conquerors.

The Chicanos' historic loss of the economic power inherent in the land of the Southwest underlay the manifestations of militant nationalism that erupted in the late 1960s: the farm worker strikes in California, the land grant struggle in New Mexico, the revolt of the electorate in Crystal City, Texas, the school walkouts in Denver and Los Angeles, and the other major events of what came to be called the Chicano movement. Though these events exploded with suddenness, they were preceded by calmer yet significant developments in the previous decade that prepared a sizable number of Mexican-Americans for the move away from Americanization. . . . [T]he 1950s and early 1960s had been the nadir in the history of Mexican nationalism in the Southwest. But even though Mexican-American organizations had generally been weakened by the assimilation of potential members into the Anglo world, several new groups had managed to establish themselves during that time. The most important of these were the Mexican-American Political Association (MAPA) founded in California in 1959 and the Political Association of Spanish-Speaking Organizations (PASO or PASSO) founded in Arizona in 1960 and most influential in Texas. These two differed from the League of United Latin American Citizens, the G. I. Forum, and other earlier groups because the new organizations believed in activating the political power of Mexican-Americans for the overall good of Mexican-Americans. Earlier groups, more assimilationist in perspective, preferred a defensive posture, protecting the rights of Mexican-Americans in the name of all U.S. citizens. While the difference may seem subtle, the new emphasis on self-interest rather than universality prepared the way for the rebirth of Chicano nationalism. . . .

On 16 September (Mexican Independence Day) 1965, César Chávez's predominantly Mexican-American National Farm Workers Association (NFWA) voted to join a grape strike initiated in Delano, California, by the Filipino Agricultural Workers Organizing Committee (AWOC). Because of their greater numbers, Mexican-Americans soon dominated the strike and later controlled the United Farm Workers' Organizing Committee (UFWOC), which came into being as a result of the merger of the two original unions. This strike was to lead to the first successful agricultural revolt by one of the poorest groups of Chicanos in the Southwest. Interestingly, this revolt was led by a man who believed in nonviolence, democracy, and religion; who had little faith in government programs; and who distrusted the very Chicano nationalism he inspired.

Chávez, whose grandfather was a "pioneer" in Arizona in the 1880s, was born near Yuma in 1927. "Our family farm was started three years before Arizona became a state," Chávez once remarked. "Yet, sometimes I get crank letters . . . telling me to 'go back' to Mexico!" As a result of the depression the family's land was lost in 1939 because of unpaid taxes, and the Chávezes migrated to California where they became farm workers. After years of such work and a period in the navy, César Chávez joined the Community Service Organization which, though overwhelmingly Mexican-American in membership, stressed the acquisition and exercise of the rights of citizenship by the poor of all ethnic groups. This early influence later helped Chávez gain widespread support for the farm workers, even though it prevented him from becoming a true spokesman for Chicano nationalism. After ten years in the CSO, Chávez in 1962 decided to organize farm workers on his own when the CSO decided the task was beyond its range of activities.

Shortly after the NFWA voted to strike, Chávez appealed to religious and civil rights groups for volunteers. By doing so, he converted a labor dispute into a social movement, and expanded his Mexican-American and Filipino base of support by including all others who wished to help. At the same time he nonetheless acknowledged that race was an issue in the strike. Chávez encouraged nationalism among the farm workers because he knew it could be a cohesive force against the Anglo growers who were accustomed to treating racial minorities as inferiors. Indeed, the Virgin of Guadalupe, the patroness of Mexico, became one of the chief nationalistic symbols used in the movement's demonstrations. Luis Valdez, playwright and propagandist for the farm workers, described her significance:

> The Virgin of Guadalupe was the first hint to farm workers that the pilgrimage [to Sacramento in the spring of 1966] implied social revolution. During the Mexican Revolution, the peasant armies of Emiliano Zapata carried her standard, not only because they sought her divine protection, but because she symbolized the Mexico of the poor and humble. It was a simple Mexican Indian, Juan Diego, who first saw her in a vision at Guadalupe. Beautifully dark and Indian in feature, she was the New World version of the Mother of Christ. Even though some of her worshippers in Mexico still identify her with Tonatzin, an Aztec goddess, she is a Catholic saint of Indian creation—a Mexican. The people's response was immediate and reverent. They joined the march by the thousands, falling in line behind her standard.

Thus, through the Virgin, Chávez and the Chicano workers linked their struggle to their aboriginal Mexican past.

Although the Mexican symbols used by the movement were generally associated with Mexico proper, Chávez was also aware of the Chicano farm workers' indigenous background in the Southwest. He had a personal interest in the history of the California missions and in their treatment of the Indians, the first farm workers. Chávez believed that though the missionaries had indeed used coercion on the Indians, they had saved them from far worse treatment at the hands of the secular authorities and the settlers. They had done this by making the missions sanctuaries where the Indians could work the land communally and by forcing the settlers to treat the Indians as human beings. As a result, Chávez once commented, "The Spanish began to marry the Indians . . . they couldn't destroy them, so instead of wiping out a race, they made a new one." The relative autonomy of the missions, politically and economically, together with the Franciscans' belief in the equality of all human souls, permitted the Indians a certain amount of security and even on occasion complete acceptance through intermarriage with the settlers. Like their Indian predecessors, twentieth-century farm workers, in Chávez's eyes, could only gain their rightful place in society if they believed in their own racial equality with other men and established themselves as an independent political and economic force capable of challenging the new owners of the land.

Chávez fully realized what the historic loss of the land had meant to the Indians and to their Mexican successors. The "Plan of Delano," a Mexican-style proclamation stating the discontent of the farm workers and the aims of Chávez and his movement, reminded society of the oppression Southwest Mexicans had endured: "The Mexican race has sacrificed itself for the last hundred years. Our sweat and our blood have fallen on this land to make other men rich." Chávez knew that the power of the Anglo growers rested on their ownership of the land, and he also realized that Chicanos and the other poor would ultimately achieve full equality only when they had recovered that land: "While . . . our adversaries . . . are the rich and the powerful and possess the land, we are not afraid. . . . We know that our cause is just, that history is a story of social revolution, and that the poor shall inherit the land." Though Chávez stated this belief publicly, he knew land reform was a distant ideal, and he was much too practical to make it a goal for his union. Despite this, the growers claimed that such statements, together with the symbols of Mexican nationalism, revealed Chávez to be communistic and un-American. One rancher remarked,

> Mr. Cesar Chavez is talking about taking over this state—I don't like that. Too much "*Viva Zapata*" and down with the Caucasians, *la raza* [the Latin American race], and all that. Mister Cesar Chavez is talking about *revolución.* Remember, California once belonged to Mexico, and he's saying, "Look, you dumb Mexicans, you lost it, now let's get it back!"

Despite such distortions and in spite of his actual encouragement of nationalism, Chávez feared the divisive effects it could have within the movement. Since the growers were quick to exploit such divisiveness, he would not allow intolerance to split the ranks of his Chicano, Filipino, and liberal Anglo supporters. He was especially concerned that Chicanos not let their incipient nationalism get out of hand: "We oppose some of this La Raza business. . . . We know what it does. When La Raza means or implies racism, we don't support it. But if it means our struggle, our dignity, or our cultural roots, then we're for it." Because of this guarded attitude, however, Chávez could never become a fully committed advocate of Chicano nationalism. His struggle after all was economic, rather than cultural; his concerns were those of the poor as a whole, rather than more specifically Chicano issues, such as bilingual education. On the other hand, Chávez showed Chicanos that their cultural problems could not be solved by politics alone, since these problems were economic at their source:

> Effective political power is never going to come, particularly to minority groups, unless they have economic power. . . . I'm not advocating . . . brown capitalism. . . . What I'm suggesting is a cooperative movement.

Such power lay in numbers and could best be harnessed if minority groups joined together with liberal Anglos in a broad interracial consumer movement.

During the grape strike, Chávez demonstrated how a cooperative movement could generate economic power, enough power to force the capitulation of the growers in 1970. His major weapon was a grape boycott extending beyond the Chicanos' Southwest, throughout the United States, and even into Europe. Since he had made the strike a moral and civil rights movement, many outsiders were willing to cooperate in the boycott. Within the UFWOC itself, . . . Chávez made the workers understand that the struggle was for human equality, not merely for better wages and working conditions. As a result, in practical terms, the UFWOC itself became more a cooperative than a trade union: "It . . . developed for its members a death benefit plan; a coöperative grocery, drug store, and gas station; a credit union; a medical clinic; a social protest theatre group . . .; and a newspaper. . . ." Such cooperative policies together with the nonviolent, mass protest methods of the civil rights movement (methods Mexican-Americans had earlier disdained to use) effectively countered such traditional grower tactics as the employment of strikebreakers from Mexico. After the grape growers agreed to sign contracts with the UF-WOC in 1970, the farm-worker movement in the succeeding decades became an ongoing force as the union entered the lettuce fields, fought for the renewal of old contracts, and expanded to other parts of the nation.

"Across the San Joaquin Valley," proclaimed the "Plan of Delano" in 1966, "across California, across the entire Southwest of the United States, wherever there are Mexican people, wherever there are farm workers, our movement is spreading like flames across a dry plain." Within a short time the farm-worker front of the Chicano movement had indeed spread to Arizona and Texas, but, more important, other fronts of the movement had opened independently throughout the Southwest in other sectors of Chicano life. One of these fronts was the renewal of the land grant struggle in northern New Mexico. . . . [A]fter the Treaty of Guadalupe Hidalgo, Mexicans in the Southwest were gradually deprived of their lands by an Anglo-American legal and economic system that constantly challenged land grants made under previous governments. In his investigation of problems resulting from the land grant issue during the 1960s, Peter Nabokov wrote that in northern New Mexico:

> These ancestral holdings had originally been awarded to single people or to communities of at least ten village families. A man had his private home and a narrow rectangular plot which usually gave him access to river water. But the community's grazing and wood-gathering acreage, called *ejido*, was understood to be held commonly, and forever, a perpetual trust. A large percentage of the New Mexico *ejido* lands had been put in the public domain by the surveyors general of the period 1854–1880 because they recognized only claims made on behalf of individuals, not communities.

During the twentieth century much of this "public domain" was turned over to the Forest Service, which in turn was given the authority to lease the lands to private individuals and companies for the use and development of natural resources. Unfortunately for the long-settled small farmers of northern New Mexico, large out-of-state corporations, engaged in mining, logging, and tourism, received preferential treatment in their dealings with the Forest Service. The impoverished small farmers, on the other hand, were gradually denied their grazing rights by an agency that was unconcerned with and even hostile to their needs; in her study of the problem, Patricia Bell Blawis observed that "while logging firms contracted with the Forest Service for immense areas on their ancestral land, the grantees were forbidden to cut stovewood without a permit." Thus, according to Blawis, in the twentieth century the imperialism of the nineteenth continued surreptitiously: "The Forest Service is evidence of the colonial policy of the Federal government. . . . Through this Service, resources of the West are exploited by Washington, D.C. and its friends." . . . [T]he native Mexicans had in the past reacted violently to this colonialism: between the 1880s and the late 1920s, for instance, at least two groups of nightriders, Las Gorras Blancas and La Mano Negra, had burned buildings, torn down fences, and committed other such terrorist acts to protest the seizure of their lands. During the late 1960s such violence flared again.

In 1963 the militant Alianza Federal de Mercedes (the Federal Land Grant Alliance—always popularly known as the Alianza, even though the official name changed several times) was incorporated under the direction of a dynamic leader named Reies López Tijerina. Tijerina, whose great-grandfather had been robbed of his land and killed by Anglos, was born in Texas in 1926; he lived and moved throughout the Southwest and beyond as a farm worker and later as a poor itinerant preacher. During these wanderings, he came to believe that the problems of his people had resulted from their loss of the land, for as he later stressed, "the ties of our culture with the land are indivisible." As a consequence, he became interested in the land grant issue, spent a year studying the question in Mexico, and in 1960 settled in New Mexico where he felt there was the best hope of recovering the grants. After organizing many of the heirs into the Alianza, Tijerina unsuccessfully petitioned the U.S. government to investigate the land titles for violations of that portion of the Treaty of Guadalupe Hidalgo that guaranteed the property rights of Mexicans in the Southwest. He had also requested the Mexican government to look into the matter, but Mexico, having gradually become economically dependent on as well as ideologically aligned with the United States since the 1930s, had not and would not support any radical claims made by dissident Chicanos. Rebuffed in his efforts to get consideration through regular legal and political channels, Tijerina turned to civil disobedience.

In October of 1966 Tijerina and other *aliancistas* occupied the Echo Amphitheater, a section of the Carson National Forest that had once been part of the land grant of San Joaquín del Río de Chama. Since the original Spanish and Mexican grants had permitted the villagers a good deal of autonomy, the *aliancistas* declared themselves the Republic of San Joaquín and elected as mayor a direct descendant of the original grantee. When several forest rangers attempted to interfere, they were detained by the "republic," tried for trespassing, and released on suspended sentences. By allowing this, Tijerina hoped to challenge the jurisdiction of the Forest Service over the land, thus forcing the land grant issue into the courts, possibly as far as the Supreme Court. Also, the declaration of autonomy would make public the Chicanos' need for self-determination, their need to escape a whole range of problems caused by their incorporation into U.S. society. Not least of these was the war in Vietnam, which even the traditionally patriotic *nuevomexicanos* were beginning to oppose: "The people," as Tijerina had once remarked, "generally feel that our sons are being sent to Vietnam illegally, because many of these land grants are free city states and are independent." The "liberation" of the Echo Amphitheater had been a dangerous act, but as the increasingly radical Tijerina declared during the occupation: "Fidel Castro has what he has because of his guts. . . . Castro put the gringos off his island and we can do the same." Unfortunately for the Alianza, Tijerina would later serve two years in prison for assault on the rangers at the Echo Amphitheater; furthermore, the courts would refuse to admit discussion of the land grant issue.

During May of 1967, according to Nabokov, "private northern landowners . . . began suffering from the traditional symptoms of unrest—selective cattle rustling, irrigation ditch and fence wreckage, shot-up water tanks, and arson." Although there was no evidence the Alianza had committed these acts, the authorities actually feared that guerrilla warfare might break out in northern New Mexico. When Tijerina revealed that his group planned to have a conference on June 3 at Coyote, a small town near the San Joaquín grant, the authorities anticipated another occupation and prevented the meeting by declaring it an unlawful assembly, blocking the roads to the town, and arresting any *aliancistas* who resisted. This proved to be a mistake, for it brought on the very violence the authorities had feared. Feeling that their right to free assembly had been violated, the *aliancistas* decided to make a citizen's arrest of the district attorney responsible for the police action. On June 5, in the most daring move of the contemporary Chicano movement, Tijerina and about twenty other armed *aliancistas* attacked the courthouse at the county seat at Tierra Amarilla. In the ensuing shoot-out two deputies were wounded, the courthouse was occupied, and the Coyote prisoners were freed. Finding that the district attorney was not present, the *aliancistas* then fled the town with two hostages.

The reaction of the authorities brought the cause of the Alianza to the attention of the entire nation. Imagining "a new Cuba to the north," the state government in Santa Fe sent out four hundred National Guardsmen to join two hundred state troopers in an expedition into northern New Mexico that included the use of helicopters and two tanks. After a few days Tijerina was captured and charged with various crimes connected with the raid, though he was subsequently released on bail. Once in the national spotlight, Tijerina elaborated on the issues and goals of the land grant struggle, issues that were important to Chicanos throughout the Southwest; "Not only the land has been stolen from the good and humble people," he commented, "but also their culture. . . ." And he remarked, "A major point of contention is that we are being deprived of our language. . . ." Tijerina also argued that in addition to property rights, the cultural rights of his people were guaranteed by the Treaty of Guadalupe Hidalgo. Once the guarantees of this treaty were honored and discrimination was ended, Indo-Hispanos, as Tijerina often called his people, would take their rightful place as intermediaries in the pluralistic Southwest:

> We have been forced by destiny to adopt two languages; we will be the future ambassadors and envoys to Latin America. At home, I believe that the Southwest is breeding a special kind of people that will bridge the color-gap between black and white. . . . [Moreover w]e are the people the Indians call their "lost brothers."

While the many charges against him were being handled in the courts, Tijerina continued his activities with the Alianza and also participated in the interracial, antipoverty Poor People's March on Washington in 1968. In 1969, however, the Alianza was deprived of Tijerina's leadership when he was imprisoned for the Echo Amphitheater incident. Suffering from poor health, he was paroled in July 1971, but on condition that he no longer hold office in the Alianza. Deprived of his full leadership and lacking the organized economic power of an institution such as the United Farm Workers, the Alianza lost much of its drive, and not until 1979 was it able to convince the government to give even nominal reconsideration to the land grant issue. Nonetheless, Tijerina and the Alianza did rejuvenate the ethnic pride of a good number of *nuevomexicanos.* Though many Hispanos considered Tijerina an outsider, many others joined his organization, and in doing so reaffirmed their ties to Mexico through reference to the Treaty of Guadalupe Hidalgo, and to their Indian ancestors through acceptance of the facts of *mestizaje* (Indo-Hispano intermarriage). In New Mexico no longer could "Spanish-Americans" easily deny their background. No longer could Spanish-American politicians, who had generally held a representative number of positions in government, ignore their economically depressed constituents without opposition from Chicano militants around the state—for increasingly among *nuevomexicanos* the image of the Spanish Southwest was giving way to the image of Aztlán.

The person most responsible for the adoption of the term "Aztlán" by the rapidly spreading Chicano movement was Rodolfo "Corky" Gonzales, leader of the Chicano community in Denver, Colorado. In modern times the term was first applied to the Chicano homeland in 1962 by Jack D. Forbes, a Native American professor who argued that Mexicans were more truly an Indian than a mestizo people; his mimeographed manuscript, "The Mexican Heritage of Aztlán (the Southwest) to 1821," was distributed among Mexican-Americans in the Southwest during the early 1960s. The term gained popularity, but was not universally accepted by the Chicano movement until, in the spring of 1969, the first Chicano national conference, in Denver, drafted "El plan espiritual de Aztlán," a document that declared the spiritual independence of the Chicano Southwest from the United States. Paradoxically this sentiment was expressed in a city never legally within the confines of Mexico; however, like arguments for Puerto Rican independence presented in New York, this declaration from Denver signified the desire of a minority group for independence from the colonialism that had subjugated its native land and that continued to affect the individuals of the minority no matter where they resided within the United States.

Born in Denver in 1928, Corky Gonzales was primarily a product of the urban barrios, even though he spent part of his youth working in the fields of southern Colorado. He managed to escape poverty by becoming a successful boxer. As a result of the popularity gained from his career, he became an influential figure in the barrios and was selected to head various antipoverty programs in the early 1960s. By 1965, however, he had become disenchanted with the antipoverty bureaucracy. He concluded earlier than other Chicanos that the War on Poverty was designed to pacify rather than truly help the poor. Had he read it, he would have agreed with a later comment made by a Chicano editor when government and foundation money poured into northern New Mexico in the aftermath of Tierra Amarilla:

> They're trying to create *Vendido* power (sellout power) . . . trying to bring Vietnam to New Mexico and trying to create "leaders" the system can use as tools. But it hasn't worked with the Vietnamese and it's not going to work with Raza here in the United States.

Disgusted with the strings attached to funds from the government and foundations, Gonzales organized the Crusade for Justice, a community self-help group. Through their own fund-raising efforts, the members established a barrio service center, providing such assistance as child care, legal aid, housing and employment counseling, health care, and other services especially needed in poor urban areas. The Crusade was, moreover, outspoken in its concern for Chicano civil and cultural rights.

More than Chávez and even more than Tijerina, Gonzales felt that nationalism was the force that would get Chicanos to help one another, and that the success of his Crusade exemplified the possibilities of self-determination. Although his participation in the Poor People's March of 1968 revealed his belief in the necessity of interracial cooperation, at heart he felt that Chicanos would have to help themselves and would do so if they became aware of their proud history as a people. Of Chicanos in his state, he once said, "Colorado belongs to our people, was named by our people, discovered by our people and worked by our people. . . . We preach self-respect . . . to reclaim what is ours." Regarding the region as a whole, he commented, "Nationalism exists in the Southwest, but until now it hasn't been formed into an image people can see. Until now it has been a dream. It has been my job to create a reality out of the dream. . . ." The Crusade was part of that reality and so was the Chicano Youth Liberation Conference, called by Gonzales to bring together Chicanos from throughout the nation, but especially from the cities, where 80 percent of all Chicanos lived. In Gonzales urban youth found a leader, unlike Chávez or Tijerina, who had successfully attempted concrete solutions to city problems. Consequently, 1,500 Chicanos from many different organizations attended the conference of this urban nationalist.

As if in exhibit of the problems of urban Chicanos, the week before the conference riots broke out in the Denver barrios, resulting from events that began with a racist remark made by a teacher at a local high school. A student and community protest led to confrontation with police; according to Gonzales, "What took place . . . was a battle between the West Side 'liberation forces' and the 'occupying army.' The West Side won [police suffered some injuries and damage to equipment]." Although Gonzales opposed violence and tried to stop the rioting, he clearly felt the trouble was justified and was proud that Chicanos were capable of defending themselves against the government he believed had made internal colonies of the city's barrios. After the riots, the conference convened in an atmosphere permeated with nationalism and proclaimed the following in "El plan espiritual de Aztlán":

> Conscious . . . of the brutal "Gringo" invasion of our territories, we, the Chicano inhabitants and civilizers of the northern land of Aztlán, from whence came our forefathers, reclaiming the land of their birth. . . . We [who] do not recognize capricious frontiers on the bronze continent. . . . we declare the independence of our mestizo nation.

In that proclamation the Chicano delegates fully revived their people's traditional image of the Southwest and clarified it for their own time: the Southwest was the Chicano homeland, a land paradoxically settled by an indigenous people who were subsequently conquered. Furthermore, these people were now seen as native, not merely because their Spanish ancestors had settled the land hundreds of years before, but because their Indian ancestors had resided on the land thousands of years earlier, tying it permanently to Indian and mestizo Mexico.

With this image of the Southwest, the Chicano delegates established a context for a variety of demands that would gain impetus in the near future. Before long in the name of Aztlán and its people, activists would demand restitution from the United States for its conquest of the region and for its economic, political, and cultural oppression of the Southwest Mexican population. From the institutions of the United States, Chicanos would reject token representation and poverty programs with strings attached; from state and national institutions they would expect unrestricted compensation; over local institutions they would demand control. With such control, Chicanos hoped to establish bilingual/bicultural education, promote their own arts and customs, tax themselves, hire their own police, select their own juries, sit on their own draft boards, and especially found cooperatives to prevent further economic exploitation. Thus, the separatism at the conference, while expressing itself in the ideal of complete political independence from the United States, more importantly would promote the pragmatic goal of local autonomy. Gonzales's Crusade offered a practical example of how such autonomy might be gained. Another practical means, discussed at the conference, was the creation of a third party independent of Democrats and Republicans, especially in local elections. Many of these ideas found a national forum in the Chicano Youth Liberation Conference. This was Gonzales's major achievement. While his Crusade for Justice continued its work in Denver, as an organization it never spread far beyond that city. However, the delegates to the conference returned to their homes throughout the Southwest inspired by the urban nationalism that the Crusade exemplified. . . .

In urban areas, students from high school through graduate school had been the major force behind the Chicano movement at least since 1968. In the spring of that year Chicanos in five East Los Angeles high schools walked out of classes to protest conditions in the schools that resulted in extremely high drop-out rates. This led, over the next few years, to a series of walk-outs in one city after another, as Chicano students and instructors throughout the Southwest demanded new schools, more sensitive teachers, and bilingual/bicultural education. Although Chicano student groups had been organized before 1968, the activism of that year put those groups into the forefront of the urban movement. In the colleges and universities of the Southwest, these groups successfully demanded Chicano studies and affirmative action programs, programs that would help produce the first group of Chicano college graduates committed to the cultural survival of their people. Even before they had graduated, these students became involved in off-campus groups to organize the poor and uneducated in the barrios and rural towns. . . .

As time passed, campus groups that in 1967 had given themselves names such as the United Mexican American Students and the Mexican American Student Confederation became more militant. After many walk-outs and after Corky Gonzales's Chicano Youth Liberation Conference in 1969, most campus groups changed their names to El Movimiento Estudiantil Chicano de Aztlán (MECHA—The Chicano Student Movement of Aztlán), revealing their increasingly radical nationalism. At the Second Annual Chicano Youth Conference in the spring of 1970, representatives of student and other youth groups, reflecting their disenchantment with the United States, declared their opposition to the war in Vietnam. Many Chicanos were no longer proud of the fact that they, as a people, were once again dying in a U.S. war in disproportionately high numbers; moreover, they opposed dying in a war fought against a people they believed were victims of the same colonialism they themselves were experiencing. To demonstrate their opposition, a national Chicano anti-war rally was planned for August 1970 to be held in East Los Angeles, the barrio with the largest concentration of Mexican-Americans in the nation. Unfortunately, the rally became a riot when the police attempted to break up the demonstration and only succeeded in provoking the participants into the worst mass violence in East LA since 1943. For months thereafter violent protests erupted periodically, and the number of police on the streets of East LA visibly increased. Rarely had the colonial status of Chicanos seemed so evident.

After 1970 the open confrontations of the previous five years became less frequent as the Chicano movement entered a period of consolidation. Having had many of its hopes and grievances dramatized, the Chicano community was gradually able to take advantage of the advances the movement had attained, especially in education and self-awareness. With a renewed pride in their culture, Chicano intellectuals set out to express a world view that had long been suppressed. That their image of the Southwest as Aztlán was an important part of that world view was clear from the titles of many of the publications that appeared as Chicano culture experienced a renewal in literature, art, and social thought. A scholarly quarterly entitled *Aztlán: Chicano Journal of the Social Sciences and the Arts* was first issued in 1970 by Aztlán Publications at the University of California, Los Angeles. A bibliography by Ernie Barrios published in 1971 bore the title *Bibliografía de Aztlán.* In 1973 Luis Valdez and Stan Steiner edited a work called *Aztlán: An Anthology of Mexican American Literature.* Two novels, *Peregrinos de Aztlán* (1974) by Miguel Méndez M. and *Heart of Aztlan* (1976) by Rudolfo A. Anaya, also carried the ancient name of the Southwest. As if to secure that name for posterity, *Aztlan: The Southwest and Its People,* a history for juveniles by Luis F. Hernández, was published in 1975. Many other works with less obvious titles also reflected the rediscovered Chicano image of the Southwest. Among the most important was . . . *Occupied America* (1972) by Rodolfo Acuña. In this history of Chicanos, Acuña interpreted the tradition of the lost northern homeland according to the modern theory of colonialism, a theory that made the image of Aztlán more meaningful to contemporary Chicanos.

Needless to say, not all Mexican-Americans accepted the image of Aztlán. Among the masses the images of the Spanish Southwest and the American Southwest continued to predominate during the 1970s, and into the 1980s, largely because these were still promoted by the educational system and the mass media. Through bicultural and Chicano studies programs, Chicano intellectuals worked to change this situation. However, a small group of Mexican-Americans conversant with the affairs of their ethnic group refused to abandon borrowed images of the Southwest, usually because their lives had been formed within those images or because those views continued to help them accommodate themselves to the standards of Anglo society. Congressman Henry B. González of San Antonio, Texas, for example, had built his political career around the integrationist civil rights movement of the 1950s and early 1960s; as a result the nationalism of the Chicano movement struck him as nothing less than reverse racism. Since González accepted the integrationist melting pot ideal, he also perceived his region as the American Southwest, to which his parents, like European arrivals on the East Coast, had come to join the "nation of immigrants." Thus, in an address to Congress in 1969, he remarked:

> As it happens my parents were born in Mexico and came to this country seeking safety. . . . It follows that I, and many other residents of my part of Texas and other Southwestern States—happen to be what is commonly referred to as a Mexican-American.

Since his background only "happened" to be Mexican, González could see little importance in notions such as Aztlán and vigorously opposed Chicano militancy. . . .

Even though borrowed images of the Chicanos' place in the Southwest persisted, by the late 1970s some of the new group of educated Chicanos were in positions where they could reveal the image of Aztlán to the general public. For example, Tony Castro, a graduate of Baylor University, spent several years writing for various major newspapers around the country and was then hired in the late 1970s as a regular columnist for the conservative *Los Angeles Herald Examiner.* Devoting most of his columns and later his special reports to Chicano issues, Castro repeatedly exposed the generally conservative readership of that newspaper to the Chicano image of the Southwest:

> The Chicano has been here since the founding of California and the Southwest. His pre-Columbian ancestors wandered here from the north, migrating farther south and establishing the great civilizations of the Maya, the Toltecs, the Aztecs. . . . [Yet] Mexican-Americans . . . have been the conquered people, strangers in their own land. . . .

Young professionals like Castro who were willing to argue for their people's rightful place in the Southwest and the United States were the most successful product of the 1960s movement. . . . [E]ducational improvement had been a major goal of the movement; consequently during the 1970s education was the area where Chicanos made their greatest strides. With Chicano college enrollment having tripled by 1978 (despite a leveling off of progress by that time), more teachers, social workers, writers, social scientists, and others influenced by the nationalism of the 1960s were echoing that nationalism, albeit with caution, from new positions throughout the Southwest.

Despite the emergence of this educated, nationalistic leadership, the progress of Chicanos as a whole was uneven in the 1970s and stagnant in the early 1980s. They continued to fit the description of a colonized people. In California, for example, where Chicanos were most heavily concentrated and where opportunities were often considered best, "Hispanics" over the age of twenty-five had completed high school at only 56 percent of the rate at which Anglos had gained the same level of schooling. And financially, the median Hispanic family income was only $16,140 or 71 percent of the equivalent white family income (1980 U.S. Census figures). While these figures did indicate some improvement over the 1960s, the gains were threatened by a backlash that persisted into the 1980s. Many of the educational and consequently the income gains of Chicanos had come as a result of affirmative action programs, compensatory programs that gave minorities preferential treatment in schooling and employment. These programs were attacked in the courts as reverse discrimination in case after case by Anglos who, though they failed to destroy the programs, managed to impede their effectiveness. Also, programs in Chicano studies and bilingual/bicultural education, while surviving, constantly met opposition from those who regarded them as contrary to the tradition of the nation of immigrants who learned English and forgot the old country. Given the fact that their educational and income gains were so recent, it is no surprise that Chicanos had accumulated little personal wealth and had made little progress toward recovering the means of production in their southwestern homeland.

This continuing lack of economic power in the 1970s and 1980s caused Chicano gains in the political arena to be inconclusive at best. While U.S. presidents generally appointed an increasing number of Chicanos to positions in their administrations, these appointees usually found themselves beholden to their benefactors and isolated in government with little real power to help their people. Even those Chicanos elected to political office could rarely represent fully the interests of their people, since as politicians they generally owed their elections to the Anglo-controlled coalitions that funded their campaigns. In many cases, of course, the politicians themselves continued to be ideologically traditional. For example, in 1974 Arizona and New Mexico elected as governors conservative Raúl Castro and moderate Jerry Apodaca, the first southwestern governors of Mexican descent since Octaviano Larrazolo fifty years earlier. If traditional electoral politics had been the best way to the improvement of Chicano life, the election of two Mexican-American governors should have brought significant social change for Chicanos in those states, but this did not happen because the ideological frame of mind and the political structures within which the governors worked were developed to protect the status quo. . . . [E]ven the radical La Raza Unida party often found the traditional structures impregnable. Without such a radical organizational base, individual Chicano politicians, regardless of any personal nationalism, found themselves coopted by a system that defended the Anglo owners of the means of production. Many newly educated Chicano leaders in other fields found themselves bound by the same strictures. Since their salaries were bestowed on them by the system they often opposed, nationalistic Chicanos could not easily put their more radical beliefs into practice. Thus, though new leaders were more conscious of the forces in control, they were not yet in a position to topple neocolonialism in the Southwest.

This situation, however, failed to prevent Chicano nationalists from voicing their disapproval of the neocolonial practices of the United States. In Latin American affairs, for example, many Chicanos had long since become disillusioned with North American motives; President Johnson's armed intervention in the Dominican Republic in 1965 had shown the United States to be as imperialistic as ever. In 1973 North American cooperation in the overthrow of a democratically elected Marxist government in Chile convinced more Chicanos that the United States was more concerned with its economic interests than it was with democracy or social change in Latin America. In the early 1980s U.S. opposition to the new government of Nicaragua and to the leftist guerrillas of El Salvador caused renewed fears among Chicanos of possible U.S. military intervention in Central America. . . . Mexicans in the United States had always seen their fate as closely tied to that of other Latin Americans, and as a consequence a significant group now believed continuing neocolonialism in Latin America to mean continuing neocolonialism in the Southwest. Quite naturally, Chicanos were most concerned with relations between the United States and Mexico, relations which intellectuals now interpreted as between metropolis and "neocolony."

José Angel Gutiérrez in 1971 remarked concerning Chicanos and Mexico, "The Rio Grande never has separated us and never will." During the 1970s and 1980s the growing dependence of Mexico on the United States would verify Gutiérrez's statement. Although the Mexican Revolution had been fought in part to free the country from foreign, specifically North American, economic domination, by 1978 the United States was once again the major investor in and chief trading partner of Mexico. Similar to the situation during the Díaz dictatorship, the Mexican government was stable, but the economy was erratic—at times superficially prosperous, but ultimately deeply troubled. Unfortunately most of the wealth was once again accruing to foreign investors and to the few Mexicans belonging to the middle and upper classes. The masses, burdened by one of the highest birth rates in the world, continued their struggle with poverty and, as in the past, looked to the north for employment. The most important pattern in Chicano history during the 1970s and 1980s was the renewed migration of Mexicans into the Southwest. Composed almost entirely of undocumented workers, commonly called illegal aliens, this movement was the largest yet from Mexico. Though estimates of their number, based on apprehensions of the undocumented by the Immigration and Naturalization Service (INS), varied tremendously, the actual figure was undoubtedly in the millions.

The arrival of so many undocumented workers presented problems for Chicanos; nevertheless, it could be argued that the migration was beneficial. As in previous migratory waves, the new arrivals competed with U.S. Mexicans for low-paying jobs and low-cost housing; they seemingly depressed wages and helped cause unemployment; they occasionally served as strikebreakers, and sometimes competed with Chicanos for aid from the government. Since the undocumented generally settled in the southwestern barrios, Chicanos not only bore the brunt of competition from the newcomers, but were also exposed to renewed Anglo-American xenophobia. With the appearance of so many un-Americanized newcomers, the Anglo notion that all people in the barrios were foreigners once again seemed plausible. As a result, harassment of Chicanos by INS agents increased, and some employers became more cautious about hiring anyone who looked Mexican since that person might be an undocumented worker. During the 1970s and 1980s, the illegal alien question, of all issues concerning Chicanos, was by far the most commonly discussed in the Anglo communications media. Though the undocumented were usually discussed in terms of a social problem, for example as an alleged tax burden on the citizenry, these terms usually hid a very real Anglo fear that the Southwest was being culturally and racially reconquered by Mexicans—a fear not entirely unfounded.

"There is a distinct possibility," wrote one openly racist Anglo, "if the legal and illegal seepage of Mexican genes across the Rio Grande and the high Mexican-American birthrate continue at present levels, that Mexican-Americans will regain their lost territories of Alta California and Texas . . .—not by violence or minority politics but simply by exercising squatters' rights." In October of 1977, this fear of Mexican invasion was so aroused by the media that the Ku Klux Klan announced it would conduct its own armed surveillance of the boundary to assist the undermanned Border Patrol in arresting illegal aliens. With the tacit approval of certain officials in the INS and of the San Diego (California) police, some Klan patrols were planned, but this activity ceased after strenuous protests from Chicano and other minority groups. Their nationalism having been revived during the 1960s, most U.S. Mexicans no longer disassociated themselves from their fellows across the border; they were no longer willing to stand by, as they had in the 1930s and 1950s, and watch Mexicans mistreated simply for lacking proper documents. Even though undocumented workers competed directly with Mexican-Americans, most Chicanos now felt their common national heritage outweighed their practical differences. Indeed, this feeling was strong enough that Chicano activists threatened to form their own armed patrols to counter the Klan's.

That Chicanos had to some extent readopted their Mexican imagination was evident from the similarity of their image of the Southwest to the image of the region perceived by the undocumented. "Undocumented workers," reported Grace Halsell, author of *The Illegals*, "do not feel they commit a crime in traveling north from Mexico. They call it going to *el norte*. As far as the Southwest is concerned, 'we are the legals, the Anglos the illegals,' one Mexican said." In spite of the artificial international boundary, many Chicanos now realized more than ever that both they and Mexicans belonged in the Southwest, and that the fate of Chicanos in that region would always be influenced by people from Mexico. Because of this, as long as Mexico existed in a neocolonial relationship with the United States, the Chicano barrios and hamlets in the Southwest would continue to be internal colonies of the United States. Deprived of a living by a Mexican economy profiting North American investors and a domestic elite, undocumented workers would continue to pour into the Southwest to provide capitalists with cheap labor and consumers with lower prices. Since the undocumented would continue to compete with Chicanos at the bottom of the economic ladder, Chicanos would continue to have a difficult time climbing out of poverty, especially given the cooptation, discrimination, and other forms of subjugation traditionally used in the Southwest to keep the Spanish-speaking colonized.

In the past Mexican-Americans had at times supported efforts to seal the border against their competitors from Mexico, but after the 1960s many concluded that, besides being practically impossible, sealing the border would not eliminate domestic forms of subjugation and would only deprive the Mexican poor of desperately needed income. Many Chicanos concluded it was immoral to deny employment to the undocumented, especially when many were friends and relatives. For this reason, in fact, some Chicanos by 1979 were quietly hoping for a completely open border. Journalist Richard Reeves noted:

> I'm convinced that the real Chicano position on undocumented workers is total amnesty . . . , and a totally open border. . . . No one will say that . . .—but many people said things like this . . . : "We know where the undocumented workers are—they're sleeping on the couches in our living rooms. . . . They're family and they're just trying to feed their families back home."

Moreover, the undocumented and other recently arrived Mexicans provided Chicanos with the best hope that their culture would survive in the Southwest. Because of the newcomers, Chicanos were forced to maintain their language and culture or suffer a breakdown in barrio communication.

In fact it was the new influx of people from Mexico, together with the emergence of an educated nationalistic leadership, that made Chicano activists in the late 1970s guardedly optimistic about the future, despite the obstacles set up by the dominant society. Of course, they had no illusions that they were about to establish a politically independent Aztlán, nor did they then wish to do so. Several years earlier, this idea had been considered and rejected for obvious reasons. "Would a separate state be viable?" journalist Armando Rendón had asked in 1971. "My guess is that the United States Government would act very quickly to suppress Chicano efforts toward this end." While such a utopian course of action would never be permitted, by the late 1970s

Chicano activists were optimistic that more practical social plans would have to be taken seriously by Anglo society, for that society could not continue to ignore the fastest growing minority group in the nation. Given the perpetually high Chicano and Mexican birth rates, Chicano voting strength was growing by the year; if the newly nationalistic leadership ever organized that power, Anglo supremacy throughout the Southwest would be challenged as it had been in Crystal City [Texas]. Faced with such a possibility, Anglos would have to make concessions because, as columnist Tony Castro commented, "The Mexican-American in the Southwest today is like a Palestinian in the Middle East. An accommodation has to be made."

The analogy with the Palestinians had some merit because, being a dispossessed group, Chicanos continued to have the potential for violent rebellion. That potential became a reality on May 7, 1978, when Houston Chicanos rioted in response to news that city policemen responsible for the death of a young Chicano the previous year had received light sentences for their crime. The Houston riot served as a warning that if Chicano optimism about the 1980s were to become disillusionment that decade could see more violence than had the late 1960s. The analogy with the Palestinians was appropriate in at least one other way—in the mid-1970s the fate of Chicanos began to be influenced by oil. At that time a major oil discovery was made in southern Mexico, and though there was a good deal of controversy concerning its exact size, speculation that the discovery might equal the reserves of Saudi Arabia caused everyone involved to reconsider the relations between the United States and Mexico, and consequently the relations between Anglo-Americans and persons of Mexican descent.

In the late 1970s some North American businessmen began to consider the advantages of a common market including the United States and Mexico, a common market that, according to Carey McWilliams, would "permit the free movement across their borders not only of all commodities—particularly oil and gas—but also of people." In their need for petroleum, some North Americans were beginning to consider the idea that the boundary between the Southwest and Mexico might indeed be artificial. In return for increased supplies of energy, North Americans were beginning to think about legalizing the seemingly inevitable migration of Mexicans into the Southwest. Such a concession to the Chicano image of the region, while not eliminating the neocolonial status of the Mexican and Chicano masses, would certainly improve their condition by providing economic opportunities for the former, and numerical and cultural strength to the latter. The thought of this is what made Chicano activists optimistic about the future of Aztlán. While such concessions would not end neocolonialism in the Southwest, they would permit Chicanos to entrench themselves until revolutionary changes in the general society of the United States could allow true self-determination.

However, the guarded optimism of the late 1970s decreased as the 1980s proceeded. In the United States the backlash of the former decade increased with the introduction of conservative federal policies on such matters as the enforcement of civil rights laws; moreover, the economic position of minorities suffered during a period of recession and slowed government spending. Declining petroleum prices left Mexico unable to repay huge loans secured with its oil discoveries, and this development stifled idealistic hopes of a common market between the two nations and of swift progress toward equality between Anglos and Chicanos in the Southwest. Significant recovery of control in the region, the myth of Aztlán, seemed as far off as ever. As a result, for the foreseeable future, the Chicanos' image of the land as lost, and of themselves as dispossessed, would continue to have credibility.

The (Relative) Decline of America

Paul Kennedy

By almost any reckoning, the United States, at least since World War II, ranked as an international power rivaling the hegemony once enjoyed by the world's greatest empires, whether Rome, imperial Spain, or Victorian Britain. In recent years, however, America's global ascendancy and confidence have been declining in the face of economic competition from Japan and the coalescing strength of the European Economic Community (the world's largest trading unit), which is moving toward full economic coordination in 1992. America's "decline" relative to these new economic centers of gravity is noticeable in industrial production, commerce, and agriculture. The United States has moved from being the world's greatest creditor nation to being the world's greatest debtor nation in a matter of a few years. America's "century" seems to be in eclipse. However, the nation's growing uncompetitiveness vis-à-vis other advanced—and advancing—nations, says Paul Kennedy, J. Richardson Dilworth Professor of History at Yale University, ought not yet be seen as a certain sign that another of history's "Great Powers" has forever fallen from the ranks of the mighty. Declarations of America's death, à la Mark Twain, have been greatly exaggerated. True, the United States is no longer in a position to fashion a unilateral grand design for the world at large either in political or in economic terms. Yet prospects for the future are not especially dim if the nation can find means to liberate itself from anachronistic, restrictive myths while cultivating a clearer perception of the "larger facts about international affairs." The most important of these is that all superpowers eventually have declined relative to their political and economic rivals. It is their inevitable fate. Some, however, have managed the matter of their relative decline more intelligently and gracefully than others.

In February of 1941, when Henry Luce's *Life* magazine announced that this was the "American century," the claim accorded well with the economic realities of power. Even before the United States entered the Second World War, it produced about a third of the world's manufactures, which was more than twice the production of Nazi Germany and almost ten times that of Japan. By 1945, with the Fascist states defeated and America's wartime allies economically exhausted, the U.S. share of world manufacturing output was closer to half—a proportion never before or since attained by a single nation. More than any of the great world empires—Rome, Imperial Spain, or Victorian Britain—the United States appeared destined to dominate international politics for decades, if not centuries, to come.

In such circumstances it seemed to American decision-makers natural (if occasionally awkward) to extend U.S. military protection to those countries pleading for help in the turbulent years after 1945. First came involvement in Greece and Turkey; and then, from 1949 onward, the extraordinarily wide-ranging commitment to NATO; the special relationship with Israel and, often contrarily, with Saudi Arabia, Jordan, Egypt, and lesser Arab states; and obligations to the partners in such regional defense organizations as SEATO, CENTO, and ANZUS. Closer to home, there was the Rio Pact and the special hemispheric defense arrangements with Canada. By early 1970, as Ronald Steel has pointed out, the United States "had more than 1,000,000 soldiers in 30 countries, was a member of 4 regional defense alliances and an active participant in a fifth, had mutual defense treaties with 42 nations, was a member of 53 international organizations, and was furnishing military or economic aid to nearly 100 nations across the face of the globe." Although the end of the Vietnam War significantly reduced the number of American troops overseas, the global array of U.S. obligations that remained would have astonished the Founding Fathers.

Yet while America's commitments steadily increased after 1945, its share of world manufacturing and of world gross national product began to decline, at first rather slowly, and then with increasing speed. In one sense, it could be argued, such a decline is irrelevant: this country is nowadays far richer, absolutely, than it was in 1945 or 1950, and most of its citizens are much better off *in absolute terms*. In another sense, however, the shrinking of America's share of world production is alarming because of the implications for American grand strategy—which is measured not by military forces alone but by their integration with all those other elements (economic, social, political, and diplomatic) that contribute toward a successful long-term national policy.

The gradual erosion of the economic foundations of America's power has been of several kinds. In the first place, there is the country's industrial decline relative to overall world production, not only in older manufactures, such as textiles, iron and steel, shipbuilding, and basic chemicals, but also—though it is harder to judge the final outcome at this stage of industrial-technological combat—in robotics, aerospace technology, automobiles, machine tools, and computers. Both areas pose immense problems: in traditional and basic manufacturing the gap in wage scales between the United States and newly industrializing countries is probably such that no efficiency measures will close it; but to lose out in the competition in future technologies, if that indeed should occur, would be even more disastrous.

The second, and in many ways less expected, sector of decline is agriculture. Only a decade ago experts were predicting a frightening global imbalance between food requirements and farming output. But the scenarios of famine and disaster stimulated two powerful responses: the first was a tremendous investment in American farming from the1970s onward, fueled by the prospect of ever larger overseas food sales; the second was a large-scale investigation, funded by the West, into scientific means of increasing Third World crop outputs. These have been so successful as to turn growing numbers of Third World countries into food exporters, and thus competitors of the United States. At the same time, the European Economic Community has become a major producer of agricultural surpluses, owing to its price-support system. In consequence, experts now refer to a "world awash in food," and this state of affairs in turn has led to sharp declines in agricultural prices and in American food exports—and has driven many farmers out of business.

Like mid-Victorian Britons, Americans after 1945 favored free trade and open competition, not just because they held that global commerce and prosperity would be advanced in the process but also because they knew that they were most likely to benefit from a lack of protectionism. Forty years later, with that confidence ebbing, there is a predictable shift of opinion in favor of protecting the domestic market and the domestic producer. And, just as in Edwardian Britain, defenders of the existing system point out that higher tariffs not only might make domestic products *less* competitive internationally but also might have other undesirable repercussions—a global tariff war, blows against American exports, the undermining of the currencies of certain newly industrializing countries, and an economic crisis like that of the 1930s

Along with these difficulties affecting American manufacturing and agriculture has come great turbulence in the nation's finances. The uncompetitiveness of U.S. industrial products abroad and the declining sales of agricultural exports have together produced staggering deficits in visible trade—$160 billion in the twelve months ending with April of 1986—but what is more alarming is that such a gap can no longer be covered by American earnings on "invisibles," which are the traditional recourse of a mature economy. On the contrary, the United States has been able to pay its way in the world only by importing ever larger amounts of capital. This has, of course, transformed it from the world's largest creditor to the world's largest debtor nation in the space of a few years.

Compounding this problem—in the view of many critics, causing this problem—have been the budgetary policies of the U.S. government itself.

A continuation of this trend, alarmed voices have pointed out, would push the U.S. national debt to around $13 *trillion* by the year 2000 (fourteen times the debt in 1980) and the interest payments on the debt to $1.5 *trillion*

FEDERAL DEFICIT, DEBT, AND INTEREST
(In Billions)

	Deficit	Debt	Interest on debt
1980	$59.6	$914.3	$52.5
1983	$195.4	$1,381.9	$87.8
1985	$202.8	$1,823.1	$129.0

(twenty-nine times the 1980 payments). In fact a lowering of interest rates could make those estimates too high, but the overall trend is still very unhealthy. Even if federal deficits could be reduced to a "mere" $100 billion annually, the compounding of national debt and interest payments by the early twenty-first century would still cause unprecedented sums of money to be diverted in that direction. The only historical examples that come to mind of Great Powers so increasing their indebtedness *in peacetime* are France in the 1780s, where the fiscal crisis finally led to revolution, and Russia early in this century.

Indeed, it is difficult to imagine how the American economy could have got by without the inflow of foreign funds in the early 1980s, even if that had the awkward consequence of inflating the dollar and thereby further hurting U.S. agricultural and manufacturing exports. But, one wonders, what might happen if those funds are pulled out of the dollar, causing its value to drop precipitously?

Some say that alarmist voices are exaggerating the gravity of what is happening to the U.S. economy and failing to note the "naturalness" of most of these developments. For example, the midwestern farm belt would be much less badly off if so many farmers had not bought land at inflated prices and excessive interest rates in the late 1970s. The move from manufacturing into services is understandable, and is occurring in all advanced countries. And U.S. manufacturing *output* has been rising in absolute terms, even if employment (especially blue-collar employment) in manufacturing has been falling—but that too is a "natural" trend, as the world increasingly moves from material-based to knowledge-based production. Similarly, there is nothing wrong in the metamorphosis of American financial institutions into world financial institutions, with bases in Tokyo and London as well as New York, to handle (and profit from) the heavy flow of capital; that can only increase the nation's earnings from services. Even the large annual federal deficits and the mounting national debt are sometimes described as being not very serious, after allowance is made for inflation; and there exists in some quarters a belief that the economy will "grow its way out" of these deficits, or that government measures will close the gap, whether by increasing taxes or cutting spending or both. A too hasty attempt to slash the deficit, it is pointed out, could well trigger a major recession.

The positive signs of growth in the American economy are said to be even more reassuring. Because of the boom in the service sector, the United States has been creating jobs over the past decade faster than it has done at any time in its peacetime history—and certainly a lot faster than Western Europe has been. America's far greater degree of labor mobility eases such transformations in the job market. Furthermore, the enormous American commitment to high technology—not just in California and New England but also in Virginia, Arizona, and many other places—promises ever greater production, and thus national wealth (as well as ensuring a strategic edge over the Soviet Union). Indeed, it is precisely because of the opportunities existing in the American economy that the nation continues to attract millions of immigrants and to generate thousands of new entrepreneurs, and the capital that pours into the country can be tapped for further investment, especially in research and development. Finally, if long-term shifts in the global terms of trade are, as economists suspect, leading to steadily lower prices for foodstuffs and raw materials, that ought to benefit an economy that still imports enormous amounts of oil, metal ores, and so on (even if it hurts particular American interests, such as farmers and oilmen).

Many of these points may be valid. Since the American economy is so large and diverse, some sectors and regions are likely to be growing while others are in decline—and to characterize the whole with generalizations about "crisis" or "boom" is therefore inappropriate. Given the decline in the price of raw materials, the ebbing of the dollar's unsustainably high exchange value since early 1985, the reduction that has occurred in interest rates, and the impact of all three trends on inflation and on business confidence, it is not surprising that some professional economists are optimistic about the future.

Nevertheless, from the viewpoint of American grand strategy, and of the economic foundation necessary to an effective long-term strategy, the picture is much less rosy. In the first place, America's capacity to carry the burden of military liabilities that it has assumed since 1945 is obviously less than it was several decades ago, when its shares of global manufacturing and GNP were much larger, its agriculture was secure, its balance of payments was far healthier, the government budget was in balance, and it was not in debt to the rest of the world. From that larger viewpoint there is something in the analogy that is made by certain political scientists between America's position today and that of previous "declining hegemons." Here again it is instructive to note the uncanny similarity between the growing mood of anxiety in thoughtful circles in the United States today and that which pervaded all political parties in Edwardian Britain and led to what has been termed the national efficiency movement—a broad-based debate among the nation's decision-making, business, and educational elites over ways to reverse a growing uncompetitiveness with other advanced societies. In terms of commercial expertise, levels of training and education, efficiency of production, and standards of income and (among the less well off) living, health, and housing, the number-one power of 1900 seemed to be losing its superiority, with dire implications for its long-term *strategic* position. Hence the calls for "renewal" and "reorganization" came as much from the right as from the left. Such campaigns usually do lead to reforms here and there, but their very existence is, ironically, a confirmation of decline. When a Great Power is strong and unchallenged, it will be much less likely to debate its capacity to meet its obligations than when it is relatively weaker.

In particular, there could be serious implications for American grand strategy if the U.S. industrial base continues to shrink. If there were ever in the future to be a large-scale war that remained conventional (because of the belligerents' fear of triggering a nuclear holocaust), one must wonder, would America's productive capacities be adequate after years of decline in certain key industries, the erosion of blue-collar employment, and so on? One is reminded of the warning cry of the British nationalist economist Professor W.A.S. Hewins in 1904 about the impact of British industrial decay upon that country's power:

> Suppose an industry which is threatened [by foreign competition] is one which lies at the very root of your system of National defense, where are you then? You could not get on without an iron industry, a great Engineering trade, because in modern warfare you would not have the means of producing, and maintaining in a state of efficiency, your fleets and armies.

It is hard to imagine that the decline in American industrial capacity could be so severe: America's manufacturing base is simply much broader than Edwardian Britain's was, and—an important point—the so-called defense-related industries not only have been sustained by Pentagon procurement but also have taken part in the shift from materials-intensive to knowledge-intensive (high-tech) manufacturing, which over the long term will also reduce the West's reliance on critical raw materials. Even so, the expatriation from the United States of, say, semiconductor assembly, the erosion of the American shipping and shipbuilding industry, and the closing down of so many American mines and oil fields represent trends that cannot but be damaging in the event of another long Great Power coalition war. If, moreover, historical precedents have any validity at all, the most critical constraint upon any surge in wartime production will be the number of skilled craftsmen—which causes one to wonder about the huge long-term decline in American blue-collar employment, including the employment of skilled craftsmen.

A problem quite different but equally important for sustaining a proper grand strategy concerns the impact of slow economic growth on the American social-political consensus. To a degree that amazes most Europeans, the United States in the twentieth century has managed to avoid overt "class" politics. This, one imagines, is a result of America's unique history. Many of its immigrants had fled from socially rigid circumstances elsewhere; the sheer size of the country had long allowed those who were disillusioned with their economic position to escape to the West, and also made the organization of labor much more difficult than in, say, France or Britain; and those same geographic dimensions, and the entrepreneurial opportunities within them, encouraged the development of a largely unreconstructed form of laissez-faire capitalism that has dominated the political culture of the nation (despite occasional counterattacks from the left). In consequence, the earnings gap between rich and poor is significantly larger in the United States than in any other advanced industrial society, and state expenditures on social services claim a lower share of GNP than in comparable countries except Japan, whose family-based support system for the poor and the aged appears much stronger.

This lack of class politics despite obvious socio-economic disparities has been possible because the nation's overall growth since the 1930s has offered the prospect of individual betterment to a majority of the population, and, disturbingly, because the poorest third of American society has not been mobilized to vote regularly. But given the different birthrates of whites on the one hand and blacks and Hispanics on the other, given the changing composition of the flow of immigrants into the United States, given also the economic metamorphosis that is leading to the loss of millions of relatively high-paying jobs in manufacturing, and the creation of millions of poorly paid jobs in services, it may be unwise to assume that the prevailing norms of the American political economy (such as low government social expenditures and low taxes on the rich) would be maintained if the nation entered a period of sustained economic difficulty caused by a plunging dollar and slow growth. An American polity that responds to external challenges by increasing defense expenditures, and reacts to the budgetary crisis by cutting existing social expenditures, runs the risk of provoking an eventual political backlash. There are no easy answers in dealing with the constant three-way tension between defense, consumption, and investment as national priorities.

Imperial Overstretch

This brings us, inevitably, to the delicate relationship between slow economic growth and high defense spending. The debate over the economics of defense spending is a heated one and—bearing in mind the size and variety of the American economy, the stimulus that can come from large government contracts, and the technological spin-offs from weapons research—the evidence does not point simply in one direction. But what is significant for our purposes is the comparative dimension. Although (as is often pointed out) defense expenditures amounted to ten percent of GNP under President Eisenhower and nine percent under President Kennedy, America's shares of global production and wealth were at that time around twice what they are today, and, more particularly, the American economy was not then facing challenges to either its traditional or its high-technology manufactures. The United States now devotes about seven percent of its GNP to defense spending, while its major economic rivals, especially Japan, allocate a far smaller proportion. If this situation continues, then America's rivals will have more funds free for civilian investment. If the United States continues to direct a huge proportion of its research and development activities toward military-related production while the Japanese and West Gemans concentrate on commercial research and development, and if the Pentagon drains off the ablest of the country's scientists and engineers from the design and production of goods for the world market, while similar personnel in other countries are bringing out better consumer products, then it seems inevitable that the American share of world manufacturing will decline steadily, and likely that American economic growth rates will be slower than those of countries dedicated to the marketplace and less eager to channel resources into defense.

It is almost superfluous to say that these tendencies place the United States on the horns of a most acute, if long-term, dilemma. Simply because it is *the* global superpower, with military commitments far more extensive than those of a regional power like Japan or West Germany, it requires much larger defense forces. Furthermore, since the USSR is seen to be the major military threat to American interests around the globe, and is clearly devoting a far greater proportion of its GNP to defense, American decision-makers are inevitably worried about "losing" the arms race with Russia. Yet the more sensible among the decision-makers can also perceive that the burden of armaments is debilitating the Soviet economy, and that if the two superpowers continue to allocate ever larger shares of their national wealth to the unproductive field of armaments, the critical question might soon be, Whose economy will decline *fastest*, relative to the economies of such expanding states as Japan, China, and so forth? A small investment in armaments may leave a globally overstretched power like the United States feeling vulnerable everywhere, but a very heavy investment in them, while bringing greater security in the short term, may so erode the commercial competitiveness of the American economy that the nation will be less secure in the long term.

Here, too, the historical precedents are not encouraging. Past experience shows that even as the relative economic strength of number-one countries has ebbed, the growing foreign challenges to their position have compelled them to allocate more and more of their resources to the military sector, which in turn has squeezed out productive investment and, over time, led to a downward spiral of slower growth, heavier taxes, deepening domestic splits over spending priorities, and a weakening capacity to bear the burdens of defense. If this, indeed, is the pattern of history, one is tempted to paraphrase Shaw's deadly serious quip and say: "Rome fell. Babylon fell. Scarsdale's turn will come."

How is one to interpret what is going on? And what, if anything, can be done about these problems? Far too many of the remarks made in political speeches suggest that while politicians worry more than they did about the nation's economic future, they tend to believe that the problems have quick and simple-minded solutions. For example, some call for tariffs—but they fail to address the charge that whenever industry and agriculture are protected, they become less productive. Others urge "competitiveness"—but they fail to explain how, say, American textile workers are to compete with textile workers earning only a twentieth of American wages. Still others put the blame for the decline of American efficiency on the government, which they say takes too much of the national income—but they fail to explain how the Swiss and the Germans, with their far higher tax rates, remain competitive on the world market. There are those who want to increase defense spending to meet perceived threats overseas—but they rarely concede that such a policy would further unbalance the economy. And there are those who want to reduce defense spending—but they rarely suggest which commitments (Israel? Korea? Egypt? Europe?) should go, in order to balance means and ends.

Above all, there is rarely any sense of the long-term context in which this American dilemma must be seen, or of the blindingly obvious point that the problem is not new. The study of world history might be the most useful endeavor for today's decision-makers. Such study would free politicians from the ethnocentric and temporal blinkers that so often restrict vision, allowing them to perceive some of the larger facts about international affairs.

The first of these is that the relative strengths of the leading nations have never remained constant, because the uneven rates of growth of different societies and technological and organizational breakthroughs bring greater advantage to one society than to another. For example, the coming of the long-range-gunned sailing ship and the rise of Atlantic trade after 1500 were not uniformly beneficial to the states of Europe—they benefited some much more than others. In the same way, the later development of steam power, and of the coal and metal resources upon which it relied, drastically increased the relative power of certain nations. Once their productive capacity was enhanced, countries would normally find it easier to sustain the burdens of spending heavily on armaments in peacetime, and of maintaining and supplying large armies and fleets in wartime. It sounds crudely mercantilistic to express it this way, but wealth is usually needed to underpin military power, and military power is usually needed to acquire and protect wealth. If, however, too large a proportion of a state's resources is diverted from the creation of wealth and allocated instead to military purposes, that is likely to lead to a weakening of national power over the long term. And if a state overextends itself strategically, by, say, conquering extensive territories or waging costly wars, it runs the risk that the benefits ultimately gained from external expansion may be outweighed by the greater expense—a problem that becomes acute if the nation concerned has entered a period of relative economic decline. The history of the rise and fall of the leading countries since the advance of Western Europe in the sixteenth century—that is, of nations such as Spain, the Netherlands, France, Great Britain, and, currently, the United States—shows a significant correlation over the long term between productive and revenue-raising capacity on the one hand and military strength on the other.

Of course, both wealth *and* power are always relative. Three hundred years ago the German mercantilistic writer Philipp von Hornigk observed that "whether a nation be today mighty and rich or not depends not on the abundance or security of its power or riches, but principally on whether its neighbors possess more or less of it."

The Netherlands in the mid-eighteenth century was richer in absolute terms than it had been a hundred years earlier, but by that stage it was much less of a Great Power, because neighbors like France and Britain had more power and riches. The France of 1914 was, absolutely, more powerful than the one of 1850—but that was little consolation when France was being eclipsed by a much stronger Germany. Britain has far greater wealth today than it had in its mid-Victorian prime, and its armed forces possess far more powerful weapons, but its share of world product has shrunk from about 25 percent to about three percent. If a nation has "more of it" than its contemporaries, things are fine; if not, there are problems.

This does not mean, however, that a nation's relative economic and military power will rise and fall in parallel. Most of the historical examples suggest that the trajectory of a state's military-territorial influence lags noticeably behind the trajectory of its relative economic strength. The reason for this is not difficult to grasp. An economically expanding power—Britain in the 1860s, the United States in the 1890s, Japan today—may well choose to become rich rather than to spend heavily on armaments. A half century later priorities may well have altered. The earlier economic expansion has brought with it overseas obligations: dependence on foreign markets and raw materials, military alliances, perhaps bases and colonies. Other, rival powers are now expanding economically at a faster rate, and wish in their turn to extend their influence abroad. The world has become a more competitive place, and the country's market shares are being eroded. Pessimistic observers talk of decline; patriotic statesmen call for "renewal."

In these more troubled circumstances the Great Power is likely to spend much more on defense than it did two generations earlier and yet still find the world to be less secure—simply because other powers have grown faster, and are becoming stronger. Imperial Spain spent much more money on its army in the troubled 1630s and 1640s than it had in the 1580s, when the Castilian economy was healthier. Britain's defense expenditures were far greater in 1910 than they were, say, at the time of Palmerston's death, in 1865, when the British economy was at its relative peak; but did any Britons at the later date feel more secure? The same problem appears to confront both the United States and the Soviet Union today. Great Powers in relative decline instinctively respond by spending more on security, thereby diverting potential resources from investment and compounding their long-term dilemma.

After the Second World War the position of the United States and the USSR as powers in a class by themselves appeared to be reinforced by the advent of nuclear weapons and delivery systems. The strategic and diplomatic landscape was now entirely different from that of 1900, let alone 1800. And yet the process of rise and fall among Great Powers had not ceased. Militarily, the United States and the USSR stayed in the forefront as the 1960s gave way to the 1970s and 1980s. Indeed, because they both interpret international problems in bipolar, and often Manichean, terms, their rivalry has driven them into an ever-escalating arms race that no other powers feel capable of joining. Over the same few decades, however, the global productive balances have been changing faster than ever before. The Third World's share of total manufacturing output and GNP, which was depressed to an all-time low in the decade after 1945, has steadily expanded. Europe has recovered from its wartime batterings and, in the form of the EEC, become the world's largest trading unit. The People's Republic of China is leaping forward at an impressive rate. Japan's postwar economic growth has been so phenomenal that, according to some measures, Japan recently overtook the Soviet Union in total GNP. Meanwhile, growth rates in both the United States and the USSR have become more sluggish, and those countries' shares of global production and wealth have shrunk dramatically since the 1960s.

It is worth bearing the Soviet Union's difficulties in mind when one analyzes the present and future circumstances of the United States, because of two important distinctions. The first is that while it can be argued that the U.S. share of world power has been declining faster than the Soviet share over the past few decades, the problems of the United States are probably nowhere near as great as those of the Soviet Union. Moreover, America's absolute strength (especially in industrial and technological fields) is still much greater than that of the USSR. The second is that the very unstructured, laissez-faire nature of American society (while not without its weaknesses) probably gives the United States a better chance of readjusting to changing circumstances than a rigid and *dirigiste* power has. But its potential in turn depends upon a national leadership that can understand the larger processes at work in the world today and perceives both the strong and the weak points of the country's position as the United States seeks to adjust to the changing global environment.

Although the United States is at present still pre-eminent economically and perhaps even militarily, it cannot avoid the two great tests that challenge the longevity of every major power that occupies the number-one position in world affairs. First, in the military-strategic realm, can it preserve a reasonable balance between the nation's perceived defense commitments and the means it possesses to maintain those commitments? And second, as an intimately related question, can it preserve the technological and economic bases of its power from relative erosion in the face of the ever-shifting patterns of global production? This test of American abilities will be the greater because America, like Imperial Spain around 1600 or the British Empire around 1900, bears a heavy burden of strategic commitments, made decades earlier, when the nation's political, economic, and military capacity to influence world affairs seemed so much more assured. The United States now runs the risk, so familiar to historians of the rise and fall of Great Powers, of what might be called "imperial overstretch": that is to say, decision-makers in Washington must face the awkward and enduring fact that the total of the United States's global interests and obligations is nowadays far too large for the country to be able to defend them all simultaneously.

To be sure, it is hardly likely that the United States would be called upon to defend all of its overseas interests simultaneously and unilaterally, unaided by the NATO members in Western Europe, Israel in the Middle East, or Japan, Australia, and possibly China in the Pacific. Nor are all the regional trends unfavorable to the United States with respect to defense. For example, while aggression by the unpredictable North Korean regime is always possible, it would hardly be welcomed by Beijing—furthermore, South Korea has grown to have more than twice the population and four times the GNP of the North. Also, while the expansion of Soviet forces in the Far East is alarming to Washington, it is balanced by the growing threat that China poses to the USSR's land and sea lines of communication in that area. The recent sober admission by Secretary of Defense Caspar Weinberger that "we can never afford to buy the capabilities sufficient to meet all of our commitments with one hundred percent confidence" is surely true; but it is also true that the potential anti-Soviet resources in the world (the United States, Western Europe, Japan, China, Australasia) are far greater than the resources lined up on the USSR's side.

Despite such consolations, the fundamental grand-strategic problem remains: the United States today has roughly the same enormous array of military obligations across the globe that it had a quarter century ago, when its shares of world GNP, manufacturing production, military spending, and armed-forces personnel were much larger than they are now. In 1985, forty years after America's triumph in the Second World War and more than a decade after its pull-out from Vietnam, 526,000 members of the U.S. armed forces were abroad (including 64,000 afloat). That total is substantially more than the overseas deployments in peacetime of the military and naval forces of the British Empire at the height of its power. Nevertheless, in the opinion of the Joint Chiefs of Staff, and of many civilian experts, it is simply not enough. Despite a near-trebling of the American defense budget since the late 1970s, the numerical size of the armed forces on active duty has increased by just five percent. As the British and the French military found in their time, a nation with extensive overseas obligations will always have a more difficult manpower problem than a state that keeps its armed forces solely for home defense, and a politically liberal and economically laissez-faire society sensitive to the unpopularity of conscription will have a greater problem than most.

Managing Relative Decline

Ultimately, the only answer to whether the United States can preserve its position is *no*—for it simply has not been given to any one society to remain permanently ahead of all the others, freezing the patterns of different growth rates, technological advance, and military development that have existed since time immemorial. But historical precedents do not imply that the United States is destined to shrink to the relative obscurity of former leading powers like Spain and the Netherlands, or to disintegrate like the Roman and Austro-Hungarian empires; it is too large to do the former, and probably too homogeneous to do the latter. Even the British analogy, much favored in the current political-science literature, is not a good one if it ignores the differences in scale. The geographic size, population, and natural resources of Great Britain suggest that it ought to possess roughly three or four percent of the world's wealth and power, all other things being equal. But precisely because all other things are never equal, a peculiar set of historical and technological circumstances permitted Great Britain to possess, say, 25 percent of the world's wealth and power in its prime. Since those favorable circumstances have disappeared, all that it has been doing is returning to its more "natural" size. In the same way, it may be argued, the geographic extent, population, and natural resources of the United States suggest that it ought to possess 16 or 18 percent of the world's wealth and power. But because of historical and technological circumstances favorable to it, that share rose to 40 percent or more by 1945, and what we are witnessing today is the ebbing away from that extraordinarily high figure to a more natural share. That decline is being masked by the country's enormous military capability at present, and also by its success in internationalizing American capitalism and culture. Yet even when it has declined to the position of occupying no more than its natural share of the world's wealth and power, a long time into the future, the United States will still be a very significant power in a multipolar world, simply because of its size.

The task facing American statesmen over the next decades, therefore, is to recognize that broad trends are under way, and that there is a need to manage affairs so that the relative erosion of America's position takes place slowly and smoothly, unaided by policies that bring short-term advantage but long-term disadvantage. Among the realities that statesmen, from the President down, must be alert to are these: that technological and therefore socioeconomic change is occurring in the world faster than it has ever before; that the international community is much more politically and culturally diverse than has been assumed, and is defiant of simplistic remedies offered by either Washington or Moscow for its problems; that the economic and productive power balances are no longer tilted as favorably in America's direction as they were in 1945. Even in the military realm there are signs of a certain redistribution of the balances, away from a bipolar and toward a multipolar system, in which American economic and military strength is likely to remain greater than that of any other individual country but will cease to be as disproportionate as it was in the decades immediately after the Second World War. In all the discussions about the erosion of American leadership it needs to be repeated again and again that the decline is relative, not absolute, and is therefore perfectly natural, and that a serious threat to the real interests of the United States can come only from a failure to adjust sensibly to the new world order.

Just how well can the American system adjust to a state of relative decline? Already, a growing awareness of the gap between U.S. obligations and U.S. power has led to questions by gloomier critics about the overall political culture in which Washington decision-makers have to operate. It has been suggested with increasing frequency that a country needing to reformulate its grand strategy in the light of the larger, uncontrollable changes taking place in world affairs may be ill served by an electoral system that seems to paralyze foreign-policy decision-making every two years. Foreign policy may be undercut by the extraordinary pressures applied by lobbyists, political-action committees, and other interest groups, all of whom, by definition, are prejudiced in favor of this or that policy change, and by the simplification of vital but complex international and strategic issues, inherent to mass media whose time and space for such things are limited and whose raison d'être is chiefly to make money and only secondarily to inform. It may also be undercut by the still powerful escapist urges in the American social culture, which are perhaps understandable in terms of the nation's frontier past but hinder its coming to terms with today's complex, integrated world and with other cultures and ideologies. Finally, the country may not always be helped by the division of decision-making powers that was deliberately created when it was geographically and strategically isolated from the rest of the world, two centuries ago, and had time to find a consensus on the few issues that actually concerned foreign policy. This division may be less serviceable now that the United States is a global superpower, often called upon to make swift decisions vis-à-vis countries that enjoy far fewer constraints. No one of these obstacles prevents the execution of a coherent, long-term American grand strategy. However, their cumulative effect is to make it difficult to carry out policy changes that seem to hurt special interests and occur in an election year. It may therefore be here, in the cultural and political realms, that the evolution of an overall American policy to meet the twenty-first century will be subjected to the greatest test.

Nevertheless, given the considerable array of strengths still possessed by the United States, it ought not in theory to be beyond the talents of successive Administrations to orchestrate this readjustment so as, in Walter Lippmann's classic phrase, to bring "into balance . . . the nation's commitments and the nation's power." Although there is no single state obviously preparing to take over America's global burdens, in the way that the United States assumed Britain's role in the 1940s, the country has fewer problems than had Imperial Spain, besieged by enemies on all fronts, or the Netherlands, squeezed between France and England, or the British Empire, facing numerous challengers. The tests before the United States as it heads toward the twenty-first century are certainly daunting, perhaps especially in the economic sphere; but the nation's resources remain considerable, *if* they can be properly utilized and *if* there is a judicious recognition of both the limitations and the opportunities of American power.

America as Idea

Barbara Tuchman

All myths are not bad. In the introduction to this volume, we develop historically the concept of the positive usefulness of myth as well as its pejorative aspects. In the short essay that follows, the late Barbara Tuchman, one of America's most distinguished historians, focuses on the idea of America based on the positive mythology found in such sources as the Declaration of Independence, the Constitution, selected Supreme Court decisions, and legislative statutes. Included in the idea are the salutary, ringing concepts of the natural rights theory and various civil and human rights. Tuchman identifies certain major stumbling blocks in the historical development of the idea but feels that during the first 100 years of our national history the positive clearly outweighed the negative. She also quite correctly points to an evident retrogression during the second century of the nation's life. However, the idea of America persists—the positive use of myth continues—and some solace can be taken from that. But also inherent in the essay is a call for eternal vigilance and active concern if we as a nation are to continue to progress toward meeting Lincoln's challenging, mythic vision of America as humankind's "last, best hope."

The United States is a nation consciously conceived, not one that evolved slowly out of an ancient past. It was a planned idea of democracy, of liberty of conscience and pursuit of happiness. It was the promise of equality of opportunity and individual freedom within a just social order, as opposed to the restrictions and repressions of the Old World. In contrast to the militarism of Europe, it would renounce standing armies and "sheathe the desolating sword of war." It was an experiment in Utopia to test the thesis that, given freedom, independence, and local self-government, people, in Kossuth's words, "will in due time ripen into all the excellence and all the dignity of humanity." It was a new life for the oppressed, it was enlightenment, it was optimism.

Regardless of hypocrisy and corruption, of greed, chicanery, brutality, and all the other bad habits man carries with him whether in the New World or Old, the founding idea of the United States remained, on the whole, dominant through the first hundred years. With reservations, it was believed in by Americans, by visitors who came to aid our Revolution or later to observe our progress, by immigrants who came by the hundreds of thousands to escape an intolerable situation in their native lands.

The idea shaped our politics, our institutions, and to some extent our national character, but it was never the only influence at work. Material circumstances exerted an opposing force. The open frontier, the hardships of homesteading from scratch, the wealth of natural resources, the whole vast challenge of a continent waiting to be exploited, combined to produce a prevailing materialism and an American drive bent as much, if not more, on money, property, and power than was true of the Old World from which we had fled. The human resources we drew upon were significant: Every wave of immigration brought here those people who had the extra energy, gumption, or restlessness to uproot themselves and cross an unknown ocean to seek a better life. Two other factors entered the shaping process—the shadow of slavery and the destruction of the native Indian.

At its Centennial the United States was a material success. Through its second century the idea and the success have struggled in continuing conflict. The Statue of Liberty, erected in 1886, still symbolized the promise to those "yearning to breathe free." Hope, to them, as seen by a foreign visitor, was "domiciled in America as the Pope is in Rome." But slowly in the struggle the idea lost ground, and at a turning point around 1900, with American acceptance of a rather half-hearted imperialism, it lost dominance. Increasingly invaded since then by self-doubt and disillusion, it survives in the disenchantment of today, battered and crippled but not vanquished.

What has happened to the United States in the twentieth century is not a peculiarly American phenomenon but a part of the experience of the West. In the Middle Ages plague, wars, and social violence were seen as God's punishment upon man for his sins. If the concept of God can be taken as man's conscience, the same explanation may be applicable today. Our sins in the twentieth century—greed, violence, inhumanity—have been profound, with the result that the pride and self-confidence of the nineteenth century have turned to dismay and self-disgust.

In the United States we have a society pervaded from top to bottom by contempt for the law. Government—including the agencies of law enforcement—business, labor, students, the military, the poor no less than the rich, outdo each other in breaking the rules and violating the ethics that society has established for its protection. The average citizen, trying to hold a footing in standards of morality and conduct he once believed in, is daily knocked over by incoming waves of venality, vulgarity, irresponsibility, ignorance, ugliness, and trash in all senses of the word. Our government collaborates abroad with the worst enemies of humanity and liberty. It wastes our substance on useless proliferation of military hardware that can never buy security no matter how high the pile. It learns no lessons, employs no wisdom, and corrupts all who succumb to Potomac fever.

Yet the idea does not die. Americans are not passive under their faults. We expose them and combat them. Somewhere every day some group is fighting a public abuse—openly and, on the whole, notwithstanding the FBI, with confidence in the First Amendment. The U.S. has slid a long way from the original idea. Nevertheless, somewhere between Gulag Archipelago and the featherbed of cradle-to-the-grave welfare, it still offers a greater opportunity for social happiness—that is to say, for well-being combined with individual freedom and initiative—than is likely elsewhere. The ideal society for which mankind has been striving through the ages will remain forever beyond our grasp. But if the great question, whether it is still possible to reconcile democracy with social order and individual liberty, is to find a positive answer, it will be here.

The Care and Repair of Public Myth

William H. McNeill

In some measure, the preceding set of readings contributes to the demise of many strongly held historical myths. And so it should be. For in a society that claims to cherish a fundamental freedom of the mind, the time for revision is always now. Old myths that sustain archaic, anachronistic beliefs and values lead a society to no good end. Yet at the same time, public myth is the *sine qua non* of any society. Without the ideological agreement that usable and revised myth spawns, a sense of cultural community is lost. Stories containing a people's image of itself in history are prerequisites for an essential, coherent, and prevailing order. Thus does myth hold potential to both distort and debase; yet it can both energize and elevate. Given myth's impact on a culture, the study of public myth and its complexities, says Professor Emeritus William H. McNeill of the University of Chicago, is a deserving topic in its own right. Subscribing to the view that myth is the cultural heart of a society, McNeill concludes that a "viable balance between mythmaking and mythbreaking" must be found in America. Discredited myths need to be replaced by a new generation of operational beliefs. Inherited political faiths may well be in need of repair and a new era of ideas and ideals needed. The American capacity for achievement and common purpose is at stake. As in religion, faith is fundamental. America's "civil religion"—its fundamental cultural stories and beliefs that motivate the nation to high levels of action and accomplishment—demands no less.

I

Myth lies at the basis of human society. That is because myths are general statements about the world and its parts, and in particular about nations and other human in-groups, that are believed to be true and then acted on whenever circumstances suggest or require common response. This is mankind's substitute for instinct. It is the unique and characteristic human way of acting together. A people without a full quiver of relevant agreed-upon statements, accepted in advance through education or less formalized acculturation, soon finds itself in deep trouble, for, in the absence of believable myths, coherent public action becomes very difficult to improvise or sustain.

Myths, moreover, are based on faith more than on fact. Their truth is usually proven only by the action they provoke. In 1940, for example, when

Hitler had defeated France, the British public continued to support war against Germany partly because they "knew" from schoolbook history that in European wars their country lost all the early battles and always won the last. This faith, together with a strong sense of the general righteousness of their cause, and fear of what defeat would bring, made it possible for them to persist in waging war until myth became fact once more in 1945.

Clearly, without British actions in 1940, World War II would have followed a far different course. Russian and American resources might never have coalesced with Britain's to create the victorious Grand Alliance of 1945. Germany, in short, might have won. Yet no merely rational calculation of relative strengths and military capabilities in June 1940 would have supported the proposition that Great Britain could expect to defeat Hitler. Action, irrational in the short run, proved rational in the longer run. Myth is what bridged the gap, remaking the reality of June 1940 into the reality of May 1945.

On the other hand, Hitler and his followers, too, were guided by their own set of myths. But their belief in Germany's racial superiority, no matter how firmly embraced and enthusiastically acted upon, brought only disaster. So belief by itself is not enough. Complex constraints operated in human affairs, only partially understood even by the wisest. Consequently, human hopes are never fully realized, and unforeseen side effects continually throw up new problems that redirect action even in the most routinized situations. It is in directing and redirecting action that myth comes into play. Conversely, when actions undertaken in accordance with accepted ideas fail to achieve anything like the expected result, it is time to reconsider the guiding myth, amending or rejecting it as the case may be. As a result of this process, the British national myth survived World War II with little amendment, whereas Germany's suffered a wrenching discontinuity.

Liberalism, Marxism, and the various technocratic ideals of social management that have proliferated so remarkably since World War II all constitute living myth systems, subject to amendment or rejection in the light of results, just as Nazism was. But the feedback between myth and action proceeds smoothly and effectively only when destruction and reconstruction of agreed-upon general statements about the world remain more or less in balance. Discrediting old myths without finding new ones to replace them erodes the basis for common action that once bound those who believed in a public body, capable of acting together.

How can a visible balance between myth making and myth breaking be assured? How can a people know what to believe and how to act? How indeed?

II

The classical liberal recipe for the care and repair of public myth was to rely on a free market in ideas. The United States is committed to this principle by law and to quite extraordinary degree also in practice. By allowing dissenters of any and every stripe a chance to express their views, liberals from the seventeenth century onwards hoped and believed that a kind of natural selection among myths would prevail. When, as is commonly the case, inadequate evidence obstructs fully rational choice, the upshot of action based on tentative or provisional belief would still suffice to permit the people to choose—eventually—what to believe and how to act.

The efficiency of such a free market obviously depends on how long it may take for the process of testing and confirmation—or rejection—to work itself out. In rapidly changing conditions, when more and more dimensions of social life are in motion and become subject to deliberate manipulation, there may not be enough time to test new formulations before they must again be altered to match newer and ever-changing circumstances. Worn-out old myths may then continue to receive lip service, but the spontaneity and force attainable when people truly believe and hope and act in unison will surely seep away.

In some fields, the free market in ideas works very well. This is conspicuously the case in natural science, where myth, tested by action and revised in accordance with results, continues to achieve spectacular success. It may seem whimsical to equate scientific theories with myth, but if one accepts the definition of myth offered at the beginning of this article, surely the shoe fits. Scientific theories *are* statements about the world believed to be true, and many of them also provide a basis for action, as our extraordinary technology attests. Moreover, no scientist any longer thinks that any actual theory fits reality so closely that revision and amendment will never be needed. No formula, whether mathematical or verbal, is immune from correction. Thus Newton supplanted Aristotle and Descartes, and was in turn corrected by Einstein, whose reign may soon be coming to a close if contemporary physicists succeed in formulating some new synthesis among the strong and weak forces their experiments have discovered.

Continual and fertile interplay between myth making and myth breaking in natural science stands in striking contrast with human affairs, where successful myth making is in short supply. This is not simply because effective social myths must go beyond observed facts. That is just as true in physics and the other natural sciences, where theory regularly runs beyond observation, guides perception and, frequently, directs experiments as well. For it is only where they have a theory to test that scientists can know how to filter out the various background noises that obscure experimental results when such guidance is lacking. Thus fact and theory interact in natural science in almost as strong a way as in human society.

Yet the natural and human worlds are not the same. Their great difference arises from the sensitivity of human behavior to symbolic stimuli. Physicists, after all, need not concern themselves with how particles of matter or energy will react to general statements they make about the world: whereas anyone describing human behavior knows that if what is said seems to be true, it will make a difference in how human beings who believe it will act. Such reflexivity therefore makes social myths different. They are more powerful to create and to destroy what they purport to describe than the formulations of the physicists, whose myths affect only the observation of behavior, not the behavior itself.

In human society, therefore, belief matters most. Evidence supporting belief is largely generated by actions undertaken in accordance with the belief. This is a principle long familiar to students of religion. In Christian terms, faith comes first, works follow. The primacy of faith is equally real for the various civil religions that since the eighteenth century have come to provide the practical basis for nearly all of the world's governments. Democratic elections legitimate governments when enough people believe that periodic elections are the right and proper way to choose who shall rule. For the same reason, divine-right monarchy, caliphal leadership and submission to the Son of Heaven were once effective too. But when assent becomes halfhearted or is actively withheld from such myths, obedience becomes irregular, the predictability of human action diminishes, and the effectiveness of public response to changing conditions begins to erode.

This, it seems to me, is our situation today around the globe. Democratic myths confront the reality of organized private interest groups operating in the interstices of empire building among rival branches of vast and ever-growing governmental bureaucracies. This makes the electoral process increasingly irrelevant to encounters between officials and citizens, even in countries like our own in which elections are not affected by armed intimidation at the polls or limited to candidates approved by a single party.

The audio-visual mass media, by opening a path into private homes where aspiring candidates may sell themselves to the voting public, do even more to insulate the electoral process from administrative realities. In the United States a candidate who secures access to TV has already won half the battle; subliminal empathy does the rest, slightly affected by the plausibility of promises to satisfy everyone, dismantle the bureaucracy, fight crime and safeguard peace. In other countries political salesmanship takes less extravagant forms. There, party organizations or governmental officials set more severe limits on access to mass media, and on programmatic statements attacking constituted authorities. In poorer lands, where TV screens have not yet spread into private homes, political campaigns are still likely to focus in the old-fashioned way on public meetings and private deals with locally based leaders of whatever sort—party functionaries, tribal chieftains, employers, landowners or whoever else matters in getting things done. But everywhere TV acts to undermine the electoral process, tending to reduce it to a popularity contest among tinsel personalities.

Communist countries have restricted the political impact of mass media by limiting what can be said in public to a narrow party line. But that policy runs into difficulties of its own. Apart from a widespread loss of credibility, the heavy weight of the police regimes that enforce restriction on public debate blatantly contradicts the anarchic brotherhood promised by Marx's vision of post-revolutionary communism. Consequently, as revolutions recede in time, the gap between reality and expectation becomes more difficult to explain away.

III

Political institutions are therefore not working well on either side of the Iron Curtain. Inherited political faiths are in danger of losing their credibility. The incipient stage of such a change is difficult to recognize or measure accurately; yet withdrawal of belief may suddenly come to matter more than anything else in foreign and domestic affairs. Revolutionary situations, like that which recently boiled up in Iran, register the collapse of old belief; but a successful revolution, like every other collective action, must invent or revive its own myths. Stability, predictability, control are otherwise impossible. The body politic cannot endure without agreement on truths that can be used to guide and justify public action.

To be sure, the United States is not in a revolutionary situation. Nonetheless, discrepancies between old myths and current realities are great enough to be troubling. They seem to widen every day, yet serious effort to revise inherited public myths remains largely the province of revivalist sectarians.

In times past, such situations have sometimes given great leaders the opportunity to reshape a nation or to remodel a state in response to a new vision of what was right, proper and possible. World War II and its aftermath gave this kind of scope to such diverse figures as Charles de Gaulle in France, Konrad Adenauer in Germany, Mao Zedong in China and Tito in Yugoslavia. Before that, the depression of the 1930s called Franklin D. Roosevelt and Adolf Hitler into action. Maybe our current difficulties will find a similar resolution in one or more of the most deeply affected countries. What is needed is a suitably charismatic figure with a vision of past and future that millions will find so compelling as to make them eager to join in common action to achieve newly articulated purposes.

Nevertheless, though the niche may be empty and waiting, no one can count on its being filled. Great public figures do not arise in a vacuum. They personify and give voice to ideas and ideals already scattered about and accepted by at least some segments of the public that responds to their call. The great leader's role is to put a coalition of new ideas into action, often by dint of overlooking logical discrepancies. When the resulting mix commands enough support to generate effective common action, logical shortcomings scarcely matter. The people who follow the great man's lead have, in effect, revised their mythical system and can therefore persist as an effective public body for as long as the new myths and action based on them continue to yield acceptable results.

But where do political leaders' new ideas come from? Tito and Mao drew on Marxism, Adenauer revivified a Catholic, corporatist tradition that had suffered near total eclipse in Bismarck's Germany, while De Gaulle combined Gallicanism, technocracy and a personal sense of mission that perhaps derived as much from his name as from anything more tangible. Such traditions are themselves human creations, of course, being largely the work of intellectuals and men of letters, packaged by historians for use in schools and other public places and then transmitted and sustained by educational, religious and other cultural institutions.

In a time such as ours, when inherited myth systems are in disrepair and no great political leader has yet emerged, historians, political scientists and other academics who are paid to educate the young and think about matters of public importance ought to feel a special responsibility for proposing alternatives to accepted ideas. Only so can they hope to trigger a successful reorganization of public myths that could command the support of informed and critical minds. To leave the field to ignorant and agitated extremists is dangerous. That, after all, was how Hitler came to power. Yet American historians are doing so today with clear conscience and from the best of motives.

Pursuit of truth has been the overriding ideal of our universities ever since the professionalization of research in academic institutions began about a century ago. Challenging prevailing myths without regard for the costs arising from the disintegration of belief therefore became professors' special calling. Intellectual honesty required as much, and methodological rigor demanded special attention to anything that failed to conform to mythical prescription and expectation.

Hence the enthusiasm for revisionism. Careers have been made and schools of historians have flourished on the strength of their discovery of flaws in received notions about the American nation and its government. By uncovering the sufferings of the poor and oppressed, revisionists discredited older ideas about the unique virtue and perfection of American society. They showed that liberty and democracy did not assure equality after all. Assimilation to a Yankee model of behavior did not guarantee happiness either, even for the most enthusiastic converts from other cultural backgrounds. Still other iconoclasts challenged the belief that foreigners differed from us simply because they had fallen behind the progress of the United States and only needed a little capital and know-how to become as rich, free and fortunate as Americans were supposed to be.

No one is likely to reaffirm these discredited notions today, even though public rhetoric often assumes the reality of such myths without expressly saying so. Politicians and journalists really have little choice, since suitably revised national and international myths are conspicuous by their absence.

Instead, the main energies of the historical profession have gone into detailed research, often focusing on the experience of groups formerly excluded from historians' attention, i.e., on one or another of the ethnically, sexually and occupationally oppressed segments of society. Frequently, the effect of such scholarship is to substitute a divisive for a unifying myth, intensifying the special grievances of one group against others.

Truth and intellectual honesty are no doubt served by noting the yawning gaps between democratic ideals and social practice. They would be even better served if historians found it possible to fit their new data and sensibilities into a wider perspective in which weak and strong, oppressor and oppressed would all find a place. In such a history, of course, the things that unite human beings would have to come to the fore. This might even provide a matrix for mutual understanding and more effective public action. Yet macrohistory is commonly deemed unscientific, and this despite the example natural scientists have given of how to react to new, discrepant data by revising theory to embrace old and new in a single formula believed to be true.

The main reason for eschewing macrohistorical synthesis is the mistaken notion that generalization inevitably involves error, while accuracy increases with detail. Getting at the sources and staying close to them seemed a sure way to truth a century ago when academic departments of history were set up. Industrious transcription of dead men's opinions therefore became the hallmark of historical scholarship. It still provides a convenient substitute for thought, despite historical quantifiers and other methodological innovators. Yet an infinitude of new sources, each of them revealing new details, does not automatically increase the stock of historical truth. More data may merely diminish the intelligibility of the past, and, carried to an extreme, the multiplication of facts reduces historical study to triviality.

The truth about foreign affairs, for example, does not reside solely or chiefly in the texts of diplomatic notes filed away in foreign offices. Search of supplementary sources like newspaper files, TV scripts and private papers will not do much to remedy the defects of diplomatic history based on faithful transcription and comparison of official documents. The reason is that all such research assumes that the situations within which human beings act are obvious and unchanging, so that only operational details that passed through the consciousness of the actors at the time need to be attended to.

But this is not the case, and historians actually know better. States are not eternal; nations emerge and pass away. Alterations in communication nets change the way governments and peoples interact, and patterns of power transform themselves all the time in ways of which contemporaries are only dimly aware. Yet changes of this kind commonly matter more for understanding what happened than anything that can be discovered by consulting additional past opinions as recorded in sources hitherto unexplored. Industriousness in archives may merely obstruct vision of the larger patterns whose evolution matters far more than new details of particular transactions.

To move from detail to perception of larger patterns is not achieved by accumulating more and more instances. Appropriate concepts are needed. Each change of scale requires its own vocabulary to direct attention to the critical thresholds and variables. Finding the right things to lump together and the right words to focus attention on critical transactions is the special work of human intelligence—whether applied to history or to everyday encounters with the world. Nearly everything is done for us by the language we inherit that generalizes and organizes the flow of sensory experience with every noun and verb we employ. But myth makers and myth breakers are entrusted with the task of adjusting and improving received ways of understanding and reacting to the world. As such, they are supposed to think more persistently and perspicaciously than others, making whatever change may be needed in inherited words and concepts so as to take account of new experience.

Finding the right vocabulary to focus attention efficiently is a difficult matter. The history of human thought records some of the more successful efforts that have been made. As a result of centuries of struggle to come to grips with the complexity of things, we now have many separate sciences, each with its own vocabulary. These actually describe the same reality at different levels of generalization. Thus, for example, no one doubts that atoms, molecules, cells and organisms simultaneously occupy terrestrial landscapes, and we have appropriate sciences for each. We also know that complicated ecological relationships exist among the separate organisms and populations of organisms that share any particular part of the earth. However complicated the relation may be across these diverse levels of organization, it is not the case that small patterns are automatically truer than large patterns, or that error inheres in a description of the ecosystem but is absent from formulas that apply to atomic interactions. Indeterminacy extends to the atomic and sub-atomic level too, as twentieth-century physicists agree.

Historians, however, through their idolization of written sources, have commonly allowed themselves to wallow in detail, while refusing to think about the larger patterns of the past which cannot be discovered by consulting documentary sources. They have consequently undermined inherited myths that attempted to make the past useful by describing large-scale patterns, without feeling any responsibility for replacing decrepit old myths with modified and corrected general statements that might provide a better basis for public action.

IV

If historians persist in dodging the important questions of our age in this fashion, others are sure to step into the breach by offering the necessary mythical answers to human needs. The question then becomes what groupings will take form and gather strength around such myths. So far, sectarian fissiparousness seems the dominant trend. Religious syncretism and revival, whether Muslim, Christian, Hindu or Buddhist, achieve success largely by cutting true believers off from the corruptions of civil society around them. Secular forms of sectarianism seem at a low ebb by comparison, thanks to the wearing out of both the Freudian and the Marxist faiths.

Tides in myth making and myth breaking are, of course, unpredictable and have often taken sudden, surprising turns. Recent events in Iran remind us of how precariously old and new systems of ideas coexist. Yet I, for one, am not prepared to abandon a secular and ecumenical faith in the power of human minds to decipher the world.

Several points seem clear to me. One is that troubling encounters with strangers constitute the principal motor of change within human societies. Ecumenical world history ought therefore to be specially sensitive to traces of past cultural interactions. This has the immediate effect of escaping the Europe-centered bias we have inherited, for any plausible view of the human adventure on earth quickly discovers that the dominance of European civilization is a matter of recent centuries. European expansion since 1500, indeed, appears to be analogous to what happened before when Middle Eastern, Mediterranean, Indian and Chinese civilizations each in turn attained skills superior to those known elsewhere, and for a few centuries were therefore able to influence others within the interacting circle of the Old World.

Whoever admired or feared the skills in question set out to acquire them or else sought to strengthen local society against their threat. Either way change resulted, often of a far-reaching kind. Comparable but less well-established patterns of cultural efflorescence and outward flow can be discerned among pre-Columbian Amerindians. African history, too, begins to become intelligible—though still dimly—in terms of diffusion of skills of the kind recorded more fully by the literate civilizations of Eurasia.

A second obvious proposition is that the national history of the United States fits into the pattern of world history not as an exception but as a part. More specifically, the rise of the United States was an important segment of the global phenomenon of European expansion that dominated most of the earth from shortly before 1500 to shortly after 1900. The U.S.S.R., too, is a monument to the same process, having been built by pioneers who moved eastward and overland rather than westward and overseas as in the case of the United States. This geographical difference had important consequences for the fashion in which the repertory of European skills and institutions was altered and adapted on the two frontiers. But such differences ought not to obscure what was common to all European frontier societies, East and West, and also in such diversified places as South Africa, Australasia and South America.

Placing our national experience within the panorama of world history will require us to give up both the original Puritan vision of creating a "city on the hill" uniquely pleasing to God, and its variously secularized versions that continue to dominate our national self-image. Manifest Destiny, translated into an aggressive, hard-nosed pursuit of national advantage in the tradition of Theodore Roosevelt and his successors, is as unsatisfactory a guide to action today as is the universalistic legal-moralism associated with Woodrow Wilson and his political heirs. Limits to our national power need to be recognized more clearly than either of these traditions admits. The plain fact is that the wealth and power of the United States vis-à-vis the rest of the world have diminished since 1945, and we must get used to this elemental fact. The best way to start is to recognize that the American way of life is no more than one variation among many to which humanity adheres.

This need not diminish personal and collective attachment to inherited values and institutions. Recognition of humanity's cultural pluralism might, indeed, allow us to react more intelligently to encounters with other peoples than is likely to happen when we are either aggrieved and surprised by their persistent, willful differences from us, or else remain self-righteously impervious to the possibility of learning something useful from people who diverge from us in enduring, conspicuous ways.

Finally, it seems no less evident that currents of cultural interaction have, since 1914, begun to run in new directions from those that dominated the world during the preceding four centuries. How to understand the contemporary scene requires more detachment from everyday events than we can easily achieve. For a while after World War II, the bipolar diplomatic pattern of the cold war seemed to ratify the existence of rival and opposing Soviet-U.S. spheres of influence. But Japan's economic rise, together with heartfelt Third World aspiration toward a more perfect emancipation from imperial tutelage, and complex crosscurrents within old Europe that extend, sometimes, to Russian and American societies as well, makes that simple bipolarity now seem inadequate in spite of President Reagan's efforts to make it the key to all else.

Perspective arising from the course of future events may be necessary before observers can discern the pattern of our time as clearly as we can recognize past patterns of interaction among the peoples and cultures of the earth. Nonetheless, seeing contemporary foreign affairs as a continuation of long-standing processes of cultural encounter will surely teach us not to expect the various peoples of the earth to wish to be like us any more than we wish to be like them. It should teach us also to expect local variation in the expression of even the most universal human aspirations. The fact that nearly everyone prefers wealth and power to poverty and helplessness does not therefore assure any uniformity in the way different peoples will choose to pursue the common goal. Nor are material goods everything. Beauty and holiness are also widely disseminated ideals, and the desire for membership in a supportive community of comrades is an even more universal and, often, passionate desire.

V

The most problematic of all these human aspirations is how to define the limits of comradeship. This, indeed, is where humanity's myth-making and myth-destroying capacity comes elementally and directly into play by defining the boundary between "us" and "them." Broadly inclusive public identities, if believed and acted on, tend to relax tensions among strangers and can allow people of diverse habits and outlook to coexist more or less peacefully. Narrowed in-group loyalties, on the other hand, divide humanity into potentially or actually hostile groupings.

The choice is awkward because advantages do not lie wholly on one side. Sectarian groups, their faces set firmly against the larger world, are far more supportive to their members than variegated, pluralistic societies can be. Nations, for the same reason, provide their citizens with more vibrant public identities than transnational and global organizations will ever be able to do. What humanity needs is balance between a range of competing identities. A single individual ought to be able to be a citizen of the world and hold membership in a series of other, less inclusive in-groups simultaneously, all without suffering irreconcilable conflict among competing loyalties. But that could only occur if conventional limits to jurisdiction somehow stabilized relationships among all the multitude of possible in-groups. Such stability has perhaps been approached in times past when some territorially vast empire brought order of a kind to parts of the globe, but it is no recipe for our foreseeable future.

Instead we must do the best we can to survive in a world full of conflict by creating and sustaining the most effective public identities of which we are capable. Cultural diversity is and always has been characteristic of the human species. No sensible person would wish or expect to see uniformity instead. Ordering diversity is, nonetheless, difficult. Violence played a large role in times past, by defining geographic boundaries and modes of interaction among diverse communities. Violence is sure to remain among us, heirs as we are of hunting bands that became the most skillful of all predators. But wisdom can sometimes restrain violence, or channel it into less damaging forms of behavior than preparation for atomic war.

Apart from the practical value which serious myth making aspires to, the reality of world society in our day constitutes an intellectual challenge that can be met only by rising to the grandest mythical plane of which we are capable. Only so can the world we live in become intelligible. Inherited ideas—whether dating back to pagan Greece, Christian Europe, 1776 or 1848—are simply inadequate, and there is no use pretending otherwise. There is still less sense in pretending that all we need is more detail. What we need is an intelligible world, and to make the world intelligible, generalization is necessary. Our academic historians have not done well in providing such generalizations of late. Thoughtful men of letters ought therefore to try.